MAO

A BIOGRAPHY

MAO

ROSS TERRILL

HARPER COLOPHON BOOKS
Harper & Row, Publishers
New York, Cambridge, Hagerstown, Philadelphia, San Francisco
London, Mexico City, São Paulo, Sydney

This book is dedicated to the flair for leadership
which is craved in some countries today, and equally
to the impulse of ordinary people to be free from
the mystifications of leadership.

Map on pages xii–xiii by Paul J. Pugliese

A hardcover edition of this book is published by Harper & Row, Publishers.

MAO. Copyright © 1980 by Ross Terrill. All rights reserved. Printed in the United States of America. No part of this book may be used or reproduced in any manner whatsoever without written permission except in the case of brief quotations embodied in critical articles and reviews. For information address Harper & Row, Publishers, Inc., 10 East 53rd Street, New York, N.Y. 10022. Published simultaneously in Canada by Fitzhenry & Whiteside Limited, Tornoto.

First HARPER COLOPHON edition published 1981.

ISBN: 0-06-090859-9   (previously ISBN: 0-06-014243-X)

84 85 10 9 8 7 6 5 4 3 2

Contents

Acknowledgments   *ix*

1. Prologue   1
2. Childhood (1893–1910)   4
3. Knowledge for What? (1910–1918)   18
4. Wider World in Peking and Shanghai (1918–1921)   37
5. Organizing (1921–1927)   59
6. Struggle (1927–1935)   92
7. A Grip on the Future (1935–1936)   122
8. Fighting Japan (1936–1945)   140
9. The Sage (1936–1945)   159
10. A Ripening Peach (1945–1949)   175
11. "We Shall Put Aside the Things We Know Well" (1949–1950)   198
12. Remolding (1951–1953)   212
13. Building (1953–1956)   224
14. Doubts (1956–1957)   241
15. Tinkering with the System (1958–1959)   260
16. Russia and Beyond (1958–1964)   278
17. Retreat (1961–1964)   289
18. The Furies of Utopia (1965–1969)   303
19. A Tall Thing Is Easy to Break (1969–1971)   332
20. Nixon (1972)   354
21. Fractured Vision (1973–1975)   366
22. An Arrow Near the End of Its Flight (1976)   400
23. Epilogue   424

Bibliographic Note   *435*
Reference Notes   *438*
Index   *471*

Acknowledgments

I am profoundly grateful to Robert Manning, editor of *The Atlantic Monthly*, for suggesting that I write this book, and for many other reasons.

In the digging and checking, I was helped on particular points by Liang Tsan-tang, and Huang Chin-hsing.

Drafts were executed (no pun intended) at the typewriter by Madge Slavin, a long-time helper, Barbara Sindrigis, and Catherine Cornish.

Edward Friedman of the University of Wisconsin, Robert Oxnam of the Asia Society, and Donald Klein of Tufts University, gave me sound advice on aspects of the whole book.

Some of the work was done while I was a Research Fellow at the Australian National University, for which stay I am grateful to Vice-Chancellor Anthony Low, Director Wang Gungwu, and Contemporary China Center head Stephen Fitzgerald.

I have talked of their impressions of Mao with Eugenio Anguiano, Couve de Murville, Stephen Fitzgerald, Ganis Harsono, Huang Hua, Henry Kissinger, Kukrit Pramoj, Winston Lord, Etienne Manac'h, Arnold Mononutu, Sunario, Gough Whitlam—and a number of others, many Chinese, some East Europeans, some Asians, whose names I do not have permission to acknowledge.

At Harper & Row, I have benefited from the care and vigor of Dolores Simon, William Monroe, Lisa Morrill, and especially from Amy Bonoff's blend of effervescence and clear-eyed rationality.

On the path of my friendship with Simon Michael Bessie, the publication of this book is, I think, a special step.

Chinese Words

Chinese characters—which are pictures as much as words—have been romanized in this book in the *pinyin* way, used by the Chinese, and increasingly by foreigners. Exceptions are the Reference Notes (see the explanation on page 438) and the following places and names well known to foreigners in their pre-*pinyin* form: China, Canton, Peking, Tibet, Hong Kong, Chiang Kai-shek, Sun Yat-sen.

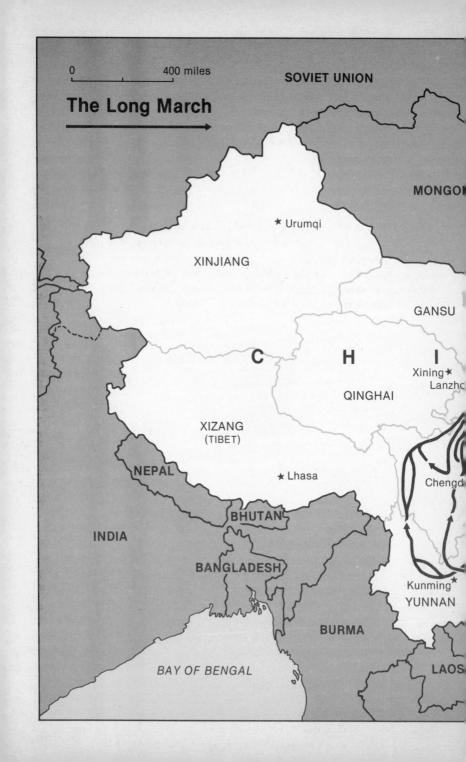

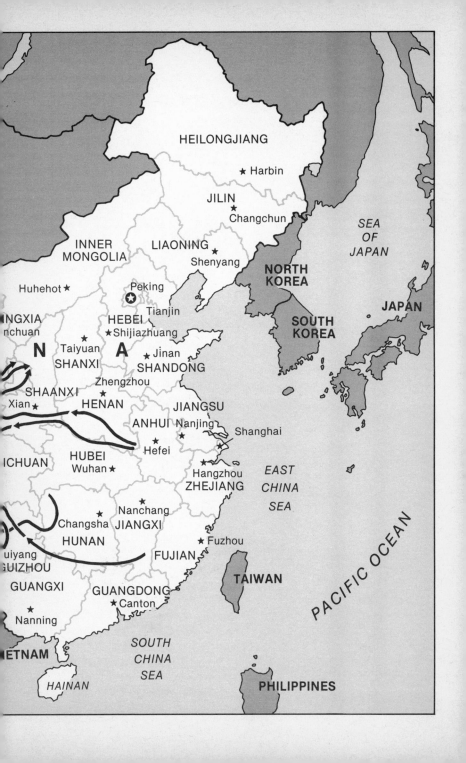

1

Prologue

Mid-parted black hair over a calm face, delicate hands, a gaze that bored into its target. Curiously flat-topped ears which gave stability to the head. Mole on the chin which was almost a relief from the broad pale face with no wrinkles. "A typical big Chinese," one Burmese who knew him and other Chinese leaders summed up. "Not handsome, like Zhou Enlai, but benign."

Over 82 years Mao Zedong's appearance changed a bit but not much. The youth looked slightly anxious. The leader in office seemed pretty well satisfied with himself. He grew fat and lost the air of an earnest intellectual. The hands found it easier to know what to do with themselves. "He looked like a sea elephant," said a Thai leader who saw him in the last years, "all very broad and splendid."

Always the same was the sense of a man in focus. Self-contained. Giving the impression of thinking of six things at once. Mao never lost the duality of being a taut wire of pure mind, yet also sensual as a cat.

Dry enough to bamboozle a visitor with a classical quotation or fry him in the heavy oil of silence. Earthy enough to startle another visitor by reaching into his baggy trousers to deal with lice. Top half of the face suggested an intellectual: immense forehead, questing eyes, longish hair. Bottom half was that of a sensualist: plump lips, chubby nose, round and childlike chin.

Mao did not move with grace; he was a lumbering type of man. Agnes Smedley, an American feminist whose passions were both political and personal, tried to get Mao to sing and dance in the 1930s—as she readily got other Communist leaders to—but gave up in disgust. "Pride prevented him from trying to dance." Sanzo Nosaka, a Japanese Communist-in-exile who knew Mao in the same period, said his dancing looked like someone doing exercises. The rhythm in Mao was not physical.

Mao's outward jerkiness was not misleading. The balance in his being, if it existed, came from a clash of opposites. He was part tiger, he said of himself, and part monkey. The ruthless side and the quixotic side each took its turn.

His handwriting suggests a man who chose his moods and bothered little about rules. The characters are of all sizes and they swirl about; it is not "good" calligraphy by the standards of the gentleman scholar.

Because Mao was complex, people never knew what current from his depths would surface at any moment. Though he was a calm man, his moods were finely pitched, and he had a temper. Edgar Snow, the reporter from Missouri who saw a lot of Mao, as early as the 1930s, said he was never neutral or passive about anything.

It is not surprising that Mao did not often evoke affection—less so than Zhou Enlai, the executive officer who was content to stand in Mao's shadow; or Zhu De, the leathery, very fallible, wide-grinning chief of the Chinese Communist army (both of whom Ms. Smedley *did* dance successfully with).

"I just could not communicate with Mao," said an Indonesian who dealt with both Mao and Zhou Enlai. "With Zhou—but not with Mao—there was discussion, you knew where you stood."

Mao was born in 1893 and he died in 1976. In that period almost everything in China seemed to be turned upside down. An empire fell. Wars came and went like tramcars. Millions died. Close comrades fell from grace. The torch of struggle was passed to fresh generations, who did not feel its warmth as Mao did.

Mao lived on. Against all odds, and into an era when he came to seem more like an ancestor than a politician, the farm boy survived. He never lost an arm or a leg or an eye—was never once wounded—in decades of battle which destroyed the *ancien régime* of one fifth of mankind and brought violent death to three quarters of his family.

In his personal physical unity was wrapped up the story of the Chinese Revolution.

What lens to apply to Mao Zedong? Peasant rebel? He coaxed riffraff from Hunan's rice fields and Jiangxi's green hills into a shoestring army that wrenched the right to rule from China's landlords.

Military commander? He said his bowels never worked so well as during a battle.

Poet? He seldom finished a battle without turning aside to express in verse his excitement at the exhilaration of struggle and the beauty of China's mountains and rivers.*

---

* Nor was he always modest about his fairly good poetry, written in a classical style which he forbade China's youth to emulate. "Who says we haven't any creative workers?" he exclaimed in a 1942 speech. Pointing to himself, he added: "Here's one right here!"

Latest in a long line of Chinese patriots who reached outside China for the means to renew an ailing China? From Europe he borrowed—not machines or religion or the blueprint of a liberal constitution—but communism. With skill and flexibility he brewed it as medicine to revive a patient, China, that was felt to be sick unto death.

Emperor? He taught three generations to laugh in the face of taboos and authorities held in awe by Chinese people for two millennia. Yet he ended up, maybe to his own despair, as a mirror-image Son of Heaven whose every syllable was truth and law—terrible proof that the Old World lives on to haunt the New.

2

Childhood (1893–1910)

A boy with a shock of black hair gleaming in the sun and baggy blue pants sat on a bamboo platform in a rice field. He was slender but tall for one not yet at puberty. His big eyes seemed full of dreams. His simple task was to scare birds away from the tender seedlings.

Strong blue hills enfolded a cultivated valley. Mud houses with rice-stalk thatch roofs broke the verdure. A stone bridge sat on the belly of the valley. Only the dog-eared book beside the boy on the bamboo platform spoke of anything but tranquil nature and the routine of an Asian farm at the dawn of the twentieth century.

The farm boy's family name was Mao, which means "Hair." His given name was Zedong which means "Anoint the East."

On a small rise by a green wooded slope was the four-room family home where Mr. Mao ruled with a rod of iron. He was a small, thin, sharp-featured man with a mustache and a deep anxiety at everything around him. The three-acre farm was his castle in a world of which he was wary.

Zedong was born in this solid and serene clay-brick house, and now as he gathered strength he was becoming a source of tension beneath its high wooden beams.

It was night. The air was hot and still and rent with the cry of crickets. No one spoke or moved and the valley seemed nature's alone. But a faint yellow dot picked out one wall of Mr. Mao's abode. Inside the glassless window Zedong defied the night, which in rural China was strictly for sleeping. He was bent over a Robin Hood–type saga of old China called *Story of the Marshes*. His sweating yellow face was close to a tiny oil lamp, its flame the size of a bean, and half covering both was a quilt to hide the glow. Mr. Mao did not like his son to read books or waste vegetable oil.

The scene was the bank of a pond that separated Mr. Mao's house from the rest of the village. People dressed in visiting clothes stood around the lo-

tus-covered pond in awkward silence. The tranquillity of the valley was be-
lied for the moment because Mr. Mao was in the grip of his hard-edged
temper. Before him a flushed Zedong was the center of attention.

A quarrel had just erupted inside the house. Father denounced the boy as
lazy and useless in front of a parlorful of guests. Zedong swore at him and
ran out of the house. Both parents went after Zedong and the guests ebbed
out in vague pursuit. When Zedong reached the edge of the pond he said he
would plunge in if his father came one step nearer.

Mr. Mao's brute rage was stayed and argument took over from assault.
Mr. Mao now asked only that Zedong say he was sorry for the insults and
kou tou to seal his obedience. (The *kou tou* in old China was an elaborate
prostration on both knees with the head lowered nine times to the ground.)
Zedong's flaming defiance in front of guests had gained him points; the
peace terms were a compromise. Zedong apologized, but he only did a part
kou tou (on one knee) and Mr. Mao promised not to beat him.

*   *   *

The Mao family was better off than most in the village of Music Mountain (Shaoshan). Mr. Mao rose from poor to comfortable during Zedong's
boyhood in the early 1900s. His three acres in 1904, when Zedong was ten,
had become four acres three years later. His household consumed about 2¼
tons of rice per year and he had 3½ tons left over for sale. He hired a second
laborer and began to make money by shrewd trading in grain and pigs and
by tight-fisted usury. He acquired a pool of capital and started to buy mort-
gages on other farmers' land. The Mao farm came to look quite well set up,
with a cowshed, a storage house for grain, a pigsty, and a small mill.

The clay-brick dwelling itself had been built by Zedong's grandfather in
1878, but it got bigger and smarter as Mr. Mao ground his way to security.
Eventually it accommodated two families—the Zous and the Maos—and
Zedong saw the Mao wing get a tile roof while the Zou wing still made do
with thatch.

Zedong's upbringing was secure. Other boys of the same era could expect
less than Zedong got. He did not go hungry. His clothes were few but they
were not rags. His mother put order and dignity into the life of the household. Zedong's big problem was his father. His yearnings were of the spirit.

Music Mountain offered beauty and peace. It was at that time hours
away—travel was by foot—from any towns. It seemed to have made its own
arrangements with a well-disposed nature. The several hundred families,
many linked by the spreading spider web of the name Mao, were few
enough so that hills and trees and crops set the tone of Music Mountain.

Red soil at the feet. The silver water of flooded fields, flecked with young rice shoots, gleaming under the sun like a giant's mirror flawed with a thousand scratches. Bamboos with their fastidious leaves framing the smoky blue mountains behind. Pines standing shoulder to shoulder on high as if sternly defending the slopes which gave them virility.

The peasants showed their humility before nature by their choice of place names. Music Mountain's name stems from a legend about an ancient emperor who took rest here and made music on a peak that towers over the valley. The nearby Xiang River gives its name to the two towns nearest Music Mountain, and also serves the locals as a nickname for the whole province.

No newspaper reached Music Mountain. News came by word of mouth. The village was insulated by a lapse of time between any event and the arrival of a report on it. If an edict came from the court at Peking, it would be read out aloud to a village meeting and a copy stuck on the school building. Just as the Mao home sat by itself without any close-by neighbors, so were the 2,000–odd villagers almost a world unto themselves.

Music Mountain was Zedong's world; he never went more than 22 miles from it until he left it for good at 16.

*   *   *

South of the Lake (Hunan) is a rich and lively hinterland province full of legend and color and the smoke of battle. Hunanese like to tell you that their homeland is 70 percent hills, 10 percent water, and 20 percent planted land. It is a nice summary of why South of the Lake is how it is.

Leaping mountains line the borders on all sides except where Lake Grotto Hall marks the northern limit. Hence the rugged spirit, the recurrent rash of bandits given shelter by the hills, and the touch of the crafty and the frugal that are all found in South of the Lake and its people. Zedong grew up to write poems and prose in which mountains were images of the noble and the wild and the invincible.

Lakes and four big rivers help give South of the Lake its nickname, "land of fish and rice." Zedong from the age of 6 became fond of swimming and he later built almost a world view around the act of plunging into water and defying currents.

The lowlands of Hunan are a great larder for the mouths of China. "If the harvest is good in Hunan," an old phrase has it, "the whole realm is satisfied." This populous plain is equally rich in political tradition. The province capital of Changsha (Long Sands) has often led the way for China in business and the life of the mind.

Music Mountain lies not among Hunan's high ranges, yet not quite on the plain either. Zedong imbibed some traits of the hilly frontier: earthiness, a spirit of rebellion, Robin Hood romance. He breathed in something of Hunan's lowland tradition: love of books, a good sense of organization, care for public affairs. If it is true that Hunanese blend the elemental quality of the hills with the smooth instincts of the town, then Zedong grew up a true son of Hunan.

In Mr. Mao's house, the plain décor was lit up by red peppers which hung in clusters from the roof beams. Mr. Mao like most Hunanese liked to fire his food with these grenades of spiciness. So Zedong began in this house his lifelong love affair with hot food.

Other Chinese have to watch out for the fire and obstinacy of the Hunanese. But they do not deny that the fieriness goes along with courage. "China can be conquered," runs a saying known all over the country, "only when every Hunanese is dead."

The people of South of the Lake fight and curse and state their views with gusto. These folk with broad foreheads, deep-set eyes, and pink cheeks are China's Prussians. Zedong did not grow up to be wishy-washy.

*　*　*

The calm in Music Mountain was deceptive because swift change was afoot beyond the hills. Up in Peking, China's last dynasty was gasping. China was backward. For all its glories, the Empire contained not one meter of railroad when Mr. Mao faced his future in 1880.

China was being carved up like a melon by a more advanced Europe. Within a few months of Zedong's birth in December 1893, Japan got into the act; Nippon's defeat of China in 1894 jolted the Chinese elite from anxiety to panic.

And non-Chinese social ideas, flowing in accord with the direction of power, began to impinge on China as they had never previously done. Just before Zedong was born, China's first resident ambassador abroad put out a book about his experiences in England, which amazed the Confucian elite by its revelation that sophistication existed outside China. When Zedong was a toddler of three, the first Chinese students ever to study in Japan set sail.

Forces of dissent rose like a flood tide against the semi-alien Manchu government. In Mr. Mao's youth the Taiping peasant rebels nearly toppled the dynasty before being wiped out with European help in 1864. The first decade of Zedong's life saw the first big political reform movement designed to revamp the dynasty. It was a damp squib, though, since by now reform was not enough.

Before Zedong was one year old, Sun Yat-sen (1867–1925) wrote a petition that marked his own shift from reform to revolution. It laid out battle plans for dismantling old China. The old elite schemed to resist change: was not a train engine fueled by feeding children into its smokestack, it was murmured, was not the theory of combustion an insult to the fire gods? Zedong was born into an era when old China was doomed.

* * *

Before father and son began to clash, Zedong was raised gently in the Chinese way. He was not smacked. Pants split open at the seat allowed him to answer nature's call at will with no adult intervention.

He scrambled after crickets and played at knucklebone. He gurgled with delight to get a red egg and see incense burned when the Empress Dowager (1835–1908) had a birthday.

He cast an eye at the bronze statue of Buddha sitting on a blackwood table in the living room. He gazed up without comprehension at the slogans about harmony and filial piety written on strips of red paper over the doorways. He began to wrestle with the pictographs of the Chinese written language, and sucked in from those around him the flattened Hunan accent, which substitutes *f* for *h* ("Funanese").

Mr. Mao like any peasant was happy when his first child turned out a "diamond" rather than a "tile." A tile (girl) could not be an heir and was less useful in the fields than a diamond (boy). Mr. Mao had received only two years of schooling and at 16 he had joined the army to escape hard times on the land. Still, it was logical to send Zedong to school, even though most children in Music Mountain never had this chance. A degree of literacy would fit Mr. Mao's "diamond" to keep the burgeoning farm's accounts and write deeds and contracts. A dose of the Confucian canon would help mold the clay of a pampered infant into the brick of a filial youth.

The private school in a part of the village called South Bank was indeed a traditional one in which no non-Chinese breeze blew. The "five books" of Classics ruled as the Bible rules in a Protestant Sunday school. Zedong began school when eight, and he remarked dryly years later: "I hated Confucius from the age of eight."

Zedong and some of his classmates read banned books at their little wooden desks and covered them up with a Classic if the teacher came near. They were tales of war and banditry—*Story of the Marshes, Romance of the Three Kingdoms, Journey to the West*—which did more than anything else in Music Mountain to color Zedong's mental world.

Not terribly subversive, they had nevertheless been outlawed at times by the Manchus. The Confucian establishment frowned upon such sagas because they could serve the literate population—the way they served Zedong—as an alternative literature.

By the time he left the school at age 13, Zedong had become hostile to the line and code contained in the Classics. But he first turned against this ancient moral philosophy of order and propriety because it was taught as a cult of obedience. The children were required only to be parrots. They shouted out the cryptic and archaic maxims while swaying in rhythm like junior Holy Rollers of the Orient.

As Latin texts have been in the modern West, the Analects of Confucius were no doubt a great force for masturbation.

Nor would that have been their only counterproductive feat. Confucian precepts of deference toward those in authority aroused in Zedong a hatred for the two adults who hemmed him in: teacher and father.

Both men beat Zedong, which made him burn with fury. Ideas he did not yet have, but an intense sense of justice existed in him. He was willful before he became a rebel, a boy of passion before he became a man of revolution.

His sense of justice showed up first in his dealings with people at school. He felt sorry for a poor boy who brought no lunch and he regularly divided his own between the two of them. His mother was puzzled that he ate so much in the evening. When Zedong told her of the fate of half of her carefully prepared lunch, the kindly soul thenceforth sent her son off each morning with two lunches instead of one.

The boy's sense of justice made him far from meek. At the age of 10 he had a brisk fistfight with an older classmate; this upset his mother, for whom nonviolence was a sacred absolute.

After two years at South Bank he knew the ritual for reciting from the Four Books and the Five Classics: rise and walk to the teacher's desk, face away from the teacher, then spout the maxims. But one morning Zedong drew a line against formality. When his name was called he did not budge from his tiny stool.

"If you can hear me well while I sit down," he ventured to the stunned teacher, "why should I stand up to recite?"

Pale with anger, the teacher ordered Zedong to bend to the time-honored procedure. The 10-year old dragged his stool to the teacher's desk and sat looking at him in calm defiance. The enraged teacher pulled at Zedong to raise him upright. Zedong writhed free and marched out of the school. Like the rebels in *Story of the Marshes*, he took refuge in the hills.

The boy struck out for "the city" (whatever that meant to him at the time). But he succeeded only in circling Music Mountain and never moved three miles from it. A search was mounted. Zedong would not return, because he feared that the teacher would surely beat him and his father would not miss the chance to do the same.

After three days someone from the Mao household found him. A bit subdued, he came home.

Years later the ex-pupil recalled this trauma in terms more of politics than of pathos. "After my return to the family," he said to Edgar Snow, "to my surprise conditions somewhat improved. My father was slightly more considerate and the teacher was more inclined to moderation. The result of my act of protest impressed me very much. It was a successful 'strike.' "

The bright Zedong learned the Classics well, even as he learned to hate their message. He soon began to shoot classical quotes like arrows at his father during their quarrels. In the China of the early 1900s, to be soaked in the Four Books was no longer a guarantee of docility.

* * *

Zedong left school at age 13 because the jobs he did on the farm before and after class were not enough to satisfy Mr. Mao. The father had suffered commercial loss through his own mistakes in calculating with the abacus; Zedong was trained in arithmetic and could serve to plug this gap in the business. From the age of 5, Zedong had done boy's work like weeding, gathering wood, watering the buffalo, and picking beans. Now he became an adult laborer by day and his father's bookkeeper after dark. The "diamond" was going to pay off.

Proximity produced extra sparks between father and son. Zedong outwitted his father and fazed the irate miser with calm obstinacy. He hated having to go round the village collecting payments due to the increasingly prosperous Mr. Mao. Once he sold a pig for his father and on the way home gave the proceeds to a poor beggar.

The father could be seen sitting by the stove in winter grumbling about Zedong's errant ways, or plunged into moody silence with his long Chinese pipe gripped tight in his mouth. He once lost a lawsuit because his opponent impressed the court with an apt classical quote. Zedong could now wield these slippery maxims too. Was the boy unfilial? But the canon also laid down that a father must be kind and affectionate.

One morning Mr. Mao pounced on Zedong as he read a novel beside a tombstone in a corner of the farm. "So you've decided to stop work?" rasped Mr. Mao with an angry glance at the two empty manure baskets at Zedong's side. "No, father, I am only having a little rest." Mr. Mao accused Zedong of having carried no manure from the pigsty to the fields during the entire morning. In fact, Zedong had already moved five or six baskets. A stand-off occurred. But in the late afternoon Mr. Mao found his son again reading a non-Classic by the tombstone.

He upbraided Zedong for being so tainted by "bad books" that he no longer took any notice of his father's admonitions. "No, father, I do listen to you. I do everything you tell me to do." Mr. Mao's mouth hung open in unhappy shock when he found out that Zedong had carried no less than 15 baskets since lunch.

"I will work regularly on the farm," Zedong said, "but I want to read my books as well."

At the same time Zedong had his lapses (no doubt more of them than the available accounts of his boyhood chose to reveal). Once he got lost in a book and allowed an ox to wander off and eat a neighbor's vegetables.

Mrs. Mao was plump and kind-eyed, a contrast to her thin, sharp husband, and she was as soft and accommodating as he was harsh and driven. Physically the likeness between Zedong and his mother was strong. Both had big vulnerable eyes, an open smile, a way of walking and gesturing that suggested largesse and even romanticism.

Mrs. Mao indulged her eldest son, and he never lost his deep affection for her. Zedong was the only child in the house during the crucial early years and he did not have to share with others the attentions of his mother (or that of Mr. Mao's father, who was part of the household until he died when Zedong was 14).*

Mrs. Mao's family was a simple one from a county not far to the south. Like most people in Music Mountain, she could not read or write. And like most others she was a Buddhist. Before and during his school days, Zedong used to go with her to sing hymns and appease the gods at the Buddhist temple on Phoenix Hill high above the valley.

Mr. Mao did not believe in Buddhism and this bothered Zedong. At the age of nine, he discussed with his mother the problem of his father's impiety and how the two of them might deal with it. "We made many attempts then and later to convert him," Zedong recalled years afterward, "but without success. He only cursed us."

Sure that his father always put avarice above all other motives, Zedong observed that considerations of prudence—not a change of heart—later gave the old man second thoughts about religion. One day he was out collecting money and met a tiger on the road. The tiger fled in surprise. Mr. Mao's relief outweighed even his terror. "From then on," Zedong noted, perhaps unfairly, "he showed more respect to Buddhism and burned incense now and then."

The birth of a third boy in 1905 may have mellowed Mr. Mao a little. Certainly the old man treated Zetan, born 13 years after Zedong, more kindly than he treated his first "diamond." But Zedong's own struggle with

*A second child, Zemin, was born in 1896, three years after Zedong.

his father went on unabated and the household was painfully polarized.

Zedong joined forces with his mother in efforts to curb Mr. Mao. They furtively gave away rice to a villager in dire need. They allied with the hired laborer to defeat Mr. Mao's stingy ways. They conspired eventually (with the help of Mrs. Mao's relatives) to get around Mr. Mao's opposition to any further education for Zedong.

Zedong saw the household as being divided between his father ("the ruling power") and a coalition of himself, his mother, his next brother, Zemin, and the laborer ("the opposition").

But the opposition was split on tactics, for Zedong's resolve and cunning soon left his gentle mother in the tactical shadows. He made a habit of directly confronting his father and she did not approve of that. "It is not the Chinese way," she objected. Mrs. Mao was also upset that Zedong's Buddhist faith was being undermined by the ideas he was getting from books, and by the impact of events that began to impinge on tranquil Music Mountain.

For the boy at school the mother was his anchor and he was fiercely loyal to her. But the adult laborer arrived at new points of reference and the influence of his mother—though not his affection for her—declined in his last two or three years in Music Mountain. Zedong was at war with "the Chinese way."

Some members of a peasant secret society called Elder Brother Club burgled the Mao home. "I thought it was a good thing," Zedong recalled years later, "because they stole things which they did not have." It was not only his father who dissented from the boy's unconventional ideas. "My mother could not accept my view," Zedong confessed.

Mr. Mao had a scheme for dealing with his dreamy-but-tough son that was typical of the era. He found a girl and forced the 14-year old Zedong to marry her. Poor Zedong was aghast. For some reason, he politely endured the stiff and dreadful ceremony—the frightened little bride was unveiled for a first inspection like a newly bought package—and he even did a full deep *kou tou* before each guest in the accepted manner. But he refused to live with the girl, who was six years his senior, and said he never laid a finger on her.

The boy's idea for dealing with his tyrannical father was also typical of the time. He tapped a wider mental and social world to dilute the narrow familial world of the farm.

School had equipped Zedong with the precious ability to read. He tracked down, like a cat after mice, every book available in Music Mountain. Into his hands came a short one about the threat to China from imperialism. It began with a sentence that Zedong was to recall with emotion decades later:

"Alas, China will be subjugated." He said of this pamphlet's impact: "After I read this I felt depressed about the future of my country and began to realize that it was the duty of all the people to help to save it."

A plea for reform and technical advance called *Words of Warning in an Age of Prosperity* introduced Zedong to the idea that China should borrow secondary things from the West in order to save the essence of its own civilization. This book by a reform-minded comprador gave him a conviction that for China's sake he should get out of Music Mountain and soak up more knowledge.

* * *

One day, not long before he finished at Music Mountain school, Zedong and his classmates met a group of bean merchants walking in from Changsha. They had left the city because the famine of 1906 had led to big food riots. Crowds had driven the province governor out of the Manchu yamen. The authorities recovered themselves, a new governor arrived, and a bloody counterattack ensued. The heads of many rebels were cut off and put up on poles as a warning to others.

For days the school was abuzz with talk of this thunderclap from beyond the hills. Nearly all Zedong's friends took the side of the rioters. The incident burned into Zedong's broad brow for life, for he made a link which he says even his classmates did not. "Only from an observer's point of view" did they seem to him to sympathize. "They did not understand that it had any relation to their own lives." But Zedong had seen a universe tremble. "I never forgot it. I felt that there with the rebels were ordinary people like my own family and I deeply resented the injustice of the treatment given to them."

Revolt even stirred within Music Mountain itself. Some members of the peasant Elder Brother Club—now quite strong all over South of the Lake—found themselves in a dispute over rent payments with a Music Mountain landlord. The angry landlord sued his tenants and won the lawsuit after crossing the magistrate's palm with silver. Led by a blacksmith named Pang, the group of Elder Brothers rioted. They were pursued by troops of the provincial government and took refuge on nearby Liu Mountain. The landlord spread the story that the rebels had sacrificed an infant as they raised the banner of revolt. The Elder Brothers were soon rounded up and Pang's head was cut off.

For Zedong history had leaped off the pages of *Story of the Marshes* to stalk his own village. He heard Pang called a "bandit" just as the peasant leader Song Jiang was called a bandit in the thrilling old novel. The benign hills now seemed like barricades, as they had often been in history. Zedong had made another connection. "The first hero of the peasants in my mind," he later reflected, "was Pang the blacksmith."

Soon Mr. Mao himself became one of the targets of revolt.

A food shortage hit Music Mountain, in Zedong's seventeenth year, when the winter rice supply was all eaten before the new rice was ready for harvest. Hungry eyes turned toward the granaries of traders and landlords, and hungry lips shaped the slogan "Free Rice at the Big Houses." Mr. Mao's "Big House" could hardly be immune; he was after all still selling grain to Changsha as hunger mounted in Music Mountain. Angry villagers seized one of his shipments and ate it.

"I did not sympathize with him," said Zedong of his furious father. The connection of ultimate force for Zedong had been made: His nasty father was a local linchpin of the unjust social order of old China. Mr. Mao had been getting richer; the boy had noticed that. The old man was a lion in the path of China's true salvation; the adolescent now drew this chilly conclusion.

Zedong's terrible words about his father took on their full meaning: "I learned to hate him." He had linked his life as a boy with the life of his times.

Looking back 26 years later, though, the grown man recalled a lack of full approval of the rioters. "At the same time I thought the villagers' method was wrong also." Perhaps he simply had been shocked at seeing his family assailed. Perhaps he was reading back into the incident his later conviction that mere revolt is barren without an overall political strategy.

*   *   *

Quarrels between Zedong and his father over further study grew bitter by 1910. Mr. Mao had a plan to install Zedong as an apprentice at a rice shop in the county town of Xiang Tan, some 22 miles away. Zedong was not dead set against this—he felt the town would bring welcome opportunities—but he really wanted to be a full-time student in a modern school that taught "foreign" subjects. In a quiet and respectful way he raised this desire with his father. Mr. Mao's only response was a loud and raucous laugh. Zedong was wounded; after this he and his father did not speak to each other for some time.

Using a family link on his mother's side, Zedong went off to do self-study for six months in the home of an unemployed law student in Xiang Tan. Although he yielded to his father's pressure to come home again—he may also have had money problems in Xiang Tan—this half year of reading, listening, and arguing drove a last nail into the coffin of his existence as his father's grown-up "diamond."

Sixteen-year-old Zedong made quiet and effective plans. From relatives on his mother's side and friends of the family he borrowed five dollars here and ten dollars there. One night at dinner Zedong looked straight into his father's eyes and declared: "I have decided to study in the East Mountain Higher Primary School."

"Do you mean what you are saying?" blazed Mr. Mao. He had the one last shabby card of money to play against his willful son: "Perhaps you have won a lottery ticket this morning and have suddenly become rich?"

When it dawned on Mr. Mao that Zedong had scraped up some money, he bared the teeth of his avarice to the full. If Zedong went off to this school in the town of Xiang Xiang, the miser rasped, money would have to be found to pay an extra laborer to do the work he had been doing.

Zedong was not going to let contempt unsteady him now. He borrowed more money from a relative (on his mother's side) who esteemed education and had helped other members of the family to go to school.

When the topic came up anew, Zedong played his father like a trout. He cut short the old man's self-pitying complaints with a curt query: "How much would a laborer cost?" The miserable Mr. Mao said twelve dollars a year. Zedong put an envelope into his battered hand. "Here are the twelve dollars. I shall leave for East Mountain tomorrow morning."

At dawn Zedong arose to pack his personal things. Mrs. Mao watched him prepare with an anxious eye but few words. Apart from asking him if he needed anything more to take with him, she only said, "Are you going to say good-bye to your father?" Zedong replied, "No, I am not."

Soon after dawn he walked out of Music Mountain. The pole over his shoulder was familiar, but no baskets of manure hung from it on this cool, golden morning. At one end was a bundle containing tunics, two gray sheets, and a mosquito net. The other end supported a basket reserved for *Story of the Marshes* and *Romance of the Three Kingdoms*. He knew little else but Music Mountain. He would never live in Music Mountain again.

* * *

Was Zedong a full-blown rebel after 16 years in Music Mountain?

A moral sense that came largely from his mother, together with a social sense fed by reading, turned Zedong toward iconoclasm within the context of a stuffy school and a tyrannical household.

Mr. Mao was an unpleasant man. He beat Zedong often, shamed him before others, mocked at his driving desire to learn from books, did his best to wither the boy with a sense of his own alleged "laziness" and "uselessness."

Tradition held that a son should be deferent even if the father was a monster. Zedong flouted this. Yet other features of the boy's response to his father are striking. Zedong did not simply forget his family, as thousands of young rebels of the era did; he was to keep in touch with members of his family and receive help from various of them, and he spoke of his family as "ordinary people" with whom it would be possible to identify in the face of gross injustice.

Nor were the tactics Zedong employed on the farm extreme. He often made a compromise with his father, he submitted to the painful "wedding," he did not walk off the rice fields and join the Elder Brother Club, he remained under Buddhist influence for most of his years in Music Mountain, and when he left it he still believed in the monarchy.

Not far to the east of Music Mountain another boy who would later rise to the top of the Chinese Communist Party grew up at the same time as Zedong. Young Zhang Guotao got on smoothly with his wealthy and well-educated father. Yet he too became a rebel.

In Zedong's life the household of Mr. Mao and the school at South Bank were not random boxes of oppression. They were psychological agents of a larger pattern of rigid hierarchy in Chinese society.

Yes, Zedong hated Confucius from the age of eight. But "most of my classmates," he recalled, were equally bored by the Classics.

The youth of 16 had become a very Chinese kind of rebel in a very particular moment of historical change. He was not a neurotic. He lashed out less at his father than at what his father stood for. His rebelliousness was of a shrewdly calculated type.

Not all of Mr. Mao's demands on his son were excessive in the light of Chinese cultural ways in that era. Zedong was repelled by his father's authority in part because he felt it was serving bad, doomed goals. How could China be saved if households and villages were divided like this? What a fate for Chinese women if the patriarchy of Music Mountain was to remain the norm!

Zedong's "individual character" as a rebel fitted like a hand into the glove of a "social character" of rebellion being woven all over the country. The rebel himself coolly subsumed the individual struggle into the larger social one: "The first capitalist I struggled against was my father."

Yet the tensions between Zedong and his father were psychological as well as social. Social "oppression" was not the whole story of Mr. Mao's impact on his eldest son. Neither of Zedong's brothers got into the trouble with their father that Zedong did, one notes, and both of them were given the education that Zedong could not get his father to agree to.

Zedong dramatized his father's mean and authoritarian deeds,* out of a need to protect his own deep sense of pride.

---

*Some authors have stated that the phrase "I learned to hate him"—a breathtaking one on the lips of a Chinese boy of the early 1900s—was omitted from Chinese editions of Mao's autobiographical reminiscences to Snow; however, the various Chinese editions of this passage which exist in the Harvard-Yenching Library all contain the sentence ("*Wo xue le hen ta*").

Mr. Mao's ruthless ways—though not his aims—curiously enough found as deep a lodgement in Zedong's life as his mother's softer ways did.

Although there was a psychological closeness between Zedong and his mother, the boy did not possess many of her character traits. Nor did his relation to his mother remain so close after three other children arrived to share her attentions, and after Zedong learned ideas that Mrs. Mao thought harsh and strange.

Zedong took away from Music Mountain an inner compulsion to vindicate himself in the eyes of his father. To grow into a fuller, better version of his father, in the service of worthier goals.

Behind Zedong's expressed hatred of his father was an unacknowledged identification; he was driven to become an authoritarian like his father, and on a far grander scale.

Mr. Mao did not understand his son very well. Zedong felt scorn for him and struggled against him in a calculating—not a desperate—way, with much success.

At the same time, the "virtues" that Mr. Mao tried crudely to plant in his son proved to have appealed deeply to Zedong. "Laziness is the grave of life," he would soon remark, as if echoing his father.

"I used the rebuttal that older people should do more work than younger," he later recorded, of his anger at Mr. Mao's charge of laziness, "that my father was over three times as old as myself, and therefore should do more work." But Zedong did embrace the virtue insisted on by his father: "*And I declared that when I was his age I would be much more energetic.*"

Neither parent guided Zedong toward a philosophy of social revolution. That was to be almost a natural possession of the educated of his generation.

The boyhood at Music Mountain explains the *success* of this revolutionary and the *type* of revolutionary leader he became.

New ideas and the condition of old China made Zedong a rebel; the trials of the household in Music Mountain made him an extraordinarily resolute one.

3

Knowledge for What?
(1910–1918)

A few minutes from home on the 15-mile walk, Zedong ran into a neighbor. Wang was startled to see the youth wearing new cloth shoes and socks, which were not daily dress in Music Mountain.

"Little Mao, how fine you look with your shoes on," began the hard-bitten Wang. "I am going to school," Zedong replied with pride. He started to explain his sacred mission, but old Wang roared with laughter until his leathery face shone with tears. He mocked the youth for his desire to go to a "foreign school." He needled him as to whether Mr. Mao could possibly have approved of this madness.

Zedong lost his composure. "You're just old-fashioned and out of date," he shouted, and then trudged on.

With his two bundles of luggage on a bamboo pole, he walked through the black lacquer doors of East Mountain Higher Primary School. The brick structure surrounded by a moat and a high circular wall made him think he was entering a temple (the largest edifice he'd ever seen in Music Mountain was its Buddhist temple).

He crossed the white stone bridge across the moat and reached a lofty gate in the wall. He was taken for a porter! Zedong lacked experience from which to borrow social grace for this unpleasant moment. The scale of things was a shock by itself; he had never seen so many children together at one spot in his life.

Shrill taunts rent the air: "East Mountain is a school, not a lunatic asylum"; "A bandit is trying to get into our school." With tense steps he walked on. Boldly he sought out the headmaster's office.

"Sir, please will you allow me to study in your school?" Some quality of peasant character seemed to come through with his question. The headmaster gripped his long brass-and-bamboo pipe. For a moment he found nothing to say. He merely asked the grave youth his name.

"My name, sir, is Mao Zedong."

Mao's quiet passion had raised one eyebrow of the headmaster's interest. He allowed the boy to argue point for point against the objections to his enrollment. Sixteen years old? No mathematics or geography yet? Such clumsy handwriting?

Another teacher who was present spoke up for the young farmer. By the time Mao left the office and rejoined the circle of sophisticated beasts who had snapped at his self-esteem, he had won a trial admission for five months.

* * *

A measure of the gap Mao had to bridge in adapting to East Mountain after the rural numbness of Music Mountain was that only here did he learn that the Empress Dowager and Emperor Guang Xu were no longer living—though both had died two years before.

A cousin called Wen (mother's side of the family) was already a pupil at the school. He helped Mao a bit. But with only two boys from the mainstream did Mao seem to become friends: a pair of brothers named Xiao, from a wealthy landed family, whose paths were to cross his over several years.

Mao had pressed himself on the school as an outsider and he spent most of his time with the few other outsiders: boys who also did not speak the standard county accent;* boys whose patched clothes marked them off from their finely dressed fellows.

One crucial trait made Mao an outsider even among the outsiders. His age and size far exceeded that of every other boy in this tribe-conscious school. Now tall even for his 16 years, he towered over classmates four and five years his junior.

Most of the pupils were elegant, snobbish young gentlemen. Mao was a son of the soil. He was not from a poor family, but he was from a rural and unsophisticated family. His hands were rougher than those on adjacent desks and his face more sunburned than most others. Mao spoke slowly and with stress. The smart boys around him chattered like machine guns.

So little did he fit in that one fellow pupil offered him a job as his servant.

Mao was slender and he walked with a loping stride. His head soon developed an intellectual look. His hair grew long and tousled even though a pigtail remained at the back. All in all he was quite handsome in an unkempt way. He already had both a sensual *and* an aesthetic streak.

*Nearly all the pupils hailed from Xiang Xiang and spoke its accent. There were even warring factions which corresponded to subdivisions within the county. "I took a neutral position in this war," Mao said sadly of the infighting, "because I was not a native at all."

If Mao was a bit crude, he was genuine. East Mountain meant for him not a social trip, or the next step up a preset ladder to a good position, but a serious effort to learn what living in Music Mountain had robbed him of access to.

*   *   *

The school premises were neat and well-heeled, a far cry from the dust and thatch of Music Mountain. Here was a comfortable slice of upper-class Chinese life.

Yet the minds at East Mountain were starting to latch on to new doctrines that would soon be subversive—of elite tradition, and of the social order in Music Mountain too. Science was taught. Reform was praised. National feeling was nurtured with a pep talk at each morning's roll call on China's plight before hungry foreign powers.

The pupils' gowns with colored waistbands covered bodies soon to be broken on the wheel of social strife set spinning by these ideas.

Work was Mao's only real friend. An ironic result of those childhood agonies at the school in South Bank was that he had become good at the Classics! He wrote powerful essays in the old style. In this way he built up capital badly needed to set against his weak points and impulsive acts.

Learning about the reform politics of the time led him to the idea that knowledge could remake the world.

Typically, he reached outside the school curriculum for two key works. Cousin Wen put him onto some issues of *Journal of the New People*, edited by Liang Qiqiao, the leading political writer of the day. Also *Reform Movement of 1898*, a manifesto of the last-ditch upsurge of reform, by Kang Youwei, its preeminent philosopher. These books gave Mao his first strictly political ideas.

A teacher who had studied in Japan made the strongest mark on Mao, even though English and music, the two subjects he taught, brought Mao low grades. The lure of proud Japan was the reason. Mao loved the tales and poems of Japan's glory in the wake of its defeat of Russia in the war of 1905. "I knew and felt the beauty of Japan, and felt something of her pride and might."

Here was his first vision of the non-Chinese world. It started him toward a lifelong conviction that Japan was China's close young brother.

The theme of warfare also marked Mao's first steps in world history.

One evening after sports were done and the bell was summoning the sweating pupils to the study room, Mao ran into Emi, one of the two Xiao brothers. What was the book in his hand? Mao asked. It was an anthology called *Great Heroes of the World*. Mao, with his vacuum-cleaner approach to books, inquired if he might borrow it. For the next few days Mao dwelt with this book as one dwells with a fresh mistress.

When he got it back, Emi Xiao* found his book marked up like a galley proof. Mao had penciled circles and dots (the Chinese equivalent to underlining) beside the paragraphs on Napoleon, Washington, Peter the Great, Gladstone, Lincoln, Catherine the Great, Rousseau, and Montesquieu.

"We need great people like these," Mao said fervently to Xiao. China must be made rich and strong "so as not to follow in the footsteps of Indochina, Korea, and India." He quoted the scholar Gu Yenwu (1613–1682): "Every common man has a hand in determining the fate of his nation."

Opening *Great Heroes of the World* he read aloud to his fellow pupil—who was not used to sitting at the feet of Mao—a sentence about George Washington: "Victory and independence only came to the U.S.A. after eight long bitter years of fighting under Washington."

Like a gleam from over the horizon, the West had been noticed by young Mao. Then as later, it fascinated him less for its own sake than for what lessons it might hold for China. America had had a revolution; what about China?

Mao loved to read about China's ancient emperors—more great men to feed his appetite for heroes—and two of them stuck in his mind for life: Qin Shihuang, strong-man unifier, and Han Wudi, military-minded founder of the dynasty bearing his name.

Pupils came to respect Mao's grasp of *Romance of the Three Kingdoms* and other sagas; they liked to iisten to his retelling of their best episodes. But Mao took the novels as historical fact and this horrified everybody. He argued with the history teacher about it. He cursed any pupil who agreed with the teacher's standpoint, and threw a chair at one. He hated to be criticized, as he conceded when he looked back on his schooldays years later.

He even went to see the headmaster about the novel. When this learned man also burst the bubble of Mao's faith that *Three Kingdoms* was the gospel truth of the Warring States era, Mao drew up a petition to the mayor of Xiang Xiang asking that the headmaster be replaced and tried to browbeat his puzzled classmates into signing it.

Mao was a rigid boy. He lacked a safety valve of flippancy. He was naïve and obstinate on these novels which had meant so much to him in the rice fields at Music Mountain.

The incident over *Three Kingdoms* made life at East Mountain worse for him. At the same time it foreshadowed Mao's later intellectual style: the

*His formal name was Xiao San; I use his semi-Western nickname, by which he was widely known (he took it from Rousseau's *Emile*) to help distinguish him from his brother, Xiao You.

oblique approach; persistence; scorn for anyone who saw a matter differently.

Mao got high grades, and the headmaster allowed him to stay on beyond the trial period of five months. Yet his success at books, consolation for his social unhappiness, was itself a coin with two sides. It made some pupils despise his narrow zeal all the more. He began to think of leaving.

At East Mountain Mao had gained a wider vantage point. Now he wanted to travel around South of the Lake and to see Changsha.

Two visits to Music Mountain—at Chinese New Year and at term's end in early summer—only increased his sense of the need to back his own judgment. His father was more mellow but still lacked vision. "When will you end your studies and become a scholar," he asked Mao, "and get honor for your ancestors?"

* * *

Mao took his pole and bundles and left Xiang Xiang in September 1911; Emi Xiao, dissatisfied with East Mountain for his own reasons, went with him. They walked to Xiang Tan, where Mao applied to a senior primary school. But he was turned down as too old and tall.

Mao had a fall-back plan. He had asked a teacher at East Mountain to smooth a path for him at a middle school in Changsha. Xiao and Mao squeezed onto the third-class deck of a river steamer bound from Xiang Tan to the capital. To Mao's surprise and pleasure, he was admitted without fuss to this fine school meant for Xiang Xiang natives.

Xiao recalls Mao "speechless with excitement" at the bustle of Changsha. Hot, flat, and dusty, Changsha was then home to 800,000 people. Opened to foreign trade in 1904 as a Treaty Port, the city was booming, but it was also a ripening plum on the tree of anti-Manchu revolution.

Mao saw a newspaper for the first time. He had learned to cherish the printed page as a window on history. But here it was speaking of current events!

Strength of the People was an organ of Sun Yat-sen's nationalist movement. Mao read in its cluttered vertical columns of an unsuccessful uprising at Canton. It was led by a Hunanese revolutionary called Huang Xing. "I was most impressed with this story," Mao recalled, "and found *Strength of the People* full of stimulating material."

Under its stimulus Mao wrote an article of his own. "It was my first expression of a political opinion," Mao said of this eager piece which he posted to the school wall, "and it was somewhat muddled." He urged a new government that would be part reformist and part revolutionary. Sun Yat-sen for president, Kang Youwei for premier, Liang Qiqiao as foreign minister! (No less naïve than if an American youth, out of a zeal for unity, urged a government made up of Ronald Reagan as President, Ralph Nader as Vice-President, and Eldridge Cleaver as Secretary of State.)

Heroes were still 17-year-old Mao's cup of tea.

But the monarch was no longer on Mao's list of heroes. In a radical plunge, Mao became one of the first pupils at the school to clip off his pigtail.* He then joined with a fellow rebel to track down ten other pupils who had entered a "pact to cut pigtails," but who backed down at the last moment. The two of them forcibly took the shears to their classmates' pigtails and reaped ten more for the anti-Manchu cause.

* * *

History gave Mao only four weeks at Xiang Xiang middle school. In October 1911 the revolutionaries moved against the Manchus in the city of Wuhan. China's creaking last dynasty was falling after 267 years. Within a month the revolutionary army had taken seventeen provinces. The Manchu era was over.

The mood on Changsha's wide shady streets was dazed and excited. Politics spilled out of the old mold but didn't yet acquire new contours. Schoolbooks were forgotten for the moment. Students wrote not classical essays but slogans to demand a perfect future.

A spokesman for the revolutionary forces came to Mao's school and spoke to the pupils on the promise of the new era. Mao was so stirred that he decided to "join the revolution." After five days to think out his exact course, he enlisted in the Hunan revolutionary army.

Mao's pay at the garrison in Changsha was seven dollars a month. Two went on food. Most of the rest bought newspapers, which he pored over like holy scripts. These publications were left wing by definition; the medium was a message, for the newspaper was a brand-new instrument in Chinese politics.

In the *Xiang River Daily News* Mao read about a Socialist Party just founded by a Hunanese who had studied in Japan. Other writings also broached "socialism" as a newfangled idea for reorganizing society. It was Mao's first meeting with the term.

Socialism then meant social reform with vague collectivist overtones. Marxism was not even a spot on the horizon. But Private Mao was enough

*The pigtail, or queue, was a mark of a Chinese man's loyalty to the semi-alien Manchu dynasty.

moved to fire off letters to various ex-classmates about this attractive notion. Only one wrote back.

*   *   *

All through history the semi-intellectual has been the most potent person in an inchoate political situation. In the army Mao began to reveal himself as a semi-intellectual. Not only because he was bigger than his fellow pupils did he decline to join a student regiment, but also out of ambivalence toward the world of education.

Mao was scared of the impact school had had on him. He was more of an educated gentleman than, as Mr. and Mrs. Mao's son, he wanted to be. He liked being a token scholar among the illiterate soldiers. "I could write," he looked back, "I knew something about books, and they respected my 'great learning.'" He would draft letters home for them, and read out bits from the papers.

Mao bought his water from peddlers who brought it to the barracks, though the other troops carried it themselves from the public well at White Sands. Half aware of his twilight status, Mao simply remarked: "I, being a student, could not condescend to carrying water."

His father had not, for all his tyrannical authority, succeeded in making Zedong a plain farm laborer.

"Thinking the revolution to be over," Mao recalled of the spring of 1912, "I resigned from the army and decided to return to my books." Sun Yat-sen had reached an agreement with Yuan Shikai, a shady strong man with his feet in Republican China and his heart in old China. The military phase of the revolution had ended.

Mao formed no attachment to army life. He did little or no fighting and passed the time on chores for officers. He was in the army because he felt it had a role to play in the coming of a new China. "If the people are weak," he remarked to a friend, in a stark rejection of Confucian moralism, "what is the use of perfecting their virtues? The most important thing is to be strong."

Both company and platoon heads urged him to stay on. But when the army ceased to ring with the call of the moment, he suddenly left. School pulled back the 18-year-old semi-intellectual.

But which school? Mao was not sure, so he scanned the education advertisements of *Xiang River Daily News* and other papers. And how to pay the fees? The message from Music Mountain was that Zedong ought to have a job by now.

The ex-soldier took a bed in a cheap boardinghouse for natives of Xiang Xiang and began the first, and last, spell of sheer drift in his life.

*   *   *

An ad for a police school appealed to Mao. But he also liked one that offered a course in soap-making; a clean, uplifting touch for China? For both
these schools he registered, only to drop out before classes began.

For two more schools he registered, believing they might have sufficient
appeal at Music Mountain to coax some tuition out of his father. One was a
law and administration school, the other a commercial middle school.

Mao said of his letter to his father asking money for the first: "I painted a
bright picture for them of my future as a jurist and mandarin." Without
waiting for word from Music Mountain, the irresolute youth lost interest in
both these schools—and yet again lost his registration fee.

Like a cushion that bears the marks of the last person to have touched it,
Mao had in rapid succession taken the advice of a variety of ex-classmates.
But he had clinched nothing. Using ten fingers to try to catch ten fleas—the
phrase is his—he watched the fleas run on regardless.

Soon Mao had to target one flea. He paid his dollar to register at a senior
commercial school. Mr. Mao agreed to pay the fees—"My father readily
appreciated the advantages of commercial cleverness"—and young Mao sat
down to learn economics.

His preliminary investigations must have been vague, for it turned out
that many lectures and textbooks were in English. Not good at languages,
he knew only the rudiments of this tongue which East Mountain school had
tried to teach him.

"Disgusted with this situation," Mao related, "I withdrew from the institution at the end of the month and continued my perusal of the
advertisements."

Short of a dollar, more untidy than ever, Mao sat about in the wooden
teahouses of Changsha's humid, teeming streets, and read the papers with
his big slow eyes. What to do?

For a while Mao took a quizzical attitude to life around him. He saw two
sides to everything. He turned in on himself (with thoughts we have no way
of knowing). He sat on the balcony of life and watched the vain rush below.
"I am the universe," he jotted down in a Taoist muse.

With friends he went off to enjoy a huge bonfire. Exploding in flames was
the ammunition of the Hunan government's army. A year before he had entered this army with his own heart ablaze. But now he commented only on
the fun of the spectacle: "It was better than firecrackers."

*   *   *

Three student friends came upon Mao one day at the top of Edifice to
Pierce the Sky. He was gazing at the roofs of Changsha from this seven-

story tower on the city wall: intense, still, alone. Mao snapped out of his dream and the four went off for tea and watermelon seeds.

The three youths were socially a cut above Mao—one of them used to lend him money—and they probably also knew more than he did about politics in the worldly sense. One called Tan ("Talker"), son of a high official, said the end of the monarchy meant "We could all be President."

When another student put Tan down by making frivolous remarks, Mao stirred himself from silence: "Let him talk. I am very interested—let him talk." Tan went on to explain how learning was less important in a political leader than the will to struggle. Mao became as absorbed by this idea as he had been in gazing at the red roofs of Changsha.

Behind a screen of vague indecision, the drifter seemed to be hatching the beginnings of a world view.

He got his foot in the door of another school—First Middle School of Hunan—but he left after six months. He had grown self-confident toward schools. He topped the list of candidates in the entrance exam to First Middle School.

A bit smugly, perhaps, Mao made a dual criticism of the school that tells much about the character of young Mao: "Its curriculum was limited and its regulations were objectionable."

One teacher lent Mao an absorbing book on Chinese official history, *Chronicles with Imperial Commentaries*, which proved a springboard for his next move. Liking these edicts and emperors' memos more than the fare offered in class, he decided on a season of self-study.

As if six months was his natural span of attention, Mao then became a hermit in Hunan Province Library for half a year.

*   *   *

He would arrive as the library's doors opened in the morning and leave when they swung closed at the end of the day. A pile of books beside him, he was like a sphinx with bowed head, leaving the reading room only to buy a pancake or a meat dumpling for lunch.

He gorged on history and geography of the modern West. For variety he turned to novels, the poetry of his own country, and Greek mythology. He tackled the key works, recently translated into Chinese by the reformer Yan Fu, of Adam Smith, Herbert Spencer, John Stuart Mill, and Darwin. Also those of two philosophers he had met in *Great Heroes of the World* at East Mountain—Rousseau and Montesquieu.

He gazed at a map of the world on the library wall. Never before had he seen a map that showed China as but one nation, arrayed with dozens of others, and not as a Middle Kingdom with a dim periphery added as a courtesy to non-Chinese.

He joked to Emi Xiao that in Hunan Province Library he had been "like an ox let loose in a vegetable garden." He later judged this half year among books to be a high point of his life.

A bit of a monkey when he had to work with others, Mao could be a tiger when tossed back onto the resources of his own will.

Each night Mao returned to the boardinghouse, a club for Xiang Xiang natives that was full of ex-soldiers, students, and flotsam in transition, and hung around watching life go by.

A big fight broke out one evening. Soldiers set upon and tried to kill students. Mao, it seems, was still a bit of a Taoist, not an up-front citizen. "I escaped by fleeing to the toilet," he said of that bloody night, "where I hid until the fight was over."

*   *   *

Rent cannot be paid with zeal for books, and soon money problems drove Mao back to reading the advertisement columns. He hit upon teaching. An announcement for a teachers' training school he found "attractive." No fees to pay. Cheap bed and food. A career as a teacher, to boot.

Two of Mao's friends were also urging him to enter this school. They wanted Mao's help at the entrance exam. Mao obliged and wrote three essays. "I did not then think my act of substituting for my friends an immoral one," he recorded. He saw it as a matter of friendship. He also took pleasure in wielding his literary talent, as he had done among the soldiers.

All three essays won a place at the school.* Consent and dollars came from Music Mountain. With an amused awareness of his flighty period, now ending, Mao recalled 23 years later: "I managed to resist the appeals of all future advertising."

Politics had turned sour. Yuan Shikai was so bankrupt of purpose that he tried to restore the monarchy, with himself repackaged as emperor. Amid the tensions between this toy-gun neotraditionalism and the flickering radicalism of Sun Yat-sen's uncohesive alliance, war lords crept to the fore. In Changsha one of them murdered the two radical leaders who had come to power in Hunan on the morrow of the 1911 revolt. By the summer of 1917 China had two governments: a war-lord affair at Peking and Sun's struggling regime at Canton.

Japan encroached, but there was no one to pull the levers of national resistance. War lords at home plus foreigners banging on China's flimsy outside doors brought fresh suffering—Hunan lost half its pig population within ten years—and a wave of pessimism among the intellectuals.

---

*Mao actually began at Fourth Teachers Training School, but this was merged within a few months with First Teachers Training School, and lost its separate identity; by autumn 1913, then, Mao was a student at First.

China had tossed off the shell of the old but could not yet grasp the heart of the new.

The timing of all this was not bad for Mao. He was of necessity still on the balcony, not yet in a position to *do* anything about China's mess. It was a golden opportunity to get a good education and he seized it.

* * *

Mao joined four hundred other students in blue woolen uniforms amid the pillars, arches, and courtyards of a two-storied copy (of a Japanese copy) of a British colonial compound.

Like all colleges in China, First Teachers Training School (FTTS) was new, but it was well-heeled and its excellent teachers carried on Hunan's rich scholarly tradition.

An outer wall announced FTTS's motto: "Seek Truth from Facts." The facts were as eclectic as the architecture. Mao found himself reading Chinese history before lunch and German philosophy by siesta time.

Still thin, he seemed to half consist of his large, grave eyes. The hands and hair and shoes now bespoke a young intellectual. A long gray gown had replaced the coarse square tunic.* His speech and gestures remained deliberate. He did not become the voluble, snappy type of Chinese student whose hands compete with his mouth. At meetings he said little.

Mao sorted his way through a banquet of courses. Diffidence gave way to mastery—not yet of ideas, but of situations and of the tools to hone ideas.

"There were many regulations in the new school," Mao observed, "and I agreed with very few of them." At FTTS he trod a fine line between brilliance and disgrace. Reading a book in his dorm far into the night, he got a quilt too close to the oil lamp and started a small fire that charred a few bunks. Moved by the plight of a fellow student who found a marriage arranged over his unwilling head, he marched off to try to talk the parents out of their neat scheme.

It seems that at FTTS Mao was less often called Zedong than Runzhi, a nickname that means "the fertilizer" or "the lubricator."

What Mao despised—still-life drawing, natural sciences—he would not stir a finger to, suffering a grade of zero or close to it. What he liked—writing essays on literary and moral themes, and social sciences—he did with such flair and zest that he would often get a grade of 100.

It was not Mao's style to merely opt out of the sterile course in still-life drawing. He had to thumb his nose at it. In a drawing exam he scrawled an

---

*Though his bedding—each student supplied his own—was a peasant-style wraparound quilt, unusual at the school.

oval on the paper, titled it "Egg," and then left the hall. One day, with a brevity designed to permit him to leave class early, he merely drew a straight horizontal line with a semicircle above it and called it "Half Stone, Half Sun" (an allusion to a famous poem by Li Taibo of the Tang dynasty). He failed in still-life drawing.

Mao wrote passionate essays in the informal style of his reformer hero Liang. But the Chinese teacher, nicknamed Yuan the Big Beard, "despised Liang Qiqiao, who had been my model, and considered him half literate."

Yuan also said Mao was arrogant to put the date at the end of every piece he wrote. Once the teacher tore off the dated last page of a Mao essay as the whole class looked on. Mao rose, seized Yuan by the arm, asked him what the hell he was doing, and tried to march him off to the principal's office to "settle the issue reasonably."

Curiously, the youth who rebelled at most constraints did not rebel at being remolded to classicism. "I was obliged to alter my style," he said a bit disingenuously. Actually he took with spirit to the classical forms, favoring especially the tricks of the skeptical scholar Han Yu (768–824).

"Thanks to Yuan the Big Beard," Mao remarked to Edgar Snow twenty-two years later, "I can today still turn out a passable classical essay if required." (The "if required" comes with a sting, for Mao had by then begun his crusade against *other* people's old-style writing.)

So in literary style Mao reached backward, just at a time when in politics he moved rapidly ahead of the reformers. He dethroned Liang Qiqiao in a pincers movement of Classics and Revolution.

*   *   *

Mao's core education at FTTS consisted of moral philosophy plus newspapers—a lifelong double love.

Like most youths, Mao learned as much by example as by exhortation, and his ethical model from 1915 was a man with a rare skill for making disciples. A gentleman with a subversive streak—he spoke up for the right of widows to remarry, which shocked Changsha society—Yang Changji was a vessel of old China in the grip of the currents of new China.

Yang's ways were patriarchal—"Confucius" was his nickname, he read his lectures from a script, he did handicrafts—but he planted seeds that bore radical fruit in the minds of a generation hungry for meaning.

Yang revered Confucianism of the Song period (from the tenth century). But he had also spent four years in Britain and Germany drinking in the theories of Kant, T. H. Green, and other European idealists. What tied the two together was a belief in Mind and Will. Take thought, dare to act, and what is born in your mind will recolor the world. It was individualism, no doubt about it, but in the cause of social betterment.

No live mentor—unless it was Stalin, from a distance, in the 1930s and 1940s—ever made as much of a mark on Mao as this Chinese Ph.D. from Edinburgh. So roused was Mao by Yang's ethics class that he wrote 12,000 words of comment on the 100,000-word textbook *System of Ethics*, by the minor neo-Kantian F. Paulsen. At Yang's residence on Sundays Mao and other favored students would sit in silent awe throughout lunch. Mao later married Yang's daughter, whom he first met at those shy Sunday luncheons. As teacher, friend, father-in-law, Yang was well placed to make an impact on Mao.

On paper Mao served back Yang's moral athleticism. One enthusiastic essay, "The Energy of the Mind," received the fancy grade of "100 plus 5." Mao was thrilled with this result and told many people of it.

"A man of high moral character," the ex-student said much later of his professor. It was a rare accolade because it was free of class analysis.

Late at night Mao pored over Changsha and Shanghai newspapers in the school library. Other students would come to him for a weekly report on the crumbling situation in China and the latest twist in World War I.

For each tidbit from Europe—Verdun, Hindenburg's tactics, the harnessing of taxis in the defense of Paris—Mao would dig up an illustrative parallel from China's own history. He was a consultant in comparative "living history" (the term he used to describe the value of newspapers).

When any fellow student came searching for Mao, he would be advised to "look in the newspaper room."

Mao used part of his tiny allowance from Music Mountain to buy a personal copy of one paper (a habit his father called "wasted money on wasted paper"). He used to clip off the blank margins of this paper and tie the strips of newsprint together. On close inspection it turned out that Mao's strips were covered with the handwritten names of cities, rivers, mountains. Keeping a Chinese atlas and a world atlas at his elbow as he gorged on the news, he looked up each geographical name mentioned and then wrote it out.

Yang bent over his handicrafts: a moral therapy. Mao scanned newspapers: a door to social action that would later take him beyond Yang's moral universe to a life of violence. For the moment, German idealism and keen citizenship fitted well enough together, for a youth who still sat in a library.

*   *   *

It was in keeping with Yang's way that he should introduce Mao to the Society for the Study of Wang Fuzhi, a seventeenth-century patriot and philosopher of public service, as well as to *New Youth*, a magazine that jabbed the rapier of modern Western ideas through the ribs of China's rigid traditions.

Like Yang, Mao never lost his moorings in China's own civilization. If he jumped at Western ideas, he grasped them only as pills and Band-Aids for the sick Chinese body politic. "A country is an organic whole," Yang wrote, and Mao came to agree with the sentiment, "even as the human body is an organic whole. It is not like a machine, which can be taken apart and put together again."

Yang was a threshold figure of modern China. He was carried around Changsha in a three-man sedan chair, yet he swore by the discipline of taking cold baths and going without breakfast. Mao, though anti-feudal, drew from Yang a faith in rebirth by heroic effort.

He embraced a cult of the physical as his first means of trying to channel rebellion into social change. Flourishing the slogan "A civilized spirit, a barbarian body," he took cold baths in order to get rid of sedan chairs.

Mao (with friends) climbed the hills around Changsha, swam in icy ponds, took only one meal each day for a long period, soaked in the sun—he thought it would irradiate him with energy—and slept for much of the year in the school courtyard rather than in the dorm. All this to toughen himself.*

"Body training," as Mao called the physical feats, was far more unusual in China than in the West. For Mao it was more than a way to get fit. Why did he shout poems of the Tang dynasty into headwinds? Not only to train the voice, surely, but in exhilaration at will pitted against all resistance.

"To struggle against Heaven, what infinite joy!" Mao wrote in his diary, "to struggle against Earth, what infinite joy!"

That is the version in a translation of Emi Xiao's memoir. But the original Chinese has a third line, which some Marxist mind thought it wise to edit out: "To struggle against Men, what infinite joy!" The secret was not just hard bodies, but a sharper will to social struggle.

One night Mao burst into Cai Hesen's place soaking wet in the middle of a storm. He had just run down from the top of Changsha's famous Yue Lu mountain. Why, he was asked. Because Mao wished to get the feel of a sentence he had come across in the ancient *Book of History:* "Being sent down the great plains at the foot of the mountains, amid violent wind and rain and thunder, he did not go astray."

With Xiao You, the smart, smooth brother of Emi Xiao, Mao made a walking tour, in his second summer at FTTS, through five counties of South

*Nevertheless—and how much in character it was!—Mao despised the 10-minute period of formal physical exercises with dumbbells and wooden cudgels, and even wrote satirical attacks on these "mechanical" training sessions. Mao preferred to invent physical "tests" of his own.

of the Lake. This "wander and study" tour was inspired by a story he read in *Strength of the People* about two students who walked all over China as far as Tibet.

Mao and his friend took no money. They wrote clever couplets on scrolls for local gentry as a way of getting fed and housed during six weeks and 300 miles of trudging that taught Mao quite a bit about his province.

Mao, at 22, brought muscle and pen together. His first published article, "A Study of Physical Culture," came out in *New Youth*. He signed it "Mr. Twenty-eight Strokes" (it takes twenty-eight marks with a pen to write the three characters for "Mao Zedong").

The piece was strident: "Exercise should be savage and rude. To be able to leap on horseback and to shoot at the same time; to go from one battle to the next; to shake mountains by one's cry and change the colors of the sky by one's roar of anger; to have the strength to uproot mountains like Xiang You and pierce the target like You Chi—all this is savage and rude and has nothing to do with delicacy."

The argument was a chain of three links. Physical exertion is a celebration of the will, which is the link between body and mind. To steel the body is in the last analysis to prepare to fight. "The principal aim of physical education," Mao wrote, "is military heroism." The muscles and the fight and the joy are all for the Chinese nation's sake.

"Our nation is wanting in strength," ran Mao's first sentence, and the rest of the article explained how to meet the need.

There were no politics yet in Mao's lust for life. Only a Promethean sense of himself, face to face with a China that needed renewal. "I believed I could live for 200 years," he later recalled himself having said at this time.

It was as a student organizer that Mao pulled together the threads of his life at FTTS. From 1915 he became a prominent activist in the student union, and in 1917 he topped the list of 34 students elected (from an enrollment of 400) to run its affairs. To augment the union's budget, he hawked snacks in the street.

He stirred the union to fight red tape and harass the stuffy and corrupt principal—whom Mao called "Mr. Turn Back the Clock"*—though he trod the brink of expulsion in doing so. (Yuan the Big Beard, of all people, helped defend him; Mao's resolution won respect even from those it bruised.) He mobilized it to barricade the school against soldiers of both Hunan and northern war-lord armies who eyed the campus as a spot to squat and loot.

The union, with Mao to the fore, led protests against Japan's "Twenty-

Fu gu pai, literally "restore-the-old type."

one Demands" and other foreign acts of bullying against China. Mao now saw a dark side to Japan. He read a book, *Know Shame,* about the Japan-China crisis and on its cover he wrote: "To avenge this awful humiliation will be up to our generation." In a letter to a friend he asked: "How could our nation with a population of 400 million tolerate bullying by a nation of 3000 islands?"

Under the union's wing he began a night school for Changsha workers. "We are not wood or stone but men," he wrote in a street announcement for this poignant try at adult education. "We must seek a little knowledge if we are to be effective members of society." A style of work had filtered out of his personal experience. "You can wear any clothes you want," the announcement added. "Notebooks and all materials will be supplied free."

Mao had forgotten that few potential students could *read* his noble announcement.* He went knocking on doors to recruit students. Even so, the school lasted only a few months. Mao struggled valiantly. When the physics class sagged, he tried to revivify it by promising the students: "We will tell you how an electric light is able to shine and how steamboats and trains are able to move so fast."

During his senior year Mao took a step that showed his new confidence and a first touch of political ambition. "Feeling expansive and the need for a few intimate companions," he later recalled with marked disingenuousness, "I one day inserted an advertisement in a Changsha paper, inviting young men interested in patriotic work to make contact with me. I specified youths who were hardened and determined, and ready to make sacrifices for their country."† The last line of the advertisement was a quotation from the ancient *Book of Poetry: "Ying* goes the cry of a bird in search of his companion's voice."

Mao got only "three and a half replies." (The "half" was from Li Lisan, later a famous Communist leader with whom Mao clashed; Mao merely said dryly of Li's "noncommittal" reply: "Our friendship never developed.") Yet this seemingly naïve quest for patriotic youths led to momentous activity. Soon Mao put together a fully political organization called New People's Study Society (NPSS). It was the first red beacon in Hunan's sky.

"There are two kinds of people in the world," Mao observed one day to Emi Xiao. "Those who are good at individual things and those who are good at organization. There are more of the former than of the latter. However, everyone has his strong points."

---

*Mao kept a "Daily Record" of the night school's progress, written in *classical Chinese!*

†Other evidence makes it plain that Mao merely pinned his ad to a wall in a Changsha street. A newspaper picked it up and thought it worth publishing. Mao headed his original leaflet: "An Advertisement for Friends by 28 Strokes."

The genius of the organizer, Mao felt, lies in being able to meld together the strong points of an assortment of people. He should not show up, or carp upon, the weak points, but inspire a coalition of all traits that are positive. Mao's father failed to do that; Mao would succeed.

* * *

Mao graduated from FTTS in June 1918. Like others in his circle, he was socially afloat even as he attained inner strength. He was not only a dissenter; he was a misfit.

The reformers of the 1890s were dissenters too, yet they had an accepted niche within the society of their time. Liang Qiqiao was an outsider intellectually but not so in the warp and woof of his personal existence.

For Mao's generation old China was no more in one piece—even to be fired at. The Classics had little meaning in an era of war lords. Nor could Mao find his identity as a Westernized Chinese, like the Honolulu-educated Sun Yat-sen. He was nether fish nor fowl.

Yet Mao had turned his personal life around. He had ceased being blown about by other people's whims and had taken control of his own hours.

Mao had been a resounding success at FTTS. Yang ranked him as third best—Xiao You was first, Cai Hesen, also Mao's friend and later a meteor in the Chinese Communist Party (CCP), was second—among the thousands of students he taught at Changsha. In his last year, fellow students chose Mao as the school's model (the principal would not have done so!) for ethical quality, courage, and eloquence in speaking and writing. "A wizard," one fellow student called Mao; "a brain," wrote another.

His own views were emerging. He was lynx-eyed for the honor of China. He believed in individual self-assertion. And he had rejected the reformism of his previous heroes, Liang and Kang; something new must come, he now felt, in a thunderclap of change.

"How can China come to have a great philosophical and ethical revolutionary like Russia's Tolstoy?" Mao burst out one night in the home of Cai Hesen as the NPSS was being formed. "Who will purge the people's old thoughts and develop their new thoughts." But would new thoughts bring a new society?

Mao in these years rarely uttered the word "revolution," and when he did he meant by it only a sweeping away of the old. He was still only 24, after all, and malleable enough so that a teacher's influence—even Yuan the Big Beard's, not to speak of Yang's—could mark his mind for life.

Mao's style was to be a clarifier, and to be against any whiff of self-indulgent complacency. He was the knife in any situation. He would challenge and probe and test and defy.

During five and a half years at FTTS he wrote no less than one million words of analytic, opinionated notes in the margins of books or in copybooks. "Absurd," he would often inscribe in a margin, or "This doesn't make sense."

He loved the phrase "study-and-question" *(xue wen)*; to learn is to probe, he used to impress on Emi Xiao. When he conducted an interview with each of the "three and a half" respondents to his appeal for friends, he did not begin with a single word of greeting, but demanded to know right away what books the youth had recently read.

One day Mao visited the home of an NPSS friend who was rich. The youthful host broke off the political conversation to call in a servant and discuss the purchase and price of some meat. Mao was so irritated at the intrusion of housekeeping trivia upon the larger issue of China's future that he cut dead his friendship with the affluent youth.

Mao was a knife with himself no less than with others. His approach to self-cultivation was summed up in his habit of taking his books off to busy South Gate, not far from FTTS, there to study in the noisiest possible place as a test of his own concentration. It was one small way to be a hero.

If he couldn't yet shape the world around him, he *could* shape himself.

Unprogrammed, yes, but not alone.

At East Mountain Mao had stood out from others, but his isolation was bleak. By 1918 he still stood out, but his separateness was a vantage point for influence. Others were ready to follow him; his quirks were reborn as strategies. The pupil had become a leader.

Mao had been persistent. He had also pole-vaulted with the times. Tradition and authority, even at FTTS, were being stood on their head because they had lost credibility with a restless new elite-to-be. Mao was only a student leader. His radical plot was merely to take cold baths. But the nature of the times clinched a link that Mao himself perhaps could not yet see. Education; the body; a political revolution.

The three were linked because, given China's mess, knowledge was for action, and action would mean sweat and the gun. To be a student rebel and a physical fitness zealot at FTTS during World War I was by its own logic to take a big stride toward Marxism—rather Leninism—even though there was not in 1918 a single Marxist doctrine in Mao's tousled head.

He was a bundle of contradictions, to be sure. Literary solutions would not cure real life ills. Tradition and modernity could not sleep the whole night through in one bed. Wouldn't a cultivated individual bursting with energy in the end be a mere fly dashed against the wall of China's collective agony?

The future would pass a sword through these contradictions. Meanwhile

Mao had a credo. He had scribbled it in the margin of his copy of Paulsen's *System of Ethics*: "Wherever there is repression of the individual, wherever there are acts contrary to the nature of the individual, there can be no greater crime."

*   *   *

Mrs. Mao was ill with tuberculous inflammation of the lymphatic glands. Zemin, the middle brother, brought her from Music Mountain to Changsha for medical treatment in April 1918; Zetan, the youngest brother, was already in Changsha, where Mao had obtained for him a place at the primary school attached to FTTS.

In October Mrs. Mao died at 52 years of age. "More than ever," Mao said of his mother's death, "I lost interest in returning home." Briefly he went back to Music Mountain for the burial of his mother. A very large number of people attended the funeral.

Mao found that his father had saved enough money to be busy replacing the thatch roof on the family house with smart new tiles.

Mao wrote a Sacrificial Eulogy to his mother. It was in the old style and made up of Buddhist and Confucian sentiments in about equal parts:

The highest of my mother's virtues was her universal love.
She was kind to all human beings, whether closely or distantly related.
Her compassion and kindness moved the hearts of everyone.
The power of her love came from true sincerity.
She never lied or was deceitful.

Then Mao allowed himself a direct remembrance:

When we were sick she held our hands, her heart full of sorrow,
And she admonished us, "You should strive to be good."

4

Wider World in Peking and Shanghai (1918–1921)

Just short of his 26th birthday, Mao left his home province for the first time.

In *Romance of the Three Kingdoms* there are Three Heroes. Mao and two other students of Professor Yang modeled themselves on the same idea (*san ge hao jie*). Xiao You was one of them; the third was Cai Hesen, a militant youth from the home district of Mao's mother.

Yang left Changsha in 1918 for a prized chair at Peking University. From the capital he wrote to the "three heroes" about how work-study in the West could help save China. The New People's Study Society discussed the letter. Cai went up to Peking to represent Changsha in the scheme to go to France. Mao and 20 others followed in the autumn of 1918, first on foot, by boat as far as Wuhan, then in a train.

Mao had wanted to go to Peking anyway. With Yang as his bridge, *New Youth* magazine as his vehicle, he had moved to the fringes of the New Culture movement. "It has two principles," he said to Emi Xiao of the Peking-based magazine. "One is to oppose the old-style language [*gu wen*]. The other is to oppose the old moral teaching."

Peking looked grand but Mao's personal situation was the opposite. Like any college student who becomes a big fish in the small pond of school, he now felt the pain of being a small fish again. Until he could land a job, he was without money.

At first he slept in a hut with the gateman at Professor Yang's big house near Back Gate. Later, with seven other young Hunanese idealists, he rented a tiny room in a courtyard house in Three Eye Wall district.

The eight of them slept in a smelly row on the stove-cum-bed *(kang)* that is a feature of homes in the north. Mao recalled these nights as a sardine: "I used to have to warn people on each side of me when I wanted to turn over."

Peking was more expensive than Changsha. Buying fuel for the *kang* strained the octagonal purse. An overcoat each was out of the question. They bought one among the eight of them (the garment was as foreign to Hunanese as a fur to Floridians) and took turns wearing it in the bitter cold that soon gripped Peking.

How to get a job in this alien place? He went to ask the help of Professor Yang. Poor as Mao was, good schools in Hunan had given him contacts and skills. Yang wrote a note to the head of the library at Peking University. Was there a niche for a needy student involved in the work-study movement?

Reading *New Youth*, Mao had come to admire two authors above all. "They became for a while my models," he said. One of them, Professor Li Dazhao, turned out to be the university's chief librarian.

Mao got a job in the periodical room at eight dollars a month. The tasks were as lowly as the pay. Tidy the shelves; clean the room; write down the borrowers' names. For a man of 26 with a diploma from a teachers' training college, it was a nonjob.

In the eyes of Peking University, Mao was not the noted student from Changsha, but only two pale slim hands that kept magazines in their place. "My office was so low," Mao noted, "that people avoided me."

Busy at his three-drawered table under a high window, or padding among the shelves in his faded blue gown and cloth shoes, his big eyes missing nothing, Mao recognized—from the names in his register book—leading lights in the New Culture movement. "I tried to begin conversations with them on political and cultural subjects," he recalled poignantly, "but they were very busy men. They had no time to listen to an assistant librarian speaking southern dialect."

Mao's status was equally low elsewhere in the university. Lectures he could audit only if he kept his mouth shut. Once he ventured a question to Hu Shi, then a well-known radical, later a famous liberal and Chiang Kai-shek's ambassador in Washington. He inquired who the questioner was. Finding out that Mao was not a registered student, the radical-chic professor refused to talk to him.

But like a leech Mao stuck to any good thing around him. Avid to get a foot in the door of intellectual circles, he joined the Journalism Society and the Philosophy Society. Apt choices, for newspapers and moral ideas were his chief mental enthusiasms.

He met new people—among them Zhang Guotao, the boy from a landlord family just over the hills from Music Mountain—though none of them became intimates.

North China is not south China. Mao's twenty-five years had been lived completely within the world of the south. Hunan's ways of living are at least as different from Peking's as are Florida's from Montana's. Beyond the problems of environment—harsh winter, a different accent, dishes insufficiently spicy—there was a larger issue of psychology.

The north was the seat of the bureaucratic tradition. Here were mandarins who assumed a coolie never had a thought in his sweating head. They seemed terribly removed from the spirit of the folk who tilled the fields in Music Mountain.

Mao felt very local in 1918–1919. His lifelong ambivalence about the Peking way of life was born that winter.

Yet Mao made his own Peking. Keeping often to himself, he made a private magic of the city and its environs.

It was from a literary and antiquarian angle that he found a Peking he liked. He wandered in the parks and palaces. In the Western Hills and at the Great Wall he touched the stones of old China. Gazing at ice crystals hanging from the willows that lean over North Lake, he relived lines from Zhen Zhang, a Tang dynasty poet who had marveled at the same winter-jeweled scene. The Hunanese farm youth found a deeper identity within this time-dwarfing civilization.

The capital was in weekly political agonies but Mao seemed tuned to more elemental things. "The innumerable trees of Peking aroused my wonder and admiration." The Changsha iconoclast was edged out, for a season, by the dreamer who loved poems and misty hills and tales from China's past.

Mao decided not to go to France. Cai Hesen and other friends from Changsha sailed; Mao saw obstacles to joining them. A preparation for the trip was study of French, and Mao proved poor at it. Though the scheme was subsidized, each student was expected to put up a reduced fare, and Mao was already too much in debt to nudge his better-off acquaintances further.*

There may also have been the tug of Ms. Yang. Mao had been seeing the daughter of his old professor on visits to the comfortable Yang home and at meetings of the Journalism Society. Yang, a journalism student, had no plans to go and work in a French factory.

At bottom, Mao stayed home because his *will* to go abroad was not

* Mao's awkwardness and impecuniousness were reflected in an incident during a discussion in China Youth Association circles. "It's no good always sitting around talking about things," Mao burst out. "One must act. Give me your clothes and I'll wash them . . . big bundle or small, the price will be the same. After three days you'll get them back and pay me the money." No one said a word. Eventually the wife of one student found her tongue and joked that Mao, as a gentleman, wouldn't be able to wash clothes well. Another student, afraid that Mao was getting embarrassed, said: "Tomorrow, come and do my laundry. We'll see if you can do it well or not." Mao did the job—and no doubt appreciated the money.

strong enough. The obstacles were allowed to stand because Mao did not really believe the key to his—or China's—future lay in the West. His mind was on the legends, the beauty, and the recent humiliations of China.

Allowing for a strange double quality of modesty and primness in the statement, we can accept Mao's own reason for passing up the voyage to Marseilles: "I felt that I did not know enough about my own country, and that my time could be spent more profitably in China." The decision was the fruit of an attitude already fixed. At the same time it had consequences that were to intensify Mao's nativism.

Meanwhile, in Tianjin, 120 miles to the east, a young man called Zhou Enlai made an opposite decision and sailed for Europe.

* * *

The Chinese Revolution began in a library. A doctrine was needed to give direction to the formless revolt against the old. One had long existed—since Karl Marx sat in another, British library, when Mao's grandfather was a boy. Bits of it had even been translated into Chinese not long before World War I. But only with the Bolshevik Revolution did the doctrine come alive for Chinese minds.

Marx was one thing. An interesting theory with a message mainly for the advanced countries. Lenin was quite another cup of tea. If backward Russia could make a Marxist revolution, and if imperialism by its own logic was going to provoke socialism (as Lenin said it would), might not China be part of the action? Maybe those difficult essays by Marx were worth a more careful look? So after 1917 a few keen Chinese hunted down Marxist articles and pamphlets in Mao's library.

Mao could read to his fill without buying so much as a daily paper—a boon for his pitiful budget—and for the first time he read Marx and Lenin.

Yet Mao failed to get hold of Marxism that winter. The idea that bubbled highest in the cauldron of his mind was anarchism. He read more Kropotkin than Marx. He understood the passionate Russian more readily than the systematic German.

Like any anarchist, Mao knew better what he was against than what he was for. As yet he had no intellectual weapon to attack militarism and imperialism with. In personal terms too, anarchism was a fit doctrine for the unconnected existence Mao led that winter.

In the spring of 1919, Peking erupted in a student demonstration—to be called the May Fourth movement—that brought to a peak all the themes of *New Youth*. But Mao was out of step. He was in one of his clouded moods, when resolve does not quite surface. He turned in upon himself at the very moment when a public cause gripped the Peking student body. He left Peking, alone, and for an unexpected destination.

As the students tore strips off Confucianism, Mao went to visit Confucius's grave in Shandong Province.

"I saw the small stream where Confucius's disciples bathed their feet," he related, "and the little town where the sage lived as a child." He climbed sacred Mount Tai. He inspected the birthplace of Mencius. The tour took him through territory—Liang Shan county—where his heroes of the novel *Story of the Marshes* had performed their exploits.

As the radicals in Peking declared the Old a heap of refuse, Mao indulged himself at founts of the Old. On May Fourth the first mass movement of intellectuals in Chinese history took shape, to burn tradition and to defy Japan's arrogance toward China. But Mao was in touch only with the hills and walls of China.

After stops at the holy places of Confucianism, Mao continued—by train, once he ran into a student friend and borrowed enough for the ticket—to Xuzhou, where he poked into haunts made famous in *Romance of the Three Kingdoms*, and to Nanjing, where he walked around the ancient city walls. He was robbed of his only pair of shoes and had to borrow yet again for a ticket to Shanghai.

The journey seemed to eclipse the goal—to get to Shanghai. Mao said his purpose was to see off a work-study group bound for France; this he did at the Shanghai docks. However, he did not travel from Peking with any of the group, and his own pilgrimage to feudal high spots took several weeks.

Clear at any rate that Mao had not found Peking gripping enough to stay there longer than six months.

Shanghai was a toehold of the West that had emerged from World War I as China's biggest city (2 million people). It was a city with business in its blood. Mao did not take to Shanghai; it had no tombs and shrines and mountains to intrigue him.

He went to see his second "model" from the pages of *New Youth*, Professor Chen Duxiu, a literature scholar from Peking who had moved to Shanghai in 1917 under the whip of war-lord repression. A seed was planted for future contact, yet this first meeting set neither man on fire.

Mao walked the streets, read newspapers, looked up Hunanese friends.

His mind was straying back to events in Changsha. It came as good news when the group organizing work-study in France gave him money to go back to Hunan. Mao wrapped up his cloth packets in April 1919 and made the complicated foot-train-steamer journey to Changsha.

* * *

For a while Mao was very hard up. He found a bed at a hostel of Hunan University meant as a way station for potential enrollees. Soon he took on some part-time history teaching at a primary school run by the teachers' college from which he had graduated. Mao had too many *causes* to really want a regular job.

So his body made do at a level below conventionality while his mind soared above conventionality. His big feet shuffled about in straw sandals, a cheap substitute for shoes, fit only for summer weather. He ate mainly a mush of broad beans and rice. He relied on others in his usual unblushing way.

It turned out that the north had left its mark on him. Silent in Peking, he now had a lot to say in Changsha. His first venture was a public lecture on the newfangled idea called *Ma-ke-se zhu-yi* (Marxism), which he knew a bit about but only a bit.

During the second half of 1919 Mao became a spearhead for New Culture and anti-imperialism—May Fourth's twin themes—in the Changsha area. Chief target was the war-lord ruler of Hunan, Zhang Jingyao, a caricature of the half-feudal, pro-Japan fudger that made May Fourth students see red.

Mao took the lead in the Changsha wing of May Fourth with two well-run undertakings. As the sun baked Changsha in June, he helped bring to birth a United Students Association of Hunan.

The social atmosphere of this student movement has never been quite matched for ardor; not in China, nor in the U.S. during the 1960s. Schools were closed half the time (ideological "truth" pushed out factual truth). All night long manifestoes were drawn up for yet one more demonstration the next day. Toothbrushes in pockets, carrying umbrellas with towels wrapped around them, students fanned out from Changsha to link up with the like-minded elsewhere. Nearly everyone was in a state of war with his or her family. Crudely printed little magazines appeared, with titles that conveyed the mood of uplift: *Awakening, Women's Bell, New Culture, Warm Tide, Upward, Strife, New Voice.*

By the standards of the 1960s these students were not modern at all. Most of them were gentlemen in gowns who did not squirm to give orders to a servant. Yet if they had one foot in tradition, their words were virulent against tradition. Like some evangelical Christians in the U.S., they lived the life of everyone around them, but snorted with disgust at the polluting threat of it all to their clear pure inner light.

A student cut off two fingers as his personal protest against Governor Zhang's brutal methods. Thirteen-year old Ding Ling, later to be one of China's best short-story writers, led her class to the chambers of the Hunan Provincial Council to demand for women the equal right to inherit property. The younger they were, the fewer doubts they had.

Mao spoke to a rally on the theme "Use National Products: Resist Japanese Goods," not facing the fact that Chinese products were inadequate to the people's needs. He organized teams of girls—from the start he brought women into the heart of the United Students Association of Hunan—to inspect Changsha shops and browbeat the owners into destroying Japanese imports.

Mao later recalled that "No one had time for love." It was true that women and men slept chastely side by side. An hour or two's repose after a night of political busyness did not lend itself to caresses. Mao, "three heroes" member Cai Hesen and his bright and pretty sister Cai Chang, swore a triangular oath never to marry.* All three broke it and Mao broke it three times.

It is not that the trio were insincere. Rather they were operating on a number of levels at once and—like the evangelicals in the U.S.—they did not blush to live within contradictions. They *thought* they had no time for love. But love crept in; often it gave the flavor to all they were doing.

The students' social situation made them a bundle of contradictions. They were a humiliated generation. The breakup of the old had made them rootless. The travail of their nation had made them desperate.

Being terrorists against old China required a boldness that ran away with itself. A group hurled a soft melon carefully filled with dog shit on the head of a pompous official making a public appearance. The crowd laughed. A spell was broken. The dirty melon had done wonders. It was not that difficult to call a bluff on the China of 1919.

*　*　*

During this stormy summer Mao, acting for the students' association, founded, edited, and wrote large portions of a weekly which he characteristically named after nature: *Xiang River Review*. Two thousand copies of the *Review*'s first issue were sold in a single day and five thousand copies of subsequent issues were printed (a big print run for Hunan in 1919).

The magazine set its type where its mouth was. Expressing a cultural aim of May Fourth, it used "plain talk" (*bai hua*), the language much as it is spoken, rather than the rigid archaic form (*wen yan*). The change was like replacing the language of the King James version of the Bible with that of *Jesus Christ Superstar*.

It was true, as even Professor Hu Shi said, that Mao was an arresting writer. His paragraphs, drafted on thin, red-ruled paper, were blunt and vivid. His avid newspaper reading bore fruit in detailed illustrations for each point.

"The movement for the liberation of mankind has shot forward," editor

* While a student of Professor Yang's, Mao once made a note that he heartily agreed with the view of two philosopher brothers of the Song dynasty that "a man isn't worth talking about if he is not able to overcome the twin crises of money and sex."

Mao declared in his inaugural piece. "What are the things which we should not be afraid of?" He gave an answer which showed the supermarket nature of his mind at that time: "We should not be afraid of Heaven, of gods, of ghosts, of the dead, and of war lords and capitalists."

In a Chinese paper we find a recollection of Mao the editor—too rosy, yet informative—by a fellow teacher at the primary school.

> He often had to write at night, as he was busy with many callers during the day. The room he occupied at Xiu Ye Primary School was next to mine, separated by only a thin partition. Often, when I woke up in the night from my sleep, I could see him writing, oblivious of the oppressive heat of summer and the harassing bites of mosquitoes. After he finished writing his articles, he had to go to the printing press to give instructions and then do the proofreading himself. Sometimes he would take a number of copies to sell them in the street. It was a hard life for him then. The pay he received from Xiu Ye Primary School was only a few dollars a month, and he had nothing left after paying for his meals. His personal effects included an old mosquito net, an old cotton-padded quilt, an old bamboo mat on which he slept, several books, which he also used as pillows at night, and a long gown, of some grayish material, and white trousers, which were the worse for wear.

Mao wrote an article called "Great Union of the Popular Masses" which summed up his views. It was eloquent, populist, and patriotic. Not a bit Marxist, it was nevertheless sharply different from his "Study of Physical Culture" of two years previously.

Mao began with a dire diagnosis: "The decadence of the state, the sufferings of humanity, and the darkness of society have all reached an extreme." He no longer saw steeled individuals as the solution. Such self-cultivated monks—first among them Mao Zedong—would be needed to *lead* China's climb out of darkness. But Mao did not broach leadership in "Great Union of the Popular Masses."

He rabble-roused for the widest possible support. He called people from all strata to join hands and "shout" against oppression. The union was to be part mystical and part organizational. Solidarity was the key. The 1911 revolution had not involved the ordinary people—the next one must.

Marx was mentioned ("the German, Marx") in order to be compared unfavorably to Mao's favorite anarchist ("the Russian, Kropotkin"). Mao said the standpoint of Marx was "extremely violent." The more moderate standpoint of Kropotkin might not yield overnight results. But its supreme virtue was that it "begins by understanding the common people."

The piece was revolutionary, but in the Changsha of 1919 Marx seemed no more logical as theorist in chief of revolution than a half-dozen others. Mao had a vision of a more just social order. He had a sharp organizational instinct. But he did not yet have an ideology.

Mao had in mind a series of unions that would converge into a revolutionary tide. Their cause was simple: "to resist powerful people . . . who harm their fellow men." Women, rickshaw pullers, peasants, students; everyone was there—and the categories did not follow class lines.

As Mao took up the plight of these groups—speaking in the first person for each—he was most excited by that of students:

> Our teachers of Chinese are such obstinate pedants. They are constantly mouthing expressions such as "We read in the Book of Poetry" or "Confucius says," but when you come down to it, in fact, they don't understand a word. They are not aware that this is already the twentieth century; they still compel us to observe "old rites" and follow "old regulations." They forcibly impregnate our minds with a lot of stinking corpselike dead writings full of classical allusions.

At school Mao had called the bluff on teachers who were out of touch. Now he would do the same in society at large. "If we can only give a shout together," he vowed, "we will shatter the force of history which habit is."

The article won praise from Professor Li Dazhao's own magazine, *Weekly Critic* ("It is an unexpected pleasure to see such an excellent brother periodical"). It inspired the formation in Changsha of an unwieldy coalition called Hunan United Association of All Circles.*

In starting to publish his views Mao crossed a threshold. One thing to read and study and write 10,000 words of notes in the margins of a textbook. Quite a fresh thing to take a stand in public. This was action, it was confession, it had consequences. Mao was no longer merely exploring the world around him, but taking steps to shape it.

It was one of war lord Zhang's habits to extinguish left-wing magazines as a janitor turns out lights during an energy crisis. An armed detachment arrived one midnight at the Graceful Xiang Printing Company. The *Review* was dead after five issues and its parent, the United Students Association of Hunan, was stamped out the same night.

Small magazines were then like birds that flew by and were gone. Mao soon joined himself to the flight of another one, *New Hunan*. Run by medical students of Yale-in-China, equally a voice of May Fourth, it was short of help during the summer months and welcomed Mao as editor. Begun in June, taken over by Mao in August, it died the same death as the *Review* in October—but not before attracting some more favorable leftist national attention for Mao's pen.

---

* Mao's *Review* column on Western affairs was always vigorous and sometimes quaint. "The only way out" for Germany was to unite with Russia, Austria, and Czechoslovakia in a "Communist republic." He commented on the French prime minister after Versailles: "Clemenceau, that ignorant old man, still holds onto his thick gray-yellow pamphlet [the Paris Peace Treaty] thinking that, names signed on it, it is as solid as the Alps."

* * *

He was well enough launched now as a political writer that his pieces were taken by *Great Welfare Daily*, the leading Changsha paper. Suddenly there was a fresh cause to write about.

A Miss Zhao of Changsha was to be married. She did not like the man chosen for her. But all four parents—her father was a spectacle-maker, the young man's father ran a curio shop—insisted on their carefully arranged match. Came the wedding day. Dressed in her finery, Miss Zhao was borne aloft in a bridal sedan chair. The stiff parade marched off toward the groom's home. In a flash, Miss Zhao pulled out a razor from under her petticoats and slit her throat.

Within two days of the tragedy, Mao was in print with "A Critique of Miss Zhao's Suicide." Eight more articles by him on marriage, family oppression, and the evil of the old society peppered the columns of *Great Welfare Daily* over the next two weeks.

As so often, Mao dug from his own life the root of a social conviction.

He blamed society. "The circumstances of an event provide all the causes of its occurrence." Even in translation his prose thumps down: "The circumstances were the rotten marriage system, the benighted social system, thought which cannot be independent, love which cannot be free." He called Zhao's bridal sedan chair a "prisoner's cart."

One sniffs between the lines of these nine articles Mao's own arranged marriage and his mother's meek submission to a man for whom the term "male chauvinism" would be the understatement of the Chinese Revolution.

Mao assumed a paternal air with his "Advice to Boys and Girls on the Marriage Problem." In another piece he begged his readers to "shout" and thus bring down the house of cards that is superstition. Boldness as its own reward was already one of his beliefs. "Everyone regards predestined marriage as a sort of 'beautiful destiny.' *No one has ever imagined that it is all a mistake*."

He began his lifelong opposition to suicide in any situation. "If in the end one does not succeed, one's energies are wholly spent and one dies in battle like the lost jade, this after all is true courage and the sort of tragedy which satisfies most." To kill oneself as Miss Zhao did was not to oppose the corrupt old society. It was to affirm that doomed order, to fit in with it. Struggle, do not commit suicide, Mao laid down.*

Mao swiped at shrines to female chastity, which were in those days thought impressive: "Where are the shrines for chaste boys?" asked the

---

* The nine articles were not Marxist. Like "Great Union of the Popular Masses," they have been omitted from the crystallized wisdom of Chairman Mao's *Selected Works*.

man who was almost certainly still a virgin. Next thing, he had girls out in the street cajoling housewives to reject Japanese goods, and drumming up support for a strike to thwart war lord Zhang.

In Mao's mind the link went back to the name of his New People's Study Society. The women's movement was a bid for new people. But Mao was coming close to the viewpoint that a *new society* was the ultimate goal.

Mao and his friends were on a collision course with Zhang's Hunan regime and December 1919 brought the crunch. Zhang's troops used swords and rifle butts to disperse a crowd making a bonfire of Japanese goods at Education Square. Late-night planning meetings followed one after the other. Mao wrote a manifesto urging the overthrow of pro-Japan, feudal, butcher Zhang.

Thirteen thousand students and their allies signed Mao's document. A Changsha-wide strike began; the issue was joined. Zhang was not overthrown—though his regime was bruised—and the trail was hot for Mao and other leaders.

Mao decided to leave Hunan: to escape Zhang, who now felt a personal fury for him, and to seek support in anti-war-lord circles outside Hunan for the anti-Zhang cause.

*　*　*

Mao went back to Peking. Four months there were a time of harvest for him, though not in fully expected ways.

It was the New People's Study Society that sent Mao north, as head of a 100-person Delegation of Petitioners for the Dismissal of Zhang. Mao had assignments, too, from *Great Welfare Daily* and other organs. He wasn't penniless this time.

After a ten-day stop in Wuhan—where Mao took voluminous notes on local conditions—the group arrived in Peking in time for an anti-Zhang rally of one thousand people at the guildhall of Xiang Xiang county. Mao came up with a slogan for the rally: "The Hunan people cannot live unless Zhang departs."

Mao rented part of the old and crumbling Fuyu lamasery on North Avenue by the moat of the Imperial Palace. He slept in the main hall of the unheated temple, under the eyes of gilded Tibetan gods. His desk for night reading and writing was an incense table made eerie by the glow of an oil lamp. A mimeograph machine—chalice of the new era of political organizing—stood by the incense table. It formed the plant for what the young provincial politician grandly called Common People's News Agency.

Mao did not achieve much for the anti-Zhang cause. Peking was a wider world in the grip of larger concerns: the downward spiral of a "national" government headed by a glorified war lord; global gyrations after Versailles; echoes of the Bolshevik Revolution; the playing out of May Fourth's themes. Mao knocked on many doors but often got a glazed look when he broached Hunan's affairs.

Mao's first Peking harvest was Miss Yang. Eight years younger than Mao, Yang Kaihui was a slight girl, with a round face and a very pale complexion for a Chinese. Mao's affection for her had grown during his previous stay in Peking. Now things advanced a stage further.

Professor Yang died a month after Mao reached the capital, and the loss seemed to clear Mao's way to physical intimacy with Kaihui.

The life of the couple began as a "trial marriage," which Professor Yang might not have liked, but in Peking they did not set up house together. They met amid the statues in Mao's feudal chamber on North Avenue, or at the warmer and more comfortable Yang family home. When spring came they would go for a pony ride along the ridges of the Western Hills and find a quiet niche. It seems that their first child was born less than one year after that Peking spring.

The Mao-Yang match, in the spirit of May Fourth, was born of free choice by the two parties, which had been rare in old China. The actual ceremony of marriage, a year or so later in Changsha, meant so little to them that no one recalled it. Even Mao, talking to Edgar Snow in 1936, could not put an accurate date on it.

Miss Zhao in Changsha had not lived to carry forward May Fourth values. Miss Yang opted for a struggle to express them in a political movement. The dead Miss Zhao had stirred Mao's pen; the living Miss Yang stirred his loins. Yang redeemed Zhao's suicide, joining flesh with spirit, helping Mao during the 1920s to match the pen with the gun.

*   *   *

At his incense table in the lama temple Mao read the *Communist Manifesto* (in translation, as he had to read everything that mattered to him). This time the ideas of Marx and Engels hit home. It was partly that the *Manifesto*—the first part of it appeared in Chinese in November 1919—was the most compelling of the Marxian works so far in Chinese. It was partly that the Russian Revolution, as analyzed by Professor Li Dazhao and others, had put a new sheen on Marxism in the eyes of a Chinese.

Russia became a beacon for Mao, as France was for English radicals of the 1790s. The theories of Marx he grasped only gradually. But the Bolshevik success got to his gut.

He declared his enthusiasm for the new Russia to a young lady, who rejoined: "It's all very well to say establish communism, but lots of heads are going to fall." Mao came back excitedly: "Heads will fall, heads will be chopped off, of course, of course. But just think how good communism is! The state won't bother us anymore, you women will be free, marriage problems won't plague you anymore!"

Marxism came to Mao as an idea about how history moves from one stage to the next.

Mao had little idea of the social future that revolution would usher in. Nor had he focused on the nuts and bolts of organizing the seizure of power. *But he did in 1920 embrace Marxism as belief in China's rendezvous with Russian-type revolution.*

Thus would the nation be saved, backwardness be conquered, the energies of a cowed people released, the will of May Fourth heroes given a proper social outlet.

*   *   *

Marxism is never merely transmitted, like an instruction or a disease, from one historical situation to another. It is reborn in the new place. So in Mao's case. The mental seeds of his brand of Marxism existed as he became a pro-liberation child of *New Youth* magazine from 1916. Marxism as a live hope for revolution in China came as a vision from St. Petersburg. Assimilation of the doctrines of Marx and Engels and Lenin occurred only as a third stage.

"Three books especially deeply carved my mind," said Mao of his second winter in Peking, "and built up in me a faith in Marxism." As well as the *Manifesto* there was one of Kautsky's works and *History of Socialism* by Kirkup. The second two did not give Mao a very pure dose of Marxism.*

But Mao had the "faith." From the summer of 1920 he considered himself a Marxist and thereafter he never wavered from that self-identification. Anarchism, reformism, utopianism, were all squeezed out as frameworks for his political thought.

That Mao did not swallow Marx and become a new creation overnight is clear from his continued preoccupation with the movement for Hunan autonomy. In April he left Peking and one reason was that he could do little there for Hunan.

Following her father's death, Yang Kaihui had moved with her mother back to Changsha. Mao vaguely planned to rejoin her there when he could, and when the Hunan political mood permitted.

For the moment he wished to talk over his new Marxist faith with Profes-

---

*Lenin, at least, had long since written Kautsky off as an anti-Marxist; Kirkup's rag-bag book has no ideological cutting edge.

sor Chen. Selling his winter coat to buy the train ticket, he set off for Shanghai, with an unsorted basket of aims.

*   *   *

Mao was hard up so he washed and ironed and delivered clothes for taipans and rich compradors.

As a laundry helper he was paid twelve to fifteen dollars a month. About eight dollars of this went on tram fares to take the finished garments back to mansions and hotels. If he seldom smiled on Shanghai later in life, one can guess why.

Mao tried to enlist Chen Duxiu's help on Hunan issues, but the revolutionary professor had bigger matters on hand. Russian advisers had arrived in China, sent by the newly founded Communist International, to consult Li and Chen about concrete steps toward a Bolshevik organization in China.

Chen was that spring the greatest single Marxist influence Mao ever knew. "His own assertions of belief," Mao said later of this ex-Peking iconoclast, "deeply impressed me at what was probably a critical period in my life." No doubt the laundry added to Mao's Marxist education by helping him see what Marx meant by the term "proletariat."

Mao went down to the docks to say farewell to a work-study group of Hunanese bound for France. The sun gleamed on the muddy ripples of the Whangpu River. Horns and shouts and the clatter of cargo filled the steamy air. Mao was wearing a gray cotton gown now almost ivory after much pounding in the wooden tubs of his own laundry.

Before sailing, the group held a meeting of the New People's Study Society in nearby Pansong Park. Mao spoke. He offered the slogan "To Transform China and the World." The meeting appointed him to return to Changsha as Hunan chief of the work-study program. A group photo was gravely taken. Everyone strolled back along the banks of Wusong Creek to the French cargo ship.

Girls were among those sailing. It had been a major contribution of Mao's to build up female participation in the program. "Each one you take with you," he had said to a Hunan friend who was leading a female group, "is one you save." His hatred of old China was focused, once more, in his feelings about the plight of women.

One student expressed regret that Mao was not also sailing for France. Mao responded: "The revolution cannot be postponed till your return from abroad."

Mao was alone on the sloping jetty facing the group lined up at the rail of the ship's fourth-class deck. Before turning back toward the city he called out: "Study hard to save the country."

* * *

A virtual civil war had been going on in Hunan, but in the summer of 1920 it ended with the ouster of Zhang by the more progressive Tan Yen-kai. Mao went back to Changsha full of political plans to take advantage of a newly liberal mood.

The man Tan chose to take over the troubled First Teachers Training School happened to be one of Mao's old teachers. This educator soon made Mao director of FTTS's primary school, Xiu Ye, where he'd taught a class while editing *Xiang River Review*. Moreover, now that Cai Hesen and other Hunan stars were busy in French factories, Mao was unchallenged leader of the New People's Study Society.

The pay was good at Xiu Ye and the directorship had prestige. Mao quickly showed that he did not value austerity for its own sake. He settled with Miss Yang into Clear Water Pond house, a quiet and elegant ex-land-lord's residence set in a garden. The rent was twelve dollars a month, the same as his entire wage at the Shanghai laundry, 50 percent above his wage at the library of Peking University. In outward trappings Mao was part of the Changsha establishment.

The period 1920-1921 was a time of aligning thought and action. It brought a new focus to his political life. It also brought pain to certain of his relationships.

He pushed ahead with May Fourth–type projects. He started a Young People's Library and (with others) put back together the United Students Association of Hunan. Visiting Music Mountain for a few weeks, he brought the torch of New Culture to his home county by establishing an Education Promotion Society. He wrote and edited at *Popular Daily*, a semi-official educational organ, after a friend of his, He Shuheng, gained control of it and pulled it to the left.

Helped by a girl he was fond of—another one of Professor Yang's best students—Mao set up a Cultural Bookstore to seed Hunan with left-wing literature. "The people of Hunan are more starved in the mind than in the stomach," ran Mao's announcement about the shop.

Mao wangled three rooms at low rent for the Cultural Bookstore from Yale-in-China. He received financial support from Kaihui's mother. He even got war lord Tan to write the signboard for the shop in his fine brush strokes, and to preside over the opening ceremony. Subversion and the sta-tus quo rubbed shoulders for an afternoon.*

The bookstore did well and grew seven branches in other towns. In its early days the best-selling items (all in Chinese) included Kirkup's *History*

---

*Mao set up a cotton mill in an effort to raise funds for the left-wing cause, but it did badly.

of Socialism, a pamphlet that introduced Marx's *Capital, A Study of the New Russia*, and the magazines *New Youth, New Life, New Education,* and *Labor Circles*.

Mao added pro-Russia spice to May Fourth themes. With He Shuheng of *Popular Daily* he started a Russian Affairs Study Group and a scheme for work-study in Russia. Under the influence of his Marxist faith, he tried to get a handle on labor union organizing. Prompted by Comintern advice, which reached him by letter from Shanghai and Peking, he began a Communist cell. Also a branch of the Socialist Youth Corps, an anteroom for looking over potential Communists.*

When He Shuheng was fired from the Education Bureau in May 1921, and the radicals at *Popular Daily* were booted out with him, Mao appointed many of them as teachers in his own primary school. If there was a strike, students made up its core. Schoolteachers were the red thread holding together the broadening flaps of Mao's Marxist tent.

FTTS itself was crucial to the network. Mao recruited new followers by the month from its classrooms, relied on its salaries for the bread and butter of several co-leaders, used the fine facilities of its Alumni Association for meetings, raised gifts of ten dollars a head there for his Cultural Bookstore, had young people going in and out of its library as if it were a bus station. FTTS was like an extended family for Mao the budding Communist.

Mao's own family members were sucked in too. Mao's father died in 1920 of typhoid at the age of 52—an event Mao seldom mentioned except to remark that few people attended the funeral—and Mao quietly took up the reins as his heir. He arranged for Zemin, the second brother, to go to FTTS, and Zetan, the third boy, to get into a good middle school. His adopted sister, Zejian, he placed in a teachers' training school in the nearby city of Hengyang.

All three were before long working directly under Mao in Communist organizations. Mao at times ordered them around as if he had stepped, all too fully, into the shoes of his father.

Mao was no longer alone. He wrote and received a stream of letters from co-workers in Shanghai, Peking and France. He was a big fish in the medium-sized pond of Changsha. Around the province he had reliable ties. He lived as man and wife with Kaihui, who was soon pregnant.

*   *   *

*One early member of the corps and one of the first Hunanese to go under the Russia work-study scheme to the University of Toilers of the Far East in Moscow was a studious boy from a landlord family in Ning Xiang county. He had graduated from First Teachers Training School five years after Mao. The two had met on work-study affairs during Mao's first winter in Peking. His name was Liu Shaoqi.

Mao's main writing for 1920 was a series of articles in favor of making Hunan an independent republic. The last twitch of Mao's localism? Yes, but a vigorous twitch, and a mirror to the whole man.

While at the laundry in Shanghai, he had linked up with a Hunanese activist who edited a weekly called *Heaven Asks*, and with the Hunan Society for the Promotion of Reform. Now that Tan was governor, Mao and others wanted him to secure self-government "and not again allow the tiger [Peking] to enter the house."

Mao's articles on this topic were on his old wavelength of liberation. No Marxist note was struck (the pieces are not in Mao's *Selected Works*). Nor were social goals for a future separate Hunan set forth. A burden was simply to be lifted from the back of Hunan.

The argument Mao made was an application of the argument against imperialism. He used "foreign" to mean "non-Hunanese." He urged a string of "27 little Chinas" because "big statism" is an evil which hinders the "natural development" of grass-roots life.

Mao's idea, to be sure, was that once the 27 provinces got their house in order, a larger and more glorious China would then exist. "This is just like the road from division to unity followed by America and Germany."

Yet for one who was already a fierce Chinese nationalist, his embrace of the smaller cause was astonishing—and judged mistaken by some of his left-wing friends.

"For 4,000 years of history," he lamented, "Hunanese have not straightened their backs. They have vomited more than breathed. Hunan's history is just a history of darkness. Hunan's culture is just a culture of ashes. This is the result of 4,000 years of Hunan's subjugation to China."

Peking, with its feeble "national" government (and its frigid winters and scorn for a southern accent) was certainly taking a beating.

By the spring of 1921 Mao had lost his zeal for Hunan self-government. A war lord was a shaky base for a radical's hopes. Tan was replaced in November 1920 and the new ruler squeezed out any notion of liberation of the people from the self-government cause.

Within weeks Mao led an assault on the provincial parliament, tearing down scrolls and banners from its elegant walls. He had learned a lesson in the limits of reform politics. He would have to organize *outside* existing political circles.

* * *

Xiao You saw Mao again after a work-study stay in France. They talked into the night. Both wept, for they found a gulf had come between them. Mao was pro-Russia. Xiao was not. Mao spoke for strong authority. Xiao feared for individual freedom.

Mao was bent on organizing to seize power. Xiao was still at heart a pedagogue. He said to Mao: "Mighty struggles such as that of Liu Bang and Xiang You [two rival politicians of the Han dynasty] are, in the eyes of Christ and Buddha, like two street urchins fighting for an apple."

Mao merely rejoined: "What a pity that you disagree with the theory of Karl Marx." The old unity of the New People's Study Society as a band of brothers was a thing of the past.

Amid a snowstorm in early 1921 the NPSS held a climactic three-day meeting in the rooms of the Cultural Bookstore. Mao urged the goal of "transformation," as against "reform." He argued for the method of the Russian Revolution, as against "several dozen years of education."

He was opposed by most of those who had been in France, and by those who were still in France and sent their views by letter. It seems that he lost the battle, for he declared that the NPSS had "fulfilled its historical mission."

But in a sense he won the war. He switched his base. He took his like-minded faction into the Socialist Youth Corps and tossed away the NPSS like a husk.

The May Fourth movement had split in two. The issues were those that divided Mao and Xiao. A debate in *New Youth* circles during 1919 already summed them up: "Isms" or "problems"? Was the task of the intellectual rational analysis of particular problems? Or was it to show the way to action by designing an overarching ideology?

Professor Hu Shi led a liberal wing of May Fourth, which stuck to "problems" and kept a detached stance toward politics. Professor Li Dazhao led a Marxist wing, which insisted on one all-embracing "ism."

Never much doubt that Mao would be on the side of "isms."* He wanted a split. If tying May Fourth to a particular ideology meant breaking it up, then the break was a great thing. Another split loomed too.

Anarchism was "in" by 1920. A number of groups were well stocked with bright young people who believed only in utter freedom: Rains of Hunan Poetry Club, Health Book Society, Youth Society, and (strongest of all) the Workers Association.

Mao knew the creed well—it had seduced him in Peking in 1918–1919—but in his mind Marx had edged out Kropotkin. He fought brutally against the Workers Association.

Mao threw the book of Marx-Lenin against its leading lights, using Engels's *Socialism: From Utopian to Scientific*. He cajoled. He ridiculed the

* Hu, eschewing ideology, called for a "government of good people"—it was the same idealistic eclecticism that had once led Mao to urge Sun as president, Kang as premier, and Liang as foreign minister.

impulse to "abolish the state in 24 hours." He threw the stones of sabotage. And each time he saved a lamb from anarchism he brought him into the tight fold of the Socialist Youth Corps.

Isolated and a bit alienated in Peking, he had leaned toward anarchism. Now that he was in his stride as a key leader of the Changsha left, he saw anarchism as a vexing indulgence.

* * *

In the summer of 1921 Mao took a boat north; the trip was a culmination of ten months of organizing in Changsha.

As a preparation there had been the Marxist and Russia clubs to draw in talent. Then a split in the NPSS. A Socialist Youth Corps for the faithful. Now came the big time.

Over the preceding months Mao had received many instructions from the provisional Communist unit coalescing in Shanghai, and from senior Marxists in Peking. He had made one secret trip to the port city for a planning session in September 1920.

Now Mao was going back to Shanghai as one of Hunan's two chief Marxists—both schoolteachers—to join eleven others from five other provinces plus Japan at the First Congress of the Communist Party of China.

Oddly enough, Mao traveled as far as Hankou in a shared cabin with Xiao You, the two of them arguing as friends through the night, as Mao plowed his way through a book called *An Outline of the Capitalist System*. Did a firm friendship matter more than discretion? It is more likely that a touch of the old Adam remained in Mao.*

The thirteen disciples sweated their way to the French Concession and claimed their reserved bedrooms at Boai Girls' School (closed for the summer). They were mostly young—average age 26—and there was not a worker or a peasant among them. Almost all were a cut above Mao in social origin.

Sessions began in mid-July behind the black lacquer doors of a gray and pink brick villa on Joyful Undertaking Street. A discreet house, with no ground-floor windows, it was owned by a brother of one of the Shanghai delegates. The delegates—plus two Russian envoys from the Comintern—sat on round wooden stools at a living room table littered with teacups and documents.

Mao looked his age now, at 27. His mouth was more set and there was a dark delta under the eyes. To one delegate, Mao in his long gown of native cloth looked like a Taoist priest from a Hunan village.

---

* It was also odd—were there arguments over who should represent Hunan?—that the departure of Mao and He for Shanghai was thought to be "abrupt" by some Changsha radicals.

Mao was remembered for continually shrugging his shoulders as he conversed. And for a combative streak: "He delighted in laying verbal traps into which his opponents would unwittingly fall by seeming to contradict themselves. Then, obviously happy, he would burst into laughter." This can be irritating to other people who think they have something important to say.

He often appeared unwashed and his manners could be rough. "You could scrape away a pound of dirt or more from his neck and body," one colleague reckoned. In a restaurant he would wipe spilled food and wine off the table with the sleeve of his jacket. He would wear shoes without socks, or with socks hanging down over the shoes (a recurring feature of his dress over many decades).

For Mao this was in one sense an exciting week. He had been aiming for it. "Though there be a 'theory,'" he had observed when pushing Hunan autonomy, "if there is not a 'movement' simultaneously arising, the goal of that theory will not be achieved." And he had come to believe that the movement should be Bolshevik style. Now he sat down at a table with two Bolsheviks.

The thirteen Chinese had come for various reasons, above all because the Bolshevik success had stimulated their radical thinking. Such a congress would not have occurred in 1921 but for Soviet inspiration and help.

But Changsha is not the same as China, let alone Moscow. Would the ideas of the inner core be in line with what Mao, the local politician, had hammered out?

It seemed a sign that the Hunan team stood at a tangent to the mainstream when the congress decided that He Shuheng, Mao's companion, was insufficiently Marxist to be a delegate. Mao, with great sensitivity to the feelings of his fellow Hunanese, found a pretext for asking He to leave by telling him of an urgent job in Changsha that required immediate personal attention.

The mood in the villa was low key. The delegates, some confused, all hot and tired, many at cross-purposes, did not have a sense of a historic occasion. Mao was by no means the leading light at the fairly casual sessions (in later years he said strikingly little about the meeting).

Was the First Congress of the Chinese Communist Party an anticlimax? In some ways it may have been. Neither Professor Li (still in Peking) nor Professor Chen (in Canton) attended.

Nearly all the thirteen were very vague Marxists indeed. They represented a mere 57 Communist cell members in all of China! No reason to expect they would be moving mountains overnight.

They were by no means tried and tested members of a team with a common outlook and style. One delegate stayed at the luxurious Great Eastern Hotel, instead of at the girls' school, and spent most of his energies on shopping and on his beautiful wife.

Nor were the thirteen quite their own masters. The shape and timing of the meeting was fixed mostly by the Comintern and the absent Li and Chen.

What especially made Mao brood was that the views expressed around the living room table were not in harmony with the *roots* of his own thinking.

Two lines emerged. The dominant one stemmed from the Comintern and won the support of the able Zhang Guotao (the boy from the other side of Music Mountain's hills). Organize the urban workers; overthrow the capitalists; establish a dictatorship of the proletariat; spurn any link with Sun Yat-sen's above-the-ground Nationalists.

The losing line was gradualist. A stage of public education was needed; the Chinese city workers were still too few to overthrow the capitalists; cooperation with Sun was possible for the anti-imperialist and anti-war-lord cause.

What ghosts from the past must have whirled before Mao! Whom to organize? Soft methods or hard? He knew a bit about these two dilemmas. Why, then, did he not take a strong stand for either side at Joyful Undertaking Street?

Simply because he had mixed feelings. The Soviet model was his new passion. Yet it sat unstably on top of deep prior convictions.

In Changsha, beating back the anarchists, he had felt sure of the doctrine. Doubts he swept under the rug out of zeal to get a political party off the ground. But in Shanghai his new-found dogmatism seemed to shrivel a bit.

Would his Hunan comrades—sixteen of the fifty-seven were in Mao's Changsha stable—understand the Moscow mind set? Would the new concepts sell in Music Mountain? Mao hadn't yet digested the un-Chinese meat of Bolshevism.

*   *   *

One day the discovery of a suspicious visitor made it plain that the secret police of the French Concession were hot on the congress's trail. A plan was made to move to a scenic resort not far south of Shanghai. The meeting would resume on board a hired tourist boat at South Lake.

Xiao You was in Shanghai en route back to France. Strange as it may seem, he and Mao (at Mao's suggestion, according to Xiao) took the train together to South Lake. The congress delegates were all on the same train, but they did not travel as a group, and Mao chatted with Xiao and then at South Lake took a hotel room with him. As they unpacked their bundles, Mao was still urging Xiao to come to the meeting.

The congress did its business while drifting gently on a gaudy 16-meter pleasure boat. Delegates ate South Lake fish dishes between resolutions to formally found the Communist Party of China, and to affiliate with the Comintern and make monthly reports to its headquarters in Moscow.

Very late that night Mao went back to the hotel, pushed back the mosquito net, and climbed into the bed he shared with Xiao. He was hot and sweaty but he would not take a bath.

"The delegates are not a bad lot," said Mao as one Changsha man to another. He seemed to be pondering the wider world he had entered. "Some of them are very well educated and they can read either Japanese or English."

Mao made a remark of uncanny foresight to Xiao: "If we work hard, in about thirty to fifty years' time the Communist Party may be able to rule China." But predictions cook no potatoes at the time they are made. Xiao was unimpressed, and fearful of the authoritarianism that might be involved.

Next morning Mao did not rejoin his congress colleagues. Having slept late, which he liked to do, he joined Xiao in a sightseeing trip to Hangzhou. They spent a day amid the gardens and hills and temples that surround West Lake.

Yet they quarreled. Xiao admired the splendors. Mao cut him down: "This is a criminal production. Many people use their money for criminal purposes." They stayed only one night in Hangzhou.

Mao soon returned to Changsha to take up his work as secretary for Hunan of the infant Communist Party. He never saw Xiao You again.

5

Organizing (1921–1927)

Everything had changed and yet—for a while—much was the same. One meeting in Shanghai could not shake the pattern of politics in Changsha. Nor did it lead Mao to turn his back on his favorite causes. He had some new baggage after the CCP's First Congress, yet he walked a familiar May Fourth path.

Mao was head of the Hunan CCP but there wasn't much to be head of. He could do his own thing, which was education-plus-organization. He tried to pour the new Communist wine into Hunan's tested radical bottles.

Changsha was still his beat. His writings of 1921–23 appeared mostly in the local *Great Welfare Daily*, not in Party or national organs. The 1921 and 1922 articles all had the flavor of May Fourth enlightenment about them. Mao had not even burned his bridges with the anarchists.

The network at First Teachers Training School held up. Being a Communist did not stop Mao from teaching at its primary school. Under the FTTS aegis he started one of his beloved night schools. To it came graphite workers, electric company staff, rickshaw pullers, vegetable hawkers, and railwaymen. Mao was known in the FTTS quarter of Changsha as "Mr. Mao of the Night School."

Mao also launched a "make-up class" (*bu-xi ban*) for unschooled rural folk over the age of 18 who wanted to study arithmetic and Chinese. This brought country bumpkins into FTTS's spacious halls. They were bronzed and smelly. They wore clothes as coarse as tents. They munched loudly on baked cakes and fritters during class.

Some at FTTS wished to get rid of these fish out of water. In defense Mao tried to charm the head of his alma mater, and he loftily observed that clothes and eating habits were "trivial matters." His tactic of smiles and scorn was hard to beat. He won the day for his make-up class.

The finest bloom in the garden of Mao's educational projects was Hunan

Self-Cultivation University. It was set up during the fall of 1921 in the love-ly chambers of the old Wang Fuzhi Society. At the peak of its two-year life the school had 200 students. Mao's brother Zetan was one of them. Mao rounded up his friends from New People's Study Society to teach. Kaihui also lent a hand.

In fact there was little teaching. The idea was to read, discuss, and re-examine one's daily existence in light of what was learned.

One of the aims, to be sure, was to propagate Marxism. The school pub-lished an ardent little monthly called *New Age*. In it Mao wrote two of his first articles with any Marxist flavor: "Against Idealism" and "Marxism and China." Mao explained that the magazine would not be a "literary de-partment store" like ordinary college organs. It would bend in a fixed direc-tion. The young organizer's teeth were trying to close shut on a settled doctrine.

Yet Mao was still a pedagogue first and an ideologue second. He believed education would uplift "old hundred names"—a Chinese term for the com-mon man—and as a teacher he was earnest.

Mao wrote few pieces more interesting in the early 1920s than the school's founding announcement. Written in August 1921, it was picked up by the important Shanghai magazine *Eastern Miscellany* in early 1923.

Mao's acid view of mainstream education led him to coin the term "schol-arly lords." In Chinese (*xue fa*) it is an echo of "war lords." The scholarly lords lack human feeling (*gan qing*). They make learning a commercial transaction. They teach by turning on a hose and telling the students to drink.

At Mao's school, potential students, instead of facing an entrance exam, were asked to "Give your critique of society" or to "Set out a philosophy of life." Lectures were few. The idea was to "read and ponder" by yourself. The learning process became a collective search for relevant light. Mao was a fork prying students from comfortable positions. History with its urgent message for China was the taskmaster at Self-Cultivation University.

Just as the school used an elegant building, so it borrowed what was worthwhile from established education. Mao said he would bind three good things together: Thorough research methods from the old Chinese acade-mies. Up-to-date teachings of the modern schools. A daily regimen to fit the real-life human personality.

The school was successful. Yet only for an elite that knew what it wanted. The CCP in Hunan drew many recruits from its classes on history,* geogra-

---

* Mao himself taught the class in ancient history, believing that the study of China's past would spur the students' patriotism.

phy, literature, and philosophy. But many "old hundred names" found the reading too voluminous and the ideas hard to grasp.

The artisan of the early 1920s who was able and willing to study world history at night was not an ordinary man. Mao had not yet reached the masses.

* * *

In one respect the congress at Shanghai had influenced Mao. He paid more attention than before to the labor movement.

The year 1922 brought an upsurge of the Chinese labor movement. The small band of Communists had a lot to do with it. They (and the Comintern which backed them) took it to be the wave of China's future. Marx had put his finger on the industrial proletariat. His Oriental disciples could do no less. Mao had his doubts, but he joined in.

Mao came back from Shanghai with two hats. He was province secretary of the CCP. He was also province head of the Labor Secretariat, which was the infant CCP's key project. Anyuan was his first battlefield.

Anyuan in east Hunan is a modest town. But its large coal mines, opened up at German and Japanese initiative in 1898, made it a toehold of China's belated industrial revolution.

A painting of the 1960s showed young Mao striding intrepid under swirling clouds to uplift the miners of Anyuan. Larger than life, dignified in a white gown, he looked like a clergyman bringing the truth to heathen.*

Mao's four trips to Anyuan from late 1921 to early 1923 were not like this at all. The work was tentative and difficult. Some of it misfired. And Mao was not a solo performer.

Walking to Anyuan along the railroad, Mao did wear a white gown. But he took it off once he saw the town. Anyuan was grimy.

The 12,000 miners were deadened by 15 hours of work a day in bad conditions. Within a four-mile radius there were 24 Christian churches, yet only one small medical station to serve 6,000 workers. The place was Dickensian. There was no May Fourth excitement to it at all.

Mao kept a low profile. He stayed in a miner's house, had a look at the pits, filled his notebooks.

The miners all stood up when he entered a room to talk to them. This awe did not fit the task at hand. The social gap yawned. Mao felt dislocated in spirit. Had he ceased to be a son of the soil and become an imposed guardian of Moscow's truth?

Mao persevered. His brother Zemin went with him on a second visit. This

* So much so that a reproduction of the painting was hung at the Vatican in 1969 above the caption "Young Chinese Missionary."

time Mao looked rumpled in grass hat, lumber jacket, and grass shoes.

For some weeks in December 1921 the two of them lived in a restaurant. Each foggy morning they tramped out to coax the miners. "History is in your hands" Mao kept saying to the black faces and tired eyes.

His theme at Anyuan was anti-fatalism.

A CCP cell was formed. A Workers Club, too, and the inevitable night school. This last did not work well and Mao soon replaced it with a very useful day school for the miners' children.

At the blackboard Mao learned to use simple illustrations. He took the Chinese character 工, which is the first part of the term for "work" or "worker." The top horizontal line, he explained, is the sky; the lower one is the earth. The vertical stroke that joins them is the working class. Workers stood upon the earth but reached to the sky! Theirs was the universe. Professor Yang might have winced, but it wasn't a bad teaching device.

By Mao's third trip, in September 1922, the mood of Anyuan was stormy. This was due in part to the objective misery of miners who were treated less as persons than as things. It was also due to the increasingly successful injections given by the intellectual doctors from Changsha.

Mao was in charge but he was not the chief operator. As important was Li Lisan, the "noncommittal" youth who had "half answered" Mao's 1917 newspaper ad for friends. Until 1921 Li had been in France on work-study.

Crucial was the youth from a landlord family who had been studying in Moscow—Liu Shaoqi. Liu was the hero of a successful strike in the fall of 1922. It made Anyuan a red banner for much of China, and ushered in the Hunan Federation of Labor. Mao was named the federation's chief: Liu had helped put a new feather in Mao's cap.

The Anyuan setup was impressive but anomalous. China had only 2 million industrial workers in a population of more than 400 million. The Anyuan Workers Club was a bastion in a desert. "Long Live the Workers," a slogan Mao took to Anyuan, had a brittle tone to it in the China of 1922.

Here were reading rooms, co-ops, a network of workers' councils. No fewer than 60 percent of Anyuan's workers joined the CCP-sponsored club. Parades lit up May Day. Festivities unrolled on the anniversaries of the October Revolution, Lenin's birthday, even of the birthday of Liebknecht, the far-away German Marxist.

Anyuan was a base to warm the cockles of the Comintern's heart. (The club indeed was nicknamed "Little Moscow.") It seemed a model outpost of what was then called the world revolution. But where would it all lead? The miners had won better wages and conditions. What was the next step?

*   *   *

Mao wrote almost nothing during 1922. He was too busy stoking up one organization after the other.

Clear Water Pond was now his office. It was the headquarters of the Hunan CCP and a clubhouse for Changsha's long-haired leftists. Until the early hours, lights from the low house shone out on surrounding vegetable plots which the Communists kept up to give the villa an air of innocence.

Mao tried to keep his privacy. He did not live among documents and tea mugs as some Communists were happy to do. Ms. Yang and he retreated from Clear Water Pond to the mellow rooms used in part by the Self-Cultivation University. It was a comfortable residence. Mao's mother-in-law lived with them in a pleasant room of her own. Mao's first son, Anying (Heroic Shore), was born during 1921. Family life was not swept away by the rush of work.

By 1922 there was a change. Whether because of family strains, or to be nearer his office, he again lived at Clear Water Pond.

Mao led a strike of Changsha's 6,000 construction workers (who complained that the only food they could afford was two meals of porridge a day). He put on rough clothes to pretend he was a worker, blew a whistle to get the rank-and-file to shout slogans, led a group that burst into a wealthy contractor's home at dinner time and proceeded to analyze the difference between the food on his table and their own diet.

The Governor's aide, suspecting that he was not dealing with an ordinary construction worker, asked Mao to give his name. Mao dodged the query by launching into a discussion of Adam Smith.

He had talks (which he does not mention) with the Comintern agent Maring who passed through Changsha in November 1921. He helped found unions of stonemasons, barbers, textile workers, tailors, and typesetters. He went south to Hengyang, where his adopted sister had paved the way for him to start a Party cell at Third Teachers Training School.

He threw himself into a typesetters' strike against his own writing outlet, *Great Welfare Daily*. This may have destroyed his tie with the editor, for after this he wrote little or nothing in the paper.

In the hard life of Changsha's 9,000 rickshaw pullers Mao took a particular interest. He lent CCP backing to their successful drive for a reduction in the rent they paid to the owners of the city's 3,100 rickshaws. At a night class he ran for the pullers, Mao used another picture play on the character for "work." He wrote 工 on the blackboard. Beside it he added 人. The two together mean "worker." Mao then put up 天, which means "sky." With a smile he showed the rickshaw pullers how placing 人 directly beneath 工 made 天. The lesson: when united, the workers' strength soars to the sky.

Some pullers qualified to join the Party. Mao held a little ceremony for them by South Gate. He draped the CCP flag on a banyan tree. The chosen pullers came forward one by one, raised the right hand and repeated after Mao: "I will sacrifice myself, carry out class struggle, obey the organization, strictly guard secrets, never rebel against the Party. . . ." A glint of satisfaction in his eye, Mao handed to each recruit a Party certificate and an envelope of study documents.

It was a reversal of a time-honored order. The lowest worker, no more considered part of politics than was a melon or a cat, climbed aboard a party that saw itself as the locomotive of history. From the gutter to pretension, one might say.

North in Peking, a little while later, Agnes Smedley sat down to dinner with some patrician Chinese. As dishes piled up and wine flowed, one cultivated type exclaimed: "There are no classes in China. Marxists invented the idea. My rickshaw coolie and I can laugh and talk like old friends as he pulls me through the streets." Smedley shot back at him: "Would you be his friend if you had to pull him through the street? Or if he revolted?"

Peking in the 1920s knew nothing of Mao. Yet Smedley had put her restless finger on Mao's cause. In a way he *was* inventing classes. And what a potent invention—to show rickshaw pullers that they were not part of nature but, through class struggle, part of history.

Mao apparently went to Hangzhou for a meeting of the CCP's Central Committee in April 1922. He was prominent, and yet he was not. "The leading participants," recalled the Comintern agent of the Hangzhou talks, "were Chen Duxiu, Li Dazhao, Zhang Guotao . . . and one other, a very capable Hunanese student whose name I do not recall." Bright, but still a local.

*   *   *

By 1923 the Hunan labor movement had reached a watershed. On the one hand it flourished. It was the strongest in China. Mao—leaving Anyuan mostly to Li, Liu, and his finance-minded brother Zemin—planted seeds over much of the province.

He organized unions. He sparked more than a dozen major strikes. Now and then he quietly spawned a new Party cell. The work grew. Within two years 20 unions with 50,000 workers were formed in Hunan. The carefully selected ranks of the CCP in Hunan grew from ten in mid-1921 to 123 a year later. As each new union was started Mao would try to place a CCP cadre as its secretary.

On the other hand there was little *national* strength to the labor movement. A crisis on the railroads brought this home.

As in most industries—for much of the capital was foreign—anti-imperialist feeling had deepened industrial tensions. Railroad workers were the most advanced of any industry. In north China, railroad work was the cradle of the infant CCP. At Shanghai's instruction Mao turned to the Canton-Hankou railroad. The CCP saw it—with the Anyuan colliery—as the presumed spearhead of a proletarian revolution in Hunan.

Mao followed the Anyuan model. Around Changsha's New River Station he felt at home and the work went well. He would hold sessions in teahouses and sometimes invite railwaymen to Clear Water Pond for a night of planning.

At Yuezhou to the north, Mao's work was for some reason less sound. The ringing slogan "Workers are the mother of world happiness" was not enough to bring success.

A strike was launched in September 1922. The trains lay in the yards like dead snakes. Mao orchestrated telegrams of support for the strikers from other unions and cities. But the northern war lord who controlled Hankou turned troops against Mao's workers at Yuezhou. Losses were terrible. The steel tracks shone red with blood.

Despite counterthrusts, and some gains, the last word was with the war lords. By February 1923 the Canton-Hankou railwaymen had been crushed. The governor of Hunan outlawed unions. The proletariat seemed far from revolution.

Suddenly 1921–1923 seemed a finished phase. In April 1923 Mao fled Changsha to escape arrest as an "extremist."*

He left without Kaihui. She was pregnant again and her mother was taking care of her. The previous two years had been the longest stretch of time Mao would ever spend with his first chosen wife.

Mao had a lot to think about as he tramped into the countryside. Had he really believed that the urban workers *were* on the brink of revolution? If not, was the CCP less than all-wise?

The Party was puffing busily down the urban road. Its general secretary was still Professor Chen, who was Marxist enough to see little hope in a rural road. Those returned from study in Europe—like Li and Liu—did not consider the possibility that revolution in Asia might be another cup of tea from that in Europe.

Yet China's proletariat was far less than one percent of the Chinese people. The CCP was still mainly a circle of intellectuals. Many active unionists did not know what the term *Ma-ke-se zhu-yi* (Marxism) meant.

Moreover, the war lords had the guns. It seemed suicidal to defy them. It

---

*The Hunan governor was asked in an interview many years later, in Taiwan, why he didn't kill Mao when he had a chance to, as he killed many other radicals. "I didn't know," he replied with a smile, "that he was going to turn out so high-powered."

seemed pathetic to reason with them—which Mao did in a Classics-quoting talk with Hunan's governor in December 1922.

* * *

Mao did not attend the Second CCP Congress in July 1922. It is a curious story. He was already staying in Shanghai as the delegates gathered for the meeting there. He explained: "I forgot the name of the place where it was to be held, could not find any comrades, and missed it." It is hard to believe that he could locate no contact in all of Shanghai. It seems that Mao was not fully tuned to Party affairs in the summer of 1922.

His passion seemed bottled up. Labor unions had become his life. For their sake he sacrificed his writing, left his teaching post at the primary school, and had to flee Changsha.

Yet urban organizing did not draw out Mao's strengths. He had never worked in a mine or factory. The soil he knew, but not machines or industrial routine. He had not been to Europe, where the vision of world revolution through an uprising of the proletariat was vivid.

Somehow he did not fit the labor movement scene as well as Zhang Guotao (the landlord's son who spoke English), or Li Lisan (returned from France), or Liu Shaoqi (returned from Russia).

He did not quite believe, as Liu did, that the onward march of industrial organization would lead, as if by force of gravity, to the gates of socialism.

The issues of wages and hours did not arouse Mao like the bride's suicide or his father's avarice toward tenants.

A nativist streak held Mao back. Russian advisers were all the rage. But was a new China on the make? Were the stones and fields and daily life of beloved China going to be changed by ticking off the items on the Comintern's agenda?

* * *

The task was to find allies. Mao knew this. His essay "Great Union of the Popular Masses" had shown his inclination for a broad coalition. But in 1919 Mao had been a free spirit writing what he pleased. By 1923 he was a member of a disciplined team. Its leaders had more clout than he. Its headquarters were 800 miles away in Shanghai.

As it happened the CCP was itself having second thoughts about the 1921–1922 policies. The line born at the First Congress was sectarian. Here was a puny band of 57 gathering its skirts about it. Moscow thought this pretentious.

Maring, the Dutch-born salesman for Bolshevism, tried on the Comintern's behalf to bring about a change. The Second Congress in 1922 toyed with Maring's ideas, yet in practice the line did not change. But events in Canton soon gave Maring ammunition.

Sun Yat-sen, head of the Canton government since 1917, was driven out of his own lair by a war lord. Sun—eccentric, passionate, malleable—was at a loose end. The West had not been generous to him. War lords had turned against him. Moscow stepped in.

In January 1923 a marriage was arranged. Sun signed an agreement with the Soviet envoy Adolf Joffe in Shanghai. The CCP and the Nationalists were to join hands. CCP members would enter the Nationalist Party (NP) as individuals. The CCP would maintain its separate existence. But organizational leadership of the "national revolution"—a new term on CCP lips—would lie with the Nationalists.

It was a fateful step. Moscow was delighted; it was the Comintern's first success in putting its own stamp on the Chinese Revolution. Not everyone in the CCP was delighted.

For Mao a new phase began. After ruminating for a while at Music Mountain, he reported to Shanghai. He stayed in a room provided by the Party amidst the commercial bustle of a foreign-ruled enclave (delicately called the International Settlement). He gave his colleagues an analysis of the work in Hunan.

In the summer of 1923 he went to Canton for the first time. The CCP gathered at its Third Congress to plan for its life with Sun. "There must be a great revolutionary union," Mao said during the meeting. "One cannot fight alone." He quickly became an enthusiast for the link with Sun's Nationalists.

The southern city was an eye-opener for him. Here was a Treaty Port with a foreign presence that hinterland Hunan did not have.* Its raucous ways were a shock for a measured Hunanese. Mao was lost before the Cantonese dialect.

On the other hand, this was south-of-the-Yangze China. In climate and food and habit Canton was more to a Changsha man's taste than was Peking. Mao took to wearing the wooden sandals in which Cantonese clip-clop through their city's alleys.

Why was Mao keen for the link with the Nationalists?†

At Canton the reasons were two. Mao had long thought that the struggle for a new China was an anti-imperialist struggle. The Nationalists in 1923 were anti-imperialist. Indeed this issue was the logical—maybe the sole—

*Hunan had no foreign factories; the Changsha elite, lacking in virtue as Mao found it, had nevertheless kept out imperialists.

†Zhang Guotao was against it. Professor Chen favored it because he thought China was not yet ready for revolution.

common denominator among the emerging triangle of Sun-Moscow-CCP.

Mao was in favor of the broadest possible array of Chinese strata against the foreign mauling of China.

Nor—in the second place—was Mao in a position to stick his neck out. A congress vote was taken on whether to turn over control of the labor movement to the ruling organs of the NP. Mao at first balked at this. Were his precious unions to be handed over to an outside authority that, so far as Hunan went, existed only on paper?

But when the majority swung the other way Mao changed his tune. He went along. He had to do so. Uprooted from his Changsha base, he needed to make his way in the national CCP network.

The congress elected him to the 14-member Central Committee of the Party. It made him head of the Organization Department, in place of ultra-leftist Zhang Guotao. For this work his base became Shanghai. His articles of 1923 were mainly published not in Hunan organs but in the CCP's national *Guide*.

Mao was now a functionary in a national team. His career as an educator in Changsha was over. His post as head of the Hunan Federation of Labor was turned over to a co-worker. He cleared his things out of Clear Water Pond house. He would never live in Hunan again.

But two important ties with his province remained. Music Mountain still had a corner in his heart. And Kaihui did not shift house from Changsha. Late in 1923 Mao heard by letter that a second son had been born. The parents called him Anqing (Bright Shore).

*   *   *

For much of the next year Mao lived in Shanghai. It was the city of the CCP's birth. It boasted by far the biggest proletariat of any Chinese city. And in Shanghai imperialism was as omnipresent as the cry of hawkers and the foghorns off the Whangpu River.

One day Mao ran into a Changsha classmate just back from study in Europe. Mao wore his faded Chinese gown and straw shoes. The classmate sported a Western suit and tie. "You'd better change your clothes," Mao said with disdain. The classmate was puzzled. "I'll show you why," Mao continued.

He walked his friend along the embankment as far as the gate of the Bund Garden. To the iron fence was attached a list of regulations for the park. One forbade picking flowers. Another said dogs were not allowed to enter. A third read: "No Chinese, excepting work coolies, are admitted."

The gap between Mao and the work-study returnees was never quite bridged. Hinterland type as he was, Mao could not get used to the idea of

Chinese having to crouch before Westerners in the Treaty Ports.

In midwinter Mao went south again to Canton. The occasion was the First Congress* of the Nationalist Party under the ailing and now pro-Russian Sun. At and after it Mao plunged even deeper than before into work for the NP. Just 30, he made his first mark in a political organization broader than a Marxist sect.

At the congress Mao spoke up for Sun's vague and un-Marxist "three principles of the people." He was one of ten Communists elected to the ruling executive of Sun's party. With two other Communists he was put on an elite 19-man body to review that party's new constitution.

He was given important responsibilities in the Shanghai unit of the NP. Within a month he had been made head of the Nationalists' Organization Department, based in the port city.

Mao went back to Shanghai in early 1924 with a spring in his stride. He held the organization portfolio for each of the two parties. Driven out of Hunan, he had needed a fresh start. He found it in the salad days of the CCP-Nationalist "united front."

Mao was working with new people, among them Mikhail Borodin and his team of Comintern agents.

Borodin was not yet 40 when he came to work in China in 1923, but he knew Lenin and was much respected. Under the regimen of the united front he was an adviser to both the CCP and the Nationalists. Visitors were admitted to his villa in downtown Canton only upon flashing an enamel badge depicting the NP flag attached to a gold chain.

Tall, with a flowing brown mane and a sagging mustache, Borodin paced his lavish office in a Sun Yat-sen tunic over high boots. He spoke no Chinese but excellent English (his American wife was a relative of Buster Keaton).

In Canton, Mao sometimes talked with the chain-smoking, gesticulating Russian. He listened to the well-spun theories and Soviet-derived advice. But he was too removed from Borodin's world to be convinced by anything the eloquent Bolshevik said.†

Few of the Russians spoke any Chinese and they did not know China well. True the October Revolution was the spark of world revolution. But would its flesh-and-blood representatives actually be able to do the job?

If Mao did not stand in awe of the Comintern missionaries, as Li Lisan did, he did not fight them either, as Zhang Guotao did. He remained de-

---

* The Nationalist Party was founded in 1912—and even before that it existed as the Alliance Society—but only after its reorganization, following the Sun-Joffe Declaration, did it hold a congress in the style of a tightly organized party.

† Borodin said he found Mao "excessively self-assured."

tached toward the brisk young advisers from Moscow. (Another young Asian Marxist in Canton at that time was more impressed with Borodin. This thin, tubercular figure in a European white linen suit spent much time in Borodin's villa. He had been hunted out of French Indochina and the Chinese Nationalists granted him asylum. His name was Ho Chi Minh.)

Mao also got to know the Nationalist leaders. Sun he met in a glancing way at Canton. His boyhood hero, now in the last year of his life, seemed diffuse. "He wouldn't allow others to argue with him," Mao complained, "or to offer their own views."

In Shanghai there were two high Nationalist officials whom Mao saw much of. Wang Jingwei and Hu Hanmin were both able, fluent politicians. Mao felt and seemed a homespun provincial by comparison with them.

Wang and Hu seemed to Mao rather vain and wordy. The two of them (together with a military officer called Chiang Kai-shek in Canton) were all would-be heirs to the mantle of Sun. The "national revolution" was in their smooth hands. But if these were to be the politicians of the new China, would it really be new?

If Mao had doubts, the CCP establishment was not excluded from them.

Professor Chen looked less good close up. He was number one man in the CCP. He had been the chief Marxist influence upon Mao. He remained straightforward and modest, which could not always be said of the Russians or the Nationalist prima donnas. But Mao wondered what had happened to the sharp edge of Chen's iconoclasm.

A detail spoke volumes: Chen as a Shanghai man wore a Western suit; Mao wore his rough Chinese gown.

When the CCP's Central Committee met at Shanghai in April, Mao for some reason was not present. Zhang Guotao said in a tone of disapproval that Mao was "busy with his work in the Nationalist Party." It seems that he was on a trip to Hunan, which included a stop at Anyuan colliery.

Meanwhile Mao kept quiet about his misgivings. The NP work absorbed him. So loyal was Mao to the Nationalist cause that Li Lisan maliciously called him "Hu Hanmin's secretary."

The Nationalists took a step in February which especially appealed to Mao. A Peasant Department was set up. The CCP had never done this. It was one more reason for Mao to be keen about the united front. And it soon led to work which helped launch Mao on a momentous new road.

One trip Mao took in 1924 was to Hong Kong. He and Zhang Guotao had labor union business to see to in the British-run appendage to Guangdong Province. They took a boat from Shanghai through the brilliant blue waters of the South China Sea. On board, a gang of hoodlums cornered Mao and Zhang. Waving knives, they demanded money. Mao would not buckle under. He wanted to fight. It showed his courage and his combative turn of mind. Zhang reasoned with Mao that the amount of money demanded was not worth a showdown. Only with difficulty and the help of others did he finally restrain his peppery Hunan colleague.

Mao was politically less left-wing than Zhang, but when personally challenged he was more fiery.

*   *   *

During 1923 and 1924 Mao's writings reflected his way of life. In *Guide*—organ of the CCP—he wrote short pieces about current politics. They were biting, but bare of theory.

Two things stood out about the 1923 items. Mao called merchants the key to national revolution. One wonders what his brothers in the Hunan Federation of Labor thought of that.

And he was always staunchly anti-imperialist. In an essay on "The Cigarette Tax" he mocked at the knee-shaking government in Peking, which fawned on the foreign powers. "If one of our foreign masters farts," he snapped, "they think it's a lovely perfume."

But these articles did not dig into history or soar toward philosophy. Mao had let go of the themes of liberation. Increasingly his bureaucratic work kept his nose closer to detail than is congenial to liberationists.

Yet there was a strong thread of consistency. He still believed in the people as an almost mystic entity. It was the merchants' (hoped-for) readiness to follow the people's interests that qualified them for a state of revolutionary grace.

And throwing off imperialism was as before the top item on Mao's agenda. In Mao's mind, if not in unfolding actuality, the united front with the Nationalists probably seemed a step toward a "Great Union of the Popular Masses" to revivify China.

The peasant issue was just a feather of a cloud on the far horizon. It had been no part of May Fourth's themes. China's rural 85 percent were a silent majority of which the CCP had taken no notice. It seems that not a single peasant was a CCP member in 1924. Nowhere *in the world* were peasants then thought to possess a talent for revolution.

Mao had spent the past 14 years in towns. He had moved among students and workers. As part of that new life he had shaken off most of his telltale rural ways. Nothing in the CCP encouraged him to think rurally.

At Canton during the CCP's Third Congress came the first sign that Mao had started to think politically about the peasantry. He urged his skeptical colleagues to weigh the peasants as a possible part of the revolution. He even broached Chinese history—instead of only Bolshevik precedent—and noted its rich tradition of peasant rebellion.

But this was an eddy and nothing came of it. The only peasant organizing was being done by a magnetic man called Peng Pai. He was a landlord's son who had changed sides to champion the rural poor. In east Guangdong Province he started peasant associations. The work went well and the NP took heed of it.

Peng was named head of the NP's new Peasant Department. Under him a Peasant Movement Training Institute was set up in Canton during July 1924. Here was the first school in Chinese history—perhaps in all history—to train farmers for political revolt.

Peng was the pioneer. But Mao was among the first colleagues Peng sought out to give him a hand. In August 1924 Mao spoke, at Peng's invitation, to the first class at the Peasant Movement Training Institute. His passion impressed the trainees. The institute in turn appealed to him. His visit was the thin end of a wedge that would cleave deep into China's future.

Back in Shanghai things did not go well. It was as if Mao's days with Peng in Canton brought into relief what was wrong with his bureaucratic months in Shanghai.

Style of life was one problem. Mao was not among those who find full satisfaction in answering the call of whatever documents land upon the "in" tray. He was an uneven worker. Some complained at his irregularity and his tendency to disappear on a trip. But these were only symptoms.

A more serious problem was summed up by Li Lisan's jibe that Mao was so much in the Nationalists' pocket as to be merely Hu Hanmin's secretary. Storms were brewing within the NP as Sun battled liver cancer. Those with eyes to see knew that anti-communism was bubbling in its fractious ranks.

Yet Mao had eyes only for the united front. "All work must be done in the name of the Nationalist Party" he insisted during the summer of 1924. Few CCP colleagues agreed.

The strain told on Mao. He had trouble sleeping—rare for him—and his health slipped. This added to his ineffectiveness within the CCP. By late 1924 he was on the out at Party headquarters. Impossible any longer for him to be a trusted bridge between the CCP and the NP.*

He dragged himself to Shanghai for the CCP's Fourth Congress in January 1925. He was morose during the sessions he attended. He played so small a part that some have wrongly written that he did not go to the Fourth Congress.

What little he said was about the peasantry. But the mood of the congress was as city-oriented as it was suspicious of the NP. The communiqué at the end of the meeting linked the word "peasant" at each mention by a hyphen

---

* After he returned to Shanghai in February 1924, Mao wrote virtually nothing for publication during the rest of the year. His next writings, in 1925, appeared mainly in a new organ of the NP, *Political Weekly*, of which he was named editor.

to the word "worker," as if the former would be naked alone.

The outcome for Mao was a formality. He was knocked off the Central Committee.

Mao was exhausted. And he was in a cul-de-sac. In his autobiography he glosses over the tensions. He chooses to not even mention the Fourth Congress. "I had become ill in Shanghai," he blandly sums up. "I returned to Hunan for a rest."

Mao was good at changing gears. This skill served him well all through his life. If he could be impulsive, he also knew how to retreat. The hour called for withdrawal. He would go back to his roots.

* * *

More than some of his colleagues, Mao kept a realm of private life. The farm at Music Mountain was his. He did not renounce it or sell it. His memories of the past were not as bitter as all that.

The money that his father's farm yielded Mao traded for freedom. If he wanted to veer off on his own—the Party regardless—he had the funds to do so. If he needed to offer meals to peasants in return for an interview, again the money was there.

Quite often when in Changsha, Mao had gone back to Music Mountain for a break. Now in early 1925 he went for an extended stay. For half a year he pulled back from Treaty Ports and documents and committees and struggles in the office.

Mao used the farm for political meetings and its profits, in part, for the Communist cause. To the folk of Music Mountain he must have seemed his father's son. He was a landlord, if a red one. He made the old serve the new.

And he turned blood ties into political ties. All of the family worked for the cause—unusual in the senior ranks of the early CCP.

Zemin, now 27, had carried on the work at Anyuan and was about to become head of the CCP's Publishing Department in Shanghai. Zetan, 19, had just joined the CCP. He had been busy at Mao's old student activities in Changsha. The adopted sister, Zejian, was organizing in the Hunan town of Yuebei. Kaihui herself, a CCP member since 1922, had been doing education-plus-organization in Changsha and Yuebei. For a while she had worked in Shanghai, but not with Mao.

The marriage seemed less close now than it had been in 1921 and 1922. "In our last letters were misunderstandings," ran one line in a poem Mao sent to Kaihui in late 1923, and after that time they did not spend much time together.

Beyond his immediate family, Mao mobilized many relatives. In the Chinese records of his stay in Music Mountain the name "Mao" recurs like the chorus of a song. Mao deals with Mao Fuxuan, Mao Yuanyao, Mao Xinhai, Mao Yueqiu, and many others. The clan link served him well.

Chinese New Year of 1925 saw a reunion at the family hearth. Kaihui and the two young boys were there. Zemin came home; maybe Zejian as well. The overlapping of clan and cause must have given them strength.

Yet they would have been superhuman not to feel a tug of contradiction in the situation. Led by Mao, they lived with the contradiction. They did not merely scorn pre-Communist ties. They seemed to find Music Mountain a place to rally themselves for the soon murderous work of revolution.

For a few weeks Mao puttered around the farm, chatted with neighbors, took walks in the valley, dabbled at spring planting alongside his hired laborers.

But in February Mao stirred to action. He left Music Mountain and criss-crossed the county and beyond. He stayed in peasant homes and drained facts and opinions from everyone he met.

His notebooks were full. It was the kind of firsthand investigation that Mao reveled in. His walks amid the green hills seemed to dissolve the frustrations of Shanghai.

The difference in mood from his boyhood days was one between day and night. The peasants of Hunan had had enough. They were on the march. Grumbling had become revolt.

Rent was now being withheld. Ragged poor peasants were gate-crashing elegant feasts in ancestral halls. Magistrates were starting to bend before the opinion of peasant unions.

Mao quickly moved from study to coordination. He did not originate the peasant organizations of Hunan. He was not a hero to the grass roots in the manner of Peng Pai, before whom peasant women in Guangdong held their children aloft so that they might remember they had once seen the "king of the peasants."

But as he traveled, Mao put the seal on peasant unions and even—heresy to Shanghai—Party cells. He was talking of communism amid rice and mud and thatch. He was making a connection to China's no longer silent majority. By the end of 1926, thanks in large part to Mao's stimulus, half of Hunan's 75 counties had peasant unions. Two million peasants belonged.

Within Xiang Tan county Mao set up some 20 evening schools. The aim was general education—the Chinese call it raising the cultural standard—with a political message tossed in. He liked to begin a Chinese lesson with the words "hand" and "leg." Nature gave the same number of hands and legs to every human being. All wealth is created by these members. How absurd, then, that the rich seldom use hands or legs. . . .

As an individual Mao had come full circle—from the soil to the soil. He had left Music Mountain a rebel in 1910. But that iconoclasm was only a boy's dark suspicion that the straitjacket of his life was unjust.

In 1925 Mao saw rebellion not as one tortured soul's refusal to conform but as a whole people's search for a new future. He could laugh at his former bitterness toward his father. The real issue was so much broader. It was not psychological but political. His father now seemed less a monster than a relic.

Mao had finally recovered from his education. Return to Music Mountain speeded his digestion of a decade in urban classrooms. His new attitude to "foreign schools" summed up the adjustment.

On holiday trips home he had stood up for schools like East Mountain and First Teachers Training School against village folk's criticisms. But by 1925 Mao had reversed himself. "I realized that I had been wrong and the peasants right." He now favored the old-style Chinese schools over foreign schools. He was no longer fighting his father. He saw things in larger proportion. He made a quiet turn toward nativism.

It was in an attic above Mao's parents' bedroom that a Music Mountain branch of the Communist Party of China was solemnized with its first thirty-two peasant members in August 1925. What Shanghai headquarters thought of this way of pursuing revolution is not recorded.

*   *   *

In a Shanghai textile mill a Chinese worker was casually killed by a Japanese foreman in mid-1925. A protest demonstration was fired upon at British orders by police of the International Settlement. Ten were killed and 50 wounded.

The incident was like a lighted match thrown near a powder keg. A cycle of protests, shootings, and strikes unrolled in many cities. The strike in Hong Kong went on for sixteen months—the longest in world history—and the once despised rickshaw pullers of Peking hung little placards on their vehicles: "No English or Japanese."

New was the impact on peasants. For the first time villages sounded a mass cry against imperialism. The CCP grew like a vine in the tropics. In January 1925 its membership was a tennis-club 995. By November it was a mass-party 10,000.

Revolution suddenly seemed more than a phrase in a radical sect's minute book.

Exactly at this time, the Nationalists reached a fork in the road. Sun died in the spring; weeping throngs saw him buried in Peking, wrapped in the red, blue, and white NP flag. Could any successor walk a tightrope as he had done? The scramble for the soul of the NP was on by summer.

Mao returned to the regular arena in the fall. His new-found issue—the peasant upsurge—was to dominate the scramble.

The governor of Hunan had his dagger out for the tall 31-year-old radical who hung around villages. In the countryside Mao was safe enough—war lords weren't awesome in the hills. But he took the risky step of going into Changsha. The governor picked up his trail. Troops were sent after him. Mao fled to Canton.

The external force of political power had overcome, for the moment, the more fundamental force of social change.

Apt that, after months of writing committee memos in Shanghai during 1924, Mao wrote a poem as a coda to his quickening months in Hunan during 1925.

"Changsha" is a poem of nostalgia mixed with sober hope. It recalls college days:

> . . . crowded years and months of endeavor,
> Young we were, and schoolmates,
> In high assurance, fearless,
> Pointing the finger at all things . . .

Mao feels a loss of some old certainties:

> Under the unmoving sky a million creatures try out their freedom
> I ponder, I ask the boundless earth,
> Who rules over destiny?

The whole poem is embedded in the affairs of nature. It ends with a flash of confidence:

> Do you remember
> How, reaching midstream, we struck the waters,
> And the waves dashed against our speeding boats?

Will not youthful strength, transmuted to other forms in those over 30, retain its power for changing situations?

Mao reached Canton as the rains began in October. He had been away from the lush city on the Pearl River for nearly a year. He had changed. So had the united front.

It would be interesting to know how Mao went about explaining to colleagues what he'd been up to for nine months. They must have cast on him the anxious eye reserved for those who have been in eclipse. All we can say is that he took his time. He tried no dramatics. He resumed work within the system.

This meant mainly the NP, for he now held higher posts in it than in the

CCP. He was a member of its ruling body—no longer of the CCP's.

Mao became editor of *Political Weekly*, the main organ of the NP. In late 1925 he showed his keenness for the job by peppering its pages with some 15 pieces from his own pen. All of them were a continuation of the radical commentary on current politics that he had written in *Guide* and elsewhere during 1923. No fruits yet from the Hunan villages.

Mao had a second important job in the NP. He was number two man in the Propaganda Department. Since its chief was busy as premier of the Canton government, Mao masterminded the communication of the Nationalist message.

But it was Mao's third job that glinted with a future. The fifth class of the Peasant Movement Training Institute began in October 1925. We find that Mao gave numerous lectures at it. Hunanese students mysteriously leaped to forty percent of the total. Mao's hand was even more plainly to be seen in the presence in the class of his own brother Zemin.

Mao was rising like a meteor at the institute. He had emerged from eclipse with his new message *as a teacher*.

That Mao's work within the NP blossomed was remarkable, since CCP-NP relations were going from tense to bad.

Maybe the united front could never have worked. At any rate, it had ceased to work by the spring of 1926. A right-wing group—named "Western Hills Group" after the spot near Peking where it first met—had emerged within the NP. It wanted no truck with the CCP.

The Party's weightiest left-of-center leader was murdered in Canton just before Mao arrived in flight from Hunan. Western Hills money probably pulled the trigger.

The tide against the united front was stemmed for a bit at the Second Congress of the NP in January 1926. It met amid fanfare in downtown Canton at a moment when leftist mass organizations in south China were surging. The first act—as at all NP meetings—was for the assembly to bow low three times before a portrait of Sun and then hear his testament read aloud.

Mao was to the fore. He spoke up in debates. He was reelected an alternate of the Executive Committee with a healthy total of 173 votes (Wang Jingwei had a maximum of 248 votes; the senior Communist, Professor Li Dazhao, had 192). He was put on the NP's Peasant Committee.

Mao showed his new thinking in his report on behalf of the Propaganda Department: "We have concentrated too much on the cities and ignored the peasants."

He was right. Yet it seemed a cry in the wilderness. The NP was more an army than a political party. And the core of that army was landowning officers. How could the NP lead the kind of rural revolt Mao had half seen and half summoned in Hunan? Surely the Nationalists would be more its target than its guardian?

At the congress the Western Hills men were badly outnumbered. Their breach of discipline was debated. They were against the united front—how to punish them for this? Mao was on the side of leniency.

What was Mao up to? If he had seemed right wing at the Second Congress of the NP, much more was to follow.

Chiang Kai-shek, using the gun, was winning out in the race to succeed Sun. He wanted to switch onto an anti-Communist path once he had draped a few strips of Sun's mantle around himself.

In March 1926 Chiang struck at the united front. An incident over the gunboat *Sun Yat-sen* provided the peg for a coup. He arrested Communists (one of them was Zhou Enlai). He shackled the labor unions where the CCP was strong. He outmaneuvered Wang Jingwei's left-of-center faction within the NP. Wang meekly left for Europe on a "study tour." Chiang bestrode a Canton government that had veered to the right.

Yet Mao was by no means through with the NP. True, the Nationalists removed him from control of their Propaganda Department. Yet he soon stepped up to a new post. While Canton's prisons were full of his comrades, he became director of the sixth class of the NP's Peasant Institute. It began in May and went on through October.

Mao was the only CCP figure to be head of an NP project during those unhappy months.

*   *   *

The institute was housed in a graceful old Confucian temple in the center of Canton. Mao loved to see traditions turned on their head in this way. He lived at the institute in a small room of his own, sleeping on a plank bed without a mosquito net (which only the poor and the masochistic did in Canton).

On the shelves of a bamboo bookcase were the notes from his stay in Hunan. They formed the basis of his 23 hours of lectures on "The Peasant Question in China."

Of three other courses he took personal charge. In "Methods of Teaching in the Countryside" he gave nine hours of lectures. He dabbled in his great love of geography. And he began a course of independent study, being still skeptical about authority in the classroom. He started a new workshop on hygiene. He broke new ground by taking the class on a field trip to Haifeng, where Peng Pai had turned beasts into men.

He picked his own staff of fifteen teachers. Most were down-to-earth types with field experience. Yet for lectures on military campaigns he chose the mandarin-like Zhou Enlai (now out of prison).

Zhou was many things that Mao was not: easygoing, dashing, gregarious, a conciliator. At 27 he still looked boyish—Mao had had an adult gravity about him even in his teens—and his ways bore the marks of his years in Japan (1917–1918) and France and Germany (1920–1924). Raised in a household of books and gentility, Zhou had stepped down the social ladder to join the revolution as an act of moral choice. He did not, yet, nor did Mao, know much about military campaigns.

That summer in Canton saw the start of a Mao-Zhou partnership that—after some rocky moments—would survive beyond all expectation: Zhou the landlord's son not long back from Europe; Mao the homespun son of the soil who had been in China's hinterland.

The Northern Expedition—about to begin—was in Chiang's eyes a military operation to unify China by grabbing power from war lords in the north. For Mao it was more than that.

Mao expected a social convulsion as the Nationalist armies moved through villages on the brink of uprising. He was correct. His aim was to train a national peasant leadership to direct the convulsion.

Halfway through the institute session Mao made a limited comeback in the CCP. A dawning concern with the rural situation led the CCP leadership to bring Mao on board again.

At a Central Committee meeting in July 1926, a Peasant Department was at last set up. Mao was named to head it. This apparently gave him a seat once more on the Central Committee. By the end of the year *Guide* had published him again—two essays on peasants.

Yet the rural initiative by no means passed to the CCP. Incredibly enough the CCP's Peasant Department was established in the metropolis of Shanghai. Meanwhile Mao was busy teaching for the Nationalists at their institute in Canton. He went briefly to Shanghai twice, but the center of gravity of his peasant work was still in the NP rather than in the CCP.

This explains why Mao got out on a political limb.

For most CCP leaders the thorny issue of the mid-1920s was how the CCP could pursue the benefits of the united front without ceasing to be an independent party.

For Moscow, equally, the united front was the pearl of great price in China. To be sure the CCP was Russia's baby. But the Russians were in no danger of overestimating the infant's capacity. For now, the NP seemed far more important. Say China, and the Kremlin would say united front.

Mao was different.

NP-CCP relations were not the key to Mao's out-of-line conduct. The *methods of action* issue did not preoccupy him.

What did preoccupy him was a *constituency* issue. Who was the revolution for? And what spark could ignite the vast body of China to a fire of revolution hot enough to melt the old and fashion the new?

Mao's answer came from Hunan. The revolution was for the poor and the vast majority of them were rural folk. It was for the 90 percent of the people in the counties around Music Mountain whom Mao judged to be poor or middle peasants. The spark would rise in the countryside, for landlord oppression was fiercer and far broader than that of urban taipans. In Mao's mind this was now a basic truth. All questions of political method were secondary.

No surprise that he stuck with the NP longer than his CCP colleagues. For in the mid-1920s the Nationalists took the peasantry more seriously than the Communists did.

Consider what Mao was up against at Shanghai. Professor Chen scholastically reasoned: "Farmers are petty bourgeois . . . how can they accept Communism?" Liu Shaoqi condescendingly purred that the proletariat must "take the peasants by the hand" and lead them forward to the revolution.

Moscow was a bit nearer, but not that much, to Mao's basic truth. Maring had a scorn for peasants that recalled Marx's remark about rural idiocy. But Maring had left China for good in 1923. Its eye on rural stirrings, the Comintern found a basis in Lenin to take seriously the revolutionary potential of the peasantry by early 1926.

Yet Mao's logic was not the Comintern's. He favored the NP's Northern Expedition. Moscow did not (on this issue Mao and Chiang saw eye to eye).

The Russians wanted the peasants to join in the revolution under the firm control of the patiently crafted united front. They feared that a march north by NP armies might induce a social unraveling that the landowning NP officers could not control. (And how right they were.)

Moreover, Moscow was cozily in bed with three big northern war lords (including the one who had massacred the railwaymen in 1923). Stalin wanted his war lords and his NP also. A confrontation between the two was not his idea of a China policy that served Soviet interests. It might force a distasteful choice between revolution in China and aggrandizement of the Russian state.

But whence the spark? Each new revolution is an unrehearsed act of creation. A nicely balanced plan based on the latest triumph in some other place seldom succeeds. The spark leaps from nowhere. Original, outrageous.

Mao saw and wanted a social convulsion that would knock the file cabinets of Moscow and Shanghai out of business. In the end, in a way, he got it.

* * *

In Canton during February 1926, Mao published "Analysis of the Classes in Chinese Society." Half a year later as he went north there appeared his "The National Revolution and the Peasant Movement."

"Who are our enemies? Who are our friends?" This was Mao's starting point in "Analysis." He sketched the position of the various groups in the special conditions of China. The urban workers were few. Bullying by imperialism made sure that some of the Chinese bourgeoisie would sympathize with revolution. The rural poor would give crucial weight to the revolution.

"They *need* a revolution"—Mao was basing himself on observed fact rather than on Marx's doctrine.

Yet in "Analysis" Mao still saw the tiny industrial proletariat as the "leading force in our revolution." He managed to fit the wine of peasant power into the bottles of proletarian supremacy.

The September article was another story. It said the peasants are the key in every way to the revolution. *They* feel the greatest weight of oppression. The compradors prevail only on the seacoast and along the rivers. "Not comparable to the domain of the landlord class, which extends to every province, every county, every village."

Mao went further. Compradors merely follow the lead of war lords. And war lords are "chosen by the landlord class." His argument was an economic one. "Ninety percent of the hundreds of millions of dollars the war-lord government spends each year is taken, directly or indirectly, from the peasants who live under the domination of the landlord class." In other words, power in China stems from the land.

"The political aims of the urban workers," Mao ventured, "are merely to seek complete freedom of assembly and of association. They do not immediately seek the political destruction of the bourgeoisie." He had at last given voice to the doubts he felt in Changsha about the muscle of the labor movement.

"As for the peasants, on the other hand," he continued, "as soon as they arise they run into the political power of those village bullies, bad gentry, and landlords who have been crushing the peasants for several thousands of years. . . ." Hence their militancy.

Mao drew the natural conclusion. "If the peasants do not arise and fight in the villages to overthrow the privileges of the feudal-patriarchal landlord class, the power of the war lords and of imperialism can never be hurled down."

It was a startling conclusion. The revolution would stand or fall with the peasants. Only their stirring could bring down the whole creaking edifice of old China. Even the struggle against imperialism depended absolutely upon them. With this article Karl Marx sank into the rice paddies of Asia.*

Mao had shown his hand. Here was what he had learned and resolved in Hunan during 1925.

* * *

Like a magnet the villages drew Mao back. The sixth class of the Peasant Institute ended in October 1926. There was nothing else in Canton to claim him. But he did not go to Shanghai to run the CCP's Peasant Department of which he was head. He came home to Hunan. He would deal with the rural challenge not from a city office but on the spot.

Much was happening in Hunan. The province was living up to its reputation as a pivot in China's affairs. The Northern Expedition had reached Changsha in the late summer of 1926. Hunan was now ruled by a war lord painted over in Nationalist colors. At the same time the peasant unions were virtually taking over swaths of the countryside.

A storm was brewing between these two forces and Mao would soon be in its eye. He seemed to be brooding, half aware of coming troubles. After a phase of activity—he went probing the villages of Zhejiang and Jiangxi and reported in *Guide* that the peasants were "rising like clouds," and he gave the main speech at the first big rally of the Hunan Peasant Union—Mao went off to unwind at Music Mountain.

He had often gone there in winter, when rooms that were not home were at their least hospitable. A pattern recurred. Exactly as two Januarys before, retreat in his home valley led on to a fact-finding tour of the surrounding villages. He spent 32 days in five counties.

This time Mao did not have to wander around like a minstrel looking for customers. Five million Hunan farmers were now unionized. His task was less to stir up than to draw a picture of the total scene and show it to the nonrural world.

This he did brilliantly. Edgar Snow's *Red Star Over China* was not the first classic of the Chinese Revolution. That was Mao's *Report on an Investigation of the Peasant Movement in Hunan*.

Mao saw landlords being paraded in tall paper hats by crowds beating gongs. The most hated types he found already locked up in county jails; their foul deeds included hoarding grain to keep the price up—exactly what

---

* I have given Mao's actual words in some detail because Peking has drawn a veil of obscurity over "The National Revolution and the Peasant Movement." It has not been published in the *Selected Works* or anywhere else in the PRC.

Mao's father did in 1906. Other landlords had left their property and fled like dogs.

Peasants formed spear corps to enforce a new kind of order. Children swiftly drank in the fresh morality. At play, Mao noticed, one child angry with another would stamp its foot and cry: "Down with imperialism!" He heard a peasant shame a bully: "Hey, you local tyrant, don't you know [Sun Yat-sen's] Three People's Principles?"

Society was being turned upside down. The smash and bounce of it stunned even this rebel who had been on leave of absence from the epicenter of rebellion. Awe pushed his pen: "Every bit of the dignity and prestige built up by the landlords is being swept into the dust." His excitement gave the *Report* a style epochs removed from the usual NP or CCP document.

Mao exulted in excess. He thought it great fun that peasants burned basketfuls of mah-jongg sets in an effort to stamp out gambling. It did not bother him that some ordinary folk *like* to play mah-jongg.

He reported with glee—and no qualm—that the fallen landlords had started to label the upstart peasants "emperors." He did not try to conceal the quip of a brought-low gentry: "Today it's a world of committeemen. You can't even go for a piss without bumping into a committeeman."

Mao saw sedan chairs smashed. He noted breezily that peasants "detest the people who use this conveyance." Did he cast a thought back to his revered Professor Yang in Changsha who was carried to college every morning in a sedan chair?

Of course the revolution had changed. One thing to call for a new society. Another thing to have your sedan chair smashed from under you.

Mao joked about Lord She, a character in a story of Liu Xiang (77–6 B.C.). This aristocrat adored dragons and had his palace decorated from floor to eaves with drawings and carvings of them. A real dragon heard of Lord She's love for the species and visited him. The man almost died of terror.

"To talk of 'arousing the masses of the people' day in and day out," Mao concluded, "and then to be scared to death when the masses do rise—what difference is there between this and Lord She's love of dragons?"

Or between this and the sedate radicalism of Mao's father-in-law?

Pedagogy was receding in Mao's order of priorities. He had turned against the foreign schools that had smoothed his way to a wider world. He would now consider a Professor Yang useless as a political ally.

Report failed to mention the leading role of urban workers in the revolution (Peking discreetly added this for the *Selected Works* in the 1950s). But these pages, if not Marxist, were acidly radical.

Mao classified the farmers into poor (70 percent) and middle (20 percent) and rich (10 percent). As social science it was rough. But as a lever for change it was clever. To make the poor conscious of their poverty is the first step toward revolution.

Mao declared—it was half observation and half exhortation—that the most poor are the most militant. It was an old theme of his. The first shall be last and the last shall be first. This is what Mao meant by revolution in 1927. He was making a "shout" on its behalf.

* * *

Once more Mao had to click back to the urban political world. Carrying a dog-eared manuscript of his report, Mao went to town for a meeting of the NP's Central Executive Committee. It convened in an exciting atmosphere at Wuhan in March 1927.

Wuhan became part of Mao's life for the rest of 1927. Capital of Hubei (North of the Lake), this industrial city is a bastion of central China. It stands on the rail route that joins Peking and Canton. Equally it guards the water route down the Yangze (Son of the Ocean) River from Chongqing to the sea at Shanghai.

In their modern green uniforms and cork helmets, the armies of the NP had reached Wuhan in December 1926. A government of left-of-center Nationalists, plus a few Communists, tried like a juggler to control unruly balls tossed by China's quickening revolution. Chiang Kai-shek was out of harm's way to the east at Nanchang. By the spring of 1927 Wuhan was the precarious seat of the Chinese revolutionary movement.

Both the CCP and the NP—now like a couple with one eye on each other and one eye on divorce—moved their headquarters to Wuhan.

The NP found a nice villa for Mao. Built by a merchant, it had gray brick walls that kept out the hubbub of the street. An interior courtyard was surrounded by rooms mellow with dark vertical boards.

Kaihui came up from Changsha to share it with Mao. Her mother also arrived with Mao's two boys and stayed for some months. A third bedroom of the villa was occupied by Peng Pai, the rural organizer from Guangdong Province. There was even a study for Mao. In it he put finishing touches to his pages on the peasants of Hunan.

He taught part time. Nearby, in a sprawling mansion of red pillars and airy archways, a branch of Canton's Peasant Movement Training Institute had been set up. It was a joint NP-CCP venture. Here during the first half of 1927 Mao lectured to peasants from Hubei, Hunan, Jiangxi, and a few other provinces.

Mao found the Wuhan political weather cloudy. Professor Chen did not like *Report*. Only part of it was published in the *Guide*. The full version—

with its praise of what Chen said were "excesses"—had to find a home in the Hunan organ *The Militant*.

In town were Mao's old Anyuan associates, Li Lisan and Liu Shaoqi. They had come to spearhead the labor movement in China's second industrial city. They thought Mao had a rural bee in his bonnet.

Mao had been criticized in the CCP as a rightist. Now he looked like a radical. Indeed he was a radical. His days as a darling of the Nationalists were nearly over.

Stress did not dry Mao up artistically. He meandered on two hills—called Tortoise and Snake—that face each other across the Yangze. On Snake Hill he found a hoary edifice that captivated him. The Yellow Crane Tower was built in the third century. Mao sat there and ruminated.

As if to lodge himself again within China's high culture, he wrote a poem in the Classical style:

> Blurred in the thick haze of the misty rain
> Tortoise and Snake hold the great river locked.

His mind was on nature and the past.

> The Yellow Crane is gone, who knows whither?
> Only this tower remains as a haunt for the wanderer.
> I raise my glass to the surging torrent,
> And the tide of my heart swells with the waves.

Had he put the villages of Hunan behind him? Not really. He was switching back and forth between worlds. The knack gave him resilience.

*   *   *

Mao's issue—the surge of the peasantry in south China and what to do about it—was the issue of the hour. At a succession of meetings it was debated. Mao was a key participant because his *Report* was being passed around as the hot potato of the season.

Yet most of the leaders of the Wuhan regime had no vivid sense of the boiling Hunan situation.

When he eventually spoke up Mao alarmed the NP leaders. He wanted the peasants to confiscate the land (by simply refusing to pay rent for the fields they tilled). He argued for this within both the NP's executive and its newly established Land Committee.

The snag was clear in his speech to the latter: "The militarists in Hunan are exploiters of the peasants." Mao had a point. But those very militarists were hand in glove with the Nationalists.

Within Guangdong Province the NP could be radical with little cost. But during the march north it was suicidal to be so. For a large number of the officers who were serving the NP north of Guangdong owned land.

Mao knew he was on the verge of a break with the NP.

He scornfully quoted military leaders who denounced the peasants for having "simply gone red." He rejoined: "But where would the national revolution be without this bit of red?" The national revolution was fragmenting.

Hunan was not typical of China. Mao had come back from Music Mountain with a vision of irresistible peasant power. It would have been a terrible mistake to imagine, in 1927, that as Hunan went so would China go.

Mao's former boss in Shanghai, the NP leader Wang Jingwei, wrote Mao off as a firebrand. Even a close pal from Changsha—a Communist and Mao's own choice to head up the NP in Hunan—told the Land Committee that Mao's plan for confiscation would lead to "an immediate struggle between poor and rich peasants."

The favored policy of the hour, among Nationalists and Communists alike, was to restrain the "excesses" of the peasants for the sake of preserving the NP-CCP united front* and pressing on with the Northern Expedition.

Mao lived in his villa and went to committee meetings. But this politicking seemed a sideshow. Beyond Wuhan, China was polarizing. The united front on the banks of the Yangze was a fragile bamboo soon to be snapped by a strong gale from down the river.

Chiang Kai-shek dealt the *coup de grace*. He had long given up on the link with the Communists. By the sword—the only political method he was comfortable with—he tore it apart once and for all.

On reaching Shanghai, Chiang massacred the left (Zhou Enlai escaped death by a hair's breadth). It was a grim revelation of the inner meaning of the Chiang version of the Northern Expedition. For the Shanghai left had fought against northern militarists in order to keep the city safe for Chiang!

Elsewhere in south and east China, war lords were springing back to crush radical organizations. A raid on the Soviet Embassy in Peking produced a harvest of leftists. One of them was Mao's old boss Professor Li Dazhao.

Mao learned that Li had been slowly strangled to death—an excruciating fate—by the forces of war lord Zhang Zuolin, and that his Cultural Bookstore in Changsha had been smashed up by the militarists. The lights were going out.

The CCP held its Fifth Congress in teetering Wuhan. An NP delegation attended for the first time. Mao prepared himself without enthusiasm.

---

* Mao himself was to do just that a decade later; see pages 163, 165, and 192.

Things went even worse than he expected. With 60,000 members, the CCP was at the height of its grass-roots power. But at the top it had lost its way.

The main problem was that Moscow clung to the CCP-NP united front as to a totem pole. Professor Chen was not happy with this policy, but he went along with it.

Mao's views on the land issue were savaged. His colleagues were so displeased with him that they took away his right to vote. He spoke little. He must have realized that he would lose his post as head of the Peasant Department. But when the ax fell (a specialist on Russian literature named Qu Qiubai replaced him) Mao was depressed. He went to no more sessions.

As the congress droned on to disaster, Mao lounged at his villa and made long walks by East Lake and on Snake and Tortoise hills.*

* * *

Under Comintern instruction, the CCP was being marinated ready for Chiang Kai-shek's oven. For the peasant issue had caught up with the left-of-center NP. Having to retreat on that issue, they handed the future of the NP to Chiang. It was now either peasant revolution or Chiang plus war lords.

The CCP itself chose neither!

The left-of-center NP in the end chose Chiang. During July it turned against the Communists in Wuhan. A terror against the left was mounted here as over much of China. By midsummer the Chinese Revolution seemed at an end.

Events in Hunan set off the slide to the right. During May some military officers under the war lord governor turned their guns on the left. Mao went south to rally resistance, traveling in disguise on a freight train.

In Changsha, soldiers marched to union and student offices and shot unarmed occupants to the cry "Long Live Chiang Kai-shek." Thirty thousand people were slaughtered in Hunan that summer. Mao was lucky not to be one of them.

A bit desperate, Mao tried everything. He rallied workers and peasants to fight against repression. But he also thought it worthwhile to have a personal meeting with the governor to urge reason on this twilight figure.

Incredibly enough Professor Chen—and Moscow—still hoped to repair the united front. Chen ordered Mao out of Hunan and off to Sichuan. Mao either disobeyed Chen or made him change his mind. He stayed on like a

---

* M. N. Roy recalls Mao being very restless in Wuhan. He would drop into a meeting for long enough to make trenchant remarks, then leave abruptly, saying he "could not live comfortably" in Wuhan "when the peasant masses were suffering" down in Hunan.

fireman amid flames. His break with his old god was all but total. But what Chen could not do the Hunan war lord could. He ordered Mao's arrest—and Mao went back to Wuhan.

Word reached Mao of terror in many places south of the Yangze that had been strongholds of the left. Strikers were beheaded on the spot. The middle of Shanghai was decorated with bamboo cages in which dangled the heads of the executed. Communist girls were killed by bullets fired up the vagina from the guns of cursing soldiers. Mao wept at the suffering.

In the countryside, students who had come to ally with the peasants were burned alive in kerosene. Leftists were bound to trees and put to death with a thousand cuts into which salt and sand were periodically rubbed. Slicing of victims was revived in a war-lord salute to feudalism. Foot muscles were gouged out.

Mao got back to Wuhan from Hunan in time for a bitter spectacle. Borodin was busy packing in his four-story villa with its elevator and damask wallpaper. He was closing the books on a portfolio—the Chinese Revolution—that Moscow had made his for four years. "It's all over" was his benediction as he left for Russia.

For Mao—but not most CCP leaders—Soviet revolutionary prestige retreated as surely as Borodin's train. Meanwhile Chiang sent a cable from Nanjing to congratulate the Wuhan NP on its patriotic act of slicing out the cancer of communism from its body politic.

If the summer was tragic, the autumn was grotesque. For the CCP lurched from one extreme to the other.

It abandoned timid collaborationism—too late—for blood-and-thunder insurrection, which was too early.

And it wrapped military extremism in a package of moderate politics—for Stalin was still months away from writing off the NP.

Mao was caught up in the reversal. He showed no more mastery than anyone else did in a doomed situation.

The CCP met in special conference. Professor Chen had gone off to Shanghai in despair at the July 15 break between the CCP and the Wuhan regime. In his absence the mood was to embrace everything he would have rejected. The button was pushed for a rash of uprisings in town and village alike.

Mao was to lead the attack in Hunan. It was to be called Autumn Harvest Uprising.* Mao was like a man in a daze. He hurled himself hither and thither, but the strategy seemed either mistaken, or not one he truly favored, or both.

---

*Autumn was a tense time—hence judged apt for revolt—because peasants had to hand over grain for rent and loan repayment to hated landlords. The peasants were also free from work after the harvest.

Pathetically enough, the new line was also Moscow-inspired. In June, Stalin had suddenly demanded a militant policy for the CCP. The absurdity of it was that the tyrant, from 4,000 miles away, insisted the CCP go on supporting the Wuhan regime at the same time. By now that was, as a Chinese saying goes, like playing a lute to entertain a cow.

So in August and September the CCP marched toward suicide. It began armed sallies *under the NP flag!* The first was at Nanchang, led by Zhou Enlai. It did not succeed. But in a distracted mood the CCP went ahead with uprisings that were military operations without a political logic to them.

Amid the chaos a special meeting of CCP leaders took place in early August. Mao attended the ragged sessions in the 100-degree heat of a Wuhan attic. A rump of eleven men overthrew Chen as head of the Party. In his place rose Qu Qiubai, the literary scholar who had succeeded Mao in the peasant portfolio.

So Professor Chen went into the rubbish tin of history. Mao later blamed him heavily for the horrors of the NP link. Too heavily, for when Mao spoke in 1936 he did not want to blame Stalin, who was the bigger culprit.

Mao's comment on the two chief resident Comintern aides was harsh. "Borodin stood just a little to the right of Chen." It was true that Borodin trusted the NP far too long. On M. N. Roy, the Indian who had played a role from 1925, Mao was hardly warmer. "He stood a little to the left of both Chen and Borodin, but he only stood." Fair enough. Roy's fiery talk could not solve the problem that Moscow was too far away, and too possessed of its own interests, to run a revolution in China.*

* * *

Mao moved left. Like everyone else in the post-Chen CCP, he turned to the gun. Unlike most of the others, he at last rejected the NP; "we really cannot use the NP flag," he wrote from Changsha to the CCP office, as he prepared for the Autumn Harvest Uprising.

And on the land issue he was still out on a radical limb.

The insurrections went off and died like so many firecrackers. Mao's did little better than anyone else's. It was not only that Mao's new leftism was not yet a digested whole (he had supped too long with the NP; the peasant

---

*If M. N. Roy's reminiscence is to be believed, both he and Borodin found Mao enigmatic:

Mao came to Hankow, where I met him for the first time. It was after midnight. We were in the midst of a heated discussion in the Politburo of the Communist Party. Borodin himself was present, sitting next to me. A tall man with a swarthy broad face and longish straight hair thrown back on a high forehead walked in calmly but haughtily. "Mao Tse-tung," Borodin whispered. He took no notice of me or even of the all-powerful Borodin. We two foreigners looked at each other. Borodin remarked in an undertone: "A hard nut to crack; typically Chinese."

armies could not do miracles overnight). It was also that Qu had embraced a varying type of leftism.

Qu wanted to start in the cities. Mao still believed that the center of gravity of the Chinese Revolution was in the countryside. And Qu thought a wave of mass violence could give the left power. Mao was chewing over a slower, more organized, building-blocks approach to using the gun for gaining power. But for the moment he half went along with Qu.

The die was set. Mao went through with his Autumn Harvest Uprising. He held planning sessions at night in a Changsha suburb. He devised his own new flag—to the CCP's irritation—which depicted a hammer and sickle contained in a star. Using his old contacts all over Hunan, he raised troops for an assault that would end up capturing Changsha.

He took the town of East Gate near the Jiangxi border and won a few small victories. But defeat glared at him like the Hunan sun.

Many things went wrong. Mao's troops were a varied lot and some ended up fighting each other. After the summer repression the mass base for a radical campaign was reduced (the Hunan CCP had lost three quarters of its 20,000 members since May). It was a nightmare for Mao to revisit the scenes of his former unions and schools and meet little but death and desertion.

When the mass movement was at its height, in 1925–1926, the CCP was as cautious as a judge. When it was dashed, in mid-1927, the CCP burst into radical flames. Such was the tragedy of modern China's first attempt at social revolution.

The chaos at CCP headquarters was crippling. Mao argued with the Party Center throughout his uprising. He was judged too concerned with armies. He was said to lack faith in the masses. His units were accused of having "soiled their own diapers" when things did not go well.

In reply Mao accused the Center of a "contradictory policy of neglecting military affairs yet at the same time desiring an armed surge of the masses." Coordination was poor. Reinforcements from outside Hunan did not exist.

Eventually it was Mao, not Changsha, that was captured.

During a dash to Hengyang in quest of miners for his army, he was nabbed by landlord troops. He was marched toward a compound to be shot. As the end approached, Mao was calm and shrewd. First he borrowed money from a fellow prisoner and tried to bribe the escort in charge of him to let him go. This plan apparently misfired.

Within 200 yards of the compound he decided to make a bolt for it. He was still thin enough to move like a flash. He escaped the bullets and reached the cover of tall grass around a pond.

The escort troops came after him. They enlisted farmers to search the grass. Mao crouched in silence and devout hope. A couple of times the soldiers came so close that he could have reached out and touched them. Half a dozen times he gave up hope and felt certain they had seen him.

Dusk bailed him out. The troops ended the search and went off for dinner.

All night long he walked across hills and through scrub. He was barefoot. The escort had taken away his shoes—as booty, and because superstition had it that a victim with shoes on as he died would spawn a ghost that would pursue the executioner in revenge.

Bruised and tired, Mao wandered in a region he did not recognize. Eventually he met a farmer whom he was able to persuade to shelter him. Mao regained his bearings. He still had seven dollars left over from the bribe attempt. With these he ate and bought the two things he most needed at that low moment of the Chinese Revolution: shoes and an umbrella.

Mao rejoined what was left of his troops. But the Autumn Harvest Uprising was a fallen soufflé. Mao's relations with the CCP would now be worse than they had ever been. He decided that he might as well be hung for a sheep as a lamb. He refused to attack Changsha. It seemed foolish to toss his remnant of troops to destruction.

Like clockwork the CCP leadership demoted Mao. He was put off the Central Committee. Even the Hunan segment of the party removed him from its ruling body.

But Mao did not get the news of these dark bureaucratic frowns. He had turned his back upon cities and all established organizations. As the chill of October eclipsed a terrible summer, he led 1,000 pathetic survivors to a craggy no-man's-land on Hunan's eastern border.

He was going to use the gun *his* way.

6

Struggle (1927–1935)

Mao walked toward the hills—the only place to go. On the way he made stops to speak to his 1,000 unhappy followers.

By the time he reached a town called Home of the Literati (Wen Chia) Mao had fixed on a plan. He wanted to go to the hills as the peasant rebels of *Story of the Marshes* had done. He had a way to pick up the pieces of the revolution. Did his men dare to follow him?

Some did. Others in the rank and file fell away because the outlook was so bleak. Homesickness was a common pain. There was a yen to get back to farming. And a hunch that fighting for the Nationalists would be more rewarding.

At Three Bays village Mao's troops gathered in an old temple that gave refuge from the autumn rains and the red clay mud which made playthings of their straw sandals. Mao spoke for hours. He explained his idea of an army—but to some it sounded more like a political study group than a military unit. He urged democracy in the regiment—but some officers felt this would obliterate due distinctions.

It did not seem a time for controversial proposals, yet it was Mao's way to be bold when at a low ebb.

The CCP was shattered. A few months before it had some 50,000 members; now it had 7,000. The left-of-center Nationalists had either evaporated into hot air or gone into exile outside China. Most of the leaders of the Hunan and Guangdong peasant movements were dead or soon to die.

Mao had lost no fewer than 90 percent of the worker-peasant force that mounted the Autumn Harvest Uprising just one month before. The 10 percent who remained were being asked to embrace a strange new plan in return for nothing but sweat and tears. They must have surmised that Mao was in disgrace with the CCP leadership. Was this aberrant leader worth the price he asked?

Mao himself must have had doubts. Though the news of his dismissal from all Party offices did not arrive for another three months, he knew it was coming. The disapproval of Shanghai—the Central Committee had perversely gone back there, like ants drawn to honey, regardless of the environs—was one thing and bad enough. Worse was that the Hunan CCP, Mao's own creation, had equally denounced him.

His mind must have ached with regret for the sufferings of the summer. He was separated from Kaihui and from everyone he was personally closest to. He was thin and worn, and his eyes were clouded. His hair was like a medieval broom. His clothes were in tatters and full of lice.

Yet if Mao had doubts he did not talk about them. His granite will showed itself during these weeks. It made of a dark winter a turning point toward mastery.

Food would be short. Soldiers' pay would be small since the sparse hilltop offered few landlords to be expropriated. Few of his officers were Communists and a number were likely to leave. One or two were so incensed by the idea of democracy in the army that they apparently tried to kill Mao during the trek from Three Bays.

But Mao was unshakable. With Hunanese obstinacy he had set his course. Inner sparks kept him moving forward. The shape of a totally new strategy had emerged in his mind after the failure to capture cities. He wanted to try it out.

Other sparks flashed from a defense mechanism. There was no point in going back to make contact with the CCP Center, which now thought so ill of him. Better to make a virtue of his isolation.

Nor did it occur to him to go into exile to Europe, as many prominent leftists did in 1927. Mao's choice of words in commenting on this trend showed how rural his own orientation was: "Many Communist leaders were now ordered by the Party to . . . go to *Russia or Shanghai or places of safety.*"

Mao seemed to have put his last dollar on nature. It was almost as if he had a secret life-giving link with the craggy peaks he had chosen to inhabit. Maybe Mao's bit of the CCP, binding itself to the soil, could be renewed by nature's own cycle.

*   *   *

Mao settled on a fog-obscured summit called Well Mountain. It is a grand but barren world of its own. Mao had chosen it with a peasant's and a politician's shrewdness. The idea was simple. His own remnant was weak. But the enemy must have weaknesses too; how to discern them and play upon them?

The war lords were not a united force. As they contended against each other—the more so to keep up with the maneuvers of the foreign powers in China—they could not at the same time control the far reaches of China's localized farm economy.

And the enemy was weak at the belly. He held the towns, but food came from the villages. If China was what it ate, the Communists should put down roots in the rice paddies.

But one more point was crucial: steel. The rebels must never again be without the means of hour-by-hour defense.

Mao said that the CCP must *build up a regular army* in the countryside. The Party would really become *an army* for a considerable period. Only after having dwelt for a long time in the countryside, and securing full control of it, would the Armed Party pluck off the cities as the last act of the revolution.

This was not Marxism as then understood in Europe—or in Shanghai. But it came to be Maoism as later understood in China—and in Africa and Latin America too.

*   *   *

It was when Mao grasped the gun that he got his act together.

Busy at organizational tasks in Canton and Shanghai through the early 1920s, Mao had paid almost no attention to military affairs. He never wrote on the subject. He was a revolutionary, yet he had apparently never shot a person dead.

Nor did his turn toward rural affairs from 1925 bring a sharp change in this regard. The Hunan *Report* contained no analysis of military power.

After the CCP-NP split of mid-1927, Mao had taken up the gun. So had all his CCP colleagues (after Professor Chen went back to his study in Shanghai). But the aim had been to take cities. And the hastily formed units were far from being a regular army.

Well Mountain was far more than a good lair. Here Mao built a novel kind of power.

Urban ways receded to the background in a double sense. Mao now began to live among the peasants, and not until 22 years later would he again settle in a city. And the chief order of business was violence. Mao now became a general. "The struggle in the border area is exclusively military," Mao said frankly. "The Party and the masses have to be placed on a war footing."

May Fourth had its first true political harvest on Well Mountain. What a paradox! That movement of 1919 had been one of students in cities; it had wrestled with Confucius and shouted against imperialism. What had it to do with the gun and the rice paddy?

Struggle by heroes. If Mao lost Professor Yang's Promethean vision in the thickets of bureaucracy from 1923 to 1926, he gave it flesh and blood on Well Mountain during 1928. "Conscious activity is a distinctive trait of man," Mao observed, "especially man at war."

Only in a one-dimensional sense had the students of May Fourth been steeled heroes. On their marches they carried not guns but toothbrushes. They were fiery in words alone. Mao's true originality lay in bringing three levels together: the gun, peasant power, Marxism. In none of the three was Mao the pioneer. But in combining them into a strategy, he was.

Mao did not seem like a military man. He did not strut. He cared little for outward form, or discipline in the usual military sense. He looked more comfortable with a book than with a gun.

Mao made the gun an expression of a humanistic world view. Until his death he believed that in war people count more than weapons. The secret was simple: war is a branch of politics because winning support from the people is indispensable to both.

It was on Well Mountain that he offered his famous image* of the army as "fish" and the people as "water." War always has a context, and it is always crucial. The gun is useless if the trigger puller is not the missionary of an appealing cause.

It was a startling idea in an era of war lords. But it was also a very old idea. In China the warrior was always supposed to be a moralist. The warriors in *Story of the Marshes* did not replace moral struggle with violent struggle—the sad dichotomy accepted in Western theories of war—but kept up their moral struggle in the midst of war. They *argued* with the enemy! Mao was the same. Over 50 years he never lost his keenness for arguing with the enemy.

Back in the era of May Fourth, two paths to a new China beckoned Mao, each blazed by a professor he revered. One said "process." Chen Duxiu had come to believe the Marx-Lenin laws of historical development: feudalism ... capitalism ... socialism ... communism.

In reaching for Marxism, what Chen grasped was really a science of social change. Cities were the place, urban workers were the key. The contradictions of capitalism would eventually multiply, the revolution would merely be harvest time.

The second path said "will." Li Dazhao gave Marxism a moral and impulsive twist. Whatever the neat symmetry of the agenda, it was *the Chinese* who must sculpt socialism. Most Chinese were peasants and a new China would be born as villages transformed themselves.

In Mao's first years as a Marxist, he had gone along with "process." La-

*The image existed in traditional Chinese literature.

bor unions, cities, the Bolshevik precedent. He had waited like a clerk at history's gate for the "high tide." He had done time in the anteroom of organization. It was Professor Chen's period.

But Well Mountain was another cup of tea. In the struggle to create a new politics, that winter of 1927–1928, the sculptor was pretty much alone with his clay. Will could not but eclipse process.

"We ought to work in the fields," Li Dazhao had written to the intellectuals in 1919, "then the atmosphere of culture will merge together with the shadows of the trees and smoke of the village chimneys. . . ."

*   *   *

There were only 2,000 inhabitants in the scattered villages of Well Mountain. Their life was frugal. The red earth was thin and rock was everywhere. The wheel did not exist. Fire was made by banging stones together.

"Cousin, what is your name?" Mao would say on meeting a shy or suspicious farmer. He was wise to be polite and cautious. Politics on Well Mountain had a coarser grain and more variegated colors than city politics.

There were secret societies. There was tension between long-time inhabitants and Hakkas (Guest People) originally from the north. There were local gentry with links to war lords and Nationalists down on the plain. And Mao was an outsider.

Like a craftsman he had to work by nuance. He could not beat a big drum for land reform, with so little land as the target. He was wedged between landlords and bandits. The two almost bred on each other—peasants squeezed by landlords had little choice but to roam as bandits—and the class structure resembled that in no CCP memo or previous Mao essay.

Mao reveled in the challenge to be flexible and ingenious. The "monkey" in him came out of its cage. The CCP's lawful wife, the proletariat, was far away. In its absence Mao took bandits as his political mistress.

He made a deal with two notorious bandit chiefs, which gave him 600 men and 120 rifles. He filled his army with drifters and vagabonds. Within two years the majority of the burgeoning Red Army were these lumpen elements (*you min*), looked down upon by worker and peasant alike.

Mao turned to riffraff because he had little else. Yet he did not quite regard them as riffraff. "They are all human beings," he said of the *you min*, "and they all have five senses and four limbs." Class to one side, the *you min* were oppressed human beings. Mao felt he could remold them.*

The work was many-sided. There were battles to be fought as Nationalist

---

*He wrote to Shanghai in 1928 that he intended to "intensify their political training so as to bring about a qualitative change in these elements" (the *you min*). Interestingly, the words from "so as" onward are omitted from the 1950s Peking version of what Mao wrote in 1928.

units began to make raids. There were social policies to be devised. How tough to be with landlords? Could a tax be imposed with impunity on the rank-and-file farmers?

Mao did expropriate landlords—it was a less bad way of getting money than taxing the ordinary farmers in the early stages—and some of them he had shot at public meetings. But he bent over backward not to alienate middle elements. He hit the big tyrants but wooed everyone else.

He formed militia and Red Guards to complement the regular units. And he mounted his hobby-horse of education. There were classes for cadres. Classes for soldiers. Classes to teach the leathery farmers to read and write a few characters.

Textbooks didn't exist. Paper was so short that teachers wrote lessons in the earth with a twig.

Mao flowered in the face of the all-round challenge. His features became less taut than at Wuhan the year before. His face was more fluent, more alive with purpose and response. It began to take on a look of authority.

If his father had been "white" squire of Music Mountain, Mao at 34 had become "red" squire of Well Mountain.

* * *

At the CCP Center there had been changes but no improvements. Moscow had become displeased with Qu Qiubai; Li Lisan replaced him at the Center.

For Li an entire metaphysic lay behind the phrase "high tide." The prospect of this almost suprahistorical upsurge, like that of the second coming of Jesus for some Christians, made the present moment different from what it seemed to the unbelieving eye. The failures of 1927 notwithstanding, he favored more such sallies of blind hope.

Li began to rein Mao in. In March 1928 he sent an envoy from the Hunan Party who arrived at Well Mountain with more criticisms and instructions than there are hairs on a cow's hide. The results for Mao were grave.

News of his dismissal from all posts did not shake Mao much. That it was four months old must have taken away some of its sting. But the envoy also assailed Mao's social policies. The Party Center felt there ought to be more "burning and killing" of class enemies. "Workerization" should be the watchword in Party and army (but whence the workers?).

Mao *was* a bit rightist on Well Mountain. Out of necessity. And because to haul in diverse types and remold them was his way (he was indulgent enough to call his two bandit chiefs "faithful Communists").

Mao was ordered to go to southern Hunan and fight pitched battles against war-lord forces. He had no choice in the matter, for Well Mountain had been subordinated to the Party office in Changsha. The costs of moving south were high. Well Mountain was occupied by the enemy—though regained a month later—and Mao's army was reduced by half.

*   *   *

The CCP sent another envoy to Well Mountain, with very different results. The aim was again to correct Mao. But the envoy was a man of less than total predictability. He did not rebuke Mao but joined him in a partnership that changed the face of China.

Zhu De arrived in April 1928. The ultra-left line of the CCP had led him a merry dance of defeat in south China. His troops were few. Still, he had been instructed by the Central Committee to criticize Mao for behaving like the bandits in *Story of the Marshes*. Mao was too military-minded, Shanghai felt. He was trying to operate like a Robin Hood on behalf of the masses, instead of inspiring the masses to rise in their own high tide of revolution.

To Zhu De's officers, Mao looked unmilitary. They recalled him as a tall, intense man in a faded gray Sun Yat-sen jacket. His hair rose high in a tangle. He was unshaven, his beard covering the mole on his chin. The palms of his hands, it was noticed, were hot and pink and shiny.

He was unassuming. Before Zhu himself arrived, Mao was quite happy to sit down—over a mug of hot water—for preliminary talks with second-level leaders.*

Mao and Zhu met and embraced by a mountain stream at the village of Water Hole. They merged their forces into a new army of 10,000 men. This was the real birth of the Red Army, as the Communist forces came to be known.

The two leaders had much to talk about (once before they had seen each other—it was hardly a meeting—at a CCP conference the previous year). Even more important they had a battle to fight, for a war-lord force was attacking. They repulsed it together.

Mao and Zhu were like each other in some ways but not in others. Both were of rural origin and could talk to farmers without it seeming a gesture. But neither in style nor in theoretical grasp was Zhu as much of an intellectual as Mao. Mao had a streak of Zhu's earthiness, but he was not an open book as Zhu was. Zhu was a very brilliant but uncomplicated soldier. Mao made himself a soldier out of a vision that went beyond soldiering.

Zhu quickly looked up to Mao as a thinker; the rebuke he had brought on

*The chief political commissar of Zhu's forces was Chen Yi, later to be Mao's foreign minister, and one of Zhu's most brilliant young officers was Lin Biao, who became close to Mao, and then almost his nemesis, 40 years afterward.

Shanghai's behalf died on his lips. Mao, in turn, needed Zhu's prodigious military talent. Mao always preferred to handle grand strategy himself while leaving concrete operations to others; now he could do that.

So each drew strength from the other at a precarious juncture in the CCP's fortunes. From their encounter a spark of resistance to Li Lisanism flashed out from Well Mountain. The couplet "Zhu-Mao"* was born—and two decades later there were tens of millions of Chinese who believed it was the name of a single hero.

Mao now had a co-worker. He had won devoted followers in Changsha. He had done his share of looking up to higher figures: Professor Yang at college, Professor Chen during the May Fourth period, Hu Hanmin in the Shanghai office of the NP. But how well would Mao work *with an equal?* Zhu was the first test.

* * *

Mao made a political workshop out of each unit. Not by setting up a political department, as Shanghai told him to do, but by forming committees of rank-and-file soldiers who raised each other's consciousness by talking about politics. Was a campaign under way against the troops of a group of landlords? The committees would rap about how landlords had scarred the lives of the peasants.

Mao insisted on a Party cluster in each squad, a Party cell in each company, a Party committee in each battalion. This dissolved the Party from a far-flung abstraction into a daily presence, and brought it to the campfire and to the hands that held the rifles.

Officers were forbidden to beat men. Accounts were open for all to inspect. After each battle Mao held a free-for-all meeting. Anyone could speak up and officers could be criticized, or praised, by name. Officers were sometimes demoted as a result of sentiment built up through an evening's discussion. Thus did Mao the teacher, and Mao the moralist, create a new military spirit.

Chinese armies had only asked for a soldier's body, never before for his mind!

It seemed to capture the psychology of democracy. Each man came to feel part of a shared crusade. This made some old-style officers hate Mao. They were ready to fight for a future goal called democracy, but they did not wish to see democracy within the army there and then.

Mao also laid down a new way for soldiers to move among the populace.

---

*Contemporary accounts give the couplet in that form—rather than the later "Mao-Zhu"—indicating that Zhu was considered the more powerful of the two in the late 1920s and early 1930s.

For Chinese soldiers it was the custom—as Mao learned when he was a student at Changsha—to treat the society around them as a larder for their every need.

To loot and rape was part of the job. Week by week the wary villagers on Well Mountain learned that Mao had rolled back the ways of millennia. Soldiers helped farmers with the early sowing; cut firewood for the infirm; returned a scythe borrowed from a farmer; *paid* for cabbages requested from another farmer; spent a night within reach of young girls but did not molest them! Earth and heaven seemed to have changed places.

Mao was demonstrating the difference between an army of occupation, which the Chinese people were all too familiar with, and an army that was to the people as fish are to water.

Mao never went to a military academy, as many others in the Red Army did.* All he had was six months experience as an orderly for the officers of a Changsha garrison. Like the farmers, Mao had not liked what he had seen of armies.

Not being a soldier, he turned himself directly into a general. He reasoned that an army must always have a *purpose* and that its way of life should befit its purpose. As a general, Mao was great because he was an outsider with an angle of vision that was not purely military.

Can we speak of Mao as a democrat? He gave the People's Republic of China a political system that was far removed from democracy. But while hacking his way to power, he was a democrat in his belief in the ultimate power of the people.

He thought everyone had some good points, and that in overall terms people were fairly equal with each other. He was sensitive to the point of view of the outsider: the misfit (as Mao had been at East Mountain school); one with no claim on others (Mao's situation in Peking in 1919–1920); one without qualifications (as Mao nearly always was). And he had the organizational wisdom to see that good results come only when grass-roots opinion is consulted.

*   *   *

Mao needed all the strength Zhu could give him, for he was between two grindstones. Li Lisan in Shanghai thought him wishy-washy. But the terrified gentry on Well Mountain, not finding Mao at all moderate, called in Nationalist troops against the red bandits.

Mao insisted on two points at key meetings in the township of Maoping.

*For instance, Zhou Enlai (Whampoa), Lin Biao (Whampoa), Peng Dehuai (Hunan Academy), Zhu De (Yunnan Academy). Cf. Mao's remark many years later: "I never read any treatises on strategy. . . . When we fight, we do not take any books with us."

One he called "concentration of forces." There is a time to fan out and attack, but it comes only when you are strong. For the moment, the Red Army was in Mao's judgment too weak.

The second was a point of style, which yet went beyond style. Mao saw politics and fighting as the two sides of a single coin. "Everyone fights and everyone does political work."

Mao stood for an armed Marxist movement—gun and book together—that would take root in the villages and move to the cities as a final climax of revolution. The very fact that CCP headquarters were still in Shanghai pointed up the basic clash between this view and Li Lisan's view. Li's CCP was an urban network of intellectuals, not at all a Party-army.

At first Mao had not envisaged such a long-term role for Well Mountain. The base had not begun in triumph but in retreat. It was an experiment founded on negative lessons from the recent past. But gradually Mao realized that red power *could* exist in the mountains, even if the NP continued to rule much of China from Nanjing.

"A base area is to the army," Mao summed up, "as the buttocks are to the human being." Without a chance to sit down and rest, a person would soon collapse from exhaustion. The same with the Red Army in the China of 1928.

The Maoping line remained in the air as a fine theory. Mao could not fully put it to the test. All summer he had to fight against the Party Center. Armchair firebrands in Shanghai and Changsha were prodding him to leap like a salmon with the "high tide."

The issue came to a head in July. Two envoys of the Hunan CCP came to press Li's familiar aims. Subdue Mao. Get him to push ahead with uprisings.

Mao scrambled for support. He put together a meeting which voted against obeying the order to march south. The Hunan envoys came up with two trump cards. Zhu De was ready to go along with them. And many soldiers who hailed from south Hunan were eager to be near their home districts. The march began in defiance of Mao.

The results were disastrous. Battles were lost. Troops deserted. Towns that had been held by the reds fell to the enemy. Mao dashed south to persuade Zhu De to come back to Well Mountain and stick with the Maoping strategy. He succeeded, but found that much of Well Mountain had fallen in his absence.

No high tide had appeared in south Hunan. It was a time for building and teaching, not for adventures into the secure urban lair of war lords and Nationalists.

The envoys from Changsha mocked: "How can there be Marxism in the mountains!" From Marx's angle of vision there could not be. But China was Mao's unwavering angle of vision. Moscow and Shanghai might be helpful in winning power, or they might not. The mountains would be crucial.

Mao and Zhu got most of their home mountain back by October 1928. The struggle to do so probably forged their link closer. Zhu was rueful about his southern campaign, and increasingly impressed with Mao's mind.

Maybe there was something to the "buttocks" image after all? Were Mao's moderate land policies perhaps wise in the end? Mao was still frowned upon by Shanghai. But locally he had reaped a moral victory. By the end of 1928 he was effectively top man in the rather fragmented Hunan CCP.

Meanwhile the Sixth CCP Congress met in Moscow. There was nowhere in China safe enough to hold it. None of the congress's resolutions was as eloquent as that stark fact. Nor as important as the reality that it took five months for reports of the congress to reach Well Mountain.

The Sixth Congress elected an ultra-left Politburo. Li Lisan ruled it. No one would have proposed the absent Mao for the Politburo, any more than they would have proposed a vote of thanks for the terrible Russian food served between congress sessions.

Still the congress (apparently at Russian prodding) did say that rural base areas were a valid step toward revolution. That was new, and it stilled some of the *fundamental* criticism of Mao's Well Mountain venture. At least Mao found himself back on the Central Committee.

Yet the Sixth Congress was at daggers drawn with Mao's methods. The rural bases were seen as no more than the anteroom in which to await the high tide. Urban workers were still cherished as the chosen few (*very* few!) of the revolution. The idea of filling the CCP with riffraff was thought worse than filling it with nothing.

Did Mao ponder the record of his role at CCP congresses? Six of them had now taken place. At two (the first and the third) he had played his part. At two (the fourth and the fifth) he had been on the sidelines. Two of the six he had missed altogether.

Mao found himself again caught up in a triangle. Earlier in the 1920s, it had been a triangle of CCP–Moscow–Nationalists. Now it was CCP (in Shanghai)–Moscow–Well Mountain.

The CCP was an organization whose members seldom met together. The largest of its congresses—the fifth at Wuhan—had gathered only 80 people. The Party organized and advanced and struggled *by letter*.

Months would sometimes elapse between the writing of a letter and its receipt. Policy A would be supplanted by Policy B, under instructions just received from Shanghai, at the very moment when Shanghai was penning a letter reembracing Policy A. As likely as not, another letter would be on its way from Moscow which contained a ringing endorsement of Policy B.

In retrospect it seems amazing that these pedants were actually trying to win power over 450 million people.

At times Mao benefited from the medieval pace of communications. He did not hear of the ultra-left line of November 1927 until four months later. This gave him a season of freedom.

Yet he sometimes lost troops because letters took so long. He did not hear of the *criticism* of the ultra-left line in Moscow in mid-1928 until November. Meanwhile he felt under pressure from that line, and went along with land policies that lost the Red Army much support.

Mao was often provocative on paper. Yet in inner-Party struggles an eloquent pen did not always serve one well. When colleagues joined him in the field—as Zhu did—they found him compelling. But his tone on the page raised hackles. He seemed to be announcing truths and this irritated those who didn't agree with them. His skill with aphorisms was a two-edged sword. It made his meaning vivid. But colleagues do not like aphorisms if they can turn none themselves.

Mao's axioms and his imagery may have seemed arrogant if only because they stood out from the gray complexity of the usual inner-Party prose.

* * *

Mao drew his family members tightly around him. Difficulties in his public life prompted an extra need for intimates. This had happened several times at Music Mountain. Now it was the same on Well Mountain—except for a dramatic casting change in the leading role.

Mao's siblings came to pull their weight. Brother Zemin somehow detached himself from the headquarters of the CCP at Shanghai (where he had been doing well, despite the Party Center's anti-Mao point of view) and loyally joined Mao's backwoods experiment. Zetan came up from the Hunan lowlands. It was he who performed the delicate task of meeting Zhu De on Mao's behalf as Zhu first approached from the south. Both brothers served Mao solidly over the next few years. As a consequence their wives were arrested at least once.

The adopted sister, Zejian, gave even more to the cause of Well Mountain than the men. She had been a Hunan leftist activist all her adult life. From late 1927 she shuttled in precarious circumstances between Well Mountain and the plains. In 1929 a Nationalist hatchet man caught and killed her.

Kaihui was in Music Mountain with the two boys.* It would have been difficult—but probably not impossible—for her to have come to Well Mountain. Maybe she had to choose, in the circumstances, between being with Mao and being with the boys. She stayed with the boys. The Nationalists nabbed her while she was on a visit to Changsha in 1930. She was tortured and killed.

For the last three years of her life Kaihui never saw Mao. There is no evidence at all that Mao spurned Kaihui; indeed he retained lifelong affection toward her. But there is also no doubt that he fell deeply in love with a high school girl in mid-1928.

He Zizhen was 18 years old when she caught Mao's eye. She was bright and lively. One of Zhu De's commanders wrote down his impressions of this "revolutionary lovemate" (*ai lu*) of Mao's. She was attractive but also refined. She spoke in a clear and measured way. Her eyes were a "pair of crystals." To meet her "gave you a feeling as sweet as honey."

Zizhen was also politically minded. Her father was a small landlord with enough progressive instincts to run a bookstore that sold left-wing items. Ms. He joined the CCP in 1927. She even lent a hand in the Nanchang Uprising in August of that year.

One evening in June 1928 Mao spoke at a Party meeting. Aptly enough, it was at the township of Forever New. Zizhen was secretary of the township's branch of the Communist Youth League. She was present at the Party meeting. Mao chatted with her after the meeting broke up. Together they ate a late supper of two chickens and two bottles of wine.

A couple of days later Zizhen spent all day helping Mao at his work. This time she stayed the night. At breakfast the following morning Mao apparently made no bones about his catch. "Comrade He and I have fallen in love," he announced to colleagues.

A few days afterward another officer had a planning meeting with Mao. Business over, he smiled and breezily offered Mao his congratulations. Mao laughed and inquired: "Who told you?"

"It's the happy news of the camp. No one *doesn't* know of it. But how about inviting me to a celebration?"

Mao arranged a feast.

The affair was sudden. It had the allure of youth to spark it. It seemed to express the new fluency that Mao had found on Well Mountain. There was gusto and boldness to him now, despite the odds against him in wider arenas.

*Some sources mention a third child of Mao's marriage with Kaihui, but the evidence on this point is inconclusive.

Soon a new popular song was heard across the ravines of Well Mountain:

Commander Zhu is hard at work, carrying rice through the ditches,
Commander Mao is hard at work—making love.*

For the next few years Mao was constantly with Zizhen. Their meeting heralded a creative period for Mao (as that with Kaihui had done eight years before). She soon bore him two children (as Kaihui had during their two years of fulfillment together in Changsha).

A new wife and a new life again coincided.

In one respect Mao's tie with Zizhen differed sharply from the one with Kaihui. The 18-year-old was wholly a child of the struggle. Mao had met Kaihui under the shadow of her father, whom Mao looked up to in a way that went beyond politics. Zizhen did not have this other dimension (Mao apparently never met her parents). She was just an eager Communist girl. It was exhilarating for Mao to clasp in his hands such a new-cut gem.

On Well Mountain few knew of Kaihui. Mao apparently spoke little of her or of his three sons. Still, Mao married Zizhen only in 1930, after word had arrived of Kaihui's execution.†

* * *

Mao left Well Mountain early in 1929. The reasons were practical and not philosophical. He left one base to try and set up a better base.

There was pressure from the Party Center to move south and stir up visible revolution. There were Nationalist attacks on Well Mountain which made of every freezing night a life-and-death struggle. There were ultra-leftist errors in land policy, which cut the Red Army off from the good will and food production of middle-level villagers. And General Peng suddenly arrived.

Peng Dehuai became one of the great figures of the Chinese Revolution.

---

*Some Chinese sources hostile to Mao suggest that Zizhen soon became sexually dissatisfied with her older, constantly busy partner. Mao, understanding Zizhen's point of view, is said to have written a poem giving expression to this sadness, and showed it to Zizhen:

I am just eighteen, hair not yet white,
Cornered on Well Mountain, waiting for old age. . . .
An orderly comes to the door and says
'Commander Mao is busy at a meeting'
I have only my pillow, against the lonely shadow,
My grassy bed grows cold as the night wears on. . . .
I should have married an elegant man, and drawn enjoyment from the hours.

If Mao wrote these lines, he most successfully held back his own style in order to speak with Zizhen's voice.

† Zhu De also took a new wife (his fourth) during the Well Mountain period. Like Mao's, Zhu's wife was a teen-ager plucked from the ranks.

But his arrival with 1,000 men was not entirely welcome. It strained the food supply.

Mao decided to move into Jiangxi (West of the River). This green, hilly province appealed to him and Zhu De for a package of reasons. By embracing another province they would get the nit-picking Hunan CCP out of their hair. Zhu had a gold mine of contacts in the Jiangxi NP (he had held hands with them all too long). And the Jiangxi establishment had less tax money and foreign aid with which to fight the reds than did the right wing in Changsha and Canton. Peng was left behind to hold Well Mountain.

A terrible march in single file along icy ridges began in January. Each of the 4,000 soldiers (the one hundred women included Zizhen) carried one pound of cooked rice. Their cotton clothes were full of lice but not of warmth. Their makeshift headgear made them look like the customers of a rummage sale. There were no medicines. More than 2,000 of the troops lacked a rifle; they carried spears.

Mao was a scarecrow: thin, ragged, hair hanging to the shoulders.

After two stops the rice was all gone. The 4,000—less a few who had already died of illness or starvation—trudged on. Without a battle, hundreds more would soon starve. Yet without another meal soon, very few could fight another battle. In time they found the enemy. The third night out from Well Mountain they overpowered a Nationalist garrison. They ate that night.

Mao advanced but at a cost. Before reaching the warmer south he lost scores of men dead from exposure. There were times when the Red Army men tore branches off trees to arm themselves against the foe. At the town of Big Surplus—in country rich with tungsten—Mao made the very human error of letting his wretched troops linger too long in an oasis of relative comfort. The enemy caught up with them and killed hundreds.

It was Chinese New Year when Mao and Zhu reached the small town of Rich Metal (Ruijin), in Jiangxi. The local regiment was in the midst of a New Year's banquet, having just returned from what it thought was a victory over the "Zhu-Mao bandits." The mood was festive. Red candles on the trestle tables matched the red paper of New Year greetings pinned by every doorway of the barracks. Wine flowed. Chopsticks were busy. Laughter soared.

Bullets all of a sudden rent the air. The revelers gaped. "Zhu-Mao bandits" manned each door. At gunpoint they marched the entire regiment out of the barracks and locked it up in an ancestral temple. "We finished the New Year feast for them," Zhu De recalled with a laugh.

Soon Mao had a base established at Rich Metal. He had lost half his men since marching down from Well Mountain. But he had a chance to put flesh on the bones of his ideas about a "war of agrarian revolution." For the rest of 1929 he used the gun to try and turn south Jiangxi red.

When a town fell, Mao put his stamp upon it. He had Communist slogans painted on walls. He held meetings to explain the Red Army's origin and purpose. People's councils (soviets) were set up. Sometimes they lasted and sometimes not.

The Rich Metal region was less poor than Well Mountain; the furniture of Mao's daily life became a shade more affluent. Food was better. Clothes could be replaced. Some medicines were available.

When the Zhu-Mao forces captured the town of Long Bank (Changding), they found themselves in charge of many sewing machines. On them, workers stitched the first standard uniforms the Red Army had known—gray-blue, with leggings and a cap topped with a red star.

*   *   *

Mao was back among rice paddies and green hills. Yet the logic of his situation was not the same as in Hunan during the mid-1920s. He now had a safe area to operate in, which he had sadly lacked during the Autumn Harvest Uprising.

The Red Army could not be the instrument pure and simple of revolution—Mao was not a Napoleon—but its force was essential to the revolution. It would *secure* the revolution.

If only Li Lisan could wait for the seed to ripen! In twenty years Mao would do just what the impetuous Li wanted to do now—march the Red Army into China's teeming cities.

Being on the move did not reduce Mao's tribulations with the CCP in Shanghai. A snowstorm of letters with ultra-leftist instructions caught up with him.

Li Lisan had lost none of his talent for being bloodcurdling from an office desk. He had interpreted the decisions of the Sixth CCP Congress to suit himself (as Mao was to do). Now as throughout 1929 he fired away: treat cities as the key; do not build bases; do not carry out land reform—it would be premature; scatter the Red Army into roving bands. And he instructed Mao and Zhu to leave their troops and come to Shanghai for consultations!

Zhu was angry. Mao was calm. Both disobeyed the spirit of Li's policy as they conformed when possible to its letter. For a year they got by with such fudging.

The wonder, perhaps, is that Mao never bolted from the CCP: In 1924 (when scorned as "Hu Hanmin's secretary"). In 1927 (when the Fifth Congress went against the land policy he believed in). In 1928 (when he was told to leave Well Mountain). Now in 1929—and at one or two moments yet to come.

He stayed within the fold because he still had a burning belief in the coming of a Marxian revolution. He was flexible to the brink of opportunism in his methods, yet his goal remained communism.

Moreover, Mao could not have gone it alone with a mere province or two as his kingdom. China is vaster than Europe; the population of Hunan alone in the 1920s was equal to that of the whole of France when the revolution of 1789 occurred. An eventual victor in the fight for China's future would need links that made him a truly national force. Mao and Zhu without the CCP were not in 1930 such a force.

Mao was going the local route, but he was not localistically minded.

Had Mao bolted from the CCP in the late twenties or early thirties, few would have followed him. He was seen as an impressive figure, but only at the middle levels of power.*

It is unlikely that he thought of himself as a savior of China. He had his own views, and quite often they were out of line with the Party Center's. Yet it is striking that Mao exerted a lot of effort, and made numerous compromises, in order to stick with the CCP structure.

* * *

In 1929 Mao fell ill with malaria. For three months he was very sick and at times he hovered between life and death. Quinine could not be obtained in Jiangxi. With difficulty and painful slowness it arrived from Shanghai by messenger (two men set out with the precious bottles; one was beheaded en route, one got through).

Mao rested in a cottage in the high reaches of Fujian Province, beyond the eastern border of Jiangxi. His life was probably saved by a Christian doctor, Dr. Fu, whom the Red Army had won over to its cause, and who had acquired his first name—Nelson—on being converted at a British Baptist mission in Long Bank.

That Li Lisan's influence was a major problem for Mao in Jiangxi was demonstrated by the behavior of Zhu De during Mao's illness. As if rudderless, Zhu began to half obey Li. He went off from Rich Metal at the head of "roving bands" to "arouse the masses."

God knows what anguish Mao felt on hearing of Zhu's futile compromise with Shanghai. At any rate Zhu's missions bore little fruit. A few months later he was back in line with Mao.

*The second Maoping conference elected a body—the Second Special Committee—to rule CCP affairs in the Hunan-Jiangxi border area. Mao ranked fifteenth in a list of nineteen.

At the end of 1929 Mao sprang back. From illness and despair over Zhu he recovered to plan a crucial meeting in the Fujian market town of Maiden Field (Gu Tian). Prone on his straw bed in the hills, he drafted the now famous Gu Tian Resolutions.

Mao was like a juggler keeping several balls in the air at once. He was arguing with Li on familiar issues.

He also had strong views about how the army should be run; his attack on "the purely military viewpoint" looked like a pained but determined swipe at Zhu De. "Military affairs," Mao insisted, "are merely one means of carrying out political tasks."

And local figures loyal to the Party Center were a problem for Mao. The Gu Tian conference was no triumphal march. It was a power struggle from start to finish, and in order to prevail, Mao finessed some cherished principles. He veered toward order and discipline.

The Red Army was not the band of brothers it had been on Well Mountain. Officers and soldiers were no longer grouped in a single cell for political work. Officers who had few political principles, and even fewer political ideas, had been made Party members just because they were officers. Mao criticized policies like this and yet he sometimes went along with them.

His main stress in the Gu Tian Resolutions was on order. He hit "ultra-democracy" and "absolute egalitarianism." Officers may be allowed the perk of riding on horseback.... Headquarters should be allotted larger rooms than the rank and file....

He tossed in a new thought which looked like a slap at Li and other, younger returned students. One mark of a worthy Party member was that he "must have no desire to get rich on foreign gold." So much for those who went off to study on foreign scholarships. So much for Party leaders who spent half their time on the Trans-Siberian train.

He had by no means lost his vision, as he showed in a letter written to Lin Biao (then a rising young officer), and later baptized as "A Single Spark Can Start a Prairie Fire." Apart from its ringing faith in the future, this letter of January 1930 made clear Mao's respect for concrete circumstance.

He was at this time fairly optimistic. The hope for revolution was as palpable as "a child about to be born moving restlessly in its mother's womb." Had Mao embraced Li's high-tide metaphysic? It happened that Li and the Central Committee were now pessimistic. Mao chided them for it, but his reasons were more striking than his optimism as such.

The struggle hinges on the total situation. Its ups and downs must be plotted not only on the graph of one's own strength but on that of *the enemy's* strength. A simple point and yet a basic one.

In early 1928 Mao had been cautious—for the war lords were not feuding among themselves—and he had been amazed that Shanghai wanted him to strike out in all directions. By 1930 he favored bold action. For now Chiang Kai-shek was being assailed by two sets of war lords, and Japan was putting pressure on China.

In March 1930 a grotesque note was struck by the lumbering bureaucracy of the Comintern. Its bulletin *Imprecorr* published an obituary of Mao! He was declared dead of tuberculosis, farewelled as a "pioneer of the Chinese proletariat."

This lapse was hardly the gravest of the Kremlin's errors in China.

As 1930 wore on, Li Lisan began to resemble the toad who puffed itself up to a gargantuan size and then burst. His oddly personal tug of war with Mao shook the ground from under everyone's feet.

In an ironic way Mao's success in Jiangxi made his problem with Li worse. Even Li was impressed with the Red Army's expanding influence. The Zhu-Mao force—technically the Fourth Red Army—was easily the most formidable weapon the left now had in all of China. This did not make Li a convert to Mao's idea of long-term rural bases. He called it "a joke" to try to set up a regime "in the mountains."

However, Li did want to *use the Zhu-Mao army* to further his idea of an assault on some major cities. Suddenly he won the authority to begin.

General Peng marched on Changsha. He held it for ten futile days and was then driven out. General He Long (his life would soon intersect with Mao's) was sent toward Wuhan, but he failed to capture that key metropolis.

Mao and Zhu aimed at Nanchang. They occupied the Jiangxi capital for a useless 24 hours. The workers did not rise. The Nationalists did not collapse. War-lord troops did not desert in large numbers.

In the sad futility of the march on Nanchang, Mao's only consolation was that Li's line had been proved bankrupt.*

But as the dust of defeat swirled, Li played one more card. One month after Peng had lost Changsha, Li told him to try again and ordered Mao and Zhu to join him for the campaign. The Red Army force exceeded 20,000—the biggest concentration of Communist troops ever—and the

---

*From the time he left the Fujian-Jiangxi border area for the attack on the cities, Mao must have been dubious about the expedition. As he left Long Bank, he penned a verse that seems ironic:

> A million workers and peasants rise up
> Sweeping Jiangxi straight toward Hunan and Hubei—
> To the Internationale's stirring strains
> A wild whirlwind swoops in the sky.

Well, not quite a million . . . hardly a whirlwind . . . Did a non-Chinese song *really* stir Mao so much?

stakes were high. For twelve days Mao went along. But the Nationalists had planes, heavy artillery, and gunboats. . . .

Mao gave up. He disobeyed Li (and carried Peng and Zhu with him). He voted against error with his feet; he returned to south Jiangxi.

Li had burst. Within two months he lost all Party office. Like Qu Qiubai before him, he was summoned to Moscow to lick his wounds in the stable— later in the prison—of his mentors.

It was in the aftermath of the attempt on Changsha that Kaihui and Mao's adopted sister were killed. His two sons were saved but he was not to see them for many years. His farm was seized by the Nationalists, who for good measure desecrated the graves of his parents.

No more rent payments for Mao. No more retreats at his farm for the "red squire." Mao had confiscated many landlords on Well Mountain and in Jiangxi. Now he found out what it was like to be confiscated.

In a curious way Mao savored his fame (and notoriety) in Music Mountain. He later mused to Edgar Snow about his image there. "Local peasants believed," he said in a reference to the early 1930s, "that I would soon be returning to my native home." It seemed a bit indulgent.

Mao had more to add: "When one day an airplane passed overhead, they decided it was I. They warned the man who was then tilling my land that I had come back to look over my old farm, to see whether or not any trees had been cut. If they had, the peasants said, I would surely demand compensation from Chiang Kai-shek." Mao always felt a tug from that secure local world.

* * *

Li's chief critics were not those who had suffered from him. It was a new group—not long returned from study in Russia—that pecked at the corpse. Mao to his credit looked ahead. He had other fish to fry. And fresh enemies to contend with—28B.

"The 28 Bolsheviks" were a group of bright leftist Chinese students in Moscow—smiled on by Stalin because they took an anti-Trotsky stand— whose mentor was the rector of Sun Yat-sen University where they studied. Rector Pavel Mif also became Stalin's favorite adviser on the Far East, which soon propelled him from the groves of academe to the alleys of Shanghai. He became the Borodin of the early 1930s.

28B were good at theory and bad at most other things. Certainly they lacked experience. The two stars—Wang Ming and Bo Gu—were 24 years old when in 1931 they took over control of the CCP from Li Lisan.

Both were as different from Mao as it was possible for Chinese to be. Wang was the suave son of a landlord. Bo's father had been a county magistrate of old China. Both were slick products of Shanghai schools. Both had left China for Russia in their teens (at that age Mao had not even left Hunan).

They came back from Sun Yat-sen University in 1930. Amazing as it seems, they assumed supreme power in the CCP at a Central Committee meeting in Shanghai as 1931 began. Mif had done his stuff.

As if to greet the return of Wang and Bo to China, Mao wrote a crisp little essay called "Oppose Book Worship." Its theme summed up the difference between "Marxism in the mountains" and Marxism imbibed in Moscow. Mao's slogan was "No investigation, no right to speak."

For a while Mao was better off than since 1926. Li Lisan was out of the way. The CCP began to smile a bit more on rural work—though its headquarters were still in the French Concession of far-off Shanghai. Mao was put on the Politburo in September 1930 (first time since 1927).

The Jiangxi base in which Mao was political boss was doing well. By the end of 1930 it covered 19,000 square miles and folded 3 million people to its new way of rule. The fiasco of the attacks on cities added to the prestige of the Jiangxi and other red rural bases.

Li's "joke" came true. Ministers materialized in the mountains. By a decision to form a "soviet regime" as an alternative government for China, the CCP crystallized its new rural emphasis. In the post-Li atmosphere Mao could not but be its key political figure.

Mao had to deal with one nasty piece of unfinished business from his three-year battle with Li. Followers of Li in south Jiangxi who did not like Mao or his ideas revolted against him. The dissidents may have been infiltrated by an "Anti-Bolshevik Corps" which the Nationalists had set up for just such a purpose.

Mao was alarmed. He acted swiftly. He imprisoned several dissident leaders at the town of Rich Field. That brought the revolt to a climax. Thousands surged to Rich Field to try and free the prisoners. Fighting occurred that involved thousands of armed men over several weeks. It was the first major incident within the Communist fold.

Mao won, but in victory he was not magnanimous. He went against his own maxim for in-house feuds: "Cure the illness and save the patient." Hundreds and maybe thousands he had shot. The incident made Mao more secure if less loved.

One day there arrived to see Mao a visitor who announced himself as an old classmate. It was Emi Xiao from East Mountain school. Xiao had thrown in his lot with the Communists (unlike his fastidious brother, Xiao You, who drifted into and then out of the Nationalist camp, and later devoted himself to cultural pursuits in Europe). Mao invited him in for an evening of talk.

The two of them discussed the problems of teaching the illiterate to write characters. The conversation seemed like an echo from Mao's pre-gun life. Yet it also foreshadowed his post-gun life. The stability of the base area gave him an opportunity to think like a teacher again. It was his bent. He would come back to pedagogy as to a favorite pipe.

*　*　*

The Jiangxi regime under Mao ushered in a season of libertarianism. Divorce was as emotion-free as posting a letter. Marriage was a question of love. Producing children was not in itself a badge of merit.

Mao's policy of easy marriage and easy divorce was as revolutionary as any policy he had ever embraced. In old China the lowest classes did not find it easy to marry; Mao was shocked to find in his Jiangxi investigations that only 10 percent of rural vagrants and only one percent of hired rural laborers were able to find a wife. And in old China divorce was almost impossible and totally so for a woman.

After Mao's new laws came into effect, there began a veritable merry-go-round of marriages and divorces. Girls treated local soviet offices as marriage bureaus, encamping there until harassed cadres had found men for them.

Couples married in the morning and divorced by nightfall.

Members of the Communist Youth League sponsored dizzy rounds of promiscuity in the name of "combating feudalism."

Mao seemed to have unleashed the "freedom to love" about which he wrote in 1919 after the bride's suicide. Yet, as the new and the old battled, Mao took a middle position which revealed a fundamental point about the Chinese Revolution. He wanted married bliss for everyone. He did not want orgies, youthful marriage, singleness, or such excesses.

Some of his policies were stricter than many of his colleagues would have liked. He would not reduce the minimum marriage age below 20 for men and 18 for women, as he was pressed to do. He insisted that a Red Army wife* could divorce her husband only with his consent, or if she had not heard from him for two years.

He made a freely chosen marriage bond the possession of ordinary peasants. But he did not favor the "glass of water" sexual views of some Bolshe-

---

*As distinct from a civilian wife. This distinction foreshadowed Mao's shift to a less liberal position on marriage, divorce, and sex in Yanan; the tougher line of the late 1930s was justified in terms of the needs of the war against Japan.

vik intellectuals of the 1920s. The peasants were to be given a place on the plateau of conventionality, not set loose upon the high peaks of sexual adventure.

This accorded with Mao's temperament. He believed in the solid rural virtues. He was not the type of May Fourth intellectual for whom bold social experimentation was an excitement that provided its own justification. His marriages to Kaihui and Zizhen had been steady in the circumstances. It is true that the marriage ceremony meant little to him—he lived with each before getting around to marriage—but once the bond began it was cozy until outside factors brought a drastic change.

Mao's Jiangxi marriage laws exactly reflected that experience. Two people who had started living together were regarded as married, whether or not they had taken out papers. This did away with the very notion of an illegitimate child—a drastic step in China. At the same time the whole aim of Mao's laws was to enthrone stable household love as the norm and the right of all.

Mao had demonstrated the irony of the eventual social impact of his revolution. The coming to power of the CCP changed everything, because it changed the "who" of Chinese society. It changed little, insofar as it retained the "how" of Chinese society.

* * *

Chiang Kai-shek was on the warpath to root out Communists. In a way it was tit for tat, after Li's drive on Chiang's cities.

But it was Mao and Zhu who had to face Chiang's fury. They turned back three Nationalist efforts to encircle them between December 1930 and July 1931. Their victories against high odds are among the glories of military history.

Mao chose the tactics. The enemy was lured in (to hill terrain which the Nationalists did not know well). Trading space in this way, Mao won control over timing. He watched the enemy spread itself out. He waited for a weak spot to become apparent, then he pounced with as many men as he could spare. This strategy he called "pitting ten against one."

The tactics were flexible. They enabled Mao's army to make use of its excellent fish-in-water relationship to the farmers around it. And they were a simple necessity for a heavily outnumbered force. In the first encirclement campaign Chiang threw 100,000 men against Mao's 30,000. In the second he counted 200,000 against Mao's 30,000. For the third effort—Chiang flew in fury to Wuhan to take personal charge of it—he had a massive 300,000 men at his disposal and Mao had but a fraction of that.

The results were the best tonic Mao had had for years. Tens of thousands of Nationalist troops ended up on the Communist side. Many NP generals were killed. Not a few defected to Mao. The Zhu-Mao forces gained more rifles than they had ever set eyes on. They found in their possession some strange machines which they did not recognize or know how to operate—radio sets.

In the summer of 1931 Mao wrote one of his most lyrical poems. The title "Against the Second 'Encirclement' Campaign" seems flat for such exciting lines:

> The very clouds foam atop White Cloud Mountain,
> At its base the roar of battle quickens.
> Withered trees and rotten stumps join in the fray.
> A forest of rifles presses,
> As the Flying General descends from the skies.
>
> In fifteen days we have marched seven hundred li
> Crossing misty Kan waters and green Fujian hills,
> Rolling back the enemy as we would a mat.
> A voice is heard wailing;
> His "Bastion at every step" avails him naught!

Mao and Zhu might roll back Chiang, but rolling back 28B was another glass of *maotai*. The year 1931 was a mixed bag for Mao. He put people's war to the test and it worked. But the situation within the CCP was ominous.

Mao had been enjoying room for maneuver due to freakish circumstances. CCP headquarters were far away in Shanghai. The Jiangxi soviet regime was a novel form of power. For a time it had a life of its own, removed in most respects from Party authority. The mood of military crisis in 1931 worked to prolong its autonomy.

All this was reflected at the First National Soviet Congress in Rich Metal. The 610 delegates—it was the largest conference the Communists had ever put together—paraded in an opening ceremony at dawn on November 7, 1931, the fourteenth anniversary of Lenin's triumph.

28B were a force at the congress, yet they could not dominate it. Mao was elected Chairman of the Soviet Republic of China. (This fragile regime bound in hopeful cooperation all the several dozen soviets—mostly tiny—in south central China). It was by far the fanciest title that had ever come his way. He was head of a government, though most of China did not hear of its, or his, existence, and he was hemmed in by two vice-chairmen—Zhang Guotao, the landlord's son with whom Mao always seemed to disagree, was one of them.

In Shanghai, Wang and Bo, with a nod from Moscow, consolidated their rule over the CCP's quaintly formal structure. A logical next step was taken in 1932. CCP headquarters moved from Shanghai to Jiangxi, where the CCP spirit was most alive. This was a blow to Mao. "From 1931 until 1934," he later claimed, "I had no voice at all at the Center."

* * *

What did 28B have against Mao? The issues of contention were the same old two: military strategy and land policy. In backward China it was the gun and the peasant masses that weighed heaviest in the scale of the revolution's future. 28B were not far removed on either military or land policy from the book-based bombast of Li Lisan.

In the eyes of 28B, Mao was a peasant guerrilla. His army seemed tainted with riffraff. His flexibility in tactics—"the enemy advances, we retreat . . . the enemy retreats, we pursue"—seemed to them to disregard the possession of territory. "Seize key cities," they cried, as if 1927 and 1930 had never happened.

All in all, 28B saw Mao as a peasant rebel from off the pages of *Story of the Marshes*, not as the leader of an army of the proletariat in Bolshevik mold.

In Jiangxi Mao adjusted his land policy to fit the demands of his policy of people's war. The "fish" needed the "water." Confiscation should be practiced in moderation. Middle-level farmers must not be alienated. It was very easy—within the cloisters of a Communist Party—for 28B to throw up their elegant young hands at this. Mao had embraced "a rich peasant line."

Of the CCP's first ten years 28B had no memory. From it they had no wounds. On the other hand what they said was not *untrue*. Their criticisms were in some cases technically well founded.

Mao did weave feudal realities (e.g., the clan) into the tapestry of his rural dominion. Mao was not yet well versed in Marx and Lenin. His mental world *was* in part that of *Story of the Marshes*.

Even on language Mao fought with 28B. He thought it arid to merely transliterate "soviet" and "Bolshevik" into Chinese. To ordinary farmers they were Greek. Many took *su wei-ai* (soviet) to be the name of a person. *Bu er shi wei ke* (Bolshevik) is more un-Chinese than the knife and fork. Mao used the term "Bolshevik" as little as possible, and for "soviet" he chose a phrase with a concrete meaning for ordinary Chinese: "council of delegates of workers, peasants, and soldiers" *(gong nong bing dai biao hui)*.

But to 28B Mao's ear for what would sell among the villagers was proof of his uncertain grasp of Marxism.

By 1933 Mao had been squeezed from policy-making (though he held on to his governmental title). A fourth encirclement was attempted by no fewer than 400,000 of Chiang's troops, but Mao was not in charge of repulsing it.

Zhou Enlai was. At a conference in Capital of Peace (Ningdu) during August 1932, he had replaced a discredited Mao as the Red Army's chief political commissar.

In these years Zhou was not on Mao's side. He believed in positional warfare, summed up in the call to "halt the enemy at the gate." He felt Mao was eccentric. Bitter words flew between the two of them at the conference in Capital of Peace. Certainly Zhou was less inclined than Mao to swim against a tide as surging as that of 28B.

The reds turned back Chiang's fourth effort. It is a vexed issue of CCP history whether Zhou's 28B-inspired methods were responsible for the victory, or whether the residual influence of Mao-Zhu strategy was responsible. Anyway the success added to Mao's isolation. His "timid guerrillaism" was henceforth considered as outmoded as the spinning wheel in an era of automation.

A post-campaign meeting was held in April 1933. It drove nails into the coffin of Mao's military reputation. Mao did not attend. His malaria had flared up again. Once more a setback led to the sickbed.

The Christian doctor arrived and ordered Mao to a hospital for four months. He got better in less than that. Soon he was rebuking Nelson Fu for ordering dishes that were too lavish: "We must not forget that there is a war." It was the doctor's turn to look as if he had malaria. "Suddenly," Fu reminisced, "my face went as red as a beet root."

*   *   *

The year 1933 saw the first article from Mao's pen for quite a while, and "Pay Attention to Economic Work" was one of his first ever on that topic. Having lost control of military affairs to Zhou Enlai, Mao applied himself with an apprentice's intensity to civil affairs at the grass roots.

He went about the soviet area on a horse. He counted the piculs of grain. He organized salt-smuggling squads to filch what could be had from Chiang's territory. He listened to farmers as he had not done since Well Mountain days.

The Central Committee had mounted a drive to build the Red Army to a strength of one million men (in early 1933 it had less than half a million). Around each base it planned earthen walls that would be "bastions of iron and fire." Mao hinted that such a build-up of the army would rob the farms of needed manpower. He thought the walls would lock the reds into positional warfare. "What is the real bastion of iron?" he inquired in a report on questions of livelihood. "It is the people."

Japanese aggression began to darken the Chinese scene once more. Like a cloud in front of the sun, it put the CCP-Nationalist fight in an odd light. What were they really fighting about? Could it possibly be more precious than the sheer physical preservation of China against a foreign foe?

"Manchurian Incident" was the delicate name for Tokyo's first stride across the prone body of its massive neighbor. Its initial result was to distract Chiang a little from his sport of exterminating reds. Its long-term impact was to be weighty indeed.

Mao's nationalism had not ebbed. Almost alone of the CCP leaders, he talked anti-imperialism to peasant gatherings. One of the worst things about the Nationalists, he warned, was that they were in league with foreigners and would open the door to control of China from the outside.

It made people laugh at the time—the few beyond Soviet China who heard about it—but a decade later it looked like a stroke of genius: Mao and Zhu in April 1932 declared war on Japan. Not that they were to see a Japanese for years. Not that they controlled more than a fraction of China's population (their writ ran only among 9 million).

But Mao had a vision.

His aim was not an abstract socialist scheme. Not a repetition of the Russian Revolution, as if "another October" could alone define what was being sweated for in the Jiangxi hills. Not in any vivid sense was he dreaming of world revolution. China was the bottom line. If China was in peril, nothing was more important than saving it. Without *China*, all talk of revolution would be mere gabbling by deracinated intellectuals.

Mao began to gravitate toward a plan for a united front against Japan. He did not have the power to do more than cogitate upon it. The Central Committee issued no declaration about fighting Japan. Indeed, 28B were so free from any taint of nationalism that they considered Japan's attack on China significant mainly as the start of a joint imperialist assault on Russia!

A tragedy occurred in Fujian Province in December 1933. An excellent Nationalist unit, the Nineteenth Route Army, led by Cai Tingkai, turned against Chiang Kai-shek. Cai wanted to fight Japan and not China's own Communists. He put out feelers to the CCP.

The CCP dithered. Attitudes toward the Fujian rebels ranged from lukewarm to hostile. Wang Ming from his lair in Moscow denounced Cai: "I'll shake his hand only if I can spit in his face." Before the CCP lifted a finger to help Cai, Chiang managed to wipe out the heroic Nineteenth Route Army.

Mao must have sympathized with Cai. He wanted a united front against Japan that would be broad enough to include all non-Communist patriots who weren't reactionary. Looking back in 1936, he said the CCP was wrong not to have united with Cai.

Yet Mao did not go out on a limb for Cai. Indeed he sharply criticized him for seeking a "nonexistent third way" between communism and reaction. The point is Mao lacked the influence to go against the tide and win— and he never fought when he knew he could *not* win. He went along. He sacrificed Cai in order to cling to the bit of power he still had in the Jiangxi regime. It was an episode that Mao looked back upon with unease.

*   *   *

Mao dragged himself to Rich Metal for a Second National Soviet Congress in January 1934. He was Chairman of the soviet regime—if by now a mere paper tiger of a chairman—so he had to proclaim the meeting open. He stared down the hall filled with 1,000 delegates and bedecked with red and green flags. He saw the slogan "Only the Soviets Can Save China." A salute of gunfire and a rash of firecrackers began proceedings.

Mao gave a short, lame speech which said nothing. All the decisions of the congress had been pre-made at a Central Committee meeting which Mao either missed or made no mark upon.

A fifth encirclement was already under way, but Mao was hardly more than a spectator. The battles were planned by Germans. Chiang in his zeal for a final solution had turned to Hitler for help; he was now advised by Generals von Seeckt and von Falkenhausen. A CCP in the grip of 28B was almost equally eager to fawn on foreigners; resistance to Chiang was directed by Otto Braun, a German Communist who was the Comintern's latest gift to the Chinese Revolution.

The congress was awash with Wang Ming's frothy optimism. The Braun-run battles had not gone badly until then. Mao had to swallow his doubts about the positional warfare that was being practiced. He was a lame duck as he presided over the congress. No one was surprised when it deposed him from the chairmanship. But it was a cruel jolt for Mao that he did not remain even a member of the government (Council of People's Commissars) of which he had been chairman for three years.

Chiang began to achieve the goal of encirclement that had eluded him for three years. The dream of "halting the enemy at the gate" could easily turn into a nightmare if the enemy were to get through the gate. That is what happened. It showed the folly of positional warfare. Braun valued territory above troops. He lost both.

Spring brought no joy to Rich Metal in 1934.

Von Seeckt built blockhouses and motor roads to link them. The plan worked because the Communists also chose to tie themselves down. The CCP was too weak and ill-equipped for such a strategy; the Red Army was not mobile enough to hit vulnerable NP units one by one. The Nationalists were able to effect a terrible economic blockade on the trapped and poorly supplied Communists.

By August the CCP had lost all but six of its seventy counties. Even Long Bank was in NP hands. Many Red Army officers were dead.

Mao could do little. He said little. He was put in a state of "house arrest" as understood in the West—holed up in a cottage on a hill at Yudu (To the Capital), west of Rich Metal, from midsummer 1934.

One night an officer of Zhu De's army came to chat with Mao. He brought wine and a chicken, delicacies indeed during that bitter season. They feasted.

They sank into wicker chairs in the courtyard of Mao's cottage to sip the rest of the wine. As the conversation turned to fond reminiscence, Mao sighed and said to this officer whom he knew well: "Alas, this is no longer the world of the comrades of Well Mountain."

Mao tried to go back to books. He made desultory notes. He wrote verses that were a retreat to ever-faithful nature. He taught his "bodyguard" to read. But he could not free his spirit from the terrible march of events beyond the pretty hills. Once again he fell ill at a bleak moment.

His temperature hit 105 degrees. This bout with malaria was almost as serious as the death-jousting bout in 1929 (though Bo Gu dismissed it as a "diplomatic illness"). From sometime in August until the end of September he lay gravely ill. On top of malaria he developed a spastic bowel complaint. He must have wondered if his body could ever spring back for another day.

The summer hung still and doomed.

Dr. Fu came to Yudu with his box of tricks. One day Fu brought a stewed chicken for Mao to eat. Mao—an undemanding patient who kept saying that a nurse rather than a doctor would have been adequate for him—refused the chicken. Something professional in him (how forced? how sincere?) made him less inclined to accept Dr. Fu's chicken than he had been to accept the army officer's. He made Fu eat the chicken alone.

Mao rose with resolve from Fu's sickbed. He found a world in pieces when he left Yudu at the end of September. Yet chaos offered a rogue's opportunity.

Chiang won the fifth campaign so handsomely that he almost *did* rid China of the "scourge of communism." The CCP decided to abandon Jiangxi.

Mao felt it was done with "unjustifiable haste." However the decision was not his but that of Bo Gu and Braun. The Red Army remnant was to walk northwest in the hope of joining a soviet under He Long in Hunan.

28B could not but be abashed by the bitter turn of events. So Mao was able to creep back to a position on the military council set up to direct the retreat. It was a mini-comeback. Mao was less blameworthy at least than almost all of his colleagues.

The Red Army was like a boat without a rudder on a heaving sea. The 100,000 men (plus a few hundred women) did not know where they were going. Many of them must have thought they were going nowhere but to their deaths. Not a few had a mind to defect if a chance arose.

So the Long March began.

Two weeks later a radio message was sent from Moscow telling the CCP to pull out from Jiangxi.

Mao managed to take with him, in addition to the three-day supply of rice that each person carried, a horse that was booty from an earlier victory over a Nationalist unit, an umbrella, and a bundle of books.

He did not carry with him the small battered bag—his hallmark in the eyes of his colleagues—that normally contained his documents and maps. This was strange. Those around him took the bag's absence as a sign of Mao's pessimism. He would have had it close to him if he saw himself on the brink of wielding power.

7

A Grip on the Future (1935–1936)

If the far reaches of the tide began to turn in Mao's favor, only a sharp eye could have discerned it during the grim weeks that closed out 1934.

It was true that his adversaries within the Party had lost some wind from their sails (though Bo Gu and Otto Braun were still in charge as the Long March began). But in relation to China as a whole the Communists seemed no more portentous than a few mosquitoes on the hide of a rhinoceros.

Most people outside the CCP (and surely some inside it) thought that its number was virtually up after the failure of 1927 and the dismantling of its Jiangxi base. The first miserable months of the Long March did nothing to change such an expectation.

It was heartbreaking for Mao to walk out from under the government structure of which he had been chief. Moreover, those who remained—in theory their task was to harass the Nationalists, but in practice they were not expected to survive—were disproportionately Mao sympathizers rather than 28B sympathizers.

One of them was Mao's brother Zetan, whose presence in any situation had come to seem like Mao's shadow. In 1932 and 1933 the discrediting of Mao resulted in Zetan's censure, and he was by Mao's side during the period of virtual house arrest in 1934.

Within five months Zetan was captured and executed (together with the hapless ex-leader Qu Qiubai, who had remained in Jiangxi mainly because he was ill with tuberculosis).

Mao also left behind his two small sons by Zizhen. The Red Army's rule was that only children old enough to march could join the exodus. Mao's pair of toddlers were put in the care of an obscure peasant family. He never saw them again.*

---

* After 1949 there were sporadic efforts to locate the two children, and some people in China believe that Zhou Enlai succeeded in this task and watched out for their welfare. But the two offspring—who would today be in their forties—have never surfaced by name.

Zizhen was one of thirty-five wives of CCP leaders who started and finished the Long March. She was pregnant with a third child as the march began; the child had apparently been conceived during Mao's house arrest. The trek proved cruel for Zizhen's body; in effect it also shattered the marriage.

Gunther Stein, a British journalist who visited the Communists after the Long March was over, asked Mao if he had ever found himself in a minority and unable to prevail. "Yes, I have been in the minority," Mao answered. "The only thing for me to do at such times was to wait." In 1935 his chance came.

The Long March took on shape and logic as it went along. No one even called it a "Long March" until well after it had finished; at the start it was no more than a bitter retreat.* "We intended to break out of the encirclement and join up with the other soviets," Mao later told Robert Payne. "Beyond that, there was only a very deliberate desire to put ourselves in a position where we could fight the Japanese."

The overriding point of the march at each of its stages was to survive the murderous assaults of the Nationalists. Within that daily imperative the marchers faced four consecutive tasks: to break out of the Jiangxi cul-de-sac; to join up with one or more of the other Communist soviets farther west; to reestablish a successor regime to Jiangxi somewhere in China; and from that new base to fight Japan on behalf of the entire Chinese nation.

Only over the first task did the CCP leaders not quarrel among themselves. Indeed the disunity was so corrosive that a fifth task of the Long March—not articulated directly and yet vital—was the establishment of new leadership for the CCP. The Long March was to separate the men from the (Bolshevik) boys.

*   *   *

For Mao's own 30,000 troops—the First Front Army, which made up about one quarter of the long marchers—the first great encounter occurred on the banks of the Xiang, river of Mao's boyhood dreams. It brought the inner-Party politics of the CCP close to a showdown.

The CCP apparently lost as many as 50,000 men before Chiang's vastly more capable military machine and in the face of his accurate prediction of the Red Army's northwesterly route. In agony, the wounded stuffed clothes into their mouths to muffle their uncontrollable screaming.

The Nationalists had carved away nearly half of the Red Army. So costly was the crossing of the river that Mao decided to begin a fresh challenge to the leadership of Bo Gu and Otto Braun.

---

* Edgar Snow found in the spring of 1936 that "25,000 *li* march" was still the term used for the epic trek.

The stark fact was that the Red Army could not achieve its plan to link up with He Long's soviet in northern Hunan. Chiang had made arrangements to meet them with a force six times the strength of their own. In this situation Mao stepped into the breach with a fresh plan and a devastating set of criticisms of 28B.

The Red Army should go southwest into Gweizhou (Noble Land), a province where the enemy was weak. Then it would link up with an existing Communist army in northern Sichuan Province. This idea of Mao's prevailed, against Otto Braun's wish to bear north.

At the same time Mao boldly spoke up at meetings in December 1934 and blamed the terrible losses at the Xiang River on two wrong tactics. The route laid down by Bo Gu and Braun was a mere straight line. This had enabled Chiang to lie in wait for the Red Army.

And Mao complained that the Communists had not used the weapon of the feint, which their constant movement made logical, nor shown sensitivity to local sentiment or awareness of topographical quirk.

Mao also felt that the Red Army had been traveling too heavy. It carried all the trappings of a government shifting from one city to another: mules and donkeys staggered beneath the weight of furniture, printing presses, and a veritable archive of documents.

Mao's struggle with 28B on this point touched a fundamental issue. Was the CCP a state temporarily on the move (28B's view)? Or was it a slowly ripening movement in calculated diaspora, going back to the soil as a first step in a building-blocks approach to the attainment of national power (Mao's view)?

One detail spoke volumes about 28B's style: during the opening months of the march the Red Army possessed virtually no accurate maps. With all the equipment and documents they *did* insist on carrying, Bo and Braun did not think to carry an adequate key to their own movements. (When a young Swiss missionary was captured, and accused of aiding the Nationalist cause, he eased his plight by helping Red Army commanders read a French map of Jiangxi Province!)

Of course, 28B lacked even a fraction of the military experience that Mao and Zhu had built up over nearly a decade. Bo had not seen a shot fired in battle by the time he became leader of the CCP in 1932; as the march began he was only 26 years old. Nor had Braun—though he was the Comintern's military adviser to the CCP—been militarily trained or fought in a war. And Braun *spoke no Chinese*!

Mao at 42 was an old man by comparison with the 54 percent of the marchers who were under 24. Only 4 percent were over 40. There were even some 11- and 12-year-olds who served as buglers, orderlies, water carriers, messengers, and general mascots. Dr. Nelson Fu declared that in his judgment 90 percent of the eager, naïve, peasant long marchers were without sexual experience.

* * *

The early losses fell due to 28B's account, and Mao could not be blamed for them. In fact Mao's influence within the CCP was quickly rising. He did not win power overnight, but he steadily accreted it in the weeks following the battle of the Xiang River.

He began to get his way on policy. Documents were burned, furniture was tossed into ravines, surplus guns were handed out to reliable local farmers, and the much-streamlined transport column made itself less of a target by marching only at night.

Each upcoming move was explained to the troops and summed up for them in a catchy slogan. In many villages mass meetings were held to explain the Red Army's mission and seek recruits. Soldiers with artistic talent were encouraged to work up song-and-dance routines to captivate local audiences. All this bore Mao's touch.

Once a company was put on top of two conspicuous mountaintops and ordered to display itself in open spaces so as to seem more numerous than it was. The Nationalists indeed took these busy soldiers to be the bulk of the Red Army; one triumphant NP radio message intercepted by the Communists said "the main Red Army is bottled up." Meanwhile a much larger Communist force attacked the Nationalists in the rear.

The results of this very Maoist feint were handsome. "The whole campaign," one general recalled, "was like a monkey playing with a cow in a narrow alley."

Such tactics enabled the Red Army to cross the 220-meter-wide Wu River, rapid in flow and cradled in piles of sheer rock, and so enter the heart of Guizhou Province. As if he had detected that his true opponent was surging to the top, Chiang flew in to the provincial capital to take personal charge of the effort of 200,000 special troops to stop the Red Army from approaching, through Guizhou, the rich prize of Sichuan. The Mao-Chiang confrontation was taking shape.

The Red Army took the wealthy old city of Zunyi (Follow Duty). It was done by a neat trick of the kind that gave the Zhu-Mao forces a reputation for magicianship (the Red Army needed to use its mind: in Guizhou it was outnumbered 100 to 1 by assorted hostile troops).

First the Communists captured a village ten miles from Zunyi and took prisoners, who were the key to the stratagem. Red Army interrogators alternately charmed and browbeat these men. They were given silver dollars.

They were earnestly told of the superiority of the "soviet way" (as Chinese socialism was then characterized).

Soon the Communists had stripped from them every last scrap of information about the garrison in Zunyi—and also their uniforms. The next part belongs to the history of Chinese theater as much as to that of Chinese warfare.

That night the Red Army marched noisily upon Zunyi in the guise of Nationalist troops returning from an engagement! They were dressed in Nationalist uniforms. They spoke phrases in local dialect. They even brazenly used buglers to herald their approach.

In the darkness of a foul night they were taken for friends upon arrival at the gate towers and during their initial dialogue with garrison guards. They explained that they had lost their company commander in a battle with the Reds. Before doubts arose in the minds of the guards, the Communists were inside the the city gates, where they raised bayonets with the shout: "We are the Workers and Peasants Red Army of China."

Mao slept till late the next morning in the elegant upstairs chambers of a minor war lord.

For twelve days he had a soft bed and a good rest in a graceful town of parks and palaces. Much of Guizhou was "liberated" (a new term) from a war lord, and the Red Army now lay poised to encircle Sichuan.

Mao also became leader of the CCP in Zunyi. In that same home of a minor war lord, he called a conference without delay. At it he turned the tables on 28B and gave a new definition to the Long March.

*   *   *

Mao did not command a strong faction of his own. Nor was he part of the two that existed: 28B, and the cadets from Whampoa Military Academy, of whom Zhou Enlai was among the best-known.

Mao was a credible leader because he had, together with Zhu De, a fine record in the early anti-encirclement battles in Jiangxi. But he triumphed *when he did* because 28B had manifestly failed, and because some key CCP leaders could see this and were ready to swallow their doubts about Mao.

Zhou played a key role at the Zunyi conference. After Mao and Zhu De had spoken, and Bo Gu had stoutly defended himself, the crucial fourth speech was given by Zhou. He swung to Mao's side. "He has been right all the time and we should listen to him," Zhou said of Mao. He offered his own resignation from the Military Council and urged that Mao be made its head.

After Zhou's move, 28B never regained the initiative. And after Zunyi, Zhou was never again to raise a fundamental challenge to Mao's leadership or ideas.

Mao's new power was essentially military. And for the duration of the Long March at least, the gun was the key to overall power. He was top man in the CCP, and it seems that henceforth he chaired the Politburo.* This gave him far more authority over the generals of the Red Army than he had enjoyed on Well Mountain or in Jiangxi. Zhu De remained commander in chief of the Red Army, and continued to be in fairly constant agreement with Mao.

Mao walked out of the Zunyi conference with a list of resolutions that read like a summation of all his favorite military ideas.

- Being weaker than the enemy, the Red Army was to concentrate its forces for selected decisive battles.
- Battles were to be avoided when victory was not certain; there was nothing wrong with a strategic retreat, when it led to a counteroffensive at a moment of the Red Army's own choosing.
- The enemy was to be lured in deep; giving up territory was not necessarily bad from a military point of view.
- The Red Army was an evangelizing team as well as a fighting force; deviance was to be handled by education rather than by an intra-army secret police; every soldier was to be told the aims and dangers of every move.

At a mass meeting in the city's Roman Catholic cathedral, held to explain the resolutions, Mao tossed out a slogan for the coming months: "March north in order to fight Japan."

The twelve days at Zunyi transformed the Long March from a ragged military retreat into a political mission with a national as well as a revolutionary purpose.

It also became clear that the Chinese Revolution had emerged from under Moscow's shadow. Stalin now had larger fish to fry than the wandering CCP. Nor could he conceive of revolution being made by a rural-based army.

Even more important, the CCP was for the first time led by a man who was not in awe of Russia. It was no accident that power gravitated to Mao precisely when access to Moscow was difficult, and when communication between the Comintern and the CCP shrank almost to vanishing point.

Mao still looked up to the October Revolution. Thirty years later—when he no longer had any reason to speak better of Russia than his convictions

---

* Mao did not become secretary general of the Party; Zhang Wentian, a member of 28B but critical of Bo Gu and Braun, took that job. Mao's prize was the chairmanship of the Military Council; in this slot he effectively replaced Zhou and Braun.

In 1935 there did not exist the office of Chairman of the CCP, later to be the supreme position in the Party. Yet the office of secretary general was no longer the supreme position, as it had previously been. The fuzzy leadership structure of the CCP after Zunyi is reflected in official Peking histories; they refer simply to Mao as having attained "the leadership."

warranted—he told André Malraux that one reason for marching to the northwest was "the possibility of contact with Russia." But for Mao the center of gravity of the Chinese Revolution was in China's own villages.

Within the Party and the army, moreover, Mao's organizational methods added up to a rejection of Stalinism. This was especially true of his faith in the remolding of people, and of his flexible, nativistic, and mind-over-matter military tactics.

*   *   *

Mao's ultimate aim was to reach the north of Shaanxi Province, and from there to fight the Japanese. Meanwhile he would try to link up with Zhang Guotao's army in northern Sichuan, and set up a soviet in that fabulous province.

Mao looked almost spruce as the march resumed. A bodyguard noticed that he had acquired tailored gray tunics while in Zunyi.

He had a horse but he seldom rode it except when exhausted. At two points he became too ill with malaria even to sit on his horse. He slumped in a sedan chair borne by a pair of soldiers.

In his personal bundle there was always the umbrella and the books. The titles changed as the march progressed, but *Story of the Marshes* was there throughout. No evidence exists that he carried with him any works by Marx or Lenin.

He often worked through the night, but sometimes he reverted to type and slept in his hammock until midmorning. He could always count on several young men as aides, including a secretary, a paramedical helper, and a bodyguard who was also a sort of bush valet.

The bodyguard, a man in his twenties called Chen Changfeng, only gradually learned of Mao's precise demands and solitary ways. Mao would require boiled water instantly when a stop was made for the night. He would insist on being kept awake if the situation called for all-night work. Chen had to quickly make ready a work place—a cave or even a clean rock.

Sometimes Mao found a bit of luxury falling into his lap. His staff took great delight in arranging for him to sleep and work for a night or two in a landlord's house with a courtyard, straw on the bed, and a desk that boasted stationery and a telephone.

For Mao a new find of cigarettes was enough to light up even the grayest day. Some reports even had his men exchanging opium for cigarettes with troops they were supposed to be fighting. When no tobacco was available Mao showed his ingenuity by testing out all manner of pungent leaves as a substitute. Otto Braun joined him in these risky experiments; the search for a good smoke was probably the one shared enthusiasm of the fussy German and the calm Chinese.

The last light of a setting sun made the sky a crimson carpet, and changed Mao's jacket from gray to orange. Under a full moon, a snarl of rocks suddenly resembled a brace of jousting dragons. On a night as black as pitch, a column of troops made torches from pine branches to warm and light their path through a gorge, and the slopes took on a ghostly grandeur.

Moments like these Mao pinned down on paper in his poems. He felt "the sky three feet above me." He saw the pelting snow as "three million white jade dragons in flight." A river in flood he depicted as "turning men into fish and turtles." A range of hills seemed to him to "charge like wax-hued elephants."

Mao truly found himself on the Long March. Despite acute discomfort, the challenge of localities he was not familiar with, a brush with death, one more wrenching feud within the Party, and several moments when the very survival of the Red Army seemed in doubt, the trek of six thousand miles over ten months brought out his awkward genius.

Paradoxically, this was not one of his phases of retreat into private ties, but rather a time of public fulfillment. He was alone and yet bound up in a collective mission. Although Zizhen made the Long March, she was hardly Mao's companion for these ten months. Detailed memoirs by those who served Mao closely do not even mention her. Nor was Mao in intimate touch with his surviving brother, Zemin, who looked after money and documents and equipment.

On the other hand Mao seldom wrote more poems than during the march. "On horseback, one has the time," he said nostalgically twenty years later. "One can search out rhymes and rhythms; one can reflect." The verses expressed a merging of nature with history which, in the end, was the secret of Mao as revolutionary and as the first Oriental Marxist theorist.

He saw the hills as part of the array of battle:

> Mountains!
> Like great waves surging in a crashing sea,
> Like a thousand stallions
> In full gallop in the heat of battle.
>
> Mountains!
> Piercing the blue of heaven, your barbs unblunted!
> The skies would fall
> But for your strength supporting.

Mao seemed to find in the soil a verification of the revolution. It was as if the life and topography of the eleven provinces that the march traversed provided a new authority—replacing Moscow's—for the changes Mao was intent upon making to the face of China.

As the march ended he even invoked a range of mountains for an image of the world peace that lay beyond China's own revolution:

> To Kunlun now I say,
> Neither all your height
> Nor all your snow is needed.
> Could I but draw my sword o'ertopping heaven,
> I'd cleave you in three:
> One piece for Europe,
> One for America,
> One to keep in the East.
> Peace would then reign over the world,
> The same warmth and cold throughout the globe.

Mao was an explorer, between battles, of the vast reaches of his nation. He saw temples and hills he had read about two decades before. Once before he had left south China, to go to Peking, but he had not felt a free spirit there. Now he traveled as his own boss; he made the terrain his own by treating it as the crucible of his new style of revolution.

The truest images of Mao in 1935 are of the poet with eyes cast far; of the strategist poring over a map with a farmer's shrewdness and a general's vision; of a leader, not being close to family or friends, who talks philosophically with his eager young bodyguard, or takes fifteen minutes to teach his secretary a few new Chinese characters.

Most of his great moments were solitary, yet also as public as the mountains. During his year as the Moses of China he communed with the land and did not seem to need the intermediate ties of wife and friend and counselor.

* * *

Sichuan turned out a tougher nut to crack than Mao expected. Chiang was on the spot to fussily direct massive anti–Red Army operations. "The fate of the nation and the party," he telegraphed to his officers, "depends on bottling up the Reds south of the Yangze." A number of war lords also roused themselves to an unusually vigorous defense.

And Zhang Guotao let the Red Army down—in Mao's eyes—by abandoning his soviet in northern Sichuan and heading pessimistically for the no-man's-land of Tibet. This meant Mao could get no help from Zhang's excellent Fourth Army in his drive to move north across the Yangze. It enabled Chiang to squeeze Mao's marchers inside a network of formidable rivers.

One fatiguing effort to enter Sichuan took the Red Army to the township of Maotai, home of the fiery rice wine that is China's contribution to world inebriation. The Communists found themselves in a distillery lined with one hundred vats that each contained twenty piculs of the opaque brew.

Red Army youths were not used to luxuries of this (or any other) type. Some of them thought the liquid in the vats was for bathing; they soaked their tortured feet in it! Otto Braun knew better and quickly became merry. Some Red Army men lost a bit of their inexperience in that distillery. For by the time the Communists had left Maotai, not a drop of "foot water" remained.

The Red Army evaded Chiang's squeeze only because of Mao's brilliant feints. It now seemed best to loop west into Yunnan (South of the Clouds). Mao pretended to attack the capital of Guizhou, where the Chiangs had installed themselves in high comfort to await final victory. "We shall win the battle," Mao observed as he dispatched the diverting unit, "if we can lure the enemy troops out of Yunnan." This the Red Army did, and in April 1935 Mao led his pilgrims into Yunnan.

Mao met a blaze of spring for which this area bordering Vietnam is famous. Paddy fields were alive with new shoots, between round hills lit up by wild flowers and butterflies. But he had to be content with a swift taste of the march's first warm weather. For Chiang, like a bee after the honey in Yunnan's blossoms, had zoomed upon the provincial capital of Kunming (Manifold Brilliance) with more than 100,000 fresh troops at his fingertips.

Mao made another feint toward Kunming. This gave him a break for the crucial crossing of the Yangze—here called Golden Sands River—that demarcates Yunnan and Sichuan to the north. The Golden Sands descends at a rate of eighteen feet per mile through hills of rock. Chiang felt certain he had the Red Army pinned against its inhospitable banks. He ordered the burning of all ferryboats at points near the Red Army's route.

But Mao's cunning made up for what his army lacked in men and guns. As a unit under Lin Biao performed the feint toward Kunming, and another laboriously began to build a bamboo bridge under Chiang's gaze, Mao dispatched a battalion to a ferry point well to the west. Here the use of disguise, worthy of the old novels of peasant revolt that Mao never tired of rereading, enabled the Communists to begin an audacious crossing of the Golden Sands.

A vanguard, dressed as policemen, Nationalist scouts, and travelers on tax business, negotiated the turbulent waters in a bouncing craft. They strolled into the garrison compound, found the troops deep in games of mah-jongg with their guns resting harmlessly against the walls, and disarmed the whole place. The scheming yet unsubtle Chiang had not thought to burn the boats here. Over the next nine days six large ferries took the Red Army over the Golden Sands and into Sichuan.

The Red Army had entered an area inhabited by non-Han—so-called minority—tribes whose ways were as wild as the terrain they occupied. Toward them Mao was at once principled and hyper-flexible.

He insisted that his troops treat the tribespeople with respect. Even the rapacious Lolos (a tribe of the Yi people) were paid in silver dollars for every chicken and ounce of grain the Reds acquired.* This stemmed from Mao's sincere belief that the non-Han minorities had been poorly treated in old China and should be made full partners in the socialist China coming up over the horizon.

But Mao also played the tribes off against each other. The outrageous methods he used recalled his deals with bandits on Well Mountain, and foreshadowed the unblushing balance-of-power tactics of the PRC's foreign policy in the 1970s.

Mao sized up that there were White Lolos and Black Lolos, and that each hated the other no less intensely than did Red Chinese and Nationalist Chinese. It suited him to lean to the Black Lolos. He argued to them that not all Chinese were bad, any more than all Lolos were bad. He proposed that the Black Lolos and the Red Chinese stand together against their common enemy, the White Chinese (Chiang Kai-shek).

Soon one of Mao's generals was draining a bowl of chicken's blood to swear an oath of brotherhood with a local chieftain; and kowtowing before a Lolo empress to ensure that after he had given her two hundred rifles and a thousand silver dollars, she would graciously allow the Red Army to claw its way across her appalling realm.

If this was Maoism, at least it worked, regardless of what 28B might think about it; several hundred Lolos joined the Red Army and made the rest of the trek to northwest China.

The last major river crossing of the Long March was possibly the most redoubtable in all military history. Chiang was determined to keep the Communists west of the Dadu River, where they would likely perish in the snows of eastern Tibet. At this river even the heroes of *Romance of the Three Kingdoms* had been said to meet defeat, as had the great Taiping leader Shi Dakai in the 1860s. Both stories were well known to Mao. Both rebel movements he admired.

Chiang, who had flown to Chongqing to again personally direct the extermination of the Communists, also knew about the two celebrated rebel movements. He despised both. His airplanes dropped leaflets on the Red Army saying that Mao was about to "go the way of Shi Dakai" (the Tai-

*One of Mao's associates (who lost both legs on the Long March) remarked later to Edgar Snow's wife: "These Lolos were first-class confiscators, and we were not too much amused to find someone who could do this much better than ourselves."

ping chief was put to death by slicing after his defeat).

The Dadu is too fierce to be generally navigable. Even a ferry crossing is a rash gamble with the rapids. The only bridge was firmly in Nationalist hands.

Luding Qiao (The Bridge That Lu Built) looks like a piece of acrobat's equipment. It consists of thirteen chains—cemented into rocky cliffs on either side—that run across the rapids at a height of 200 feet. An infinity of planks lies side by side on top of the giant chains.

The Nationalists, by way of welcome, had removed every plank from the half of the bridge on the Communist side. Only the sparse, forbidding chains remained. To minimize extra preparations of such a kind by the enemy—Mao believed that delay had cost past rebel armies dearly—the Red Army men covered the last eighty miles of their approach to The Bridge That Lu Built in a fantastic twenty-four hours.

The suicidal task of an advance group was to swing forward like monkeys from chain to chain, with grenades and Mausers strapped to their backs. Then, if still alive, they were to approach and assault the Nationalist bridgehead across the planks of the second half. Of course most of them perished, falling into the water after being hit by Nationalist bullets. But five of the first batch of twenty-two got far enough to begin hurling grenades into enemy ranks.

Spirit somehow triumphed over matter that afternoon at the Dadu. Others followed the five survivors; momentum gathered. The Nationalists, stupefied, tried everything. They began pulling up the planks on their side of the bridge. When that was too slow they tried to ignite the wood in a fire of paraffin.

But Mao's men were surging as if gravitation had become a horizontal force. More and more troops swung from under the chains—the bullets were fewer now—and ran across the flaming planks with bloodcurdling shouts. As if broken by the mad heroism of the Reds, the enemy ran pell-mell from their positions even before the jaws of defeat closed upon them. About a hundred Nationalist troops asked to join the Red Army on the spot.

All of the volunteers who led the crossing of the Dadu were under twenty-five years of age.

*   *   *

The next order of business was to link up with Zhang Guotao's Fourth Front Army. Nature and non-Chinese tribesmen made it far from easy. The struggles of midyear rammed home to Mao that Chiang was not his only problem.

The Great Snow Mountain range brought a sharp change of clime and altitude. Darkness came at midafternoon. Rice did not exist, and the available corn upset most stomachs. During the frequent storms, hailstones the size of potatoes poured from the sky. At heights of 16,000 feet, hundreds of the lightly clad troops, especially the thin-blooded southerners, collapsed from exposure and sank forever beneath rifts of Sichuan snow.

To make matters worse, tribesmen of the Fan people murderously rolled boulders down mountain slopes to express their displeasure at the Red Army's intrusion.

Mao tried to cheer up the men with poems and stories. He had learned somewhere a recipe for a warming drink—a brew of boiled hot chilies and ginger—which he peddled to the freezing soldiers. But the hardships, and perhaps anxiety over the coming reunion with Zhang, wore Mao down and he got malaria again.

Mao's own view of health gave the central role to the spirit. With two doctors on the Long March—Nelson Fu and Ji Pengfei (later to be the PRC's foreign minister)—Mao raised the topic of psychosomatic illness. He expressed the belief that at times people can live on nothing more than a furious hope.

That he ruminated aloud on extraphysical factors in illness is suggestive in light of the striking coincidence of Mao's own bouts of sickness with setbacks in his work.

It had been true in 1923 in Shanghai (in the face of criticisms of his pro-Nationalist attitude); during the Fourth Congress of the CCP a year later (when he lost his place on the Central Committee); on retreat to Music Mountain in the winter of 1925 and again in 1926 (amid growing tensions over estimates of the role of peasants in the revolution); at the end of 1929 (as pressures from Li Lisan mounted); and in the summer of 1934 (when clashes with the policies of 28B led to his virtual house arrest).

Now once more, as he brooded about Zhang Guotao, anxiety was the harbinger of illness.*

One day a stone friendlier than those of the Fan tribesmen landed at the feet of a Red Army man. Around it was wrapped a piece of paper with the scrawled message: "We're Fourth Front Red Army troops. Forty li upstream at Inien is a rope suspension bridge where you can cross." The rank and file were elated.

Mao was not. For he was about to face a challenge from a man who—the Zunyi meeting notwithstanding—considered himself the leading figure of the CCP.

It had been eight years since Mao saw Zhang. He had not missed him.

---

*Mao confessed to Liang Shuming, at Yanan in 1938, that now and then he fell victim to nervous exhaustion (neurasthenia).

Neither man liked 28B, though Zhang had been to Moscow and knew Russian. Both were of an older school than the boys of 28B. Their distrust for each other antedated 28B.

At their first meeting in 1918 it had been clear that they were far apart in style and background. Zhang the landlord's son was a registered student at Peking University as Mao hung around anxiously on its fringes. Zhang remained attuned to the urban labor movement long after Mao had rooted himself in the countryside.

The Long March brought out fresh differences. Zhang thought Mao lapsed into "guerrillaism." He dismissed the idea of the CCP's leading a national resistance against Japan as a pipe dream. He considered the Zunyi conference an "arbitrary" proceeding whose decisions ought to be reviewed.

Mao complained, for his part, that Zhang did not believe in the idea of soviet bases. He judged that Zhang had twice let the Mao-Zhu forces down by "fleeing" from a base. In his eyes Zhang's Fourth Front Army had little Communist spirit and was thick with elitism.

Banners and posters and a speakers' platform were set up by a roadside in far west Sichuan. In teeming rain Mao waited for the arrival of Zhang. An entourage of thirty men on horses galloped toward Mao.

The gut source of the Mao-Zhang tension was manifest in those handsome horses. Zhang's forces were more numerous (50,000) than the Mao-Zhu forces (45,000). And they were fitter and better equipped. Compared with the experiences of the Long March, after all, the hideaway life of Zhang's men had been a holiday camp.

As Zhang drew up Mao murmured with a nervous laugh to someone beside him: "Don't envy the horses." He may have recalled to himself that his branch of the Red Army had eaten not a few of the small supply of horses that ever came its way.

Zhang recounted the incident in a different way. "As soon as I saw them, I got down from my horse and ran toward them to embrace them and shake hands with them."

A pro-Mao officer recalled: "[Zhang] came riding in with his mounted bodyguard of thirty men, like an actor coming onto the stage. Zhu and Mao rushed forward to meet him, and he waited for them to approach him. He didn't even meet them halfway."

So be it. Certain it is that Mao and Zhang felt uneasy about each other and the character of each other's army.

That evening Mao, Zhang, and other leaders dined together. Zhang noted with a loser's attention to form that the dinner table pursued no serious conversation at all: "They were not even interested in listening to my account of the Fourth Front Red Army."

The wily Mao unnerved the ponderous Zhang with small talk. Himself an ardent chili eater, he floated the proposition that loving chili and being a revolutionary went together. It is possible that Zhang was not fond of chili. His memoirs offer a rather humorless parting shot: "[Mao] was refuted by Bo Gu . . . who did not eat chili."

If this was the moral low point of the Long March, there were reasons for it. Two armies were trying to merge, each with its special traits, experience, and bundle of ambitions. To the center stage came issues that had been forgotten for months: quirks of personality, institutional pride, the future civilian dreams of the poor soldiers.

Mao and Zhang had each shaped an army with a personal imprint, and neither wanted to lose control of what he had wrought.

*   *   *

As for the future, Mao wished to press north and fight the Japanese. Zhang preferred to stay in the west (which he had come to know well) and build more strength.

A climactic meeting of the Politburo was held during August at the township of Maoerkai. This area is heavily Tibetan by race. Mao was quartered in the two-story wooden home of a Tibetan family—the ground level for animals and the second for humans—and the Politburo met in a Lamaist temple.

It was clear that Mao had a majority, but equally so that Zhang commanded the CCP's best fighting force. A compromise emerged. The two armies were to march north *in separate columns.*

A dramatic twist occurred in the execution of this plan. Tensions were so deep that Zhang found an excuse—the difficult terrain—to go west instead of north. For his part, Mao departed from western Sichuan with a strange abruptness. It is very likely that he feared an actual attack on his army by Zhang's superior force. In any case he rated the feud at Maoerkai as among the most critical moments of his career. He could not cope with Zhang at all.

Proof of how wrenching the split had become was that Zhu De went west with Zhang. Mao must have been staggered at this turn of events. He later claimed that Zhu went along only at gunpoint. Zhang asserts to this day that Zhu joined him of his own free will, out of irritation at Mao's pretensions to military genius.

The truth lies somewhere in between.

Zhu's motives were mixed, as seems proved by his refusal in later years to talk about the episode. One of them may have been his desire as a Sichuanese to remain in his own bailiwick. Another was possibly a desire to retaliate against Mao's high-handed ways.

But the heart of Zhu's concern was probably the split itself. He may well have been the author of the compromise policy of splitting into two columns, and have decided to go with Zhang as a way of heading off the devastation of a fight between the first and fourth armies.

At any rate, after a year with Zhang (whose forces fared badly), Zhu returned to the saddle with Mao in Yanan, and thereafter said remarkably little about Zhang.

Unless Zhu went with Zhang by prearrangement with Mao, which seems unlikely, Mao must have suffered mental as well as physical pain in the trek north from Maoerkai.

The grasslands of Gansu Province were in themselves one of the Long March's chief horrors. Mao lost thousands of troops to sinking mud, hunger, and the hostility of the first local populace (the Man minority) to be impervious to all of his rich array of tactics. The queen of the Man hated Chinese so much that she threatened to boil alive anyone who helped the Red Army.

For the first time, the long marchers had to kill and steal to get decent food (otherwise the staples were pine cones, fungus, and grass). "This is our only foreign debt," Mao remarked later, "and someday we must pay the Man and Tibetans for the provisions we were obliged to take from them." There is no sign that this was done.

Mao's curious remark may have been bitterly ironic. Some of the harshness of the PRC's handling of Tibet in the 1950s was probably due to memories of how Tibetans treated Mao's men in 1935.

The Long March ended lamely. Mao entered Shaanxi just south of the Great Wall, after crossing the Six Twists Mountains. A small force under a Communist already in the area, Xu Haidong, welcomed the haggard remnant.* Mao stepped forward and inquired quietly: "Is this Comrade Haidong?" It was. The horror and heroism of the Long March were over.

Mao had crossed twenty-four rivers and eighteen mountain ranges, in weather now tropical and now frigid. He had arrived in the loess† country of the northwest with only 10 percent of the troops who had left Jiangxi one year before.

In the emotion of the moment Mao said only: "Thank you for taking so much trouble to come and meet us." For the first time in his life he slept that night in a cave cut in the side of a loess hill.

---

* It had settled in Shaanxi as a throw-off from the Jiangxi soviet of the early 1930s, joined forces with a Shaanxi peasant movement that had developed in the 1920s, and been enriched by the leadership of sixteen Shaanxi youths whom Mao had taught at the Peasant Institute in Canton during 1926.

† Loess is powdery yellow soil that centuries ago blew down to China from what is now the Gobi Desert.

* * *

The Long March had "made" Mao as a man who joined ideas with action. It had put him on the brink of being China's most promising political leader. And it had provided him with a steeled team who were to stand together with him virtually until the Cultural Revolution of the 1960s.

True, the Long March had been a retreat. And at the end of 1935 the outlook for the CCP was still full of uncertainties. Yet the march had a deep impact, far beyond its physical result of transporting the Red Army a distance equal to twice the width of the U.S.A. It was for Mao's China what the Exodus was for Israel. From a heterogeneous crowd it forged a potent movement that believed deeply in its cause.

The journey was a missionary feat. Passing through territory that was home to 200 million people, the soldiers spoke of their cause. Mao insisted that if a one-night stop permitted nothing else, at least it allowed time to teach some peasants to write the six characters that translate as "Divide the Land."

The marchers took on the aura of prophets. Each fresh act of heroism seemed to validate the Word about tomorrow's socialist China.

All new social systems must start out with ideals—capitalism in its springtime was no exception—and Communist China's were born amid the sweat and blood and ice of the Long March. They stirred all subsequent builders of the new order to a sense of duty. For a season Mao was the Moses of his time.

The Long March would not have succeeded without the daily bravery of the young soldiers, who were idealists because there was nothing else to be. Luck played a role too; war lords in Guizhou and Yunnan could have smashed the Red Army had they focused on the task. But the third indispensable ingredient was the drive and skill of Mao.

The stroke of political genius in Mao's leadership of the Long March was his vision that the CCP's chief task should henceforth be to spearhead national resistance to the Japanese assault. Such a cause brought all the elements of "Maoism" into an interrelated whole. It suggested the northwest as destination. It filled the vacuum of the CCP's raison d'être after the miserable collapse of the Jiangxi base. It unlocked the Communists from a cage of sectarianism, and made them patriots in the eyes of millions of Chinese who did not know Marx from the moon.

Mao got to the top of the CCP not purely through organizational skill, nor in any way by Moscow's blessing, nor yet by evolving a fresh application of Marxism. He rose by being single-minded and ruthless, and because he put some simple psychological and social truths into action.

The ideological formulations would come later, when Mao had time to think them through.

For now Mao had taken the CCP to the soil. He felt more deeply for China than for anything or anyone. This enabled him to do something that 28B could not do: make the Chinese Revolution truly Chinese.

While on Six Twists (Liu Pan) Mountains, with Shaanxi only days away, Mao wrote a poem which looked to the future:

> The sky is high, the clouds are pale.
> We watch the wild geese flying south till they vanish;
> If we reach not the Great Wall, we are no true men!
> Already we have come two thousand leagues.
>
> High on the crest of Liu Pan Mountains
> Our banners idly wave in the west wind.
> Today we hold the long cord in our hands;
> When shall we bind fast the gray dragon?

"Gray dragon" is the name of an eastern constellation of seven stars. In Mao's verse it meant Japan. Dealing with the Japanese was indeed an overriding task for the next decade, and the Long March proved to be a springboard to the fray.

8

Fighting Japan (1936-1945)

In the northwest Mao had a chance to build. He had a formula; "Yanan Way" was soon a phrase with a world of meaning.

Shaanxi in the 1930s was a land of suffering, ignorance, and low expectations.

Peasants wore blue denim and a towel wrapped around the head. What they scrounged to eat had little in common with a southern diet. Many of them did not know the location of Peking, or who the Japanese were.

In the famine of 1928-1929 at least 3 million starved in Shaanxi; Mao found entire villages without a single child under six years of age.

One man told Edgar Snow that he saw peasants pull down the walls of their houses and sell them in order to pay the tax collector, and another that he personally followed a pig as it moved from owner to consumer and saw six separate taxes paid on the transaction.

Latter-day imperialism of the sort that aroused Mao's ire in the south had not penetrated to the northwest. Mao found no Western "exploiters" in Yanan. On the other hand, Shaanxi Province had always been a strategic spot for China's northern relationships. This was one reason why the loess country now became the epicenter of CCP activity.

Mao's formula was to fight Japan on behalf of the entire Chinese nation, and to forge Communist strength from inside this national struggle.

Because the Communists fought Japan tenaciously, the Red Army grew like a vine in the tropics over the next three years. Because Mao was a passionate nationalist, as well as a Communist, he won a victory that Chinese communism could not have won without him. Because he would brook no opposition to his own idea of a "Yanan Way," he ironed out every un-Maoist wrinkle from the broadening fabric of the CCP.

Headquarters was first at Baoan (Protected Peace). Then in January 1937 it was safe to move to the larger and more secure town of Yanan

(Eternal Peace). Mao's Yanan was essentially a training and coordination center for the CCP's guerrilla war against the Japanese.

Yanan is three thousand years old. Until Japanese planes bombed its buildings into rubble in 1938–1939, it retained its ancient form as a walled town cradled by dusty hills. As buildings fell, wall caves multiplied.

A wall cave is really no more than a hole in a hill, with a front in the shape of an arch, done in a latticework of paper windows. The floor is of gray stone and the rear wall is a patched-up surface of the yellow hillside.

Mao lived in four such caves during his ten years in the Shaanxi outpost.

He had known better houses, and worse. One of his three whitewashed rooms he set aside as a study, with candles on the desk, a flask of wine within reach, and bookshelves that held almost no works of foreign origin.

His small luxury was a wooden bathtub. He insisted on a southern-style bed, a four-poster, with a mosquito net. He never got used to the platform, half stove and half bed, on which northern peasants sleep, though he tried it at Baoan.

Japanese bombing drove Mao from his first cave. A second he abandoned because an auditorium was being hammered into existence nearby and the morning noise kept a late sleeper from half his night's rest. The third cave was in a date orchard, whose tranquil groves also contained the offices of the Central Committee. As the war intensified, Mao wanted to be closer to the offices of the Military Affairs Commission, so he moved his household once more.

In front of each cave was a leveled patch with an easy chair or some stone stools, and Mao generally kept a small vegetable plot of his own.

The texture of Mao's daily life and work changed for the better. Fighting was over for him as a constant direct experience. There were bombings now and then, especially after 1939, but it would be ten years before he would again be on the front line of battle.

The local people spoke a recognizable Chinese, which was reassuring after months in western China, where Mao heard the gabble of a hundred dialects but hardly met anyone who could speak Mandarin. There was virtually no rice to be had in north Shaanxi, so Mao ate golden-colored millet as his new staple, with goat meat as an occasional bonus.

Mao sent his eager bodyguard to school. "You've been with me six years now," he said to Chen Changfeng, "and you haven't had much opportunity to study." Chen claimed he was so upset at the prospect of leaving his boss that he wept into the water basin he was bringing in for Mao's morning wash.

Mao no longer needed a personal bodyguard and man Friday. He had a large office staff. He did not, in Yanan, turn to an illiterate youth for late-night philosophic chats. He soon had a new wife, and many visitors, and some close friends.

If Chen wept for the broken spell of his intimate bond with Mao, the pads and pencils that Mao handed him as he took his leave to enroll in class summed up the routinized life which would replace it, for both of them.

* * *

Japan and Russia were now rejuxtaposed on the screen of Mao's world view.

He first heard of Russia as an exploiter of China, long mired in autocracy. Then after the October Revolution the new Bolshevik Russia seemed to him the hope of the world. Yet Mao came to disesteem most of Stalin's advice to the CCP, and his rise to power was a victory of a son of the soil over the awe-struck pro-Russianism of 28B.

Mao's first vision of Japan was a heroic one. It shone as the Asian power that showed Russia to be decrepit in the war of 1905. Even after Japan began its long career as the bully of an incapacitated China, Mao continued to believe in the brotherly potential of the China-Japan relationship. Yet by the end of the 1930s Mao was the high priest of anti-Japanism. It seemed to be the measuring rod for his every judgment.

Mao's anti-Japanism in truth ran no deeper than a calculation as to how China might survive.

The point about Japan and Russia, for the Mao of the late 1930s, was that it would be Japan, not Russia, that would secure China for the CCP.

Japan helped the CCP unintentionally, to be sure. In contrast, Moscow's declared intention was to bring about a socialist revolution in China. But Mao was interested only in results. Without Stalin's aid to the Chinese Communists in the 1920s, Mao would in all probability still have become leader of the CCP. But without Japan's attack on China in the 1930s, Mao would not have become supreme leader of China in 1949.

* * *

During 1936 it became clear that Mao was bent on a revival of the united front with Chiang Kai-shek. The arrangement that had led to such a bitter reversal in 1927! With the group that had murdered his first wife, his brother, his adopted sister, and half of his close friends! A cooperation between two armies that had been killing each other like insects for a decade!

There were several reasons for Mao's veer toward common action with Chiang. One of them was straightforward love of country. During the Long March he had become wistful for national unity, as in a Promethean poem written in early 1936. The lines have the modest title "Snow." They are not modest. But if they are expansive, it is as much on China's behalf as on Mao's own.

> North country scene:
> A hundred leagues locked in ice,
> A thousand leagues of whirling snow.
> Both sides of the Great Wall
> One single white immensity.
> The Yellow River's swift current
> Is stilled from end to end.
> The mountains dance like silver snakes
> And the highlands charge like wax-hued elephants,
> Vying with heaven in stature.
> On a fine day, the land,
> Clad in white, adorned in red,
> Grows more enchanting.
> This land so rich in beauty
> Has made countless heroes bow in homage.

Mao switches from the glories of nature to the glories of the will. He mentions four esteemed Chinese emperors (who reigned during the dynasty from which part of their name is drawn) and even the formidable Mongolian conquerer of China:

> But alas! Qin Shihuang and Han Wudi
> Were lacking in literary grace,
> And Tang Taizhong and Song Taizu
> Had little poetry in their souls;
> And Genghis Khan,
> Proud Son of Heaven for a day,
> Knew only shooting eagles, bow outstretched.
> All are past and gone!
> For truly great men
> Look to this age alone.

The verse drips with Mao's sense of personal destiny. The heroes of the past are all gone. They do not count as the sun rises on a new arena of battle. Is Mao alone the trustee of China's beauty?*

---

* The final two lines seem to have been inspired by *Romance of the Three Kingdoms*. In this favorite novel of Mao's the formidable Cao Cao, half hero and half villain, says to a Han scion called Liu Bei: "The only heroes in the world are you and I."

Yet "Snow" is a very nationalistic poem. It was China's beauty that inspired in Mao the extraordinary belief in the present moment as more glorious than any in four thousand years of history.

Mao wrote the lines while on the brink of putting together a united front of all people who would resist Japan. His dream of heroism occurred at a time when the highest cause was China itself, and the threat was greater than any since that from Genghis Khan.

The heroes that came to Mao's mind did not include Lenin, or George Washington, or any Western figure. They were all Oriental, as well as all dead.

Marxists have often stumbled on the rock of nationalism. Possessed of the idea that class is the key to ultimate human loyalty, they have been confounded by the tenacity of national feeling. Hence the failure of the Second International as the clouds of World War I gathered.

It was not the least of the reasons for Mao's success in the 1930s and 1940s that he never made this mistake.

Every time Mao sent a cable to the Nationalists during 1936, he had one eye on the reaction of the Chinese people. The double task was to shame Chiang and rally the masses.

Was Mao sincere about a fresh united front? He certainly did not believe that the CCP and NP could share the future. Or even that they could fuse to form a single government for the duration of the war.

But Mao *did* believe that the CCP and the NP could join together in the sense of both concentrating—in their own separate fashion—on the anti-Japanese struggle, and doing each other no decisive damage so long as marauders remained in China's house.

There was a disarming frankness about Mao's remark to Snow at Baoan: "We cannot even discuss communism if we are robbed of a country in which to practice it."

And there was an extraordinary fulsomeness to his assertion in an interview with Agnes Smedley: "The Communists . . . are most passionately concerned with the fate of the Chinese nation, and moreover with its fate throughout all eternity."

Chiang tried to be a patriot. Yet the nature of his political legitimacy made him less nationalistic than Mao. His NP lacked roots in the peasant majority of China. As if to fill the vacuum of support, the NP sought foreign backing. In the end, Chiang turned his back entirely on the Chinese, and put himself with a self-pitying shrug into the arms of the United States.

And Uncle Sam was too much at a tangent to the situation to be able to save him.

Mao was shrewd in his playing of the anti-Japanese card. He was also lucky that Japan attacked *when* it did—at a point of uncertainty in his own anti-Chiang strategy. Yet neither factor, nor the two together, would have prevailed if the fight on China's behalf had not touched the deepest layer of Mao's being.

The united front was a double game. But then Mao had a double conviction. The whole point of Marxism, in his mind, was to be medicine for the sick man of China. There was never any question of putting a higher value on the medicine than on the patient.

At the same time, Mao preferred his brand of medicine to Chiang's, and was prepared to fight for it, as the Long March showed, and the renewed civil war of the late 1940s would yet show. He believed that the very choice of medicine was an index of love for the patient.*

Mao's messages of appeal to minorities and outlaws in 1935–36 had the dual quality of shrewdness and passion for China that made his united front policy a success. He challenged the Mongolians to "preserve the glory of the era of Genghis Khan" by taking the hand of the CCP. He urged the Moslems to ensure the "national revival of the Turks" by doing the same thing.

Before the Elder Brother Club he truly bent over backward:

> The Elder Brother Club has always been representative of the organizations of the resolute men of our nation, and of the broad masses of peasants and toilers. ... Its members have been considered as "inferior people" or calumnied as "bandits," and it was denied a legal existence. The treatment inflicted on the Elder Brother Club by the ruling class is really almost identical with that inflicted on us! In the past, you supported the restoration of the Han and the extermination of the Manchus; today, we support resistance to Japan and saving the country. You support striking at the rich and helping the poor; we support striking at the local bullies and dividing up the land. Our views and our positions are therefore quite close—especially as regards our enemies and the road to salvation.

Mao's handbills to this secret society ended: "Let the Elder Brother Club and the whole of the Chinese people unite to strike at Japan and to restore China." The future friend of Richard Nixon was nothing if not flexible.

* * *

Half the story of Chiang's failure is told in a speech he made while Mao was calling for a united front.

"Don't talk about the Japanese menace now," the haughty Generalissimo said at Xian in October 1936, while on a visit to the northwestern city to

---

* An aspect of Mao's attitude to the united front was revealed in a quip at an open-air rally in 1938. "When the Nationalists are wrong we have to criticise them," he said with a smile. "In the past we used the machine gun to criticise them. Now we use the pen and the tongue."

plan a sixth "bandit suppression" drive. "Anybody who speaks of fighting Japan now and not the Communists is not a Chinese soldier. The Japanese are far away. The Communists are right here."

The Communists were even nearer than Chiang knew. Two months later, after a mind-boggling sequence of events, Chiang was Mao's prisoner near Xian.

Mao had put Chiang on the spot with a series of proposals during 1936. One consequence was a restiveness among Chiang's own generals.

For Zhang Xueliang, son of the famous war lord Zhang Zuolin, Chiang's anti-communism and foot dragging against Japan became impossible to stomach by autumn. This bright and emotional man was head of the Man-churian army, whose men were particularly anti-Japanese because their homes in the northeast had been overrun by Japan armies from 1931 onward.

Zhang got in touch with the Communists. A tacit understanding grew be-tween the two sides; during 1936, three thousand of Zhang's troops, sensing which way the wind was blowing, went over to the Red Army.

Then one December night Zhang surrounded a temple north of Xian where Chiang was elaborately quartered. He fired on it and killed thirty of Chiang's entourage.

The nimble Generalissimo escaped barefoot in his nightshirt—leaving his dentures behind him—and after scaling a wall and hurting his back he reached a nearby hill. One of Zhang's officers found him crouching in pain and fury inside a crevice.

Chiang stiffly reminded the officer that he was his commander in chief. The officer bowed politely and rejoined: "You are also our prisoner."

Mao and his colleagues faced a tricky decision. Zhang Xueliang's aim was also Mao's—to mobilize China against Japan. But how best to handle their eminent captive in pursuit of that aim?

Some CCP leaders wanted to keep Chiang in prison indefinitely, and even to try him publicly as a traitor. Mao had other ideas. He wished to use this moment for a show of magnanimity that would give him a moral victory *as a patriot* over the nominal leader of China.

"We didn't sleep for a week, trying to decide," remarked Zhou Enlai (who was for leniency).

As the CCP leaders eyed the hot potato before them, an unbelievable ca-ble arrived from Moscow. Stalin's view was that the kidnapping of Chiang must have been a Japanese plot, and that Zhang and the CCP should re-lease him at once and unconditionally. It seems that Mao flew into a rage on seeing the cable. He tore it up, he cursed, he stamped his feet.

This was the last occasion on which Stalin gave a direct order on a basic matter to the CCP. That Mao was upset—he did not merely burst into laughter, a great weapon of his—shows that he was far from despising Stalin. Still, Mao disregarded the instruction from Stalin, and the crisis added to his mental reservations about Moscow's wisdom and sincerity.*

After dozens of talks between the three parties—Zhang, the CCP, and Chiang and his formidable wife—the outcome of the "Xian Incident" was a compromise that was surprising on its surface.

Chiang flew back to Nanjing a free man. Zhang went with him and was soon Chiang's virtual prisoner. But in return Chiang had given up the pretense of unique governmental authority in China.

Within months a united front of the NP and the CCP was in being, spurred by the "Marco Polo Bridge Incident," which began Japan's large-scale assault on China, and brought on the fall of Peking and Tianjin in August 1936.

The Red Army was reborn as the Eighth Route Army, formally part of China's overall armed forces. The northwest soviet ceased to be an alternative government, bent on replacing that in Nanjing, and became the Border Region. At subdistrict level the name Communist Party was abandoned in favor of Anti-Japan National Salvation Association. Mao was paid a salary—five dollars a month—from Chiang's treasury.

Chiang regained his dentures, but only part of his grip upon a nation that had followed his ordeal as no event in China had ever been followed before. Chiang the man won the victory of his release. But the CCP as a movement won a new stature in the eyes of the nation for releasing him.

Never more than at Xian did Mao show his superiority over Chiang. He took the long view, and left it to Chiang to fuss over immediate gain. He remained calm (except when reading Stalin's cable) and made Chiang's panic seem ill-bred. He shrugged off the formalities of the situation, while Chiang tried to hang on to every last shred of a generalissimo's rights to protocol.

*   *   *

Yet the Xian Incident showed, as in a mirror, that the CCP had by no means put intra-Party squabbles behind it, and that 28B had not been crushed out of existence at Zunyi. No colleague got to the verge of overthrowing Mao—though two would have loved to do so—but there was much sniping from the wings.

Mao as a leader always liked to feel himself in a middle position between

* It may be true, however, that the cable from Moscow helped tip the scales against the hard-liners who wanted to put Chiang on trial. Liu Shaoqi indicated that these hard-liners were numerous by citing the incident as a case where "the minority turned out to be correct"; and Molotov later claimed the Russian *démarche* saved Chiang's life.

dissent on both left and right. That was his position during the formation of the second united front. His swear words for the extremes of dissent were "capitulationism" and "closed doorism."

Chieftains of the first group were the unstable Zhang Guotao (he had once been so "closed doorist" as to be a speck on Mao's far left horizon); and Wang Ming, who as boss of 28B had come back after six years in Moscow, where Chiang was considered the hope of Asia. They wanted a full coalition with Chiang.

Mao shrewdly put the boy who loved candy under lock and key in the candy store—he soon made Wang Ming head of the CCP's united front department, based in Chiang's capital.

Exponents of the "closed door" drew from Mao a hostility that was all the more striking since none of them could, like Zhang or Wang, bid to match Mao as leader of the CCP. These zealots wished to put Chiang on trial and maybe execute him. They ruled out any kind of cooperation with the NP as going against the logic of class struggle.

Mao disliked their lack of a sense of the national danger. He felt they were applying the concepts of Marx and Lenin mechanically, without taking sufficient account of China's unique traits. He thought them Trotskyist— and he always took a dim view of Trotsky.

Many earnest leftists favored "closed doorism" simply because the land reform carried out by the peasant movement in Shaanxi had been a boon for the ordinary farmer. They feared that a fresh deal with Chiang would dilute the CCP's social program. This it did. Mao unblinkingly gave the nod to salvation of the nation over reform of the land.

Mao was even more hostile to the "closed doorists" than to the "capitulationists." Indeed, until 1941 he invested more hope in the new link with the Nationalists than was warranted. Not because he trusted Chiang personally, but because he overestimated the importance of the CCP in Nationalist eyes.

Mao already believed that the future was his. But Chiang still thought the CCP could soon be wiped out. He did not take the Communists as seriously as Mao calculated that he would.

Mao's methods of fighting the Japanese came to be known as "people's war." People's war turned Chinese military tradition on its head. Far from treating war as an esoteric craft of specialists, it threw the task down to the people.

Mao and Zhu had gone some way down this path on Well Mountain and in the heyday of the Jiangxi soviet. But now they trod a grander stage. And what a cast of characters there was to direct! Such emotions to play upon and channel! A people's war was truly that when the subject matter was not merely the dispossessed part of the populace—as a decade earlier—but the full array of the Han race.

"The people" entered the Chinese Revolution on the day that Mao, the chief revolutionary, spoke for China by forging the anti-Japanese united front.

Behind Japanese lines—which meant increasing chunks of China as Chiang's government retreated westward—the Communist guerrillas were the only effective anti-Japanese forces until 1941.

Moving among the people as fish in water, the Communist armies grew to record strength. The Eighth Route Army (ERA) counted 400,000 men by the spring of 1940. CCP membership grew from 40,000 in 1937 to five times that number by 1940.

Chiang could not match the fish-in-water role of the red fighters. Nor could he exercise any control over them, for they were mostly split up into roving bands of only a thousand or so.

The effect of the war on the NP and on the CCP was staggeringly different. As the NP was pushed into western China by Japan's advance, CCP bases behind Japanese lines in the north and the east went from strength to strength. By 1940 fifty million people lived within Mao's base areas of north China.

The origin of the term "liberation" as now used in the People's Republic of China gives us a clue to Communist success. When the reds spoke of liberation, ordinary Chinese took this to mean liberation from the Japanese. Yet Mao already had in mind its emerging meaning as a social liberation from the landlords, taxes, usury, war lords, and Confucian elitism of old China.

And as the CCP's attainment of power.

The reds heavily tilted the odds toward a coming social liberation by their conduct and by their very nature as an army of poor peasants. Mao applied his army to the national cause which Chiang shared. But somewhere within the spirit of that army was a promise of revolution.

To Chiang it was a threat. Yet the Generalissimo was trapped by Mao's unopposable tactic of a united front.

Many foreigners observed with astonishment the stoic heroism of the red armies. Chiang was supposed to provide ammunition and supplies to the Eighth Route Army, but after 1939 he sent nothing. Nor did Russian aid reach any Chinese armies other than Chiang's own. The ERA lived by the enemy and off its wits.

Agnes Smedley watched a grotesquely wounded soldier beg for medicine. None existed. All she could give him was her last sleeping pill. Blood transfusions were unknown. Clothing was so poor that troops waded barefoot across frozen streams, breaking the ice with their feet as they went.

Smedley traveled with one unit that fought all day and had no food to eat when the battle was over. Millet was on hand, but the unit had no money to pay for it, and the commander would not allow it to be taken without payment.

On this cruel evening the commander began to lecture his men on Mao's "3-8" jingle from Gu Tian. A number of the three "major rules" and eight "lesser rules" are about taking nothing from local people if money is not given. To Smedley's stupefaction, the night ended with this hungry unit singing the "3-8" jingle in soaring tones. "Their voices were like a string orchestra," she recorded.

All this from men who could not read or write; who burned Japanese yen because they had no conception that anything other than Chinese yuan could be money; who beheld a locomotive for the first time as an American teen-ager might assess a stegosaur; and who, on a rare visit to Xian, lined up like boys at a hamburger stand for a turn at flicking an electric light switch to watch a bulb glow at the command of their fingers.

Mao, the military man who was not a military man, understood that armies are part of the society that appoints them. For an ERA man, to rape could be to humiliate the sister of the man fighting alongside. In making the ERA out of China's dispossessed—and giving it an idea to fight for—he made people's war serve his side of the struggle.

The ERA's advance parties soon had peasants hunting down Japanese as one might hunt snakes. Children were rescued from a life worse than a dog's, fed, taught to read, given work to do as messengers or medical orderlies. Naturally they became Communist believers.

ERA news singers, in the manner of medieval minstrels, offered an account of the latest battle in rhyme to the accompaniment of drums and clappers. Posters of the CCP leaders were left behind to regale the drab villages. That of Mao gave him a long bony face like a horse.

*   *   *

In a burst of writing during the first half of 1938, Mao set out most of the military ideas that he had been trying out since he first took up the gun in 1927. He wrote *Basic Tactics*, which was a manual for officers, *Problems of Strategy in the Anti-Japanese Guerrilla War,* his classic statement of the meaning of people's war, and an overall view of World War II from China's angle of vision, *On Protracted War*.

One of his bodyguards watched in fascination the writing of *On Protracted War*. Mao sat in his cave at a desk. Candlelight gave a sallow look to his pale face. For two days he did not sleep, he ate only bits and pieces, and a mop of the face with a washcloth was the only cleansing he allowed his sweating body. A rock lay beside his notebook; when his hand grew numb from continuous writing he squeezed the rock to relax the fingers.

After five days the sheets of paper filled with his unruly characters were piling up. But he had lost weight and his eyes were bloodshot. His staff counted it a major victory when he deigned to eat any of the dishes they repeatedly prepared for him. Rare is the politician who gets so carried away at a writing job.

On the seventh day Mao suddenly leaped up in pain; the fire in the brazier had burned a hole in his right shoe as he was lost in composition. He drank a glass of wine and sat down to push his brush a little further toward the end of *On Protracted War*. On the eighth day he had a headache and felt faint and a doctor arrived to reason with him. But he went ahead and on the ninth day finished this essay which fills eighty printed pages.

Then he sent it around to Liu Shaoqi's cave for comment.

Mao's military essays were vivid, China-centered to the point of chauvinism, and viscerally hostile to left-wing extremism.

He insisted on close factual investigation before judgment. He mocked those who dwelt on the parts, at the risk of being caught unawares by the whole. He counseled patience to impatient leftists who expected a soup to be ready to eat the moment they tossed in its ingredients.

In order to maximize surprise (one of the few weapons the weak have against the strong) he employed the dualisms of traditional Chinese military thought: offensive and defensive, mobility and base position, delay and sudden swiftness, concentration and dispersal of forces.

He uttered his famous maxim "From the barrel of a gun grows political power."* This did not mean that military matters were to dominate political. On the contrary, Mao believed that an army's work is pointless without an overarching goal. But Mao had learned in the 1930s that in China's backward conditions, the Communists must have an army of their own in order to win independence of political action.

Even as Mao spoke of the gun his eye looked beyond the gun. He was an anti-warrior, yet he believed that in the China of his day war was the true test of political legitimacy.

He unpacked war into its irreducible human components: "We are men, the enemy are made up of men, we are all men, so what should we fear?"

He was shrewd enough to make a virtue out of the Communists' weak-

---

* This is a literal translation of the Chinese words *Qiang gan zi li mian chu zheng quan*. I believe it a more accurate rendition than the usual: "Political power grows out of the barrel of a gun." The Chinese does not imply that all political power stems from the gun; the subject of the maxim is gun, not political power.

ness: "Oppose the strategy of striking with two fists in two directions at the same time, and uphold the strategy of striking with one fist in one direction at one time."

He argued on political grounds against those who never wished to go on the defensive: "In every just war the defensive not only has a lulling effect on politically alien elements, but it also makes possible the rallying of the backward sections of the masses to join in the war."

His vision was far-reaching and also arrogant: "Mankind's era of wars will be brought to an end by our own efforts, and beyond doubt the war we wage is part of the final battle."

Mao saw three phases of the war against Japan. During the first—already near its end—the Japanese would be on the offensive and much Chinese territory would be lost to them. Mao did not panic at such losses. It was good to lure the enemy in deep. The Japanese would make mistakes. They would be surrounded by a vast and hostile populace.

A long second stage would ensue, marked by a certain equilibrium between the two sides, and by nibbling guerrilla warfare behind Japanese lines. This would so weaken the enemy that a third stage would occur; the Chinese would be able to go on to the offensive, replacing guerrilla tactics with conventional large-scale battles.

All this is pretty much what occurred between 1937 and 1945, except that Communist guerrillas were by no means the only force that weakened Japan during the second stage.

Much of Mao's military writing in Yanan was based upon the civil war experience of the 1920s. But there were new themes. He was less sectarian during the national crisis of the 1930s than he'd been during the partisan rural bouts of the 1920s.

He began to talk like a world statesman. For the first time in his life, Mao in Yanan followed world affairs as part of his daily agenda of work. He needed to. It benefited his cause to depict the Chinese struggle as part of a global crisis.

Mao foresaw the potential value of the Western democracies' anti-German effort for his own resistance to Japan. His pen was eloquent on the need for a universal fight against fascism. He felt worried at occasional signs of Western weakness: might these not lead Chiang in desperation to make a deal with Tokyo? He paid tribute to the British and American war effort in its vigorous phases. In a word, Mao was giving his united front ideas a worldwide application.

He began to speak of the significance of China's convulsion for the underdeveloped world. Of Africa and Latin America he had little sense, but he detected an emerging Pan-Asian movement for liberation against colonialism. India cropped up in his talk and his essays, a first suggestion of his later vision of revolution throughout the Third World.

*   *   *

Mao had not formed attachments with non-Chinese. Fewer than had other CCP figures.

Comintern agents were virtually the only foreigners Mao had ever dealt with. And these—from Borodin to Braun—he thought ill of and did not relax with. But the Westerners (mainly Americans) he met in the 43rd and 44th years of his life were quite another cup of tea.

China has a tradition of sucking the outstanding foreigner into its way of life. Jesuits in the seventeenth century came to convert the Chinese, but stayed to be half Sinicized themselves—and even to play a role at the Chinese court—until the Pope became alarmed and put a stop to this reverse evangelization.

Yet seldom before, and not since, have foreigners been participants in Chinese events as much as they were in the pre-1949 history of the CCP. First the Comintern aides in the 1920s. Then the Western sojourners in Yanan during World War II.

One day at 3 P.M. the British journalist Gunther Stein went to Mao's cave for an "interview." Mao talked until dinnertime. Then the pair of them went out and dined under an old apple tree, Mao still chain-smoking, Stein still putting down on paper a flow of information on the CCP and its goals in the midst of World War II.

After dinner they resumed talking in the cave over glasses of wine. Noticing that the table on which Stein was resting his notebook was rickety, Mao went out and fetched a flat stone from the garden, and knelt down and placed it beneath the offending leg. Several times during the evening Stein rose to leave. Mao would not hear of it.

For twelve hours at a stretch Mao talked with this sharp but not at all famous newsman. "At three in the morning," Stein recalled, "when I finally got up to go, with a bad conscience, aching limbs, and burning eyes, he was still as fresh and animated and systematic in his talk as in the afternoon." *

Agnes Smedley would call on Mao—and he on her—and she would slap him on the back and even try to teach him to dance. "I would send a note to Mao Zedong to come and chat," Smedley recalled, "and he would soon enter, bringing a sack of peanuts."

Mao shrewdly addressed the Western world through such visitors as Stein

---

* A couple of days later Mao saw Stein in the street and said to him: "I had to consult comrades Zhu De and Zhou Enlai about all I told you. They approved."

and Smedley. He also used foreigners to address the Chinese people. In the spectacular case of Edgar Snow he did both.

In spending hundreds of hours with the talented adventurer from Missouri, during the summer of 1936 and later, Mao in addition formed his first easy relationship with a non-Chinese. He once took off his trousers in the company of Snow—and Lin Biao—to be more comfortable for a long chat on a hot day.

In *Red Star Over China* and other works Snow told a story that most Chinese did not know—Mao had no chance to exploit the Chinese press in the 1930s—and the translation of his work helped Mao become known in his own country.

Mao also got a feel for America through his relationship with Snow, and that turned out to be important a few years later.

Mao found in an idealistic young American reporter the first non-Chinese he was prepared to open up to. He was under no illusion that a foreigner could share his goal of a socialist China. But in his Yanan cave in the 1930s he did believe that a non-Chinese could *understand* his goals. Otherwise Mao would not have taken the step—unusual alike in a CCP leader and a Communist leader in any country—of telling an American the story of his own life.

*   *   *

When Snow talked with Mao, hot-pepper bread or a compote of sour plums would often be brought in by He Zizhen. Mao's wife had changed for the worse as Mao had risen to power in the CCP.

The coming of three children had turned her from a bouncy political comrade to a quiet housewife.* Twenty pieces of shrapnel had lodged in her soft flesh during a bombing raid as the Long March passed through Guizhou. She had become a scarecrow to look at and a victim of nervous disorders as well.

One evening during 1937 Mao dropped in for dinner at the cave of Agnes Smedley. The only other guests were Nym Wales, wife of Edgar Snow, and Lily Wu, a pretty actress who was bold and "Shanghai" enough to wear lipstick and long hair in the pre-Communist style.

Before the night and the wine were finished, Mao and Lily were leaning close to each other and holding hands. Mao had taken emotional leave of Zizhen and was available for a new storm of the heart.

It was not Lily Wu but another actress, a little less pretty and a lot more single-minded, who gave Mao his new storm.

---

* And maybe the fact that none of them were boys had depressed her; feudal discounting of women was not as dead in CCP circles as official rhetoric suggested.

One day he gave a speech at the Academy of Art. In the audience, as far to the front as the existence of a separate block of seats reserved for cadres permitted her to be, was a bright-eyed girl who had recently arrived in Yanan from Shanghai. She applauded loudly, she asked the welcome kind of questions, and she ended up in a tête-à-tête with Mao on "ideological issues."

Mao was not the first CCP leader into whose presence Lan Ping (Blue Apple) had thrust herself. But after that meeting at the Academy of Art she had no need to keep her signboard out any longer.

Blue Apple—this was not her original name and it would not be her last—came from a poor family. (In this she was unlike Zizhen and almost all of the CCP notables.) She had had a miserable childhood at the hands of a father who beat his wife and daughter with a spade. She had found her way into the Shanghai theater, and through a veritable waterfall of love affairs.

Like many other young artists and students from eastern cities, she headed northwest out of excitement—on some level of her being—at the challenge of a new way of life in Yanan.

The pattern of her encounter with Mao was reminiscent of the Communist Youth League meeting near Well Mountain in 1928 that had led Mao out of an earlier lonely phase. But the two girls who put themselves in evidence were not at all similar.

Blue Apple was quite pretty, if less gently so than Zizhen. She had dark, clever eyes and she was masterful in deploying her emotions to get what she wanted. She never gave herself without reserve to a cause larger than herself. Rather she shopped around in the wider world for ammunition to use in her personal struggle for fame and power.

Mao moved briskly, if not without difficulty, toward a third marriage. It seems that Blue Apple as well as Mao had a living spouse. Hers was far off in Shanghai. Mao's was all too near. In small-town Yanan, Zizhen quickly heard of Mao's appreciation for Blue Apple. She reacted bitterly and perhaps violently.

Moreover, the Party could not be as indifferent to Mao's private life as it had been when Mao met Zizhen on remote Well Mountain. Mao was now too well known.

The Central Committee debated the issue. Feelings ran high. Who was this pushy movie girl with no solid political background? Should a veteran of the Long March and mother of three be forced out to make room for her?

But Mao was adamant. He muttered a threat to "go back to my native village and become a farmer." The Party acquiesced with one condition that was to prove a sleeping tiger: Blue Apple must remain a housewife and play no role in public affairs.

One can fall out of love even with a heroine when the magic moment passes. In exchanging a worn mother for a newly arrived film girl, was Mao putting behind him the bleakness of the Long March?

The match certainly offered the excitement of opposites: Mao the rural boy, fond of China's traditions, whom politics and war now consumed; Blue Apple the rootless actress, ignorant of the Chinese Classics, a butterfly who had fluttered from plant to plant in the hothouse of Shanghai culture.

During his personal crisis Mao spent an evening with Agnes Smedley in her cave. At one point he switched the conversation from world affairs to romantic affairs. Had Agnes ever loved a man, he inquired, and why, and what did love mean to her? Soon he began reciting a poem of his own in memory of Yang Kaihui, his first wife, who had died seven years before.

It was an unusual personal display on Mao's part. No doubt it expressed some conflict of values within himself. (Alas, the sterling Ms. Smedley was ill-equipped to tap Mao's emotions further. Her mind was on jeeps and bandages and Nazism.)

Meanwhile Blue Apple seemed to have decided that attack was the best means of defense. She chose for herself a grandiose new name, Jiang Qing, which means "Green Waters" (or river) but has also—by virtue of its sound—the second meaning "Pure Waters." "Green Waters" seemed apter; this woman had the murky depths, the allure, and the catlike icy charm that the phrase conjured up.*

In China even Communist history is full of clannish twists.

Mao's youngest brother took Zizhen's young sister as his second wife. Zetan had first married in 1925. His wife was arrested in 1930, together with Mao's first wife and his adopted sister. Although Zetan's wife was later released—the Nationalists rated him a smaller fish than Mao, so his wife fared better than Yang Kaihui—Zetan did not resume the liaison with her. His new marriage with He Yi, He Zizhen's sister, was a brief one, for Zetan was executed in 1935.

But like a ghost from the family closet, He Yi made her presence felt in 1937–1938. She had married again and come to Yanan. She and her new husband made a fuss about Mao's "abandonment" of Zizhen. It availed nothing. He Yi's husband was transferred to the south of China—while He Yi remained assigned to a post in Yanan—and this was probably a way of

---

* In a 1972 interview, Roxane Witke found Jiang Qing sensitive when asked about having chosen yet another name in Yanan: "She reacted swiftly, as if I had trespassed in a private realm."

stilling the clamor that the couple were making against Mao's marriage to Jiang Qing.

In early 1938 Mrs. Zhang Guotao found herself in the city of Xian en route to join her husband in Yanan after nearly a decade of separation. At army headquarters she was allotted a room which contained two simple wooden beds. In the second bed lay a slight, pale, sickly woman of about thirty. Who should it be but He Zizhen!

It was the wife of Zhou Enlai who formally introduced the wives of the CCP's two feuding titans: "This is He Zizhen, who is Chairman Mao's lover." *

The two women talked and Mrs. Zhang discovered that "love" was hardly an apt term for the current relationship. "Zedong treats me badly," Zizhen claimed. "We bickered and had a fight. He grabbed a bench and I grabbed a chair. Oh, it's clear we're finished."

Mrs. Zhang tried to persuade Zizhen to return to Yanan. But the sad creature felt it better to go on to Moscow for medical help, as Mao had planned she should do.

According to Mrs. Zhang, who is biased against Mao but cannot be dismissed as a witness, she herself went to see Mao about the matter on reaching Yanan. By her own admission, Mrs. Zhang blazed at him angrily. "It's all your fault," she declared. "You should write her a letter straightaway."

Mao did not blow up at Mrs. Zhang—as he might well have done, for this wife of his rival was poking her nose into delicate territory. He listened and said nothing. Later on Mrs. Zhang ran into Mao again and he reported: "I've written a letter to He, but she won't return."

It is indeed unlikely that Zizhen wished to return, and quite likely that she was by now a difficult woman to deal with, for reasons not mainly her own fault.

He Zizhen did go on to Russia, accompanied by her third daughter who had been born on the Long March, and by Mao's first son by Yang Kaihui, the 17-year-old Anying.

Anying and his younger brother, Anqing, had been through scarifying times since Mao last saw them at Music Mountain in 1927. After their mother's torture and murder in 1930, the Party and their maternal grandmother tried to bring them up. But being the offspring of "Communist bandits" did not make for an easy life.

They sold newspapers in Shanghai. At one point they found a place to

---

* The term "lover" (*ai ren*), which came into use within CCP circles during the early 1930s, means both wife (or husband) and, less frequently, girlfriend (or boyfriend).

sleep in a deserted temple, outside which they posted a sign: WE TELL STORIES—ONE PENNY."

It is striking, though it was perhaps only natural, given Mao's absence and the grandmother's role, that in the early 1930s they went by the names Yang Yunfu and Yang Yunshou, taking their mother's maiden name.

Once Mao had settled in Yanan, both boys were sent there, though neither lived in Mao's home. Anqing was placed in a peasant's home. So was Anying until his departure for Moscow.

That Anying traveled with Zizhen to Russia suggests that Mao had by no means cast his ex-wife beyond the realm of his responsibility. But Zizhen's condition did not improve. She beat her daughters mindlessly, and before long she found herself in an asylum near Moscow.

In the late 1940s she was transferred to an asylum in Shanghai. It seems Mao never saw her again after 1938.*

Moscow never made use of its knowledge of He Zizhen's experiences, or of her presence on Soviet soil, to criticize Mao for his treatment of his second wife.

By 1939 Mao was living with Jiang Qing and in early 1941 their first daughter was born. Once more Mao sat lightly to formal procedures. Nowhere is it recorded exactly when Zizhen divorced Mao—Jiang Qing said the initiative was not Mao's—or when Jiang Qing married him.

The striking assertiveness of Mao's new wife seemed borne out by the name given the baby of 1941: Li Na. Li was Ms. Jiang's original surname and Na was the given name of a Shanghai actor who once fell in love with her.

---

* In 1979 Ms. He was still alive, out of the asylum, and being mentioned again by the official press after decades of silence.

9

The Sage (1936–1945)

In appearance Mao now betrayed the wiliness—for some who met him it amounted to a sinister air—that had propelled him to the top. He had become deliberate in manner. He could be oblique in his glance and smile.

Sometimes he would gaze at a person he was speaking to, head at an angle, as he weighed the impact of what he had just uttered. All the while he would puff with puckered lips on a cigarette and suck in the smoke with a loud rasping noise.

Some foreigners were so intimidated that they left the room without remembering anything of what Mao had said to them.

The steel inside Mao was hidden by a laconicism that some took for effeminacy. "We were sorry to note that in appearance Mao seemed an effeminate type," intoned the Americans Claire and William Band.

A similar impression was gained by Agnes Smedley, who had rubbed shoulders—and more than shoulders—with every conceivable type of man: "The tall forbidding figure lumbered toward us and a high-pitched voice greeted us. Then two hands grasped mine; they were as long and sensitive as a woman's. . . . His dark, inscrutable face was long, the forehead broad and high, the mouth feminine. Whatever else he might be, he was an aesthete."

"He neither grasps nor shakes your hand," she complained, "but takes it in his own and pushes you away."

Smedley's standard among CCP leaders was the earthy stud which she believed Zhu De to be. But if this Maid Marian of world revolution wanted more from Mao than political conversation, her hopes were dashed before she descended onto her stool. "I was in fact repelled by the feminine in him and by the gloom of the setting. An instinctive hostility sprang up inside me. . . ."

Smedley soon woke up—as did Snow, who at first found Mao "grotesque"—to a crucial point: Mao was no longer an open book to be judged on sight. He was on the way to becoming a sage. And a sage can be subtle and self-indulgent.

In Yanan we see Mao in midcareer. His eyes had switched from past battles. He ruled a swath of territory. He began to see himself as the next leader of China. Rather self-consciously he was arranging himself in the cockpit of power. And as a man in his forties, he felt like doing what he pleased.

A touch of the prima donna came to Mao the man.

He had lost the eager look. His eyes no longer shone out from the face like saucers; they had taken their place within a face of Buddha-like solidity.

Mao allowed the various colors of his personality to clash with each other. Though he headed a complex organization, he was also a man who liked to turn in on himself for long periods. He was gregarious only at calculated intervals. He did not care—maybe did not even notice—if people found him "sinister" for the rest of the time.

Mao was both secure enough in his own being and firmly enough in the saddle as CCP leader to be a law unto himself in matters of style.

In a community that considered a short haircut part of one's uniform, Mao let his grow until he looked like a musician. Smoking and sleeping late were taken to be signs of indiscipline, yet Mao smoked like a chimney and seldom rose before noon. Though he headed an army, his salute resembled an absent-minded brushing of the brow, and his shambling gait was that of a farmer.

In his writings Mao urged that any criticisms be made with modesty and self-restraint, yet he could lose his temper with a colleague, shouting and cursing like a trooper, until the victim would flee blushing from the room.

And Mao had coolly taken a glamorous new wife in the face of raised eyebrows in the Party. Frequently aloof as he was, he had set up a bustling household, as virtually no other CCP leader had, with Blue Apple's vivacious presence, and his own and his brother's children running in and out of the study.

Mao grew fat in Yanan. His old teacher from the teachers' college in Changsha, Xu Teli, now in charge of education in the base area, stayed lean. Like Mao, Xu had been a zealot for physical fitness and Spartan ways in Hunan twenty years before. Xu kept this up in Yanan. In his sixties, he swam in cold rivers, refused to own an overcoat, and ate like a sparrow.

But Mao felt himself beyond any particular regimen. He did all the things that Xu regarded as temptations of the devil. There was more—and less—than personal slackness to Mao's spreading style.

The exceptional man does not break rules merely because he finds it difficult to observe them. He does so because he feels a sense of mission which obviates all rules. The rulebook is a crutch which a man who has found his own strength can do without and yet be a man of monklike discipline. So it was with Mao in Yanan.

Smedley with a touch of naïveté asked Mao's advice on her plans to finish a book she was preparing on Zhu De's life; it was 1937, just a year after Mao had related his own life story to Snow. "I asked Mao Zedong which he thought more important for me to do—remain in Yanan and write Zhu De's biography, or go to the front and write of the war." It is a pity that she did not record Mao's facial expression as he replied: "This war is more important than past history."

An *imperial self-image* was taking shape in Mao. He felt the mantle of Chinese history on his shoulders—that is why he lost some of his old spontaneity—and his streak of vanity grew stronger.

It was less the case of a politician growing fat and indulgent in office than of a sage becoming aware of his place in the pageant of the ages. Mao did not grow fond of luxury and he remained personally fearless.

Still, a cult arose around him. Regardless of who triggered it and why, its existence changed Mao's daily life, and eventually changed the man himself.

Portraits of Mao began to appear. His calligraphy was displayed in public places. Two transcendent nouns were hung on him: Lin Biao in 1938 (and others later) spoke of Mao as a "genius"; Emi Xiao in 1941 (and others too) called him "our savior."

By the mid-1940s a visit with Mao had lost the informality that Snow and Smedley knew. The summons to see him would come as a sudden excited announcement. Guards with fixed bayonets stood at his door. A bustling staff put a distance between Mao and the visitor. And Mao stopped going to *other* people's caves.

The building up of Mao's image was to a degree the consequence of the war effort. In all major countries the war leaders became a bit larger than life. The cult of Mao did not exceed that of Stalin, Churchill, or Roosevelt.

In China the logic of boosting Mao was especially compelling in that the CCP, maneuvering always against the NP, needed a figure to be offered to the Chinese nation as a match for Chiang Kai-shek.

The town of Yanan was small enough for Mao to be able to sniff its mood. A range of people knew him. Ordinary folk could frequently see "the Chairman" stroll through the town's dusty lanes. In such circumstances the cult did not go beyond human proportions. It had not yet become a religion, under the spell of which people cry and bow even though they know nothing of the god they would adore.

Mao's authority in Yanan was functional; he was still a believable man.

Even when he drove he was not veiled from view. His "car" was a Chevrolet van on which was written: "Ambulance: Donated by the New York Chinese Laundrymen's National Salvation Association." He would sit in the front seat, looking like the driver's helper.

Incessantly Mao wrote and spoke at meetings. He had a Word to give and the community was encompassable enough for him to offer it directly.

He had had plenty of ideas in the years before Yanan, but only wisps of power. Into the 1950s he would have the power, but the vast bureaucracy of the biggest nation on earth would then eclipse his voice as teacher. The excitement of Yanan was that he *both taught and ruled.* It made the Yanan era Mao's golden age as head of the CCP.

As a political leader Mao was part soldier, part intellectual.

He had taken up the gun and spent a year walking the breadth of his land. Chinese rulers had never done that. He sat in a study and worked out his own ideas. Few modern rulers of a major nation—de Gaulle was one—have done that.

His style had none of the feudal touches that were still the norm among Chinese war lords: sedan chair, Confucian sacrifices, opulent homes, receiving visitors—as one Shandong war lord did—while in bed with a concubine.

At the same time Mao seemed more traditionally Chinese than 28B, or Chiang, or the leaders of the Democratic League (a leftish third force which stood between the CCP and the NP). He often wrote with a brush. He still liked to sink his mind into the archaic realm of Chinese historical novels.

"I have yet to see a Western suit or a formal long gown in this region," wrote Israel Epstein, an American journalist, after a tour of the northwest in 1944. Mao wore neither. He (and other officials) appeared in the same baggy pants and square jacket peasants wore.

The standard cotton clothes seemed to reflect a new brand of citizenship: classless and in a way traditionless. The Yanan spirit was certainly not foreign. But neither did it have any precedent in China.

Something new had sprouted among the dusty hills.

* * *

Yanan was Mao's 100 days, and 1,000 days, and more. A stable regime existed that could almost be called *his* regime. In budding form "Maoism" in all its aspects began to appear.

Jiangxi had been a tenuous affair by comparison; there Mao had seldom been able to do as he wished, and his socialist ideas were neither fully developed nor favored by CCP figures more senior than he.

Mao proved that he was not just one more war lord, for whom the gun was a cause, and power a destination. A social vision led him to sculpt a social order which won the praise—often the enthusiasm—of those who trekked to the loess hills.

If mere power had been Mao's aim, he would not have gone ahead, as he did in Yanan after his power was secure, to try and remold the souls of the ninety million Chinese who called him ruler by 1945.

On the other hand, Mao's notion of "remolding" was fearsome, and it owed much to his boyhood traumas. He was proving to be an authoritarian personality, driven to be everything that his father had been and found young Zedong incapable of being.

Visitors to Yanan sensed the cheeriness and mateship of a Boy Scout camp. There was evident that disregard of material hardship that a shared purpose engenders. Wealth did not bring its burdens, nor hierarchy its anxiety. People felt, for a time, that they were building a new world with their own hands.

Foreign observers later disagreed among themselves as to whether Mao had long been bent upon communism, or was once a mere "agrarian reformer." There was really no mystery about the matter. In Yanan he was not practicing communism. But he had not budged one inch from communism as his postwar goal.

Because the problem of the hour was Japan, Mao suspended class warfare in favor of drawing all possible social groups into a crusade that was led by the CCP but essentially nationalist in nature.

Land policy was the key. Confiscation came to an end the moment the united front with the Nationalists was agreed upon. Rent was kept moderate—before the reds took over it had run as high as 60 percent of the value of the land—but it was also guaranteed. This proved a shot in the arm alike for the economy and for morale.

Mao's tax policy also won the hearts and minds of the majority. For a while there was virtually no taxation at all (Mao's government was being subsidized from Chiang's treasury under the terms of the united front). When tax was later imposed it was so progressive that less than 20 percent of families paid anything at all.

Throughout the Border Region elections were held. A "three thirds" system was adopted at each level of the administration. Communists filled no more than one third of government offices. One third were reserved for non-CCP leftists. One third went to those Mao described as middle-of-the-roaders.

These measures did not amount to Western democracy—though Communists were occasionally outvoted in administrative bodies—but they transformed the communal psychology of the northwest. The secret of the Yanan spirit was participation.

No elections had ever been held on the basis of universal suffrage in China before (in those of the Jiangxi soviet, "exploiting classes" had been excluded).

It is true that voters had no choice between competing sets of leaders. Yet the fact that ordinary peasants could refer to "our government" was entirely novel. Mao had achieved a mutation in the attitude of Chinese to their rulers. Every man, woman, and child was tucked into a cocoon of collective responsibility. A *sense* of democracy seemed to exist.

* * *

Mao the semi-intellectual began to show an acute ambivalence toward intellectuals. As a mood of disappointment with the Nationalists grew in the big cities, students, writers, artists, and others flocked to the northwest. They sought a new role. Lively and patriotic Yanan seemed to offer it.

Mao was proud that men and women of ideas found his base a magnet. He welcomed them, not least because Chiang had cold-shouldered them.

Yet Mao did not attach great weight to the role of intellectuals in his struggle, and he untiringly resisted their desire for extra freedom.

A mixed attitude of scorn and fascination toward the literati showed that two skeletons from the cupboard of the past still existed in Mao's subconscious.

Mao had not forgotten, it seemed, the cold reception Peking University had given him in 1919. It left him with an obsessive desire to put intellectuals in their place at every opportunity.

Mao had hated his father. Yet in the end the ghost of his father dwelt very close to Mao's soul. His father did not like to see Mao reading a book; young Mao rebelled against such narrowness. But something in Mao wanted to scoff at book learning just as his father had done at Music Mountain.

Perhaps Mao's father had influenced him, after all, more than his mother had, if subconsciously. His mother was an ally against the threat of his father. But his father was a *model* that some level of Mao's personality strove to emulate.

Old Mr. Mao insisted on physical labor. Young Mao resented having to work in the fields. Yet Mao at Yanan (and thereafter) hustled the intellectuals out of their studies to do physical labor.

Old Mr. Mao had been an autocrat who criticized his son for laziness. Now that Mao's socialist philosophy had taken shape, it turned out to be centered on the exaltation of will.

In all these ways old Mr. Mao seemed to have been not only an oppressor of his son, but, through his son's subconscious desire to be what his father wanted him to be, a shadow of oppression on those who were "rectified" by Mao Zedong at Yanan.

One bone of contention was sex. In Jiangxi, Mao had been a libertarian—by Chinese standards—on love and marriage. But in Yanan he took the hard line of a leader who asks every ounce of energy for the national cause and thinks sexual activity, other than his own, is a waste of energy.*

On this and other matters Mao came up against the views of a bold woman who was literary editor of Yanan's newspaper *Liberation*. Ding Ling was a vivacious and outspoken writer from Mao's own province of Hunan.† In the 1930s few wrote more movingly than she of the tug of war between private and public values.

In her personal life she practiced promiscuity with the flourish of one who believes it to be a trump card of socialism. She had been part of more than one *ménage à trois*. She was an open fan of Kollantai's libertarian book *Three Generations*. "Undisciplined guerrilla warfare" was her light-hearted term for sleeping around.

Mao became quite intimate with Ding Ling in Yanan. Some had expected that she, rather than Jiang Qing, would become his third wife. Perhaps Ding Ling was too much her own woman to bow to a Mao who was fast becoming a Leninist.

In his personal life Mao was no slouch in answering the urge for a fresh bout of love. But what he practiced he did not care to make easy for all. The sage of Yanan did not believe that socialism meant a new fluidity in sex relationships.

His marriage law of 1944 was no less family-minded than those of Stalin's Russia. Divorce was made more difficult than before, and virtually impossible for a woman whose husband was a soldier in the anti-Japanese war.

When a group of ten students who had come north to join the Communist side formed a Free Love Club, Mao had them arrested.

He had grown more cautious for a number of reasons. All aspects of the CCP's social radicalism had to be toned down to fit the bland texture of the united front.

Second, the peasants of Shaanxi were more backward than those of Jiangxi. They were the "water" in which the "fish" of the CCP's armies had to swim. Their conservative ideas could not be slighted.

---

* The switch was like that made in Russia's early post-revolution years, from Ms. Kollantai's unshackled view—sex should be as casual as drinking a glass of water—to the family-minded view of Stalin's state juggernaut.

† We met her earlier (see page 42) as a precocious participant in some of Mao's May Fourth activities in Changsha.

And war had its own logic. "Our" collective effort became all; "my" whims were as nothing. National war proved a great leveler of tastes, a merciless furnace for the fragile artistry of an individual's quirks.*

Mao's own marital ups and downs had also closed his mind to libertarianism. He had been questioning himself about the meaning of love (as in the dialogue with Smedley). The collapse of his affection for Zizhen came when he was well over forty. He now seemed to feel the need for a long-term companion.

With Jiang Qing he began a shared life that was to last, in its own way, for more than thirty years. He settled down. Children became part of his daily life. Sex as "a glass of water" had run dry.

And he inclined to think that what happened to him set a norm for others.

Ding Ling criticized Mao and the CCP for their retreat on the women's issue. She marked International Women's Day in 1942 with a stinging little essay called "Thoughts on March Eighth." It questioned whether the CCP (to which she belonged) was any longer in the vanguard of sex liberation.

Unlike Mao she looked down on marriage. Though Mao had just climbed into a nest of domesticity with Jiang Qing, Ms. Ding dared to broach the especially acute fate of leaders' wives.

If a female comrade does not marry she is blamed, Ms. Ding pointed out. Yet if she does marry, either it is said that by taking a job she neglects home duties, or else her life sinks beneath the weight of childbearing and she is equally criticized for failing to be an active citizen of the new socialist society.

Mao's Yanan had become a male chauvinist club with a few pushy women added in special positions. The ratio of men to women was almost like in an army—eighteen to one. According to Mao's old female friend from the springtime days of liberation in Changsha, Cai Chang, there was not a single woman of working-class origin in the whole of Yanan (but she had "forgotten" Jiang Qing!).

Mao took the opportunity soon after Ms. Ding's angry essay to make an ironic gesture to this woman whom he liked but found annoying. Seeing Ms. Ding arrive for a session of group photos of literati, he leaped up from his own seat in the middle of the front row and offered it with elaborate courtesy to the obstinate feminist. "Let our woman comrade take the center seat,"

---

* Constraints on liberty that were defense-related became a fact of life in the PRC. In Mao's last years an Australian girl, resident in the city of Xian, fell in love with a Chinese boy. The pair wished to marry. Despite intervention by the Australian prime minister, Peking for a long time denied permission, on the ground that the boy was the son of a military man. Only after Mao's death was permission granted.

he murmured as he did so. "We don't want to be rebuked again on March eighth."

*　*　*

Mao battled the intellectuals from the garrets of Shanghai over the issue of how politics and art should relate.

"Art for art's sake" Mao ruled out. Every piece of intellectual work must serve the clear-cut purpose of hastening the liberation of China. This view put him in tension not only with Ding Ling but with most of China's left-wing minds. They resisted him when he set out his hard Leninist line at a series of talks at a "Yanan Forum on Literature and Art."

Mao hurled several mental grenades into the packed trenches of the Yanan intelligentsia.

He derided the "clamor for independence." This had to do both with theory and with naked power politics. "Truth" and "love" have no meaning apart from the concrete class struggle of the moment. The writer is a cog in the grand "machine" of the Party's cause (here Mao was drinking from Lenin's glass).

"As soon as a man talks with another man," Mao declared, "he is engaged in propaganda." A crude notion, yet it came from a once creative strain in Mao. Study is a weapon to change the world, he had felt as a young man trying to push ahead in Changsha. Now in Yanan he saw writers and artists for whom intellectual work seemed a mere personal preference. They had not, like him, entered the world of letters out of a driving sense of ideas as wheels of advance to a new society.

Like Rousseau, he wished to recall the sophisticates to simpler and more ardent ways.

Mao insisted, as men of power tend to do, that criticism from intellectuals would undermine national security in the face of an enemy threat. Several values underlay his argument.

The solid backward peasants of Shaanxi seemed to him infinitely more useful to the war effort than the quibbling intellectuals from the east coast. He accommodated the peasants; hence the moderate land policies of these years. He felt no similar need to accommodate the men and women of letters.

"Opinions should not be allowed to become conclusions," he announced to the writhing literati of Yanan. In other words, you only have the freedom to be correct. An opinion, if incorrect, is *not allowed* to become an openly stated conclusion.

Mao as a youth had felt that browbeating was a proper weapon in the service of truth. He had never found it easy to respect the right to err. In Yanan such instincts began to take on the full force of state policy.

Mao also required intellectuals to depict only the bright side of life in their works of art. Fiction should offer "a higher plane" than exists in "everyday life."

These views were not swallowed without complaint in the 1940s. *Talks at the Yanan Forum on Literature and Art* began a running feud between Mao and many of China's creative intellectuals that lasted for the rest of Mao's life.

*   *   *

In all realms—not only culture—Mao laid out fresh doctrine at Yanan. Maoism was born. It was hardly the child of an immaculate conception—idea uniting with idea. Rather it came as a by-product of one more fierce battle for survival.

By early 1942 Japan was Mao's overriding worry. Tokyo had mounted a "burn all, kill all, destroy all" counterinsurgency drive—America's in Vietnam resembled it—against the Communists. The damage done to the red areas was all the more because the CCP-NP united front had shrunk to little more than a scrap of paper.

Chiang, far from subsidizing Mao's Border Region, had put a tight blockade on it. Would there be enough space and people for "people's war" to be valid much longer?

Within the CCP, Mao had fewer feuds at the top to cope with than during the Long March, but more severe problems at the grass roots.

Zhang Guotao was no longer a thorn in Mao's side. He had limped into Yanan in 1937,* most of his army and all of his prestige lost in the wastes of Tibet. Mao calmly let Zhang wither on the vine. The deflated rival built a nice house on the outskirts of Yanan, lectured a bit at Resist Japan University, and looked after himself carefully as always.

When Zhang saw Mao for the last time a petty charade ensued. The occasion was a children's song and dance show at the School for Cadres Children. Zhang's son was a pupil at this institution (an outcrop of elitism on the plateau of Yanan egalitarianism). The boy was known as a talented singer and actor; naturally he had a role in the pantomime.

But to Zhang Guotao's fury the boy was cast as a horrendous villain and traitor called Zhang Mutao.

Mao was present, enjoying the performance along with other leaders. According to Zhang, Mao joked as he watched the villain being hissed: "A per-

---

*With him came Zhu De; though ill at ease on his arrival, Zhu quietly took up with Mao where he had left off.

fect fit to have the son of Zhang Guotao play the role of Zhang Mutao."

Mao's old rival thereupon rose, tore the mask from his son's face, and led the boy from the hall, shouting in anger: "Barbarians! Wicked people! Worse than beasts!"

Soon afterward Zhang slipped out of Yanan and joined the Nationalist cause. Mao never saw him again (he lived for many years in Canada until his death in 1979). Mao may have had a malicious tongue, but he did not kill, harm, or even purge Zhang, who remained in senior office until he switched sides.

Mao also took a cool approach to his second great rival of the 1930s. Wang Ming returned at last from Moscow in 1937. His sniping at the united front from a "capitulationist" standpoint bothered Mao for two years. But he was too closely identified with Stalin—it was presumed that he drafted the appalling cable that Stalin sent to Mao during the Xian Incident—to be a focus of loyalty during a national crusade.

"Are you a Chinese or a Russian?" Wang Ming was asked in exasperation by a Nationalist colleague during a clash at a united front meeting. Moreover, his silky shift from ultra-leftism to support for a joint government with Chiang had made him seem a bit of a "radish" (red outside but white inside). After 1939 he ceased to count in the power structure of the CCP.

Mao was not vindictive toward 28B's standard-bearer.

Wang Ming went on speaking his mind. He remained on the CCP's Central Committee through the 1940s and 1950s. (So did Bo Gu, until his death in 1946.)*

*   *   *

Success had swollen the ranks of the CCP with young newcomers who were less tough than the Long March veterans. That the united front worked brilliantly for the CCP from 1937 until 1940 meant, paradoxically, that Mao had a quiet crisis of raison d'être on his hands. Patriots had flocked to him. But in a crunch—and by 1942 Mao realized he would prob-

*Wang Ming would have found the price of unsuccess far higher in his favorite foreign capital than he did in Yanan—as he could have been reminded by the fact that 70 percent of the members of the Soviet Communist Party's Central Committee were arrested and shot in the two years 1937 and 1938.

We can probably trust the following account by Wang Ming to suggest the flavor of the Mao-Wang relationship in the late 1940s. The pair of them were arguing about Russia. In came Wang's wife. "I've been looking for you all over," she said, "and it turns out that you two are arguing again. Better come home for supper." Jiang Qing, who had been listening in a corner, agreed with Mrs. Wang: "How marvelous that you've come. . . .These two old cockerels are impossible; they no sooner meet than they start to fight. . . . Get hold of yours and take him for his supper, and I'll get hold of mine and take him for his supper, so they can't fight any more."

ably have to fight the Nationalists again—would they support his Communist goals?

When darker days arrived in 1941, Mao's economic problems required him to tax poor peasants for the first time. He even ran a lottery with fat prizes in 1942. Was his honeymoon with the masses over?

Because of the scattered character of the red outposts, the CCP functioned as a government. This bred bureaucracy. Also careerism on the part of those who took the Border Region regime to be an end in itself.

Committees multiplied. Small Caesars popped up. Three different colors of cotton tunic came into existence to denote steps on the ladder of seniority. The Yanan spirit was no longer the effortless instinct of an inspired community.

In these circumstances Mao pulled together the doctrine of Maoism—a stone that could kill more than one bird. It put the final seal on Mao's success in rising above all rivals in the CCP.

It provided pithy teaching material for a "rectification" (as Mao called it) of the Party's style of work.

And it gave the Chinese Revolution an ideology made not in Moscow but at home.

"Theory has not kept pace with revolutionary experience," Mao said coyly at a rally of a thousand Party workers that kicked off his Rectification drive. In Yanan the victor of repeated struggles looked back at his own methods and found the time and motive to dignify them in the robes of philosophy.

On the Long March there had been no energy—nor even paper—for the writing of political essays. By the 1940s, Mao had read quite a lot of Marx and Lenin and Stalin; their names sprinkle his Yanan pages.

Yet there was a paradox about Mao's new habit of quoting the European masters. The more he read them the less they awed him. Mao was quoting Marx and Lenin and Stalin to buttress or prettify a structure of thought that was as much his as theirs.

*　*　*

"If you want to know the taste of a pear," Mao wrote in an essay that he grandly called *On Practice*, "you must change the pear by eating it yourself." Maoism meant thinking with the fingers.*

Mao put *experience*—rather than matter—at the core of the process of knowing. It was an odd brand of materialism, which might have raised one of Marx's bushy eyebrows.

*It seems likely that Mao's "pear" aphorism owed something to a Zen Buddhist saying widely known in old China: "Only the man who drinks the glass of water knows if the water is hot or cold."

Mao was criticized by 28B for "narrow empiricism." But he unrepentant-
ly clung to a pet formula expressed in another speech during the Rectification drive: "If you have not investigated, you have no right to speak."
Maoism meant a good pair of boots.

The tours of the native son in Hunan Province—plus the courage to stand
by what he had seen—had led to an acceptance of the peasantry as the
backbone of China's revolution.

Mao raged against Party officials (there were many of them) who treated
Marxist doctrine as a collection of holy tablets and forgot about the listener
it was intended to sway.

"Releasing the Arrow Without a Target," Mao dubbed this failing in a
talk which became his famous essay *In Opposition to Party Formalism*.
Maoism meant heeding the audience as well as mastering the message.

One day Mao noticed on the Yanan town wall an anti-Japanese slogan.
The eagle eye of the semi-intellectual saw that the two characters for
"worker" had been written with a literati's affectation. The part of the character *gong* that is a straight line had a zigzag in it, and three embellish-
ments had been added to the foot of the character *ren*. This made the slogan
obscure to ordinary people. Mao in a speech tossed a coil of angry sarcasm
around the fancy penman.

Here was his plea for knowledge that would count.

> Cooking food and preparing dishes is truly one of the arts. But what about
> book knowledge? If you do nothing but read, you have only to recognize three
> to five thousand characters, learn to thumb through a dictionary, hold some
> book in your hand, and receive millet from the public. Then you nod your head
> contentedly and start to read.

Mao the populist was in full swing. His anti-scholasticism made him sound
like his father:

> But books cannot walk, and you can open and close a book at will; this is the
> easiest thing in the world to do, a great deal easier than it is for the cook to
> prepare a meal, and much easier than it is for him to slaughter a pig. He has to
> catch the pig . . . the pig can run . . . he slaughters him . . . the pig squeals. A
> book placed on a desk cannot run, nor can it squeal. You can dispose of it in
> any manner you wish. Is there anything easier to do?

The pedagogue took over with a series of prescriptions.

> Therefore, I advise those of you who have only book knowledge and as yet no
> contact with reality, and those who have had few practical experiences, to real-
> ize their own shortcomings and make their attitudes a bit more humble.

Instead of worshipping "ready-made books," Mao suggested that Communists should go out into towns and villages and fashion oral histories of

China's actual life. Bandits and "well-known prostitutes" would make good topics for oral biographies.

At the same time Mao was Confucian enough to think that the written word *is* potent. He told cadres to weigh the gravity of firing off paper missives to a public that still looked upon writing with awe.

"If a man fails to wash his face for a day or two," Mao reasoned, "it is certainly not a pretty sight, but still there is really no great danger involved. It is different in writing essays and giving speeches." Maoism meant self-conscious dialogue with the masses.

All this was a swipe at 28B. Mao spoke of "seventeen- and eighteen-year-old babies"—Wang Ming and Bo Gu were much younger than he—"taught to nibble on *Capital* and *Anti-Duhring*." He even accused them of not being revolutionaries.

"The relation between Marxism-Leninism and the Chinese Revolution is the same as between the arrow and the target." But "some comrades" merely fondle the arrow, murmuring "excellent arrow, excellent arrow," and do nothing about it.

"The arrow of Marxism-Leninism must be used to hit the target of the Chinese Revolution," Mao continued. "If it were otherwise, why would we want to study Marxism-Leninism?" Mao went even further down the path of China-centered pragmatism: "Marxism-Leninism has no beauty, nor has it any mystical value. It is only extremely useful." Maoism meant pruning the German philosophy from Marx's radicalism and lodging it in the soil of Chinese pragmatic philosophy.

"Your dogma is less useful than shit," he announced to the haughty far-leftists who were his main object in the Rectification drive. "Dog shit can fertilize the fields; man's can feed the dog. But dogmas? They can't fertilize the fields, nor feed a dog. Of what use are they?"

Mao simply terrorized the type of CCP official who thought it an achievement to be able to recite from memory the rules of the Soviet Communist Party. He likened such mistaken zealots to bamboo: "sharp mouth, thick skin, hollow inside."

It was just like the young Mao at East Mountain school. He had disliked the glib sons of gentry who took books for granted as casual weapons for their own social advancement. Now he criticized Party formalists who treated Marxist texts in a similar way.

* * *

The term Mao used for his adaptation of Marx's ideas to Chinese conditions—"to make Chinese"—is a curious one to use of Marxism. As a theory of society was Marxism so "European" at its birth that it had to be "Sinified"? Mao thought so.

"There is no such thing as abstract Marxism," he wrote in 1938, "but only concrete Marxism."

To put Marx's ideas into the Chinese language was already to give them a fresh twist.* The term for "proletariat"—"class without property" (*wu chang jie ji*)—does not sound to a Chinese ear like the urban working class alone.

"A world of Great Harmony," Mao's lively vision of China's future, seems an amazing phrase to use for "Communist society," since its two characters (*da tong*) denote a utopian golden age believed to have existed in ancient China and to have been lost!

Some of Marx's conclusions Mao rejected. Instead of accepting the German's five stages of historical development for the non-Han parts of western China, Mao came to believe that slave society could lead to socialist society, skipping over the feudal and capitalist stages.

Others of Marx's conclusions Mao accepted as headlines but modified by adding fine print underneath. Yes, the city workers must "lead" the revolution. But the peasants would be its "main force."

Mao drew on Marx, but Maoism was not to prove the same as Marxism.

Of the 158 items in Mao's official *Selected Works*, 112 were written in the northwest. They included all his main philosophic pieces. In them the tone of voice was that of the sage.

"Consider this speech carefully," he intoned at the end of one lecture. "It is my hope that you will actually cure your own disease."

Even when he was being modest the effect was somehow of a giant insisting that he is a pygmy. "I myself am groping in the dark about these things," he wrote in a preface on methods of study. "To continue as a primary school student—this is my ambition." The bubbling verve of Mao's voice in the Hunan *Report* of fifteen years before had given way to the voice of a would-be teacher to the Chinese nation.

* * *

As World War II wound down, Mao called a CCP congress. It was the first since the Sixth Congress, held at Moscow in 1928. Mao had missed that one, being on Well Mountain at the time.

The Seventh Congress was a triumph for Mao and for Maoism. From "Moscow 1928" to "Yanan 1945" was a long journey in time, space, and the ebb and flow of the Chinese Revolution.

"A congress of unity, a congress of victory," Mao aptly called the meeting in a Yanan orchard. It got under way just as Franklin Roosevelt died, and as Hitler killed himself amid the rubble of Berlin. Delegates were cho-

---

*Recall that Mao never read Marx in German; the Marx he met had already been poured into the mold of Chinese thought patterns.

sen from the 1.2 million members of what was now the world's second largest Communist Party.

They sat on wooden benches before a row of plants and a huge photo of Mao. Two dozen red flags stood for the number of years the CCP had existed. Each pillar in the hall was hung with a huge "V," to identify the CCP with the Allied triumph over fascism.

Some of the slogans on the gray-brick walls, fruits of Mao's drive to reshape Marxism along Chinese lines, carried a whiff of Confucian moralism.

"Persist in the Truth, Correct Your Mistakes," ran one paper strip. "Of One Heart, Of One Virtue," cried the back wall.

A new Party Constitution proclaimed the "Thought of Mao Zedong" as the ideology of the Chinese Revolution. It did not mention Stalin's name.

Moscow now recognized that Mao had won out against Wang Ming, but Mao did not return the favor and bow a knee to the north.

Mao summed up the Party struggles which he had lost in the early period and won since the Zunyi conference. The text of his resolution was polite to the Soviet Union. But at no point did it acknowledge Soviet assistance for *any post-1927 phase* of the Chinese Revolution.

Mao was elected to the new office of Chairman of the CCP.

He listened to praise from Wang Ming, Bo Gu, and others who had resisted him. He heard Zhang Guotao dubbed a "war lord."

He did not blush as Liu Shaoqi—now second only to Mao in the Party—mentioned his name 105 times in a single speech, and declared that "our great leader Mao Zedong . . . has raised our national thinking to an unprecedented height."

Mao was uncharacteristically genial and almost offhand as he raised teacups with the delegates. Upstairs from the meeting hall was a Ping-Pong room, where the "unity and victory" of the sessions gave way to the disunity of winners and losers. Mao took up the paddle. He was not a classy player. But he could lose his Ping-Pong games "with great equanimity," a colleague noticed.

10

A Ripening Peach (1945–1949)

For Mao the late 1940s was a time not for theory but for swift maneuver, as power hung tantalizingly before him like a ripening peach.

Decisions tumbled out of him. He flirted with the U.S., then turned away in bitterness. He fought again with Chiang's Nationalists, and won with an ease that amazed even himself. He put the seal on a sullen marriage with Russia.

America was as vivid to Mao as China was to Roosevelt—a dim light in the distance. Scraps of reading had built up in his mind a favorable picture of the U.S. as a land that Washington had rescued from British bullying.

Russia and Japan were a presence; America was but an idea.

All that had changed by 1944. Mao needed the U.S. to defeat Japan. Yet Uncle Sam was now at his door in ugly guise as Chiang's sponsor. And Mao had begun to ponder the role of America in a postwar Asia of which he expected China to be the centerpiece.

In Yanan Mao's curiosity about America captivated the American journalists whom he met and quizzed. Now that he had access to international news stories, he dissected America with the attention of a broker reading stock tables.

He saw a few American movies. *The Grapes of Wrath* he thought splendid. Betty Grable made him shudder. A picture about GI's fighting in Italy called *A Walk in the Sun* made him marvel at the happy-go-lucky style of U.S. soldiers—were they at war, or were they on a picnic? Charlie Chaplin he liked immensely.

In the summer of 1944, a C-47 plane full of American soldiers and diplomats fluttered down over Yanan's loess hills. Mao bumped out to the airport in his ambulance-limousine to greet the "Dixie Mission."

He shook hands with a U.S. government official for the first time in his life.

As he met Colonel David Barrett, Second Secretary John S. Service, and others, his gaze was wary but not without expectation. A dialogue began between Mao and Roosevelt's assorted representatives.

Behind the Dixie Mission's trip to Yanan was the desire of General Joseph Stilwell, U.S. theater commander in the East, to evaluate the Communists' capacity to help the U.S. complete the defeat of Japan. "Vinegar Joe" thought well of the CCP and wanted closer collaboration with it to galvanize the war effort.

Mao seemed to be pro-American in 1944. He felt—not foreseeing the use of the A-bomb—that U.S. forces would have to land in China to beat Japan. He was in favor of this. He came to like the free-wheeling style of his American visitors. He even agreed with the American proposal to place a U.S. general in command of the entire Chinese war effort (Chiang did not agree).

He sprinkled his talks with Dixie Mission members with the word "democracy," as if it were a value shared between Yanan and Washington. But Mao had not become an admirer of democracy as known in the West. "Anti-fascism" was all Mao meant when he spoke of democracy in an international context.

The 1950s would show that Mao had a stiffly Marxist view of the U.S.'s destiny.*

---

* Mao's simplistic Marxist view of American society had already come out in a 1947 talk with the Canadian journalist Mark Gayn:

Mao said a little impatiently:

"The trouble with you liberals in the West is that you misunderstand the social and political currents in the United States. The American toiling masses have had enough of capitalist oppression and injustice. They want a better life, a democratic system. When the next depression comes, they'll march on Washington and overthrow the Wall Street government. Then they'll establish a democratic regime that will cooperate with democratic forces all over the world, including China."

I told Mao that the picture of the American toilers marching on Washington to overthrow the Wall Street government did not fully agree with what I knew of American society.

Mao said, "I'll give you an example that will prove my point. Have you read 'Thunder Out of China' by Theodore White and Annalee Jacoby?"

I said I had.

"Would you agree," he asked, "that this book is quite critical of Chiang Kai-shek and of the Kuomintang misrule and corruption?"

I agreed.

"Don't you think," he asked again, "that it's quite fair to us?"

I did think so.

"Who published the book?"

I told Mao it had been distributed by the Book-of-the-Month Club, and when Mao asked if this was a capitalist enterprise, I conceded that, yes, indeed, the book club was very much a capitalist undertaking.

"All right, then," Mao said triumphantly, "there you have the answer! Why would a capitalist firm publish a book critical of Chiang Kai-shek and fair to us but for the pressure of the American toiling masses who are friendly to China and who demand to know the truth?"

Informed Americans were dismayed at the vanity, corruption, and sheer ineptness of Chiang's Nationalists. Mao's thoughts about American policy also centered on the Nationalists.

Beyond defeating Japan, he wanted Roosevelt to stop pouring dollars and supplies into Nationalist hands. Otherwise the CCP's battle with Chiang would be long and bloody.

Mao tried to convince the U.S. of the CCP's grip upon the future. If Washington could be led to see that Chiang was doomed by his lack of support from China's peasant majority, perhaps civil war might be avoided. If America would accept that the CCP was now a co-equal with the NP, a coalition government might be formed. Mao believed that within such a coalition, he would triumph over Chiang as the dawn banishes the night.

Mao found it no easier to convince Roosevelt that the CCP was fast eclipsing the NP than he found it to convince Stalin.

*   *   *

Mao didn't realize until too late what a bag of snakes the China issue was within American politics. Chiang and his wife had seduced some key Republicans to 100 percent support for the Nationalist cause. So Roosevelt had to tread carefully with Chiang.

In China, "Vinegar Joe" had differences with General Claire Chennault, who wanted, not to work with Mao, but to finish Japan off by a flourish of air power. And Roosevelt's bulldozer from Oklahoma, Major General Patrick Hurley, was on the warpath against the China specialists on Stilwell's staff and in the State Department.

Poor Mao was bewildered. No one had told him that Americans dealing with China spent 70 percent of their time sparring with each other and 30 percent on China.

Patrick Hurley came to Yanan in late 1944. Mao drove out to the primitive airport to meet Roosevelt's personal representative. Hurley announced himself with a Choctaw war whoop that sent the dust swirling. Crisp and martial—it was said of him that he could strut sitting down—he wore an officer's uniform dripping with medals. Mao walked quietly forward in his shapeless cotton outfit and cloth shoes.

"Mouse Tongue," one staff aide heard Hurley say as he greeted Mao Zedong. Another listener thought the booming envoy said "Moose Dung."

Mao and Hurley stuffed themselves into the ambulance. Seldom had the cause of international understanding faced a stiffer test.

As they crossed the Yan River, Mao described how the stream rises in winter and dries up in summer. Hurley responded that in Oklahoma rivers get so dry in the summer that it is possible to follow the course of a school of fish by watching the cloud of dust it raises.

They came upon a peasant beating a mule forward with a stick. Hurley put his head out the window and offered the peasant some advice in English: "Hit him on the other side, Charlie!" Mao managed to wedge in the remark that he had tended mules himself when a boy in Music Mountain. Hurley explained that he used to be a cowboy, peppering his account of that life with the cry "Yahoo!"

"The fellow's a clown," Mao told Zhu De later, and from that moment on "The Clown" was Hurley's nickname in Yanan.

Ignorance was Hurley's biggest problem. He knew no more about China or Marxism than Mao knew about the Choctaw war whoop. He did not even understand his friend Chiang.

Mao and Hurley worked out a plan for an NP-CCP coalition. Mao was quite pleased with it. They both signed it. But in Chongqing the Nationalist leaders laughed at the five-point plan.

Mao had been prescient to wonder aloud to Colonel Barrett if Chiang had really approved, as Hurley said he had, the gist of the five points before Hurley brought them to Yanan.

Hurley had the manners of a tank, but intellectually he was as weak as a cushion. Within days he had changed his mind about the five points. For the next year—until he resigned in a huff and explained the sagging fortunes of the NP by saying the State Department was pro-Communist—he kept U.S. policy pro-Chiang.

Mao played one more card. Talks at the top level seemed the only way. He asked to come to Washington.

His message was passed in January 1945 to the Dixie Mission office in Yanan for transmission to the "highest United States officials." It said that Mao or Zhou, or the two of them together, were prepared to come to the U.S. if Roosevelt would receive them as the spokesman of a primary Chinese party.

Mao asked that if Roosevelt would not invite him, the request be kept secret; this was to avoid electrifying Chiang, with whom the Communists were still in sour negotiation.

Hurley killed the message. It went first to Chongqing, where the Oklahoman had become U.S. ambassador. It never got to the "highest United States officials," except in unrecognizable form as part of a complaint to Roosevelt about furtive links between Colonel Barrett and the CCP. Mao waited in vain for a reply.

Ten weeks later Mao learned that Service had been recalled to Washington. He immediately invited the young American diplomat for half a day of conversation. He no doubt surmised that Service was going back to make arrangements for a Mao-Zhou visit to Roosevelt. (Service himself did not know the reason for the summons home.) Mao could not have been more wrong.

By midsummer Service was under arrest, charged with leaking secrets to the left-wing magazine *Amerasia*. Mao was disturbed. Roosevelt had already fired Stilwell, at Chiang's insistence, and now Hurley was mowing down all those American officials who believed Mao would bulk large in China's future.

Mao wrote an article called "The Hurley-Chiang Duet Is a Flop." His flirtation with America, like Roosevelt's life, was almost at an end.

The Oklahoman and the Generalissimo had made inevitable a new civil war between the CCP and the NP, had almost handed the future of China to Mao, and had pushed Mao toward a closer link with Russia than he had ever had or wanted.

Everything that Hurley and Chiang said they stood for was soon to go under.

A flicker of new interest in cooperation with the U.S. seemed to stir in Mao in the autumn when he had the nasty experience of seeing Russia sign a treaty of friendship and alliance with Chiang's government. But it could only be a flicker, for Washington was now supinely at Chiang's beck and call.

Mao lost America four years before America "lost China."

Barrett got caught between Mao and Hurley. After Hurley went back on the five-point plan, the hapless colonel was dispatched to see Mao in case something could be salvaged. Mao lost his temper and fumed against the "bastard" Chiang.

"If you Americans," he shouted, "sated with bread and sleep, want to curse the people and back Chiang, that's your business. I'm not going to interfere."

In his anger he made a prediction that stood up well through the tragedy that was about to unfold: "Back him as long as you want. But remember one thing. China is *whose* China? It sure as hell is not Chiang Kai-shek's; it belongs to the Chinese people. The day is coming when you will not be able to prop him up any longer!"

When Barrett went to report to the "Genbassador"—a title used by a fed-up staff for the boss who liked to straddle the military and diplomatic worlds—Hurley likewise flew into a rage and called Mr. Mouse Tongue a "motherfucker."

The texts that Hurley had handed to Mao in Yanan owed much to the phraseology of the American Revolution. "Writ of habeas corpus" Mao had probably never heard of. "A government of the people, by the people, for the people" is not an easy phrase to render in Chinese. Hurley was leaning on the U.S. Bill of Rights to define the values he thought a postwar coalition should adhere to.

Was Mao repelled? No, his reaction to the first round of talks with Hurley was favorable. The irony—and the tragedy—was that the man who invoked for Mao the American Constitution was also the man who later whipped the rug from beneath Mao's feet.

To learn the tenets of American democracy in this way did not predispose Mao to put much trust in U.S. ideals during the 1950s and 1960s. When his *Selected Works* was published, most of the warm references to the U.S. in the 1940s had been weeded out.

If Mao *had* come to Washington, he might have convinced Roosevelt of his grip on the future. That would not have prevented a Mao-Chiang showdown; but the Chinese civil war would not have lasted three years and killed three million people.

Chiang would not have been backed until the end—indeed, beyond the end—and George Marshall would not have had to mediate with one hand tied behind his back.

Probably Mao would have defeated Chiang regardless of anything Marshall could have done, even with both hands free. But the shock in America would have been less, the "loss" not so keenly resented, if Mao had in 1945 come in the door of the White House as a political leader, instead of hovering in America's imagination as a distant god of fate.

Mao's first trip outside China would have been to the U.S., at age 51, not, as it turned out, to Russia at age 56. His relations with the U.S. over the next 25 years would have been less mired in bitterness, less punctuated by war and threats of war.

* * *

The war was over but there was little peace. Tension came to a head over the modalities of the Japanese surrender. The CCP and the NP vied with each other to seal the enemy's defeat; to take the guns from the Japanese was to take control of the future. Outraged cables flew back and forth between Mao and Chiang on this matter.

For the moment Chiang had the advantage; Mao had to bend. Both world powers were on the side of the NP. U.S. logistical aid to Chiang put him a step ahead of the CCP in taking over from the Japanese. Moscow's treaty with Chiang's government made Mao fear that civil war against the NP might be long and tough.

So Mao decided to go to Chongqing to talk with Chiang. "My humble self is most willing to come to Chongqing to discuss national peace and reconstruction," he cabled to Chiang in traditionally polite phrases. "Your younger brother is preparing to come."

Some of the Communist leaders were against the trip. Without an American guarantee of his safety in Chiang's realm, Mao would not have gone.

The still-ebullient Hurley flew up to Yanan to fetch Mao in August 1945. Mao climbed into an airplane for the first time in his life. He openly entered territory ruled by Chiang for the first time. Flying south, Hurley gave a commentary on the state of the world. Mao wrote a poem.

For once in his life Mao was not hatless. He emerged from the plane wearing a topee, which someone had suggested as a safety measure. His look was wary and distant.

Chongqing (Weighty Celebration) had been the Nationalist base since Hankou fell to the Japanese in 1938. A city perched on hills above the Yangze, it was a new sight for Mao.* He stayed in a comfortable house on a narrow lane in Red Cliff district. Chiang put an American car at his disposal.

The heat was a change for Mao. For eleven years he had lived north of the Yangze. Yanan is dry in the summer—though frigid in winter—while Chongqing is a steam bath.

It had been eighteen years since Mao entered a city as other than a bandit. As at Wuhan in 1927, his presence was legal. Visitors called. Newspapers mentioned his name without cursing.

He ran into old friends and old enemies. Toward them all he showed largesse, murmuring patriotic sentiments, exchanging literary morsels handwritten on scrolls. He leaked his poem "Snow" to *New China Daily*. (It was the first of his poems to be published in a major organ.) All Chongqing read of his love for China's mountains and his sense of his own destiny.

Chiang and Mao had not seen each other for two decades. They shook hands.

One looked Prussian, the other Bohemian. Chiang's jacket was nicely pressed and covered with decorations. Mao's was rumpled and plain as if picked up from a pile of hundreds (though he was wearing a new pair of leather shoes).

Chiang looked like a rod of steel; Mao looked like a bamboo.

*On the Long March he saw parts of Sichuan Province, but not its capital.

Not quite true—as has been said—that Chiang was tense and Mao calm. No one who chain-smokes, as Mao did, is entirely calm—though Mao exhaled as slowly as it is possible to do.

Mao kept calm with Chiang because he knew he could outwit him, and because he believed his cause (personalities apart) would win out over Chiang's. In part for the same reason, Mao was candid while Chiang was secretive.

After forty-three days Mao and Chiang signed a piece of paper. The Generalissimo affixed his signature in square characters; Mao wrote his in flowing characters.

The agreement solved none of the fundamental questions: could the NP and the CCP truly share power; would the Red Army have to disband if a coalition came into existence? But arrangements for a national assembly were gingerly set in train, and some territorial lines of division were agreed upon.

As the two enemies clinked glasses, each was smiling to excess, while others at the banquet table seemed too riveted by the unlikely spectacle to manage more than a quarter smile.

Mao went as Chiang's guest to see a classical opera almost on the eve of his return to Yanan. In the middle of the show a message reached the Communist group. Zhou Enlai left his seat in great agitation.

Shots had been fired at Mao's car, parked outside the theater, and one of Mao's aides was dead. Pale and angry, Zhou sought out Chiang's chief negotiator to express his indignation.

Mao stayed in his seat. He loved Chinese classical opera—though after gaining power he would stifle it—and he meant to enjoy every minute of this one. When the show was over the leaders gathered for a farewell reception. Had Mao forgotten the attack on his car? Smiling broadly, he raised his glass and proposed a toast: "Long life for Mr. Chiang Kai-shek!"

Mao never saw Chiang again after that night at the opera.

How could Mao and Chiang have trusted each other? Mao did not trust Chiang. "There are no straight roads in the world," he remarked to some aides after he got back to Yanan. His approach to Chongqing had been a curved one. He did not think negotiation with Chiang could succeed in the sense of ending the Nationalist-Communist struggle. He made the trip because the international situation forced him to; Russian and American backing (in varying ways) for the Nationalists meant that Mao had to handle Chiang with a certain respect.

He also went to Chongqing because the "old hundred names" of China did not want a civil war and Mao could not afford to seem against peace.

And he went in order to show his strength. That Chiang had to invite him was more important to Mao than the content of the talks. China—and the world—received a timely reminder that Chiang had a rival, already ruler of one hundred million people, with an army of one million men at his command.

"The sky cannot have two suns," Chiang insisted to his aides. But Mao had made the point that the Chinese sky offered a *choice* between two suns.

Mao despised Chiang. "Chiang Kai-shek has lost his soul," he would soon sum up, "is merely a corpse and no one believes him anymore." Yet Mao kept his feelings under control while in Chongqing.*

Some Communists had no stomach for negotiation with the man who had fought them from 1927 until 1937, and had begun to do so again. Others were so fed up with war that they made themselves believe negotiations with Chiang could succeed—Zhou may have been one of them.

Mao's subtlety cut across both questions. The world is in flux, he maintained. Nothing is quite what it seems. The present moment is real, but what lies ahead is also real. Indirect methods are essential if one is to both respect the present and grasp the future.

Marshall came to Yanan in early 1946, for one last effort to narrow the gap between Mao and Chiang. Zhou, who escorted him, had not given up hope in Marshall's mediation. Zhou was always less inclined than Mao to dismiss the possibility of a straight road, which is why Marshall found him a more straightforward man.

Mao expected little. Unlike one year before, he seemed detached; he moved through his role in the negotiations like an actor.

He must have had his tongue in his cheek when he toasted Marshall: "Let us all cheer the durable cooperation between America and China, between the Communist Party and the Nationalist Party."

Marshall was sincerely proceeding, in deep fog, down a straight road. Ready to depart at Yanan airport, he asked Mao when he would be prepared to go and talk with Chiang again. "I shall go whenever Chiang asks me," Mao replied, as distant as a mountain. He could find a way of agreeing with Marshall's emotional declaration: "I can tell that an unprecedented era of progress awaits China."

Mao did not meet an American official again until three wars and four U.S. Presidents later.

All mediation having failed, Marshall soon left China, and by autumn

* Wang Ming claims Mao was in a state of nervous exhaustion after the Chongqing encounter, suffering dizziness, palpitations, and insomnia; unfortunately it is not easy to trust Wang Ming's words on this topic.

1946 Mao and Chiang were at each other's throats for a final round. Both went back on agreements.

"When two 'can't-see-whys' come together," Mao observed, "they fight."

*   *   *

The next three years were good for Mao. His military plans worked. His political predictions made him seem like a magician with an abundance of rabbits in his hat.

The Politburo had its disagreements—on land policy and on the timing of seizing power—but these did not turn into debilitating feuds. Administrative ailments were mostly due to the swellings of success.

In 1946 the Nationalists held all of south China and the sparse far west. The Communists were strong in the north. Mao's armies had one third the men of Chiang's and one fifth the arms.

For the first year Mao chose to go on the defensive, as Chiang charged around. By early 1947 the world believed that the CCP was withering on the vine.

Especially when in March Mao abandoned Yanan. Some of Mao's colleagues wanted to stay and fight for the town. Moscow thought the decision to leave was wrong and saw defeat looming for the Communists.

Mao was unsentimental. "It is after all only caves," he said of Yanan. He was bent on an ancient Chinese strategy: "Empty cities don't matter. The aim is to destroy the enemy's army."

Chiang flew to Yanan in triumph, like a cop who goes to kick over the pots and pans of a criminal's lair. He predicted that only three more months would be needed in order to finish off the People's Liberation Army (PLA). Three months later his own armies were being chewed up, bite by bite, as he shouted orders at the empty cities.

Mao was in villages again; he carried a gun again.*

This time he rode on a well-looked-after horse. Fine quality cigarettes somehow reached him from the east coast. He had radios and a good telephone system.

A year on the move took the fat off him, though the food was generally not bad. On a usual day he ate some meat, with millet, and perhaps turnips or cabbage. During one week there was nothing to eat but gruel made of

---

*After leaving Yanan, the CCP leadership divided itself into two. Mao took Zhou and Ren Bishi—a Hunanese, close to Mao, who would have been a top leader of the PRC if he had not died in 1950; Zhu De went with Liu Shaoqi.

flour and elm leaves. "Delicious," Zhou Enlai politely called this stuff. It is not recorded that Mao, who liked spicier fare, praised the gruel as he swallowed it.

Once Mao became badly ill and the evidence suggests that the ailment was the Parkinson's disease that was later to fell him.*

His telegrams were studded with concrete instructions. He worked in a team with others—he had to, for the unit commanders were his executives—and seldom went to commune alone with mountains.

As Mao's life was less austere than on the Long March, so his style of leadership was more conventional. Much of his time was spent closeted in meetings with Zhou and others, as secretaries ran in and out of the cave with radio messages from the front.

He managed to keep Jiang Qing and the two girls born in Yanan with him in a fairly close-knit traveling family circle.†

There were no fresh basic ideas. Nor did he write a single poem, at least that he allowed to reach the public. Typically his only verse was a footnote to another's effort. One morning a bodyguard was inspired to write by the sight of the sun rising like a fiery ball out of the purple mists over the Yellow River. But he got stuck. Mao heard the poem read, declared: "Unfortunately it has no ending," and added three lines of his own.

Mao used a pseudonym—"Li Desheng," the given-name part of which means "obtaining victory"—as the fame of his own name grew.

He chatted with an old man who had never seen a radio before. Wang was about to smash up the wooden box for firewood. "Li Desheng" explained as much as he knew about electromagnetic waves. "Don't make kindling of one if you see it around," he admonished. "I won't burn it," old Wang rejoined. "I'll keep it to hear Chairman Mao speak."

Mao began to exude a sense of his own power. His writings claimed to speak for China ("If this is not done, the Chinese people will deem it most improper").

After a big victory at Panlung, Mao and Zhou sat on stools under a tree to listen to the report from the Communist broadcasting station. From a battery radio on an upturned vat came the emotional voice of a girl announcer. She put steel in her voice when she spoke of Chiang, warmth when she spoke of Mao. Said Mao to Zhou: "That is the way to make a clear dis-

---

*In 1964 Mao remarked of the year 1947: "At that time I had contracted a disease whereby I could not write." He had to dictate his cables and essays to Jiang Qing.

†This did not stop Mao seeing other women, and probably having an affair with one. "Sex is engaging in the first rounds," Jiang Qing once remarked, "but what sustains interest in the long run is power"; other women, too, were drawn to Mao by his growing power in the 1940s.

tinction between hate and love! We ought to train more announcers like her."

Settled for a while in a village, Mao would emerge from his cave at dusk and sit on a stool with a "Learn English" manual. He still lacked flair for foreign languages, but the dealings with Americans in 1944–45 had made him want to tackle America's language. A self-image of the postwar statesman seemed to be taking shape.*

One memoir gently compares Mao unfavorably with Zhou for industry: "Sometimes, to ease the load of heavy responsibility from the Chairman's shoulders, Zhou went to bed still later than the Chairman, and rose still earlier." By Peking standards, that was a sharp comment.

Yet it is interesting that no one—not even Zhang Guotao—ever hinted that Mao lacked personal courage.

* * *

Mao fought an intense duel with NP general Hu Zongnan. Hu had taken Yanan after Mao left. He married there, having sworn not to marry until he had captured Mao's headquarters.

Mao's men numbered no more than 20,000, to Hu's 230,000. He wove around north Shaanxi, causing Hu to overextend himself, and to drain troops from other theaters where the PLA was hard-pressed.

Mao had his troops sing: "Keep men, lose land; land can be taken again. Keep land, lose men; land and men both lost." Not caring about territory, and hiding from Hu much of the time, he often sat around with his staff talking about novels. He even edited the diaries that he'd encouraged his guards to keep as a way of improving their writing.

Hu's 230,000 spread out far and wide. They did not enjoy good ties with the peasants, as Mao's "fish" did. With Hu lured in and lulled, Mao stirred. "Hu came in like a fist," he summed up. "We forced him to open like a hand; now we are cutting off the fingers one by one."

Mao went on the offensive all over China in late 1947. What he did to Hu, the PLA did to the NP throughout north and central China.

"The people are our bastion of bronze." Mao's words had seemed boastful but turned out to be true. The Communists had the populace; the Nationalists had only territory. An American military observer stated that by

---

* In the 1950s and 1960s, English dropped off the list of Mao's priorities. He apparently felt defensive about having chosen English—rather than Russian, or Arabic, or Spanish—as a language to study in the late 1940s. Memoirs published in Peking in the 1960s spoke of Mao studying "a foreign language" during the civil war. They never said it was English.

1947, "70 percent of the peasants in north China were Communist-oriented."

In Manchuria Chiang learned a nasty lesson in the uselessness of commanding buildings but not hearts. His trains set out from one city to the next, only to find that the Mao-inclined peasants had carried the rails off into the hills. Chiang held the stations alone! It summed up the civil war. Men won over machines.

Extra boon for Mao that a bandwagon effect occurred in the cities. "Food, Peace, Freedom" was the slogan of a new student movement. It was anti-Chiang, because the Nationalists were giving the people none of these things.

In peasant caves, Mao was a long way from this mini-May Fourth movement. But his way had often been to harness, rather than fully jump into, the activities of the intellectual avant-garde. Same in 1919, when the cry for a new world went up just as he ruminated at Confucius's birthplace. Same in 1935, when an anti-Japan student movement erupted in Peking while he was far off in Yanan.

Yet Mao immediately saw the importance of the urban surge against Chiang in 1947. "A second front," he called it—the first being that of the armed struggle.

Mao proved his flexibility by fighting big battles in the spring of 1948. He had never been against such confrontations *except* when he knew he was too weak to win them. Now he was strong. Suddenly the war was being fought not in Mao's enclaves but in the Chiang government's territory.

Chiang had written a book, *China's Destiny,* which foreshadowed his total victory. Now a movie version seemed to race across the screen of China's imagination, at unnatural speed, and in reverse. Each new frame showed disaster for the Nationalists. Half of Chiang's troops tied up on garrison duty. . . . Communist "bandits" suddenly looking like Chinese boys fighting for their country. . . . Chiang shouting at a general who had just lost half his army. . . . Mao in contemplation, his face as serene as Buddha's. . . . Chiang hopping in and out of planes. . . . Mao walking through villages.

By November 1948, the PLA outnumbered Chiang's armies; it was all over bar the curses and the cheers.

In his excitement Mao wrote prose that was almost poetry. "They heave great sighs," he said of his enemies. "They wail about a crisis, and no longer show any sign of joy."

Mao did not straightaway move on Peking after taking Manchuria. This led Chiang to believe that he could not do so. But Mao had his reasons. The time allowed the PLA to rest. It made the Nationalists more and more demoralized as they contemplated their predicament. And it permitted Lin Biao and his fellow commanders to surround all of the 500,000 NP troops in the area and plan a stage-by-stage demolition.

Meanwhile Mao wrote a message to the Nationalist commander urging him to cease resistance. "Think it over!" he admonished in the tradition of the warrior-moralist. "If you feel this is right, then do it. If you still want to fight another round, you can have it, but you will be finished off anyway." The Nationalist decided to fight to the end.

The PLA moved on Tianjin and lesser cities first—contrary to NP expectations—and took them one by one with almost German efficiency. Li Lisan and Otto Braun would have been overjoyed at the spectacle, had not their un-Maoist error—seeking the right thing at the wrong time—long since removed them from the cockpit.

*   *   *

By the spring of 1948 Mao's victory became palpable. He shed his caution of 1946–1947 as a snake sheds a skin whose job has been done.

Some of Mao's colleagues had held a lower expectation of victory over Chiang than Mao himself. "We cannot be defeated," General Peng Dehuai apparently said in 1946, "but it is probably true that we cannot win."

It was felt—almost certainly by Liu among others—that the Communists ought to be content for the time being with separate regimes in north and south China. To cross the Yangze, according to this prudent view, would not only be contrary to Stalin's advice, but likely to provoke Truman's unwelcome intervention (100,000 U.S. troops were in China in 1948).

The Mao of 1948 scorned such pessimism.

"Thirty to fifty years" had been Mao's estimate to Xiao You, as they took a boat to Shanghai in 1921, of how long it would take for the CCP to win power. "One and a half years of fighting," he predicted in the summer of 1946. "July 1951," he said in the spring of 1948. "Another year or so," he declared in late 1948, and *that* turned out about right.

Chiang became a peace-maker. Messages full of smooth words came out of Nanjing. But now Mao was the one who did not want to share power. His terms were as stiff as the bayonets of the advancing PLA. His only real answer to Nanjing came when the PLA marched down from the green hills and took the lovely city in April. "Southern Capital" had fallen and soon the south fell too.

Mao wrote his first poem in a while. He spoke of a peak just east of Nanjing that the ancients styled a dragon. It hovers over the city, likened by tradition to a tiger.

> Over Mount Zhong a sudden storm has arisen,
> A million courageous warriors cross the great river.
> The crouching tiger and the coiled dragon are more
>   majestic than ever in the past,
> It is a moment of heroic triumph, heaven and earth
>   have been overturned.

The poem ended with lines that seemed to come from the tiger within Mao:

> Let us gather up our courage and pursue the broken foe,
> It is not fit to seek praise by imitating the
>   Tyrant of Chu.
> If heaven had feelings, heaven too would grow old,
> The true way that governs the world of men is that
>   of root-and-branch change.

"True way that governs the world of men" was a very Confucian turn of speech. But the second part of the line put Confucius off the agenda; no Confucian ever used political power for root-and-branch change.

Mao had been reading *Aesop's Fables* and found in "Evil for Good" a logic for ruthlessness. The farm boy found a snake frozen by cold. Taking pity, he nursed it. Revived by warmth, the snake reverted to its usual ways and bit the poor farm boy. Mao quoted the boy's dying lament: "I've got what I deserve for taking pity on an evil creature."

The monkey within Mao was permitted no tricks at this moment of reckoning. The Tyrant of Chu had spared an opponent only to be destroyed by him. The opportunity for root-and-branch change had come; no wisps of sentiment would stop Mao from grabbing it.

Mao hurled his victory into Chiang's face:

> "To whom should the fruits of victory in the war of resistance belong?" he inquired. "It is very obvious. Take a peach tree, for example. . . . Who is entitled to pick the peaches? Ask, who planted and watered the tree? Chiang Kai-shek, squatting on the mountain, did not carry a single bucket of water, yet now he stretches out his arms from afar to pick the peaches. He says, 'I own them as the landlord. You are my serfs, and I won't allow you to pick any.' We say, 'You never carried any water, so you have no right to pick them!' "

* * *

Mao was now an actor in the realm of world politics. His trip to Chongqing in 1945 made him known. His success on the battlefield during 1947 made him feared.

On the walls of his office in Yanan he had hung portraits of the Big Four: Chiang, Churchill, Roosevelt, Stalin (in the order of the Western alphabet, as they generally seemed to be in Yanan). This line-up had put China among the concert of great powers.

By 1948 Mao felt that he had all but replaced Chiang as China's leader. (He had begun to order Chiang around; "we absolutely will not permit you to do it," he said of the Nationalist plan to set free a notorious Japanese war criminal.) In his own mind this put him into the world arena. Came an incident which made it clear that he was correct.

Britain sent a frigate up the Yangze as if the Orient were still John Bull's backyard. The *Amethyst* headed for Nanjing, at once to show the flag and to carry cigars and port to the British Embassy in that teetering capital.

But the Yangze valley was no longer in Chiang's hands as assumed by a London grown used to mastery over pliant Chinese. Mao's men shot at and crippled the *Amethyst*. Twenty-three Britons were killed. For 101 days the frigate lay like a sick fish because its captain refused to sign a document confessing to having "criminally invaded Chinese waters."

The House of Commons bristled with indignation. Churchill called the PLA's action an "atrocious outrage." Mao replied with the simple point that a sovereign country could not allow foreign boats to sail up and down its rivers at will. The "bandit" now spoke for China.

"A foreign government which wishes to consider establishing diplomatic relations with us," Mao declared in a statement that aroused the British but seems only logical today, "must sever relations with the remnant Nationalist forces and withdraw its armed forces from China."

Stalin's contribution to Mao's victory was to urge him to give up just as he reached the brink of power. "We considered that the development of the uprising in China had no prospects," the Russian admitted later, "that the Chinese comrades should seek a *modus vivendi* with Chiang Kai-shek, that they should join the Chiang Kai-shek government and dissolve their army."

Mao correctly felt that postwar Asia was taking a shape that outstripped the vision of the Big Four. His later distrust of "superpowers" was due in part to the fact that in 1948 the great powers showed no sign of welcoming him to their club.

Chiang moved south to Canton. The U.S. ambassador did not follow Chiang this time. Nor did the envoys of the other major countries. They all stayed in Nanjing—with one exception. The envoy of the U.S.S.R. went to Canton, clinging to Chiang's white bones as north China turned red under Mao.

Mao invited Ambassador Leighton Stuart to come and talk. It was a footnote, in mirror image, to Mao's own attempt to go to Washington and talk with Roosevelt in 1945. Mao had decided that China would look to Russia for the time being. But still at stake was whether or not Mao's China would have businesslike ties with the U.S.*

But Stuart dithered, and Washington was quarter-hearted about Mao-Stuart talks.†

In 1945, when he was weak, Mao would have come to Washington. The U.S. did not ask him. In 1949, he was strong and did not have to *go* anywhere. But he did invite a U.S. official humbler in seniority than himself to come to him. Again the U.S. was not very interested.

In 1945, Washington saw Mao as too weak to bother with. Just four years later, it saw him as too strong to get anything from.

Mao became bitter. Soon he ordered tough and peremptory treatment for U.S. consular personnel in north China; accused of being "spies," many were bundled out of the country.

The last contacts the Americans had with the Communists in Nanjing were not pleasant. "Huang Hua said frankly they looked on U.S.A. as an enemy," Stuart noted in his diary. The frail ambassador went back to the U.S., where he soon suffered a stroke. Mao said good-bye to him with "Farewell Leighton Stuart," the nastiest essay he ever wrote about the U.S.

He looked back on Marshall's mediation as an effort to "gain control of all China without fighting." He called Chiang's regime a "U.S. colonial government." The lines were acidic, recklessly anti-American, laced with quips from old Chinese books.

Mao could not hide a certain resentment that the U.S. was rich while China was poor. He hated U.S. charity even more than U.S. weapons. "The Americans have sprinkled some relief flour in Peiping, Tianjin and Shanghai to see who will stoop to pick it up."

U.S. arrogance toward its clients made him recall a fisherman in the Zhou dynasty (1122–255 B.C.) who held a bare rod without hook or bait three feet above the water while declaring: "The fish that is destined to be caught will come up."

With a line from the ancient classic, *Book of Rites,* he warned those Chinese who might still wish to hold out a hand toward Uncle Sam: "He who swallows food handed out in contempt will get a bellyache."

There was a wound in Mao beneath the shell of bravado. He threw contempt at the U.S. with the stridency of one who believes he has been treated contemptuously. "Why can't we live without the United States?" he cried in a voice too loud to suggest a sense of security.

---

* As Zhou had put it to Marshall in 1946: "Of course, we will lean to one side, but the extent will depend on you."

† The U.S. never made public Mao's invitation to Stuart.

Why did Mao attack the liberals—Stuart, Acheson—yet pay little attention to the McCarthy rightists? The American liberals were Mao's main enemy because their attractiveness to Chinese liberals raised a question about Mao's pro-Sovietism.

Some "third force" people, even some Communists, looked up to American democracy. And they felt the U.S. (so far away, after all) was a lesser evil than the U.S.S.R. Mao was making a foreign policy point to hit a domestic target: "making use of the mulberry to point to the ash," as a Chinese saying has it.

Chiang had known for a long time that he could not survive without the U.S. He spent 1949 trying to ensure that Uncle Sam—and a supply of gold—would stand between himself and a Mao who chased him from city to city. He moved five times during that year and in December he left the mainland for Taiwan.

Stuart told his diary: "CKS on Formosa raises many problems." Neither Stuart nor Mao knew then *how* big the problems would be.

* * *

Did Mao win, or did Chiang lose? Both occurred. Chiang himself admitted in 1948—to an NP meeting—that the CCP had been more dedicated than the NP and had served the Chinese people better. The PLA outfought and outwitted the Nationalist armies. The Chinese economy fell to pieces in Chiang's uncomprehending hands.

The two failures were really one: Chiang's constituency was too narrow.

"A people's war is not decided by taking or losing a city," Mao told the American reporter Anna Louise Strong when she asked him about the loss of Yanan, "but by solving the agrarian problem." Mao beat Chiang because he understood, as Chiang did not, the social significance of war in the green and brown vastness of China: you win when you have won the "old hundred names" of rural China.*

Mao did not turn the people off by conscription and grain levies, as Chiang did. His cadres did not spend half their time feathering their own nests, as Chiang's did. He did not depend on foreigners for support, as Chiang did by 1948. (*After V-J Day* Chiang received $3 billion in U.S. aid; in the same period Mao received no foreign aid at all.)

Mao won the backing of intellectuals who found that Chiang's brittle declarations of allegiance to the Free World went along with shrinking liberties in his own backyard. Of Chinese patriots who looked around and saw their

---

* Mao, though more uncompromising toward Chiang than Liu, was "softer" on land policy than Liu. "Haste will do no good," he testily reminded Liu in a telegram that argued for going easy on small landowners. Making the "water" healthier for the "fish" to swim in, Mao's moderate social policies helped the PLA crash through to victory against Chiang's armies.

nation going to rack and ruin under Chiang. Of anyone who preferred a vague hope for the future over a patent disgust at the present.

Chiang was shrewd only within the bounds of each successive crisis; his mind had no reach. Mao took the long view of a man who has studied the forces of history.

Chiang was a vain man often sidetracked by the shadow of things. Mao was (in the 1940s) a dry man interested only in the substance of his goals.

Chiang was merely a military man. Mao was a man of ideas for whom the gun was one instrument. In 1943, when the CCP was still weak, Chiang could have reached an agreement with Mao favorable to himself. But he did not understand, as Mao did, the relation between politics and war. Seeking *only* a military solution to the problem of communism, he lost both his armies and the Chinese people.

Mao found in *Dream of the Red Chamber* an image for Chiang's view of his army. A character called Jia was born with a piece of jade in his mouth. "The root of his life," it had to be worn around his neck day in and out. If he lost it he would lose his wits. Mao saw Chiang's army as a totem meant to shield him from the external world.

Mao's own idea of an army was different. Basically it was the people mobilized. Not a mechanism; nor a mystical thing. Simply one of the modes of political struggle. Mao could never *lose* his army—as if it were Jia's piece of jade—but Chiang was haunted by a fear of losing his.

* * *

By mid-1948 more than 3 million people belonged to the CCP and 2.5 million to the PLA. The army had to be divided up into field, regional, and guerrilla forces. Problems of discipline and coordination arose. Mao wrote dull memos like "On Setting Up a System of Reports."

On Well Mountain, Mao had been a shepherd to his sheep. Now he commanded one of the world's five biggest armies. Methods could not be the same.

A city existence brought way-of-life dilemmas that had never before faced Mao's rural band. Mao had won the battle for power; at the same time he began to lose ground in the battle for purity. His ambivalence about bigness grew. He began to suspect that more could be less.

The monkey would not allow the tiger to have all that its force seemed to command. And the role of teacher—which at Yanan he had nicely combined with that of leader—seemed to slip away from him.

In April 1948 the PLA retook Yanan. But it did not—could not—retake the Yanan spirit. Mao dictated a telegram to congratulate the Yananese on their return to the fold. He never revisited Yanan.

Mao scarcely showed himself as Liberation came. He seemed almost bored by the outward forms. He sat in a back room and made decisions. These were mainly how, and in what order, to pluck the fruits that hung temptingly around him.

As 1948 drew to a close, Colonel David Barrett lunched in Peking with John Melby, who was also from the U.S. Embassy in Nanjing. It was a perfect day. A steady sun lit up the persimmons. But a rumble of artillery rattled the chopsticks. The PLA had reached the Western Hills which overlook the flat, square calm of Peking. Shells were falling on Peking airport.

An NP general, holding on to the city by a fingernail, sent a delegation outside the city walls to talk with Mao's peasant warriors. A surrender was arranged, robed in the term "coalition." This no longer meant shared power. It was merely a symbol for manipulation by the CCP. The NP general handed over Peking and also 200,000 troops.

Mao's tactics had saved the city from a lot of destruction. By delaying so long, and taking so many other cities first, he made it unlikely that the Nationalists would fight for Peking. Mao rewarded Chiang's general for being reasonable by making him Minister of Water Conservation.

Soon the PLA padded in like rural boys arriving for a Saturday outing in the city. Cloth shoes; gawking expressions; uniforms like pajamas. Some tried to light their cigarettes from light bulbs.

A loudspeaker preceded them with a slightly sanctimonious cry: "Congratulations to the people of Peiping* on their liberation." Some spectators took the soldiers' pink farm-boy complexions for a mark of exhaustion after a long trek. Others gasped to see that the tanks, jeeps, and heavy artillery that rolled silently by were nearly all American.

"Chiang is our quartermaster," Mao used to joke, and he had been right.

Portraits of Mao and Zhu De were held aloft. Zhu was grinning and Mao was impassive. Walls and telegraph poles were flecked with mimeographed handbills about "New China." The *North China Daily News,* organ of Chiang's Ministry of Information, overnight became Mao's *People's Daily.*

Peking editors were wise to swiftly toe the new line, for few things did Mao supervise more closely than the printed word.

He commissioned articles. He demanded the galley proofs of important pieces, and marked changes in his own swirling characters. He wrote scores of newspaper columns himself, never signing them. And for years he hired and fired press people as if they were his kitchen staff.

---

* Peking had been China's capital for some 500 years. But when Chiang—who like Mao had mixed feelings about north China—set up his capital at Nanjing in 1928, he changed the name Peking (northern capital) to Peiping (northern peace). Upon the formal establishment of his regime, Mao rebaptized the city as Peking. Since then the CCP has looked upon "Peiping" as a swear word that denotes Chiang's era.

The world began to look different from Peking, as Peking began to look different from the rest of the world.

*   *   *

Peking was turning red, yet its citizens had never set eyes on the chief painter. Did he really exist, asked the ignorant, when seven weeks after the Nationalist surrender Mao still had not arrived. Had Peking been so cold to him in 1918–1920, wondered the better-informed, that he had decided to base his new regime elsewhere?

Then one day a rumor flew through the alleys that Mao was on the way. His plane had just taken off from Shijiazhuang (Stone Homestead), 160 miles south, the first city in north China to fall to the PLA.

People's Daily printed its first extra. "CHAIRMAN MAO HAS ARRIVED IN PEIPING," the newsboys cried in piercing tones. The headline was four inches high in red ink. Customers clawed the newsboys to get a copy of the single sheet. It sold out in forty-five minutes.

Do-gooders and the left were thrilled at the turn of events. The rich were bitter and afraid. Rickshaw pullers chatted evenly about the prospects. Everyone speculated about Mao's nature and his priorities.

At Peking University a porter called Guo paused to reminisce with a librarian. "He used to work right in this room, at that desk over there, checking out newspapers and magazines." Librarian Wang stared at the spot. "Yes, I remember. It's thirty years since I saw him last. In his photographs he looks heavier. . . ."

The pair of them went upstairs to look at the cubbyhole where Mao used to study in his time off. Guo pointed with the handle of his broom: "There it is. On that very chair he sat thirty years ago, reading all day long."

Wang addressed the universe: "Who could have known . . . ?" Maybe he wished that he'd looked after Mao a bit better in 1920, taken more pains to track down books for Mao to devour.

Wang was right about Mao's being heavier. "You've put on weight," said a visitor who had seen Mao just four years before. "The reactionaries caused me to get thin," Mao beamed with a victor's good humor. "Now that they've been chased away I am filling out."* Sleep was part of the story; when he went to bed earlier, he got fatter.

When Changsha fell—or did it rise?—a telegram of celebration reached Mao. It was from the brother of his early wife, Yang Kaihui. Five days later Mao replied at some length. He gave Mr. Yang some family news. Both

---

* In fact, Mao's body did wax and wane in rhythm with the presence of enemies. Through the years of struggle he was fairly thin. In Yanan he put on weight. During the civil war he lost it. After 1950, he never again had a lean and hungry look.

Mao's sons by Kaihui were in Peking. Anqing was at school. Anying was using his Russian in translation work at the CCP offices. "They both want to see their grandmother," Mao added.

He arranged for his two sons to visit Hunan. On separate trips, Anying in 1950 and Anqing in 1951 went to the grave of their mother, and made the rounds of the Yang family. Mao got in touch with Chen Yuying, the nurse-maid from his days with Yang Kaihui at Clear Water Pond in Changsha. Four times she came up to Peking at Mao's invitation. Mao spent long sessions alone with her.

* * *

Mao did not feed the excitement in Peking by going into the streets. He went straight to the Imperial Palace and settled in—books, tobacco, worn garments, Jiang Qing and all.

It was a striking choice of home. The ax fell on much that was old in Peking over the next four months. Walls and gates came down like scenery after the end of an opera. Craftsmen were diverted from making *objets d'art* to making soap. Almost all foreign embassies were required to leave the graceful mansions of the Legation Quarter and establish themselves in a sterile suburb.

Yet Mao did not build himself a Stalinist bungalow; he lived where the emperors had lived.

The "house" was a Ming dynasty pavilion. It occupied a quiet corner of the grounds of the Forbidden City, heart of the dynasties. Its golden tiles curved up to an apex beneath a plane tree's spreading branches. Red pillars stood like sentries around the walls of dark brown wood.

Outside Mao's windows were bronze dragons, mouths open too wide, snarling some message from the past that no one in the Peking of 1949 was in a position to hear. White stone steps led up to a wide glass door in four parts with curtains draped discreetly on the inside.

The place was called South and Central Lakes and Mao could see the porcelain-blue waters of the fish-laden lakes from his front door.

The interior was plain and elegant. Mao did not favor flowers or any other decoration. Very tall ceilings lent a sepulchral air. Tall windows threw down light as in a cathedral.

Carved wooden screens and long silk hangings set a sparse tone. Lamps were hoisted like street lights ten feet above capacious armchairs. Books were stacked flat in piles, as old Chinese books are arranged. Amid them stood the *Encyclopaedia Britannica,* perhaps a tool for Mao's periodic attacks on the English language.

A tea mug and a magnifying glass stood out on Mao's cloth-covered

His work chair was wicker, so that his shirt would not stick
summer.

bedroom did not look very different from the study. On one side of
wooden bed was a vast bench piled high with books.* On the other was a
spittoon. Clothes hung on stands like doctors' robes.

Outside the window lay a vegetable plot. Mao would wander out to tend
the beans in moments of rumination. This the emperors did not do.

Mao's mind's eye must have taken many a snapshot of "liberation." Who
raised the red flag over his farmhouse in Music Mountain? Was there a
struggle at *Great Welfare Daily* in Changsha? How was the PLA received
as it marched by Snake and Tortoise hills to take Wuhan?

Liberation *from* quickly became a past memory. "Chinese Communist
Party in power" was the blunt, disturbing new meaning of the word "liber-
ation." Enormous as his part had been in removing the old burdens from
China's back, Mao would now be judged by what he would do in office *for*
China.

"Will the tattered clothes change Peiping," Mao mused as he took up the
reins, "or will the change run in the opposite direction?"

---

* "I cannot go to sleep unless I read myself to sleep," Mao once remarked to Prime Minister
Tanaka of Japan.

11

"We Shall Put Aside the Things We Know Well" (1949–1950)

Mao, at 55, came out of his study to proclaim the People's Republic of China and hoist its flag on October 1, 1949.

A tank rolled ahead of Mao's car as the parade slowly ate up the Boulevard of Lengthy Peace. It was a Sherman, No. 237,438 W14. It had come from Detroit to Shanghai as a U.S. gift to help Chiang exterminate Mao. Sherman 237,438 W14 had served the Free World for a season. Now it clattered its way by the Imperial Palace into a different world.

Mao stood in a new suit high on the Gate of Heavenly Peace. A blowup of Sun Yat-sen beamed an involuntary blessing toward him from the south. Millions of people, organized in positions at the Square of the Gate of Heavenly Peace by numbers written on the flagstones, heard Mao sum up what had made him run: "The Chinese people have stood up . . . nobody will insult us again."

Mao wrote a thank-you note. Despite the press of business, the government made plans for a Monument to the People's Heroes, and Mao did an epigraph for it. "Eternal glory," ran the lines in usual war-memorial style, "to the heroes of the people who laid down their lives . . ."

The struggle of "the past three years" was saluted, and a second stanza honored that of "the past thirty years." Surprisingly there was a third: Mao thanked all those "who from 1840 laid down their lives in the many struggles against domestic and foreign enemies . . ."

Mao had given *the Opium War as the base date for the revolution.* He was recalling not just three years' fight against Chiang, and three decades of the CCP, but one hundred years of abjectness before the non-Chinese world.

The Communist era was not treated as its own separate slice of time, but as a culmination of the entire anti-imperialist era. None of Mao's colleagues, I think, would have written the epitaph in such a way. The monument with Mao's epitaph stands—a granite stalk in the bare ninety-eight acres of the Square of the Gate of Heavenly Peace—as Mao's plea for legitimacy in the Chinese history books.

Mao in a speech recalled that the hero of his school years, Kang Youwei, whom he had urged as prime minister in 1911, "did not and could not find the way to achieve his utopian vision of a Great Harmony." Mao had found the way. "The only way," he said in a reversion to Marxist words, "is through a people's republic led by the working class."

Here was Marxism offered as a tool for implementing a dream as old as the hills of China.

Kang had understood the goal, Mao implied. Mao was doing to Marx what Kang had done to Confucius. Kang asserted that values for life in the modern world could be found in Confucius, if you read him properly. Mao asserted that Marx's idea of communism did exist in China's past; as a goal it had been unattainable because no one, prior to the CCP, had found the means to get from there to here.

Moscow must have been alarmed. Mao had lifted Marxism from its lineage in Europe and given it a Chinese birth certificate.

Mao put the West in its place too. "The era in which the Chinese people were regarded as uncivilized is now ended." He declared that Chinese culture eclipsed all that the West any longer had to offer. The level of understanding of the modern world of "Acheson and his like," Mao claimed, "is lower than that of an ordinary soldier of the Chinese People's Liberation Army."

* * *

"We shall soon put aside some of the things we know well," Mao observed wistfully in mid-1949, "and be compelled to do things we don't know well." Village days were over; so was life with the gun. Ahead were new things: budgets; squabbles between regions; fights among lieutenants; a honeycomb of bureaucracy; the moral problems that belong to success.

Mao's tasks were clear-cut for a while. Some territorial mopping up remained to be done. Still "unliberated" were Taiwan, Hainan—an island of bananas and balmy breezes near Vietnam—and Tibet. There were also borders with half-a-dozen nations which the colonial era—as its parting shot at new China—had left in a messy state.

Mao had no intention of touching Hong Kong, a golden goose which could yet lay many an egg for the fatherland, by remaining outside though within reach of the fold.

Production had to be spurred. China had been at war for twelve years, and half at war for years before that. Factories were decrepit. Transportation was a joke for a nation of China's 9.6 million square kilometers. Virtually no steel was being produced in the late 1940s.

And the 550 million had to be joined in a network of organization. This was the cutting edge of the Communist Party's encounter with that large part of China that still lay beyond its mystique. Nothing could be written on the blank piece of paper to which Mao—in a troubling image—likened the Chinese masses, unless the paper was firmly in place before the calligrapher.

This was no ordinary change of government. A new U.S. government is faced with, and its power to act is limited by, an array of social and bureaucratic institutions: from the federal civil service to Wall Street, from the churches to the "Fortune 500" and the universities. Mao's new government, by contrast, was bent on changing the social and bureaucratic system. He was going to melt down every institution in China—even those hitherto not thought of as political—and recast each one in a socialist mold.

To get China moving, Mao needed energy from all reaches of society. Eleven of the twenty-four ministers in his first government were non-Communists. Fourteen political parties were admitted to a role in the first act of the PRC. Mao scared almost no one in 1949–1950.

Unless they read with care what he wrote. "New Democracy," Mao called the phase of national recovery. For its duration private enterprise could coexist with that of the state. But he meant New Democracy to be a stage, not a fixed pattern of society. He never hid that "Transition to Socialism" would follow it.

Transition to Socialism had its *method* and it was to reach a *class goal*.

Mao laid down the method in "On the People's Democratic Dictatorship," a meaty pre-inaugural speech. He had used "people" instead of "proletariat" in offering a Chinese version of Marx's "dictatorship of the proletariat." It was not a sleight of hand. Mao's revolution *had* been a broader one than Lenin's, for a clear reason. Non-Chinese had bulked large among the CCP's enemies, so a wide spectrum of Chinese supported the Communists. Say "imperialism" and the echo came back "people."

On the other hand Mao was not using "dictatorship" merely as a textual bow to Marx. He meant it as a method for recasting Chinese society. "Democracy for the people," he blandly announced, "and dictatorship over the reactionaries." Everything—far too much—would hinge on who belonged to the "people" in changing times.

On the class goal Mao was also quite frank. The flag that he hoisted to found the PRC showed five yellow stars on a red background. One star is bigger than the others. The five stars—which shine above the Gate of Heavenly Peace—stand for the five classes which Mao included in the New Democracy compromise. But the big star is the proletariat.

*   *   *

Two months after the PRC was founded Mao packed his bags for his first trip outside China. He went to Moscow to meet Stalin and formalize the PRC's "leaning to one side." He felt ready to put in an appearance—decades after all his top colleagues had done so—at the fountainhead of Communist power.

Mao, at 56 the Marxist boss of 550 million Asians, was to broach the future with Stalin, at 70 the pope of worldwide Marxism.

By the time Mao came back to the Forbidden City he probably regretted the nastiness of "Farewell Leighton Stuart." For it was a tough visit to the frigid Soviet capital. "Stalin was not willing to sign a treaty," Mao recalled. "After two months of negotiations he at last signed."

In Moscow Mao first glimpsed the non-Chinese world. He gazed unappreciatively at the Bolshoi Ballet. He tried to eat the abundant slabs of fish and meat which to a Chinese seem underprepared.

Mao faced the hauteur of Stalin who still had not grasped the magnitude of the CCP's victory. "Another Tito" was one of the Soviet leader's swear words for Mao in 1949. "Margarine Marxist" was another. It seemed a proof of anxiety—rather than a result of the borscht and the vodka—that Mao once more became ill in a moment of pressure.

Stalin's interest in China was not compatible with Mao's view of China's destiny. Stalin saw socialist China as a new pupil to be given a place in his Marxist class, alongside Poland and Hungary and the others. He expected new China to honor—and supply goods to—the Soviet fatherland just as East Europe did.

Mao saw his revolution as *sui generis*. He felt that he had fired a shot that would ring for decades throughout the non-European world. It was not easy for him to align his pride in China with the need to maneuver in a complex world not of China's making.

Stalin at times kept Mao waiting like a message boy. For days at a stretch Stalin had no contact with Mao; and since Stalin did not order anyone else to talk to Mao, no Russian dared to go and see him. Mao, feeling isolated, at one point threatened to pack up and return to China.

Mao wrung a mere U.S. $300 million in credits (for five years) out of his hosts. It was to be repaid with Chinese goods and raw materials, plus one percent interest. Such aid was less than Moscow gave to Poland, twenty times smaller than China, and about one third the value of the equipment the Soviet armies took home with them from Manchuria in the late 1940s.*

It also happened that the ruble was devalued by 20 percent just as Mao arrived back in Peking, which sliced $60 million off the meager $300 million.

Stalin exacted a price for his credits. Mao agreed to three distasteful things. Until 1952—as it turned out, until 1955—Russia was to retain control of parts of Manchuria: its two sea gateways, Dalian and Port Arthur, and its Chinese Eastern Railway. Joint-stock companies were to be set up to exploit minerals in the western deserts of Xinjiang. And Outer Mongolia, which Mao had hitherto spoken of as China's, was recognized by the PRC as a sovereign nation.

Mao looked troubled and he was. These concessions touched the core of his national pride. And it was a loss of face to receive a loan ten times smaller than the amount that (according to Indian government sources) he had hoped for.

For the first time since he became Party leader, Mao faced criticism from Chinese who wished to be tougher with Stalin than he was being. *Why Lean to One Side?* was the title of one skeptical pamphlet that found its way from hand to hand. Some in Peking openly resisted the alliance with Stalin under the tactful slogan: "Victory is possible even without international help."

Mao was a subtler man than Stalin. But Stalin had more experience of the world than Mao. And playing on foreign turf, Mao was less masterful than when the game took place amid the old books and red pillars and overhanging trees of the Forbidden City—as it would with Khrushchev.

What Mao did get—a Treaty of Friendship, Alliance, and Mutual Assistance—turned to ashes in his mouth within a dozen years. Some figures in Peking—not top CCP colleagues but intellectuals—were soon to murmur, "I told you so."

Stalin bested Mao. Thirty years on—the planned duration of the treaty—the trip to Moscow does not shine as one of Mao's achievements.

It had been out of the question ever since the Long March that Mao would take any more orders from Moscow. And since the Rectification of 1942–1943, his socialism was separate in spirit from that of the U.S.S.R.

Wouldn't a Soviet China be under Moscow's control? Snow asked Mao in the 1930s. Mao replied, in a joust of rare rakishness, that if such could occur it was "also possible to build a railway to Mars and buy a ticket from Mr. H. G. Wells."

Yet in 1949–1950 Mao felt he had no alternative but to bow a knee be-

---

* Over the entire period of the China–U.S.S.R. alliance's effective life,1949–1960, Soviet aid to China totaled only U.S. $1.5 billion—less than 40 percent of U.S. aid to Chiang's tiny Taiwan over the same period.

fore Stalin. He had lost America, he needed security in the north and a guarantee against Japan, and he could do with $300 million not available elsewhere.

Mao also felt in awe of Stalin.

His awareness that he thought more of Stalin than Stalin thought of him did not make him turn against the pope of Marxism. Certainly there had been enough recent reasons for Mao to doubt Stalin. Moscow had clung to Chiang until long after Marshall had written him off.* Stalin was at least an indirect help to those in the CCP who were willing to make a deal with Chiang in 1948.

Still, Stalin had been a better friend to Mao than Truman and Attlee (skepticism being less bad than hostility). Moscow recognized the PRC twenty-four hours after its proclamation. If Stalin was the last major leader to acknowledge that Chiang had lost the mainland, he was the first to acknowledge that Mao had won it.

Stalin's actions in Manchuria were not anti-CCP, as sometimes viewed, but they were based on a breath-taking underestimation of the CCP's grip upon the future. When Stalin looted the factories of Mukden (now called Shenyang), he did not dream that Mao would rule the city within a couple of years.†

Soon after Mao's trip to Moscow, Stalin took a liking to pineapple. "Get off a message to the Chinese," he ordered Malenkov, "that I'd like them to give us an area where we can build a pineapple cannery." Khrushchev gently warned Stalin that the CCP did not like foreign factories on Chinese soil. "This is sure to offend Mao Zedong," said the man who later became a specialist in doing just that.

Mao did not like Stalin's idea but his cable was a mild one: "If you are interested in canned pineapples, then give us a credit loan and we will build the cannery ourselves. We will then pay back your loan with the produce from this cannery." Stalin cursed and fumed. No Chinese pineapples graced the Kremlin's tables.

Yet Mao never wrote Stalin off, as he wrote off so many others.

---

* As late as August 1949, Stalin was negotiating with the Nationalist government to try to fudge some privileges in Xinjiang Province.

Mao's New Year Message for 1949, "Carry the Revolution Through to the End," refers to "certain persons" who were working "artfully" and "assuming the guise of beautiful girls" to dilute the final surge of revolution; these apparently included Liu and Stalin.

† Mao had trod gingerly on Manchurian issues. His old foe Li Lisan, long in Russia, entered Manchuria with the Soviet troops in 1945. Mao did not prevent Li from assuming quite high Communist Party posts there in the late 1940s.

At the same time Mao was careful to keep the CCP's nerve center well away from Manchuria with its "Moscow boys." After leaving Yanan, he did not set up his capital in Mukden, as he might readily have done, but kept his regime on horseback for a time.

It was a measure of Mao's oddly dogged respect for Moscow that in 1950 he toned down his own claims to be an original Marxist thinker, in order not to risk casting a shadow upon Stalin. He even asked Stalin to send a bright Soviet Marxist to Peking to screen the Mao *Selected Works* before they began to go to press in 1951.

In Mao's 60th year the news arrived of Stalin's death. "The greatest genius of the present age,"* Mao called the Russian tyrant. On the other hand, he did not fly to Moscow for the funeral. He was the only Communist leader in the Soviet bloc not to do so.

Both reactions counted. Mao admired Stalin *and* he felt that he alone had the stature to be the world's next Stalin. By staying away from the funeral,† Mao seemed to elevate himself above the remaining Soviet-bloc leaders.

Years later, Mao refused to criticize Stalin in public, even after Stalin had been unfrocked by his own colleagues.

* * *

Mao's first great acts of state were a marriage law and a land law. Both struck a body blow at old China. Both seemed to bestow individuality on the hitherto undifferentiated Chinese masses.

Mao sought to give the peasant a free choice of spouse, and a piece of land for himself.

But setting people free to be individuals was not Mao's final goal. He had a fresh grand design in mind, for which the Chinese masses would again be furnishings, as they had been of feudalism's grand design. Mao did not intend to turn China into a land of Jeffersonian small cultivators.

To smash the landlords and divide up the land among the tillers was a first step. It was a big step—almost like a religious conversion—for the Chinese peasants whose chains fell off. The rural poor, unleashed, murdered landlords by the hundreds of thousands.

Yet this was a storm, not a change of climate. Tillers would soon have to pool their land into a commune.

Politically Mao was still a paternalist. China was too backward to make one sure leap to modernity. Reaching democracy and equality—values Mao embraced—was going to be complicated indeed.

A marriage law and a land law could not overnight put an end to the intractable distinctions of old China. Guardianship would still be the order of the day.

---

* His statement, "The Greatest Friendship," is not included in Volume V of Mao's *Selected Works*, which covers the year 1953.

† Zhou Enlai went instead, and served as the only foreign pallbearer. Mao's wife was at the time in a Moscow hospital—clad in garments of a deep green which had been custom made for her on Stalin's personal orders—but she neither went to the funeral nor had any direct contact with the Russian leaders.

*   *   *

A China that we can almost recognize from looking at the PRC thirty years later took shape in 1950. The stage props that belong to dual rule were in place. In the foreground were cardboard organizations to fit every stage and station in life: women's federation, youth league, labor congresses, Young Pioneers. In the background was the Party—omnipresent, like the Church in a Catholic country.

Going to meetings, as to mass, became the badge of one's new life. Some weary committee-goer may have wryly noted a passage from Mao's Hunan *Report*. "A world of committeemen," Mao quoted a landowner as complaining of the new peasant associations in 1927; "you can't even go for a piss without bumping into a committeeman."

"Philosophy," said a label in one section of every bookstore. Behind it were the works of Marx, Lenin, Stalin, and Mao. What else could philosophy mean after Liberation? The quest was over; the answers lay on the shelves.

In parts of Sichuan Province, as late as 1948, people had never heard of Mao Zedong. China is big. Extending a net of rule across it took years, even though Mao had got a head start by controlling part of north China for fifteen years.

Ideology captured the *words* of China with neat finality. China was at last being ruled by "the people." Peace was everywhere threatened by "imperialism." The U.S.S.R. was the world's showcase of "democracy." The first volume of Mao's *Selected Works*—two million copies came off the presses in 1951—provided the set phrases.

Tongues, if not souls, fell into line.

At one of the numberless "lane" meetings in Shanghai, an illiterate old woman was required to express her opinion on the draft of the new Constitution. In Shanghai dialect "constitution" and "magician's trick" are pronounced the same. The whole discussion seemed to the old woman to be about "supporting the new magician's trick." As the eager priests of communism pressed her, she drew herself up and declared: "During my 73 years I can recall having seen only one magician's trick. The People's Government which is now about to perform a magic trick, therefore, has my support. I am determined to witness it." The priests were so furious that the meeting was kept in session half the night—until the old woman managed to utter some enthusiastic words about the Constitution.

*   *   *

The monkey in Mao, out of sight during the 1940s, returned to disperse a fart or two in the golden temple of accomplishment.

"When a man reaches old age, he will die," Mao remarked to an august

Party audience, "and the same is true of a party." The axiom may have shocked some. Mortality is not always a polite topic, least of all among Communists talking of their Party.

"Revolutionary dictatorship and counterrevolutionary dictatorship are by nature opposites," Mao said in reference to the class rule he had introduced, "but the former was learned from the latter." Indeed, then can it be all good? Was there a touch of wistfulness for the anarchism which Mao had left behind?

Leaders of the New Democratic Youth League came to see Mao. "Be more independent," Mao told them, though every other voice around them seemed to be saying the opposite. "The revolution has brought us many fine things but also one thing that is not so good," he burst out. "Everybody is much too active and enthusiastic, and often getting tired out." He ordered his visitors to make sure that "all students be given an additional hour of sleep."

Too many committees after all? Mao went on to say just that: "Meetings for activists are too frequent and should be reduced."

The young cadres showed him a draft of their proposed constitution. One article laid down: "Don't gossip behind people's backs." Advised the man who had been learning about the gap between paper and performance: "You may prohibit backbiting, but actually it won't work."

"The true admiration the masses feel for their leaders," he remarked, "derives from what they come to know of them in the course of revolutionary practice." How could young cadres attain stature, then, now that the battles of the revolution had all been won?

Success changed the nature of Mao's leadership. The paradox was that as the Party gained control of China, Mao found it harder to control the Party.

Alike at Yanan and during the civil war, Mao ran a tight ship in the sense that he led personally. "Once we entered the cities," he remarked in a post-mortem years later, "we were dispersed, each devoting himself to his own sphere."

"Practically nothing comes to my ear in Peking," Mao soon complained, "and therefore I shall go on tour from time to time." The *scope* of work in a nation of nearly 600 million people required a maze of intermediate levels between Mao and the grass roots.* Its *compartmentalization* gave Mao a sense that he was losing control.

---

* Mao, like Rousseau, believed only in direct community. "I don't believe in elections," he once remarked. "There are over 2,000 counties in China, and if each county elected two people there would be more than 4,000 people; and if they elected four people there would be 10,000. Where is there a place big enough to hold a meeting for so many? How could one know that many people?"

On the eve of victory Mao had talked readily of "total power" and of China falling "into the hands of the Chinese people." Total power was to prove an elusive thing. Nor was it easy to define "people." Mao in 1949 had by no means foreseen the full shape of the 1950s and 1960s.

His first rude surprise was the Korean War.

* * *

One hot June day in 1950 Mao gave a speech about "two trials" thrust on China. "The trial of war is already basically over," he said before dwelling on the trial of land reform. Next day he pushed through the same government forum a resolution about soldiers going back to their home provinces for assignment to civilian jobs.

And the day after that, North Korean troops moved into South Korea.

Tibet and Taiwan were the only two places where Mao had expected a further role for the PLA (Hainan island having been taken by a neat amphibious operation in the spring). No PLA units were in a state of readiness in the northeast area that adjoins Korea.

The world has learned that even small countries often make wars all on their own, and in retrospect we can see that the two Koreas caused the explosion of 1950 essentially by themselves.

If Stalin encouraged Kim Il-sung, the North Korean leader, proof of that has never surfaced. Certainly Mao was not on close enough terms with Kim (whom he had never met) to have laid joint plans with him in early 1950. Korean Communists looked up to Moscow, not to him.

But when the war occurred, it engulfed Mao all too deeply.

Mao grew up to take Korea for granted as a sideshow of the Middle Kingdom. He thought of it mainly as a place where Japan marauded, as in China, and from 1945 as one more link in the chain that Truman seemed bent on rattling at China's doorstep.

Yet if Mao had no great respect for the Korean nation, he thought it an important place for China's interests. Geography wills it; the China-Korea border snakes 500 miles along the Yalu and Tumen rivers.

As General MacArthur grew expansive in his war aims, Mao conveyed his position to the U.S. through the Indian ambassador in Peking. It was not hawkish but it was clear-cut: China would step in if MacArthur took the war to or over China's border.

MacArthur did just that. When he bombed bridges at the Yalu, in October, Mao hurled 250,000 troops into Korea on Kim Il-sung's side. China and America were at war.

Mao did not intervene mainly to save Kim's regime. Some of his "internationalist" colleagues may have wanted, well before October, to take such a step of solidarity with the embattled Kim.* Stalin, too, probably wanted earlier, rather than later, Chinese intervention; very convenient for the Kremlin to have China do the fighting, while Russia merely supplied arms.

Mao's calculations were based strictly on China's own security.

He paced his study for a sleepless night or two before deciding to intervene at all. And when he did join the fray, it was by stages, with attempts at negotiation before each fresh commitment.

Mao sent Chinese troops into Korea only after the U.S.A. deployed the Seventh Fleet in the waters between China and Taiwan, after U.S. officials publicly linked the Taiwan and Korean issues, and after MacArthur urged Chiang's army to join the war.

Mao the slouching semi-intellectual; MacArthur the booming, can-do activist. But they both believed in the Middle Kingdom as Asia's pivot.

Mao's eldest son, Anying, had gone to Moscow with his stepmother and his mentally troubled brother, Anqing, just as Mao began a new life with Ms. Jiang. Throughout World War II Anying was a student. He tried to fit himself into Soviet life—though he roomed not with a Russian but with the son of the Italian Communist Party leader Luigi Longo—while his stepmother passed her days in a mental asylum, and his brother Anqing mostly played chess and dallied with a Russian blonde.

Anying returned to China in 1945. Mao talked to him in Yanan and decided that he knew enough about books but not about farm work. So Anying left Peking to scrape up manure, put it in bags, and train donkeys to carry the stinking bags, in a village of Henan Province. His student hands became a mass of blisters.

Mao was pleased to see his son learn chores that Mao himself had been required to do *before* becoming a student. There were echoes of Mao's father's treatment of Mao in Mao's treatment of Anying.†

After Anying left farm life—for translation work which utilized his fluent

---

* This would probably have had disastrous consequences for the U.S. forces in Korea. A U.S. commander in Korea—who had also been the chief of the Joint U.S. Military Advisory Group in China—later said that if Mao had intervened in Korea just twenty-four hours earlier than he did, he (General David Barr) "would not have brought out a single man from that disaster."

Yet it was also true that some of Mao's colleagues didn't want to intervene in Korea at all.

†There may be some truth in the claim of Soviet scholars that Mao was irritated at some of the ideas Anying had picked up in Russia, and that Anying criticized the "cult of the leader" which surrounded his father. They say that Anying was required to "write an explanation" of his inconvenient views, and that for a time he was forbidden to come to Mao's house without written permission.

Mao must have been shocked to hear that both his sons, while in Russia, were found not to be able to read and write Chinese well, and had to be sent to a school for the study of the Chinese language, as well as to the Comintern School at Ivanovo.

Russian—Mao would quiz him about rural minutiae ("How many tou of ground millet can be obtained from one tou of unhusked millet grown in soil that has been loosened twice?").

Mao felt his son should learn about war as well as pigs. He asked General Peng Dehuai to take Anying with him to the Korean front.

One day U.S. planes bombed the headquarters of the PLA's Second Army in the Korean hills. It was a direct hit and most of the staff were killed. Among the mangled bodies was Anying's. At 29 he was dead, not of blisters but of bombshells.

Peng did things in Korea that Mao disapproved of: set up his own channel of communication with the Russians; forsook Mao-type guerrilla warfare for positional warfare and "wave" assaults; launched big offensives which led to terrible Chinese losses just after MacArthur's dismissal, when the time was ripe for negotiations, In some recess of his mind Mao may have made a link between Peng's bombast and the death of Anying.

In a way Peng was Mao's MacArthur. But whereas Truman fired his headstrong general, Mao "contained" his for eight more years.

Mao both won and lost in Korea. He prevailed in that MacArthur's yen to strike at the "source"—Mao's China—went unsatisfied. The fine performance of the PLA in Korea also made a deep impact in Washington.

Had Mao not flashed an amber light in Korea, China and the U.S. probably would have fought a war in the Taiwan Straits in the 1950s. Perhaps, as well, on the fringes of Indochina in the 1960s.

Yet the Korean War cast dark shadows on Mao's life and work. The death of his son hung in his mind.

The war effort cost China a lot of money. "Last year," Mao said in 1952, "what we spent on the war to resist U.S. aggression and aid Korea more or less equaled our expenditures for national construction."

And the enhanced role of the PLA in Chinese politics that the Korean War brought about helped lead to a terrible clash between Mao and Peng later on.

Other shadows were even longer.

One day in the fall of 1950, two Americans still living in Peking watched a crowd standing by a bulletin board near the library of Yenching University. Excerpts from *U.S. News and World Report* and *Collier's* (as translated in *People's Daily*) were the featured attractions. The Chinese crowd was seething.

The *U.S. News* piece included a map of North Korea and the Manchurian part of China, with arrows pointing from Korea to various Chinese cities and the flight distances noted. The *Collier's* excerpt also had a map aglow with arrows leading into China, from Taiwan, Korea, Japan and Okinawa. Both maps had been published in the U.S. *before* Mao sent Chinese troops into Korea.

Such items created for Chinese onlookers the kind of atmosphere that existed in the U.S. during the Cuban missile crisis.

The slogan "Resist America Aid Korea" soon saturated China. Lines of communication between Americans and Chinese were cut, as by a power failure. Chinese intellectuals who had been open-minded about the "Land of Gentlemen"—as Mao now ironically called America—froze overnight. "Spies" and "counterrevolutionaries" were hunted like rabbits. Ideas, songs, paintings that were part of the unexamined fabric of life in 1950 became "subversive" by 1951.

The Korean War brought on the PRC's McCarthy Era.*

The Korean War saved the regime of Chiang Kai-shek. It brought an American reembrace of the Nationalists, which had seemed out of the question six months before. It ensured that the red and white banner "Ten Thousand Years to Chairman Mao" would not be hoisted on Taiwan during Mao's lifetime.†

In Mao's mind there crystallized a view of Uncle Sam scheming for a triple assault on China: from Korea, Taiwan, and Indochina. Washington gave it plenty of encouragement. It lasted fifteen years as the centerpiece of Mao's outlook on Asia.

And the Korean War lodged a germ in the stomach of the Mao-Stalin relationship.

"When our revolution succeeded," Mao remarked years later to some Party leaders in Chengdu, "Stalin said it was a fake." Mao went on to electrify his listeners with a frank summing up of what then ensued: "We did not argue with him, and as soon as we fought the war to resist America and aid Korea, our revolution became a genuine one to him."

As Stalin learned respect, Mao learned distrust. If Mao "did not argue" with Stalin in 1949–1950, the new prestige China won amid the rubble of Korea made him more inclined to speak up against Moscow—in private.

Mao had become clear about two things. The Russians were mean; in-

---

*A catch in the analogy is that Mao's China was under threat. If McCarthy never found a single Communist in the U.S. government, Mao did have on his hands large numbers of people who supported Chiang and the U.S. On the other hand, the repression in China was far worse than McCarthyism.

†For Mao, an exasperating pattern in American policy seemed to repeat itself in Korea. In 1944–1946 he had faced the problem of detecting which American voice should be relied on. It was the same in 1950. Should he be reassured by Truman's cautious words, or alarmed by MacArthur's messianic words? Most of his wrestling with the Korean issue occurred before Truman lanced the boil of insubordination by firing MacArthur. The experience helped him to appreciate Kissinger's crisp authority twenty years later.

credibly, the Chinese paid full market price for every Russian gun and grenade the PLA used in Korea—they even paid the living and travel expenses of Soviet journalists sent to Korea to cover the war.

And Mao realized that alliances are not made of granite.

Would Stalin have defended China if Mao had not jumped into Korea with 250,000 troops, and MacArthur in his ebullience had driven north into China? We cannot say. But Mao wondered about it.

What *did* happen was that Mao took all the risks. China went in and fought on Kim's side, as Russia sat back and spoke for Kim's side.

Years later, in the midst of a talk about the need to strike a balance between struggle and conciliation, Mao mentioned the war. "There should be compromises," he remarked. "Did we not compromise with the Americans at the 38th parallel in Korea?"

12

Remolding (1951–1953)

"Chairman Mao gave us land," said a newly possessed family. Land reform. The very term made some grown men tremble, others cry with joy.

China is its villages and no Chinese government had ever penetrated each village as Mao's government began to do. The change was not an economic or a technological one. A Chinese village looked—still does—much like a village in other parts of Asia.

It remained a place of the bent back, the scythe, rising at daybreak, maddening localism, the hoe which a tiller of 2,000 years ago would have recognized, engulfment with the cycle of birth, marriage, and death, simple entertainments in which costume and action are the only indispensable ingredients.

The change—as when Mao took part in stirring up rural Hunan thirty years before—was organizational and psychological. The burdens of tax and rent fell off the backs of the poor. To own land no longer meant to have power over others. Farming step by step became a team, not just a father-and-son, effort.

And Chairman Mao came to be viewed as a new "good emperor" used to be viewed.

There was a biblical gravity to the "settling accounts movement" which handed out landlords' possessions to the poor. That the Chinese peasant tends to be materialistic did not reduce, but added to, the spiritual intensity of the days of distribution. The joy at change was almost vicious.

"All you had to do to make a man talk was to heat an iron bar in the fire" a new authoritarian remarked to an American writer, of the vengeance against the rich, "but the women were tougher. They would rather die than tell us where their gold was hidden. Burning flesh held no terror for them."

Mao had never participated in hand-to-hand class retribution. His time as a rural youth was too mixed an experience for any simple surge of personal hatred to sway him. He had never starved or been enslaved. Yet although he was opposed to torture, he could not prevent it as a furious peasantry took land reform into its own hands.

The mental life of the village was remade. Authority had been like a law of nature; criticism replaced it.

Precedent had been another law of nature; new ideas rained down upon the village: class, love for the Soviet Union, struggle, turning one's life over (*fanshen*).

Peasants asked a U.S. visitor a new kind of question. "Why does Truman support old Chiang?" "Do you eat with chopsticks in America?" "What does a tractor look like?" "Does the American Communist Party have an army like ours?"

Mao's youthful concern for women's liberation bore fruit at last. Property was the key. Mao's government gave the Chinese woman the right to own land and other property in her own name.

*   *   *

Mao now lived in a city. Change in the cities came not as a roll of thunder but by nibbling.

The CCP was less well equipped to tame the cities than the villages. Its cadres were not of urban type; three million Nationalist state employees had to be held over to serve the new cause.

Yet the cities were a less tough nut to crack than the villages. The capitalists were few. They had little moral authority because they had been supping with foreigners who had exploited China. And they were upstarts, mere morning dew on the grass of a land-based social system that had been growing for 2,000 years.

Mao did not have to *destroy a class* in Peking or Shanghai or Canton. Many capitalists simply turned red when the heat went on, silently, like lobsters put in hot water.

Mao aimed to turn "consumer cities" into "producer cities." No longer would the metropolis be a mere base for foreigners to trade, and landed gentry to dally and collect rent for housing they owned, while they lived off the produce of the village. Each urban neighborhood made small new factories the centerpiece of its life.

Foreign commerce ended abruptly. Rental of property tapered off. The lights of exciting night life were switched off, less out of puritanism than because energies were rechanneled into making machine tools and bicycles and plastic shoes.

Urban consolidation was more draconian than it would otherwise have been because of tensions due to the Korean War. "Counterrevolutionaries" seemed more numerous to Mao because, with the flare-up in Korea, his victory over Chiang and the U.S. began to look incomplete.

Hundreds of thousands were either executed or put in labor camps. This was the one urban drive in the PRC's history that led to physical elimination—a word Mao himself used—of large numbers of people.

The rooting out of "counterrevolutionaries" was not done in a very Maoist way. It was a police operation like any other. And far too vast for Mao to supervise. "Cure the illness and save the patient" was not its keynote.

On the other hand Mao moved very cautiously in taking over urban industry and commerce. Much of it stayed in private hands until late 1955.

A drive to remold intellectuals, with the chilling name "thought reform movement," also given a rough edge by the Korean War, did bear Mao's stamp.

Liang Shuming was a semi-Confucian rural populist. He was no Communist, but Mao liked arguing with him. He found funds for Liang to start a small research institute.*

But in the autumn of 1953 Mao fired a rupturing volley of shots at Liang. The occasion was a session of a government committee on which Liang was one of the non-CCP members. Liang gave a speech which dissented from the CCP line on agriculture, the Korean War, and class theory.

Mao grabbed the microphone in fury.

"I suppose you think you are very beautiful," he sneered in a reference to a famous concubine of the Tang dynasty, "more beautiful than Yang Kuei-fei. But to me you stink."

Mao was so exercised that he alternated between addressing the one-thousand strong audience and turning with a pointed finger to assail Liang (still awkwardly on the platform). "[The Nationalists] were so pleased with you," Mao raged, "addressing you as Mister while maligning me as a 'bandit.' " One cannot miss the note of personal rivalry, odd as it may seem that Mao should have felt challenged by this would-be Gandhi of China.

Mao asked the committee how it could be that Liang should think himself wiser than the CCP on rural issues. "This is like showing off one's proficiency with the ax before Lu Ban the master carpenter."

Mao the semi-intellectual scoffed at the uselessness of Liang the pure intellectual. "Is he any good for providing us with products and paying income tax like the industrialists and the businessmen? No, he is not." He

_____

* At Peking University, three decades before, Mao as an unregistered student had audited classes of Liang, then a professor of Indian philosophy. Later, in conversations at Yanan in 1938, and again between 1950 and 1953, Liang probably influenced Mao in the direction of a more nativistically Chinese view of socialism.

sarcastically suggested that Liang, so eager to help the peasants, do so not by trying to cut workers' wages but by voluntarily cutting his own fat salary.

"Chiang Kai-shek is an assassin with a gun," Mao cried, "and Liang Shuming an assassin with a pen." He dwelt upon these two ways of killing people, as if in echo of the double character of his own thirty-five years of struggle. Summing up "killing with the pen," he turned toward Liang and sneered: "That is the kind of murderer you are."

The arrogance of power appeared in all its starkness: criticism was equated with murder.

Mao's intervention turned the mood of the meeting against Liang. Shouts arose from among the varnished chairs. Liang was heckled so much that he had to give up the platform. Another non-CCP figure rose to urge calm: "We should not have become so excited today."

But Mao *was* excited, and he ordered a period of self-criticism for the old ex-Nationalist who had appealed for calm.

Yet Mao insisted that Liang retain his office!* He wanted Liang to write a confession (though this would provide China with no taxes or products!). He wanted the old feudalist "as live teaching material." Such a preference for pedagogy over punishment (or pedagogy *as* punishment) had not marked communism prior to Mao.

Liang should continue on the National Committee, Mao declared in an amazing remark, "unless he himself has lost the desire to use the platform of the Political Consultative Conference to spread his reactionary ideas." He wrestled with Liang because he wanted Liang's soul, as proof of Maoism's triumph over the Chinese mind.

Mao had begun a 25-year struggle to force rough-edged reality into the smooth contours of an ideal that was—for him—more vivid than the speckled reality that hemmed him in.

"We must become religious again," Ludwig Feuerbach said a century ago. "Politics must become our religion." The author of *The Essence of Christianity* prefigured the age of secular ideologies which Mao, in his Chinese way, put himself firmly within. Chinese sages before him had sought a Great Harmony. Mao took a fresh step: he fused truth and power.

The whole point of building up an armed Party over twenty years was none other than this ancient dream of unclouded togetherness. *Of course* the intellectuals would be the chief casualties of an expedition toward a land where doctrine (*jiao*) and administration (*zheng*) were to be fused.

---

* Member of the National Committee of the Chinese People's Political Consultative Conference.

Mao as a semi-intellectual had long resented ivory-tower dwellers. He disliked their straw splitting, their detachment, their lack of passion, their clear eye of doubt, their technical mastery which exceeded his own.

Mao fused doctrine and administration, not out of mere expediency, but—and this was worse—because he deeply believed the two should be fused.

Anxiety became a way of life during the thought reform movement. Second-guessing the next lash of the mental whip became a grim parlor game. One journalist went in and out of prison in a rhythm that at first mystified him and later soured him. Back "in" on one occasion, he sat in the prison garden and told himself that perhaps it was better to be behind bars. "Outside, you were likely to be arrested; while in jail, at least you did not have this worry."

Mao wanted surrender—as from his father at Music Mountain; as at East Mountain school when he insisted on what religious believers call "unity in the truth." Any claim to detachment he judged a badge of disunity.

"An intellectual can be killed, but not humiliated," said Confucius, and Mao turned the saying on its head. He didn't kill intellectuals. But he did want their minds in the palm of his hand.

Mao sounded at times like Milton ("I cannot praise a cloistered virtue"), or J. S. Mill ("It is better to be Socrates dissatisfied than a pig satisfied"). Yet Mao did not agree with Mill that truth was a various thing. He believed in debate, not to *find* the truth but to establish in every mind a pre-existent truth.

Like Milton—and unlike Mill—Mao had a god. Truth was not the end product of a process, but an emanation from a fixed source. In this respect the Mao of middle age was an unwavering Marxist. Social thought was a matter of science, he believed in the 1950s. Like the priest in his robe, Mao was a scientist in a white coat, watching the intellectuals develop in a test tube. Sure of his formula, he added some crystals of Correct Thinking now and then, awaiting without anxiety the appearance of the predicted synthesis.

It is in this context that a favorite admonition of Mao's, "Fight self," came into focus. Mao did not merely mean "Do not be selfish," as the Bible asks. The word *si* means "private" as much as "self." Mao was telling people not to try to dwell aside from the consensus. There was no place in new China, nor mental space, for the man who thought he had his own conception of the truth.

Mao was a holist, of Chinese type. There *is* a god—the masses—he once declared. If the masses were a collective being, an entity with a single per-

sonality, the paths available were one, not multiple. People may not run off
in their own direction.*

One may even speak of "it"—Mao's masses—rather than of "them"—the
people of China. (Recall the quip about de Gaulle: he loved France, but not
Frenchmen.) To embrace pluralism was to embrace six hundred million sel-
fishnesses, for Mao. "Fight self" did not mean "Be altruistic." It meant
"Stick with the team." At once a moral law *and* a sociological principle.

"Fight self" included "Fight family authority." For the family could be a
pool of private values, an offense against Mao's effort to subsume all private
values within a Great Harmony.

Many a person broke down during thought reform at the point of being
required to denounce his or her father. Mao had no sympathy for such a dilemma. He saw filial piety as a piece of trash from old China. His own father, after all, had been in Mao's eyes both a symbol of the feudal order *and*
an ungenerous father.

So Mao saw a distinction—fine to a Western eye—between a tame sheep
and a sheep that sticks with the flock. Within the flock he wanted each
beast to speak up, be self-reliant, practice self-cultivation, not to be tame.
But life without the flock was not valid, as Mao saw it, and there was only
one flock.

* * *

Mao began a "Three Antis" drive against corruption, waste, and bureaucracy. Officials were the target. Some of them had begun to think of the new
regime as an end in itself—not Mao's idea of it.

A parallel drive to clean up economic life was the "Five Antis" Crusade
against bribery, tax-evasion, fraud, stealing government property, and using
government secrets for personal advantage. The target here was the private

---

* Running off in one's own direction, of which he had a horror, Mao called "forming mountaintops." In later life he looked back and sadly saw this lack of solidarity running like a dark
thread even through the history of the CCP.

At the Party school in Yenan, when the setting sun sank in the west and we went for a
stroll, we also divided into mountaintops. Even when we went to eat in restaurants we
divided into mountaintops. Within [each] mountaintop there was nothing that was not
talked about [but] it wasn't easy to talk to other mountaintops. In northern Shaanxi,
even when [we were] hiding from airplanes, cadres from outside and local cadres traveled separate paths. Even when we were in danger of losing our lives we didn't mix
together.

Should this separatist tendency in man be stoically accepted?

We should recognize mountaintops, admit to [the existence of] mountaintops, pay heed
to mountaintops, and eliminate mountaintops. Mountaintops have been brought about
by historical causes and regional differences.

businessman, still a regular part of the Chinese urban scene in the 1950s. The drive squeezed out extra revenue to help pay for the Korean War.

The twin drives were designed to give Mao the total control that all Marxist leaders feel a moral right to. Yet the methods used were mostly those of the thought reform movement. Not a knock on the door in the middle of the night, as in Stalin's Russia. Rather a social pressure to confess. Then an audacious effort to align private consciences with the public weal.

The "Antis" drives had the smack of Leninist organization, but they also gave off an aroma of Confucian moralism.

Mao was a product of old China as well as the author of new China's Marxism. In China the individual has never been told to pull himself up by his own bootstraps. He did not wrestle—with God, or an outsize Protestant conscience—in solitude. He was wrestled *with* in a *group*.

People in Mao's China did not become socialists by a conversion like Saint Paul's on the road to Damascus. The rebirth—if it occurred—was social. In the West we assume people can change themselves in isolation. In Mao's China no such acrobatics of the soul were expected.

Mao wrote slogans for the "Antis" drives. But he plunged less into the criticism of officials and businessmen than he did into the criticism of men of ideas.

Hu Feng was an impish poet of rustic origin who shone in the Shanghai literary sky. He was a leftist from way back (though he had spoken up against Mao at the Yanan Forum on Literature and Art). His poem "Time Begun," which celebrated the victory of 1949, was as far from being anti-Mao as it was possible to be. "Mao stands like an idol, Speaks to the whole world, Gives order to time," gushed one of its lines.

But in the early 1950s Hu began to complain about "uniformity of public opinion." He felt that Mao's Yanan *Talks* had become too untouchable. "People have made a totem of this small booklet," he objected. "Mandarins," he called the busybody organizers of the thought reform movement.

People's Daily began a procession of articles critical of Hu Feng; most were from Mao's own pen. The standard rejoinder to Hu, of course, was that public opinion is, like everything else, a class question. Under the people's democratic dictatorship, the people are permitted freedom of expression, but the counterrevolutionaries are not.* Hu was trying to float in the air high above class.

Mao went further. The enemy was not dying out as socialist construction went ahead, Mao asserted, but expanding! Nor were the people always good

* There are two Chinese terms for "people": gong min means "the citizenry"; ren min—which is being used here—means those of the citizenry who are not counterrevolutionary.

at discerning counterrevolutionaries. "The eyes of our people," Mao found himself saying, "are not keen."

Here was a first whiff of pessimism; and here was a devastating chain of reasoning.

Oneness had not been attained; intellectuals still squawked their unharmonious songs. Yet Oneness was on history's relentless agenda. The old class divisions must be reasserting themselves. What else could account for the squawking?

This provided a basis for witch hunts that made Joe McCarthy seem timid. To sing out of tune was to be a criminal, in Mao's view. "We don't have ... people like Hu Feng ... executed," Mao explained, "not because their crimes don't deserve capital punishment but because such executions would yield no advantage."

Mao happened to remark one day that some 10 percent of cadres in administrative units seemed to be counterrevolutionaries. One neighborhood sewing unit in Shenyang, having only seven members, held a meeting, in a mood of mixed fear and zeal, to discuss the possible shape of seven tenths of a counterrevolutionary!

As for Hu Feng, he was repainted out of all recognition. Just as McCarthy called anyone who had doubts about Chiang Kai-shek a Communist, so Hu's doubt about Mao's *Talks* was seen as proof that he was after all a counterrevolutionary. Soon the angular poet was found to be a "spy." That enabled the red mandarins to put him in prison. There he had a mental breakdown.

Mao was correct to suspect that Hu was the center of a circle of grumbling writers. "Because I wanted to write," one of them confided in a letter to Hu, "I read Mao's *Talks* at Yanan. But after reading them, I do not wish to write anymore."

Yet for Mao to have put the controversy into the category of class struggle was like trying to wrap a cloud in paper.

*   *   *

People's Daily began a slap-up serialization in mid-1951. The author was Mao; the book was his *Selected Works*.

The works were very selected indeed. Many of the essays quoted in this biography did not find a place in the authorized *Works*. Some from the 1920s were too lacking in Marxist content. Others from the Jiangxi period—when Mao had only a toehold upon power—contained ideas that Mao expressed but probably did not believe in. The poems were left out.*

* Perhaps because their style was too feudal and their sentiments too romantic.

What did appear had been sandpapered. Earthy images and jests had disappeared. The author was saved—by some pen that bore more than literary authority—from a number of small errors about world politics. Rendered inoperative by the editorial pen, too, were the younger Mao's ideas about how certain Asian countries might one day be absorbed into China.

A blanket of white was thrown over an army of doctrinal gremlins. Also over a number of remarks friendly to the West which Mao had made in a different season. No reference to the U.S.S.R. that was not glittering survived; even criticisms of Li Lisan were muted lest they irritate Li's mentors in Moscow.

Mao had picked up where the emperors had left off. Words were norms; what was published was what the rulers judged it healthy for the ruled to heed.

The Chinese character is more than a word. It is a semi-picture. Four strokes represent "grass"; a sign of a pig under a roof means "home"; a character meaning "day" or "bright" includes a *picture* of the sun.

To a Leninist—twin brother on this point to a Confucian—a slogan is often as useful as a tank. Few languages lend themselves to a crisp slogan as well as Chinese. Four ideograms, even two, can carry a universe of meaning, with an overtone of ambiguity that is enticing in a slogan. Mao was a master of this art.

To educated people, the ideograms are a streak of lightning that brings into view the long terrain of the past. Mao's skillful way with them made him a force to reckon with, even for those intellectuals who disliked his Marxism.

Mao's poetry created just the right impression. It could be only half understood by most people—Mao's friend Guo Moruo candidly said so—but that did not matter. A poem by the supreme leader added to his aura; it was virtually a technique of rule.

* * *

Mao shifted his main attention from political drives to economic tasks in late 1952. Soon *People's Daily* announced the start of the PRC's First Five-Year Plan. A hefty 58 percent of capital investment was to go for heavy industry (41 percent had been so allocated in Russia's First Five-Year Plan; 19 percent in the U.S.A. during the years 1880 to 1912). Moscow was to be relied upon for technical help in 60 percent of the basic construction.

It seemed a fresh tone of voice when Mao confessed one day to a Party audience that the wonders of China could grow a bit thin. "We have bragged so much . . . yet we cannot compare with a country like Belgium." Mao had been looking at the tables of steel and coal output.

Literacy was no great asset in an army of rebels. Roads were a positive disadvantage. Electricity had nothing to offer the PLA in the days before it came to include an air force and a navy. Now these things were crucial for the next leg of Mao's journey.

Mao was more pro-Soviet in the realm of socialist ideas than he had been at Yanan. In 1945 he had spoken of joining Marxism to the concrete realities of China; that did not leave much place for the Soviet model. Yet five years later a key slogan in Peking was the amazing: "The Soviet today will be China's tomorrow." Were the two socialisms to be the same after all?

The First Five-Year Plan did well. The annual rate of industrial growth was 11 percent. Iron and steel output quadrupled; coal and cement doubled. This was a period when visitors to China came away talking of China's sense of purpose. "Blue ants" to some. "A new man" to others. In either case, China seemed to be on the march.

Bridges and railways appeared. Illiteracy was almost swept away. The health of the people improved and life expectancy soared above usual Asian levels. For the first time, a large non-Western country seemed to have taken off toward industrialization.

China did not cease to be poor. Taking the economy as a whole, three things happened. In the countryside the feudal framework was smashed and fresh energies were released. First steps were taken toward industrialization. And—crucial to the spirit of Mao's China in the 1950s—the pie was cut up more equally than ever before in China.

*   *   *

A voice from the past spoke up in 1953. Zhang Guotao, now languishing in Hong Kong, wrote a portrait of his old rival, and through its bias shone some truth.

"Mao leads an irregular life and is rather nervous," Zhang related. "[He] is usually courteous in his relations with others, but he is very dictatorial and firm in his views." The staff at South and Central Lakes would have recognized their leader in these remarks.

"Although he knows how to use power in the top leadership," Zhang judged, "he has little talent for building up a large personal following except as a remote symbol." Mao was indeed discovering that being a giant in the eyes of the masses did not obviate the need to drum up support in the Politburo.

Zhang's observations count the more since he was not merely negative about Mao. "In many ways Mao is even trickier than Stalin was," wrote the man who knew them both, "but he is not so venomous." Zhang half acknowledged that Mao had beaten him through ability. "Compared with the numerous inept rulers in Chinese history," the ex-rival felt, "Mao Zedong is indeed more capable."

Like Lyndon Johnson, Mao impulsively phoned staff and colleagues in the middle of the night. He summoned specialists and grilled them for long periods, pursuing an idea regardless of circumstance. He strolled out into the garden to bounce a proposal of high policy off a security guard. He reached for his ancient books (here the parallel with LBJ breaks down) to check a precedent or find an illustration.

He would drive over to the house of Soviet Ambassador P. F. Yudin for a late night visit. Yudin was an intellectual; Mao would discuss philosophy with him until dawn. The doctrinal adjustments that some of Mao's essays underwent before reappearing in the *Selected Works* probably owed something to these night-owl dialogues.

China is the world's largest user of tobacco, and Mao over six decades smoked at least his share. Perhaps no political leader of any country has ever disposed of as many cigarettes as Mao did.

Only for one extended period, it seems, did Mao abstain. Marshal Voroshilov, visiting China after Stalin's death, told Mao that according to Soviet medical opinion Stalin would not have died as early as he did but for cigarettes. Mao gave up smoking.

Ten months later he resumed.

"It's no good," he remarked. "We work too hard; we just have to smoke."

Mao did not write many essays in the 1950s, but in no decade did he give more speeches. He was not an accomplished mass orator. Wang Ming spoke with more emotion, Zhu De with more man-to-man sincerity. Smedley said that at public meetings Mao spoke as if his mouth were full of hot congee. He permitted himself no gesture of any kind.

Yet with a small audience Mao could be brilliant. He was intense. He was blunt. He liked to make subtle allusions. These traits suited a seminar rather than a rally.

Mao's talks were given mainly from rough notes. Only once or twice during the early 1950s did he sit down and compose a major text.* In mid-1953 he took up English again, but a nasty crisis in Manchuria put an end to that. The scholar was being overtaken by the politician.

"The higher you go the less knowledge you get," Mao burst out one day to a roomful of local politicians. "Peking is not a good place to acquire knowledge." After three years in power he felt—despite the success of this period—restless about the political system.

"Pagoda" was the word used by ordinary people (when they were sure no cadre was listening) to snigger at the multileveled bureaucracy that rose above them. Mao felt like a man stranded at the top of the pagoda.

He decided to come downstairs and look around. "Practically nothing

---

* Virtually no new major pronouncement by Mao was published between 1950 and 1955.

comes to my ear in Peking," he declared to a group of finance officials in mid-1953, "and therefore I shall go on tour from time to time."

Mao also sent his own spies to the villages. Guarding South and Central Lakes was a unit called 8341. This elite force grew from Mao's pre-1949 bodyguard. Its young soldiers did everything from helping with his melon patch to keeping an eye skinned for any sign of a palace coup.

Once in 1955, and probably at other times as well, Mao turned to the ranks of 8341 for a job he needed done. He sent a number of 8341 men, representing a cross-section of China's regions, on a mission to their home villages. He wanted to know about the mood on the farms.

His 8341 eyes and ears snooped around, asked people's opinions, checked matters out with family members. Later they reported back secretly and in person to Mao. All regular channels were by-passed and kept in the dark.

Emperors used to do this. Mao's colleagues may not have approved of the chairman of a workers' party doing it.

"I spent eleven days reading 120-odd reports," Mao remarked to the Central Committee during a debate on agriculture, "making corrections and writing notes on them." He could not resist a historical glimpse at himself. "In this manner I have 'traveled all the kingdoms' and gone farther than Confucius, 'traveling' as far as Yunnan and Xinjiang."

In the 1950s Mao did not yet consider Confucius the curse of China's past. He had the status of a friendly rival.

One day Mao strolled out from his study to give a talk in the Hall of Benevolence, a lovely old pavilion within the Forbidden City that serves as the Central Committee's headquarters. One of many non-CCP figures present was Zhou Chingwen, who had been a "third force" leader in the 1940s and, like so many, had gravitated toward the CCP in 1949.

Mao was used to the fact that any audience in China would rise to its feet and clap whenever he appeared. But Mao's aides did not always trust in spontaneity. Before Mao's arrival a protocol man came up to Zhou and told him the procedure. Since Zhou was sitting near the door, he would see Mao first. The moment Mao came into view he must rise and clap. This would give a signal to the whole hall to erupt in honor of the Chairman.

So it went. Mao walked down the aisle at the pace of a snail, as Zhou recalled it. Apparently the storm of applause did not embarrass him.

If there was a touch of the sense of reaching down to the crowd in Mao, he did *go* before the crowd. At meetings he strolled around and said hello to acquaintances. He listened to long talks by others. He heard himself criticized. He dealt with questions put to him from the floor. He handled interjections.

The Mao of the 1950s was not yet a distant god.

13

Building (1953–1956)

Mao in 1954 made some changes in the outward forms of his government. They reflected inner strains during 1953.

Mao had made three compromises at the outset of the PRC's life. He gave the non-CCP parties a role in the state, even though he took a dim view of them. He allotted the PLA a share in ruling the nation, despite his firm belief in civilian control of the military. And he allowed six regional administrations a lot of room for maneuver, at the risk of weakening his personal command from Peking.

By 1954 Mao wanted a tighter ship. More central control seemed possible after the Korean truce, a certain stabilization of the urban economy, and a successful end to the trauma of land reform.

A total of 1,226 deputies met in Peking during September 1954 for the first session of the National People's Congress (NPC), a toothless parliament, separate from the structure of Communist Party authority. Mao's speech was hardly more than a page long and its main point stood out like a star against a black sky: "The force at the core leading our cause is the Chinese Communist Party." That put the NPC in its place.

Mao abolished the six regions. And he relieved the PLA of a direct administrative role. In sum, behind the new constitutional forms of 1954, the reality was intensified CCP control of the nation. "Independent kingdoms" were ruled out.

One independent kingdom in particular, that of the Manchurian leader Gao Gang, had reared up at Mao in 1953. He struck it down—but not without making himself ill, and feeling the CCP's sense of its own rectitude wobble beneath him.

Gao Gang had played a most important role in providing a secure place for the Long March to end in Shaanxi Province, and he never forgot it. The marchers arrived like "beggars in rags," he used to recall. "If I had not tak-

en Mao in then," he even boasted, "where would he be today?" A disingen-
uous streak in Gao allowed him to quote in all innocence a remark Mao had
made ironically: "Only Comrade Gao Gang makes no mistakes."

If Gao's ways were irritating to Mao, his link with the Russians was men-
acing. Mao had not been the first CCP leader to visit Stalin in the wake of
Liberation. In mid-1949, Gao Gang went off to Moscow to sign a trade
agreement with the U.S.S.R. on behalf of his northeast region. Manchuria,
China's industrial showcase, remained a Russian sphere of influence under
the terms of the Mao-Stalin agreements of 1950. Thirty of the fifty Soviet
aid projects agreed upon in 1950 were within Gao's realm.*

Years later Mao would refer to Manchuria and Xinjiang as "the two
colonies" of the period following Liberation.

Gao dealt with Stalin over Mao's head. He gave the Russians special information (not unconnected with the fact that Stalin presented Gao with a
car). In the end, according to Khrushchev, Gao was considered "Russia's
man" in China.

Stalin passed on to Mao memos of conversations about Chinese affairs
between Gao and the Soviet ambassador in Peking. "God only knows what
Stalin thought he was doing," was Khrushchev's apt remark. Most evidence
suggests that Stalin thought Gao's position was slipping in China, and that
the Soviet boss wanted to square off with Mao.

Mao had indeed hauled Gao from his regional base to a job in Peking in
1952. But Gao was still a marked man so far as Mao was concerned. The
danger of an independent kingdom in Manchuria may have receded. But
Gao (supported by his ex-Shanghai associate Rao Shushi) still sniped at
Mao.

The two clashed over economic policy at a major conference on the topic
in mid-1953. Gao was more impressed with Russian-type "one-man management" in factories than was Mao. He allegedly had "contacts" in the
PLA that he should not have. And he wished to be premier (though he did
not seek to replace Mao as Chairman of the CCP).

Once Stalin died, Mao went for Gao. He intended to drive the knife into
Gao, both to stop any future tricks by Gao himself, and *pour encourager les
autres*.

For there were others. A letter was sent to Mao by several top colleagues
urging him to "take a rest."† It may have originated in the territory of
Rao (who did not add to Mao's opinion of him by remarking that the

---

* The slogan "Ten Thousand Years to Gao Gang" was heard and seen at rallies in
Shenyang.

†Under pressure years later, one of the letter's signatories stated: "The letter was written for
the sake of Chairman Mao's health."

world's greatest political leaders had been Abraham Lincoln and Franklin Roosevelt).

And Zhu De joined in the maneuvering. "Rotating chairman" for the CCP was the military hero's suggestion—at once mild and explosive—at this time of crisis.

The showdown came at a Politburo meeting in Peking on Christmas Eve 1954. Mao assailed Gao and Rao. Both were dismissed from office. Mao then withdrew to Never Dry Mountain in Zhejiang Province. For four months he was out of sight. Officially he was "on leave."

It was a familiar pattern. Strain made him ill; he retreated for a lengthy period; he then returned to the fray with batteries recharged. But the Gao-Rao fight was the first event since Liberation that drove Mao to severe psychosomatic illness. He did indeed "take a rest," though *after* turning back the challenge to his untrammeled power.

Mao was still away brooding when the Central Committee gathered in February 1954. His absence "on holiday" was remarkable. The Central Committee had not met since mid-1950. It would not meet again until April 1955. The purge of Gao and Rao was to be formalized at this meeting. Mao maybe did not want to be there for the denouement.*

Liu Shaoqi presided. Gao and Rao were called into the room in turn and confronted with the charges against them. Gao entered. He professed his innocence of any plotting against the Party. Then he pulled out a pistol and placed the muzzle against his temple. Someone next to him struck his elbow—the bullet pierced the ceiling.

It was merely death postponed. Gao later poisoned himself in prison. He was the first high CCP man (not the last) to fight with Mao and lose his life in the aftermath.

Mao clipped Zhu De's wings after the Gao Gang affair. At the NPC session, the Chairman of the CCP (Mao) was made commander of the PLA— which was a quiet way of taking that command away from Zhu. The next year Mao conferred the new title of marshal on Zhu *and nine other PLA leaders.* "Mao-Zhu" was a partnership of the past.

That Mao lacked appetite for the denouement is made the more likely by what he said at the next full discussion of the affair that he did attend. "Man needs help," he observed as he drew on a literary quotation. " 'Although lotus flowers are beautiful, they need the adornment of green leaves.' " The thrust of this speech in the spring of 1955 was a call for mutual help, collective leadership, and a constructive attitude among comrades.

---

* Two men who were present, and who replaced the fallen Gao and Rao in the Politburo, were Lin Biao and Deng Xiaoping—of whom we shall hear much more.

Mao clearly felt bad that Gao Gang's "illness" had not been cured without the sacrifice of the patient.

Yet, the outcome being what it was, Mao could not resist sanctifying the struggle against Gao. Six months later he found a moral niche for it; Gao was one of those types who "don't want to go on making revolution." The pragmatic Gao had begun to play a role—history's teacher by negative example—that he would not have understood.

*   *   *

Who was that lounging beside a Peking swimming pool with Mao? None other than Nikita Khrushchev. In swimming trunks that strained to hold their ample forms, the two chieftains of world Marxism were in guarded debate on nuclear war.

One of the great tussles of our time had begun. Which of the two was Stalin's true heir in the international Communist movement? Whose line would prevail in the vital task of dealing with an expansive U.S.? Khrushchev was not keen on swimming—few Ukrainian peasants are—and in the short run the talks went better for Mao than for Khrushchev.

The PRC was five years old and Khrushchev was guest of honor at parades, banquets, and speeches to celebrate the birthday. Khrushchev later recalled that Mao's hospitality was almost more than could be desired. The two of them kissed each other on both cheeks. The world muttered grimly about an unstoppable Communist monolith. (In this autumn season SEATO was founded and the U.S. also concluded a treaty with Chiang Kai-shek.)

As men, the pair had little in common but a large girth. Mao was oblique; "I was never exactly sure," said Khrushchev, who was as frontal as a tractor, "that I understood what he meant." Mao liked books. Khrushchev liked corn cobs. Mao (in Khrushchev's words) "moved calmly and slowly as a bear." Khrushchev jerked around like a bull. Mao gazed down the corridors of the world's future. Khrushchev was dealing day by day with the challenge of American power.

The Peking meeting was the first Sino-Soviet summit for nearly five years. Zhou had been twice to Moscow and Liu Shaoqi once (for three months). Second-level Russian leaders had come to China. Mao in these years had not left China at all.

Though Mao did not say so, Moscow began to show him more trust and largesse after Stalin died. All sorts of issues were resolved in 1953–1954 that had previously been piling up on Moscow's "in" tray. In a startling change of attitude, *Pravda* even called Mao "a great Marxist theorist." Khrushchev's readiness to go to Peking—his first trip to Asia—seemed one more good sign.

The specific results of the summit were mostly a boon for Mao. He got more loans. He got back the two ports in Manchuria that had been under Soviet control. The Russia-China joint-stock companies, which he disliked, were dissolved *25 years* earlier than the date agreed upon at the Mao-Stalin talks. Russian statements referred to China in unprecedented terms as "an equal partner."

Yet Khrushchev left China deeply uneasy. "Conflict with China is inevitable," he told his colleagues after returning to Moscow.

Mao raised the issue of Mongolia with Khrushchev. He had agreed to Stalin's insistence on Outer Mongolia being independent—he could not avoid doing so—but he felt Moscow was treating Ulan Bator like a monkey in a cage. "We took up this question," Mao later reported, "but they [Khrushchev and Bulganin] refused to talk to us."

Culturally the meeting resembled two battleships passing each other in the night. Here was Khrushchev: "The Chinese served tea every time we turned around—tea, tea, tea. . . . And according to the Chinese tradition, if you didn't drink it up right away, they'd take that cup away and put another one in front of you—over and over again." Khrushchev, in his insularity, felt that Mao was playing games with him.

The Russian asked for one million Chinese workers to come and develop Siberia. Mao found the idea a bit offensive. Khrushchev backed down. Then (according to Khrushchev) Mao said the plan could be tried out. By now Khrushchev had cold feet. But he had to go through with his own proposal. Two hundred thousand Chinese workers went to Siberia. The scheme died an early death.

Khrushchev had the growing feeling that Mao was too clever by half. "He really knew how to put us down."

Mao and Khrushchev stood atop the Gate of Heavenly Peace for the National Day parade. Khrushchev looked like a farmer eyeing the crops. The fireworks gave more pleasure to Mao than to Khrushchev. At one point, Zhou Enlai, spotting Mao's wife, made a move to introduce her to Khrushchev. But Mao intervened. Moving swiftly across the purple balcony he led Ms. Jiang out of Khrushchev's reach. In a remote corner, husband and wife gazed at the fireworks together.

It is hard to say whether Mao did not want Khrushchev to meet Ms. Jiang or whether he did not want her to meet him.

At the poolside Mao urged on Khrushchev his view that imperialism was a paper tiger. To Khrushchev's amazement he treated the U.S. threat lightly. "I tried to explain to him," the Russian reported, "that one or two missiles could turn all the divisions in China to dust."

This 1954 exchange recalled Mao's view of the A-bomb explosion over

Hiroshima nine years before. The first reaction of the CCP was not unlike that in dozens of chancelleries. "A Revolution in the Art of War," said the Communist *Liberation Daily* in Chongqing the day after the attack on Hiroshima. Mao did not agree.

"Can atom bombs decide wars?" he asked an audience four days later. "No, they can't." Here was a bombshell of Mao's own. "Some of our comrades," he complained, "believe that the atom bomb is all-powerful; that is a big mistake." Mao was dead serious. "The atom bomb is a paper tiger which the U.S. reactionaries use to scare people," he reiterated to Anna Louise Strong, the revolution-watching journalist from Nebraska. "It looks terrible, but in fact it isn't." *Liberation Daily* had to reverse itself.

In 1954 Mao still believed that human will mattered more than weapons. For Khrushchev a thing was real if you could eat or touch it. Mao was a seer by comparison, with a massive confidence in himself, China, and the upward spiral of history toward communism. Khrushchev felt that Mao looked on him as a coward.*

Mutual sniping followed Khrushchev's visit to Mao. Khrushchev some months later hinted to Adenauer of Germany that China might become a "worrying problem for the West." Mao apparently believed the reports that reached his ears of the Russians calling the CCP a "children's Party" and a mere "patriotic Party." It wasn't quite true for Khrushchev to say to Eisenhower—as he did five years later—that he and Mao were "good friends."

The scene at the swimming pool had been a prologue to the Sino-Soviet split. How much to fear war—that was the looming issue between Mao and Khrushchev. On the eve of Khrushchev's arrival in Peking, Mao gave a clue to where he stood. As a "test of intention"—the phrase comes from the Peking side—he ordered shells to rain down on the islands between Taiwan and the mainland. The echo from those shells was to grow louder.

* * *

"Work on your own," Mao said to Jiang Qing in late 1951. It was his answer to a dilemma. Equally it led to a strange period in Mao's third and longest marriage.

The Party gave Ms. Jiang jobs of some weight in 1950. She headed the administrative section of the Central Committee offices. And the cinema division of the Propaganda Department of the CCP was in her hands.

---

* One thing that Mao and Khrushchev did agree upon was soon forgotten, to gain another life in different circumstances two decades later. Khrushchev proposed a conference on European security. Mao said this was a good idea. The Russians sent invitations to 23 European governments and the U.S. But the West was not interested. When the Helsinki conference did take place in 1975, Mao railed against it as a sellout to the perfidious Soviets (see page 412).

But "Mao's nice mattress" (as Khrushchev called her) already had more enemies than friends. Efforts were made to force her out of Party work. She appealed to Mao. But on her own admission, Mao essentially took the side of her critics. For her to work on her own was Mao's solution.

In fact, Ms. Jiang spent most of her time in bed or in Moscow or both.

She was indeed often ill in the 1950s. But Mao thought she was less ill in reality than in her own overheated imagination. He seemed to be swiping at her in a remark made at a health conference some years later: "Excessive attention to food, clothing, housing, and means of transportation are the four underlying causes of illness among high-level cadres."

Sometimes Jiang Qing was seen with Mao at a reception, but the two of them spent many months apart. Four times Ms. Jiang went to Russia for treatment between 1949 and 1957. Her total time outside China was almost three years. Though Mao went to Moscow twice during that period, they were never in the Soviet capital together.

At least one of Ms. Jiang's expeditions to Russia was very much against her own will. Yet Mao concurred with those who insisted on sending her away. During her fourth stay, in 1956–1957, she sank to a very low ebb. She wished more than anything else to come back to China. However, Zhou Enlai—who went to confer with Khrushchev in January 1957—brought explicit instructions from Mao that his wife should stay in Moscow until she had regained her health.

Maybe it is not surprising that Ms. Jiang was haunted by a possible parallel between herself and Mao's previous wife, He Zizhen, who had been sent to Russia by Mao and ended up in a Soviet asylum.

For Ms. Jiang to work by herself probably meant, in the Party's view of the matter, for her to do nothing of importance. However she set herself up as Mao's secretary. This did not seem to be a smooth arrangement, for within a year she was pushed out to Moscow. "Certain leaders" made this decision, said Ms. Jiang. But if Mao was not happy with their decision he could have vetoed it.

By her own account, at any rate, she worked for Mao off and on through the 1950s. Propped up in a special reclining bed, she scoured documents for a bright idea which she could pass on to the man whom she now referred to as "the Chairman." He sat by her bedside as she read to him from telegrams and newspapers. It is likely that she learned more than he did.

Mao never publicly referred to any help received from Jiang Qing in this period. He did nothing to bring her out of the wilderness that she was in during the 1950s. All this was certainly done in part as a result of Party pressure on Mao. The marriage had never been a very popular one in establishment circles.

In Peking Mao saw a lot of his two daughters. Both Li Na (Cautious in Speech) and Li Min (Quick in Action) lived at home. By the mid-1950s they were enrolled at students at Peking University. Li Na, apparently the brighter of the two, studied history as her father liked to do. Li Min went into the natural sciences.

In and out of the household was a nephew, Yuanxin, son of Mao's brother Zemin, who had been killed by the Nationalists in 1943.

Not present was the surviving son of Mao's marriage with Yang Kaihui. Anqing spent most of this period in a mental asylum, and Mao did not seem to take much interest in him.*

*   *   *

What shape was Mao's China taking after half a decade?

Mao talked from the Gate of Heavenly Peace of "the revolution." Having been over the horizon for so long, the revolution had taken on the aura of a cosmic event. Now it had broken into its component parts like the contents of a suitcase once unpacked.

It did not any longer seem a cause.

The revolution meant a day of work at the factory bench. It meant studying Mao's Thought. It meant a small girl teaching her grandmother the Chinese characters she had just learned at school. It meant a young idealist from Peking going as a cadre to a village, taking the message of communism to peasants who seemed to him interested only in the weather and their bellies.

The revolution was better health, long meetings, dunce caps, closed-up temples, new bridges, ration coupons, Sukarno of Indonesia coming to salute "People's China."

In the villages many small battles were still being fought, but few big ones. No landlords, no Japanese anymore. Just richer mutual aid teams gaining advantages over poorer mutual aid teams. The odd lazy farmer to be disciplined. The busybody to be coped with.

Rural China was far from being a welfare state. Incomes were not equal. There was no social insurance. You lived by working. What family you were born into still counted for much.

But everyone was wrapped together in mutual obligation even more than in the past. Socialism meant that. And it meant persistent cadres holding

---

* Mao once made a curious remark about the relationship between fingernails and childrens' character. "The first thing you must do with your sons and daughters," he told Indonesian visitors, "is to check whether their fingernails are good." As he smiled slightly, and held his own hands with the ten nails bunched together, he went on: "This way you will know whether your children can be controlled, or not."

endless meetings and telling you how to live. They were hard-working and often sincere and it was hard to argue against them. But they poked their fingers into everything.

When Mao reversed himself on population growth, and ordered birth control, cadres herded the peasants to meetings on *that*. "Why, they even tell you when to fuck," one man complained.

The words hung up for display at New Year's told a new story. Formerly you would put on your gate a motto about virtue and prosperity. Now you put up a slogan about the Five-Year Plan. Fresh, too, were the phrases coming out of the ubiquitous loudspeakers. "Ten Thousand Years to the Chinese Communist Party" was one of the commonest.

Into every train compartment girls screamed messages such as "We are approaching Peking, home of Chairman Mao." Combining the duties of disk jockey and of catechist, these announcers with piercing voices kept new China on its ideological toes.

Or did they? The main point was sociological, not ideological. People were working together in a constructive way on jobs of importance to China. What was in their hearts and minds even Chairman Mao soon found he did not know.

One day the Polish ambassador in Peking decided to test the honesty of Mao's China. Could it really be true that a new spirit existed at all levels of Chinese society? He let his wallet fall in the corridor of a hotel (where he lived). It was returned to him that evening. The forty dollars he had put in it was intact. Next morning he left the wallet on a couch in the hotel lobby. Again it came back with all its contents. The Pole was impressed.

For a third test he left the wallet in a nearby park. A local Public Security man brought it around to his room at the hotel.

In it was eighty dollars. Gomulka and the Virgin Mary! Virtue was one thing; magic quite another.

When the Public Security people found the wallet, the Pole reasoned, the forty dollars must have been gone. To hide the fact that a theft had taken place, they estimated what a Polish ambassador would be likely to carry with him, and inserted eighty dollars into the wallet before returning it.

Did a Chinese steal the forty dollars? Quite possibly. It happened in Mao's China, if less often than in Gomulka's Poland.

Mao had set China on a quest for a Oneness of outlook. He liked to hear of PLA officers washing the socks and underpants of their soldiers, to show that distinction had been thrown to the winds. The gesture smacked of his days on the road. It could never be really institutionalized in a vast, status-conscious, fairly materialistic society. Yet the possibility of a general washing a private's socks did exist; it made backwardness tolerable, it spurred people on, and made China a better place than it would have been without such occasional gestures.

Mao's China in the 1950s was a more easygoing and less cynical place than Stalin's Russia. People seemed eager. They worked with spirit and without an eye constantly on the clock. They seemed able to relax in a park or at home. Socialism had not softened the dedication of Chinese chefs.

On the other hand, Mao had not broken open the age-old self-containment of the Chinese. He had not yet stirred his people to much curiosity in things non-Chinese. China was their world. They placed it within no wider perspective.

More human than Russia, one could say, but less cosmopolitan.

Mao's China was meant to be like a family. Mao urged people to honor the new bonds of comradeship as scrupulously as the old bonds of clan had been honored. When his own son was killed in Korea, his words, at least, went along such lines. Brought the news, he made no show of emotion. After a long silence he remarked: "Without sacrifices there will not be victory. To sacrifice my son or other people's sons is just the same."*

Such a vision of China was not altogether new. "Big family" is the Chinese term for "everybody" (*da jia*). The tie between emperor and subject was considered a higher version of that between father and son. The county magistrate was known as "the father and mother official" (*fu-mu guan*). No one was really a discrete individual. Everyone had a reason to be in everyone else's pocket.

So legal institutions played a small role. Parents did not invoke the law against their children. At the same time, they denied to their children the autonomy that an appeal to the law implies.

It was the same in Mao's China. As a child felt secure in a family of old China, so did a citizen feel a certain security in Mao's PRC. The child had no rights to defense counsel and a public trial if his father accused him of wrongdoing; nor did Mao's citizens. A father's will was inseparable from his love. So was Mao's power inseparable from the prestige of his doctrine. A family—not a limited corporation—was what Mao's China aimed to be.

Was it a case of Mao versus China? Not quite, not yet.

His *methods* of going after power had been nativistic. He removed the Western suit of Marxism in favor of a Chinese gown. Instead of trying to repeat in Shanghai what Lenin did in St. Petersburg, he went to the hills as Chinese peasant rebels had done.

Nor did he pluck his *goal* from outside Chinese tradition. He thought of

---

* Remarkably enough, Anying's body was never brought back to China; he is buried on Korean soil; Kim Il-sung sends a wreath to the grave each year.

the future state of communism as a realization of the old ideal of Great Harmony.

He did not need to struggle much against religion. Castro did. So too the Poles. Even the Russians to a degree. The otherworldly sense was feebler in China than in Catholic Cuba and Poland, or Orthodox Russia.

Mao inserted himself into the Chinese spiritual tradition like a hand into a glove. Confucius did not believe in a personal God; nothing to be dethroned there. Confucius did believe in an immanent cosmic law; so did Mao.

Moral truth was as fixed as the natural order, for Maoist and mandarin alike.

Yet Mao did collide with China—with two Chinas. Seldom had there been strong *state power* in this civilization held together mostly by social bonds. Mao's Peking tied the people up in regulations as they had hardly been since Qin Shihuang did the same 2,200 years before. He knocked China into a tidy shape, in the heterodox tradition of a Chinese Legalist* who trusted in administrative sanctions more than in the established Confucian idea of moral community.

Mao also collided with the new China which he himself had brought to birth. As a neo-Legalist, he set the Chinese free from bonds and mystifications: family oppression, superstitions about the cosmos, extreme localism. But he was enough of a Chinese holist to want to bind the Chinese millions into a new design. His new state began to turn out modern citizens. For how long would they jump through the hoops of a Maoist system that owed so much to a pre-modern past?

Here was a crisis still in the future.

*   *   *

In the mid-1950s Mao sat in his study and watched China's prestige rise abroad. He did not travel. Nor did he write about foreign affairs. The volume of his *Selected Works* that covers 1950–1957 is 99 percent about domestic matters. The same lack of foreign policy discussion marks his informal talks of those years.

It was Zhou who did the traveling—to clinch China's influence at the Geneva Conference on Indochina in 1954, to win (and even kiss) nonaligned friends at the Bandung Conference in 1955—while Mao did the thinking. Mao made strides by the old Chinese recipe of doing nothing.†

---

*Legalism was a science of power that evolved through the practice of realpolitik, starting more than 2,000 years ago.

†In traditional China, *wu wei* (nonaction) meant ruling by abdicating from rule.

To be sure, China's performance in Korea won a healthy international respect for Mao. (Not a single country recognized the PRC for the duration of the Korean War. Quite a few did so, soon after it ended.) And Stalin's death made Mao look bigger by elimination. But it was above all the shadow of his achievements within China that cast itself so strikingly across the Third World in particular.

Foreigners came *to* Mao.*

Mainly they were Asian. U Nu of Burma came to pay homage in 1954 and was as impressed as he had expected to be. Sihanouk saw Mao in 1956 for the first of many times. "I like princes," Mao said to the Cambodian, "when they're not reactionary, and against imperialism as you are." Another prince—Souvanna Phouma of Laos—came also in 1956, but Mao liked him less than Sihanouk. He certainly went on supporting the neutral (and princely) forces in Cambodia longer than he did the neutral (and princely) forces in Laos.

"It was like going to the court of Louis the Fourteenth," the first Indonesian ambassador to the PRC recalled of his visit to Mao to present his credentials. "The ceremony was severe."

At ten o'clock one morning Ambassador Mononutu was received by Mao's protocol chief at a large red door in the Forbidden City. The anthems of Indonesia and China were played. Mononutu was led, his six Indonesian colleagues having to remain behind, into an old hall furnished only with porcelain Ming vases on each side and an endless red carpet down the middle. A door opened noiselessly in front of him. A second long hall, identical with the first, yawned at him. As he reached its far wall a further door somehow opened. There stood Mao, large, silent, benign.

No conversation took place. Mao and the ambassador exchanged pieces of parchment. Then Zhou Enlai, who had been hovering in the background, led the way into a side room, where Mao and the Indonesian each made brief set speeches about patriotism and peace. (Meanwhile the other six Indonesians had been whisked to another part of the palace to drink champagne and eat sweet Chinese cakes.)

Mao left after the set speeches. Mononutu found himself exiting by a different door. "I felt I shouldn't ask Mao any questions. He was like a god. If you had a real question you asked Zhou."

Mao did seem to offer himself as an emperor to Asians (not to Westerners) who came to him. Some liked it. "Benevolence was written all over his

* Sukarno complained that he had eight times invited Mao to visit Indonesia, without any sign of Mao's accepting.

face," said U Nu. Others unhappily recognized in it an age-old Chinese hauteur. "Mao never spoke to me of the Heavenly Kingdom," Mononutu said, "yet I think he believed in it."

It did not leave the Indonesian with a feeling of warmth—however much he appreciated the politeness—when in three separate meetings Mao only made such remarks as: "I am told your country is very beautiful." Even after giving full weight to the reports of those Asians who liked him, the impression remains of Mao bending downward, patronizing, bamboozling his Asian visitors.

Mao took little notice of Africa, and met few Africans, during the 1950s. One of the few statements he made about the continent was as much about China as about Africa. Learning that South Africa's proposed apartheid legislation would discriminate against the Chinese minority there, he joined black Africans in protesting the measures.

Mao in the autumn of 1955 received what could have been his first Japanese visitor since the war. Within weeks he met two more Japanese groups. He was taking a fresh look at Japan. For the next twenty years he had more meetings with Japanese than with the nationals of any other country.

In the early 1950s Mao had hoped the left in Japan would win power. He had been too optimistic. All of Asia was not going to bubble over just because China had done so. By 1955 Mao had adjusted his aim. He was shaking any Japanese hand, left or right, that could help tip the scales in Tokyo to the side of recognizing the PRC (and breaking with Chiang Kai-shek).

In mid-1956 Mao proposed to Japan a Pacific Treaty that would link China, Japan, and the U.S. Spurned in 1956, it came to birth, in spirit though not in form, in the 1970s, when Mao lined China up with Japan and the U.S. in a tacit phalanx against Russia.

Mao met no visitors from the U.S. Dulles was snarling at him, "containing" him—ironic to busy oneself containing the most self-contained major nation on earth—and forecasting that his regime would "pass away." Now and then he received a Soviet official. The Russians he *had* to deal with; quietly he compromised with them.

It was Asia (and a few other parts of the Third World) that chiefly gave illustration to Mao's image of himself in foreign affairs. The Third World was a stage on which he could be judged a hero—not less so by staying in the wings and deputing Zhou to deliver the lines.*

---

*Zhou said little or nothing when he was present at meetings between Mao and foreigners. Yet when he was alone with a foreign leader Zhou conducted business with a firm authority that throws an intriguing light on the Mao-Zhou relationship. U Nu, whose sincerity made him naive and bold by turns, on one occasion delivered a tirade to Mao's face about China's "acts of aggression" on Burma's border. Mao responded calmly as Zhou sat in silence. U Nu's own colleagues felt he had "blotted his copybook" by tackling Mao directly.

China had been oppressed—so it was with the Afro-Asian lands. China was poor and rural—as were they. China was nonwhite—in Europe even the Communists could not attain such a gut solidarity with the colored masses of the Third World.

The era of Bandung was a rich one for Mao's image outside China, as numerous Third World nations set up ties with his government.

This era found Mao at a halfway house. He had begun to play the Third World card that he knew his Russian friends could not so readily play; one day that would bring Sino-Soviet tensions. Yet in the mid-1950s he played the Third World card circumspectly.

He had a special role within the camp, as head of Asia's first great Marxist revolution and Marxist state. But he did not challenge Moscow's primacy. He did not say that the Third World was the key to world politics. He did not make the originality of China's revolution the springboard for a fresh Marxist world view. That would come later.

*   *   *

Many a leader from an ex-colony was swept off his feet by Mao's reception of him. The first thing he saw was a beaming thirty-foot portrait of himself at the start of the boulevard that sweeps in from the airport to the city. That morning's *People's Daily* had told China's millions that the visitor was a giant of the times. China was on his side against all comers, it assured him in ardent front-page prose.

The visiting leader had never seen anything as extravagant as the National Day parade by the Gate of Heavenly Peace. A huge paper-machier statue of Mao headed the floats, its hand extended as if forlornly reaching out to touch the dancing colored balloons. The foreign statesman's spirits soared with the balloons.

Banquets were mounted. Aid was pledged for economic development at home. The ultimate honor of a session with Mao sent the visitor spinning in euphoria back to his lesser sphere.

Life in prison—where many, like Nehru, had spent years—was never like this. Nor did Washington or Paris or Moscow seem quite as pleased to see one as did Peking with its orchestrated millions.

It is not surprising that—in the simpler days of the 1950s, when few

---

"Premier Zhou," U Nu inquired earnestly as the pair drove to Peking airport next day, "was I wrong to speak to Chairman Mao as I did last night?"

"U Nu," the Chinese premier replied evenly, "you and I are in the habit of meeting frequently. Instead of speaking to Chairman Mao, you might have brought your complaints to me."

"I am very sorry."

"That's all right," said Zhou with a degree more warmth. "It doesn't matter."

clouds had yet gathered over Chinese politics—many a Third World leader looked upon Mao as the lodestar for his climb toward dignity.

Sukarno of Indonesia came to see Mao in the autumn of 1956. "They hugged each other as if they'd been friends for years," a Sukarno aide recalled. The two of them stood together in a Packard convertible that moved like a tortoise through Peking. Mao half smiled and held his right hand toward the crowd. Sukarno grinned like a schoolboy and gesticulated. Pan-Asian friendship was in the air. People came within five feet of the Packard to toss flowers. The ambling cops did not stop them; no armed soldiers were visible at all.

A gun fired twenty-three shots. Mao and Sukarno were perched on the Gate of Heavenly Peace. A parade of sixteen columns began beneath them. Tanks and guns. Gongs and cymbals. Gymnasts doing cartwheels. A sea of color as the marchers held fans now this way and now that to make a tableau of flowers or slogans for bird's-eye viewing. The sun itself seemed to add its rays to the brilliance of the welcome. A crowd of 500,000 . . .

Toward 8 P.M. the night before, a housewife had made the rounds of the courtyards in Western Strip Street just by the Forbidden City. At each house she made a crisp announcement. "President Sukarno arrives in Peking tomorrow. The government has decided to mobilize half a million residents to stage a grand welcome for him." The lady was an unpaid staff member of the neighborhood committee of the area.

At one house the specific instruction that she added went like this: "You have four people in this house. The committee expects two of the four to be on Western Strip Street before 2 P.M. Your spot will be the east mouth of this particular lane. You are not to disperse until President Sukarno and Chairman Mao have passed by."

The brilliance of the welcome was not due to the sun alone.

What did the residents of Western Strip Street *feel* about Mao and Sukarno? Within limits—never gone beyond in the 1950s—feelings were not the point. It was a patriotic occasion. Residents were proud of China's new zip under Mao. . . . Each person had a social function to perform. . . . The onerous aspects were for most people bearable in the context of food and work and peace. . . .

Nehru came. It was a serious visit, for Mao was intrigued by Nehru. Nehru was less of a mystic than most Indians. He was a modern man—who did not drink urine as Morarji Desai does—and Mao warmly admired his fight against the British. Mao—who had denounced the Indian in 1949 as a bourgeois destined for the rubbish dump of history—treated him with great respect.

But he shocked Nehru with a clinical remark about nuclear war. "He

[Nehru] believed that if an atomic war was fought," Mao related, "the whole of mankind would be annihilated. I said that if the worst came to the worst and half of mankind died, the other half would remain while imperialism would be razed to the ground and the whole world could become socialist." *

Mao and Nehru agreed on most issues at the time—1954—but the exchange on war brought out a sharp contrast between the two of them. Nehru was a moralist on international affairs. Mao was a moralist only on China's affairs.

In style the pair were ill-matched. Mao thought Nehru verbose, as Chinese often find Indians to be, and as Mao had found M. N. Roy to be in the 1920s. Nehru thought Mao was cunning—a common Indian view of Chinese.†

Mao was open toward India as a nation. He respected Lenin's view that Delhi would be a pivot of the coming world revolution. Yet there was a thinness to Mao's impulse toward solidarity with any cause outside China, which made it unlikely that Mao and Nehru would walk very far together down the path of mere anti-colonialism.

Mao saw the world through the yellow-tinted spectacles of his existence as a Chinese. (Citizens of most great powers are ethnocentric, it is true, especially of continental powers like China.) Rarely in its history has China looked outside for anything it desired for itself; never until the nineteenth century did it need to do so. China was a Middle Kingdom not only in its self-understanding but in geographic reality too.

For Mao the man there were extra factors. He was bred in the hills, not on the seacoast. His formative years were not spent in any great urban center. The making of the Chairman took place deep in the hinterland.

From Yanan he saw the world—but not China—pretty much as Stalin saw it. He contorted himself the day after the Hitler-Stalin pact, as all good Communists did. His 1950s views were for the most part a steady development of the Marxist outlook he had imbibed in the late 1930s. Inclinations that did not sit well with this orthodoxy, Mao, for the time being, kept to himself.

---

* We find that in this matter as in so many others, Mao drew his confidence from the study of ancient Chinese history. He remarked to the Eighth CCP Congress in 1958: "Do not be alarmed either if there should be war. . . . Eliminating half the population occurred several times in China's history. The fifty million population in the time of Emperor Wu in the Han dynasty was reduced to ten million by the time of the Three Kingdoms, the two Qin dynasties, and the North and South dynasties." Mao went on to supply further examples of how losing half the people did not amount to losing civilization.

†I asked a Burmese who knew both to compare Mao and Nehru. "Totally different," he replied. Then, after a long pause: "If I had to deal with each of them on affairs, I would prefer Nehru."

Mao did not know the outside world firsthand. No journey shook his thinking as Khrushchev's was shaken by exposure to the U.S. in 1959, or Harold Macmillan's by his tour of Africa in 1960.

Mao knew much *about* the outside world. He continued to read books. No other world leader of midcentury—not even de Gaulle—read for himself and wrote his own talks to the extent Mao did.* History and geography were the twin pillars of his foreign knowledge. Technical questions and the ins and outs of political office interested him much less.

But the outside world was not China. Mao knew quite a bit, but there was a limit to how much he cared. He was in this respect the opposite of Lyndon Johnson, who knew little but thought it his duty to do for Asian children what the New Deal had done for tots in Texas.

For Mao, foreign policy had a single aim for the time being: to allow new China to proceed unhindered with its socialist construction. (His long-term aim I shall return to on reaching the 1970s.) He had no interest in crusades outside China.

"You come to us" summed up his attitude to every nation except Russia. As for establishing ties with "the imperialist countries," he had told his colleagues that China "need not be in a hurry" about it "even for a fairly long period. . . ." True, the great powers had not welcomed him to their club; but it was a complacent remark.

* In one detail de Gaulle and Mao were the same. They sent handwritten missives. Neither was keen on dictation. Neither used a typewriter—de Gaulle for aesthetic reasons, Mao because a typewriter and the Chinese language are as ill-suited as a spoon is for emptying a swimming pool.

14

Doubts (1956-1957)

Now and then a single year can seem like a lifetime. Nineteen sixty-eight was such a year in America and much of Europe. For China (and the whole Communist bloc) 1956 was that kind of year. It changed the rules of the game within international communism. Not since Liberation did Mao have to maneuver with such care as during the bittersweet season of de-Stalinization.

Nineteen fifty-four had been a good year for Mao. Power was consolidated; the Five-Year Plan began well; he got the better end of the stick with Khrushchev in the autumn. During 1955 he felt able to put his foot on the accelerator for a quicker advance toward some cherished goals.

Then in 1956 he met disabling cross-currents coming at him from both near and far.

"Some of our comrades," Mao barked in a broadside on rural work in mid-1955, "are tottering along like a woman with bound feet. They are complaining all the time, 'You're going too fast, much too fast.'" He thought he saw a hurricane in the villages, as he had done in 1927. "An upsurge in the new socialist mass movement is imminent throughout the countryside."

At issue was how to move toward collective farming the like of which the world had never seen. Five hundred million peasants were being induced to work with each other, under Party guardianship, rather than each for himself.

The first step had been mutual aid teams of ten or so households each—no great change from small peasant proprietorship. Next came cooperatives—joint ownership, in essence.*

To Mao this was exciting. He had lived with the land problem ever since

---

* Neither stage affected the peasant's private ownership of his own home.

the oppressiveness of his father hit him fifty years before. A solution was at hand—and he was in no mood to dawdle about grasping it. To make farming collective was to clinch socialist political power.

Not everyone agreed with him. "Big movements aren't possible from now on," Liu Shaoqi assured the farmers after land reform was fully achieved. "The main thing is to concentrate energy on economic construction." Another senior figure expressed a similar sentiment during the preparation of the new constitution of 1954: "The CCP has in the past lived by movements but in the future it must live by the law."

The Rural Department of the CCP dragged its feet. Mao had to put a bright but brittle disciple, Chen Boda,* in its number two slot to get his way there. Meanwhile, some regional figures went about dissolving cooperatives! Some 20,000 out of a total of 670,000 were ordered out of existence as failures. A widespread view, shared by Liu, was that large cooperatives would make sense only when large machines existed on the farms.

Most of the leadership thought of power as an end in itself.† A socialist government now ran China; henceforth the job was to put one foot in front of the other.

For Mao the use of power was not bricklaying, but sculpture. Liu and others did not quite have the measure of their leader.

Mao turned out a slogan for the rising tide in the countryside: "More, faster, better, and more economically." But the Rural Department fiddled with the wording of the slogan, and delayed its publication in *People's Daily* for a long time.

Mao was no Stalin in the 1950s. He could not merely shoot or shunt to Siberia those who made it difficult for him to do what he wanted to do. He had to cajole and manipulate.

One evening he had a meeting with eighty Shanghai business leaders. These men ran private companies. The CCP called them "national capitalists." Out of regard for their patriotism—and a need for their industrial skills—he had allowed them to operate fairly freely. Until now.

In his slow drawl Mao set about with brilliant success to put the tycoons at ease. "Why don't you smoke?" he asked the nervous group affably. "It won't hurt you. Churchill has smoked throughout his long life and he is in good health. In fact, the only man I know who doesn't smoke but has lived long is Chiang Kai-shek."

Mao said the national capitalists had been doing a good job. But up in Peking he'd heard that businessmen *themselves* were urging nationalization.

---

* We shall see Chen Boda rise to the top during the Cultural Revolution.
† To be fair, some also feared losses from coerced collectivization—correctly, as it turned out.

They would not want, after all, to lag behind the rest of new China in going through the noble arches of socialism. Yet Mao declared that he was not sure about it. He had his doubts. He had come to the great city of Shanghai to listen. "I have brought only my two ears to this meeting."

It was Mao's way. Of course the capitalists, like birds whose feathers drop out by the hour, could see and feel a change under way. One after the other for two hours they spoke up for a switch to state ownership. They got what they "asked for." A man who owned a company on Monday found himself its manager on a salary by Friday. Mao was reaching for a more distinctive socialist shape to industry as well as agriculture.

After this meeting a story about Mao's methods went the rounds of Shanghai's remaining executive suites. Mao called in Liu and Zhou. He had a question for them: "How would you make a cat eat pepper?"

Liu spoke up first. "That's easy," said the number two man. "You get somebody to hold the cat, stuff the pepper in its mouth, and push it down with a chopstick."

Mao raised his hands in horror at such a made-in-Moscow solution. "Never use force. . . . Everything must be voluntary." Zhou had been listening. Mao inquired what the premier would do with the cat.

"I would starve the cat," replied the man who had often walked the tightrope of opportunity. "Then I would wrap the pepper with a slice of meat. If the cat is sufficiently hungry it will swallow it whole."

Mao did not agree with Zhou any more than with Liu. "One must not use deceit either—never fool the people." What, then, would the Chairman himself do? "Easy," he said—concurring with Liu at least on that. "You rub the pepper thoroughly into the cat's backside. When it burns, the cat will lick it off—and be happy that it is permitted to do so."

Whatever the antecedents of the story, it was true that Mao disliked coercion, and considered administrative cunning a poor second best to the evocation of enthusiastic participation. That did not make him any less authoritarian about his goals.

Mao was not activated merely by an abstract vision of social togetherness. He wanted more grain and more machine tools. At this time, abundance and socialism were for him two sides of a single coin. So they were—at all times—for Liu. The special point about Mao's position was his stress on moral will.

He felt that a new spirit in the villages, whether accompanied by mechanization or not, could catapult Chinese farming to a new high form of social organization. Of course, it was a rationalization of China's backwardness. Communal spirit was, among other things, a means of coping with the absence of a material incentive for the individual.

The new spurt in agriculture was also meant to fuel an industrial takeoff. The lights of a modern socialist future gleamed for Mao as 1955 ended.

* * *

Came the Communist world's *annus mirabilis* of 1956, during which "Liberalization" was the watchword from Prague to Peking. Mao joined in the spirit of liberalization even before the first snowflakes fell on his villa in late 1955. His motivation was largely economic—*his* type of economics.

Mao took the screws off the intellectuals. He announced that they would be the "decisive factor" in putting an end to China's hated backwardness. He tossed a bone to the well-off farmers. Reversing previous policy, he made it clear in February 1956 that they would be permitted to join the cooperatives (to be outside a cooperative was to be a virtual leper).

Both groups were needed if the heady drive into a realm of abundance was to succeed. Both would be enticed to "lick the pepper off their backsides." The bitter paradox was that for neither intellectual nor well-off farmer would there be a niche in the society Mao was pushing toward. Eventually each person would be a jack-of-all-trades and the splitting of straws by overspecialized academics would be obsolete. Just over the horizon in the villages was a new order in which possession would mean little.

Yet this did not lessen the excitement of the Chinese spring of 1956.

"Ten Great Relationships" was a major speech to the Politburo in April 1956. The long text was full of policy decisions. It was also a philosophic homecoming for Mao. He had kept his big wings folded in the early 1950s. Now he put them on.

The title gave the clue. Mao did not believe in fixed, linear development. "Process" wasn't a term that came readily to his tongue. "Relationships" was. All is flux, he insisted. To see that contradictions exist at the heart of all phenomena is the starting point of wisdom. "Each age, whether the future or the present, has its own two aspects, and each individual has his own two aspects."

Nothing is stable. Fine, make use of instability. Keep each person on his toes. Find that true balance that comes, not from a neat plan, but from the ebb and flow of jostling wills.

"Walk on two legs," Mao liked to say. That summed it up. Neither leg is sufficient unto itself. The secret lies in the relationship between the movement of the two. Peeping through Mao's Marxism was the old Chinese idea of *yin* and *yang,* dark and light, female and male. It stood for the irreducible duality of all things, including Mao's own double nature as tiger and monkey.

Economics was still Mao's topic. But he was pushing toward a more *Chinese* mode of economic development.

A bit less stress on heavy industry, he decreed, a bit more on light. China could not turn into another Soviet Union overnight; meanwhile the Chinese people should be allowed to have brighter and better consumer goods. "They're draining the pond to catch the fish," Mao remarked of the Soviets one day to his trusted chief of dirty tricks, Kang Sheng. By "fish" he meant industrial production. By "pond" he meant the life of the people.

Cut back Party and government bureaucracy by two thirds, he said. It was a breathtaking, on its face unworkable, suggestion, but it showed the way Mao's mind was tending. He wanted to loosen up China's rigid bureaucracy.

In a related passage, he broached the relationship, which had long concerned him, between central control and grass-roots initiative. It was the monkey's turn: "We are now having a meeting, which is centralization; after the meeting, some of us will go for a walk, some will read books, some will go to eat, which is independence. If we don't adjourn the meeting and give everyone some independence but let it go on and on, wouldn't it be the death of us all?" He also applied this Taoist-like axiom to industry.

Mao now felt that the defense budget should be cut back. "Do you want atom bombs?" he asked the Politburo. "Then you ought to reduce defense spending and increase spending on economic construction."

"If war should break out in the future," Defense Minister Peng Dehuai said to the same meeting, "we should contribute troops and the Soviet Union would contribute atom bombs." It was a pregnant, and for Peng's relations with Mao, a fatal, formulation.

Mao viewed the defense budget from three elevations. He had begun to peer into a future in which China and Russia would no longer walk hand in hand.

In 1956 he believed passionately that economic growth was about to accelerate and that this would be the key to everything in China's 1960s.

And he was expressing his personal philosophy of defense: people's war plus the bomb. He was not enthusiastic about the intermediate level of a professional military with a vast arsenal of costly conventional weapons.

* * *

As flowers bloomed in China, guns smoked in East Europe. Khrushchev's secret speech on Stalin came within weeks of Mao's first speech on the new soft line. Mao did not like Khrushchev's speech.*

---

* Zhu De and Deng Xiaoping heard Khrushchev's stunning attack as leaders of the Chinese delegation at the Twentieth Congress of the Soviet Party. Zhu agreed with the denunciation of Stalin's *Diktat*. Deng had his doubts. A public reaction had to await Mao. The contents of Khruschchev's speech were cabled to Peking. It turned out that the politically clumsy Zhu had put his foot in it again; the shrewder Deng was vindicated.

"We were on the one hand happy," Mao remarked two years later in a talk at Chengdu, "but also apprehensive." Actually the speech shook him to his foundations. It echoed on like an irritating drumbeat behind all of Mao's moves during the rest of 1956.

Previously Mao had sworn about Stalin in private and gushed about him in public. In a 6,000-word piece in *People's Daily*, he now tried gingerly to align gut and brain. Stalin's errors were personal, Mao reasoned, not errors of the system.

In six months Mao four times received a visit from a Russian official. Seldom if ever before had he received the leaders of any nation as frequently as this. By October he was even reaching for the phone to invite the Soviet ambassador around, so agitated was he about the political explosions in Poland and Hungary.

He told Mikoyan in April that he felt "Stalin's merits outweighed his faults." This was his main point to each visitor from Moscow, as of his *People's Daily* article. For the international Communist movement to think otherwise, he felt, would be to open Pandora's box.

And would it not cast a shadow on China's Stalin? Mao did not ask that question out loud. But it was his key fear about de-Stalinization. His other objections to Khrushchev's speech were real enough. Moscow should have consulted him in advance about such a bombshell. If Stalin was so evil, what of those who worked beside him for so long? Khrushchev himself, Mao reasoned, must surely be judged either an "accomplice" or a "fool."

But neither objection mattered a chopstick compared with the supreme issue of his own power in China. Mao was more than China's Stalin. He was its Marx and its Lenin too. But his *current role* was that of a Chinese Stalin.

In a series of speeches Mao asked the intellectuals to speak their minds. "Let a hundred flowers bloom, let a hundred schools contend." The phrase was not from Marx but from early Chinese tradition.

Liu Shaoqi publicly pointed out that Mao did not think up the slogan all by himself. "There have been very many things that were not thought of by Chairman Mao," the number two man told a history class at Peking University. "He merely improved on them." It was a bold remark. (*Very* many things. What others did Liu have in mind?)

Mao took the lid off China's mental life as no Marxist party in the world has ever *voluntarily* done. And he did so *before* de-Stalinization effected a similar thing in Europe.

Mao wanted enthusiasm—not a mere nod of acquiescence—from every man, woman, and child in China, for economic and other tasks. And he believed that his China had reached a certain plateau of achievement from which new vistas could be considered.

The tiger wanted more action out of the economy. The monkey wanted a proof of how much he was loved.

Let there be reprints of Voice of America broadcasts, Mao said, and Chiang Kai-shek's speeches too. Liu eventually chimed in to urge that journalism be taken out of the state structure to make it more independent. Give the reporters by-lines, he suggested, guarantee them high salaries—"perhaps higher even than Mao's"—and then they will "speak the truth."

A lot of older, liberal intellectuals spoke their minds in no uncertain fashion. They took Mao's "Millsian" side at face value. "China belongs to 600 million people," an academic wrote in *People's Daily*. "It does not belong to the Party alone." That cry against one-party rule was the commonest blossom in the floral blaze that suddenly surrounded Mao.

A second flower was almost as widespread. A cry went up against the *total scope* of the CCP's grip on Chinese life. Men of letters wanted more space for the mind.

Mao later asked Khrushchev—whether out of curiosity, or just to irritate the Russian—what he thought of the slogan "Let a hundred flowers bloom." Khrushchev denounced it. "Any peasant knows," he riposted, "that certain flowers ought to be cultivated but others should be cut down." Khrushchev claimed: "Mao agreed that maybe it wasn't a good slogan for Russians."

It was indeed a very Maoist slogan, which expressed a dualism deep in Mao's nature. In his gut he felt scorn for the average intellectual. This was partly for Leninist reasons—these were shared by Khrushchev—and partly because of Mao's experience of "academic lords" (*xue fa*) early in life. But Mao, unlike many Leninists in China and elsewhere, thought intellectuals could be remolded.

"While uniting with them educate them" was the philosophy behind Mao's style of united front. To Stalin, on the other hand, a united front was a calculus of power, pure and simple. For Mao, what took place *within* a united front was almost as important as its overall effectiveness against the enemy of the moment.

Stalin called his wartime alliance with the U.S. and the U.K. a united front. The purpose was simply to beat Hitler and his allies; he was not trying to change the American and British social systems. Mao's united front with Chiang against the Japanese had a double point: to beat Japan and also to chip away at Chiang's position while supposedly working in harness with him.

Mao had a softer, more patient, but ultimately perhaps less compromising political technique than Stalin. And the teacher in him never died even when power was his.

At the end of 1956 Mao made a statement that he might logically have made years before: those in the CCP who had stood in his way in the late 1920s and early 1930s were Stalin's boys. That he did not say it earlier showed the strength of his lingering awe for the Russian tyrant.

To say it, even so late, was a neat move. In one fell stroke he poked a spear into Stalin's corpse *and* put a fresh feather in his own cap as the CCP's rightful chief.

* * *

Weeds appeared among the flowers. In Wuhan a big student movement arose. In the sweltering heat of mid-1956 it reached a peak with vast demonstrations at which a prominent slogan was: "Welcome to the Nationalists! Welcome to Chiang Kai-shek!"

One flower may really have been a weed. A celebrated sociologist, Fei Xiaotong, educated in England and the U.S., wrote an article in *People's Daily* that declined to embrace the rules of Mao's game. Mao's speech calling for all-out blooming was like "early spring weather," Fei observed dryly; "sometimes it is cold and sometimes it is warm." He pointed out that "blooming flowers could easily perish from the frost."

Such deep-rooted skepticism—which was widespread—was probably more disappointing to Mao than the straightforward dissent of those who asked for an open parliament and a free press.

Mao ordered the flowers cut, in part because of pressure from Liu and other colleagues. First he brandished—in a speech of early 1957—a distinction between two kinds of contradiction. Those within the ranks of the people; those between the people and the enemy. It was a slippery distinction.*
The ambiguity of it hung like an intimidating black cloud over the PRC for almost all of Mao's remaining twenty years.

Fei had been wise to be skeptical. By late 1957 many an academic who, a few months before, had spoken up with hope and self-importance rising in his chest, was now cleaning the toilets next door to the offices of those who had been less bold. Ding Ling, with whom Mao had had a hot-and-cold relationship, was scrubbing floors at the building of the Union of Writers.

"The present social system of our country," ran Mao's same speech, "is far superior to that of the old days. If this were not so, the old system would not have been overthrown and the new system could not have been set up." The tone had changed. The remark was almost plaintive. Certainly it was defensive, and not entirely logical. What had gone wrong?

---

*A hoodlum in a Shanghai park demonstrated how slippery the distinction was. When caught trying to rape a woman he defied the police with the angry question: "What do you mean by interfering? This is a contradiction among the people—it has nothing to do with you." The police, puzzled, left him alone.

Mao in his optimism had overestimated how far he had by 1956 molded China into one organic family. "The driving wind and rainburst form of mass class struggle has basically concluded," Mao had felt. But he later changed his mind. Exactly such struggle he would go on unleashing at intervals for the rest of his life, whether "class" was really at issue or not.

Mao also carried into the Hundred Flowers movement a flawed idea of free discussion. Some mental cut and thrust was needed as a safety valve against the rigidities of dictatorship, he believed, and to ensure for China a new generation of lively minds. So far so good.

But the buds were to swell and open according to a formula that the gardener held in his pocket. Free expression was not to be a quest for truth. It was to be therapy.

Not everyone in the Politburo saw the point of the Hundred Flowers call (nor had they all shared Mao's bustling mood of late 1955). Liu and others were not happy about having the structure of CCP rule criticized in public orgies. Mao alone thought it valid to invite non-CCP people to rebuke the CCP.

Even when Mao pulled back in early 1957, it was not a sharp enough reversal for some. Senior figures apparently *left the hall in protest* as Mao spoke from the rostrum in February. And a fight ensued over whether the text should be published. Liu was absent from pictures of the meeting that *People's Daily* published. So were five other members of the Politburo, including Zhu De.

A key buttress of Mao's faith in the future fell away beneath the winter snows of 1957. The change he had pushed through in the *social system* was a success. The land was collectivized; a new psychology was appearing in the villages. These transformations seemed irreversible.

But Mao had less success in molding a *political system*.

He went out on a limb to summon dissent. Then he waved it away. The result was a wary, even sullen intelligentsia. In the story of Mao-in-power, the affair of the Hundred Flowers was the first of a series of zigzags, all in search of a political system that would do the impossible. Handle conflict in a democratic way yet still within the framework of CCP tutelage. Evoke lively debate among the citizenry yet with the goals fixed in advance.

* * *

At the tense midpoint of 1956 Mao did a characteristic thing. He got out of Peking, even though the capital's weather was more pleasant in May and June than that of Wuhan, where he went. And he took to the water, even though his colleagues tried to stop him.

"Everyone has a streak of subjectivism and Chairman Mao is no exception," Deng muttered. "Despite everyone's being in disagreement with his going swimming, he insisted on doing it." It was not a case of a dip in a pool. The 62-year-old Mao swam the Yangze at Wuhan.

A first effort took him twenty kilometers through that fierce waterway. He set out from the Wuchang part of the tri-cities and landed on the shore of the Hankou part. It took him two hours. Dripping from the muddy water, he sat down to a plate of the famous Wuchang fish, then took up a brush:

> Just then a drink of water in the south,
> Now a taste of fish in the north.

Other lines of this poem hinted at the mingled daring and frustration in his heart in mid-1956:

> Let the wind blow and waves strike,
> This surpasses an aimless stroll in the court.
> Today's leisure is well spent.

He could not resist a comparison of himself with Confucius, as if he was rippling not only his physical but his political muscles:

> Standing by a stream, the Master once said:
> "Life—like the waters—rushes into the past."

Well may Mao have evoked Confucius, for his swimming did seem a bid to put him in the tradition of a ruler showing his personal worth. Mao gave a modern twist to an old pattern. Emperors had shown their worth by fine calligraphy, or by nobly turning away from lust. But never by swimming.

That Mao's mind was also on economic development was suggested by the second stanza of "Swimming." He referred to a new bridge being built between the two hills that guard each bank of the Yangze at Wuhan:

> Breeze shakes the masts
> While Tortoise and Snake hills are motionless,
> A great project is conceived—
> A bridge will fly across
> And turn a barrier into a path....
> Were the goddess still alive,
> She would be amazed by the changes on this earth.

One cannot but feel that Mao's fascination with *changing* China may have gone along with a daunting feeling that the tough old monster was not easy to coax into new ways.

Mao made a second swim while at Wuhan. It covered twelve kilometers (downstream with the current like the first one). A third swim had him weaving through the piles of the half-finished bridge. The ruler was blessing the fruits of his people's labor.

He lingered in south China (until the riot at Poznań turned Poland upside down, and a revolt began to bubble up in China's own backyard of Tibet). He turned up in his old haunts at Changsha. He swam the Xiang River.

He was trying to think things through, in detachment from the daily concerns of his office in Peking. And he was easing strain by his favorite method: merging himself with nature.

* * *

Mao was in a dappled mood when the Eighth CCP Congress met in September 1956. It was the first congress since 1945, and China's progress in eleven years had been impressive by any measure. Yet Mao could not get his own way on all points.

Delegates from fifty-six foreign Communist Parties were in the hall as Mao struck a gavel to open proceedings. In fact, China's prestige was high abroad. Passages of speeches from the rostrum that referred to China's international achievements were often applauded by the delegates. Those claiming domestic triumphs were less often applauded.

For Mao's taste the congress was too complacent. To be sure he won some victories. Defense spending was cut. Deng—whom Mao then liked—was promoted to a new and important post as general secretary of the Party. This was handy insurance for Mao against the formidable power of number two man Liu.

But the congress did not endorse Mao's "leaps" and "waves" approach to the economy. It put its trust in steady plans. Even more irritatingly, it reined in the cult of Mao. In the Party constitution of 1945 the CCP was said to be "guided by the thought of Mao Zedong." The phrase was struck out of the 1956 constitution. Of course the congress was influenced by Khrushchev's dethronement of Stalin seven months before. One more black mark, in Mao's book, against Khrushchev.

Under the surface the first big cracks in the CCP's unity had begun their terrible career. The historic faith was still intact in the congress documents. Quarrels stayed within limits. And Mao put up with criticism. (Recall only that Li Lisan and Wang Ming were allowed to be reelected to Mao's Central Committee.) But fissures existed. Two of them would within a decade yawn like caverns.*

*A third, a bit less serious, concerned Peng Zhen. He was close to Liu. Deng was promoted by Mao above him. Peng Zhen did not like this. He was never close to Mao thereafter and in 1966 Mao purged him (see pages 309 and 314).

General Peng was disgruntled. He was demoted in the Party, though he held on to the defense ministry. "I am old, out of favor and of no importance to the Chairman," Peng grumbled. It would be surprising if Mao had forgotten that his son had died in Korea while under Peng's bombastic command. At any rate it was all too clear that Mao was grooming Lin Biao to balance Peng. That particular pot would boil over in three years.

Liu sniped boldly at Mao for the first time. He had the stature to do so. Mao was now a politician with a mixed record, no longer a solitary hero carrying the whole revolution in his head as he trod the mountains.

At the Seventh Congress in 1945, Liu's report mentioned Mao's name 105 times. At the Eighth, a mere four times. The phrase "collective leadership" was never off Liu's lips. He tried to damp down Mao's ardor for political gymnastics by saying the basic political battles in China had been won and the job was now an administrative one. He said straight out what many an economic planner would have liked to shout from the rooftops: "What was done to win the revolutionary war cannot be applied to China's construction."

With nonchalance Liu explained why "thought of Mao Zedong" was taken out of the constitution: "Chairman Mao's leadership over the whole Party was established at the time of the Seventh Congress. Even if we don't talk of Mao's thought now, everyone will still know about it." Liu added a very gray remark: "Besides, if one is always repeating something so that people get accustomed to hearing it, it does not serve any purpose."*

Mao knew full well that Khrushchev's attack on Stalin had put in question his own supreme authority. Deng, then close to Mao, sounded defensive when he remarked to a Youth League audience: "Chairman Mao has never said that he could not make a mistake." The minister of communications (non-CCP) spoke up: "Socialist democracy ought to exceed capitalist democracy. The president of a capitalist country has a term of three or four years. . . . Who knows how many years Chairman Mao will want?"

Mao did think about stepping down in early 1957. He compared himself to an opera star, and wondered aloud if he was not getting too old to sing his

---

*A rare glimpse of how a CCP meeting worked came in a later fight over a passage in Liu's report to the congress. Mao did not like two sentiments in it. (Liu said the class struggle between workers and capitalists was basically over, and that the chief remaining contradiction—"between the advanced socialist system and the backward productive forces of society"—had to do with the economy.) Liu's defense was that "everything was done in a hurry" and "there was no time to revise them." Certainly Mao did not read the report in advance. And apparently Liu himself did not go over it thoroughly. Yet this report was graven in stone the moment the congress adopted it. If that could happen with a major document at the well-organized Eighth Congress, the mind boggles at what whoppers must have survived the screening process during the Cultural Revolution.

arias well. But he did not step down. He muted his demands on the machinery of Party and state, while staying head of both.

Toward Russia he was cautious from the rostrum. But behind the scenes he chided Moscow. He decided to receive Mikoyan and the Polish leader Ochab jointly. It was a mischievous deed. During the conversation he leaned heavily to the Polish side. He even praised Gomulka, whose name was a curse to the Russians.

Observed Mao to the Polish first secretary: "It seems that China and Poland have been keeping company for some time without even knowing it. It is good company and we are glad of it." Mikoyan was furious. Ochab was so encouraged that he spoke up there and then in criticism of Moscow. Mao was instigating an argument between the two foreign leaders in his own office.

Mikoyan objected to Ochab's calm analysis of the Poznań riot. Ochab retorted that Poles knew more about what was going on in Poland than Russians did. Mikoyan then exploded. "People who voice such anti-Soviet ideas can only be regarded as enemies and treated accordingly. *The same goes for those who listen to them.*"

Ochab, embarrassed, shook hands with Mao and walked out of Mao's room.

But Mao rose and went with the Pole. Mikoyan was left to splutter. Wiping off the rest of the congress, he flew back to Moscow the same day.

Before 1956 was over Mao used a word soon to be famous among Chinese typesetters. "Revisionism" should be opposed no less than "doctrinairism" should be. This was arcane but important. Stalin had been judged doctrinaire. Mao was pointing out that an opposite error existed.

It was a snowflake out of season, but that one flake would become a blizzard.*

* * *

By early 1957 Mao was like a Persian carpet-weaver who sits down with threads of various colors and does not know what pattern will appear until the rug is finished. Six threads he had to weave in relationship with each other. More weeds than flowers had sprouted in the garden. A balance should be kept on Stalin. The Polish uprising could not be condemned. The warning from Hungary must, however, not be forgotten. He must draw

*Mao said oddly to Ochab: "We also have our Gomulka in China, but he has never been expelled from the Party. The Party keeps him in the Central Committee, and while they do not always agree with him, they often ask his opinion." Was Mao making a theatrical, wounded reference to himself, and his frustrations in the CCP?

back gently from the brink of a Chinese cult of personality. And the Chinese economy must be pushed ahead with all possible speed.

For some months Mao strove to orchestrate a reasonably open debate on these issues. But the pressures in the Party against doing so were strong. And the Hungarian case had planted a seed of doubt in Mao's own mind about how far criticism from outside the Party should be allowed to go.

"Certain people in our country were delighted by the events in Hungary," Mao said in his speech on the handling of contradictions. "They hoped that something similar would happen to China." A sad statement. For Mao himself was by no means opposed to the Hungarian rebellion at first. Like a dishonest maiden, he dallied for a while, then cried rape later.

And when he turned against the Hungarian rebellion, he misapplied its lesson to China. "Capitalist restoration" *was* a possibility in Hungary. Hardly so in China. Yet Mao, haunted by Hungary, for the rest of his life spoke as if it was.*

"If what you say is right," he said with passion to a conference of communicators in March, "you need fear no criticism." But it seemed a big "if." The theory of two kinds of contradiction was a flexible tool. How could one be sure from one day to the next that one's opinions would be judged within the bounds of *non*-antagonistic contradictions?

And could Mao be sure that a middle path existed between Nagy's Budapest and Stalin's Moscow?

Mao began to pull in his horns. At home he ordered "rightists" tracked down. The student movement at Wuhan he referred to as a "little Hungary." Abroad he was soon singing the praises of Kadar, Moscow's new monitor in Budapest; twice within a year he feted him in Peking. He revealed, in talks with the Hungarian leaders, that during the 1956 crisis he had sent an urgent message to Khrushchev urging quick military action against the Budapest "revisionists."

His sympathy for Poland evaporated. In April he had announced that he would visit Warsaw during the coming summer. But he abruptly canceled the trip—it would have been the only visit of his lifetime to a country other than Russia—and by late 1957 he was talking in militant terms about the need for unity in the socialist bloc and loyalty to Moscow as its leader!

In Peking 1957 was a year of unity because Mao compromised. The economy did not "leap" in 1956 as he had hoped. His experiment in free expression within a Marxist economy lost momentum. Both setbacks made many

---

*Edgar Faure, raising the topic of Hungary with Mao soon after the uprising in Budapest, found that the topic "seemed to touch the Chairman on the raw."

of Mao's colleagues feel justified in murmuring "I told you so." Mao drew back into line with them.

But not fully. In his own mind nothing could be the same after the de-mythologization of Stalin. His awe for the Moscow-based faith was not as it had been. Something had clicked within him. He was going to walk a path that would be more unabashedly Chinese.

His doctors had not allowed him to eat eggs or chicken soup for three years because Russian doctors had said they were bad for an older person. One day the Russian doctors changed their minds, and his own Chinese doctors, like lap dogs, changed theirs. He could eat eggs and chicken soup again. Mao vowed in the wake of this incident that he would entertain no more blind faith in Russian ways.

When he had been painted with Stalin, he complained, the Chinese artists always made him a bit shorter than Stalin.

Mao did mention these pinpricks. Yet he went ahead with policies that showed his faith in Moscow's ways was not yet dead. For the moment he swept much under the rug. He had been too much in awe of Moscow; but he declined to say so.

If Liu thought the plateau of 1957 offered space to settle down, he was mistaken. Both he and Mao were preoccupied with questions of economic development. But the "how" of the economic issue would divide them. Both were shaken by the Hungarian events. But whereas Liu thought a better standard of living was the best guarantee against any such danger in China, Mao gave a higher priority to moral renovation.

In the middle of 1957—which Mao later called a bad year—he wrote a beautiful and astonishing poem. "The Immortals" was about his first wife, Yang Kaihui of Changsha. As clouds gathered around him, Mao dived away into a happy stretch of his personal past, and linked it with doom, and yet again with glory.

He addressed the lines to a woman who, like Mao, had lost her spouse to Chiang Kai-shek's sword in the 1930s. All four had known each other in the CCP in Hunan. He used a play on words to refer to Yang (the name can mean "poplar") and to the woman (whose name can mean "willow"):

> I lost my proud poplar, and you your willow,
> Poplar and willow soar lightly to the ninth heaven.

Mao then reached for an old legend about Wu Gang, who searched reck-lessly for immortality and was condemned by the gods to cut down a cassia tree on the moon. As fast as Wu Gang chopped the tree, it sprang back to its original shape, and so he had to go on chopping for eternity.

> Wu Gang, asked what he has to offer,
> Presents them humbly with cassia wine
>
> The lonely goddess in the moon spreads her ample sleeves
> To dance for these good souls in the endless sky.

Mao linked heavenly blessings with the march of justice down on earth. The "tiger" here is Chiang; the tears are of joy:

> Of a sudden comes word of the tiger's defeat down upon earth,
> Tears fly down from a great upturned bowl of rain.

It was romanticism run wild. Heaven, personal bliss, glorious deeds, suffering, all together in a jostling bundle.

"The Immortals" was not the only sign that Mao had been thinking about his first marriage. A few weeks after writing the poem he summoned to his study the nursemaid from the Mao-Yang household of the 1920s. Mao became nostalgic during his two-hour conversation with Chen Yuying. "Seeing you today, it seems as if I have seen Kaihui again." Tears welled up in Mao's eyes, according to a version of the talk made available in Peking. "Why not come to Peking every year?" he suggested. He tacked on a public rationale for his personal wish: "To see how construction is advancing here."

Jiang Qing had come back from the Russian hospital earlier in the year, but she was far from well. Mao took her on some of his trips, yet things did not go smoothly. In Nanjing it was too hot. In Qingdao it was too wet and she caught cold. Mao bundled her back to Peking, while he stayed in the northern port to plan new moves to expose "rightists."

* * *

In his 82 years Mao went to only one international conference. It was a summit of world Communist leaders in Moscow in the late autumn of 1957. Mao flew in to head the Chinese delegation. He also joined in celebrating the fortieth anniversary of the Bolshevik Revolution. And he had his second encounter with Khrushchev.

At Moscow airport he praised the U.S.S.R. warmly. Yet several times during the visit he subtly used the word "people" in order to avoid saying that Moscow had helped the *CCP*. "The Chinese people have received tremendous sympathy and generous assistance from the people of the Soviet Union."

Mao felt entitled to strut a little. Certainly he was going to make known some views that he knew Khrushchev did not agree with. But—like Khrushchev—he was in the mood for unity. He played a big role at the conference.

It is not too much to say—as some East Europeans later complained—that Mao and Khrushchev pulled all the strings between them.

Mao went out to the Lenin Hills to make a speech to Chinese students at Moscow University. "Our socialist camp should have a head, and that head is the Soviet Union." If Mao was on the international stage for one of the few times in his life, that did not mean he had lost all traits of the provincial. As he began his remarks to the students, Mao asked how many had difficulty understanding his Hunan accent. A majority put up their hands. So—to a Chinese audience—he gave his speech through a fellow Chinese who turned his phrases from Hunanese into Mandarin!

Mao at several moments during the summit deferred to the Russians. Gomulka, after a talk with him, came away mumbling of his "disappointment" with Mao's insistence on "Communist conformity." The Yugoslavs were disgusted with Mao's loyalty to the Soviet line on authority within the bloc. Nor did Mao speak up in public for his Hundred Flowers policy. He—like Khrushchev—had been cowed by Hungary.

Peace and war were on Mao's mind, in a double way. Two weeks before he flew to Moscow, the Russians had signed an agreement to help China get a bomb.

Mao might not have gone to the Bolshevik celebrations if that backdrop had not existed. His talks with Khrushchev were heavily on defense. Two days after the first session, a high-level Chinese military group quickly flew from Peking at the invitation of the Soviet defense ministry. Mao still needed Russian help.

But Mao did not agree with Khrushchev on the *issue* of peace and war. He talked of nuclear weapons lightly, as he had to Nehru in 1954. This shocked both the East Europeans and the Russians.* "The east wind prevails over the west wind," Mao declared in a phrase that was soon famous. He meant that it was time for the socialist bloc to be more assertive against the U.S. A bloc led by Russia, yes, but a more militant bloc.

Those who heard Mao felt that the Soviet "Sputnik" of recent days had impressed him deeply. On arrival at Moscow airport he remarked: "The launching of the first man-made earth satellite by the Soviet Union is no simple feat. It marks the beginning of a new era of man's further conquest of nature." There was still in Mao a touch of the May Fourth intellectual

---

*Mao's choice of words also shocked Khrushchev, who was evidently a shade less earthy than Mao. In arguing that a nuclear war could be survived, Mao apparently said: "The years will pass, we'll get fucking and produce more babies than ever before." Khrushchev was sitting beside Sun Yat-sen's widow when Mao made the remark. She laughed. Khrushchev primly summed up: "He should have watched his language." Mao was often crude in a naturalistic way. Khrushchev had his own variety of crudeness, as in the description of Jiang Qing as "Mao's nice mattress."

dazzled by the promise of science. A socialist bloc armed with Sputniks, he felt, could thumb its nose at the imperialists.

In private Mao baited Khrushchev. He urged Khrushchev not to get into disarmament talks with the West. But if Mao and Khrushchev were a meter apart on policy toward the West, they were a kilometer apart on the roots of their defense thinking.

"If the Soviet Union is attacked from the West," Mao urged on an astonished Khrushchev, "you shouldn't counterattack—you should fall back."

"What do you mean 'fall back'?"

"I mean retreat and hold out for a year, two years, even three years."

Mao was thinking of Russia's World War II retreat to Stalingrad. Khrushchev was gasping. He explained to Mao that the retreat from Hitler had been *forced,* and also that the next war would not resemble World War II because of nuclear weapons.

"If you fell back to the Urals," Mao calmly advised, "then we Chinese could enter the war." It was a case of ships passing each other in the night, in three ways.

Mao's efforts to cope with his own relative weakness against an enemy had taught him the value of a strategic defensive that was simply not part of the Russian mental world.

Mao did not fear nuclear weapons—of course he knew less about them than Khrushchev—and he believed that they are potent only if they are feared. Otherwise the deterrent does not deter.

Above all, Mao was playing for time. His aim was to build China up to be at least the equal of Russia and America. Until that time—still a long way off—it was desperately important that he prevent Russia and America from colluding together in any kind of alliance against China.

* * *

Mao talked a lot to Khrushchev about his Chinese colleagues. According to Khrushchev most of them came off badly. Gao Gang was the extreme case: "You couldn't even mention his name in Mao's presence." It was all a reflection of the frustrations Mao had been going through in Peking, though it was interesting that he now felt them sufficiently a thing of the past to be mentioned to Khrushchev.

About only one colleague did Mao enthuse. "See that little man there?" he said to Khrushchev as he pointed to a member of his delegation. "He's highly intelligent and has a great future ahead of him." It was Deng. In fact the bullet-headed Sichuanese had three futures ahead of him—two of them cut short by a Mao who changed his mind about his abrasive colleague. But that is a later story.

Khrushchev joined in the fun and told Mao that Bulganin was not doing a good job. Mao asked who might replace him. Khrushchev suggested it would be Kosygin. "Who's this Kosygin?" Mao inquired. He knew as much about him—nothing—as Khrushchev did about Deng. Khrushchev introduced Kosygin to Mao. The two went off into a corner to talk. Kosygin did replace Bulganin. Mao's meeting with him eight years later in Peking would be the last he ever agreed to have with a Soviet leader.

For all Mao's militancy on behalf of the socialist bloc in Moscow, an idea of another stripe was rising inside him. He saw a deflation of the historic faith of Marxism. "I think there are two swords," he had said back in Peking. "One is Lenin and the other Stalin." The image showed that Russia was still the cradle of his Marxist thought.

"The sword of Stalin has now been abandoned by the Russians," he went on. "As for the sword of Lenin, has it too now been abandoned to a certain extent by *some* leaders of the Soviet Union?" Mao answered his own question: "In my view, it has been abandoned to a *considerable* extent."

The qualifications he made showed that the scorecard was not yet totaled on this crucial tussle between faith and a void. "Is the October Revolution still valid?" Mao left this question hanging. It hung in a succession of varying ways over the nineteen years he still had to live.

These remarks had been made *before* he went to Moscow. While pretending to sip his vodka in the Kremlin, he played a game fully as cunning as the anxious Khrushchev darkly believed him capable of.

15

Tinkering with the System (1958–1959)

"By 1957 he was a different man," a Burmese who knew Mao from the early 1950s recalled. "He brooded more, showed signs of old age, was slower in his movements." The two of them talked atop the Gate of Heavenly Peace. "Mao's eyes were far away. He reminisced about the Korean War. . . ."

After the difficult year of 1957, Mao, on his return from Moscow, put hope into 1958 by ordering a Great Leap Forward.

He swept 500 million peasants into the soul-sharing collective life of 24,000 people's communes. He tried to more than double the speed of economic development. He got the Chinese people to believe for a moment that the revolution was not, as it may have seemed, a form of rule pressed on them from above, but a bright flower of moral choice.

"After I've stayed in Peking for a long time," he sniped at a conference of officials in the capital during January, "I feel my brain has become empty, but as soon as I leave Peking there is something in there again."

He went down to Nanning in a defiant and self-possessed mood. He swam in the Harmony River which winds through the southwestern city. He strolled among the orchids in South Lake Park. He felt in touch with the real China.

"I have said this ten thousand times, but to no avail," he burst out in anger at the persistence of bureaucratic ways during a conference in Nanning. "Anyway, I do have some seniority and I should be informed," he declared petulantly at another point.

"For two years I have not read your documents," he told his economic planners, "and I do not expect to read them this year either." He was impatient with the slow grinding of bureaucratic structures. He wanted more spontaneity from below.

It is good to pull down city walls, he provocatively told a senior intellectual who had wept when Peking's walls were razed. It is good to demolish elegant old houses. Mao was so strident that it was clear he was trying to get rid of much more than old walls. He was doing battle with a world view which he thought unworthy of the times.

Water was for Mao the symbolic element of the Great Leap Forward. "We have to wash our face every day" was his phrase in ordering a cleansing of Party ranks. "Pour cold water on them," he said of officials who were getting arrogant. He spoke of "germs" and of "washing away" stale accumulations.*

He took to the water himself. Seven times he swam sizable distances in the Yangze at Wuhan, to wide publicity. The current was a challenge; the water made the skin shine. In 1957 Mao had felt restless, like a man who has not bathed for a long time. In 1958 relief came. Mao splashed and scrubbed.

The Mao of the late 1950s never rested for long from chewing on the question of who was with him and who against him. "I am exploring now with comrades from the localities," he said at a meeting after finding out that weeds outnumbered flowers in his garden of forced growth, "just how many people actually disapprove of socialism."

The year 1958 began for Mao in 1956. The call for a Hundred Flowers had been a disappointment; the intellectuals had let Mao down. He would now trust only in the energy of the untutored rank and file.

"If young people don't put pressure on older people," he declared to a government planning meeting in Peking, "older people won't progress." The intellectuals were mostly old and grubby with the stains of pre-1949 society. Youths were arising who would be purer—"blanker"—and more ardent for a new social order.

"It's like stacking wood," the man from Music Mountain summed up to the same audience. "The last pieces to be stacked attain the top."

To a degree, what Mao did from 1958 onward had its roots in his unfulfilled ideas from earlier years. Yet he was also reacting to the Russian way, and to China's efforts up till then to echo it. Mao began to do battle, too, with a phantom: the gap that reared between what was emerging in new China and what Mao had expected would emerge.

There was one more root to Mao's tinkering with the system—a thickening sense of his own mortality.

*   *   *

"It's like raising pigs," the ex-farm boy said of his Great Leap Forward. "The bone structure is formed in the first four months." The aim of the Great Leap Forward was to "build the bone structure."

*"Germs have no superstition and are full of energy," he remarked to the Eighth CCP Congress in 1958. "They do not respect anyone. Isn't their fearless spirit much stronger than that of certain people?"

The Leap was indeed a concept of development, not a clear, agreed, detailed plan for development.

Colossal paradox that Mao, son of May Fourth, created during the Great Leap Forward a mood that was nearly religious. WE SHALL TEACH THE SUN AND MOON TO CHANGE PLACES, ran one slogan. WE SHALL CREATE A NEW HEAVEN AND EARTH FOR MAN. As workers were pressured to stay at factories through the night to fulfill swollen quotas, they saw a notice on the wall: THE ACHIEVEMENTS OF A SINGLE NIGHT SURPASS THOSE OF SEVERAL MILLENNIA.

It was naïve but it was catching. Even life in prisons did not remain untouched. For one prisoner (who later left China) the Great Leap Forward was symbolized by a letter from his wife announcing that, to spur the steel drive, she had donated the couple's iron bed to the state.

In the same prison, to help the drive to kill flies, each prisoner was given a quota of fifty per day. Extra flies could be stockpiled and used to barter for cigarettes.

Mao's spirits were lifted by the Leap. However reserved some of his colleagues were, however resentful many Chinese people later became at how their own sincere efforts had been manipulated, Mao was personally rejuvenated by the new policies of 1958.

"Our nation is like an atom," he ventured in an image that may have reflected his recent talks with Moscow on acquiring nuclear weapons, "and after the fission of the atomic nucleus of our nation, such formidable thermal energy will be released that we shall do things we never could do before."

At his office in South and Central Lakes he swatted flies. Outside his cottage in Hangzhou he nabbed the odd mosquito that crossed the path of his night walk. He regretted he was not able to catch rats (with sparrows they made up the "four pests"). "No one in the past few millennia," he remarked in a fresh comparison of himself with China's supreme sage, "not even Confucius, had the ambition to eliminate the four pests."

Mao's head was swelling along with the statistical estimates.

Did not the building of the Great Hall of the People in ten months (after Soviet advisers declared the task impossible) show that a true Communist spirit was arising in China? "Did they need material incentives?" Mao asked of the 12,000 people who put in twelve hours a day, rather than the standard eight, to build it. "Did they want a few extra yuan? . . . They didn't want them, these people didn't want them." Mao was enormously excited by this step beyond socialist morality toward Communist morality. "This is not merely 'to each according to his work,' " he declared, "but it also involves Lenin's great idea of a 'Communist Saturday.' "

One night, after visiting some factories, he wrote a verse full of enthusiasm at the vital will of the grass roots, and full of frustration at the inability of China's organization men to harness it:

> Only in wind and thunder can the country show its vigor.
> Alas, the ten thousand horses are all muted.
> O Heaven, bestir yourself, I beseech you,
> And send down men of many talents.

Another night in the summer of 1958, Mao picked up *People's Daily* and read a news item that electrified him. Schistosomiasis had been wiped out in a county of Jiangxi Province not far from Mao's old base on Well Mountain.

He was so excited he could not sleep. At dawn he got out of bed and shuffled to his desk. A warm morning breeze stirred, the first rays of sun touched his window. He fixed his eye on the southern sky and wrote a poem.

He pictured the bad old days, when snails and leeches seemed to own a dispirited land.

> The waters and hills displayed their green in vain,
> Even the ablest physicians were baffled by these pests.
> A thousand villages were overrun by brambles and men were feeble;
> Ghosts sang their ballads in a myriad desolate houses.

The present moment he viewed in expansive terms:

> Now, in a day, we have leaped round the earth
> And inspected a thousand Milky Ways.
> If the cowherd [a constellation of stars] asks about the God of Plague
> Tell him that with joy and sorrow he has been washed away by the tide.

"Farewell to the God of Plague" goes on in such images of water and growth and nature's blessing. Through it all is the Promethean vibration of the Great Leap Forward:

> Green mountains turn to bridges at our wish,
> Gleaming mattocks fall on the Five Ridges, heaven-high....

* * *

The Eighth CCP Congress went into a second session, during the summer of 1958, in a different mood from that of the first session in 1956. Mao was out of his cage.

"I once asked some comrades whether we live in heaven or on earth," he told the startled delegates. "They all shook their heads and said we live on earth." Mao the monkey had another view. "When we look at the stars from the earth, they are in heaven. But if there are people in the stars, when they look at us, wouldn't they think that we are in heaven? Therefore I say that we live in heaven as well as on earth."

Mao spun the same web of paradox in asking "Are we gods?" and "Are we foreigners?"*

There was a point to all this, and over the next decade Mao hit China with its four-sided weight. Nothing is what it seems. Flux is the only true reality. The future does not exist "out there" but must be seized within the present. Chaos is the midwife of most good things.

"In the Yangze River each succeeding wave pushes the preceding wave forward," Mao remarked one day. "All things are undergoing change." This was not so much a view of history as a denial of any view of history.

"There is no pattern for straw sandals," runs a Hunan saying. "They take shape as you weave them." For the rest of his life Mao ruled China as if he were weaving straw sandals.

Mao claimed that the Great Leap Forward "broke down superstition." He had in mind the "superstition" that foreign countries were better than China, that China must accept indefinitely its backwardness, that what seemed to be true *was* true.

Mao's definition of superstition was getting very broad indeed. In 1919 it had meant religion and thrall to ancestors; the meaning of feudal superstition was then all too clear to everyone. By 1958 it seemed to mean any shackle on the pure will of the moment.

"Those who attack the people's communes," he complained in a marginal note, "have brought out this scientific principle evolved by Marx [in *Critique of Political Economy*] as a magic power against us. Aren't you scared by this magic power?"

Was even Marx, now, one of the superstitions to be fought against?

Mao did begin to put Marx gently in his place. "Marx was also a human being with two eyes, two hands, and one brain," he reminded a Party session. "Not much different from us—except that he had a lot of Marxism in his mind."

Had not Marx failed to make revolution? Did not Lenin surpass him in this respect? "Marx never undertook China's great revolution," he said to clinch the point. "Therefore our actions have also surpassed Marx."

The Great Leap Forward did not do away with magic power. It substitut-

---

*"Man will probably change into another being," Mao also remarked. "By then the earth will no longer exist. The sun will have cooled." These thoughts may have reflected Mao's reading of Ernst Haeckel, the nineteenth century German exponent of evolutionism. Late in his life Mao said he had been strongly influenced by the ideas of "four Germans: Hegel, Marx, Engels, and Haeckel."

ed *Mao*'s magic power for that of all rival ways of thought, including part of Marx's.

*   *   *

If Mao had doubts about goals, he had fierce convictions about how to proceed. He felt that experience had taught him the secrets of political action.

- Exploiting contradictions is the way to obtain and hold on to power.
- Balance is an illusion and even bad; disequilibrium is a more creative state of affairs.
- It is by "waves" that progress is made.
- Nothing is gained if change comes by mere fiat from above, without the stirring up of the masses, whose own enthusiasm gives life to the change.
- Struggle purifies; it is not just a way of getting what you want, but the holy sacrament of politics.
- Those to be trusted are not the experts but the innocents, the amateurs, the lowly, anyone who has a heart bent to the public weal.

"When we become a modernized, industrialized, and highly cultured great power fifteen years hence," he told the Eighth Congress, "we may possibly become too cocky and raise our tail sky high." It was a strange mixture of overoptimistic prediction and awareness that success would have a dark underside to it.

The ardor of the Great Leap Forward, in the case of many Chinese, was inspired by a vision of an imminent modernized future. Steel output would rise eightfold in fifteen years. Britain would be surpassed. Cars would abound.

But for Mao the battle, as well as the goal, was of fundamental importance. If Mao was a utopian, his utopianism had to do more with the journey than with the destination. Something wonderful would happen to people's souls on the road, even if it was not too clear where the road led to.

Statistics he used as metaphor. To be sure, many exaggerated figures were given out simply because euphoria was permitted a ransom on the truth. Yet Mao's own philosophic approach to statistics also had an influence on the unbelievable documents put out during the Leap.

The Chinese language lends itself to a nonliteral view of statistics. "Ten thousand" in Chinese often means no more than "thousands" or "a great many" in English. Mao's own mind reinforced the tendency. "Ninety percent are with us." It was no more than a self-injection of morale.

Mao would say that a certain task should be done in two years, or else in four, or failing that in five. The numbers were whips, not calculations.

Mao now believed in the swing of the pendulum as a philosophic truth. In a talk on dialectics he took the example of rest and rising. "An old saying runs: 'He who has slept for a long time thinks of getting up.' Sleeping transforms itself into awakening; awakening transforms itself into sleeping." The old saying was Taoist.

One day Mao called in a scholar for a talk. It was Professor Fei, the sociologist trained in the West, who had bloomed cautiously during the Hundred Flowers. Mao did not want to give up on Fei. "Can you change a bit?" the dictator asked the citizen.

It was a poignant question, which showed that Mao was not simply a dictator.

Fei explained that he was set in his ways and caught in a circle of two hundred top Chinese intellectuals who tended to reinforce each other.

"Don't deal with that two hundred," Mao riposted. "Find another two hundred—go among the workers and peasants and search out two hundred there." Fei doubted that it would work.

"Genuine friends are to be found where there are workers and peasants," Mao burst out.

Mao hated specialists of any kind; the Leap was a celebration of the amateur ideal.

An *intellectual* specialist seemed to Mao a particularly arid specimen. The semi-intellectual loved to scorn, and yet at the same time vie with, the professors who crossed his path.

In one talk at Hankou he denounced expertise, distinction, and high rank, by listing all the historical figures who had done great things without benefit of education, office, or age. "Comrade Fan Wenlan"—he interrupted himself to turn toward a well-known scholar who was listening to the talk—"am I right? You are a historian. Please correct me if I am wrong." Without a pause Mao swept on: "Marx did not create Marxism during his adulthood or old age, but in his youth. Lenin was only thirty-two when he founded Bolshevism. . . ."

Five or six times over the years Mao made a pretense of deferring to old Fan in this way. Fan was not able—or else did not feel it apt—to say one word in reply on any occasion. Mao liked to show that he knew much history *and* to thumb his nose at the historians at the same time.

"The proletariat must create its own army of intellectuals," he laid down in a tough speech after the wilting of the Hundred Flowers, "in the same way that the bourgeoisie created its army of intellectuals." No goal mattered more to old Mao than this one.

There was a flaw in it: the intellectual vocation was linked with the rise of the middle class; it could not survive the destruction of the middle class. Farm hands did not *need* historians. Life at the blast furnace may not have *lent* itself to a subtle novel. What *use* was the study of French literature?

Mao summoned "proletarian intellectuals" into existence like a man ordering dishes from the kitchen. But they never came.

* * *

Groping for a Chinese Way, Mao took up where he had left off in Yanan. The compromises that had intervened—with domestic allies in order to win power, with Russia in order to gain time and aid—he put behind him during the Leap.

The very term for commune, *gong she*, harks back to an ideal of primitive communism as old as China itself. Any Chinese, on first hearing the phrase *ren min gong she* (people's commune), could sense its meaning without any reference to Marx or Lenin.*

"Philosophy comes out of the hills and the valleys," Mao reiterated. He had not talked that way since his struggle against 28B in the 1930s.

"The Way prevails in the state," Mao remarked to a startled audience of high officials. The term is a Confucian one for a truly moral politics. Mao relocated his Marxism within this noble, if elitist, Chinese tradition. The transcript shows that Mao's audience laughed when he introduced the Classical phrase. For some faithful Marxists it was no doubt nervous laughter.

One day a colleague pointed out gently to Mao that "there is no Marxism in Sun Zi's *Art of War.*" Mao was outraged that a Chinese Communist could dismiss so mechanically a sage from China's rich past. Shaky as his view may have been, Mao felt there *was* Marxism in Sun Zi.

Or did he really mean there was Sun Zi in Marx? And that this enabled him to use Marx while dwelling with Sun Zi?

"China has its own language," he remarked at the Eighth Congress. "The pronunciation of the words 'communism' and 'imperialism' is basically the same in Russian and English. But our Chinese pronunciation is completely different." With such a linguistic analysis he had in spirit already left the Soviet bloc; the Soviet Union was, after all, just a part of the rotten West.

In criticizing Russian economics, Mao went far toward Confucianism and away from European Marxism. "We still need to study whether the Chinese Way meshes with Chinese economic laws. *In my opinion, if it does generally speaking, that will be all right.*" He was ready to put the Chinese Way above concrete economic results. It was in the Confucian tradition to do so.

---

* This was by no means true of other Communist terms—for instance, *jie ji* (class)—which did not build on anything in the Chinese past.

It was not in accord with European Marxism, which is *based on* economic laws, which knows no "Way" that is other than a reflection of economic laws.

In asserting that everything has two sides, Mao went to extremes during 1958–1959. Doubts are good, he remarked to a gathering of local politicians, though he did not say why, and so is failure. He urged the convening of meetings to which good *and bad* people were to be invited. "If there are no bad people, there will be no good people."

"It was good for Taiwan to fire artillery shots," he told a meeting in November 1958, "for otherwise the militia could not have been organized so quickly." This comment on the Taiwan Strait crisis was like saying illness is a good thing because it gives the doctor a chance to show his prowess.

Lowliness is always a good thing, he kept on telling those who had risen high. He was delighted when a report reached his desk that a boy near Canton had stumbled on a method of exterminating destructive ants. "The whole world couldn't find a way to control the white ant," he pointed out to the distinguished delegates at the Eighth Congress, "but a young student in Guangdong who only attended middle school found a way."

Mao even began to assert that America was a good thing. "Walk on two legs," he urged a bunch of officials in November 1958, "with Russia's revolutionary fervor and America's practical spirit." A couple of months later he found a precedent for the Leap in American history. "It must be considered a Great Leap Forward," he reasoned, "to have become first in the world for over a hundred years" (*sic*).

He went so far as to remark that "extinction of the nation" was one of the apparently horrible possibilities that nevertheless should be seen dialectically.

All this was shocking to China's elite. It did not seem Marxist.* It spurned the precious Chinese (and Leninist) value of order. It did not issue in concrete policies. It contained none of the optimism that is meat and drink to Communists.

Nothing in the Mao of the Leap period seemed more outrageous than his hearty assurance that splits in the CCP were a good thing. "There are always splits in the world," he remarked to the Eighth Congress. No one could deny it. But the image Mao used suggested that splits were nature's mode of renewal. "It is merely metabolism!" he told the delegates. "Every year there are splits, every month there are splits, like the death of cells." He seemed to love the very word "splits."

---

*Though Mao felt his Leap was Marx-inspired. "I recently met a friend from West Germany," he remarked in the spring of 1959. "I said to him: 'Your Marx has completely neglected matters in his own home—he has been so busy with matters in *our* country.'"

Mao's faith in the healthiness of splits was about to be put to a terrible test.

* * *

The experiment into which Mao had bullied China did not work. An evening of euphoria gave way to a morning of dismay. Soon the Great Leap Forward looked more like a miserable lurch to one side.

As therapy, the Leap was not without benefit. Each generation must find its own excitement, and 1958 provided some for millions of young farmers. Local initiative was sparked. Communal spirit grew. The ordinary person felt anew his Chineseness. And a new framework of rural government—fusing work life and civic life—came into existence.

But as economic policy the Leap was a disaster. China lost five years on its new long march to modernity.*

Grain output fell. By 1960 there was widespread hunger for the first time in Mao's China. Grumbling in the ranks of the peasant PLA turned to minor revolt in five provinces. Mao's predictions on steel production and the time needed for agricultural mechanization proved absurdly optimistic.

A cruel cut for Mao was the resurgence of capitalist habits. As food grew short, farmers who had grain and vegetables on hand pedaled into the towns and sold them on the black market at exorbitant prices, then spent the proceeds in orgies of un-Maoist conspicuous consumption.

The ups and downs of the sparrow summed up a lot. It had been Mao's idea to declare sparrows one of the "four pests." Did they not eat precious grain? Was it not exciting to see the 600 million Chinese people, in response to a slogan offered by all-wise Peking, hunting down pests that impeded economic progress?

But the war on sparrows was not very wise, for these birds eat the enemies of grain as well as grain itself.

Insects hit China's crops like a tornado. Quietly Mao accepted a redefinition of the "four pests." The sparrow was reprieved. Bedbugs would face the fury of the masses instead! (Rats, flies, and mosquitoes held their place in the pantheon of evil.)†

The Leap was a brilliant success in that 600 million responded with impressive loyalty to Mao's summons. It was a painful failure in that Mao's schemes were brittle and ill-coordinated.

---

*Deng Xiaoping is said to have criticized Mao's Leap with the remark: "A donkey is certainly slow, but at least it rarely has an accident."

†One bizarre economy measure in the cities, introduced with impressive efficiency, was that contraceptives were to be washed out and re-used; but when they were pegged up on the washline to dry, children came and stole them, mistaking them for balloons.

Put the two together—high trust, low results—and we see why the Leap left a gaping wound in the Chinese body politic.

"My mind has changed too," Mao said a bit sadly, as criticism mounted in late 1958. He realized that the commune was too big to digest in one gulp. It required an equalization—rich villages sharing all they had with poor villages—which simply aroused too much opposition. Such a leveling "would be banditry, piracy," Mao himself admitted in an irritable speech during February 1959. So he accepted a retreat to the brigade—a smaller unit—as the operative unit of ownership for the new order in the countryside.

"The brigades *are* the communes," he snapped. It was a breath-taking juggling with words. "Everything must be done gradually," he purred like a cat which has just taken its paw out of the casserole.

One recalls the Chinese proverb: "The chicken thief is posing as a pillar of the community. He has not stolen a chicken for three days."

Whether in pique or under pressure from colleagues, Mao in mid-1959 gave way to Liu Shaoqi as head of state, while retaining the supreme job of CCP Chairman.

Mao could confess and defy in the same breath. "Whoever says that such a broad social movement can be free from any defect," he declared, "must be a wishful thinker, or a tidal-wave watcher, or a bookkeeper, or simply an antagonist." It was a wild, sweeping, defiant remark, and vintage Mao. He hated bookkeepers—they reminded him of his father. He despised those who lived in fear of the next tidal wave. He was all too quick at discerning the shape of an antagonist.

Blunt reality poked through the paper walls of Mao's optimism. A blast furnace in every backyard had seemed a marvelous way to push up steel production *and* community consciousness. Peking University built its own furnace, which gave Mao special pleasure. Perhaps he had cracked the nut of academic haughtiness open at last?

But an ugly blast furnace on the lovely campus of the university where he had been cold-shouldered in 1919 did not turn out to be an effective means to any goal. The steel it spat out was of pitiable quality. Mao's long battle to put an end to the gap between hand and brain was still not won.

The whole idea of the Leap, ironically enough, was a classic case of an intellectual trying to remake the external world by a force no stronger than his own overheated imagination.

"Even if there's a collapse," Mao mused to a meeting as the Leap sagged, "that'll be all right. We'll rebuild. The worst that will happen is that the whole world will get a big laugh out of it."

His frankness was still mixed with defiance: "If you don't join me in carrying it through, I'll go on by myself, right to the point of being expelled from the Party—even then, I'll go and file a complaint with Marx."

Amidst the strain of 1959 Mao retreated to the hills. It was just weeks after he had resigned as chief of state, days after Khrushchev had torn up the Russia-China nuclear agreement, and the eve of a terrible showdown with a key colleague. He chose Hunan.

For the first time in 32 years he saw Music Mountain. He went to the farmhouse that had been confiscated from him in the debacle of 1927.

Mao stood like a statue before a photo of his mother and father. "They would not have to die," he murmured at length, "if they were attacked by the same diseases these days." He seemed to be thinking of his own age as well as of the PRC's progress in health care. "Medical facilities were very poor at that time," added the 66-year-old Mao. "They died although they were not very old." (His father died of typhoid at 52; his mother of tuberculosis at the same age.)

Mao went to his parents' graves, which in recent years had been cared for—a traditional rite in a nation now shifting toward cremation—after having been torn up and scrawled with insults in the Nationalist terror of 1927.

A pine branch was held out to him. He took it in heavy silence. He held it to the graves and said: "Those who went before us had a hard time in order that the next generation might be happy." Then he bowed low in reverence*
before the tablets.

His words were the warmest reference he ever made to his father.

At night Mao sat alone by an oil lamp as he had done in defiance of his father fifty years before. He wrote a poem. It is a *lu shih*—an age-old form—like many of his verses. In "Music Mountain Revisited" the Leap-style boldness was by no means unalloyed.

> Like a dim dream recalled, I curse the long-fled past—
> My native soil two and thirty years gone by.
> The red flag roused the serf, halberd in hand,
> While the despot's black talons held his whip aloft.
> Bitter sacrifice strengthens bold resolve
> Which dares to make sun and moon shine in new skies.
> Happy, I see wave upon wave of paddy and beans,
> And all around heroes homebound in the evening mist.

* *Ju le i gong* was the august Chinese term used by an eyewitness to describe Mao's reverent bow.

As in other poems, Mao rejoiced at the new society that was taking shape. But for the first time his sense of triumph was flecked by a melancholy at the cruelty of *time*. He cursed not only the mean days of the past, I think, but the very march of the days.

The picture of "heroes homebound in the evening mist" added to the impression of a man painfully aware of the downward drift of his own life.

So did the arresting phrase "bitter sacrifice." Not only boldness—Mao's fond theme since youth—but also *suffering* had unlocked the door to a new society. Bitter sacrifice was the emotional pivot of the poem.

Escorting Mao at Music Mountain was an eager young local politician. He looked like a homely scoutmaster. He had been head of the CCP in Mao's home county of Xiang Tan. Mao took to him, as if reaching down for a younger hand to grasp, amid the bitter tensions with Politburo members of his own generation. The Hunan politician's name was Hua Guofeng.

Mao sought out the brother of his first wife, Yang Kaihui, and a long-time girlfriend of Ms. Yang, for an intimate talk. The talk was not publicized. But the 38-year old Hua was present at Mao's side.

Prime Minister Munnich of Hungary came to Peking while Mao was away in the Hunan hills. The highlight of his program was to be a meeting with Mao. "Somewhere in the countryside," was all the Chinese protocol chief would tell Munnich of Mao's whereabouts, "hard at work on ideological and philosophical matters." The Hungarian grew irritated. Even Stalin, "the living god," he murmured to his aides, was less mysterious than Mao.

One day as the visit neared its end Munnich, a gourmet, was in the middle of a Peking Duck lunch when he was told that Mao was waiting for him. "The boss can wait a few minutes," snapped the Hungarian between mouthfuls. "I waited long enough to hear from him." But that was not the Peking style. Munnich was tactfully overruled; within minutes he was in Mao's study at South and Central Lakes.

As if recharged by his stay in the south, Mao was polite and masterful. "We have a new president," he began, pointing to Liu Shaoqi, who stood up when referred to.* The atmosphere seemed, for the moment, all sweetness and light.

*   *   *

Mount Lu is a cool oasis of beauty 4,000 feet above the blazing Yangze valley, but Mao knew he faced trouble as he drove up to meet his Central Committee colleagues there in July 1959.

---

* Liu's perspective on Mao's stepping down as head of state is suggested by a remark of his wife's. "Daddy's very busy," she said to her children one day. "He has no time for rest. Chairman Mao has now washed his hands of the concrete affairs of state, and handed them all over to your father. You must not disturb him."

He sat in a wicker chair and gazed out over the ridges, his eyes enclosed deep into his face. Before the battle began he wrote a poem. July 1 was the anniversary of the CCP's founding, but on this July 1 his mind was reaching beyond politics.

> Perching as after flight, the mountain towers over the Yangze;
> I have overleaped four hundred twists to its green crest.
> Cold-eyed I survey the world beyond the seas;
> A hot wind spatters raindrops on the sky-brooded waters.
> Clouds cluster over the nine streams, the yellow crane floating,
> And billows roll on to the eastern coast, white foam flying.

Mao again had immortality in mind. The yellow crane is a legendary bird that does not die. A pavilion to it exists a few miles from Mount Lu. An ancient sage who attained mortality was said to fly by this hill astride a yellow crane. Mao ended "Ascent of Mount Lu" with two transcendental lines:

> Who knows where Magistrate Tao has gone?
> Could he be tilling the fields in the Land of Peach Blossoms?

Tao was a fourth century official who, like Mao, was also a poet. He retired from office before he grew old, to become a hermit and write a utopia called "Land of Peach Blossoms." Mao may have been reflecting on some past simplicities now lost, or thinking of retirement, or his own resignation as president of the PRC, or musing on a cosmic harmony that went beyond any particular social order.

Within hours he had a fight on his hands about the social order of 1959.

Defense Minister Peng Dehuai was an able, flawed man. He looked like a bulldog and had little learning and fewer graces. His forthrightness showed itself early; as a boy he kicked over his grandmother's opium stove, and was ostracized by his family as a result. His soldiers revered him, but he was not an easy colleague, as Zhu De was. Blunt where Mao was crafty, Peng did not always grasp the subtle indirection of Mao's military tactics.

"Who wrote the book you're reading?" someone asked Peng one day in Yanan. "*He* wrote it," replied Peng as he looked up from the draft of Mao's *On Protracted War*. "He also wants to publish it!" This was the essay—it quickly became a classic—that Mao wrote in nine days during 1938. "A book written by an individual can only be published in his own name," Peng said petulantly to his visitor, "but not in the name of the Central Committee."

Peng was only four years Mao's junior. They had been together since the days on Well Mountain. Peng had seen Mao make mistakes and did not regard the Chairman as higher than other mortals. He jibed at Mao's expanding girth at Yanan. He referred to Zhu De as the father of the PLA long after it had become *de rigueur* to call Mao its father.

By 1959 the atmosphere at the top of the CCP was too poisonous for Peng's freewheeling bluntness to be taken in stride by a Mao bent on a willful, unpopular new policy line.

The CCP had for decades been an organization in which human relations were paramount and casual. Mao used to sit around and chat and smoke for hours with Zhu, Liu, Peng, and others. They had shared the simple items of daily life. All this broke down gradually during the 1950s, but it was on Mount Lu that it was buried.

"I am of the view," the defense minister said to a subgroup of the Central Committee meeting, "that the people's commune has been set up too soon." This cast a shadow on Mao's fond child.

"The commune in Chairman Mao's home area has actually not brought about so big an increase in output last year as claimed." Sacred soil! "The Chairman also paid a visit to that commune," Peng went on, "and when I asked him what his finding was, he said he had not talked about the matter. *I think he had.*" This was a direct challenge to the veracity and authority of Mao.

Peng did not act alone. Allied with him were powerful military men including the chief of the General Staff of the PLA. The PLA was a peasant army, and this senior officer felt he could assure the Central Committee that the peasants were being pushed too fast by Mao's Leap.

Remnants of the old 28B group, including Zhang Wentian, who had lined up with Mao at Zunyi, also stood with Peng. Zhang had recently been ambassador to Moscow. Like Peng—who grumbled about Mao on a tour of East Europe in the spring—Zhang saw the Leap as a departure from the Moscow-based historic faith of Marxism.*

The Leap had been a mistake, said Peng and his friends, and the responsibility for it should be shared by everyone, "including Mao Zedong." Ideological phrases were no substitute for economic expertise, they insisted. Dishonesty born of euphoria was a disease in China and ought to be stamped out.

Mao was shaken. He wrote of his anguish to Jiang Qing, who was then holidaying by the sea at Beidaihe, and sent her a draft of the reply he planned to make to Peng. Ms. Jiang phoned Mao to say she was flying im-

---

* Mao was "brilliant," Zhang observed privately, but like Stalin in his later years, he was "very strong-handed in rectifying people." Peng's quiet comment on Zhang's remark showed just how bold (and accurate) the opposition to Mao could be in the 1950s: "All through our history, the first emperor of every dynasty has been at once brilliant and strong-handed."

mediately to Mount Lu to be at his side during the confrontation.

"No," said Mao. "The struggle's too acute." She came anyway, bringing her camera to take snaps of the pines and the pavilions. Willfully, she sat in on the tense sessions. Instead of calming Mao, her presence dismayed him.

Mao had not felt such stress for years. He couldn't sleep at all. The night before he was to reply to Peng he took three doses of sleeping pills, but still paced up and down waiting for the dawn. Like an Oriental King Lear, he came tormented to the morning session.

"You have spoken so much," he began vaguely. "Permit me to talk some now, won't you?" He wandered—repeating steel figures like the rosary—which showed how shaken he was.

Yet before his forty minutes were done Mao had made a shrewd speech. Peng later confessed that he himself had been as rash as Zhang Fei—an impulsive and successful hero of ancient times—but not as cunning. Mao correctly said near the end of a wheedling speech: "I am like Zhang Fei, who, although crude, was careful at times."

Mao retreated without being abject.

"The mess hall is not our invention," he observed in pretending to get out from under a leftist totem. "It has been created by the masses." He embraced a modified form of this communal dining scheme which had annoyed millions of peasants. Mao went halfway toward accepting Peng's charge of "dizziness" in a quest for the impossible.

Mao asked for solidarity. It was not characteristic of him; he liked to be a knife, not a trowel, in any situation. But he had done quite enough slicing for the moment.

"Being basically not good at construction," he confessed in a humble contribution to solidarity, "I knew nothing about industrial planning. . . . It is I who am to blame."

His choice of words in confessing error was cunning. "In regard to speed," he remarked, "Marx also committed many errors." And again: "I have seen Lenin's manuscripts, which are filled with changes. He too made mistakes."

Mao fought to rescue the kernel of his Leap from the husks of acrimony. He demanded that the failures not be exaggerated. He insisted that boldness in finding a Chinese way to communism was still what the country needed more than anything else.

He trailed his spiritual coat before the delegates, whether in pure anguish or in part merely to win the day.

One criticism of Mao for sacrificing human beings on the altar of unreachable production targets had quoted Confucius. "He who makes human images to bury with the dead," the sage once declared in opposition to

burying clay figurines of people alongside a corpse, "should have no posterity." In his sleepless nights Mao had been torn apart by this veiled accusation that he had lapsed into human sacrifice.

"Shall I be deprived of my posterity?" Mao asked the Central Committee. "After all, one son died at war and the other is insane."

It was a scarifying moment. The shadow of his remark reached into a
realm far too personal for a Chinese political meeting. (Was he also having
a crack at Peng, in whose care his son had been when killed in Korea?)

The hills were alive with rumors that if Mao dismissed Peng from office
he would have a military revolt on his hands. Now that the tide was turning
against Peng, Mao faced the rumors head on.

"If the PLA follows Peng," he said, turning to the senior military figures
present, "I'll recruit a new Red Army and start all over again." Many a
stomach churned. As he stormed that he would "go back to Well Mountain," some must have recalled his threat in 1940 to "go back to Music
Mountain" if the sniping at Jiang Qing didn't stop.

Mao wisely gave the sweating generals a way out: "But I think the PLA
will follow me." At that a number of key military figures rose and pledged
their allegiance to Mao.

Peng fought on—he was not a supple willow like Mao—even though he
did not have enough troops. He began to speak bluntly about the danger of
a "Hungarian rebellion" in China and hinted that the Soviet army would
come in if that occurred. Mao asked that the meeting adjourn.

Peng lost his very losable temper. He recalled a Mao-Peng feud in Yanan
that had gone on more than a month. "In Yanan you fucked my mother for
forty days," he shouted in a Chinese expression which I here translate literally.* "Now I've been fucking your mother for just eighteen days and you're
trying to call a stop—but you won't."

Standards had slipped. Reeling from this session of confrontation, Zhu
De was heard to mutter: "And to think we all ate out of the same dish in the
past!"

Within a month Peng was out. Lin Biao replaced him as defense minister.

Mao's victory did not come easily, and he was not able to clinch it during
the sessions on Mount Lu. He had to call follow-up meetings. He wrote earnest marginal notes on documents that flew among the leaders, and subtle
letters to divide off foes from waverers.

"Why did you get yourself entrapped in that military club?" he wrote to
Zhang Wentian. Then he struck a softer note: "Since you say you respect

*The Chinese phrase can simply be translated "Fuck you."

me, and you have phoned several times, if you want to come to my place for a talk, I am willing to talk with you."

*   *   *

It was no wonder that Mao looked gaunt on Mount Lu. Far from reaching a "Land of Peach Blossoms," he had lost some fundamental ground. His victory over Peng came at a shocking price. After the sessions he was so worn out that he gathered up Jiang Qing and took her with him to his Hangzhou cottage for a complete rest.

The struggle against Peng was more serious than the Gao Gang affair of 1954.

Gao was merely a schemer. Peng disagreed with Mao on basic policy. Gao thought Mao's personal rule had gone too far. Peng's similar view was a bigger challenge to Mao because in the meantime Stalin had been dethroned for this very failing. Gao provoked nearly all the Politburo to oppose him. At Mount Lu, Zhu De backed Peng, Liu was neutral, and almost no one in the Politburo agreed wholly with Mao.*

The ghost at Mount Lu was that of Stalin. For several years Mao had been wrestling with the de-Stalinization issue; the results came in on Mount Lu.

Mao found a Chinese way to cope with the crisis in world communism that stemmed from Stalin's death. But he split the CCP in the process.

In the winter of 1959–1960 Mao repainted Peng as a "rightist." He declared him one with the enemies of 1957. Indeed, Mao made Peng a monster of the imagination who could henceforth serve any purpose required of him.

"Truths are developed from struggles with fallacies," Mao declared during the Peng crisis. The more fallacies he could expose—or imagine—the more truth he felt well up inside himself.

---

*A remark of Mao's about the weakness of the communes may have scared his listeners at Mount Lu more than his belief in their strength. After asserting that the communes showed no sign of collapsing, he burst out: "We are prepared for the collapse of one half of them. After 70 percent collapsed, we would still have 30 percent left. If they must collapse, let them collapse."

16

Russia and Beyond (1958–1964)

"What are poisonous weeds?" Mao inquired of Bulganin during the lead-up to the Great Leap Forward. The Russian was not stimulated to a memorable reply. Mao proceeded to lecture him on the history of the tomato. "One hundred years ago the tomato was a poisonous weed in Europe." Nothing is certain—were not Jesus and Copernicus considered poisonous weeds at first?—except change.

If Bulganin was less than overwhelmed, Mao was only confirmed in his growing conviction that the Russians had lost interest in dialectics. They had come to favor a stable world. Mao was excited by a world in flux.

Was this why the China-Russia partnership went sharply downhill? It explained the *atmosphere* of the feud. And since the disagreements, once they began, were endless in type and number, it may have been the atmosphere of distrust that was crucial. Mao changed gears in 1958—for reasons that in turn went back to de-Stalinization—and soon thereafter Moscow judged him crafty and crazy.

The Russians were correct to be alarmed about the Leap. It was Mao's declaration of independence from Moscow-based orthodoxy. The talk with Bulganin about the history of the tomato was one small sign that Mao was rejecting the tradition of international communism as it had evolved under Soviet guidance. He would seek the bright red tomato of tomorrow among seedlings now judged poisonous weeds by the "undialectical" mind.

Khrushchev sensed what this would mean for Russian interests and for the unity of international communism. Deprived of a shared Marxist faith, the Mao-Khrushchev bond disintegrated like Chinese bean curd turned out of its dish.

Khrushchev came to Peking for a second time just as the Leap reached its zenith. The visit was brief (three days) and practical. Mao had been closeted for several weeks with his military advisers. The immediate issue was a tense situation in the Taiwan Strait. Behind it was the larger one of how tough to be with the United States and how to fight it if war came.

Mao and Khrushchev—flanked by their defense ministers—ostensibly talked about Sino-Soviet military cooperation. In fact Khrushchev's purpose was to restrain Mao.

"Military cooperation" is a stone that flashes a variety of colors, depending on what side it is viewed from. "We needed a radio station in China," Khrushchev later said, "to keep in contact with our fleet." He blandly recalled: "We offered to base our interceptor squadrons on their territory." Mao gave another version of the conversation with Khrushchev. "He wanted to raise a common fleet with us, to control the coast—and blockade us."

Khrushchev correctly judged Mao to be in a hotheaded mood. He feared the Taiwan Strait crisis might land the Soviet bloc in a big war. He wanted a Russian hand on the levers of decision.

Yet he still considered China a firm ally. He fully supported Mao's claim to Taiwan and gave him military aid designed for its capture.

For Mao the problems with Khrushchev ran deeper. China's sovereignty was being trifled with. China's desire to stand up against "imperialism" was no longer shared by Russia. And Mao's Leap was considered a bad joke by Khrushchev. "It's impossible to *leap* into communism," the Russian declared.

Despite Khrushchev's irritated words as early as 1954, it was Mao, more than Khrushchev, who saw the split coming, Mao who walked deliberately into its messy depths, Mao who wanted the break.

Had Khrushchev read Mao's speech to the military conference just prior to the summit, he might have tried to grapple with the Russia-China problem at a deeper level than he did. The speech was not about foreign policy— yet Russia was its theme.

"Today the dogmatists advocate copying the Soviet Union," Mao complained. "Whom, I would like to know, did the Soviet Union copy in the past?"

He wondered why it should always be a question of China copying Russia and never of Russia copying China. He railed against "blind faith in foreigners." He declared straight out that China had a "richer experience" to draw on than Russia.

Khrushchev was approaching Mao on quite a different level from this. The Russian thought he was husbanding a basically sound alliance with a junior partner.

Mao felt himself to be dealing with an identity crisis of the Chinese Revolution.

Three weeks after bidding Khrushchev farewell, Mao shelled the islands of Quemoy and Matsu. This alarmed the world, yet viewed from the Forbidden City it was a sideshow. For Mao's line in foreign policy stemmed from the new look he was trying to give to socialism *within* China.

Increasingly Mao painted the political struggle in colors from the palette of his past life with the gun. "In my view," he said a little defensively, "the rural-areas work style and the guerrilla attitude are still good. In twenty-two years of war they were victorious."

Mao rattled the sword in the Taiwan Strait at the same time that he pushed the Chinese peasants into the biggest social experiment in human history. It was not a link that most Western observers found logical. But it did make sense to this man who saw struggle as the doorway to redemption.

"Every man a soldier," became a theme slogan of the Leap. "The militia must be developed in every people's commune," Mao ordered in September 1958. "Every province must produce light weapons, rifles, machine guns, hand grenades, small and light mortars." A cloud of war hung over the Taiwan Strait, to be sure, but that was not the root cause of this military-mindedness.

Mao frankly admitted that he—not Chiang Kai-shek—triggered the crisis over Quemoy and Matsu. "A few shots" he modestly called his adventure. It was not that he wanted a real war. "I just did not expect," he confessed, "that it would kick up such a storm."*

But an external crisis was fuel to the fire of the Leap. "Besides their harmful aspects," Mao said on the same occasion, "crisis situations allow us to mobilize forces—to get backward strata and middle-of-the-roaders to prepare for struggle."

Nineteen fifty-eight was the year when an aging Mao made the first of several efforts to infuse politics with a military spirit. Of course, it was a throwback to more exhilarating days. Of course, it furrowed the brow of many a planner and alarmed Khrushchev.

"He is lame in one leg," Mao summed up Khrushchev. "He does not walk with both legs." This was his objection to Moscow's inflexibility in political and economic method. "They believe technology and cadres decide everything," he said of the Russians in a defense of his own preference for tossing issues directly to the masses.

Mao's objection to Moscow's world view was summed up in his dislike of the term "complete consolidation," which he pounced upon in Soviet documents. "In the universe and on the earth," he noted, "all things emerge, develop, and extinguish continuously, and cannot be consolidated completely."

---

*Mao himself apparently later took the view that his actions in the Taiwan Strait may have been precipitous. "If we rush," he remarked to a meeting in December 1958, "we may possibly commit errors in international matters."

This was the same philosophy that led him to abandon the steady grooves of the First Five-Year Plan for the wavelike lunge of the Leap.

It was in keeping with Mao's roguish attitude toward Khrushchev that he baptized the first commune with the name "Sputnik."

Moscow's world was a static one; Mao's was in flux. The Russians had sunk into the easy chair of the status quo; Mao could not yet approve of the world around him.

*   *   *

A year later Mao and Khrushchev met again. Further clouds had gathered over the relationship. India and China were fighting on their border and Moscow was tilting to the Indian side. Khrushchev had been supping with Eisenhower on a grand tour of the United States which Mao saw as an exercise in bootlicking. The Russians had also denounced Mao's communes as "madness."

Worst of all, the plan for Soviet help toward a Chinese nuclear weapons capability collapsed amid a spiral of mutual recrimination.

Khrushchev did not wish to go again to Peking; wasn't it Mao's turn to come to Moscow? But Mao would not budge. In a testy atmosphere, the summit got under way in Peking in the autumn of 1959.

Khrushchev had a little tactlessly flown in direct from the United States. He reached the Chinese capital in time for the tenth anniversary of the founding of the People's Republic of China. It was a festive occasion. And by later PRC standards a most international one, with Ho Chi Minh, Kim Il-sung, and many other foreign figures on hand, and Beethoven's Ninth Symphony as the theme music.

But the photos of Mao and Khrushchev together suggested a funeral more than a celebration. The eyes of both men were squeezed tight almost to the closing point. Khrushchev later spoke of "a chill that I could sense as soon as I arrived." Jiang Qing said Khrushchev's visit was "tedious and painful."

To Mao's irritation, Khrushchev praised Eisenhower as a man of peace. Then Khrushchev criticized the Chinese—seldom done at a formal banquet in Peking—as "cocks fond of fighting." Khrushchev infuriated Mao by talking of Russia and the United States as the two powers with a special joint responsibility for securing peace in the world.

Khrushchev even asked again for a radio station on Chinese soil to help keep his fleet churning through the Pacific Ocean. "For the last time, *no,*" Mao said with thunder in his voice, "and I don't want to hear anything more about it."

At Moscow in 1957 Mao had taken the initiative on the issues. Probably again at Peking in 1958, when he had Khrushchev guessing over the Taiwan Strait. But during the 1959 encounter the initiative seemed to lie with Khrushchev. Mao merely sniped from Khrushchev's rear.

"How many conquerors have invaded China?" he asked Khrushchev over tea one afternoon. "Many," he said in answer to his own question, "but the Chinese have assimilated all their conquerors." Khrushchev's doubt as to what Mao was getting at did not last long. "Think about it," Mao resumed. "You have two hundred million people and we have seven hundred million people."

During the same session Mao remarked to Khrushchev—as he had previously done only within Chinese circles—on the uniqueness of the Chinese language. "All the rest of the world uses the word 'electricity,' " he drawled. "They've borrowed the word from English. But we Chinese have our own word for it." Mao had chosen to deal with Khrushchev by tossing out broad, imponderable, unnegotiable themes.

What rankled most with Mao during the 1959 summit was that Khrushchev asked to see Peng Dehuai and came laden with a fancy gift for the purged general! This seemed to Mao to be interference in China's domestic affairs.

Khrushchev's gesture also pointed the finger of blame for the Russia-China crisis uncomfortably close, for Mao's taste, to the Great Leap, which Mao had already been tormented about by Peng and other colleagues.

Khrushchev left for home in an icy atmosphere—and without seeing Peng. No communiqué was issued. Mao never saw him again.*

Mao had had a tough autumn, what with Peng and then Khrushchev. He went (without Jiang Qing) for a holiday on tranquil Hainan island in the far south.

*   *   *

Within a year Russian aid to China ended. It seemed inevitable after the 1959 summit. Yet there were signs that Mao, overestimating his hand with a foreign partner, as he so often did, jabbing Khrushchev with one more barb than the Russian would bear, was taken aback by the speed of the sudden withdrawal of some 12,000 Soviet technicians in mid-1960.

Khrushchev shouted that drunken Chinese (a rare species) had abused the Soviet benefactors. Mao replied that Russian advisers always kept back key plans and information.

---

* "I went to Russia twice," Mao mused to a visitor in 1964, "but I shall never go there again. . . . The Russians have landed us in the shit."

Later, after Khrushchev's fall, Mao suggested to Kosygin that Moscow send Khrushchev to "study Marxism in Chinese universities."

"Better to deal with the French bourgeoisie," Mao snarled. "They still have some notion of business ethics." He had belatedly discovered that Russian products were "heavy, crude, and high-priced."

The outward civilities went on for a time. Mao turned up for the annual Soviet Embassy party to celebrate the Bolshevik Revolution anniversary in the autumn of 1960. But the Twenty-first Congress of the CPSU in 1961— the Soviet Party's first congress since the thunderous de-Stalinization congress of 1956—brought a big open fight. Albania was the topic; China was the issue. Zhou, head of the Chinese delegation, left Moscow in a huff and Mao, most unusually, met his colleague at Peking airport.

In late 1962 Mao took a step that was fatal to the worldwide Marxist church. He announced that power in the U.S.S.R. "has been usurped by the revisionists." That clinched the schism. Party-to-Party relations dried up. Nineteen sixty-three brought a stream of letters about ideological betrayal between Mao and the Russians.

All this was a way of getting the bile out of the system. In fact, the struggle at the level of ideology was just about exhausted. And it was by now a struggle for possession of a corpse—international communism.

By 1964 there was no limit to the number of horns Mao saw on the Soviet devil. "The Soviet Union today is a dictatorship of the bourgeoisie," he declared without a blink at a meeting of planners, "a fascist German dictatorship, and a Hitlerite dictatorship." Once more he reached for a comparison—lame after that with Nazism—with the Western country that he knew a bit about. "They are a bunch of rascals worse than de Gaulle."

There was only one more conceptual step that Mao could take, and he took it in the winter of 1964–1965. *Russia was worse than the United States.*

Both were bad, to be sure, in the eyes of this chauvinist from the Chinese hinterland. But Russia was more deceptive. "The Americans are bastards," he observed, "but they are honest bastards. The Russians are also liars." And the Russians were on the rise, whereas he detected that the American will to dominate was flagging.

A clue to his new thinking came in a disagreement with Deng. When Deng remarked—echoing settled policy—that Asia and the Pacific was the center of gravity of global tension, Mao corrected him and said no, Europe now was. Thus had the American threat shrunk in Mao's eyes, and the Russian one grown.

Mao did the unthinkable. He relabeled China's savior as its bully. For many of his colleagues—not only the fallen Gao and Peng—he had gone too far.

Yet on this issue Mao won support from the alleys and rice paddies. Most

Chinese do not like the Russians. Many educated non-CCP Chinese were against the Sino-Soviet alliance from the start. Even in Taiwan, Mao won grudging, private praise for having broken loose from the avaricious bear.

Nevertheless the Politburo counted most; Mao still had some battles ahead of him on the issue of Russia.

Since Mao uncorked himself so recklessly, one must ask why he had remained bottled up for so long. He later claimed that China had no choice but to follow Moscow in the 1950s. "We lacked experience," he noted. "We could only imitate the methods of the Soviet Union, though we always had a feeling of dissatisfaction with them."

That was not the whole story. Until de-Stalinization, Mao had also believed in a historic Marxist faith with Moscow as its fount.

Wisps of the faith trailed on, as occurs in many religious experiences, beyond the sharp moment of doubt. As late as 1962 Mao showed that the man who had lost faith could still be caught gazing up at the steeple. At a Central Committee meeting he laid down a pair of doctrinal points, then added oddly: "Moscow has announced that these two statements are mine." They were Maoist statements. Mao was proud of them. But still it had struck him, and somehow impressed him, that Moscow cited them as his mental offspring.

*　　*　　*

Mao took a lively interest in the world beyond the Soviet bloc during the early 1960s and he pinned down some marked successes in foreign policy. It was as if the split with Russia in 1960 took a burden off the back of Chinese diplomacy. Instead of being a junior partner in someone else's show, Mao made China its own one-man show on the broadening stage of the Third World.

Seventeen nations recognized the PRC between mid-1960 and the end of 1964. Chinese aid began to flow to parts of the Third World. China glittered in the eyes of those revolutionary movements that felt Russia aspired only to become co-boss of a stable world with the United States.

China strained a few friendships during the Leap. With his disarming ability to recognize, as well as cause, setbacks, Mao observed in a marginal note of 1962: "During the twists and turns of 1959, the whole world turned against China."*

---

* China retained the hand of faithful Albania. But a prison memoir of the period suggests that to an ordinary Chinese the size of the Balkan land made it impossible to take it seriously. "If we 600 million Chinese got together," one of the prisoners remarked, "we could sink Albania by merely pissing on it." After Mao died, official Chinese policy quickly sank to the level of that popular contempt.

Mao more than regained the lost ground in the first half of the 1960s.

"I suppose you know you are talking to an aggressor," Mao said with a twinkle in the eye that bespoke confidence, when Lord Montgomery of Britain spent a lengthy evening with him in 1960. "I have been branded as such in the United Nations. Do you mind talking with an aggressor?" *

India he did not wish to mend fences with. He insisted, against some resistance in the Politburo, on a military showdown in the Himalayas. It was in military terms a brilliant success for China. The PLA dealt the Indians a heavy blow and then withdrew like a bored champion, leaving the Indian democracy enmeshed in a finger-pointing post-mortem.

But Mao, as if demonstrating that his only foreign policy aim was to ward off the world, not to win it, did not follow up his military victory with any diplomatic drive. China's relations with India stayed poor to the end of Mao's life.

Mao discovered Africa. Prior to 1960 he had scarcely mentioned it. Even as he began to take an interest in the continent—and as China achieved striking successes there—his knowledge of it remained dim. Receiving visitors from Algeria in 1964, he had to ask them at the end of the conversation to write down the full name of Ben Bella, their president.

During the same year he had this exchange with a Zanzibari: "What is the population of Kenya? Three million?" The embarrassed visitor informed Mao that the figure was eight and a half million. Nor did Mao's questions about Zanzibar display any firmer grasp. "Is your country in the southern or northern hemisphere?" Mao inquired. "It is actually on the equator," replied the African. "Isn't it very hot along the equator?" was Mao's next question.

This naïveté (perhaps masking condescension) about Africa did not mean that Mao failed to make shrewd private judgments. Despite the huff and puff over ideology, Mao acknowledged in private the real reason why Cuba was leaning toward Russia rather than China. It lacked oil and weapons, and these things Moscow could supply.

Mao was also canny about the basic techniques of exerting influence. In 1964, Romania, edging away from the U.S.S.R., asked for a high-level Chinese delegation to visit Bucharest. Mao was cautious about making any

---

*Mao asked this bantering type of question, which was not as modest as it seemed on the surface, quite often as he grew older. "Aren't you afraid of me," he said to the Thai leader Kukrit years later, "since Chiang Kai-shek and the West have called me a bandit, a criminal, a murderer?" (A moment afterward, when Mao said he was going to die soon, Kukrit said that wasn't possible. Why, asked Mao. "Well, Chairman," Kukrit replied, "the world couldn't afford to lose a number one bad man like you." The remark "pleased Mao mightily. . . . He banged the arm of his chair, rocked with laughter, got up and shook hands with everybody in the room.")

commitments but he laid down: "It would be very important even if we only shake hands with them."

"Are we isolated?" he cried to a conference in echo of John Foster Dulles's dogged crusade to keep China out of international institutions. "I don't feel isolated. . . . Our country has some six hundred million people. Are six hundred million people isolated?"*

The "anti-China" attitude amazed him even more than it irritated him. He assured his less nativistic colleagues—and reassured himself—that the anti-China forces were not large. In 1960 a Chinese exhibition in Pakistan was besieged by anti-China demonstrators. This greatly bothered Mao and he wrote a paper about it called "On the Anti-China Question." His pride in the degree of acceptance the PRC had won jostled with his hurt that some people still seemed to hate the PRC. There was something terribly narrow about his exhortation to his colleagues to "accept the fact that about 10 percent of the world's people will oppose us intermittently over a prolonged period of time."

* * *

Within a matter of hours two big pieces of news erupted in the autumn of 1964. The first was that Khrushchev had been overthrown in the Kremlin. The second was that China had exploded its first nuclear device. Both were triumphs for Mao—and linked in his mind, for both gave a boost to China's pride and independence.

Mao's reaction to Khrushchev's fall showed traces of the ways of thought of a Chinese emperor. Edgar Snow shortly afterward asked Mao if there was any truth to the Russian view that a cult of personality had grown up in China. Some, Mao felt, but probably Khrushchev fell because he had no cult of personality at all!

It was very hard, Mao said, for the Chinese people to get out from under thousands of years of worship of the emperor. Indeed. And hard, perhaps, for even a Marxist Chinese ruler to dispense with it.

Mao kept an open mind about Khrushchev's successors, which was also a traditional thing to do. From a Marxist point of view there was little reason to think Brezhnev and Kosygin would be "socialist" if Khrushchev had been "fascist." Had not the Soviet *system* reverted to an unredeemed condition?

Yet Mao saw the coming of a new leader in more personal terms; and within four months he met Kosygin—the Kremlin's number two man—for talks.

On the night of the A-bomb test, PLA trucks drove around Peking to

---

*Mao was erratic in giving figures for China's population; cf. page 282.

drop a one-page extra of *People's Daily*. It announced the news in red characters three inches high. Next day every shop had a placard in its window: NUCLEAR BOMB SUCCESS.

An earlier photo haunted those Americans who had seen it: Mao sitting at a wooden table at the Lop Nor testing site with Qian Xuesen, the Cal Tech scientist who fathered China's bomb after being harassed by the U.S. government and finally deported in 1955.

Mao was enthusiastic for a Chinese bomb. He personally encouraged Qian and other scientists. He spoke with rare passion to foreign visitors about how China *had* to make the bomb even though the cost to living standards tore him apart.

The warfare Mao knew and believed in was people's war—war as an extension of socialist politics. For a strangely similar reason he insisted on the totally different asset of a nuclear weapons program. He desired the bomb for political reasons above military. Like de Gaulle, he saw it as a guarantee of his nation's freedom of action. Unlike most military strategists, he felt that a few bombs would be enough. Six will do, he said to André Malraux in 1965.

His aim was to "break the monopoly of the two superpowers." He denied the efficacy of nuclear weapons to achieve any worthwhile result when used. They could deter anyone who was afraid of them. But he said this did not include himself. "If you kill all the people and seize the land, what can you do with it?"

So Mao's outlook on defense—tractors plus the bomb—was a logical result of his longstanding axiom that war is an extension of politics. If anyone attacked China, he would lure the enemy in, surround him, and pounce in the fashion tried out against Japan.

The bomb had its role on quite another level. "Yes, we need them," he cried when two high economic officials raised the issue of nuclear weapons. "No matter what country it is, what bombs they are, atom bombs or hydrogen bombs, we must overtake them!"

The 1964 test buoyed Mao. He saw to it that Chinese scientists had every facility to move ahead swiftly with the nuclear program. Just thirty-two months later China conducted its first successful H-bomb test. This was fast indeed; the equivalent step had taken the United States seven years and four months, Russia four years, and the United Kingdom four years and seven months.

*   *   *

Mao uttered many criticisms of United States policy in the first half of the 1960s. He condemned the persecution of American blacks, U.S. control of the Panama Canal, and Washington's expanding network of military bases around the world—"just like an ox with its tail tied to a post—what good can that do?"

Yet he was less bitter against the U.S. than he had been in the late 1940s, if only because a decade and a half later China was less vulnerable. His polemics were sneering in tone, yet curiously detached. They did not compare in emotion with the hand-to-hand battle he had begun to mount with his latest betrayers, the Russians.

An ox with its tail tied to a post could not be as dangerous, after all, as a bear that wandered freely, its evil potential not yet understood.

Mao now expected very little from the U.S., and even began to wonder how much the U.S. expected from itself. Dim as his perception of life in America was, he brilliantly detected the unfitness of the U.S. for a sustained imperialist role.

"The United States devotes its energies to making money," he said to a gathering of intellectuals in 1956. "If nobody else picks up the sedan chair, it won't think of going on foot."

"Imperialism and revisionism have joined hands," Mao remarked at a Spring Festival talk in 1964, "and are beating at our borders." It was an amazing and revealing statement. The two isms were his mental constructs for the U.S. and the U.S.S.R. Mao felt similarly about the two powers. Seat of world revolution? Seat of world reaction? None of it. Both were simply marauders banging at China's door.

It was one more proof of his loss of the historic Moscow-based Marxist faith. It was also a portent of a new struggle within the CCP, for few of Mao's top colleagues felt in 1964 that the U.S. and the U.S.S.R. were on a moral (or any other) par.

Above all, the insouciance of Mao's statement strikes us. Let them come: "We'll return to Yanan," he said. It seemed unwise to defy both powers simultaneously and scorn the politics of using one against the other. Yet that was just what Mao was preparing to do for the second half of the 1960s.

Prudent Mao often was. Modest he never was. For him the main significance of the world's existence was as a standard for China to match and surpass.

17

Retreat (1961–1964)

From 1961 Mao drew back into himself, quizzical in mood, bowing to political and economic reality, though still full of sparks within. The Liu-Deng stress on the politics of order and the economics of results was in accord with the mood of the time. It was less that Liu and Deng clashed with Mao than that they hastened down their own pragmatic path and power accrued to them. Mao did not—perhaps could not—stop them.

As Chairman of the Communist Party, he convened *only one* meeting of its Central Committee between 1961 and 1966! In the Politburo—an unprecedented occurrence—Mao was often gently disregarded. He saw few foreign visitors for the next three years.

Mao knew of the sour feelings toward Peking that flourished in much of China. One story that came to his ears he bravely repeated at a meeting in 1962. "When I hear the rumble of a train going south," a bitter wag in Canton had it, "it sounds like 'Road is bright, Road is bright, Road is bright'; when I hear the rumble of a train going north [i.e., to Peking], it sounds like 'Hope is gone, Hope is gone, Hope is gone.'"

The change of tone was caught by the charge later made against Deng that in the early 1960s he "met Chairman Mao on equal terms and without ceremony." In the press the cult of Mao ebbed. You could read the Party magazine *Red Flag* for an hour and hardly come upon a Mao quote or even Mao's name.

Communes were in effect broken down into brigades. Private village markets were legalized. Managers were given their heads again in factories. Spontaneity was squeezed out of CCP work style. Intellectuals who had been uprooted as weeds in 1957 found fresh soil in the market garden of Liu's and Deng's bureaucracy.

But in this atmosphere the economy picked up. Mao could not gainsay it and he did not try to—at the time.

Mao in the late 1950s told several foreign visitors to "come back and see us after a period of ten years and see whether we have been right or wrong." His colleagues hardly gave the Great Leap Forward one year, let alone ten.

That Mao accepted retreat was only underlined by his tactful denial of it. "We are all good comrades," he remarked sweetly. "It is unimaginable for one to have no regrets," he added in the voice of one who has accepted a bleak outcome.

"It's a case of raising fat pigs in the hall," he told the Central Committee as 1961 began. Consolidation, in a word. The architect must not tinker with the hall anymore; it was time to make use of the hall.

"In everything we will start out from reality," Mao assured the unindulgent, even grim assembly. "We cannot transform what we do not know about," said the man who had tried to do just that.

"I am a middle-of-the roader," he said but may not have believed.

Most of the grievances against Mao stemmed from his self-assertion of the late 1950s. De-Stalinization had untied his ideological moorings. Restless, losing the faith, hemmed in by the file boxes of routine, he had struck out in a new direction.

The weed killing of 1957? Hungary had unnerved Mao. The Great Leap Forward? Mao wanted to get out of the sagging tent of international communism and find Chinese roots for his dreams. The fight with General Peng? Mao saw it half as a fight with Khrushchev's ghost.

Sniping at the cult of personality? Here was the eye of the needle at which all the threads of Chinese politics since 1956 were caught in a bunch. Mao felt that his own will embodied the Chinese Way for his era. He felt able to transcend the rules and leap across the structures.

But Liu, Deng, and others believed in the rule book and could see no safe way to obviate the structures in a land of 650 million.

"They treated me like a dead ancestor," Mao later complained of Liu and the blunt Deng. They nodded at him with eyes glazed. They applauded his words and then did nothing to implement them. They "forgot" to report to him. At a conference they would steer to an opposite side of the room from him to avoid an unsettling query or an acidic instruction.

The fight with Defense Minister Peng had left a nasty taste. Even the circumspect Liu spoke up in 1962 against "ruthless struggles" that end with "merciless blows" dealt to the losers.

The resentment against Mao for demoting Peng came to a head with an intriguing play written by the vice-mayor of Peking. It was about a worthy minister in the Ming dynasty who was fired by the emperor for making honest criticisms. Or was it?

Mao saw at once (though he held his peace for a time) that *Hai Rui Dis-*

missed from Office was a stinging commentary on his own ill-advised dismissal of Peng.

A Peking columnist wrote a story about an athlete of medium talent who, in a delusion of grandeur, boasted that he had broken the Olympic record for the broad jump. An alert reader knew very well who the athlete was.

A satire about amnesia came from the same pen. The author built up a picture of an amnesiac—without mentioning a name—as short-tempered, forgetful of his own past statements, and heading for insanity. "If anyone finds such symptoms present in himself," the piece warned mysteriously, "he must promptly take a complete rest [shades of Zhu De's advice to Mao during the Gao Gang crisis!] and say nothing and do nothing. . . ."

It was all Aesopian, as dissent typically is in the PRC, but it was very bold.*

Mao's speeches of the early 1960s were chastened in tone. He rambled less, as if conscious that he now had less rope to play with. He organized his points with an almost petulant regard for form and order.

"I don't have much to say," he would begin. Or, "Here are six points." He clogged his talk with data as if to prove that he, too, could be a dull expert if he wanted to be.

Edgar Snow, visiting Peking in 1960, asked Mao what were his long-term plans for China. "I don't know," was Mao's lame reply.

"You're being too cautious," Snow came back.

"It's not caution," Mao insisted. "I just don't know; I don't have the experience."

He could hardly hide his errors of the Leap period. In 1958 he had said China would overtake the most advanced capitalist countries in fifteen years. By 1962 he spoke of fifty to a hundred years.

Yet there were barbs in Mao's words too. "Haven't we bungled a lot in the last few years?" he ruminated to the Central Committee's only session in these years, in 1962, leaving his listeners unsure whether the remark was a confession or not.

"Those of you who do not allow people to speak," he burst out at another meeting in 1962, "who think you are tigers, and that nobody will dare touch your ass—whoever has this attitude, ten out of ten of you will fail. People will talk anyway." Mao was in full swing against his favorite target, heavy-handed officialdom.

"You think that nobody will really dare to touch the ass of tigers like you? They damn well will!"

---

*The columnist, Deng Tuo, had his "good name" restored, along with playwright Wu Han (both posthumous), in 1979.

In Mao's eyes, bureaucrats were losing touch with grass-roots opinion. Industrial managers began to strut again as if they owned their factories. Medical workers refused to work in remote villages as a comfortable urban establishment sucked them in. Officials who were supposed to do a stint at manual labor treated a trip to the rice fields as a picnic outing. All this outraged Mao.

As a man, what impressed Mao increasingly was the particular, odd, simple, unpredictable things in life.

As a politician, he lacked patience with the multitude of organizational levels that the PRC possessed.

As a philosopher, he saw no hope for the Chinese Revolution unless the cadres sincerely joined the masses in a duet of shared participation.

Even books now seemed to him just one more badge of authority. "Somebody writes them and then we have these inexperienced kids read them." Without a prior direct experience of life's tussles, "the kids" would become immobilized by stuffing themselves with secondhand knowledge.

One day some Chilean journalists came. A recent Chinese economic exhibition in Santiago had aroused great interest, one editor told Mao, as a preface to a discourse on China-Chile friendship. But Mao had other fish to fry. "It is from your mouths that I first heard that China held this economic exhibition," he said with agitation. Then he aimed a sarcastic thrust at the Chinese officials present in the room: "It seems that my bureaucratism is rather severe."

Mao in his sixties did not cease to be a complex man, but he ceased to be tolerant of the complex organization needed to reform a society of 650 million people. He wanted to be able to see everything with his own eye, to stretch out his hand and feel the texture of the Chinese Revolution.

*   *   *

In 1961, having pulled back from the front rank of rule, Mao wrote more poems than in any year of his life.

One verse was a simple cry of praise for the military virtues on which he was beginning to pin hope for a political revival. A photo of some militia women reached his desk and on it he wrote:

> How bright and brave they look, shouldering five-foot rifles
> On the parade ground lit up by the first gleams of day.
> China's daughters have high-aspiring minds,
> They love their battle array, not silks and satins.

"Reply to a Friend" was a poem of intense yearning, set in Hunan. Mao referred to a legend about Emperor Shun. When this good ruler died the princesses shed such tears that the drops, falling on bamboo, left marks which are still seen in the famous spotted bamboo of Hunan and Jiangxi provinces.

> White clouds are sailing above Mount Qiuyi;
> Riding the wind, the Princesses descend the green hills.
> Once they speckled the bamboos with their profuse tears,
> Now they are robed in rose-red clouds.
> Dongting Lake's snow-topped waves surge skyward;
> The long isle reverberates with earth-shaking song.
> And I am lost in dreams, untrammeled dreams
> Of the land of hibiscus upon which the morning sun also shines.

Mao suffused the geographic features of his native province with wisps of immortality. The princesses lived on through pink clouds cut from their robes. The waves of the lake—Xiao You and he sailed across it on Mao's way to the founding of the CCP in 1921—seemed to be knocking on heaven's door. The island at Changsha where he roamed as a youth was so stirred that its moorings on earth were put in question. Mao himself—in the closing two lines—dreamed of rebirth. Will the trammels not by then have fallen away from him?

"Ode to the Plum Blossom" stood out among all the poems of 1961. Mao said he came across a twelfth-century poem on the same theme by Lu You, and wrote his "Ode" to "counter" it.

The poem was written to nerve the Chinese arm in the emerging struggle with Russia, but Mao had himself in mind too.

> Wind and rain escorted Spring's departure,
> Flying snow welcomes Spring's return.
> On the ice-clad rock rising high and sheer
> A flower blooms sweet and fair.
>
> Sweet and fair, she craves not Spring for herself alone,
> To be the harbinger of Spring she is content.
> When the mountain flowers are in full bloom
> She will smile, mingling in their midst.

Spring was hemmed in by its negation, as Mao felt all good things were. The plum—a symbol for integrity in Chinese tradition—was lonely on its ice-clad rock. Here Mao was evoking China's isolation in the Soviet bloc, and perhaps his own isolation in China.

But if Lu You had seen only sadness on the face of the plum blossom,* Mao found for it a magnificent, though self-effacing, destiny. Because the noble blossom gave up desire ("she craves not Spring for herself alone"), it won a supreme position for itself. Indeed, the "smile" in the last line hinted at immortality.

Isolation, yes, as in Lu You; but whereas Lu You lamented, Mao groped for a redemptive joy.

* * *

Buddhism made a comeback in Mao's conversation and imagery from 1959.

"The high targets," Mao remarked as the Leap began to falter, "are Buddhist idols which we set up for ourselves to worship. Now we must smash them. . . ." He scrawled on a letter of "confession" that General Peng wrote to him after being fired: "If he thoroughly changes . . . he will 'instantly become a Buddha' [an old phrase]—or rather a Marxist."

Urging that cadres should get out of the city and regain humility among the farmers, Mao said they should "leave Peking for four months every year and seek the sutras from the working people." The image came from the novel *Journey to the West,* in which the monkey king goes off to search for the Buddhist sutras.

"Why does the monk knock the wooden fish drum when he chants his sutra?" Mao asked an intrigued Central Committee in 1962. He had again been reading *Journey to the West.* The story goes that the sutras collected in India were devoured by the black-fish demon, who spat out one word each time it was knocked. "We must not behave like the black-fish demon," Mao said. The Buddhist legend made Mao's point that Party leaders should not mince words ("spitting out one word at a time").

He took to praising religious monarchs. Was not Sihanouk of Cambodia, a prince, better than the puppet of South Vietnam, a president? Wasn't Nepal, a kingdom, a more satisfactory neighbor than India, a presidential republic?

A prim girl called Wang Hairong was studying English at Peking Foreign

---

* Lu You's poem read:

Beside the broken bridge, outside the courier station,
Alone, it blooms for no one.
The dusk is sad enough,
But now wind and rain are added.

It does not intend to display itself in the spring,
Or to arouse other flowers' envy.
Once its blossoms have fallen and been trampled to dust
Only its fragrance remains.

Languages Institute. She was Mao's niece, daughter of Zemin.* She came
to see him in 1964. To her shock he urged her to study the Bible and the
Buddhist sutras.

It was no accident that Mao began to talk of Buddhism in the wake of the
clash with Peng. As he lost his faith in European Marxism, he turned back
to Chinese tradition, and showed a new openness toward religion.† He increasingly found a precedent for all good things in China's own experience.
He began to see the past as a moral tale; not the mere fine print of Marx's
historical laws but an eternal, recurring war between good men and bad.

Wang happened to complain to Mao about a classmate who was always
reading *Dream of the Red Chamber* instead of his English grammar. Mao
seemed to stiffen:

MAO: "Have you ever read *Dream of the Red Chamber?*"
WANG: "Yes, I have."
MAO: "Which character do you like in this novel?"
WANG: "None."
MAO: *"Dream of the Red Chamber* is worth reading. It is a good book."

While his niece was busy educating herself to be a cosmopolitan, modern
woman, Mao had just read *Dream* for the fifth time.

Had she read "The Northward March," by the Tang dynasty poet Du
Fu? Wang gave a classic student's reply: "No, it's not in *Three Hundred
Poems of the Tang.*" Mao rose from his chair and went to his shelf of poetry. He found "The Northward March," passed it to the girl, and told her to
read it many times.

"What precautions should I take against its influence?" Wang inquired.

Mao was roused. "You are always metaphysical. Why should you take
precautions? No, no. You should *receive* some influence from this poem. Go
deep into it and then emerge from it."

The Mao of the mid-1960s found his niece at once too conventional (he
told her to rebel more at school) and too trendily leftist (he told her to im-
merse herself more in China's past).

Mao read more about the Chinese past in the 1960s than during any period since graduating from teachers' training college in 1918. In history he
was seeking solace.

Were not Sun Zi's feet cut off at the time he wrote his brilliant *Art of*

---

*She chose to change her name from Mao to Wang.

†Back in the 1950s, Mao had once been with the Dalai Lama at a celebration of the Tibetan
New Year. Told that it was the Tibetan custom to toss pieces of the celebratory cake to the
ceiling as an offering to Buddha, Mao threw his portion of cake aloft, but then with a mischievous grin took another piece and hurled it to the floor.

War? he asked one audience. Was not Han Fei in prison when he wrote his superb *Explanation of Difficulties?* Were not most of the 300 poems in the *Book of Songs* written as cries of rage?

Mao took to dividing the history of the CCP (prior to his own control of it) into five "dynasties"; Chen Duxiu and the others he turned into failed evil emperors. Inevitably he began to compare himself with the successful good emperors.*

Within Mao a sense grew of an impending rendezvous with a gentleman of fate—called "God" one moment and "Marx" the next.

"A while ago the imperialists said the Chinese government would collapse," he said to Algerian visitors in 1964, "but now they don't talk so big. It appears that China hasn't collapsed yet."

But the inner Mao was far from sanguine. "I myself, on the other hand, am going to collapse. I will soon be seeing Marx. Our doctors cannot guarantee how many more years I can live."

A few weeks later four vice-premiers came to discuss the Third Five-Year Plan with him. "Planning must have an objective basis," said the man who had not believed that in 1958. "I am over seventy years old," he went on, "but we cannot rely on what we see of communism shortly before we die as the basis for planning."

"When the atomic bomb is dropped," he remarked to some military officers in midyear, "there is nothing else but to see Marx; since the days of old there has always been death." He struck a note that sounded personal: "When the burden is too heavy, death is the way out."

Edgar Snow, dining with Mao, asked if a TV film could be made of the evening. "There are rumors that you are very ill," the American ventured. "Wouldn't it be well to show the world, on the screen, that the rumors are greatly exaggerated?" Mao smiled wryly. Perhaps there was some doubt about that, he countered, for in fact he was soon going to see God (*Shang di*).

Mao saw his own death coming and he accepted it. "You can't avoid dying," he said to the Algerians. "[At least] no such thing [has happened] yet in China's history."

But as the juxtaposition of his collapse and China's collapse in the talk with the Algerians showed, his own fate and China's were not easy for him to separate in his mind. He had accepted death for the man Mao Zedong. But he had *not* accepted that China might choose to depart from the Maoist

---

*The amazing poem "Snow," which he wrote after the triumph of the Long March, was published for the first time in the PRC in 1964. Its last line seemed to clinch the link between Mao's hunger for the past and his sense of a present moment to be seized: "For truly great men, look to this age alone."

Way after his death. To the military officers he observed: "Each person must be ready with successors."

*   *   *

Mao's face did not grow more interesting with the years—as Deng Xiaoping's did—but became moonlike and less responsive. There were hardly any lines; the eyes became less accessible; the hair took on no new character.

Nurses often hovered as visitors talked with him during 1964 and 1965. The stiffness, trembling, and poor coordination of Parkinson's disease had begun to bother him. Yet he did not become prudent about his health.

He heavily smoked a Chinese brand of Virginia cigarette—a dozen in the course of the evening with Edgar Snow—which by now had stained his fingers and blackened his teeth. He drank a bit of Chinese grape wine, not slowly or regularly like a real drinker, but every now and then.

"When I have a fever I will call you," ran his gentleman's agreement with the physician, "and when I don't, I won't bother you and you're not to bother me."

Disdaining specialists of all kinds, he treated his doctor like a cleaning lady. "I only follow half of what the doctor says," he declared, "and expect him to follow me in the other half."

He lived much as he long had. The style was one of simplicity in the midst of grandeur.

He hated flowers or other decorations in his room. He ate the same few peppery Hunanese dishes. He would slurp his soup and belch after a hearty meal regardless of whether his table companion was Jiang Qing or a foreign head of state.

Yet the setting of his life by South and Central Lakes was magnificent. He took an unassuming pleasure in his quarters—called Small Palace of the Fragrant Concubine under the dynasties—and he had a swimming pool to himself.

His salary in the 1960s was 430 yuan—only double what a senior technician in a factory was making. Mao had no taste for costly possessions. On the other hand, anything he really needed the Party procured for him, and it is hard to take at face value his complaint of 1964: "I can't afford to hire secretaries, but I must."

Though he seemed to have risen above mortal ranks he was still known as "Chairman Mao." A different ring from "Premier Zhou" or "Defense Minister Lin." Why a title as bland as a kitchen chair?

Red China did not, in truth, know quite how to label Mao; but it knew how *not* to label him. He was a general; but a party that controls the gun does not like to use the gaudy professional terms of the military. He became terribly like an emperor; but words could not be allowed to give external blessing to that similarity.

So it was the title Chairman, with its town-meeting severity, that Mao used as he occupied a post which for millennia in China was an assignment of heaven itself. The bland label hid the frightful misfit of a demigod at the head of the committee table.*

Mao became blunt and subjective as many old men do. He took to remarking aloud on the appearance of people who came to visit him. "All are young!" "Very tall!" "She is already more than seventy years of age!"

He would tolerate no sentiment from newcomers. Said a Zanzibari visitor in 1964: "May I be permitted to express my feelings to you? Ever since my arrival in China, I have looked forward to this day. There are no words that can express my feelings."

Mao stared at him and dryly inquired: "Have you read any Marxism-Leninism works?"

Moments later the African was again piling the politeness a little high: "Your works are very readable."

Mao brushed him aside: "I do not have many writings."

The Zanzibari insisted: "No, you have a great many."

Mao simply pulled the plug out. "Well, let us end our conversation there." With a "Good-bye," the session was over.

Mao wrote his own letters. They would often be signed "4 A.M." or "6 A.M."—the morning's proof of night toil.

And unlike many of his colleagues, he read books. In the presence of a visitor he would reach for a poem or a dictionary in order to illustrate or check a point.

"Catch a sparrow and dissect it" was one of Mao's favorite ways of tackling a problem. "Although the sparrow is small, the gall bladder and liver are all complete. Chinese sparrows and foreign sparrows are alike." Intensive study of the small gave him, he felt, valid conclusions about the large.

Policy Mao seldom talked about. Philosophy and work methods—these were his mind's favorite pastures.

Mao had seldom been good at, or fond of, speaking to mass audiences. In the 1960s he no longer tried it. His days of dialogue with ordinary people were over. He dwelt more and more in a world of long-term imagination.

At closed-door gatherings his remarks became acutely personal. He spoke about his early life. He discussed his family members—rare in a Chinese

---

*Bland as the prefix "Chairman" was, its incessant use irritated Liu. "Why is he so attached to calling himself 'Chairman'?" the head of state mumbled. "'Chairman Mao,' 'Chairman Mao.' Have you ever heard anyone speak of 'Chairman Lenin'?"

politician—and drew models from his experience for others to emulate.

Half a year is long enough to be a soldier, he advised a young visitor, not adding that this was the length of time he had spent at the Changsha garrison in 1911. He gave a sharply personal illustration for his favorite philosophic principle: "Everything is one divided into two. I personally am also one divided into two. I was a primary school teacher, [yet] I believed in the spirits."

When it came to his marriages, Mao did seem to be one divided into two. The mother of his Changsha wife, Yang Kaihui, died in 1962, and he sent a letter to the Yangs. "As to the burial," he wrote in traditional vein as a son-in-law doing his filial duty, "let her rest in the same grave with my dear wife." Rather surprisingly—for he had remarried more than twenty years before—he remarked: "Our two families should be considered as one, without distinction among the members."

Some found it challenging, and others found it merely odd, when he speculated about the far distant future. "What will Peking be like 10,000 years from now?" he asked himself at a conference in 1964. At a science meeting he ended with a cosmic poem which defies conclusive analysis ("If the Moon Goddess never marries, who can tie her down?").

"Let me ask you," he said in an effort to make everything problematic during a briefing in 1964, "when Marx was young, did he ever read Marx's works?"

Perhaps some in the audience agreed with his remark a moment later: "To talk about philosophy for half an hour is enough; if you talk longer you would not talk clearly."

Had any major nation ever been ruled by a man so detached from the meat and potatoes of policy, so intrigued by eternal things, so much the monkey with a *tant pis* attitude to life?

* * *

Could it really be true that Mao had cut loose from the tenets of Marxism? Yes it was true. To see the process of Mao's thinking we must plunge for a moment into the cesspool of Marxist conceptual infighting.

Mao found in one stroke a way both to explain past setbacks and to justify a new effort to shake the PRC to its foundations. History could move backward as well as forward!

Had he not been thwarted these past years by a new bourgeoisie? As early as 1962 he began to lay the foundations for this startling case.

For many years Mao held a subtle, and by Marxist standards quite soft, view of class struggle. He insisted that antagonistic (class) contradictions not be confused with nonantagonistic (among-the-people) contradictions. At

Yanan he rebuked 28B for putting too many conflicts into the former category.

In the 1950s he remained reluctant to brand an opponent a "class enemy." He did not put that label on Gao Gang at the time of his struggle against the "independent kingdom" in Manchuria.

Moreover, Mao had taken the view—as late as October 1957—that as socialist power was consolidated, the struggle between classes would die down.

All that changed in the wake of the General Peng affair. Mao revised his definition of class. He came to fling class around as a mere term of abuse. And he came to believe that class struggle was getting *ever sharper*.

This shift of mental gears was to turn Mao into an entirely different man for the last years of his life.*

Soon he was drawing class lines in terms of *attitudes*. "It is important to distinguish between class background and one's own performance, with emphasis on the latter."

Mao's pet idea that 95 percent of the officials were good was solemnly said to be a class viewpoint, when it is nothing more than an arithmetical viewpoint. A faction was absurdly defined as one wing of a class. *The* bourgeoisie was said to have *taken up residence* within the Communist Party!

Mao had one more doctrinal foundation stone to lay for the perverse edifice of ideology he was bent on building: the new enemy at home was holding hands with the new enemy abroad.

"Revisionism" was Mao's word for the slack outlook of Stalin's successors in Moscow. "Right opportunism" was his term for Peng's standpoint. Mao decided they were two sides of the same coin. "It would seem better for China's right opportunism to change its name," he remarked to the Central Committee in 1962, "to Chinese revisionism." How convenient.

The link between revisionism and class enemies came in 1964. "The advent of revisionism marks the ascent of the bourgeoisie onto the political stage," Mao scribbled in a marginal note. "That is the dismal truth."

His new ideas hovered like an odd but not fatal vapor over the Peking scene. Colleagues were startled at Mao's suggestion that class struggle remained fierce, as Mao himself noted, but as long as it remained a matter of words they could live with it.

"Good men who make mistakes," Mao observed during a meeting at the resort town of Beidaihe in the autumn of 1962, "are quite different from men who follow the capitalist road." It was an absolutely crucial distinction.

---

*"To draw class lines is to ferret out the bad elements." This Delphic note—without date but probably from 1964—seemed to catch Mao at a crucial moment in his shift away from a Marxist view of class. Getting rid of bad elements—a political imperative—had taken priority over the analytic task of drawing class lines.

But also a maddeningly elusive one. No one felt the need to pursue its exact meaning for the time being.

*   *   *

A poem of 1963 caught the mood of Mao newly astir. Formally a reply to a poem by an intellectual in the government, it also stemmed from Mao's feelings about his own colleagues and Moscow.

He felt that his enemies were after all just a bunch of insects.

> On this tiny globe
> A few flies dash themselves against the wall,
> Humming without cease,
> Sometimes shrilling,
> Sometimes moaning.
> Ants on the locust tree assume a great-nation swagger
> And mayflies lightly plot to topple the giant tree. . . .

An urgent will to do away with them gripped him again. Would not the cosmos itself join hands with him in the task?

> So many deeds cry out to be done,
> And always urgently;
> The world rolls on,
> Time presses.
> Ten thousand years are too long;
> Seize the day, seize the hour!
> The Four Seas are rising, clouds and waters raging,
> The Five Continents are rocking, wind and thunder roaring.
> Our force is irresistible;
> Away with all pests!

Liu and Deng (pests-to-be) were calling most of the shots, but it would have been surprising if the defiant poem did not bring a frown to the brows of this unpoetic pair of bureaucrats.

One day Mao called in his nephew for a talk. "You seem to have been classified as a progressive," he remarked to Mao Yuanxin,* now a student at Harbin Military Engineering Institute. "What is a progressive? Do you know?" Mao swept on to give the young man his own definition: "A progressive does the work of those who have fallen behind." It summed up Mao's self-image in the mid-1960s.

---

*The son of Mao Zemin, this boy had been conceived when his parents were in prison in Xinjiang Province in the early 1940s, shortly before his father was tortured to death by the anti-Communist authorities who then held sway in Urumqi. Wang Hairong, the student at Peking Foreign Languages Institute, is Yuanxin's sister.

Many colleagues seemed to Mao to have fallen behind. He would have to do their work for them—wrench their work from them in some cases—in order to keep the goal of communism alive.

"We must issue strict orders," Mao remarked elliptically. "There must be an Emperor Qin Shihuang. Who is Qin Shihuang? It is [Liu Shaoqi]. I am his aide." Did Mao mean what he said in this treacherous remark? No, in that the "aide" still had more ultimate power than the "emperor." Yes, in that Mao saw Liu's daily influence outweighing his own.

Mao's juices were flowing again. He may not have been commanding the ship, but he was very active below decks. Swimming in the Ming Tombs Reservoir near Peking during midsummer, he seemed almost jaunty.

The sage who doubted all was about to call down a naïve festival of renewal.

The man in the shadows was going to step to the dais as a demigod.

The leader who liked to bemuse his visitors with speculations on eternity still had in him a burst of Machiavellian diplomacy which would fix a place for China among the top three nations of the world.

The sulking politician who saw Liu becoming a strongman-administrator in the mold of Emperor Qin would soon knock Liu into the rubbish dump of history.

18

The Furies of Utopia (1965–1969)

André Malraux called on Mao. The French minister of culture was on a visit to Liu Shaoqi to present a letter from de Gaulle to the head of the Chinese state, but the afternoon did not quite turn out that way.

Entering a vast chamber of the Great Hall of the People, decorated not with pictures of tractors and blast furnaces but with traditional scrolls, Malraux recognized the "horselike face" of Liu and walked up to him. A cluster of Chinese ministers stood with Liu.

Near them but alone, like a trainer with his acrobats, stood Mao.

Malraux addressed Liu and handed him de Gaulle's letter. Liu did not reply; it was Mao who began talking with Malraux and his colleague, the French ambassador to China. "You've been to Yanan, I believe. What is your impression?" Throughout the afternoon Liu did not get the chance to utter a single word.

"I am alone with the masses—waiting," Mao murmured. It was as if Liu and the others were less colleagues than mere silent witnesses.

On this summer afternoon of 1965 Mao's talk, punctuated by heavy pauses and full of indirection, was pessimistic on the issues. At the same time there was a sense of mastery about him.

He seemed, in Malraux's eyes, like a bronze emperor. A stiff, overwhelming figure, like a titan of legend who has just stepped back to life from a tomb.

As the conversation turned to France's independence from the U.S., and China's from Russia, Malraux happened to use the word "allies." Mao had been still until this moment, only moving his right hand from his mouth to the ashtray at the service of his cigarette. But now he threw both hands toward the ceiling and banged them down again. "Ou-ur allies!" He rolled the Chinese words in sarcasm. "You-urs—and our-urs!"

Nor did Mao let the limousine liberals from Paris get away with any rosy statements about the condition of China. "Neither the problem of industry nor that of agriculture has been solved," he remarked. "The writers are often anti-Marxist."

The French ambassador, trying to inject some hope into the diagnosis, ventured that Chinese youth seemed sincere believers in the line Mao had laid down for them.

"How long have you been here?" Mao shot back at him.

The embattled envoy enlarged on his optimistic impression based on a recent trip through south and central China.

"The things you saw represent only one side of the situation," Mao rejoined. "You didn't notice things on the other side."

So much for a noble Gallic effort to play Voltaire at a moment when Mao, far from idealizing China, felt almost as angry about its condition as he had in the iconoclastic days of the 1920s.

Mao recalled the remark of Kosygin at the Twenty-third Congress of the Soviet Communist Party: "Communism means the raising of living standards." He snorted his disgust: "And swimming is a way of putting on a pair of trunks!" Had the world's Marxists lost sight of the ends for which power had been seized?

"Our revolution cannot be simply the stabilization of victory," Mao added to the Frenchmen.

Small wonder that Liu kept silent that afternoon.

These, then, were Mao's themes as the winter of 1965 drew near. He was a dissatisfied man. And yet a certain cockiness had returned.

He slipped away to revisit Well Mountain—after 38 years' absence—and while there wrote a poem which expressed his mood. The opening lines spoke of unfulfilled yearning:

> A long-cherished wish to approach the clouds,
> Once more, by climbing Well Mountain.

But there was audacious hope, too, in "Well Mountain Revisited."

> We can clasp the moon in the Ninth Heaven
> And seize turtles deep down in the Five Seas.

Everything depended, Mao still felt, on the will of the hero.

> Nothing is hard in this world
> If you dare to scale the heights.

"These days a Party branch secretary can be bribed with a few packs of cigarettes," Mao observed at a closed-door Party meeting, "and by marrying a daughter off to a cadre there's no telling what you can get as a reward." However high Mao's hopes were, they did not rest with the Party.

"There are at least two factions in our Party," Mao added explosively. "The socialist faction and the capitalist faction."

* * *

The immediate obstacle was Liu Shaoqi, who lived with his aristocratic, English-speaking wife in elegant quarters adjacent to Mao's. To the Chinese people Liu was by now a man of immense stature. In the Party he was viewed as a near equal of Mao's.

A part of the Chinese Revolution since before he met Mao at the Anyuan mines in 1921, he now seemed to be its chief executive officer.

A little book of Liu's, with the authoritative title *How to Be a Good Communist,* sold 15 million copies between its reissue in 1962 and 1966, eclipsing in that period the sales of anything by Mao. Editorials of the mid-1960s urged cadres to study Mao's *and* Liu's works.

Mao himself had spoken—even to foreigners—of Liu as his natural successor.

Mao's dissatisfaction with Liu came to a head over the Socialist Education Movement (SEM), a drive to sharpen political consciousness in the villages. In keeping with the radical ideas he had raised in 1962, Mao wrote a ten-point plan with class struggle as its theme.

Liu saw the SEM in blander hues—as a drive against corruption and administrative slackness, under the close supervision of the all-wise CCP.*

A third ten points appeared, as some low-level officials began to wonder if the SEM was anything more than a political football to be kicked back and forth between Mao and Liu. Mao viewed this draft as leftist in its wrappings and rightist in its content.

He came up in early 1965 with a fresh draft—swollen by frustration into twenty-three points—which boldly pointed a finger at Liu: "The key point of this movement is to rectify those people in positions of authority within the Party who are taking the capitalist road." Mao added: "Some are out in the open and some are concealed. . . ."

Liu would not endorse the twenty-three points. Mao decided to get rid of him.

Lin Biao looked more like a Boy Scout than a seasoned commander of the world's largest army. Shorter than Mao, with a nose large for a Chinese, Lin spoke in a thin, high-pitched voice, kept his cap on to hide a balding

---

*Mao and Liu had had a revealing exchange during the post-mortem on the Leap. Liu said 70 percent of its failure was due to human error, and 30 percent to floods, drought, and other natural causes. Mao commented that Liu's percentages were upside down: 70 percent was nature's fault, and only 30 percent was due to poor planning, overzealous leadership, and other man-made errors.

head, and wore a uniform that hung on him as from a hook. At 57, he had poor health, and as a public personality he was nonexistent.

But Lin was to be Mao's escort into the coming storm.

Lin had taken over the defense ministry from the fallen Peng Dehuai in 1959, and where Peng had been a bulldog at Mao's heels, Lin went along with Mao in feline smoothness.

Lin did not resist the break with Russia—as Peng did. Lin was happy to elevate ideological work to a high place in the PLA's priorities—as Peng was not. Lin did not try to treat Mao as a near equal—as Peng did with fatal results.

Even more important than the differences between Peng and Lin was the bleak conclusion Mao had drawn about the Party in the wake of the 1959 crisis. Lost on Mount Lu was the CCP's collegial authority. From then on the Party was a machine to be captured, not a holistic force supreme above all individuals and issues.

And Mao step by step came to regard his own personal authority as separable from the Communist Party's.

The PLA under Lin took on a startling role. As the Party bureaucracy treated Mao like a "dead ancestor" in the early 1960s, the military treated him as its living Caesar. Lin was an Oliver Cromwell, his PLA an Oriental counterpart to the pure and bright-eyed New Model Army.

Lin asked his armies to become a "great school of Mao Zedong's Thought." Officers formed choirs to sing of Mao's Thought and of the "Four Firsts."* *Liberation Army Daily,* the PLA paper, as early as 1962 began to publish Mao quotes boxed and in bold type on page one.

Quotations from Chairman Mao was first published by the PLA. All of its editions after 1965 carried a foreword by Lin. "Comrade Mao Zedong is the greatest Marxist-Leninist of our era," it began.

In Mao's mind Lin seemed to have already taken Liu's place. In Lin's mind Mao was his avenue into the future and Liu loomed as chief obstacle.

The surface was calm. But new realities of power were building up beneath it.

In the 1940s and 1950s it would not have been apt to speak of "Maoism" or "Maoists." While collegial authority endured in the CCP, *every* Party member was to a large degree a Maoist. Maoism was pretty much the Chinese Communist Way.

Now things were different. Mao's following had shrunk from almost the

---

*A slogan of Lin's that became a Cultural Revolution theme: put men first above weapons, political work first above other work, ideological work first above routine political work, and living ideology first above book knowledge.

whole, in the 1950s, to merely one part, in the 1960s. In a split Party he was reduced to latching on to one wedge.

But he did have a substantial wedge. Its color was khaki. Mao launched a drive for all of China to "Learn from the PLA."

What exactly would China learn from the PLA? First signs were odd. "Comrade Jiang Qing talked with me yesterday," Lin Biao told a group in Shanghai. "She is very sharp politically on questions of literature and art."

For years Jiang Qing's health had been spotty and her mood brittle. Mostly she had stayed home and looked after the two daughters. Mao had spent much time away from her. "A man with few words," was how she found him even when they were together.

But her topic—culture—was Mao's chosen weapon for the first round of the fight he was preparing for. "Green Waters" plunged into art and literature circles with a heavy baggage of resentment at her long exclusion from them.

Soon soldiers were doing songs and dances at her behest. Her terrible crusade to put China's artistic life into a straitjacket had begun.

Mao helped her. Not trusting his own CCP, he was turning, like an emperor of the Ming dynasty playing court politics, to lackeys and family for a too personalized support.

Soon his daughter Li Na was in the editorial chair at *Liberation Army Daily,* and his other daughter, Li Min, was wielding power in the Science and Technology Commission (responsible for the development of nuclear weapons) at the defense ministry.

*   *   *

Mao left Peking for Shanghai in the autumn of 1965. Jiang Qing was with him. The pair settled at the former French Club in the port city for a stay of some months. From time to time Mao took a break at his villa by West Lake in the nearby resort of Hangzhou.

It turned out to be his longest absence from the capital since he had begun to live there in 1949. For six months he was away from what he felt were the suffocations of Peking. For five of those months the Chinese people were given no clue to his activities.

The spell away from Peking was one more of his retreats, prior to a strong return with batteries recharged. He came to Shanghai to recruit some bright young intellectuals as political tools.

One day the Shanghai daily *Literary Currents* carried a heavy piece of drama criticism. That at least is what the strollers on the Shanghai Bund, opening their papers after work on November 10, thought it was.

The article was the first shot in the most amazing gunfire that any Marxist government has ever inflicted upon itself.

The Cultural Revolution had begun. Only in China could an epic of political theater begin with a dry slice of real theater.

The author of the drama column was Yao Wenyuan, a 44-year-old Shanghai essayist with a moon face and sly eyes. As drama criticism his review was stale stuff. For the play that he damned was none other than *Hai Rui Dismissed from Office*, the 1961 work by the vice-mayor of Peking.

Wu Han's play was a cunning allegory that protested Mao's own dismissal of Peng from the defense ministry. Mao had seen the barb behind it four years before. Now he felt he could hit back.

Only Mao would have made a big issue of Wu Han's play—because Mao was its target. In remarking to some Albanian visitors that the Cultural Revolution began with the *Literary Currents* article, Mao admitted that his own role in Chinese politics was its first bone of contention.

Yet Mao did have some broad and even noble motives for his "Great Proletarian Cultural Revolution." Villagers so wretched that they ate bark, he told Malraux, made better fighters than glib chauffeurs from Shanghai. He was worried about the softness of the 300 million young people born since 1949. They must be put through a struggle of their own.

Mao was also reasserting his belief that people count more than things. "Should we attach more importance to men, to things, or to both?" he asked in a directive on labor reform. It was a question that Chinese tradition had long concerned itself with and Mao gave an answer that was very Confucian. "If we do our work on men well," he concluded, "we shall have things as well." Mao was trying to reestablish, amid the shifting sands of the Chinese Revolution, a priority for social relations over economic output.

The man believed deeply in purge and renewal. "If you have to fart, fart!" he once cried out at a Party meeting. "You will feel much better for it." As in the past, it was nature that lent him the patterns of thought he felt comfortable with.

"Don't peasants weed several times a year? The weeds removed can be used as fertilizer." The sentiment was macabre in its implications. Yet Mao was rousing himself not without hope.

He was in search of immortality for Mao Zedong—but also for the Chinese Revolution.

Mao started with a shot at *Hai Rui Dismissed from Office* for reasons beyond mere wounded vanity. Like any Chinese leader, he had a healthy regard for the role of literature in cementing, or undermining, the legitimacy of a political dynasty.

Being a semi-intellectual himself, he did not quite trust the species, yet he was fascinated by it too. He had come to believe—and told an audience of economic planners so in mid-1964—that in Russia the new privileged elite had sprung first from literary and artistic circles.

"Why are there so many literary and artistic associations in Peking?" he inquired in irritation. "They have nothing to do." At the festivals, "army performances are always the best, local troupes rank second, and those from Peking are the worst."

His obsession with Russia, his chauvinism, his craving for immortality, all tumbled out before the same group of economic planners. "You have this association, that organization—it's all just a transplant from the Soviet Union . . . all ruled by foreigners and dead men. . . ."

If Mao was furious with Peking cultural officials, he also had bigger fish to fry. Shooting at the vice-mayor, he hoped to splatter some blood of accusation on the mayor.

Peng Zhen was a man of taste and stature. In some eyes he was a possible successor to Mao. His urbane, routinized ways turned Peking into a city that Mao found as soulless and self-important as some Deep Southerners find Washington.

Mao angrily refused to read *People's Daily* during these years. He preferred the army paper *Liberation Army Daily*.

Much of the Academy of Sciences in Peking, he sneered, was "a sort of fairyland where they no longer eat the food of human beings." He noted with distaste that the "antiquarians" there read precisely those journals which he himself found impossible to stomach. But the work of the academy was a prime example of the sober and specialized research that the mayor thought necessary for China's future development.

"Still at the stage," Peng Zhen snapped of Jiang Qing's simplistic, politicized pieces for the theater, "of wearing trousers with a slit in the seat" (a reference to the open seam in a Chinese child's pants which allows it to shit unannounced).

Two outlooks were about to collide.

Using a crablike technique to bring pressure to bear on Peng Zhen and the Peking establishment, Mao appointed a group that included the mayor himself to guide what he had already labeled a Cultural Revolution. Nothing could come of that, except a fight.

The mayor tried to limit the Yao article to the realm of academic debate. Mao was bent on far-reaching political change. The first wave of the Cultural Revolution was against those officials who had come to regard the edifice of PRC rule as an end in itself. A fight was just what Mao had in mind.

He watched it brew during the spring of 1966 from the vantage point of Shanghai.

* * *

Mao met with the veteran American radical Anna Louise Strong and some of her friends to honor Ms. Strong's 80th birthday, just after he had finished editing Yao's article through eleven drafts for its publication in *Literary Currents*. His mood on this cool morning was calm and obstinate.

He walked into the Shanghai reception room with Jiang Qing at his side. He inspected a bamboo carving on the wall. Quite absorbed in it, he stood there as if alone, forgetting his wife. He moved to a second carving and to a third. The roomful of guests meanwhile stood in utter silence, waiting for him to say a word, or make a move toward the waiting lunch.

Remarking that his doctors told him he should quit smoking, he lit a cigarette. He did not intend to give up, he drawled. He invited other smokers in the room to light up with him. Some did.

A few moments later he noted that nonsmokers were in the majority. "Don't be worried by that," he said to the smokers. "Go ahead regardless."

His guest of honor was a fiercely anti-Vietnam War American. Yet Mao never mentioned the Vietnam War. All his barbs about the outside world were directed at the Soviet Union.

Mao asked a half dozen of Ms. Strong's friends their views on the international scene. The answers did not stimulate him. All six people had the same view, he remarked. That suggested prior orchestration. It would be more interesting if someone had a divergent view.

The real cause of the stiffness in the conversation was that Mao's leftist visitors were merely anti-Washington, whereas he was also anti-Moscow.*

Mao had made a new analysis of international relations which put Russia and America theoretically on a par as class enemies of China. It was a confused analysis—gaily mixing up national and class factors, arbitrarily reclassifying Russia as capitalist—yet it carried the seed of a coherent new foreign policy line for China.

Mao's problem in calling a plague on both superpowers was that most of the Politburo disagreed with him.

It was clear to everyone in Peking that the U.S. was still a threat to China. Mao did not deny it. The novelty of Mao's position was that he asserted *Russia could be no help* to China in this predicament. Liu and many PLA leaders, on the other hand, still believed in the possibility of "joint action" with Moscow in the face of the American threat.

Early in 1965, under pressure from Vietnam, Mao and Kosygin met on the Russian's way back from Hanoi. Mao was full of irony about Russia at

---

*Mao's hostility toward the U.S. faded rapidly during 1964–1965. A Frenchman who spent some hours with him in September 1964 came away with the recollection: "Coloring everything is his implacable hatred of the United States."

this time. He had given up on "joint action" before Kosygin descended on Peking.

In dramatic fashion he posed a question to the Russian which put the issue beyond dispute. Would the U.S.S.R. come to China's aid if the U.S. escalated the Vietnam War into an attack on China?

Kosygin not only declined to give such an undertaking but failed to utter a single word in reply!*

With amazing frankness Mao admitted to Kosygin in the ensuing conversation that "some" of his own colleagues did not see eye to eye with him on his attitude to Russia.

Luo Ruiqing, chief of the General Staff of the PLA, refused to equate Russia and the U.S. He thought Mao had taken leave of Marxist tradition and military common sense alike. Luo spoke warmly of the Soviet Red Army and hopefully of the socialist camp. He urged "joint action" for the sake of Vietnam.

Mao engineered Luo's dismissal by a series of sharp maneuvers. Luo jumped (or was he pushed?) out of a sixth-floor window.† He was the first top victim of the Cultural Revolution.

In striking down Luo, Mao built up Lin Biao even more, for these two generals gave voice during 1965 to divergent military-political lines.

Lin was far removed from the positions that Luo had been purged for embracing: esteem for Russia, faith in the socialist bloc, a Europe orientation, a hawkish posture on the Vietnam War. Lin's own line became a faithful echo of Mao's mid-1960s view of the world.

Mao and Lin saw the global situation as an extended replay of China's own revolution. The countryside (Third World) would one day surround the cities (the West and Russia) as surely as Mao's peasant revolutionaries had surrounded Shanghai and Peking.

World politics had been made a branch of guerrilla warfare.

This looked very militant but it was not. The Mao-Lin line was dovish compared with the "joint action" line of Luo and Liu.

- The PLA should not venture beyond China's borders.
- China should fight only if the enemy came into Chinese territory.
- China was not the active spearhead of the anti-imperialist forces; the Third World in general was (the embattled Vietnamese in particular).

---

*One wonders if Kosygin's non-response reminded Mao of his own prevarication when Soviet officials pressed him in September 1941 on what military action the CCP would take in Russia's defense if Japan were to attack Russia.

†His apparent effort to kill himself failed by a wide margin and it was not long before the Red Guards were unleashed to grill and taunt the distinguished officer. Luo dragged himself, his smashed left leg a mountain of bandages, to the Workers Stadium, where 20,000 Red Guards put him on "trial."

The Mao-Lin line dripped with nationalism. In Russia's bloc China could only be number two. But as spokesman for the Third World, China could be a kind of number one, yet without the burdens of alliance relationships.

As a wedge in the socialist bloc the Chinese were hitched to a Eurocentric, goulash-communism view of socialism. Now they could march under their own banner:

- Peasants rather than Communist parties of industrial workers were the key to revolution.
- Armed struggle and not parliamentary maneuver was the way to change the world.
- Yellow and brown—not white—were the colors of the future.
- China's experience, not Russia's, was the point of reference for the Third World majority.

Meanwhile U.S. bombs were falling close to China's southern cities. It was as if, from an American point of view, Mexico was being pounded by the planes of a global adversary of the U.S. Mao kept amazingly cool about it.

He purged most of those in the Politburo who were hawks on the issue, including some who favored sending Chinese troops into Vietnam to meet the U.S. forces before they burst through China's own door.

Mao's strategic view was not changed by the outcome of the Vietnam War. He had already decided by the mid-1960s that Russia was a rising menace and the U.S. a falling one.* The U.S. failure in the rice paddies of Indochina merely gave a delayed illustration to his thesis.

*   *   *

On reaching Shanghai in the autumn of 1965 Mao wrote a truculent poem, "Two Birds: A Dialogue." An eagle and a sparrow found themselves in the midst of gunfire. The sparrow was scared out of its wits:

> "This is one hell of a mess!
> Oh, I want to flit and fly away."

The eagle was of different mettle. It asked skeptically where there could possibly be refuge.

The sparrow had in mind "a jeweled palace in elfland's hills." This gullible bird—as Mao saw it—took comfort from such falsities as the Nuclear Test Ban Treaty and Khrushchev's vision of goulash communism:

---

*Mao later made a striking remark to Chancellor Schmidt about America's performance in Vietnam. "The United States can't be considered so powerful," he said to the German, "if it gives up after losing 50,000 men."

"Don't you know a triple pact was signed
Under the bright autumn moon two years ago?
There'll be plenty to eat,
Potatoes piping hot,
Beef-filled goulash."

The eagle had the last word:

"Stop your windy nonsense!
Look, the world is being turned upside down."

The poem was anti-Soviet, to be sure, but it also spoke of flux and reversals in the order of things. A long-standing philosophic view, not mere strategic calculation, led Mao to his new foreign policy.

Kenji Miyamoto, leader of the Japanese Communist Party, came to China for earnest talks in early 1966.

The Japanese reds were Maoist enough to toss around the term "revisionism" when talking of Moscow. Yet they feared a large U.S.-provoked war in Asia. So they were on a trip to China, Vietnam, and Korea to argue for the "joint action" with Russia that now was also favored by some of Mao's colleagues.

In Peking the Japanese hammered out with senior Chinese leaders a communiqué that went part of the way toward this position. But Mao was far off in Canton, taking a respite from the March weather of Shanghai. Ominously—for some in Peking—he sent word that he wished to see the Japanese Communists on their way out of China to Hong Kong.

Mao was staying at a tranquil hot-spring resort near an army base in the hills outside Canton. The bamboos must have shaken at his language when the Japanese arrived.

No sooner had Miyamoto bent deep in polite bows than Mao began a tirade. He denounced the draft communiqué. He infuriated Deng Xiaoping, and other senior Chinese who had come south for the meeting, by shouting: "You weak-kneed people in Peking." The Japanese cringed in amazement at the scene.

Mao wanted the communiqué to call for a united front against both "U.S. imperialism" *and* "Soviet revisionism." The Japanese refused to agree. Mao then said the communiqué drafted in Peking was null and void and that there would be no communiqué at all. There was none.

Mao went on to alienate Miyamoto further by urging the Japanese Communist Party to put arms directly into the hands of the Japanese people and prepare for "people's war."

This painful scene brought an end to the close ties between the Chinese and Japanese Communist parties.

It also roused Mao to a fresh bout against those in Peking who were resisting him. Just after Miyamoto left, he forced the dismissal of Peng Zhen, the mayor of Peking.

He was adding with a prodigal hand to his list of enemies; in particular the gap between him and Deng began to widen.

*   *   *

While in retreat from Peking, Mao reread *Journey to the West*. The hero of the novel is a monkey with a red ass named Sun. He performs wonderful feats.

Sun steals and eats the peaches of immortality in the gardens of paradise. He storms the gates of hell in order to strike his name off the cosmic blacklist. He covers 180,000 leagues in one bound to reach the pillars that mark the boundary of the world, and once there pisses on a pillar to show his independent spirit.

Daring fate, Sun the monkey king has a trick for coping with adversity. He plucks hair from his body—the term for "hair" happens to be the same Chinese character as Mao's name—bites it into fragments and cries "Change!" Each piece then turns into a small monkey and he has at his side an army of supporters.

"We must overcome the king of hell and liberate the little devils," Mao remarked to a Politburo colleague in March 1966. "We need more Suns from the various local areas to go and disrupt the heavenly palace."

He—and Peking—got them before the year was out.

Mao in earlier years had always used the monkey image in a negative sense—as for fascists during World War II—but from the late 1950s he used it positively. Sun the monkey king's daring, impishness, irreverence, and infinite aspirations all suited Mao's frame of mind.

He brought this fantastic usage to a climax in 1966 by declaring that the revolutionary and the monkey king were one and the same type!

By mid-1966 Mao was ready to spring back in person to the public arena and he did so clutching a packet of surprises worthy of Sun the monkey king.

He let China know he was alive (but not where he was sojourning) by receiving the premier of faithful Albania at an undisclosed location. Then he offered proof of his physical vigor. He went to Wuhan and swam the Yangze before a battery of TV cameras.

People's Daily reported—perhaps in the spirit of the monkey king legend—that Mao covered fifteen kilometers in sixty-five minutes and showed no sign of fatigue afterward.

Mao returned to Peking to summon some real-life "little devils" to his cause, and to write in his own hand a wall poster that asked the whole nation to revolt.

So the Cultural Revolution really began.

"We need," Mao ruminated of China's future, "determined people who are young, have little education, a firm attitude, and the political experience to take over the work."

His own experience was his guide. "When we started to make revolution we were mere 23-year-old boys," he pointed out, "while the rulers of that time . . . were old and experienced. *They had more learning but we had more truth.*"

The Cultural Revolution put this idea to the test. Young people were supposed to be untainted with old ways. Their education had been purely Chinese and without distortions from the non-Chinese world. As pristine products of new China, would they not prove to have "more truth"?

In that sense the Cultural Revolution was a fresh effort to do what the Hundred Flowers had failed to do: crystallize a moral consensus.

In another sense the Cultural Revolution was a departure from anything Mao had tried before. The "political experience" that Mao wished youth to have was to be gained by a *struggle against the Party!*

This gamble, too, stemmed from the shocks of 1956–1957. At that time Mao lost his faith in the established doctrines of Marxism-Leninism. Truth and the authority of the Party were thereafter quite separable in Mao's mind. So much so that by 1966 he believed that truth could be established *over against* the authority of the Party.

For the Great Leap Forward Mao trusted the Party as vehicle. For the Cultural Revolution he did not. He called in the little devils to assault the Party.

Mao set the Red Guards loose by assuring them that "To rebel is justified" is the gist of Marxism. He invited them to "Knock down the old."

At first their targets were cultural. They smashed temples. They ransacked the homes of intellectuals and better-to-do folk for items that seemed "bourgeois" or "revisionist."

Sunglasses were unacceptable on the first score; chess was too Russian to pass the second test. Almost all books other than those of Marxist doctrine were suspect. Burning them made rousing bonfires which were fun to watch.*

---

*Edgar Snow's books were destroyed at Nanjing University.

If the Red Guards seemed at times like religious zealots, Mao had handed them an apt doctrine. His line of thought was reminiscent of the maxim "Love God and do what you like," which some Christians down the ages have believed in.

If the heart is in the right place, it presumes, then good conduct will flow as naturally as water down a slope.

Mao in 1966 gave Marxism a similar twist. He put "rebellion" in the center, where the Protestant sectarian put "love." If youth has the spirit of rebellion, the Mao of 1966 and 1967 believed, then it will do good deeds for China.

It was a mindless theory and it issued in mindless practice.

The Red Guards had their own reasons to find satisfaction in rebellion. They were a lost generation who suddenly had a sense of being found. They had been to high school, but the expectations aroused there could not be fulfilled. Neither college places nor city jobs existed for them.

A generation that had never had the chance to let its hair down now did so to an extreme. High school kids, who would not have known a capitalist if they saw one, accused veterans who had battled against capitalism for decades of being fingers on capitalism's black hand!

A group of Red Guards broke into Peng Zhen's home in the middle of the night, switched on the light in his bedroom and ordered the mayor to rise and come downtown to be criticized. "Peng Zhen's face turned ashen out of surprise," the young zealots wrote in a breathless report, "and he could not even dress himself properly."

Mao asked his old comrade Zhu De to write some articles in support of the Cultural Revolution, and later to write a self-criticism for failing to support it. Zhu declined both requests.

Zhu De was soon called a "big war lord and careerist who wormed his way into the Party." Mao was losing comrades-in-arms of decades' standing.*

The Red Guards seemed to be devoted to Mao as believers to a prophet. It was in some cases a sincere devotion. But a student of seventeen could not really share Mao's perspective on the Cultural Revolution. For him or her it was exciting to shout insults at "evil ones." It lent self-importance to travel up to Peking by special train to see Chairman Mao and "take part in revolution."

---

*In moments of frankness he seemed to acknowledge that he was isolated in the Party. "Some people say that China loves peace," he remarked to some Albanians in early 1967. "That's bragging. In fact, the Chinese love struggle." He then felt the need to add: "I do, for one."

The mechanics probably meant more than the message.

"The Central authorities constantly urged us," one Cantonese youth who eventually swam to Hong Kong recalled, "to take along Mao's *Quotations* and study them whenever there was time. What we did was take along a pack of cards and play whenever there was time."

It seemed that Mao had forgotten the difference between student politics, with all its instability and mixed motives, and the politics of administering a country of 700 million people.*

*　*　*

The pen and the gun—these were always Mao's two tools. He returned to Peking only after troop reinforcements had been brought to the city. Once home again, though, he took up the pen.

He wrote a wall poster. "Bombard the Headquarters," he headed it. The Cultural Revolution was being hampered by the Center, it said, and so the Center had to be dismantled. He took his poster to the building of the Central Committee and pinned it up on an inner door.

Mao's act had large consequences. Wall posters appeared all over China like mushrooms after spring rain. China became a news paradise unmatched in its history.

Posters were pasted to walls, pinned to trees, draped on stone lions, even spread out on the road when every other surface was filled. Peking looked like one vast bulletin board.

Huge crowds gathered to read the handwritten messages on white, yellow, or pink paper. It was all great fun for the ordinary person. He was being addressed, almost hourly, by the high and mighty, and that was flattering.

Eventually, though, the voices of the wall posters became so cacophonous, and so much the expression of hopeless feuds, that they sank to insignificance under their own weight. Small boys gathered up fallen posters to sell them for a few fen as fuel.

Mao wrote another wall poster—half poem and half political manifesto—of mingled romanticism and defiance:

*The Red Guards, limited as their own grasp of Mao's purposes was, were often amazed at the much lower limits they found among peasants.

"I asked her what was in heaven," one Red Guard said of his talk with a peasant woman in a remote mountain village of Fujian Province. "She said Mao Zedong was in heaven, constantly watching over everybody. He would know whoever was not working hard and have him punished." This was somewhat removed from Mao's call for an awareness of class struggle.

"I asked her if there were any countries besides China," the Red Guard continued. "She shook her head. I asked her if she knew the earth was round. She shook her head." Declared this envoy of Mao's new world: "Finally I could only shake my head with her."

It was not going to be easy to build a new society in China's villages.

> Shall China no longer be proletarian at the end
>   of the movement, but bourgeois? Certainly not! . . .
> Hats are flying in the air and cudgels are roaming the land.
>   We have already sustained blows and lumps
>   on the head. . . .
> What shall we see in the last period of the movement?
> The sky has been cleaned of dust.
> The surface is full of sunlight and flowers.
> And as the mountain flowers open up, the plum tree
>   blossom laughs with them.
> And if you do not believe me, just watch and
>   wait a little.

More hats were to fly, more cudgels were to strike; the sunlight and flowers were hardly to be seen.

At first the Red Guards wrote posters that merely criticized everything old. But in late 1966, Mao handed graver tasks to the little devils. He asked them to knock power from the hands of half of the Politburo. As if to anoint them for their labors, Mao met eleven million of them at ten sunrise rallies by the Gate of Heavenly Peace.

The young people wore khaki—what did the seasoned veterans of the PLA think of that?—with a red armband and the white words "Red Guard." Each one clutched a copy of *Quotations*. Waved in the air, the red covers made the square resemble a field ablaze with butterflies.

Mao contributed to the rather forced military atmosphere by wearing his PLA fatigues and cap with the red star. The floppy green garments hid a figure that was by now pear-shaped.

At none of the rallies did Mao make any kind of speech (it was frequently Lin Biao who spoke). He merely stood on top of the gate, Jiang Qing beside him (also in PLA uniform), and raised an arm. Yet hundreds of thousands wept from joy, biting their sleeves and jumping up and down in response to his mere presence.

The Cultural Revolution brought all kinds of formalization of self-expression. In a weird way, Mao revived old China's ritual in his waning years.

The philosopher who had written books wrote 200-word posters instead.

The leader who used to lecture for hours to persuade his followers of the merits of a new policy now merely appeared before them with an upraised hand and a glassy smile.

The teacher who always wanted his students to think for themselves seemed content to have them chant a phrase of adoration which they no more understood than does a child understand the catechism it repeats.

Artists signed their paintings, during the mad months of late 1966 and 1967, not with their own name—not with any name—but with the sycophantic phrase: "Ten Thousand Years to Chairman Mao."

How could Mao look at himself in the mirror each morning amid such disgusting nonsense? Had he not asked in his 1949 speech on "Methods of Work" for a "stop to flattery and exaggerated praise"? Had he not forbidden even the naming of a street after a Party leader?

Yet now his own statue stared down over every lobby, his phrases were treated like magic charms, and urban China had come to resemble the interior of a Catholic cathedral with Mao as a red Mary.

Why had Mao changed? Because in his old age he did not any longer believe in the collegial authority of the Communist Party, and his own self-image reverted toward that of a traditional Chinese ruler.

Because the cult of personality now seemed to him—as his remarks to Snow about Khrushchev's lack of a cult suggested—necessary in a backward society even within a Marxist political system.

Because Lin Biao was pushing the Mao cult, for his own purposes, and a mixture of lack of energy and lack of will prevented Mao from scotching it.

"You should be concerned about the national crisis," he told a throng outside the Central Committee building one day, "and you should carry out the Great Proletarian Cultural Revolution to the end." He needed more turmoil, for inside the building he was in danger of being outvoted.

Mao's opponents could not easily denounce his rabble-rousing methods. Was the PRC not a revolutionary regime? Were the masses not its sacred constituency, whose will was supposed to be one with the will of the government?

Liu and Deng tried to limit the scope of Red Guard activity—just as Peng Zhen had tried to keep Yao's article in *Literary Currents* within the bounds of academic debate—but they did not dare to denounce it for the anarchy that it was.

With outrageous disregard for historical circumstance, Mao likened his colleagues' "suppression" of students to that of the anti-Communist war lords of the 1920s. Doubts he covered up in a vapor of psychology. "You should replace the word 'fear,' " he said to his most senior colleagues, "by the word 'dare.' "

Many of Mao's colleagues were indeed afraid. But they were also puzzled at what kind of daring was required of them.

Deng was quietly contemptuous of the Cultural Revolution. Liu probably spoke the truth when he said he simply did not understand it. Chen Yi remarked: "I have always told comrades who were close to me that if I were to lead the Cultural Revolution there would be no Cultural Revolution."

Meanwhile, with China on the brink of civil war, the first Chinese H-bomb was detonated.

Mao wanted both nuclear weapons and political disorder. This tiger-monkey saw no contradiction between the two.* That China got both at once showed that Mao was having his way.

*   *   *

The Cultural Revolution was trying for the 75-year-old Mao.

A profusion—his secretaries felt a confusion—of documents, phone calls, and visitors from this unit and that province washed over him. Often he became impossibly tired and after a torrid night of work simply had to withdraw for the day.

Deceitful tricks reached into Mao's own apartment at South and Central Lakes. An important official at Party headquarters secreted tape recorders in potted plants in Mao's office and in sofas in his lounge.

Yet Mao did not seem to suffer as much anguish as the other principals, even those, like Zhou, who avoided being purged.

He did not go to large meetings, as Zhou did, and expend himself on oratory. He sat at his desk and solved a problem by penning cryptic comments on someone else's document.

Nor did Mao seem as torn by the breaking of old friendships, as some leaders were. He had always derived a fierce pleasure from the rooting out of what he judged obsolete. He found a note of exhilaration in death.

In early 1967 there was violence, uncertainty, and hatred in the air. Tens of thousands of people had already been killed in the Cultural Revolution. Yet Mao declared to Albanian visitors in February that he felt more optimistic about the situation than he had the year before!

Was Mao putting China through some kind of high-level therapy or was he fighting a life-and-death battle for control of China? Mostly the former, but not only.

Mao had lost quite a deal of power by the mid-1960s as compared with any period of the PRC's life until 1959. But he himself had taken the first step toward that loss of power.

His eclipse, however, went further than he found acceptable. "Deng

---

*Yet the disorder of the Cultural Revolution did affect at least the morale of some of China's nuclear scientists. Qian Xuesen, in one of his very few communications to former colleagues in the United States, sent a Christmas card to a dean of Cal Tech. It bore a traditional Chinese painting of a spray of flowers, beside which Qian had written in neat English words: "This is a flower that blooms in adversity."

Xiaoping never consulted with me," he complained, not having expected the secretary general of the Party to grow *that* independent of him.

From 1962 Mao worked out some fresh ideas designed to renew the spirit of the Chinese Revolution. These ideas—about the persistence of class struggle, the relation of culture to the economic system, and the menace of Russia—were resisted by Liu and Deng and others.

Mao decided, as he told Snow, that Liu "had to go."

Yet he was fighting a bigger, vaguer enemy than Liu and Deng. In the name of his vision of socialism as eternal struggle, he was fighting the reality of socialism as proliferating bureaucracy.

His inability to confront certain cold hard facts about the regime he had created made him invent phantoms to explain why things kept going wrong. Chief phantom was an exaggeration of the role of class in the China of the 1960s.

Mao explained to some Albanian army men what he meant by "capitalist roaders." They were people who had thrown themselves into class struggle before Liberation but did not see the point of doing so in the different circumstances since 1949. Mao had hit the nail on the head.

Indeed, he gave voice to a logical inference from his analysis that made nonsense of "capitalist roader" and such terms. "Let's just say that it is 'veteran cadres encountering new issues'!"

No doubt Mao meant some irony. But his phrase aptly identified the kernel of truth inside the absurd husk "capitalist roader."

The Cultural Revolution was not mainly a power struggle between individuals. Students at the grass roots, like marionettes lined up against each other by a hidden string-puller, used guns and killed each other. But the leaders did not fight each other with guns.

We do not have the full story of Liu's and Deng's point of view (that in itself shows us the limits of Mao's view of "blooming and contending"). But it seems likely that they felt themselves to be in a bargaining situation.

Both men lived on in their homes in the Forbidden City through months of disgrace. Both probably talked at length with Mao during that time (and they are no more likely to have used the language of *People's Daily* than are cardinals to chat with each other in the Latin of Holy Mass).*

Mao did not suddenly dismiss Liu and Deng, or lock them up, much less

---

*Deng, before leaving Peking to be reformed in the countryside, had a talk with Mao during which he expressed bitterness and defiance. Perhaps he should have been like Lin Biao, he remarked, "making meritorious achievements out of nothing," and earned Mao's approval that way.

"History will judge whether Lin Biao is correct or not," Mao replied with a smile. "You don't have to be defiant."

shoot them. Over a period of months he put pressure on the pair. From them a variety of responses was possible. For a while Deng went along somewhat with Mao's idea of a Cultural Revolution. Liu was obstinate and with great dignity chose to go down rather than embrace notions that he judged mistaken.*

Mao did not intend to turn China over to the Red Guards; he wished to stir up and steel Chinese youth—not to share state power with them. So "seizing of power" was a murky idea. A purge of some rightists, yes. A new political system, no.

One day in early 1967 Mao asked Zhou how the seizing of power was faring. "In some units," Zhou replied, "power is taken over by one group, and then another, and passes back and forth." Zhou had skirted with delicacy around the farcical character of the whole enterprise. Back and forth indeed!

Meanwhile Mao and Zhou—the real power holders—sat receiving reports of "power seizures" as if they were football games.

*   *   *

Liu was disgraced by early 1967. But this was not enough for Mao. He wanted to beat the dog in the water (a Chinese saying for truly finishing a job).

No doubt Mao feared that Liu could still become a rallying point for those dismayed at the terrible costs of the Cultural Revolution. Might Liu's steadiness be vindicated?

A startling photo was pinned up on the bulletin board of the *People's Daily* building. It showed three people in a group at the National Day celebrations for 1966. Mao was on the left. The widow of Sun Yat-sen was on the right. In the middle was Liu!

Crowds looked at the photo with a kind of guilty shock. Photos are powerful in Chinese politics and this one seemed to reverse heaven and earth. To publicize a photo of Liu at all at this stage was unusual. And *Mao* should have been in the middle!

Soon the *People's Daily* chief lost his job. He had been a supporter of Liu. With picture power he had tried to arrest the downward slide of the head of state.

Mao and Liu worked together for most of forty-five years. They were both Hunanese and understood each other perfectly in its muffled accent. In Yanan it was Liu who planned the build-up of Mao as leader and thinker capped at the Seventh CCP Congress in 1945.

*Zhou and some other leaders went along almost fully and the question of being purged did not arise.

No shred of evidence exists that Liu ever tried to dislodge Mao from the number-one spot.

The two men differed in outlook. Liu had less esteem for the peasant contribution to revolution than Mao did. He believed in Party authority as a Catholic does in the Church, and was less keen on inviting the masses to criticize the Party than Mao was.* He was by temperament given to orderly procedures and not inclined, like Mao, to a wavelike approach to economic development.†

Liu lacked Mao's soil-deep nationalism, and he did not become obsessed with Soviet failings as Mao did. Unimaginable that Mao would ever have used the internationalist form of words that came naturally to Liu's tongue: "The Chinese Communist Party is one of the outstanding branches of the World Communist Party."

For Mao nothing Chinese could be called a "branch" of something not Chinese.

Biggest difference of all: there was no "monkey" in Liu. He did not share Mao's oblique angle of vision on things. He did not see—and delight in—life as eternal flux in the way Mao did.

For Liu, history was an escalator. For Mao it was a churning sea.

For Liu, socialism was a science, to be pursued by rational steps. For Mao, socialism was a morality, not susceptible to being clinched in a final victory.

Yet these differences had not prevented the two men from working together with enormous success. (In speeches Mao had often referred to Liu warmly by his given name, Shaoqi, a rare usage for Mao when talking of colleagues.) Only the Mao of the Cultural Revolution found Liu intolerable.

What happened then? Mao came to transcend Marxism, and the idea of the Party as a Church, while Liu remained an orthodox believer.

The Mao-Liu split began to open up at the time of de-Stalinization. Mao's eventual response to the shock from Moscow—a decision to find a Chinese Way to socialism even if it was not still a Marxist way—left Liu behind in dogged orthodoxy and sheer incomprehension at the pranks of the monkey king.

Only a Mao who had lost the historic faith could have purged Liu.

---

*It is interesting that Mao was *never* secretary general of his Party, unlike virtually every other leader of a major nation ruled by a Communist Party.

†Zhang Guotao's remarks on Liu are typical. He remembered him from the 1920s as a "tall, skinny, pale young man" whom some people "found . . . a bit too glum and devoid of youthfulness." Like Zhang himself, Liu stressed "action and practice," rather than "ideology and theory." He recalls Liu once saying that he felt Mao "was somewhat illogical in his approach to problems, stubborn, indiscriminate in his choice of means, and lacking in self-culture."

Recall his own objection to Khrushchev's attack on Stalin: the actions of Stalin "bore the imprint of the times"; at stake was not just Stalin's reputation, but the authority of the Communist movement.

Liu's actions, too, bore the imprint of the times. And his reputation was hard to separate from the movement he had played so prominent a part in.

But Mao had lost all collegial sense.* He cared much less than before for the edifice of authority of which Liu was a leading buttress.

Particular issues, as always in politics, helped fuel a general discontent. During the early 1960s Liu was not as disposed as Mao to give foreign aid, or play the Third World card with large commitments to "national liberation struggles." And the two men fell out, perhaps climactically, on how the Socialist Education Movement should be carried out in the villages. But if it had not been these issues, it would have been others.

The real issue was Mao's evolution from Marxist to monkey king.

Liu proved obdurate. The split might have been arrested if Liu had the willow's suppleness, as Zhou had, but he did not. Speaking to an Albanian group in late April 1966, when Mao was starting to crack the whip for his new adventure, Liu did not once mention the words "Cultural Revolution" or even "Mao"!

Liu's most drastic step of resistance was typical of his organization-mindedness: he tried to summon a full Central Committee meeting and have Mao's Cultural Revolution reviewed. But 1966 was not a moment for the triumph of the letter of Party law; a Caesar had much of the nation mesmerized.

*   *   *

Soon after Mao put up his wall posters he began to recognize that things were going wrong. He admitted it. He may have liked the disorder—he said in August 1966 that the chaos should be allowed to go on—yet neither he nor anyone else could be pleased with the resulting death and destruction.

"The situation developed so rapidly as to surprise me," he confessed lamely to the Central Committee in October. "I cannot blame you if you have complaints against me."

The Cultural Revolution became, by the winter of 1966–1967, a series of ad hoc responses to occurrences that hit Mao with no more predictability than lightning hits a tree. And as 1968 arrived it had become, militant words notwithstanding, a rescue operation.

---

*According to Wang Ming, writing from his exile in Moscow, Mao often told colleagues that through the Yanan Rectification he "developed several close comrades-in-arms": Liu, Chen Boda, Hu Qiaomu, Gao Gang, Lu Dingyi, Peng Zhen, and Zhou Yang. Except for Gao, who had already fallen foul of Mao in the 1950s, *all of these* were victims of the Cultural Revolution!

Mao's responses grew more and more anti-leftist. The opening stage of
the Cultural Revolution, 1965–1966, had been directed against those "veteran cadres encountering new problems" (the code word was "capitalist
roaders").

The next stage, from 1967, was directed against young firebrands who
proved less good at building than at smashing (the code word was "ultra-
leftists").

The wind shifted. *People's Daily* still managed to urge rebellion. Yet between the lines was a very different admonition to law and order. Well before Liu was formally dismissed from office, in October 1968, Mao's focus
of anxiety had switched from Liu's errors to the errors of the "little devils"
who had attacked Liu and who wanted "communism now."

The turning point came in Shanghai. Militant leftists "seized power" as
Mao had invited them to. They proclaimed a "Shanghai Commune" along
the lines of the utopian Paris Commune of 1871. Mao did not approve.

He summoned to his office in February 1967 the two leaders of the Cultural Revolution in Shanghai: Zhang Chunqiao, a former journalist whose
career was closely linked with Mao's patronage; and Yao Wenyuan, the
moon-faced propagandist who had written the critique of *Hai Rui Dismissed from Office.*

Mao could hardly wait to see them. As their plane flew up from Shanghai
he kept asking his secretary if it had arrived at Peking airport yet. The supreme leader ended up waiting in the doorway for the two firebrands to enter his quarters.

He poured cold water on them. Anarchism should be avoided, he said.
Organizations must have someone in charge of them.

Shanghai leftists had been quoting a statement of Mao's from the May
Fourth period. "The world is ours," ran this cry of youth, "the nation is
ours, society is ours." Don't quote it anymore, Mao said, murmuring that he
didn't "altogether recall" using those exact words.

As for a Shanghai Commune, Mao backed out of it with a curiously thin
objection. If all China's cities set up communes would China's name not
have to be changed from PRC to something else? Would foreign countries
grant recognition to a "People's Commune of China"?

Zhang and Yao went back to Shanghai and turned down the thermostat
of the Cultural Revolution from hot to lukewarm. The Shanghai Commune
lasted just nineteen days.

The reason for Mao's change of heart was his dismay at the factionalism
of the leftists. They had excelled at knocking down. But when it came to
building, there were hundreds of supervisors and no bricklayers.

Vanity reigned. Doctrinal hair-splitting drove any ordinary person crazy.

The further left the Red Guards were, the less they deigned to link hands with anyone who seemed insufficiently pure.

The multiplication of warring Red Guard groups made the sects of Christendom seem like a monolith by comparison. Three provinces (Hubei, Hunan, Guangxi) and three cities (Peking, Canton, Shanghai) alone counted 1,417 separate Red Guard organizations among them.

In France the Revolution ate its children. In China the children nearly ate the Revolution.

Mao took trips around China. He did not like what he saw. Not only were Red Guards fighting among themselves, but Red Guards as a whole were coming into bitter conflict with industrial workers. Rumblings of discontent could be heard in the army.

Mao remarked in dismay to Zhou: "China is now like a country divided into 800 princely states."

* * *

Mao sent two senior figures to Wuhan as his personal envoys.

In Wuhan as elsewhere the first stage of the Cultural Revolution—the drive against "capitalist roaders"—had caused resentment. The Red Guards were not as popular as Mao wished or believed. The powerful commander of the military region centered on Wuhan resisted them. So did a broad front of workers from the city's many big factories.

Mao's two envoys, both ultra-leftists, came south to iron out the contention. Within a couple of days they almost got ironed out themselves.

The Wuhan commander detained the two men—both among the twenty top-ranking leaders of China at that moment—and Zhou Enlai, at the risk of his life, rushed down to intervene.

This time the Wuhan PLA commander lost; Zhou escorted him back to Peking.

Yet the Wuhan war lord's cause won: Mao had to accept the fact that the PLA was more in tune with popular sentiment than was the ultra-left.

The Wuhan incident did not check, but rather enhanced, the power of the PLA in Chinese politics. *People's Daily* chirped that the PLA had arrived on the scene to "support the left." But neither in Wuhan nor elsewhere did the PLA support the left.

In mid-1967 the ultra-left took China's foreign relations by the throat, in a showdown that shook Mao no less than the one at Wuhan.

Red Guards denounced Foreign Minister Chen Yi. They occupied his ministry. They sent cables to Chinese embassies around the world ordering fiery gestures; relations with Cambodia, Burma, and other friendly countries were badly strained.

Zhou himself was held prisoner for a couple of days. "The rotten boss of the bourgeoisie," one Red Guard group labeled the premier, "toying ambidexterously with counterrevolution." Another group wanted to put Zhou on trial. "Agreed," Mao is reported to have responded to their request, "as long as I stand with him."

To cap off their new approach to foreign policy, the Red Guards marched upon the British Mission. They burned it, taunted the grim-faced staff, grabbed some by the genitals, made one and all bow before a huge photo of Mao. . . .

Mao drew the line at this degree of unprogrammed rebellion. In the autumn of 1967 he spoke of "unity" as incessantly as a year before he had spoken of "rebelling." "Ultra-leftist," he murmured of the assault on the British.

Chen Yi got away with talking back to his captors in terms that the Mao of 1966 would have found intolerable. "I have opposed Chairman Mao on several occasions in the past," the earthy foreign minister declared, "and I'm not sure I won't do so in the future."

Chen Yi cut very close to the bone: "Marx came from Germany; a Kautsky and a Bernstein were produced there to modify him. Lenin came from the U.S.S.R.; a Khrushchev appeared there. Chairman Mao belongs to our country; there may also be someone to modify him—wait and see."

Mao did not—could not—go along with the attacks on Chen Yi. "The material isn't 'black' at all," he concluded when shown a compilation of the "black utterances" of the foreign minister; "he is by temperament frank and straightforward."

Another dimension to Mao's predicament in late 1967 was revealed when he asked for an end to the grilling of Chen Yi: "He has lost twenty-seven pounds," Mao declared. "I can't show him to foreign visitors in this condition."

Chen Yi was lucky. The storm hit him—unlike Liu—when Mao was no longer enthusiastic about the storm. Chen was salvaged because Mao needed to replace spontaneity with order.

*   *   *

At the height of the long, hot summer of 1967, Mao departed from Peking, leaving Zhou to handle some of the most terrible moments of the Cultural Revolution. He retreated to Shanghai. Then he traveled around the Yangze valley. His new line took form as he went.

"You cannot deal with cadres in the same way as you deal with landlords," he said in Hangzhou, objecting to the putting of dunce hats on officials who had made mistakes.

"You cannot be skeptical about everything, you cannot overthrow everything," he told the comrades in Wuhan, without any admission that he had recently been and done just that.

A chastened Mao was less sure than two years before that rebellion was justified. He needed to recoup. "Those who can be saved should be saved," he laid down in Jiangxi Province.

By late 1967 Mao was in favor of law and order. The "little devils" were ordered back to school. They were still to "make revolution," but in practice the reopening of the schools rendered that impracticable.

"If leftists remain uneducated," he murmured in Jiangxi, "they will become ultra-leftists."

"Can the Red Guards assume command? They will certainly be toppled tomorrow after being installed today. This is because they are politically immature . . . . The Red Guards are incompetent." Mao got out from under the genii he had invented.

The senior ultra-leftists of the Cultural Revolution group were not able to save themselves in the same way. Many were arrested before 1967 was done. Mao even began to criticize his wife as a "left opportunist."

Turning against the ultra-left, Mao chose the logical alternative ally: he asked the army to restore order. In factories, schools, and offices, the PLA took over from the "incompetent" Red Guards.

Mao made an immortal rationalization of his decision to call in the troops: "Soldiers are just workers and peasants wearing uniforms." His own maxim of earlier years would have been more to the point: "The barrel of a gun is the source of political power."

Soon a tortured new organizational form emerged. The name Revolutionary Committee conveyed nothing of its significance. The form was a triple blend of Red Guards, army men, and cadres who had reformed themselves since 1966. The reality was a three-legged monster that could go nowhere.

It wasn't very revolutionary—a cumbersome administrative structure. It wasn't a committee—the PLA leg swelled and dwarfed the other two legs.

Really the Revolutionary Committee was a thinly veiled step back toward the pre-Cultural Revolution political order—with PLA power added.

Mao appeared at a function with Zhou and Lin Biao one day in early 1968. The *People's Daily* report of the occasion included a photo with Lin standing in the middle. Zhou was to his right, Mao to his left. It looked to many Chinese as if the head of the PLA was China's man of the moment.

*   *   *

It was past midnight in the summer of 1968. Mao was in his home at South and Central Lakes. Present were two groups, two generations, two segments of the Cultural Revolution leadership.

The Politburo colleagues whom Mao had stuck by sat with him: Lin and his wife; Jiang Qing; Kang Sheng; Yao Wenyuan of Shanghai; Xie Fuzhi, the police minister, who had been one of Mao's two envoys nabbed in Wuhan; Chen Boda, the left-wing theorist.

There were also five key Peking Red Guard leaders, among them Nie Yuanzi (her given name means "atom"), a philosophy teacher who headed an extreme Red Guard camp; and Kuai Dafu, an intense, bespectacled science student who had become intoxicated with power at Qinghua University.

Mao scolded the Red Guard leaders for using violence in the factional struggles.

At the same time he mocked their lack of real power. "Nie's cannon fodder is limited in number and so is Kuai's," he observed. "Sometimes 300, other times 150 men. How can that be compared with the number of troops under Lin Biao? . . ."

He tried to switch the Cultural Revolution back to its academic beginnings: "We want cultural struggle, not armed struggle."

Mao dealt with the Red Guard leaders bluntly as a veteran politician talking to neophytes. "I am the black hand that suppressed the Red Guards," he said to these young people who had expected that "seizing power" would lead to a new political system.

He announced with crisp authority (and doubtful accuracy): "I have never made any tape recordings before, but I am doing it today. Otherwise you will interpret what I say today in the way you wish after you go home."

There were flashes of chagrin. "Too many people were arrested," Mao said of the violent phase of the Cultural Revolution, "because I nodded my head." Xie interjected that he, as the police minister, was the one to blame for excessive arrests.

"Don't try to free me from my mistakes," Mao rejoined sadly, "or to cover up for me."

Chen Boda chipped in with an admonition to the Red Guards: "Follow the Chairman's teachings closely."

Mao snapped: "Don't talk about teachings."

There was a certain guilty realization on the part of Mao (and some of the left wing of the Politburo that sat by his side) that the Red Guards had been edged onto the path of extremism by ambiguous orders from the top in 1966.

Mao permitted himself a moment or two of bitter humor. "Children are collecting big-character posters as waste paper for sale," he suddenly remarked. "How much a catty?"*

---

*A catty is half a kilogram.

The police minister had a reply: "Seven cents. The children are making a fortune."

Mao did not offer a solution to the basic issue of order versus spontaneity that underlay the Cultural Revolution. He was unable to align faith in struggle as good for the character (a question for the individual) with his awareness that millions of people struggling with each other produce chaos (a question of political order).

He gave a clear-cut instruction as China's leader: "If anyone continues to oppose, fight the PLA, destroy means of transportation, kill people, or set fires, he is committing crimes . . . and will be annihilated."

Yet he would not give up his strain of anarchism: "Let the students fight for another ten years," he burst out. "The earth will revolve as usual. Heaven is not going to fall."

The conversation drifted off politics and ended up with talk of plans for spending what was left of the night. "Kuai Dafu," Mao said like a solicitous teacher, "if you don't have a place to sleep tonight, you can go to Han Aiqing's place. . . ."

Quite soon Kuai—and Nie and most of the other Red Guard leaders— would be sleeping in peasant huts in remote parts of China, having exchanged the cultivation of revolution for the cultivation of pigs.

*   *   *

Was the Cultural Revolution the culmination of Maoism? By no means. It was a charade in a hothouse.

Mao wanted a new society. But in the Cultural Revolution he was driven less by a vision of the future than by a flight from a recent past that he did not like.

There was something obsessive about the quest for yet one more "blank piece of paper" on which a fresh lyric could be written.

Mao entered upon the Cultural Revolution armed with an intellectual diagnosis of the shortcomings of Chinese socialism. Capitalism was reasserting itself, he claimed. A battle had to be fought in the realm of ideas—a cultural revolution carried out—or else the economy might revert from socialism back to capitalism. This diagnosis was probably false.

And most of what was smashed was later restored. Liuism without Liu came back. Mao had smashed his enemies—but not his Enemy.

Mao also entered on the Cultural Revolution determined to establish more deeply his long-standing socialist values.

• Relations between people are more important than production of things.
• Struggle has a therapeutic benefit that goes beyond attaining the object of the struggle.

- Life is a battleground on which few victories are final and the low and the high change places often.

Here Mao had *some* success. He reminded China of the Maoist faith, even if he did not convert China to it.

The Cultural Revolution did not produce a new type of rule—only some new assistants to the ruler and, for a season, a new social atmosphere. It did, though, put untrammeled power back in Mao's pale and aging hands. He used it to some effect.

19

A Tall Thing Is Easy to Break (1969-1971)

Mao drove to the Great Hall of the People to bang the gavel for the start of a Party meeting that was meant to crystallize the "gains" of the Cultural Revolution. But the Ninth CCP Congress, hollow and tense, solved few of Mao's problems.

Mao gave an appalling opening talk. The congress would be one of unity, he began, and loud cheers bounced off the wood-paneled walls of the auditorium. But he devoted the rest of his speech to a vindictive caressing of all the CCP splits in the course of which he had cast aside old colleagues.

The revised constitution, thanks to Lin Biao, stated that "Mao Zedong's Thought," together with Marxism-Leninism, was the official ideology of the CCP (a sharp change from the Eighth Congress in 1956, which, in the more collegial mood of Liu's heyday, had not waved the banner of any one living man's "Thought"). The Cultural Revolution had hoisted Mao to new heights. Lin with his constant smile had been chief hoister.

Did it not follow that the Cultural Revolution had given way to a stable and harmonious Mao-Lin era?

The Central Committee elected at the Ninth Congress certainly looked like a Mao-Lin instrument. Nearly 40 percent of its members were from Hunan (Mao's province) and Hubei (Lin's), even though the two provinces contain less than 11 percent of China's population.

Yet the outlook was very mixed from Mao's point of view.

On the eve of the congress, the politically bruised foreign minister Chen Yi said to Mao with the mixture of wit and bite for which he was famous: "How can I be at the congress? I am supposed to be a 'rightist.'" Mao replied: "Well then, come and represent the right."

The remark caught Mao's wry, quizzical mood.

Unlike the congress of 1956, the Ninth Congress was held as a secret cabal of which no detailed news was given. It was a sign of the jumpy atmosphere.

And for the first time ever, a CCP congress was held without the presence of any observers from foreign Communist parties—a clue to the fact that the Mao-Lin era was built on Chinese feudal intrigue and mystification more than on Marxism as known abroad.*

Mao behaved like a Buddha—and was treated like one—in sessions that consisted of ritual rather than debate (only eleven of the 1,512 delegates spoke from the rostrum to the full congress).

In the back rooms, tensions were so great that it took more than a week to elect a new Central Committee—delegates filed past a wooden ballot box at the front of the hall in a pattern of voting that went back to Yanan days—and this body had to be swollen to twice its planned size in order to accommodate all the vying factions.

Mao had stabilized the ship after a terrible storm. And he appeared to have been accorded the status of supreme sage of Marxism that Liu and Deng had denied him at the Eighth Congress. Yet the sky had some dark patches.

More than half the delegates wore PLA uniforms. Mao had brought the army in to pick up the fragments of the Cultural Revolution; the results of that intervention sat before him at the congress.

Had Mao put in jeopardy his own principle that the Party should control the gun?

There were unresolved issues of contention, too, between some of these hard-nosed military officers and the extreme left faction which Mao's Cultural Revolution had inflicted on China.

The congress brought high office for the "helicopters"† who had risen up under Mao's patronage during the Cultural Revolution. Mao's wife joined the twenty-one-member Politburo of the Party; also added were her two Shanghai associates, Yao Wenyuan and Zhang Chunqiao; the three of them had acted as Mao's left hand during the Cultural Revolution.

Even those two firebrands of the Red Guard movement, "Atom" Nie of the philosophy department at Peking University, and Kuai Dafu of the chemistry department at Qinghua University, managed to get places as delegates to the congress.

---

*Zhou saw and objected to the traditionalistic tendencies of Mao's CCP. "The Party regulations of the Ninth Congress," he complained at a private meeting, "have a pervasive feudalistic coloration."

†Deng's derisory term for Cultural Revolution leftists who rose too quickly to high posts beyond their capacity.

Down in the middle ranks of the new Central Committee was another new face: the amiable, large-featured, shrewd-eyed face of Hua Guofeng, a methodical politician from Hunan Province whom Mao had gotten to know on his return to Music Mountain in 1959.

At the same time the congress brought Lin's followers to the fore. In a move of neat symmetry, if ominous import, Lin's wife as well as Mao's wife was elevated to the Politburo.

The god of mischief was sowing seeds for the future—for Lin's group and the Cultural Revolution left were poles apart in background and outlook. Lin rose during the Cultural Revolution, if only because so many others fell, but his link with the ultra-left was largely accidental.

Mao had leaned on the military and still needed them. But he agreed more with the Cultural Revolution leftists. For the time being he floated along with both wings and went nowhere in particular.

It seems that Mao had mixed feelings about the promotion to the Politburo of both Lin's wife and his own.

He worried that Jiang Qing was inclined to become "giddy with success"; he told her so in a letter. As for Ye Chun, the tough young second wife of Lin, who was also his administrative chief of staff, Mao soon began referring to her in rather sexist terms as Lin's "old woman" (*lao po*).

Mao was a bit less anti-feudal, in practice at least, than he used to be.

*   *   *

Darkest patch of all was that Mao had doubts about Lin Biao. He had known Lin for forty years and worked with him for more than thirty. But after 1966 the relationship between the two men was clouded by an issue that is delicate in any political system and exquisitely so in a Marxist dictatorship: the succession.

"People like de Gaulle and myself," Mao remarked to André Malraux in 1965, "we have no successors." Yet three years later a piece of paper from the Ninth Congress did announce Lin as Mao's successor.*

Before the ink was dry on the paper a process of rejection had begun to occur in Mao's mind. Each time a successor loomed—hand-picked by Mao as he had been—Mao stirred to a fresh burst of activity which undermined the rising successor.

There was more to the Mao-Lin problem than the tendency of number two men to remind Mao uncomfortably of his own coming death.

First, Lin's PLA had grown all too happy in its post-1967 role as a keystone of the political establishment. Mao was now bent on rebuilding the

_____

*Never before had a number two—not even Liu—been formally designated Mao's heir.

Party structure that he had so ardently tossed to the winds in 1966, but not all of Lin's PLA wanted to go back to the barracks.

Second, Mao felt that Lin during the 1960s developed a power politics mentality. It irritated the monkey in him that Lin spoke of "absolute authority."

Mao did not, like Lin, give top priority to safeguarding the edifice of political power at all costs. He was not inclined, as Lin was, to smother political differences by throwing down a blanket of military authority.

Third, naked ambition played a part. Mao, in a 1966 letter to his wife, had expressed irritation at the way Lin was packaging "Mao Thought" as a magical panacea. "I have never believed," he wrote, "that those little books of mine could have such fantastic magic, yet he blew them up, and the whole country followed." By 1969 Mao suspected that Lin was flattering him out of an ulterior motive.

Such are the deceptions of politics that Lin's hour of triumph, the Ninth CCP Congress, occurred after Mao had probably decided that Lin should *not* be his successor.

Poignant that both Mao and Lin held on to some key values of the Cultural Revolution—into an era when many in the Politburo did not—even as they failed to agree on implementing these values.

Both men stood to the left of Zhou and several other leaders, including key regional military commanders. Both despised material incentives in industry, for example, and in cultural policy both rejected the notion of art for art's sake.

But Lin wanted to carry on with Cultural Revolution policies *the army's way*. Mao not only distrusted Lin for his ambitiousness but felt that military methods were not a substitute for political methods.

"I approve of the traditional army style of quick and exact implementation," he said in remarks to local politicians, "but not in questions of ideology."

Mao wished to press on with open-ended revolution that would stir men's souls. Lin wished to consolidate the "gains" of the Cultural Revolution under military aegis.

Mao's summing-up speech to the congress was lame. After a crack at foreign journalists who had criticized the secrecy of the proceedings ("the reporters in Peking are not much good"), he gazed out at the assembly and murmured: "That's more or less that. The meeting is adjourned."

*   *   *

For some months Mao brooded—he made no public appearance between May and October—and 1969 looked like Lin Biao's year. Mao's one fresh remark, "Fear neither hardship nor death," on the occasion of Army Day, did not suggest optimism.

For the moment he had decided to give Lin rope to play with—or else he could not avoid doing so. Bonapartism grew in China.

The Red Guards, or what remained of them, now marched to the beat of Lin's left-inclined military machine.*

Not all PLA leaders liked Lin, or his leftism, or the idea of the army playing a direct political role. Such dissenters for the most part held regional rather than central military posts.

But Zhu De was among them. "Who do you think you are?" Lin shouted at the venerable Zhu during one of their arguments. "It was I, not you, who did the fighting."†

Mao's problem was that these unideological old-style military commanders were no more Maoist than they were Linist. They could be expected to abandon Lin in a crunch. But Mao's Cultural Revolution had appalled them. Some had begun to wonder if Mao's useful days were over.

Mao blamed Lin for the grotesque Mao cult, which made him seem more like a religious than a political leader. It was true that Lin hung the label "genius" on Mao. "One single sentence of his," Lin gushed, "is worth more than ten thousand of ours."

"Don't you think this is going too far?" Mao later claimed he said to Lin. "One sentence is, after all, just one sentence; how can it be worth ten thousand sentences?"

Mao feared that the infallibility of a god meant also the remoteness of a god. He suspected that Lin was trying to kick him upstairs to the high benches of sainthood.

One day in 1971, Jiang Qing, strolling at the Summer Palace, came upon an inscription on the walls of the White Cloud Pavilion: "Read Chairman Mao's Book, Listen to His Instructions." A harmless enough slogan.

But while the words were those of Lei Feng (a famous young martyr), the six-feet-high characters were done in Lin's calligraphy!

Jiang Qing was outraged that Lin should give the public the impression that *he* was the author of the slogan. Was he not using the cult of Mao to hoist himself up to fame?

Lin gave the cult a twist that understandably disturbed Mao. He made "Thought of Mao Zedong," rather than simply "Mao Zedong," the talisman of doctrinal rectitude. The "Thought of Mao Zedong," radio stations began to declare in 1970, "is the Brightest, Brightest Red Sun." The magic of Mao could outlive Mao, in other words, and be mediated by a fresh hand.

---

*"Atom" Nie gave expression to the connection by marrying an officer from within Lin's personal circle.

†Lin meant against Japan and Chiang Kai-shek.

Mao-Lin tension also arose over Lin's desire to appoint someone to fill the office of head of state, which Liu Shaoqi had occupied until the Cultural Revolution hit him. "Without such a post," Lin said, using a line of reasoning that showed how different his mind was from Mao's, "orders will not have due weight and people will not know who is in authority and who is not."

Lin said he wanted Mao to become head of state as he already had been in the early years of the PRC. Mao did not want this largely ceremonial job. But Lin was so persistent that Mao complained he had to declare six times that he would not again become head of state.

"If each time I said it I used one sentence," Mao later remarked in a sarcastic reference to Lin's pretended reverence for sentences from the Chairman's lips, "that is now the equivalent of sixty thousand sentences." He raged that apparently "each of my sentences is not even worth half a sentence."

Mao came to feel, and he was probably correct, that Lin was trying to coax Mao to offer *him* the top state job. Mao had no intention of doing so.

On the face of it Lin's clumsy overreaching on both the genius issue and the presidency issue was amazing. Had he not already been named in the new constitution as Mao's successor? Did the situation not call for patient modesty above all else?

But Lin chafed in the number two spot. Being in Mao's shadow, so near to the top job and yet still infinitely far from it, seemed to fray his judgment. (Not an uncommon fate for a number two man, as Anthony Eden found out in Churchill's shadow, and Hubert Humphrey in Lyndon Johnson's.)

Another problem for Lin was that many Chinese other than Mao began to doubt that he had what it takes to be Chairman of the CCP.

At the first National Day celebration after the Ninth Congress, on October 1, 1969, Lin and Mao appeared together on the balcony of the Gate of Heavenly Peace. Lin gave the speech. His thin, nasal voice carried no excitement. His head was buried in his script. Even as he read his lines, the one million people in front of the gate were calling out: "Chairman Mao! Chairman Mao!"

Many in the crowd must have wondered—and some leaders on the balcony did wonder—if Lin's tubercular figure really had in it the timbre of chairmanship.

* * *

Guns crackled on the banks of the Amur and Ussuri rivers in China's far northeast.

Russia and China, "brothers," treaty partners, and self-appointed beacons of proletarian internationalism to a world presumed to be in darkness, were at war over bits of icy wasteland.

Nearly a thousand were killed—most of them Chinese— in a few weeks of fighting on the eve of the Ninth Congress.

Mao was not surprised and he may even have felt grimly vindicated.* He had believed for several years that Russia, not America, was China's biggest problem. "Have no fear of tigers from the south," ran a Chinese proverb, "but beware even a rooster from the north." Mao took the proverb as policy.

When he launched his Cultural Revolution, the main international issue for Mao was how to deal with the U.S. The question he addressed to Russia—as during his brutal session with Kosygin in 1965—was the derivative one of whether Moscow could be of any assistance to China in the event of a Sino-American war.

By the time the Ninth Congress brought down the curtain on the rubble of the Cultural Revolution, the situation was an opposite one, to Mao's eye. Could he play the American card against Russia?

For this acute change in Mao's world view there were two reasons.

American policy was changing. Mao felt that the U.S., having struck trouble in Vietnam, would not in future cause trouble for China.

At Guam in mid-1969, Nixon indeed told the world that the era of U.S. military expansion in Asia was over.

Meanwhile Russian foreign policy was fully living up to the dark view Mao had held of it for a decade. Moscow sent tanks into Prague to put an end to Dubcek's experiment in democracy-within-Marxism. Mao promptly called Brezhnev and Kosygin "the new Czars."

If the doctrine of "limited sovereignty" could prompt the Russians to barge in and "rescue" Czech socialism, might it not spur them to try to scrape together a pro-Russian group in China, and prop it up at the point of Soviet bayonets?

Said Mao when Brezhnev convened an international meeting of Communist parties in mid-1969 and proposed a made-in-Moscow version of SEATO in the form of a collective security pact for Asia: "He is like a notorious prostitute who insists on having a monument erected to her chastity."

Mao was pitilessly tearing the Marxist mask off the face of the Russian bear, oblivious, it seemed, to the precedent he was setting for a later claim that his *own* Marxism was tainted beyond recognition by nationalism.

Not all of Mao's colleagues agreed with his startling shift of foreign policy line.

Peng Dehuai in 1959 had been one of the first to be puzzled by the vehe-

*Though it is possible that Lin Piao provoked the fighting, for reasons of political power.

mence of Mao's rejection of the Soviet embrace. Liu Shaoqi's idea that "joint action" with Russia was still a possibility in 1965–1966 damned him in Mao's eyes as much as did any other issue.

Now it was Lin Biao's turn to find out that Mao's hostility to Russia seemed to go beyond reasonable bounds.

Russia had come to obsess Mao. Part of the problem was his sincere distaste for Soviet socialism as it had evolved after the death of Stalin. Part of it was the cultural gap between Mao and Russia that had yawned so starkly when he and Khrushchev sparred. It is hard to separate the two factors.

If Mao had visited Russia back in the 1920s, as Zhang Guotao did, he may well have discovered, with Zhang, that Russian socialism *even under Lenin* was not a very appetizing dish to a Chinese palate.

By 1969 Mao's hostility to Russia also stemmed from a simple nationalistic calculation. America had peaked; Russia was on the rise. A tilt to the American side would serve China's interests.

There was, too, an irrational streak in Mao's obsession with Russia. Russia was a mirror in which Mao saw certain ugly realities that had to do less with Russia itself than with Marxism, shortcomings inside China, and his own style of rule.

He came to hate Russia for its espousal of "goulash communism"—in large part because China was too poor to permit consumer levels to be made the yardstick of true socialism.

He scorned Soviet "revisionism" as a travesty of Marxism—less because he held a clear-cut alternative view than because he was floundering in pessimism about the future of Marxism as a faith.

*   *   *

Mao was on the brink of giving up class analysis in favor of balance of power as the key to international politics.

The late 1960s line, agreed upon by Mao and Lin, was to call for uprisings around the world to "topple" U.S. "imperialism" and Soviet "revisionism." As Lin continued to cry out for upheaval, Mao turned into an Oriental Bismarck.

A clue to the change was Mao's new use of "hegemony." This ugly word differs from "imperialism," and even more from "revisionism." Not out of the Marxist phrasebook, as the other two are, it is an old Chinese term meaning little more than "power over others." *

Power, not a particular kind of social system, is its point of reference.

---

*The Chinese, *ba quan*, has an overtone of tyranny which the nearest English translation, "hegemony," does not quite catch.

Anyone who lords it over others is a hegemonist. So the door was opened to the unblushing amoralism of China's foreign policy in the 1970s.

Mao had done much to bring into being the global strategic triangle that became the hallmark of the early 1970s world scene.

Lin in 1970 was still urging a defiant, even-handed, and armed-to-the-teeth attitude toward both superpowers. It was not a subtle policy, though it did seem to spring logically from Mao's Cultural Revolution–period analysis of "imperialism" as a state of sin shared by Washington and Moscow.

Perhaps Mao was not sure about his own analysis even when he made it. At any rate, he had no intention of maintaining an equidistant posture toward the U.S. and the U.S.S.R. for an extended period.*

Lin simply did not agree with Mao's tilt toward the West. Zhou—unlike Lin, the premier knew the West firsthand—adjusted more readily. The turn toward the West gave Zhou a welcome opportunity to resume his old links with Americans, Frenchmen, and others.

Mao had to juggle a number of factors in the period following the Ninth Congress. There was the problem of Lin as his looming successor; how to ease him out of the number two spot and onto that well-stocked rubbish dump of history?

There was the awkward fact that many PLA officers still regarded the U.S., not Russia, as China's main enemy.

And there was the crucial variable of Russian and American responses to Mao's neo-Bismarckianism. How much anti-Sovietism would Moscow let him get away with? Would his pro-Americanism be reciprocated by a Washington long mired in anti-CCP emotion?

The Vietnam war did not make it easy for Mao to sculpt his new pro-West foreign policy.

Yet Mao felt that the trend of events in Indochina made a pro-Western policy for China all the more logical. He was already by 1970 less interested in the Indochinese wars than in what pattern of alignments would come in their wake.

Japan seemed a roadblock on the way to Mao's pro-West policy. How could Mao tilt toward the U.S. when Washington was the sponsor of the "Japanese militarism" that Peking painted in such alarming hues?

Yet Mao had long viewed Japan, not mainly in terms of China's bilateral relations with Tokyo, but in terms of the global strategic situation; his view

---

*To André Bettencourt, Mao had expressed his doubt that China could—as the French politician said France did—have good relationships with both the U.S.S.R. and the U.S. "This game of coming and going between Washington and Moscow," Mao remarked, was easier for France than for China; China did not have such freedom of movement.

of Japan followed from his view of the main contradiction at any given point.

As long as the U.S. was China's main worry, Japan's power was indeed a challenge to China's interests in Asia. But if the U.S. turned benign, fear of Japan could be forgotten for a generation. And if Russia should become China's main worry, Japan would be a potential candidate (along with the U.S.) for a united front against the Polar Bear.

The Polar Bear was not idle. Moscow was at least as shaken by the Amur-Ussuri clashes as was Peking. If Mao could call Brezhnev and Kosygin "the new Czars," that suspicious pair must have realized he might turn to Washington for insurance.

The Russians were also aware, however, that Lin and others in Peking were less anti-Soviet than Mao. They sought to forestall, or at least minimize, the sea change in Mao's foreign policy. They pressed for talks with the Chinese.

When Ho Chi Minh died and left a will that cast a shadow of shame on both Marxist giants for their feuding, the pressure was irresistible. Kosygin had to be received in the Middle Kingdom.

But only Zhou talked with him, when he arrived in September 1969, and that in the terminal of Peking airport. Mao would no longer see a Russian leader.

The truth was Mao did not want a settlement—of border issues or anything else—with a regime he had decided to defy until hell froze over.

His adamancy was increased a hundredfold by the fact that Lin wanted to maintain the policy of evenhandedness toward the U.S. and Russia that had been laid down at the Ninth Congress.

When Moscow in mid-1970 proposed holding the summit that had been agreed on in principle at the Zhou-Kosygin airport session, the Chinese government refused. It was a sign that Lin was losing out. Six months later the Russians suggested a nonaggression pact to Peking. Again the Chinese said no. Again Lin's star seemed to be sinking.

Lin may well have reflected bitterly that it was not he, but Mao, who was changing his line. "I believe it won't be long before these countries," Mao had said during the 1940s, in reference to countries in which the U.S. was setting up military bases, "come to realize who is really oppressing them, the Soviet Union or the United States."

That Mao saw Moscow stepping into Washington's shoes was made clear by his acid remark in 1970 (repeated by Zhou in my presence a year later): "The ghost of John Foster Dulles has now taken up residence in the Kremlin."

* * *

Mao-Lin tension came into the open at a Central Committee meeting on Mount Lu in the early autumn of 1970. For two and a half days a fight almost as grueling as that between Mao and General Peng Dehuai, at the same hill resort eleven years before, rocked the CCP's 255 leading figures and gave Mao sleepless nights.

Although Mao complained of a "surprise attack" from Lin and his "big generals," Lin, already feeling the chill wind of Mao's disapproval, was probably on the defensive.

The issues were the same: the headship of state, the "genius" question, the role of the PLA in politics, the issue of whether or not American imperialism was still a menace.

New was Mao's open and clear-cut opposition to Lin's views, maneuvers, and continued status as his successor.

The rights and wrongs of the clash on Mount Lu are hard to pin down, as Lin's version of events is not available. Lin was not as rude to Mao as Peng had been, but his conduct was more devious than Peng's.

The actual issues seemed less weighty than at the 1959 confrontation. In 1970 a big role was played by ambition (on Lin's side) and by psychological complexes (on Mao's side).

The consequences of Mount Lu were very clear. Politically, Lin was henceforth in sharp confrontation with Zhou. His coalition with Cultural Revolution leftists such as Jiang Qing began to unravel. He was soon reduced to being the head of a cabal of disaffected generals.

Policy-wise, the tide flowed against Lin on the "genius," head of state, and American issues.

Under a serene sun, on October 1, 1970, Mao was watching the National Day parade of floats, guns, balloons, and athletes from his balcony atop the Gate of Heavenly Peace. To his side he summoned two Americans then visiting Peking, Edgar and Lois Snow. *People's Daily* later published a front-page photo of Mao with the veteran journalist and his wife.

"A friendly American" was the label given to Snow, and a buttressing quote from Mao was chosen for the sacred box on the upper-right-hand corner of the page: "Peoples of the world, including the American people, are all our friends."

As Mao and Snow gazed down on the Mao statues, Mao busts, and Mao quotes, the American could not resist inquiring: "How does it *feel*?" Mao grimaced. The personality cult was a "nuisance," he later explained to Snow. It had served its purpose. Any prolongation of it would serve only Lin's purposes.

Richard Nixon would be welcome to visit China, Mao told the left-wing journalist over breakfast at South and Central Lakes, whether as a tourist or as President. That remark set the stage for a final tussle with Lin over foreign policy during the spring of 1971.

The last roadblock to a Mao-Nixon handshake was the U.S.-backed invasion of Laos by South Vietnamese forces in February. Fortunately for Mao's pro-American policy, the "incursion" achieved little. It merely demonstrated afresh the Saigon regime's feebleness, and so turned out to be a parable of Mao's emerging world view.

Mao went ahead with plans for a preparatory visit to China by Henry Kissinger, the German-born wizard who had been a student at Harvard when President Truman "lost China" to Mao.

One hears in China that Lin, in defense of the Ninth Congress foreign policy of evenhandedness toward the two superpowers, blazed at Mao: "If you can ask Nixon to China, why can't I ask Brezhnev?"

*   *   *

Mao worked out a strategy for one of the biggest—though not closest—battles of his career. It could not but be big and bloody. Lin had been elevated very high in the eyes of the Chinese public and even named in the constitution as China's next supreme leader.

He had risen up on the left-wing wave of the Cultural Revolution; difficult to repaint *this* budding renegade as a "rightist."

And Lin held the gun. Even Peng had not had firmly on his side a line-up of military leaders as senior as that which, by mid-1971, was conspiring to replace the Mao dynasty with a Lin dynasty. Not since the fight with Zhang Guotao during the Long March, indeed, did Mao have so much CCP military punch arrayed against him.

Getting rid of Lin would command its price. Mao had months in which to weigh it.

He had to move cautiously. So he first purged Chen Boda, who had become allied with Lin, to cut the bonds between Lin and the ultra-left; and then, at meetings in December 1970 and April 1971, aimed his fire at the "big generals" who surrounded Lin.

The heir apparent himself Mao pretended to "protect" and even "save."

A crucial division *within* the military, and a brilliant job by Zhou, gave Mao victory.

The PLA had long been a self-reliant, political army, living close to the soil. That changed in the 1950s, after power was won and the army underwent Soviet-style professionalization. A gap emerged between the PLA leadership in Peking and that in the regions.

The center (especially the small but growing air force and navy) became more like modern military establishments in other countries. The regions, led in many cases by earthy veterans of the Long March, remained more traditional and less impressed by the ideological fashions of the moment.

Unintended results of the Cultural Revolution sharpened the differentiation.

Mao had encouraged Lin to militarize the social order and politicize the military order. He had by this same stroke turned off many a regional military commander. By early 1971 Mao needed to change sides, and thanks to Zhou he was able to mask his defection.

Zhou and the commanders were less inclined than Mao and Lin to hold fast to the values of the Cultural Revolution. Their alliance (a rather anti–Cultural Revolution one) now saved Mao from Lin. The PLA split. Zhou, on Mao's behalf, harvested anti-Lin fruits from the split.

Mao coolly made Lin's central military establishment the third target (following Liu and the utopians) of the cannibalizing crusade that was his Cultural Revolution.

Earlier he had propagated the slogan "Let the People of the Whole Country Learn from the PLA." Now he dryly observed: "This is incomplete." He tacked on an explosive, negating addition: "Let the PLA Learn from the People of the Whole Country."

The PLA would no longer be exempt from the "dialectic" of the monkey's second thoughts.

Soon the last of the provincial Party committees were set up. This could not but mean a clipping of the PLA's wings. Soldiers had come into the political arena when the Party committees lay in ruins as a result of Red Guard smashing. Now they were being asked to give up the bright lights and go back into the trenches.

Each time Mao closed the internal door further against Lin, he opened China's external door further to America.

He convened a Central Work Conference to force self-criticisms from an inner group of Lin confidants that reached as close as Lin's wife. In the same month of April 1971 he sent a message to Washington that the way was clear—the Laos crisis had simmered down—for an American official to come to Peking in midsummer.

Just before Kissinger came in across the Himalayas the Chinese press broke out in a rash of articles about the noble CCP tradition of Party control of the gun.

As the world reeled from the shock of seeing Kissinger go in and out of Mao's door, a parallel duality colored the muted celebration of China's Army Day. Lin's friend Huang Yongsheng, the urbane chief of staff of the

PLA, gave a speech that assailed the U.S. and did not mention Russia once.

Meanwhile Mao ordered republished a 1945 essay, *On Policy,* which justified his decision at that time to negotiate with Chiang Kai-shek, and by implication also justified his new dealings with the Americans.

Then Mao, on a tour of military bases in south China to argue the case against Lin, forced a dramatic confrontation with a sullen and silent Chief of Staff Huang. "I just don't believe that our army could rebel," Mao began at a Party session. Then he apparently turned his face toward the chief of staff: "I just don't believe that you, Huang Yongsheng, could order the Liberation Army to rebel!"

On reaching Shanghai during his tour, Mao called in one of Huang's closest military colleagues and asked him: "What is your impression of Huang Yongsheng?" The officer, unaware that Mao was on the warpath, spoke warmly of his senior colleague.

Mao rejoined icily: "Huang Yongsheng is a swindler of the Liu Shaoqi type."

According to a story given credence in Canton, the sweating officer abjectly confessed his faulty judgment about "swindler Huang." Mao purred like a cat. "As pleased as if he had taken some tranquilizing pills," he earnestly gave the officer "confidential instructions" for his future role in the anti-Lin and anti-Huang cause.

By his own admission, Mao in all these ways *moved against Lin* after Mount Lu.

A part of Lin's circle grew desperate and hatched a counterplot that brought about in the autumn of 1971 a Götterdämmerung of top-level death and dismissal.

*   *   *

Lin retreated to lovely Suzhou for urgent talks among the willows and canals with his wife and his 26-year-old son, the foolhardy Lin Liguo, who had risen at nepotistic speed to be a deputy commander in the air force. Their exact conclusions at this session in the early spring are not known,* but the evolution of events suggests that they failed to reach a common mind.

The impetuous son, Liguo, together with some other Young Turks in the air force, began to plan a coup d'état against Mao. They went ahead with a crude scheme, without the agreement, perhaps even the knowledge, of Lin and his senior followers. Ye Chun—Lin's second wife and 22 years his junior—joined in as the plot skidded forward.

---

*A key document about Lin's activities, the alleged "571 Plot" outline, may have been tampered with by the Peking government.

Lin probably heard of the coup only as a *fait accompli*. Huang Yongsheng and the other pro-Lin leaders may never have been involved in it at all.

At the same time Lin was certainly obsessed with Mao and now probably hated him. He had betrayed his anxiety about the succession by remarking that Mao may well live "over one hundred years."

Liguo was trying to salvage his father's career.

The coup was code-named "571." Pronounced in Chinese it can also mean "armed uprising." The blueprint referred to Mao as "B-52." To use a term of infamy from the still-raging Vietnam War was certainly an insult. It may also have carried the overtone of alleged pro-Americanism on Mao's part.

At any rate, the image of Mao as a giant moving high above all else, striking suddenly, was not inapt.

Nor were the denunciations of Mao in the blueprint without their point (inconceivable that Mao's Peking would have totally concocted a picture that was in parts so damaging in its proximity to the truth):

- "Those who are his greatest friends today will be his prisoners tomorrow."
- "[B-52] is a paranoid and a sadist. . . . He is the greatest dictator and tyrant in China's history."
- "B-52 favors those who struggle with the pen rather than those who struggle with the gun."
- "When B-52 has decided to make someone lose face, he never stops halfway."
- "Even [B-52's] own son has been driven mad by him."
- "Our strength is still not at a maximum of preparation and the cult of B-52 is deep among the masses."

The pro-Lin conspirators had some harebrained schemes in mind. One was to have Mao killed in a traffic accident. (Was there enough traffic in the Peking of 1971 for a convincing accident to be staged?) For whatever reason, few of the Lin group's weird plans were actually acted upon.

After the fall of Lin, the Chinese government made accusations of a number of other attempts on Mao's life.

Poison was said to have been inserted into Mao's food.

A mansion in Shanghai in which he was staying in autumn 1971 was "strafed" by air force fighters.

An explosive charge was planted in Mao's train as he sped north for the climactic showdown in Peking at the end of his southern tour. (The plotter lost his nerve; Mao's entourage learned of the explosive; Mao got off the train and continued to Peking by car.)

Within hours of Lin's demise, an officer "appeared at South and Central Lakes" in a last-ditch effort to shoot Mao on the spot. (He wilted with guilt; the gun fell from his hand; he fell on his knees and begged forgiveness for his almighty crime.)

It is impossible to verify these amazing charges. Probably they are exaggerations of acts that Liguo and the Young Turks at least contemplated. It is unlikely that Lin himself made any attempt to kill Mao.

Force was used, however, at the top echelon of Chinese politics in the autumn of 1971. In one way or another, Lin and five other members of the Politburo died violent deaths in the second week of September.

At this time Mao's personal situation was insecure enough that he felt he had to move out of his residence at South and Central Lakes. He could not "sleep or eat there safely," according to Jiang Qing; the compound had been "infiltrated by the enemy."

The pair of them, with staff, moved to the Golden Seas Hotel. Because the hotel was not convenient, they later moved again, to the cavernous chambers of the Great Hall of the People.

Desire to get away from intense pressure, a recurring impulse in Mao's life, made him leave Peking in mid-August for a month-long trip in the south.

Signs of a drama moving to its climax existed once Mao arrived back in Peking.

After September 10, none of the four pro-Lin PLA leaders in the Politburo ever appeared in public again. From the next evening, all of China's top leaders were out of sight for several days—they were in urgent consultation at the Great Hall of the People. During this period air movements in China virtually ceased.

Mao had made only one publicized appearance since May Day—a meeting (not in Peking) with Ne Win of Burma—and none since early August. People began to gossip about his condition.

Foreigners noted with knowing nods that Dr. Paul Dudley White, the American heart specialist, had arrived in Peking at the invitation of the Chinese Medical Association on September 18.

CCP members, receiving a sufficient flow of sensitive information to guess at the Mao-Lin tension, were anxious on other grounds.

In Hong Kong an arresting piece of verbal gymnastics was performed. The building of the Bank of China, Peking's hand on Hong Kong's heart, had for some time borne an illuminated slogan, "Long Live the Invincible Thought of Mao Zedong." The phrase was Lin's. It was highly suitable for Lin's purposes.

In early September the red neon tubes came down. A new slogan went up:

"Long Live Chairman Mao." A slogan less suitable for Lin's purposes. The heir apparent was apparently no longer heir.

Soon an internal CCP document carried the news that Lin, having attempted a coup d'état, died when his fleeing plane crashed over the People's Republic of Mongolia. Then the Mongolians laconically announced the "intrusion" and crash over the village of Undur Khan of a Trident belonging to the Chinese Air Force.

But how did Lin really die? Is it possible that *Mao killed Lin?*

According to Peking, Lin died in the air crash which Mongolia (and its big brother Russia) reported to the world in prim, sparse terms. Heading for Russia, he had hastily boarded a plane that was not properly fueled. It did not last the distance.

As in all fine Chinese stories, a hero was involved—Lin's daughter—as well as a number of villains.

The Lin family was on holiday at the seaside resort of Beidaihe in early September. The bungled efforts to kill Mao led the Lins to retreat and consult. A plan was drawn up to flee to Moscow (where Lin had spent some four years of his life). "Little Bean" thought this was too much.

"Little Bean" (so named because of her father's lifelong habit of chewing roasted beans during battles) was a twenty nine-year-old daughter of Lin's first marriage. She was not greatly enamored of her stepmother.

She tipped off Zhou about her parents' nefarious plans.

Zhou picked up the phone and made a seemingly innocent exploratory call to Beidaihe. Lin was out of the house at a concert. Ye Chun took the call. She assured Zhou that she and her husband were merely on a quiet vacation and had no plans to fly anywhere.

After hanging up she hurtled to the concert hall to warn Lin. Something more must have gone wrong, she hissed; Zhou suspected their plan to flee.

In a convoy of cars the Lins rushed to Beidaihe airport. A guard who resisted Lin was shot by Liguo and pushed half dead out of a speeding car. Suspicious members of the fueling crew parked two huge trucks across the runway to impede the takeoff of Lin's Trident.

Lin's plane got into the air only after grazing one of the fuel trucks, detouring through a field, and using prodigious amounts of fuel in the process. An accompanying helicopter, full of top Lin colleagues and boxes of documents, including Lin's diaries, came to grief after its pilot was shot for refusing to follow Lin.

The Trident ran out of fuel 250 kilometers beyond the Chinese border and crashed and burned just east of Ulan Bator, the Mongolian capital, where Lin had planned to refuel.

Some of this may be true. It is by no means the whole truth, for it cannot accommodate some known facts. A top-level meeting took place at the Great Hall of the People *before* the tawdry scenes at Beidaihe. Mao had arrived back in Peking to chair it.

This would seem to reduce the importance of Little Bean's role.

The session at the Great Hall must have moved in some way against the Lin group. At minimum it removed them from office. At maximum Lin and some of his cohorts may have been killed, on the spot in the heart of Peking, or very soon after at Beidaihe.

"Lin didn't dare put his plot into practice," Zhou told a group of American editors in 1973. Then whose sword forced the denouement?

"Lin planned to assassinate several members of the Politburo," the CCP later claimed. Were some of his own group assassinated as punishment for the intent?

Clear at any rate that Mao had been undermining Lin for at least a year. Clear that the alleged attempts to kill Mao gave Mao sufficient ground to arrest some or all of Lin's group. Clear as well (confirmed by Peking after Moscow stated it) that some of the nine bodies found in the wreckage at Undur Khan were riddled with bullet holes.

One of the very few remarks known to have been made by Mao during the final crisis was his ominous "Let him go, he won't get far," made late on the night of September 12. It suggests that Mao had managed to cook Lin's goose at the eleventh hour.

Unclear is why Moscow would not have exploited, far more richly than it has, any hard evidence that Lin switched his loyalty from Mao to the Soviet Union. One notes that Peking made the charge that Lin had secret contacts with Moscow *only much later* than its initial secret description of the crisis to Party cadres in September 1971.

All in all, it is unlikely that Lin was a prime mover in the second week of September. It cannot be excluded that he died before, even long before, the climax of September 12. (He had not been seen in public since June 3.)

Moscow claimed that none of the nine charred bodies at Undur Khan was that of a person "over fifty years of age." A touch of Russian bluff. A team of Chinese diplomats from Peking's embassy in Ulan Bator went quickly to the scene of the fiery crash and buried the bodies. They said the bodies had been burned beyond recognition.

In calmer days, more than a year later, Kosygin told Chancellor Brandt of Germany that this was so. Pressed about the "over fifty years of age" claim, Russian sources quietly backed away from it.*

---

*Had the Russians been seeking to have Mao believe that Lin was alive and well—and talking—in Moscow?

If the Russians did find identifiable bodies and documents among the wreckage, and felt the evidence could be used to embarrass Peking, it is hard to understand why Moscow refused the British manufacturers of the Trident permission to examine the wreckage.

Everything Peking said later hinged on whether or not the corpses were identifiable. Sure that Moscow could not prove to the world that Lin was on the Trident, the Chinese history-makers were free to assert that Lin *was* on it. That enabled them to neatly cover up any grisly details of violence that occurred within China's corridors of power before the night flight into Mongolia.

The crash at Undur Khan was probably a footnote to a drama already completed in Peking.

Liguo and his Young Turks took drastic steps, including some of which Lin was later accused. Perhaps Mao ordered a defense, or a retaliation, against these steps, which in turn engulfed Lin.

His death is unlikely to have been an accident.

It could have been suicide, or a death from illness while in detention sometime before mid-September.

It was probably murder.

"He [B-52] is wary of us," ran a passage in the "571" blueprint, drawn up in the spring of 1971. "It is better to burn our bridges behind us than to sit and wait to be captured." Here was a clue to Lin's undoing. He was caught between two millstones: Mao's withdrawal of confidence in him, and the impetuous response to that colossal reverse by Young Turks within his own camp.

Mao ended Lin's career, if not his life.*

* * *

National Day 1971 passed in an eerie atmosphere. There was no giant parade—for the first time in the history of the PRC—and Mao was still out of sight. Grandstands had been erected in early September, ready for the parade and the viewing of National Day fireworks. In mid-month they were speedily dismantled.

Low-key festivities unrolled in the parks. Zhou appeared at midday to escort Prince Sihanouk on a boat trip at the Summer Palace. Three American

---

*In 1973 Prime Minister Whitlam of Australia asked Mao if Lin Biao had really been conspiring with Russia. Mao replied: "We suspected for some time that he was. He'd spent a lot of time in Russia during the war against Japan—instead of being back in China fighting. His flight north was proof of it. Then, after his death, we found documents that made the link quite clear."

Black Panther leaders were there, and a French chef who had come to China at Sihanouk's invitation. But few of the Politburo.

Zhou seemed like a host trying to pretend that a funeral is a party.

Mao was present only in the form of huge blowup photos. At Peking airport the set of fifty photos of Mao's life that had been released in time for National Day shrank overnight to thirty-nine. The eleven in which Lin appeared had been whisked away.

People's Daily did not offer its usual celebratory editorial on October 1. Nor a picture of Mao and Lin together (the ultimate in political photography during 1970–1971). Some people inside China as well as outside thought Mao was dead—or gravely ill in the hands of Dr. Paul Dudley White.

At last on October 7 Mao surfaced. He was seen on TV benignly greeting Haile Selassie of Ethiopia. At a welcoming banquet the previous evening, the Ethiopian emperor was greeted in Mao's name alone. A well-informed citizen—reading the greeting in *People's Daily*—knew this was most unusual. Haile Selassie had toasted Lin as well as Mao in his banquet speech, heard by many foreign diplomats and Chinese cadres.

People's Daily handled this thorny problem by omitting the toasts altogether from its report of the occasion. Again most unusual. The careful reader could guess that a power shakeup had occurred.

From Radio Lhasa, on October 4, was heard for the last time in China the famous, hallowed reference to the CCP "with Chairman Mao as head and Vice-Chairman Lin as deputy." Thereafter even Tibet grasped the message that Mao stood all alone without a deputy.

Amid all this, Mao's China, so long judged unworthy by dozens of other nations to take part in the international community, was voted in festive mood into a UN seat, including permanent membership of the Security Council.

Foreign embassies in Peking were advised that in their telegrams of felicitation to the Chinese government on its victory at New York it was "not necessary" to include Lin's name. North Korea, as close to Peking as any foreign government, sent a model telegram. It mentioned only Mao and Zhou.

Other governments fell into line. The world had put its seal of recognition on Lin's fall.

*   *   *

The Lin crisis was huge and costly.

Little more than two years after the "triumphant" conclusions of the Cultural Revolution, one third of the CCP's top leadership fell from grace as "Party enemies."

Never in its history had the PLA been so rocked by split and subsequent purge as in 1971–1972. The spectacle of senior officers fleeing toward Russia, and some twenty middle-level officers trying to escape to Hong Kong, was an appalling blow to Mao as the PLA's commander in chief.

On Lin's side there was nepotism, ambition, and a high-handed disregard for any role by the masses in politics.

On Mao's side there was a similar by-passing of the masses; a terrible lack of judgment, or nerve, or both, about his "boundlessly loyal" successor; and a failure to hold on to the top PLA leadership in Peking as he repudiated Lin.

The crisis diverted Mao for a year from urgent domestic problems. It drove a few more nails into the coffin of the Cultural Revolution's reputation. It fed a mounting pessimism in Mao's own mind about the future course of the Chinese Revolution.

Accusations built up of illicit foreign currency dealings, gun battles in the cockpits of Chinese Air Force planes, spy equipment imported from "decadent" Hong Kong, murder plots and poison gas and kidnapping, and a morbid fascination on the part of some PRC leaders with the ideas and stratagems of China's feudal past.

Mao's lakeside cottage at Hangzhou was bugged during the Lin crisis, according to his wife, and one Central Committee member sent a diversionary telegram to Mao to keep his mind off his immediate vicinity, where an anti-Mao group was surrounding his residence.

Another member of that ruling body was so harassed in his own neighborhood that Mao found a spare bedroom for him at South and Central Lakes, Jiang Qing also divulged, and Mao's own daughter, Li Na, was almost kidnapped by Lin agents.

A stench of intrigue and suspicion and doubt had come to stay in the corridors of Mao's Peking.

How could Mao admit to himself that sordid plots went on in his Politburo? He had discounted the purity of Marxist theory and practice more than a decade before. His loss of the historic Moscow-based faith during the epoch of de-Stalinization lay behind his acceptance of the abysmal standards of 1970–1971. A *tant pis* spirit was not that surprising in a man who was now an amoral gambler using doctrine mainly as a rapier of power.

There was a loss of credibility involved in erasing Lin's name from the PRC's honor roll of achievement. The Central Committee transmitted this sad, lame secret document:

Resolved by the Central Committee of the Chinese Communist Party: Copies of the 'Constitution of the Chinese Communist Party,' 'Documents of the Ninth Party Congress,' and 'Long Live the Victory of People's War' be turned in to the central authorities for disposal. Other works about Lin Biao, as well as Lin Biao's epitaphs and portraits, be collected by the basic levels and submitted to the county authorities for disposal.

Many a nightmare lay ahead of Mao as a result of this paper-tiger effort to cancel Lin and all his deeds.*

In a letter to Jiang Qing, Mao had tried to make a distinction between his own standpoint and that of those, including Lin, whom he felt were conniving against him. "What they want to do is overthrow our Party and myself," he claimed. "This is the difference between me and the black gang."

But it is a distinction clear only to eyes that bulge with the zeal of battle.

Lin might well have thought Mao was seeking to "overthrow the Party and myself." The phrase is chaff, after all, except for "myself," which is its kernel. What could "overthrowing the Party" possibly mean among squabbling comrades who were themselves all leaders of the Party?

The Lin affair knocked so much stuffing out of Mao that he would never again, in his remaining five years, appear in person before the Chinese public.

---

*One comparison made in the welter of anti-Lin propaganda seemed apter than any other. The Mao-Lin struggle bore a family resemblance, it was said, to the Mao–Zhang Guotao struggle. It was true. In both cases vain men were vying against each other. Zhang and Lin each built up a separate show that got in the way of Mao's show.

20

Nixon (1972)

On a crisp February day in 1972, U.S. President Richard Nixon's *Spirit of '76* touched down on the bare vast tarmac of Peking airport. It drew up before the American flag fluttering from one staff, the PRC flag fluttering from another, and a huge photo of Mao's face in between.

The President bounded out with a half smile. Zhou Enlai was waiting expressionless at the foot of the ramp. Remembering John Foster Dulles's refusal to shake hands with Zhou in Geneva in 1954, Nixon rammed his hand at Zhou's.

Within a few hours Nixon was sitting in a loose-cover armchair beside Mao at South and Central Lakes. By late evening, thanks to his mere presence in that chair, Nixon had in twelve hours done more for U.S.-China relations than any President had managed to do in the previous twenty-four years—since Marshall's mediation efforts failed.

People's Daily did not mention Nixon or his trip on the day he arrived. The six-page issue's only reference to the U.S. came in an article about the death, one week before, of Mao's American friend, Edgar Snow.

If Nixon and Snow were hardly ideological birds of a feather, it was typical of Mao's style to juxtapose them. By having the press speak only of Snow on "Nixon's day," he managed to unnerve the American side, to suggest to the Chinese people the enduring validity of his view that the "American people" were on the side of light, to convey an impressive insouciance on the eve of a great encounter, and not least to magnify the impact of the *next* day's *People's Daily*.*

---

*See page 359. Nixon no doubt felt relieved to recall that not long before leaving for China, he had written a cordial letter to the dying Edgar Snow, and referred in it to "your distinguished career [that] is so widely respected and appreciated." Mao had not realized that Nixon thought so well of the left-wing journalist. Indeed, his own tribute to Snow may have been meant to remind Nixon that Snow's voice as a "friend of China" had been a lonely one for many years.

The situation was delicate for Mao as for Nixon. He could not introduce the President to a full array of Politburo colleagues. Gaping holes left by Lin and his group had not yet been filled.

Except for Jiang Qing, who could hardly decline her husband's request to escort the Nixons to a performance of *Red Detachment of Women,* the Cultural Revolution leftists were not to the fore.

Only two members of the Politburo, other than Mao and Zhou, had more than a few words with the Americans during the eight-day visit: Ye Jianying, an anti-Lin moderate now in charge of the PLA, and Li Xiannian, another moderate whose portfolio was economics.

Mao was also cautious about drawing the Chinese public into the mood of the summit. Certain facts could not be got around. China and the U.S. had no diplomatic relations. Ordinary Chinese had been fed on a diet of anti-Americanism for twenty years.

Some military officers, in partial sympathy with Lin's point of view, were lukewarm about the talks, mindful that Washington continued to cling to Chiang Kai-shek's regime as the government of China.

Just two months before, a pamphlet dissenting from the Mao-Zhou line on the U.S.A. had gone on sale—for a few hours until suppressed—in some Peking bookstores; *Problems of Chinese-American Relations* no doubt stemmed from a PLA source that felt Russia was less dangerous, and the U.S. more so, than Mao now felt.

Mao's friends in Indochina were still locked in a relationship of daily mutual slaughter with America. China's closest ally, North Korea, on the eve of the visit declared, with Mao in mind as much as Nixon, that the U.S. President was going to Peking with "a white flag in one hand and a beggar's bowl in the other." Albania and North Vietnam maintained a silence of disapproval on the Nixon trip.

*   *   *

Mao was even more secretive than Nixon in his preparations. Not all members of the Politburo were drawn into the plans; there was more than one "William Rogers"* on the Chinese side. Peking's briefing of North Vietnam, Cambodia, and other sensitive allies, done mostly by Zhou in the middle of the night, beat Washington's last-minute efforts with Japan, South Korea, South Vietnam, and others only by a few hours.

Secrecy was enormously easier for Mao than for Nixon. Foreign policy in Mao's Peking was a subject not for journalism (how Kissinger loved China for that!) but only for ceremony.

*The U.S. secretary of state, who had been peripheral to the making of China policy.

Between Kissinger's first visit to China in the summer of 1971, through a second Kissinger trip, a further trip by General Alexander Haig and press secretary Ronald Ziegler, and a number of other advance activities, to the eve of the President's arrival, the total number of Chinese characters devoted by Peking's press to all aspects of the Nixon visit was 1,647. The few items were chastely placed at the bottom-right-hand corner of page one, like weather reports. All were severely factual; no analysis was attempted.

In characteristic Chinese fashion, one type of preparation was simply too important to be keep secret. Peking residents found, to their dismay, that at their favorite restaurants the magic touch seemed to disappear in the first weeks of February.

The best chefs had been seconded to the kitchens of the Great Hall of the People!

Mao did not deign to appear at a banquet himself, but he insisted that at these vast feeding operations, in a dining room the size of a baseball field, the Americans were served the best shark's fin, stewed prawns, and spongy bamboo shoots that the Middle Kingdom had to offer.

On leaving Washington the U.S. President compared his trip to China with his countrymen's voyage to the moon. America had no out-of-this-world flavor on Mao's palate, as China had on Nixon's. Long before Nixon had picked up the topic of China as an exotic stick to beat Democrats with in the 1950s, Washington's conduct in China was one of the variables Mao faced in his struggle to best Chiang Kai-shek.

Still Mao felt a bit out of touch. It had been a quarter century since he last dealt with American officials. He decided to brush up on his meager English.

His latest assault on English was not much more successful than the previous ones over fifty years, but it did begin long before Nixon opened his briefing books and invited André Malraux to dine and gesticulate at the White House.

In the summer of 1971 Mao was already back at his English textbook. "The two new phrases he's fond of pronouncing at present," Mao's friend Guo Moruo told me just as Mao and Kissinger met for the first time, "are 'law and order' and 'anti-Mao.' "

No doubt both phrases had come to Mao's notice during the fight with Lin.

Mao and Nixon! To a pre-1971 eye the duet seemed outlandish.

• When Nixon was in office as Vice-President, the U.S. three times threatened Mao's China with nuclear weapons.

• The U.S. more than a dozen times blocked the seating of Mao's government in the UN.

- In the twenty-two years Mao had ruled from the Forbidden City, not a single government official from either country visited the capital of the other, until Nixon sent Kissinger the previous summer.
- During 1969 and 1970 the Chinese press called Nixon "God of Plague and War," as if the prefix were a replacement for "Richard Milhous."

Yet there it was: a U.S. President was visiting Mao's Peking before a U.S. President had ever visited either Tokyo or Moscow. The eight-day stay in China was the longest visit to any foreign country by a U.S. President. It was the first time a U.S. President had ever negotiated on the soil of a nation that lacked diplomatic relations with the U.S.

And it was *Nixon* of all Presidents. His own chief of staff, H. R. Haldeman, said that "Nixon for years had been this nation's foremost enemy of Communist China."

Here he was beaming with joy alongside America's *bête noire* in the Orient. There was Pat Nixon done up in a red dress carefully chosen by her New York designer for Red China.

And Mao presiding with a grandfather's mixture of pride, hospitality, and condescension. The god of plague and war had come by with his wife for a cup of tea.

The world could be excused for wiping its eyes.

Each man had held a dim view of the other. But Nixon, once he decided to go and see Mao, felt a need to depict his mission in expansive terms. At Guam airport, en route to Shanghai, he recalled that in terms of the clock, Guam is where the American day begins. "I would hope that all of you here today would join me in this prayer," he cried, "that with this trip to China a new day may begin for the whole world."

The American party flying from Washington to Peking was provided with chopsticks to eat the Western-style airborne meals! Once in Peking, Nixon quoted Mao's poetry as if it were Holy Scripture.

Mao did not change mental gears in such a way. He hung no new moral label on Nixon. He is not known to have referred to the summit in terms as lofty as Nixon's "the week that changed the world."

Certainly he did not take to the knife and fork. Or quote from Nixon's *Six Crises*.

Yet the Chinese side was not entirely immune to the intoxications of summitry. A number of buildings and streets mysteriously changed their names a month before Nixon came.

Mrs. Nixon visited the Capital Hospital. A few weeks before, its name was Anti-Imperialist Hospital. The street north of Mao's own quarters in the Forbidden City, named by Red Guards, with dubious aptness, Street of Workers, Peasants, and Soldiers, reverted, before the Nixons glided along it, to its long-standing name, Street of the Gate of the Earth.

Still, there was a gap in moral expectation between the two partners.

True, balance-of-power politics was hardly less prominent in Nixon's motivations than in Mao's (especially if domestic politics is included). True, both men had one eye on Russia.

But Mao, a Chinese pragmatist, did not dress up balance-of-power politics in a mantle of morality; Nixon, tinged with America's idealism, did.

Mao did not expect to reach any moral consensus with Nixon. It was symptomatic that he suggested a "divided" communiqué.

The U.S. did not have in mind for the two sides to express their disagreements in such a clear-cut way as to have an "American section" and a "Chinese section" in the communiqué. But Zhou came to Kissinger one night and said Mao insisted upon it. "It is more honest," he stressed. He got his way; the Shanghai Communiqué exposed disagreements frankly.

It was Nixon who made a long journey. He sent an advance party of eighty and took with him a total press contingent of 168.

Mao stayed home. Throughout Nixon's stay in Peking he did not budge once from his quarters in the Forbidden City.

He did not go to the airport to meet *Spirit of '76.* Nor to the banquets. Nor to any of the policy talks. Zhou handled these for the Chinese side; Mao's niece, Wang Hairong, always present at them, briefed Mao after each session.

Mao did not even talk with Nixon on the telephone subsequent to the meeting of the two men, which occurred on the first of Nixon's eight days in China, or exchange any written message with him during the rest of Nixon's stay.

Despite all that, the climactic moment of Nixon's trip came in Mao's sitting room, amid his Ming dynasty books,* next door to where he slept, and read, and ate his hot Hunan dishes.

Nixon felt moved, and thought Mao was too, as he walked into Mao's book-strewn room. A girl aide helped Mao to his feet. "I can't talk very well," he murmured in reference to a bronchial condition. Meanwhile the two men clasped hands, and Mao, according to Nixon, held on to Nixon's hand for a full minute.

As he did so he joked to Nixon: "Our common old friend, Generalissimo Chiang Kai-shek, doesn't approve of this." It was an effective start, yet the Americans were in too positive a mood to take it as a point against them.

All three Americans in the room (Nixon, Kissinger, Winston Lord) im-

---

*Kissinger in his memoirs says "manuscripts lined bookshelves along every wall,"but these were actually old Chinese books, which are stored horizontally on shelves.

mediately sensed Mao's strength of will. "I am convinced that if I'd never met the man," Winston Lord remarked, "didn't know who he was, and I walked into a cocktail party at which he was present, he would draw me to him by his power."

Mao remarked on Kissinger's cleverness in slipping in and out of China in 1971 without being noticed. Nixon responded that Kissinger had been unique in his ability to travel to Paris and Peking without anyone knowing of it "except possibly a couple of pretty girls."

"So you often make use of your girls?" Mao inquired of Nixon.

There was not much talk about international politics. "Those questions are not questions to be discussed in my place," Mao said a bit haughtily when Nixon mentioned a list of countries which the U.S. and China should do something about. "They should be discussed with the premier. I discuss the philosophical questions."

Mao smiled often—"a smile both penetrating and slightly mocking, warning . . . that there was no point in seeking to deceive this specialist in the foibles and duplicity of man"—and conducted a Socratic discussion. Each topic he dealt with by an aphorism or a remark with an indirect meaning. "Actually," he pointed out to Nixon in a second reference to Chiang Kaishek, "the history of our friendship with him is much longer than the history of *your* friendship with him."

"There was no frontal brilliance as with Zhou," Winston Lord observed, "but an allusive, elliptical, seemingly casual style that was actually very subtle and skillful."

If the Mao-Nixon conversation was not of a caliber to set the world on fire—they did not negotiate, or even talk much about policy—its mere occurrence very nearly did.

American reporters correctly judged that a Mao-Nixon talk on the first afternoon guaranteed a basic success to the trip.

People's Daily devoted two pages and seven photos to Nixon's activities for that day. Chinese TV carried a ten-minute film. After that, most ordinary Chinese did not hesitate to look and smile at the American visitors, if they saw them passing by.

On both sides the change of mood seemed more abrupt than Mao's one-hour role could justify. But the reality of the change was undeniable. Mao had exerted dominion from his armchair. Had he not won a vital, if still obscure victory over the Americans for the first time in his life?

*   *   *

For Mao the "week that changed the world" was not a sudden extravaganza, but part of a strategy that had gradually evolved. For several years he had felt that America was a shrinking problem for China. When Nixon showed real interest in dealing with China, in 1970, Mao was more than ready.

A team of American table tennis players had gone to Japan in March 1971 for the world championships. China asked several national teams to come and play in Peking on their way home. Some of the U.S. players were eager to go to China. It happened that the day they left for Japan, the U.S. government fully lifted the ban on Americans' going to the PRC. The American players expressed interest to the Chinese players.

Soon a cable came from Zhou Enlai saying an invitation to the Americans was not possible. In Peking, Mao heard of Zhou's cable and disapproved. He ordered a phone call to overrule the cable.* The Americans were invited and accepted.

An important symbolic step toward Nixon's visit had been taken. And Zhou learned in a crisp way the nature of Mao's feelings on the American issue.

As he dryly put it to some American visitors months later: "Chairman Mao happened to take an interest" in improving relations with Washington. The stage manager took in good grace the shouts of the producer.

The immediate background to the Mao-Nixon handshake was America's Vietnam problem. Nixon was seeking, with great skill, to disguise America's inability to prevail in Vietnam—in a benign haze of détente with China.

If Vietnam was a spur for Nixon, it was from Mao's point of view an obstacle to Sino-American conciliation. Nixon was still in lively torment from the war; he wanted Mao's help to get this albatross off his neck. Mao wished to look beyond Vietnam, but he could not quite do so; strong pressures within the Marxist world required him to go on supporting his troublesome Indochinese friends.

In a way Mao had achieved his main aim when Nixon walked into his study.

For a quarter century he wanted America only *not* to do certain things. He worried about an attack on China by the U.S. in the late 1940s (when Washington was aiding Chiang); in 1950 (as an outgrowth of the Korean War); in 1953 (when Eisenhower was trying to pressure China into a Korean truce); in 1954 and 1958 (the Taiwan Strait crises); and in 1966 (when some U.S. generals were attracted to the idea of winning the Vietnam War by striking at China).

---

*Mao made an interesting remark to Nixon that related to this division in Peking. China had been insisting, Mao said, that major issues would have to be settled before people-to-people visits could take place. "Later on I saw you were right," he confessed, "and we played table tennis."

U.S. expansionism in Asia seemed to Mao to have stopped dead there on the rug between Nixon and himself. He was exaggerating the American decline, as we shall see, but he was correct to feel in Nixon's presence a guarantee that the U.S. and China would not fight each other again for many years.

Mao could be excused if he felt that a number of American illusions about China lay in dust beneath the feet of the summiteers.

Where was the sense of innocence that had marked U.S. forays into the Far East? For Nixon came with the cloud of Vietnam shadowing his face. Where was America's unilateral sense of mission in the Orient? For Nixon came to say that America was prepared to share the future in Asia with China. Where indeed was the Prometheanism of America's post–World War II role in Asia? For Nixon arrived on the trail of a falling dollar and asked Mao's "help" in ending the Vietnam War.

Positive cooperation, however, was not going to be easy. The U.S.-China dialogue was hardly beyond the stage of baby talk. Each side knew far less about the other's politics than is the case today.

On only one current international dispute did Mao and the Americans see eye to eye. Both supported Pakistan in its grievance against India over the amputation of East Bengal (Bangladesh).

Mao took a long-range view of Vietnam that was not possible for a Nixon still embroiled in the war. The American, on the other hand, wanted to discuss the future of Asia in the long-range terms of his "structure of peace." Mao had to remain elliptical on that, for fear of being seen to abandon his Indochinese friends.

On Russia too, time and space bore a different relation to each other for the two sides. Stunningly enough, Nixon, the visceral redbaiter, was more anxious about Russian reactions to the "week that changed the world" than Mao was. Mao was looking far ahead. His anti-Sovietism and pro-Westernism were deeper than the American side, in 1972, believed possible.

Nixon asked Mao straight out: "Which is the danger that is the most frontal for China: that of aggression from the U.S., or of aggression from Russia?" Mao's answer stressed the Soviet danger. Yet did the American side both grasp and welcome the implication?

Mao wanted Nixon to put China first in his calculations. Nixon could not reasonably do that. Twice before, Mao had expected Washington to take the CCP more seriously than it did. He felt both Roosevelt and Truman had underestimated the CCP at the end of World War II, and that Truman had also done so on the eve of China's intervention in Korea. Had Mao still not established his credentials?

Yet Mao was also to blame for the hesitancy in the Sino-American embrace. Ambivalence marked his view of America. A strong U.S. had bugged Mao's China in the past. But Mao wondered if the U.S. might not go from one extreme to the other. Was Washington capable of finding a halfway house between overweening strength and debilitating passivity?

The root of Mao's ambivalence lay in the mixed feelings he had toward the West as a young man. The U.S. was both capitalist and non-Chinese. It was hard for Mao to bring himself to rely on such a force. The U.S. was advanced, yes, but maybe also sated by its wealth and comforts. Maybe doomed by Marx's "laws" to fall even quicker than it had risen.

In his heart Mao may have suspected that if he'd been to America, as he'd been to Russia, he would have felt the same disappointment with Washington as he felt with Moscow.

Did Mao, like Nixon, dream of a "new structure of peace" for mankind? Mao seldom spoke of any truly international goals. He used the phrase "world revolution," it was true. Yet it fell short of meaning an international grand design. It meant foreign countries making revolution as China had done, or simply taking a stand against foes that were China's foes.

International relations as a *process* greatly fascinated Mao; he discussed it as such with visiting statesmen.

He held fast to a cluster of values: the constancy of change, the omnipresence of struggle, the mixed blessing of massive military establishments, the uselessness of space in itself.

He took satisfaction in seeing the plans of superpowers, "reactionaries," and others who clung to their privileges upset by these "irresistible forces."

Yet Mao did not seem to be seeking anything much, beyond the security of China, in the churning process of conflict and decay. He was a bit like a prophet looking down on turmoil from a mountain.

* * *

This was Mao's second meeting with Kissinger and he was to see him several more times. Chinese sources say he found talking with Kissinger more stimulating than talking with Nixon and—unusual in a Mao conversation with a foreign head of government—he did often draw Kissinger into the conversation with Nixon.

"Mao admired Nixon for his policy," said Winston Lord who visited Mao five times. "He drew enjoyment from Kissinger's company and exchanges."

Yet Mao thought less well of Kissinger than Kissinger thought of him.*

Kissinger during 1970 quipped that whereas in the previous Democratic

*Mao observed to Pompidou in 1973: "Kissinger likes to give briefings, and often his remarks are not very intelligent."

administration, Dean Rusk used to compare Mao unfavorably with Hitler, Nixon administration people compared Mao favorably with Hitler. An off-color quip, but then Kissinger's view of China was a distant one.

Mao apparently knew of this quip, for he observed to President Pompidou: "America has said we are worse than Hitler."

Mao knew that accidental factors largely underlay Kissinger's enthusiasm for China in 1971–1972. The opening to China was a tailor-made opportunity for Kissinger to increase his power (then still limited) within the U.S. government.

Part of Kissinger's excitement was that he had discovered, in China, a card he could play against Moscow. This meant—as later became crystal clear to Mao—that Russia, not China, was at the center of Kissinger's calculations.

With Nixon, more than with Kissinger, Mao knew where he stood in foreign policy. (Nixon schemed, yet in foreign policy he was less of a schemer than Kissinger.)

Mao saw Nixon as an orthodox right-wing politician who had acquired considerable knowledge about the world and was now leading the U.S. to adjust to the realities of the 1970s. "People say you are a rightist," Mao said to Nixon. "I am comparatively happy when [Westerners] on the right come into power." He had read Nixon's article in *Foreign Affairs,* in which the "new Nixon," prior to his election as President, showed that he had shed his anti-China obsession of the 1950s.

He viewed Nixon more indulgently than he had viewed Dulles because his lens was deep anxiety about the changed Soviet role in the world. Who better than Nixon to have on one's side against the Russians?

Left-wing people were shocked by Mao's warmth for Western conservatives. A question of perception: Mao didn't know enough about Western politics to see that a liberal Democrat or Labor Party–type stance could be a tenable one.

Also a question of predictability: Mao liked a leader from a capitalist country to *behave* like a capitalist; it confirmed his world view.

And there was the question of Mao's need for a united front against Russia: Nixon (and Edward Heath and Franz Josef Strauss in Europe) seemed more reliably anti-Soviet than liberal Democrats (and European Labor Party leaders like Harold Wilson and Helmut Schmidt).*

*   *   *

*The anti-Russian point was crucial, for in the 1950s, before his split with Moscow, Mao had not spoken well of right-wing parties in the West. He praised the Social Democratic Party of West Germany in a talk with Gunther Weisenborn in 1956. "It ought to be supported," he told the German author, "a victory by it in the election [of 1957] would be just (*zheng que*)."

Nixon was farewelled at Shanghai by Zhou—smiling this time—who then went up to Peking to talk over the "week that changed Nixon" with Mao. In the Forbidden City the visit earned an A minus.

Mao's strategic analysis of the world, with Russia seen as the central problem, had gained in the world's consciousness as a result of the summit.

On the Taiwan issue Mao got a fairly good deal. The U.S. took a large step toward bowing out of the PRC-Taiwan dispute, by stating that it "does not challenge" the view that Taiwan belongs to China and that it hoped for "a peaceful settlement of the Taiwan question by the Chinese themselves."

In the future, Nixon would angle for maximum cultural exchanges, trade, and access to China, within semi-normalization.

Mao would angle for a speedy advance to full diplomatic relations; Nixon promised him that this would come early in Nixon's expected second term as President.

In some respects both Mao and Nixon gained. A nagging obsession that China and the U.S. had felt about each other lifted like a weight from each side's shoulders. And Russia would no longer enjoy the luxury of knowing that Peking and Washington were out of touch with each other.

The lead-up to the trip provided an atmosphere in which enough nations switched their votes to give Peking a seat in the UN. Twenty extra nations recognized Mao's government within nine months after Nixon left Peking.

China's "five principles of coexistence," rejected by Washington since the 1950s, were embodied in the joint section of the communiqué. The international position of the Taipei regime began to erode as a result of the Nixon trip. And Mao did not "help" Nixon with the albatross of Vietnam to any degree that made him vulnerable to a public cry of betrayal from Hanoi.

In the long run Mao was proved correct in his view of the U.S. "The English are sly and cunning," he had said in 1958 when discussing John Foster Dulles. "The Americans are relatively short-tempered." He did not think the U.S. had the patience to play the imperial role for a long time, like the Europeans.

It was hard for anyone in the Politburo to say he had been wrong.

Yet the Nixon breakthrough came rather late for Mao's good. He would have liked to tap American know-how for the benefit of the Chinese economy much earlier. He had little time left to consolidate the new trans-Pacific bond; the Indochina situation would continue to be an obstacle to it for three of Mao's remaining four years.

And would there be time to coax Washington to loosen its grip on Taiwan, so that Mao might see a final end to the Chinese civil war before he went to "see Marx"?

In the wake of the Nixon visit Mao changed his policy toward Japan.

The Japanese took the initiative, it is true. In reaction to the "Nixon shock," Tokyo scrambled to embrace Peking and break ties with Taipei.

But the net result was that Mao stopped talking about "Japanese militarism" and adopted a cautiously positive view of Japan.

This was not simply due to Nixon's powers of persuasion. For Mao, détente with the U.S. made logical a more sanguine view of Japan, America's key ally in the Pacific. The fact remains that Mao came around to America's view of Japan.* (He was soon to urge Kissinger to be more respectful of Japan. Spend as much time in Tokyo, he urged the secretary of state, as you do in Peking. "I accepted the recommendation," Kissinger relates.)

Mao wrote a cryptic verse for Nixon and presented it to the U.S. President in honor of his visit:

> The old man sits on a stool.
> Chang-o ascends to the moon.
> Flowers are viewed from a galloping horse.

The old man on the stool was imperialism. Chang-o (a mythological character of the third millennium B.C. who flew to the moon to escape her nasty husband) was a charming image for a satellite. Nixon himself, in briefly visiting China, was the one viewing flowers from horseback.

Mao paid tribute to his guest. Nixon at least came to have a look at the Middle Kingdom, unlike a typical imperialist chieftain, who merely sits complacently on a stool.

Yet the rest of Mao's vision was disturbing for any Western leader who might wish to walk hand in hand with him.

The day of imperialism is done. Not only America and Russia, but China too, can now send satellites to the moon.

Enlightened as Nixon may be, he skates on the surface, gaining only the glimpse of reality that is possible from the back of a galloping horse.

"Nixon did not catch my meaning," Mao remarked later to a gathering of military men in Wuhan. Perhaps it was just as well. The verse, though not unfriendly to Nixon, was so quizzical that the U.S. President, had he grasped it, might have wondered if he and Mao could ever see the world in similar hues.

---

*Years before, Mao had spoken of the kind of China-Japan-West entente that now came about. "It would be a beautiful thing," he said to French visitors in 1964, "to have a London-Paris-Peking-Tokyo axis."

21

Fractured Vision (1973–1975)

Mao's long partnership with Zhou Enlai reached its height in 1972. Although Mao did not pay public tribute to Zhou—he was not in the habit of praising his lieutenants—Zhou served Mao brilliantly during the exit of Lin and the entry of Nixon.

Never had the premier been so nearly Mao's co-equal. Seldom—perhaps not since the turning-point conference at Zunyi during the Long March—had Mao needed Zhou as urgently as in 1971–1972.

Mao had to move to the right in order to defeat Lin. That led him into Zhou's arms. He made the opening toward America against some ultra-left and military opposition. Again Zhou was a logical ally.

Mao was grudging about leaning on Zhou. After all, Zhou's instincts were not his own. If the brooding, elemental Mao was a combination of tiger and monkey, Zhou was a man who had extended the mandarin tradition, which Mao hated, into the Communist era.

Far less than Mao did Zhou believe in a world of constant flux; or exult in struggle above all other values; or see all phenomena as shot through with contradictions.

Zhou did not become a man of doubts after the de-Stalinization crisis of the late 1950s, as Mao did, because Marxism had never meant as much to Zhou as it had to the more passionate, angular, original Mao.

Less impulsive than Mao, Zhou never found himself expelled from Party office, as Mao was three times, much less subjected to full-scale purge, as Liu and Deng and others were.

Zhou came to regard Mao as the towering figure of China's twentieth century. "He taught us all we know," he said with a peculiar intensity in his voice.

Yet Zhou had to be wary of Mao. He saw Mao grow dissatisfied with a string of senior colleagues. He took care to mount no challenge to the arbitrary, hypersensitive later Mao.

When Zhou criticized Mao during the 1960s, it was either in private or in Delphic terms. "Chairman Mao is an unerring man," he said elliptically at a tense, tedious Cultural Revolution meeting, "and he is very modest." To get his meaning across Zhou added: "All of us, including myself, have made mistakes." *

By late 1971, however, Zhou felt more secure with Mao than he'd ever been.

"How can there ever be absolute authority?" Zhou mused openly to an American visitor. "Mao Zedong may be an authority on some questions, but as to questions that are not in his field, how can he be an authority on them?" Zhou raised a second explosive issue. "There is also a question of time," he remarked in the course of a dawn dialogue. "You may be an authority today, but does that mean you are an authority tomorrow?"

It was true that Zhou's remarks were anti-Lin, for the phrase "absolute authority" was one of Lin's totems. But Zhou was also making a circumspect swipe at Mao's godlike status.

Zhou's boldness did not last long. Painful ructions of the mid-1970s were to prove that the prime minister would not be allowed—any more than previous number two men—to become a true co-equal to Mao. It happened that the two great achievements of 1971–1972, in which Zhou was Mao's indispensable executive officer, were soon called in question.

Lin had gone; but by 1973 Mao was not entirely happy with the anti-Lin coalition. The door had been opened to the U.S.; but by 1974 Mao was hearing criticisms about the usefulness to China of the traffic going through it.

* * *

Mao himself had urged Lin to politicize the PLA and make it a "school for the whole nation." Lin gave Mao the type of PLA he wanted, and that Peng Dehuai had failed to give him. On its back Mao rode to battle for his Cultural Revolution.

In 1972 Mao was ironically enough once again saddled with a Peng-type PLA leadership!

Xu Shiyou was typical of the regional military commanders who now set the PLA's tone. "It is not necessary to make the rich and the poor equal," the Canton commander had declared in opposing Lin's leftist rural policy, "in order to make a revolution." The anti-Lin coalition could not by its na-

---

*"We have followed in Chairman Mao's steps for several decades now," Zhou said at another of those exhausting Cultural Revolution sessions with rebel groups. "We kept quiet most of the time because we wanted to take the whole situation into consideration."

Cautious as he was, Zhou himself came in for criticism now and then. Suggestions in the media during 1969 that there really had been *twenty-nine* Bolsheviks was a swipe, from the ultra-left, at Zhou's links with 28B, Mao's opponents in the early 1930s.

ture remain for long a nest of singing birds. Xu and such men were not Mao's natural allies. Time soon showed it very clearly.

Mao had received the help of regional military commanders in defeating Lin. Now these self-possessed potentates were lining up for their pound of flesh.*

Mao, far from triumphant in the winter of 1971–1972, did not denounce Lin by name. Nor did he replace Lin with a fresh choice as his "successor" and "closest comrade in arms." If Zhou's supporters expected the honor to fall on their hero's patient shoulders, they were disappointed.

Mao seemed diffident. The end of the Lin affair was a relief, at best, not a green light for a surge of Maoist policy-making.

All the idealism, faith, and struggle of the Cultural Revolution had collapsed in Mao's hands like so many bubbles, leaving his fingers clammy with the telltale sweat of power politics.

A right-wing mood was clear in a relaxed rural policy, new postings of Cultural Revolution victims to senior jobs, a return to regular schedules and less stress on ideology in schools, adoption of material incentives under disguised names in factories, and discussions on history and other intellectual topics that were relatively free from bias imparted by current political imperatives.

Nineteen seventy-two's swing to the right must have reminded Mao of the similar swing in 1962 that followed the failure of the Great Leap Forward.

It was a price Mao had to pay for his morbid battle against his own mortality, for regaining control over the gun, and for changing his mind about the "boundlessly loyal" Lin.

One cold winter day, Mao put in a surprise appearance at the Papaoshan Cemetery of Fallen Revolutionaries. Foreign Minister Chen Yi was dead of cancer.

A few eyebrows rose at the sight of Mao attending this funeral, and speaking at length with Chen Yi's widow and children. True, he had been associated with the military veteran for 40 years. But Chen Yi had been a victim of Mao's Cultural Revolution (and lost a son in it) and Mao had only belatedly protected him.

Seldom did Mao come out for the funeral of a colleague. Why was he at Papaoshan?

Mao liked the feisty Chen, even though he did not always like his views,

---

*The irony of it was summed up by a surprise appearance, at the reception for Army Day in the summer of 1972, by the leaders of the Wuhan Mutiny of 1967! Generals Chen Zaidao and Zhong Hanhua had committed the most direct defiance of Mao's authority (Lin's too) in the history of the PRC. Now they were happily back on deck in the un-Maoist political atmosphere of *après* Lin.

and the loss of a man who always fired straight from the shoulder moved Mao, in a season when conspiracy seemed to have become the norm in Peking.

But the PLA uniforms filling the stark marble funeral parlor told a fuller story. Mao owed a debt to the military commanders. Paying tribute to the foreign minister, he was also smoothing a few khaki feathers.*

Mao did not find it easy to chop out all the pro-Lin pockets in the PLA. Some were groups of loyalists who had served with Lin in his Fourth Field Army. A tenacious few were confidants of the Lin family.

Others in the PLA who resisted Peking in the early 1970s were not pro-Lin, but merely resentful of the swaths cut into the military—tens of generals were arrested and dismissed—in the aftermath of Lin's fall.

A volley of shots rang out among the bamboos at Zonghua hot springs not far from Canton. A young woman on holiday as a guest of the government at the elegant Zonghua chalet fell down dead. It was Little Bean.

The shots that sprayed into her back came from the direction of a nearby PLA camp. No doubt a rank-and-file soldier pulled the trigger. But behind him must have been senior officers—the Canton Military Region had been a bastion of Lin's power—who did not appreciate Little Bean's "heroism" at Beidaihe in September 1971. The dead body had pinned to it a strip of red cloth bearing in yellow paint the denunciation "Treason and heinous crime" (*da nie bu dao*).

If Little Bean Lin was an exemplary citizen in Mao's eyes, that had not saved her from a violent early death.

If Mao thought Lin a "swindler," that did not deter many a PLA officer from saying a quiet word in Lin's favor (at times even in print).

If Mao had got rid of his defense minister—the third time he'd done so—that did not mean he could secure agreement on a replacement; the post was to remain unfilled for *four years* after Lin's death.

In mid-1972 Mao reached out for two unlikely and unready vehicles in order to speak his mind. Prime Minister Bandaranaike of Sri Lanka was in town. She presented a baby elephant to China's children on behalf of Sri Lanka's children and then rolled into South and Central Lakes for a chat with Mao.

In the midst of a broad-brush depiction of the world scene, Mao suddenly began to tell the amiable Sri Lankan of mayhem and murder within his own government. Mrs. Bandaranaike was puzzled as well as embarrassed. For a while—probably even as she left Mao's study—she did not know which par-

*Even Zhu De was allowed to send a wreath and visit the hospital to pay his last respects to Chen Yi's body. The man who refused to endorse Mao's Cultural Revolution had not been so publicly visible for years.

ticular "swindler" Mao was nailing into a coffin of infamy.

It was Lin. The remaining Lin sympathizers were now sufficiently cowed for South and Central Lakes to spring a few leaks. Mao was ready to bring the world up to date with his crafted version of the truth.

The "swindler" was dead. . . . He had "tried to murder me" [Mao]. . . . He had opposed the rebuilding of the Party and the opening to the U.S. . . .

Five months earlier Nixon was given no answers even to simple factual questions about the former defense minister. Now Mao was forcing information about Lin on a woman who had come to ask for economic aid, not political secrets.

Two weeks later Mao gave French Foreign Minister Schumann similar portions of the authorized version of the Lin crisis. "I applied a drop of alcohol," Mao summed up for his French visitor, "and Lin was finished." The remark did not suggest—any more than did the overall chronology of events in 1971—a conspiracy by Lin against a passive Mao.

"We have to pay an equal amount of attention," Mao purred in a document that ordered a package of moderate policies for communes, "to the interests of the state, the collective, and the individual." That this meant a veer to the right was made clear when the document went on to say editorially that in the past "artificial egalitarianism has hampered the realization of Chairman Mao's revolutionary line."

What a convenient, all-purpose rag bag "Chairman Mao's revolutionary line" could be in changing seasons!

And yet, however much the doctrinal phrase could be tossed around by officials of varying views, the man himself was still very much alive. He had paused, but not retired, from the fray. Other leaders could tease out any strand of Mao Thought that suited their purposes; Liu, Deng, Lin, and Mao's own wife had done that. But Mao alone retained the supreme power to hire and fire them all.

*   *   *

By the spring of 1973 Mao was riding the crest of a foreign policy wave.

He benignly received, one by one in his study, the leaders of many of the twenty-odd nations that recognized the PRC in the year following Nixon's trip.* He regaled them with axioms. He asked polite questions about their far-off country. He drew a veil over the desert years of nonrecognition, dealing in broad trends of history and spurning the petty coinage of blame for past isolation, pitching the conversation as if China and nation X were real-

---

*He met far more foreign leaders in the early 1970s than in any period of equal span in his entire life. Within 1973 alone he entertained, quizzed, hugged, and occasionally mystified five African heads of state.

ly old friends between whom a relaxed interaction was as natural as air or water.

Mao, who had risen to power on a bandwagon of anti-Japanism, dealt with Prime Minister Tanaka as if he were a younger brother.

Zhou brought Tanaka through the anteroom to Mao's armchair. The Chairman addressed them both with a welcoming smile: "Did you finish your quarrel yet?" Without waiting for an answer he pronounced: "Quarrels are good for you."

"We've had amiable talks," Tanaka ventured, sweeping under the rug an argument over whether the Sino-Japan war had caused China "disaster" (the word proposed by the Chinese) or merely "trouble" (the Japanese suggestion).

Mao positioned himself on a philosophic plane far above the earnest strivings of negotiation. "Truly good friends are made only by quarrels," he declared, as he waved the two premiers to their seats.

Mao advised the unprepossessing Japanese to drink little *maotai*. Tanaka rejoined, "I hear *maotai* is 65 proof, but I really enjoy it."

"It is not 65 proof, but 70," the leader of China observed. "Who gave you the wrong information?"

Mao's next words took him as far away from *maotai* as it was possible to go. "By the way, there are too many ancient things in China. It is not good to let old things bind you."

This led Mao into a soliloquy on his father, capped off by a blind turn to the topic of Japanese politics.

"When I was a child," he went on, "my father was very harsh with me, and I rebelled against him. It is said in the Four Books and the Five Classics of Confucianism that unless parents love their children they cannot expect their children to respect them. I asked my father why he was unkind to me. Not to change the subject, but you seem to have a rough time in elections in Japan, don't you?"

When Tanaka spoke of the rigors of election campaigns in Japan, Mao shook his head in wonderment and murmured: "Things are far from simple if you have to go out on the streets to make campaign speeches." The old warrior put a mental arm around the younger politician's shoulder. "Speaking on the street is a tough job," said the man who did a lot of it in Changsha a half century before. "Please take good care of your health."

"How is the parliamentary system going?" he inquired of Tanaka. The prime minister murmured, "It has its problems." Mao grandly summed up: "Japan certainly has a lot of problems, doesn't it?"

It was as if Mao had rolled back the centuries, jumping back over the terrible China-Japan war, treating as a past episode the post-Russo-Japanese war phase when Japan's leadership in Asia had won his schoolboy admiration, resuming history at the point when China was tutor and Japan was pupil.

"Zhou is a nobody before Mao," Tanaka told some Japanese politician friends on his return to Tokyo. "He behaves in front of Mao like a clumsy secretary attending an outstanding congressman."

It was an interesting comment, even if one feels that what Tanaka said of Zhou in Mao's presence was truer of himself in Mao's presence.

Mao's government was still a new boy at the UN. Far from "disrupting" the organization, as some had predicted, the Chinese representatives in New York were playing the game of paper and words and protocol in an utterly conventional way.

At the same time, the PRC became the weightiest voice at Turtle Bay for the Third World point of view on law of the sea, debts, trading structures, and other issues that pitted "have" against "have not" nations.

People's Daily gave lavish coverage to China's words and deeds in the Security Council (where China was one of the five permanent members) and other units of the world body.

Yet Mao seemed bored by the UN. Hardly for a single moment, in all his talks and conversations on foreign policy, did Mao broach the topic of the UN. He left it to the tiny internationalist wing of Peking's vast officialdom that held precarious root in the foreign ministry.

Mao had little faith in committees to discuss peace, define aggression, and deliver paper judgments on disputes between nations. He was a China-firster whose mind ran in balance-of-power grooves, not an internationalist whose mind was hospitable to schemes of cooperation.

As for tensions between "haves" and "have nots," Mao felt strongly about the moral rectitude of the Third World point of view, yet his actual knowledge of the complex economic issues involved was not detailed or up-to-date.

He seemed much more interested in the deeds of the globally striving superpowers than in the words of their Third World adversaries at the UN.

That was natural. Mao saw China limbering up to enter the big league of the superpowers, not remaining content with the tamer company of the "new nations" that crowded the little league.

Mao sat down with Kissinger for the third time as the early spring dust from Mongolia began to clothe Peking in 1973. China and the U.S. had just agreed to set up liaison offices—embassies in all but name—in each other's capital, a major step ahead.

The Sino-American link was a settled fact of life in international affairs.

Yet there were still a few voices of doubt about the Mao-Nixon handshake within China. "Some comrades say," a lecturer at a secret PLA meeting in Kunming admitted edgily, "that in the past we interpreted negotiations between the U.S. and the U.S.S.R. as a U.S.-Soviet collusion, but now we too are negotiating with the U.S." Indeed one might say so.

The lecturer (whose text fell into the hands of Taiwan spies) was quite defensive about Mao's pro-American tilt. He told his audience of PLA officers of company rank or higher that "Nixon is a man of transition" and that China's real aim was to "get in touch with the people of the United States."

What to say about Mao's isolation from the once fraternal nations of the Soviet bloc? The text alludes gingerly to the "superficial phenomenon of temporary decrease of truly socialist countries."

Like Nixon, Mao was at pains to tell his people that policy had not changed. Yet PLA officers in particular knew that China's American policy had changed—just as Americans could see that Nixon's China policy had changed.

* * *

In the Politburo new tensions appeared. Some of them were Mao's own doing.

Tactically Mao always preferred—quite apart from the strength of his convictions on questions of principle—to occupy a middle position on the Politburo's spectrum. From it he could lurch to left or right in accord with the swirl of dialectics.

In 1973, finding the anti-Lin coalition pulling him too far to the right, he felt an impulse to turn left. He rummaged in the cupboard of ideology for some ammunition to fire at colleagues he judged too conservative.

Nature played a baleful role in the new crisis brewing at the summit of Chinese politics. Doctors found out in 1972 that Zhou was very ill with cancer. This knowledge undermined the Mao-Zhou partnership as surely as the disease undermined Zhou's vigor.

Mao himself was quickly losing the physical capacity to direct the Politburo. His health fluctuated but was seldom good. For a stretch of several days he would work prodigiously. Another week his Parkinson's disease would keep him in bed, out of the picture except to sign documents and be briefly consulted on grave matters.

Access to Mao became crucial to Peking's power stakes. Who could get a signature or a nod of assent from the old man?

And this at a time when everyone in the Politburo knew that Zhou's role as Mao's bridge to the nation must come to an end within a couple of years at most.

A shock awaited the guests at the Great Hall of the People for a banquet given by Zhou in honor of Prince Sihanouk. Who should be there but Deng Xiaoping!

Mingling with the Chinese leaders, moving a little uneasily from one foot to the other, but looking no worse for his six years on the scrap heap, was the blunt and stocky powerhouse who had been one of Mao's three great *bêtes noires* of the last decade.

Here beamed the renegade, the demon, the freak, the counterrevolutionary, the Number Two Man in Power Taking the Capitalist Road, the metallic former secretary general of the CCP who used to sit as far away from Mao's chair as possible to avoid having to hear the Chairman's latest instruction.

Back like Lazarus from the political grave.*

Mao's niece Wang Hairong, the former student at Peking University, now a foreign affairs aide, took Deng's arm and reintroduced him to an incredulous knot of foreign journalists. He bowed in a courtly way and said he was glad to be back. He had been at a reform school in Jiangxi Province, he divulged like a boy explaining his absence from class.

Now he was a vice-premier, Ms. Wang explained with sweet nonchalance. Mao let it be known a few weeks later that he now considered "too harsh" the denunciation and privation to which Deng had been subjected since 1966.

Harmonious as the mood at the Great Hall seemed, Deng's reemergence was an expression of seismic forces under Mao's sinking throne.

Ailing Zhou wanted Deng back in the leadership; it was probably he who twisted Mao's arm to accept the resurrection. Yet Mao was very nearly locked into accepting Deng by the logic of the appalling fight against Lin and its fallout.

Deng had shrewdly written a letter to the Central Committee from his reform school as soon as he heard of Lin's fall. He was infuriated at Lin's treachery, he declared. Would it be possible for him to join in the criticism of Lin?

The return of Deng was one more check Mao had to write in payment for the coalition that had enabled him to topple Lin. Mao had leaned on the regional military commanders; these hard-nosed veterans were mostly Deng's buddies. Mao had opened the door to scores of high officials who had been struck down in the Cultural Revolution; Deng was (after Liu) their natural hero.

The situation into which Deng returned, however, was not a simple one of "left" versus "right." Mao's shaky health, the sporadic nature of his assertion of power, his Don Quixote–like leaps after truth, all put the skids of uncertainty under every well-laid plan from whatever quarter.

Mao was no longer capable of masterminding a sustained political oper-

---

*I have described elsewhere (*Flowers on an Iron Tree,* 1975, page 201) the electric shock that ran through a Hangzhou cinema when an audience saw in a newsreel their first glimpse of Deng's face for six years or more.

ation. He could emit a supreme instruction. He could hire and fire. He could veto.

His role was that of supreme legitimator. In any clash of opinions he could win by murmuring a phrase or scribbling a maxim. But he could not follow through (as he had done in the Cultural Revolution) and make reality jump to his maxims.

In the history of the PRC this was utterly new, and terribly dangerous. New China, the biggest bureaucracy on earth, the most highly organized large society in history, the state that was proud to call itself a dictatorship, was a dragon without a head.

Lin Biao had not done badly to code-name his boss "B-52." Mao was now indeed like a heavy bomber, capable of immense impact now and then, but in between times of little import to what went on below him.

This particular "B-52" was also known to be running out of fuel. He was near the end of his flight; only a few more bombing raids need be feared (by those likely to be hit) or hoped for (by those who wished to move in and profit from the debris).

* * *

Mao "presided" over the Tenth Congress in August 1973. *People's Daily* reported that when Mao appeared on the rostrum "cheers resounded through the hall" and the Chairman "warmly waved to the delegates." It sounded like a monarch being glimpsed, not a working chairman arriving for a meeting. And Mao gave no speech.

The congress lasted only five days, as compared with twenty-four for the previous one in 1969. Perhaps Mao could not stand the strain of coming out for more than five days in a row.

The Ninth Congress had been secret enough, but the Tenth was not even announced until it was safely over, and its place of meeting was never divulged.

Nor is there any intellectual vigor in its documents—a new Party constitution and a couple of cliché-ridden speeches. Old slogans were juggled, that was all.

For this aridity there were two reasons. That Mao lingered on, reigning but not ruling, seemed to veto intellectual creativity on the part of those around him. To come up with new policies in 1973 would have been like offering amendments to the Ten Commandments in God's presence.

And there were paralyzing tensions between a fairly dominant Zhou and those who thought as he did on policy, and Mrs. Mao and her brittle, eager friends, who scented in old Mao's iconoclastic mood their last chance to claw their way to the top of Chinese politics.

Said the new constitution: "The future is bright, the road is tortuous." In other words: We'll make it in the end, but God knows how, given the present situation.

Zhou was a star at the Tenth Congress. Some of his followers from foreign policy circles advanced in the pecking order. So did a number of un-Maoist bureaucrats—most of them Zhou associates—who had earned their reward by opposing Lin Biao. The big losers, as compared with the Ninth Congress, were leftist PLA officers.

Yet that was far from the whole story of the 1973 congress. The ultra-left forged ahead as they could not have done without Mao's wind in their sails. A handsome young ex-textile worker from Shanghai, the militant Wang Hongwen, shared with Zhou the honor of giving one of the two congress reports. "Dare to go against the tide" was Wang's theme phrase.

The congress wrapped up the Lin Biao case. Lin's faults were played upon in the usual vastly exaggerated Chinese way. He was expelled from the Party "once and for all." (Yet what does that mean in the case of a corpse? If even a dead renegade had to be expelled from its ranks, was the CCP viewing itself as an immortal institution?)

Mao refused to choose a new number two man. Lin's old job of vice-chairman of the CCP was divided among five vice-chairmen. It seemed that Mao—in resentment at his own loosening grip, or wry amusement at the shabby maneuvers his decline precipitated—wished to keep all contenders off balance.

Mao was 79, Zhou was 75. The average age of three of Zhou's four fellow vice-chairmen was almost 70. And there among them, like a boy with his five old uncles, was 39-year-old Wang.

The eerie thing was that the old guard that shaped the CCP in the 1920s was leading its last Party Congress, yet Wang and his friends (who included Jiang Qing) did not possess the mettle or the mandate to be accepted in China as the new guard.

Mao was not really orchestrating a balancing act. He was creating confusion by standing in the shadows and—whether because of senility or out of perversity—flashing signals that defied sure interpretation.

Zhou saw the mellow Mao he wanted to see. Jiang Qing, emboldened by Zhou's illness, saw an emperor whose mandate was slipping into the empress's hand.

Mao's status was measurably less than at the Ninth Congress. At times he was called simply "Comrade Mao," a term which in the late 1960s had disappeared in favor of "Great Helmsman," "Supreme Leader," "Red Sun of Our Hearts," or at minimum "Chairman Mao." Zhou quoted Lenin where he could have—and would have in the late 1960s—quoted Mao.

The Central Committee looked less of a Mao instrument than in 1969. It was bigger—319 members as compared with 279 before—which suggested a stand-off between jostling interests; and it contained fewer people from Mao's home province than had the previous Central Committee.

Lin was dead, Mao was damaged.

The Chairman had used up some of his prestige by changing his mind about Lin. It would not be impossible but it would be hard for him to again "apply a drop of alcohol and get rid of" any more senior figures in the CCP.

* * *

It was a cool day in November 1973. At the Great Hall of the People, the prime minister of Australia was talking with Zhou Enlai about Bangladesh. A protocol man handed Zhou a piece of paper. "Can we have a word in private?" Zhou immediately said to Gough Whitlam.

As the tall Australian rose to follow Zhou into a side room, a tassel of the green baize cloth on the conference table caught in his buttoned-up jacket. The entire cloth moved from the table like a skin peeling off a banana. Pads, pencils, teacups rushed in Whitlam's direction as if by gravitation.

"Mao, perhaps?" the Australian ambassador to China jotted on a pad, pushing the message toward the head of the Australian foreign ministry, who sat near him. Of course, he was right. This kind of drama attached uniquely to meetings with Mao.

"Where's the piece of paper with the questions?" Whitlam asked his brilliant young ambassador, Stephen Fitzgerald. No one could find it. Mao, as it happened, had a few questions of his own.

At four-thirty in the afternoon, two black Chinese cars whisked into South and Central Lakes through a red gateway on the Boulevard of Eternal Peace. A Chinese aide held a flattened hand at the top of the car doorway as each visitor climbed out, to ensure that no one should bump his head.

For the next hundred minutes Mao's outlook on life and politics (on the brink of his 80th birthday) was laid remarkably bare, as he sipped from a porcelain mug of tea and his smooth pale hand picked at rough patches of skin on his cheeks.

His walk was a stiff shuffle; he complained to the Australians about the condition of his feet. His hearing did not seem good. The other Chinese in the room—who included Zhou and Wang Hongwen, basking in his amazing elevation to number three post in the CCP at the Tenth Congress, just three months before—spoke more slowly than normal when addressing him.

He got up and down unaided, nonetheless. His animated hands suggested a younger man, and one with strong opinions. He was by no means so incapacitated as to make his guests feel embarrassed at being with him.

During the first half of the conversation Mao was passive and almost inaudible. Whitlam, an eager man not reticent in displaying his knowledge, did most of the talking. Mao passed most of Whitlam's questions on to his two colleagues. Zhou spoke almost as much as Mao did. Even Wang spoke once or twice.

Whitlam put to Mao some questions about the composition of the new Central Committee. Was there some fresh young blood? Were women being given a larger role? Was the Chairman satisfied with the new ruling body that emerged from the Tenth Congress?

Mao seemed either bored with the topic or too tired to say much.

Zhou and Wang pieced together some facts and figures for the Australians. Mao opened his mouth only on the issue of military representation on the Central Committee. There was quite a bit of it, he said, about 30 percent.

The Australians began to wonder if Mao was senile. Perhaps there had been a practical point behind the midafternoon preliminary drama?

Zhou carried a satchel of papers that afternoon. He rarely did so. As Bangladesh and Overseas Chinese problems were being discussed in the Great Hall, he occasionally opened the satchel to check something. He took the satchel with him to Mao's residence.

At the end Zhou did not leave with Whitlam, but remained behind, apparently to do business with Mao.

The periods when the Chairman was strong, or lucid, enough to see people and make decisions were getting less frequent. The papers in Zhou's satchel were for Mao to inspect and sign or attach his thumbprint to.

When Mao felt up to it—regardless of the time of day—a visit by a foreigner and the conduct of other business were slotted in together.

On this occasion Mao sprang to life partway through the session. After one more show of indifference—this time to a question on Taiwan's future—he put both hands firmly down on the sides of his armchair and said abruptly: "Now let me ask the questions."

It was almost as if a drug administered earlier had begun to take effect.

Mao asked Whitlam the difference between the philosophy of his Australian Labor Party and that of the Communist Party. Whitlam replied that he believed in a socialism that comes by evolution, whereas the Communists held that only revolution brings socialism.

"Oh, your outlook is Darwinian?" Mao continued. Soon he swept on to geography. "Is your Australian port of Darwin named after the biologist Charles Darwin?" *

---

*Whitlam was unable to answer Mao, but on his return to Canberra he sent the Chairman an account of how the northern city of Darwin came to be named—as Port Darwin, in 1839, it was named after Charles Darwin, though the town itself was called Palmerston until 1911—together with a "self-criticism" for failing to meet the query on the spot.

Mao was quite argumentative, resisting many ideas put to him. When Whitlam reflected on Mao's enormous contribution to modern China, Mao rejoined that his role had not been so great.

Whitlam observed that the Russians hadn't been helpful toward the CCP before 1949. Mao again qualified him. Moscow had been unhelpful "at times," he drawled.

Mao seemed to treat Whitlam's earnest objections to Chinese nuclear tests light-heartedly. "We don't mind you raising the subject," Mao said, like a father telling his son that no subject, however idiotic, is forbidden for discussion. "It's a necessary routine," he declared of protests by Australia, Japan, and other countries against Chinese tests. Mao didn't even bother to defend China's nuclear testing policies.

Whitlam protested the phrase "necessary routine." But he then backtracked. China's position could not be condemned as forthrightly as France's, he conceded. The explosions were occurring on China's own soil, not on that of colonies far from home, like France's. Moreover, China was truly threatened by nuclear-armed enemies; France was less so, and Paris enjoyed protection from America. Whitlam's effort to be conciliatory did not succeed.

Mao was roused. France was very much threatened by the U.S.S.R. It *needed* an independent deterrent. It *should have* one!

Having played adversary—as well as expressing his convictions—Mao then threw in a "Maoist" philosophic maxim that appeared to undermine his realpolitik stance on behalf of bombs as the cutting edge of national power. "Anyway, nuclear weapons are not much use," he mused. "Men still matter more than weapons."

That was not the only dose of fundamentalist doctrine with which Mao laced a laconic afternoon.

The Australian praised the PRC's internal progress. Mao demurred, and said the achievements so far were a drop in the bucket. *"But there is one good thing about China's poverty,"* he declared. *"It makes people want to make revolution."*

Mao seemed like a man who could not, or did not want to, align the various levels of his thought into a consistent pattern.

Few of Mao's colleagues subscribed to his nostalgic militancy about poverty being a virtue; none less than Deng Xiaoping. Yet Mao brought up Deng's name favorably.

He was in the middle of explaining to Whitlam that the army in China was not like the army in other countries. Take the case of Deng, "a civilian with a military background," Mao remarked.

The vice-premier had told the Australians, Whitlam related to Mao, that he had attended the Eighth Congress of the CCP, and also the Tenth, but not the Ninth. Why had Deng been absent from the 1969 congress?

Foreign visitors seldom asked Mao about the affairs of the Politburo, but the Chairman did not mind this excellent question. Deng was out of the picture in 1969, he replied, "because at that time the Lin Biao problem had not been solved."

Mao, in other words, had still been in bed with the ultra-left in 1969, and he neither wanted nor needed Deng's presence.

In 1973 Mao's attitude to the ultra-leftists was more complex. He had turned aside from them in 1970–1972. He now hankered for some fireworks from their well-stocked arsenal. But he wavered. Partly because his physical condition jumped up and down from day to day. Partly because his outlook on colleagues was now so eccentric that an embrace in the morning almost guaranteed a rejection by evening.

Whitlam remarked that Wang Hongwen was "world famous" in the wake of his meteoric rise at the Tenth Congress. "Where did you find him?" the Australian inquired.

Mao could have struck a light-hearted note; Whitlam's question had a playful flavor. But the reply was crisp indeed. *"Bu zhi dao,"* Mao grunted. The Chinese term is the sparsest possible way to convey "Don't know."

The Australians had their eyes on Mao, so we do not know what expression Wang's face bore at that moment.

Recalling the long record of Mao and Zhou in the Chinese Revolution, Whitlam noted that when the pair of them took part in the Long March, Wang had not yet been born. Wang tried to speak but was cut off both by Zhou and by Whitlam.

Toward the end of the session Wang found a chance to come back to Whitlam's remark. "I *was* born at the time of the Long March," he managed to say. "I was one year old." He added—and the protestation only seemed to accent his junior status—that since then he had been "making revolution for years, just like Chairman Mao and Premier Zhou."

Wang did not sound like the number three man in the Chinese government, nor were Mao and Zhou treating him as such.

Mao had said yes to Wang's elevation at the Tenth Congress. "Watch him," he said of Wang to President Pompidou of France just after the congress. "He has a great future." But disenchantment had begun to set in.*

Zhou was Mao's bridge to the world beyond the magic garden of his

---

*Wang knew it. In January 1974 he gave a speech (never published in China) that was a classic of wounded self-justification. No text by a CCP leader has ever quoted Mao so much as this talk of Wang's to a Central Committee study group. He was desperately trying to remind the audience that he was—or had been—Mao's fair-haired boy.

study. Yet there was a terrible irony to Zhou's protective, gently masterful handling of his boss.

Whitlam several times tried to inject an optimistic note into his awkward, revealing dialogue with Mao. He remarked that for all China's problems—which Mao had been dwelling upon—"the future of the revolution" was surely guaranteed by China's sturdy youth.

"Neither Zhou nor I will be around for the conclusion of the Chinese Revolution," Mao began in response. He declined to join in Whitlam's chime of hope. He declined to discuss the future of the Chinese Revolution in the structural terms Whitlam had broached. *Personal mortality* was his theme.

"My body is riddled with diseases," he declared.

Zhou jumped in with a smile. "He only has rheumatism in his knees," he amplified, whether in jocularity, as he wished his guests to think, or in embarrassment, or possibly in a gentle shot at Mao's self-pity.

"I have an appointment with God," Mao went on to Whitlam. He did not want a veil drawn over the bleakness of his physical prospects.

Zhou merely listened. But Zhou's appointment with God (a phrase he never used) was closer at hand than Mao's.

With Mao on that cold November afternoon were two flesh-and-blood illustrations of his tragic isolation. Zhou was nearer death than Mao. And Mao already had doubts about Wang only months after making a "helicopter" of him. The pair were number two and number three in his regime. But Mao was shuffling toward a future that would include neither of them.

Death and doubt were to deprive him of two more possible successors.

Zhou looked at his watch as a signal that the interview had gone on long enough. Mao gestured to his niece—an ideological left-hand little finger—Wang Hairong, who was sitting prim and quiet beside Zhou. "She will never let me talk for too long," the Chairman bantered. "She looks after me very closely."

*   *   *

As a tense, debilitating seesaw contest over place and policy began between the ultra-leftists and groups resisting them, all in the unlikely name of criticizing Confucius, Mao switched back and forth between three roles:

- Often he supported the ultra-leftists.
- He hedged his bets about some of them, however, and placated some moderates.
- At times he simply sat on the mountain and watched the tigers fight below.

"Every seven or eight years," *People's Daily* quoted Mao as saying, "monsters and demons will jump out." Published in late 1973, the remark was an invitation to resume the 1966 struggle against "monsters and demons."*

That Mao was too feeble, or too bloody-minded, or too uncertain in his own mind, to help the citizens *identify* the monsters and demons was a guarantee of confusion.

Mao personally kicked off the anti-Confucius drive—though no mortal could have plotted its eventual weird career—and *pi Kong* (a catchy short form for "Criticize Confucius," *pi-pan Kong zi*) became the justification for a great deal of left-wing craziness.

Phrases from the Cultural Revolution popped up like bamboo shoots after spring rain. Mao badges were again widely worn.† In Shanghai, base of the top ultra-leftists, a new magazine, *Study and Criticism,* appeared, its aim seemingly to be more red than the official CCP monthly *Red Flag.*

Inner morale fell as fast as the political temperature rose. It wasn't enough, as it had been during the two post-Lin years, to merely do your job well. Now you had to spout ideology—the more loudly and dramatically the better—and link all evils with "class enemy" Confucius.

The clue to reducing road accidents, said a broadcast from Hainan island, lay in criticizing Confucius.

The Italian film director Michelangelo Antonioni, welcomed to China with his cameras in 1972, was now called an "anti-China clown." His sober, even tedious, movie had become a "wild provocation against the Chinese people."

The attack on the "clown" from Rome was given an anti-American twist that soon became a subtheme of *pi Kong.* Americans found Antonioni's poisonous film "fascinating," sneered *People's Daily,* so it seems that "the specter of John Foster Dulles still clings on" in the U.S.

Beethoven was judged "decadent." During 1973 the Philadelphia, Vien-

---

*The leftward lurch actually began, typically, in education circles, and dates from late 1973. It was triggered by a high school graduate working on a farm in northeast China, Zhang Tiesheng, who handed in blank sheets of paper in answer to the science questions at Liaoning Province's exam for college entrance. He attached an angry letter criticizing the whole idea of exams and book learning.

Zhang's letter was read out like scripture over the radio in half a dozen provinces. *People's Daily* printed it, with a flattering preface. Soon the same paper ran on its front page a fiery article by a twelve-year-old pupil who said she'd had enough of her teacher's authoritarian ways.

"Are we children of the Mao Zedong era to be treated like slaves?" the child blazed.

The choreographer of much of this rebellion against educational authority in the northeast was Mao's nephew, Mao Yuanxin, now thirty years old and propaganda chief for Liaoning. His encouragement made it possible for Liaoning's young rebels to "go against the tide" and not suffer for it.

It was Uncle Mao in Peking who wanted Zhang Tiesheng and his ilk to attack rules, exams, teachers, and book learning. Yuanxin was his tool. Jiang Qing was the arm-twister at Mao's elbow, and his channel to Yuanxin.

†I had seen hardly any on a tour of China in 1973.

na, and London symphony orchestras had toured China and were well reviewed. But in Mao's China nothing was safe. "It is not difficult for us to perceive behind these weird and bizarre melodies," *People's Daily* now intoned of an array of European compositions, "the nasty, rotten life and decadent sentiments that these works reflect."

Old Mao (not a music fan) had evidently murmured into a receptive ear that music, like everything else, yields its secrets only to class analysis.

"To go too far," Confucius once remarked, "is as bad as to fall short." Mao didn't believe it. He saw no great merit in balance.

Yet the antics of 1974 were more, and less, than combat between Mao's idea of flux and Confucius's idea of order.

Confucius's influence did hinder the Maoist transformation of China. In the villages especially, attitudes to women, status, and the relative weight to be given to progress as against precedent, all still had a Confucian flavor.

A drive like this in Mao's China was also a sign that someone in the Politburo feared something.

And *pi Kong* was also Mao's whim. It burst upon China, like thunder, because the Man Up There willed it. But he was not able to follow it through with well-aimed rains to produce the desired harvest down below.

The drive was soon a bottle into which everyone poured whatever wine he or she chose. The brews were so various as to cancel each other out.

During 1974 Mao received more foreign dignitaries—twenty-odd—than in any previous year, while each day in his own newspapers he read anti-foreign remarks that recalled the fever of the Boxer Rebellion.

The ultra-left Shanghai monthly *Study and Criticism* mentioned Mao as often as the Bible mentions God, and yet in February 1974 Mao withdrew the magazine's right (or someone else did so in his name) to reproduce his swirling calligraphy as its frontispiece.

Were these the lurchings of a craft out of control; were they a sign of factions pushing in different directions; or were they a mirror to Mao's own inconsistencies?

Some of each, but with a good dose of the last.

"The need to shit after eating," Mao remarked, "does not mean that eating is a waste of time." This typical line, dating from Yanan, was prominently recalled by Peking's press in the autumn of 1974. Mao had given fair warning that he believed in flashing a green light one moment and a red one the next.

Jiang Qing took Confucius as a code word for anything that rode high prior to the Cultural Revolution. Zhou Enlai, in order to jump into the drive with enough enthusiasm to satisfy a Mao who now seemed distant from him, added Lin Biao's name to Confucius's!

Turning *pi Kong* into *pi Lin pi Kong,* the war-torn premier made a farce into a near-comedy. The sage and the defense minister were thrust at the long-suffering Chinese people as twin monsters of the type that—had Mao not said it?—must surely leap out every seven or eight years. One had been dead for two and a half years, the other for two and a half millenniums.

Zhou felt the entire campaign was absurd. And so it was; a painful disgrace to a great civilization. It could only occur because the Politburo was in paralysis, due to Mao's being still able to reign but not to rule.

For Jiang Qing the evolving chaos of *pi Lin pi Kong* was viewed in anti-Confucian perspective as a push to the left. For Zhou it was viewed as an extension of the anti-Lin coalition, and so a lasso around the neck of the ultra-left.

Mao favored Jiang Qing's view, but he could not go all the way with the Maid Marian of the Cultural Revolution; in any case his physical condition did not permit him to keep abreast of her maneuvers.

"Water too pure breeds no fish," Mao reminded his nervous colleagues in the winter of 1974. "A teacher too harsh has no pupils." He was capable of a nonchalant swipe against the ultra-left as well as more than one against his time-honored opponents on the right.

"Nowadays metaphysics is running wild," he said in February 1974. "There is one-sidedness." He then referred to a phrase used for the special access to education of privileged cadres' offspring. "If the criticism of 'going in the back door' is added to the criticism of Lin Biao and Confucius, it may play down the Lin-Confucius criticism." The old man had indeed put his trembling finger on a problem.

But he could not solve it. And he was still too much of a revolutionist to agree with Zhou's cynical "solution" of merely allowing the drive to spiral off as a jumble of harmless, meaningless abstractions.

Mao and the ultra-leftists differed on the question of the PLA. It was all very well for Jiang Qing, from the silk sofa of cultural affairs, to snipe at the army now that the leftist officers had been eliminated with Lin Biao. She had little to lose in the khaki corner.

Mao, as supreme leader of a country where the PLA was in some ways closer to the masses than was the Party, could not afford to alienate the military.

True, Mao gave a breathtaking jolt to the regional military commanders in the winter of 1973–1974. He switched the jobs of nine of the eleven of them. It was unprecedented; and very uprooting for these territorial titans to have to leave their bailiwick and go to a new city. It was a brilliant display of Mao's power that he brought it off with only grumbles and no shots as the response.

But one may doubt that Mao could have repositioned his growling military lions if he had not, on the eve of the move, reinstated Deng to his high posts, and had Deng not been Mao's circus master who broke the news to each lion of his new post.

Yet even Mao would not be able to do such a thing again. A year later, toward the end of 1974, he called the eleven regional commanders together at his Hangzhou residence. Some of them said they would *not attend the meeting.* Only after Mao promised policy concessions—which were unveiled at the following month's pragmatic-toned National People's Congress—did they agree to assemble with their commander in chief.

"Water can keep a boat floating," runs a Chinese saying, "but can also capsize it." The PLA was Mao's "water" from the middle of the Cultural Revolution onward. But he had to be wary lest that same water rise too high and even swamp him.

*   *   *

Prime Minister Bhutto of Pakistan walked into Mao's study in May 1974. The protocol chief shepherded each dignitary to his armchair. Bhutto sat on Mao's left, as foreign guests always did. But on Mao's right (beyond the interpreter), in "Zhou's chair," sat Deng! *Zhou was present but seated on the far side of Bhutto.*

A new seating pattern in the Forbidden City, where photos are like news reports, is the equivalent of a cabinet reshuffle in many a government.

Four days before, at Mao's meeting with President Senghor of Senegal, Zhou had been in "his" chair to Mao's right; the lesser leaders sat as usual to the foreign guest's left.

It had been that way on scores of occasions.* Zhou had not for years sat anywhere else during an official photographed meeting between Mao and a foreign statesman. But he never sat in "his" chair again.†

In mid-1974 Mao went south. It was unusual for him to retreat from Peking in the summer months; mostly he left the capital in order to benefit from the warmer clime of Hangzhou, Changsha, or Canton. More unusual still—one has to go back to 1965 for a comparison—he stayed away from Peking for eight months.

Just before Mao went south, Zhou entered a military hospital in Peking. "I am not very well because I am old," Zhou remarked. He continued to do some work. But only three times did he emerge from the hospital for a public occasion. At none of these—Army Day 1974, National Day 1974, and

---

*During Mao's spring 1974 sessions with Boumediene of Algeria, Kaunda of Zambia, Nyerere of Tanzania, and Khieu Samphan of Cambodia, Zhou each time sat on Mao's right.

†At three sessions with Mao later in 1974—with Makarios of Cyprus, Razak of Malaysia, and Heath of Britain—Zhou was present but seated in the lesser spot.

the CCP and NPC sessions of January 1975—was Mao present.*

The pair were never seen together in public again.

Behind that external fact, making due allowance for the role of illness and chance in their separation, lay the inner and terribly consequential fact that their partnership was largely at an end.

However China was being run, it was not by the old firm of Mao the architect and Zhou the builder. And in the absence of the builder, it is doubtful that the architect could create much of substance.†

One afternoon while Mao was away in the south, the building of the Peking newspaper *Brilliant Daily* rocked with recrimination. An early edition of the paper was recalled and destroyed. Its second page carried an article, "Solitary Anger," which someone very senior, risking a public snafu of the kind that is rare in China, decided should not reach *Brilliant Daily*'s readers. A new edition replaced "Solitary Anger" with five items of local news.

"Solitary Anger" was written 2,200 years ago by Han Fei of the realpolitik school. Taken together with an editorial preface by *Brilliant Daily,* however, the article was all too clearly about Mao and his court.

Han Fei was indeed both alone and angry. He was surrounded by "traitorous ministers." Courtiers fawned on him, he complained, but cut him off from the real world, and from officials he could trust. It was a "monstrous crime" for a ruler to be treated like this. And a "great mistake," the protesting essayist also said, for a ruler to permit such a parlous state of affairs.

"Solitary Anger" paints a picture of a kingdom so sunk in lies and factionalism as to be headed for destruction.

Brilliant Daily—or its first, fated edition—made sure its readers did not mistake the essay for a mere antiquarian fable. It printed the essay both in its original *gu-wen* (classical) form, *and* in *bai-hua* (contemporary) form. Han Fei's evil ministers, said the editorial preface, were like Lin Biao and "his type."

Who made the decision to publish "Solitary Anger," and who ordered its withdrawal? There are two main possibilities, and each would be testimony to the disarray of Mao's government.

It *could* have been Mao's idea to republish the essay. He, like Han Fei,

---

*For a period of eight months Mao and Zhou probably met with each other only once, when Zhou flew to Changsha on December 27, 1974 to report to Mao on preparations for the forthcoming Party and NPC sessions. Mao's poem to Zhou may have been written during this visit (see page 392).

†Stephen Fitzgerald, Australian ambassador in China, 1973–1976, felt after his meeting with Mao in late 1973 that "Mao was the ruling force in China *only* as handled, as interpreted by others—especially [at that time] by Zhou." Mao showed in 1974 that he still had the immensely important power to make a selection among the "handlers" and "interpreters."

felt he had been surrounded by his fair share of "deceiving ministers." Nor would it have been out of character for him to engage in some self-criticism by identifying himself with Han Fei's scorching panorama of pessimism.

If Mao authorized the essay—before going south—it is not difficult to imagine some (perhaps most) of the Politburo wishing to suppress it on the ground that such a public parade of disgust and pessimism was, to use the American term, not in the interests of national security.

Yet the airing of "Solitary Anger" was *probably* an attack on Zhou Enlai by Jiang Qing. Zhou was the Lin "type," during 1974, in Ms. Jiang's twisted view. She was disputing the post-Mao future with the man who was (together with his allies) the main obstacle in front of her.

The mistress of the arts, who had the power to order editors around, and who rode especially high in Peking that summer, was taking advantage of Mao's absence to hit at Zhou.

Yet—if this was the explanation—it was striking that Zhou's friends were able to so swiftly impound *Brilliant Daily's* allegorical fireworks.

* * *

A delicate personal issue intervened between Mao and the ultra-left. His marriage with Jiang Qing went well and truly on the rocks.

The ex-actress with the gleam of a future empress in her eye had already moved out of South and Central Lakes. By the time of the Tenth Congress—not a good one for her; she made the Politburo but not, as expected, the inner nine-person Standing Committee of the Politburo—she had a nice house of her own not far away.

From early 1973 onward, if she wished to talk with Mao, she had to submit her reasons in writing to a liaison officer, and receive Mao's consent before she was allowed to proceed to his residence. In the middle of *pi Lin pi Kong,* Mao at least once refused to meet her.

"It is better not to see each other," he wrote to her. "You haven't carried out many of the things I talked to you about over the years. What's the use of more meetings with you?"

Jiang Qing was not with Mao during his long stay away from Peking in 1974–1975. While the cat was away the mouse did play.

Mao's last appearance in the capital for 1974 was in June. In July Jiang Qing came into her own. *People's Daily* adjudged her an "expounder" of Mao Thought, a rare honor far beyond her previous reach. She was in charge of Mrs. Marcos of the Philippines and other foreign guests, a new role for her.

In Zhejiang Province, "instructions by Jiang Qing and Wang Hongwen" were seen. Only Mao—and possibly a number two figure—ever gave "instructions" (*zhi shi*). Speeches of hers from 1964 were glorified with a tenth anniversary feature in the media.

The last straw—for those who despised Mao's wife—was a curious historical article about the founder of the Han dynasty. The article, one of many during 1974 that spoke of great women in history, put inordinate stress on the qualities and role of Han Gaozu's wife. She was firm of purpose. She took over power after her husband's death. She won glory by carrying on his line.

Mao became fed up with his estranged wife's political activities during 1974.* "She is poking her nose into everything," he said as she rode high in that year. "She lectures people wherever she goes. Is she ambitious? I believe she is."

It was at a Politburo meeting in early 1975 that Mao finally, angrily repudiated her right to interpret any of his own views. "Jiang Qing speaks only for herself; she cannot speak for me!"

"I am too old, already 81, and in poor health," he lamented in a message to her during 1975, "and you don't even show any consideration for me." It was a pathetic cry. It was the message of a man who could not really deal with the complex emotional and political problem of an ex-lover who had high ambitions but was poised for defeat the moment he gave the signal—or died.

"I do envy the Zhou Enlai marriage," Mao added in an unusual reference to his premier's private life.

During the last weeks of Mao's eight-month self-exile from Peking, his wife gave a talk to a gathering of diplomatic personnel at the Fragrant Hills Hotel near Peking, declaring that she was speaking on Mao's behalf.

In her own muddled way she was playing the role of Mao's Mao. China wants "black friends" and "small friends" and "poor friends," ran her text, which was obtained by Taiwan spies. Mao still wanted China to have that image. But when Jiang Qing said China had no "white friends" or "big friends" or "rich friends," she was out of line with Mao's actual practice.

Jiang Qing intoned that Kissinger's "basic point of view is limited by the class interests of the bourgeoisie." Yet she noted that Kissinger believed in

---

*Some of the evidence is *ex post facto*. It was claimed by Peking after Mao's death that he wrote to his wife in July; "You'd better take care. Don't form a small faction of four people." Again in December he is said to have written to all the Shanghai ultra-leftist chieftains: "Don't form a faction. Those who do will fall."

One retains an open mind about this; it is not at all clear that there was a Gang of Four in 1974 (or even in 1976, for that matter). But that Mao criticized Jiang Qing is not to be doubted.

"maintaining the balance of power" and that he "recognized the contradictions" that existed in international relations.

Jiang Qing had expressed, in the tumble of her self-important remarks, a
duality that marked Mao's foreign policy.

In Mao's mellow eye, Kissinger's bourgeois ranking was really beside the
point.* Mao did not discuss the niceties of socialism with Kissinger; he
would not have judged the American statesman a worthy co-revolutionary.

But such ideological quibbles did not have a place in Mao's foreign policy
thinking of the mid-1970s. Jiang Qing may have got hold of Mao's words,
but hardly the fullness of his thoughts.†

Mao dealt with Kissinger (and met with him twice more in the year of
Jiang Qing's Fragrant Hills tirade) for the strategic reason that China-Russia hostility was the main contradiction and it required a pro-American tilt.

When Mao did criticize Kissinger, it was not for being a bourgeois adven-
turist, as Jiang Qing said Kissinger was, but for not being a sufficiently vigorous bourgeois to stand up against the hungry, much less bourgeois Polar
Bear.

To a degree Mao shared Jiang Qing's unease at the possibilities of con-
tamination in cultural exchanges with the West. But he emphatically did
not share the hankering of the ultra-leftists to return to Lin's policy of
"evenhandedness" toward the U.S. and the U.S.S.R.

Jiang Qing may have seen the "specter of John Foster Dulles" leering
from across the Pacific. Mao was sure it now lived in the Kremlin.

*   *   *

Colleagues were simply not sure what Mao would do next.

He had purged two successors chosen by himself. Now in 1974 he was
distant from Zhou Enlai, who had helped him get away with both these acts
of major surgery, and he had begun to think Wang Hongwen had a great
future behind him.

Toward two others in Peking's top ten Mao wavered. Jiang Qing irritated
him, but some shred of sentiment, some sense of propriety, some lingering
suspicion that the pragmatists were even worse than the ultra-leftists, stayed
his hand from purging her.

---

*Kissinger is justified, in the case of Mao at least, in his remark: "The leaders of China
were beyond ideology in their dealings with us."

†Jiang Qing revealed to her audience with self-righteous pomp that the former minister for
foreign trade, the handsome Bai Xiangguo, lost office because he "failed to withstand the poisonous snake that took the form of a beautiful woman." Mao never dwelt on a colleague's
weakness of the flesh, let alone ascribed it, as Jiang Qing did in discussing Bai, to a lack of
"revolutionary vigilance."

Deng he leaned upon. Yet he seemed to use a long spoon when supping with the vice-premier who by the end of 1974 was sitting in Zhou's chair. Deng was no doubt still "deaf"—as Mao angrily accused him of being in the 1960s—but he was now tactful enough to look at Mao when the Chairman was speaking, and not drum his fingers as if he felt it time to move on to the next item on the agenda.*

Mao sent Deng and Wang Hongwen *together* on an inspection trip. How "Lazarus" and the "helicopter" got on with each other during a tour of the provinces is not recorded. When they returned to Peking, Mao summoned them for a report on what they had seen.

His question was as morbid as his choice of an investigating team had been odd (unless it happened to be shrewd in the extreme). "After I die, what will happen in China?"†

"The whole country," replied young Wang, "will certainly follow Chairman Mao's revolutionary line and unite firmly to carry the revolution to the end." Did Mao expect such mush from his boy wonder? No one who heard Wang's talk to the Central Committee group a few days later would have expected anything else.‡

"Civil war will break out," Deng rasped, "and there will be confusion throughout the country." Mao preferred Deng's answer, according to the Communist source in Hong Kong that supplied the story.

Out of touch with many realities as he was, Mao still read *People's Daily,* which may seem masochistic. This six-page newspaper seems to have been written by a congressional committee. News is not its cup of tea. *People's Daily* does not tell; it reminds. It is (or was when Mao was alive) a daily catechism, just journalistic enough to root its eternal verities in a recent concrete morality tale. Somehow old Mao found truth in even the strident editions of 1974.

Truth that was an echo of a past *he* knew. If he read about a "two-line struggle" in a silk mill at Hangzhou, that rang true. Two-line struggles had been with him, he thought, ever since he began his long climb to power in the 1920s. He felt he knew what the line of division was. He could persuade himself that silk output would be good only if the "workers' line" won out over the "bourgeois line."

---

*Deng had been back in office only a few months when *pi Kong* began, and he was relatively tactful about the drive. In private he summed up: "Confucius is dead. His thought is out of date. Thus it should be opposed. We too will die soon. After several thousand years, our thought will be opposed too, because it will not be in line with people's thought at that time."

†Years before, when Mao told Lord Montgomery that Liu Shaoqi would succeed him as China's leader, the Briton pursued the issue of the succession. "I asked [Mao] who would come next after Liu. He didn't know or care; he himself would be with Karl Marx and they could work it out for themselves in China!" But he probably did care.

‡See page 380.

But Mao was living in the past; otherwise he could hardly have found *People's Daily* of 1974 believable. More and more Chinese people felt so.

* * *

Cars holding 2,885 dignitaries drove up to the Great Hall of the People. People in the streets guessed that the Fourth National People's Congress, a parliament that is a rubber stamp but a useful one, was finally in session. There had been so many delays that it had begun to rank as a mirage.

It looked like back to business: Zhou reemerged and cut a figure of authority; a new state constitution was unveiled that gave workers the right to strike and farmers the right to their private plots; the ultra-leftists obtained few of the new government appointments announced; Deng was promoted; and the documents of the meetings struck a note of order and stressed economic tasks.

Was it not a victory for Zhou's views; an end to the leftist festival of criticizing Lin and Confucius; a green light for Deng?

But an empty chair weighed down the auditorium; Mao was not there.

Was he gravely ill or even dead? No, for during the sessions in Peking, the prime minister of Malta and the German right-winger Franz Josef Strauss were spirited down to south China to meet him.

With or without a full grasp of the complexities of the situation in his own government, he was sulking in his tent.

The communiqué of the NPC did not explain Mao's absence. It said nothing about him at all. Nor did Mao attend a Central Committee meeting just prior to the NPC's opening.

The new constitution gave less prominence to Mao Thought than the draft of it prepared in 1970, and less than did the Party Constitution of 1969, or even the blander one of 1973. It referred to Mao Thought, and to the office of Chairman of the CCP, but not to Mao himself.

To make matters weirder, Zhou's report, but not that of leftist Zhang Chunqiao, bent over backward to quote Mao. No less than twenty-six times did Zhou's text mention Mao's name.

A few weeks earlier, Mao had talked at length with Wang Hongwen. The "helicopter" pressed Mao to give more jobs to the ultra-leftist circle. He hinted—this idea came from Jiang Qing—that Zhou was not as ill as he pretended and was very busy plotting for the future from his hospital. He cast doubt on Deng's reliability. Would Mao not agree that, in the circumstances, Zhang Chunqiao should become premier?

Mao did not endorse Wang's plan. He was prepared to make Zhang defense minister, until the one-eyed veteran Liu Bocheng and other generals jacked up against the idea. He may even have been willing to give his wife the nod as culture minister. But old Mao found that politics never ceases to be a bargaining process; too much opposition existed to such plans.

Soon afterward the Politburo met. Mao was in the chair. Factionalism was a terrible thing, he said. Everyone makes mistakes, he purred, including himself, as when he went along for so long with Lin Biao. He threw in a word of praise for Deng as a "practical man." At the same time he warned his colleagues about the recurrent menace of "bourgeois revisionism."

Mao had explained why he would stay away from the round of Party and state meetings about to commence. He was biding his time; having a dollar each way; hiding the more lurid of his doubts; letting the waters flow by unchallenged for the moment.

In his report to the NPC, Zhou probably mentioned Mao so frequently both to soothe the Chairman and to say a graceful thank you for the extra freedom his absence lent Zhou.*

It seems that Mao visited Music Mountain at this time. Chinese sources had him "in the countryside" as well as in his old home city of Changsha. As he had done several times in the 1920s, and in 1959, Mao retreated to his local soil in a season of frustration.

Again as on all the other occasions, it was in midwinter. Again he carried with him a mixture of physical ailments and political ailments. Again he went home to stoke up for a fresh blaze of activity.

> Loyal parents who sacrificed so much for the nation
>   never feared the ultimate fate.
> Now that the country has become Red,
>   who will be its guardian?

Mao wrote these lines during his quiet period in the south. The poem was, perhaps surprisingly, for Zhou.

> Our mission, unfinished, may take a thousand years.
> The struggle tires us, and our hair is gray.
> You and I, old friend, can we just watch our efforts
>   being washed away?

The job was vast, much remained to be done, and Mao doubted that those who would take over could do it. His pessimistic mood cut across any line of division between "pro-Zhou" and "anti-Zhou," or "left" and "moderate."

---

*It was interesting that a very junior ultra-leftist, less circumspect than his mentors, did criticize Mao's absence. Mao had "poured cold water on the Fourth NPC," said Zhang Tiesheng (the Liaoning student who had become famous after writing an angry letter on his college entrance exam; see note on page 382), by giving no audience to the NPC delegates, of whom Zhang, having risen like a "helicopter," was one.

Indeed it no longer made sense to ask if Mao was these days a Maoist. One day he was; the next day he wasn't.

* * *

The pragmatic mood of the NPC seemed out of date within two months. A fresh breeze from the left began to blow during the spring of 1975, spurred by a new quote from Mao: "Study well the theory of the dictatorship of the proletariat."

Probably the NPC line never won a consensus in the Politburo. Mao's absence made it even easier than usual for colleagues with differing views to "make their own Mao" out of his words. Zhou's illness added to the opportunities to jump out of line.

"Some of our comrades," Zhang Chunqiao warned, "have joined the Communist Party organizationally but not ideologically." Sounding like a trumpeter for a new Cultural Revolution, the Shanghai leftist hit out at swindlers on high who "peddle among youth" the idea that money incentive, "like bean curd, may smell awful but tastes good."

Zhang's fellow ultra-leftist Yao Wenyuan also dug up Cultural Revolution themes. Wages are too unequal. The money system is a capitalist hangover which must eventually go. New class enemies, the Shanghai essayist predicted, might use these evils to engineer a reversion to capitalism.

Mao gave some encouragement to the Shanghai pair. Both came up with new quotations from the Chairman, one of the surest signs, apart from being photographed beside him, of a blessing from him.

Industrial unrest was the only tangible result of the drive—which had the disadvantage of being at once vague and earnest—to study the baffling abstraction "dictatorship of the proletariat."* Resentment, disruption, and fighting were so bad in Hangzhou that Mao agreed to send Wang as a mediator to the lakeside city. His stay appeared to make the situation worse.

Just at this time Prime Minister Kukrit witnessed a sign of Zhou's fading authority. "Now Kukrit," the ailing premier said in his hospital suite, "go back home and tell everyone, especially your children and grandchildren, that China will never attack Thailand."

"Mr. Prime Minister," the Thai leader replied, "those are very reassuring words." Taking a long piece of paper out of his pocket, Kukrit leaned forward and asked Zhou to write down the promise in his own hand. "I'll have millions of copies made and hang them around the necks of my children and

---

*I have described elsewhere (*The Future of China*, pages 54–55) a visit made in the late summer of 1975 to a factory in Shanghai that was a pet of Wang's and tried to push to the end the logic of studying the dictatorship of the proletariat.

grandchildren—of everyone in Thailand. It will be the most valuable possession in my life."

"My hand shakes," objected Zhou, "I am too ill to write it down."

Kukrit took Zhou's excuse at face value, he told me in an interview; yet I believe Zhou's reluctance, at this mid-point of 1975, had a political component.*

Confusingly enough, the fitful left-wing breeze dropped by late summer, as the monkey in Mao stirred to take a swipe against the ultra-left!

After an inactive spell—visiting heads of government from Guyana, Mozambique, and Congo all failed to see him—Mao summoned and chaired a Politburo meeting in May. At it he criticized the ultra-left for factionalism. Zhang, Yao, and Jiang Qing all wrote letters of self-criticism to the grumbling Chairman.

As this morality play wound on, Deng began to arrange himself in the cockpit of power, and PLA officers purged in the Cultural Revolution came back like commuters at rush hour. Among them was no less a figure than Luo Ruiqing, the former chief of staff whose insufficient hostility toward Russia had made him the first senior victim of Mao's Cultural Revolution.

Mao as arbiter gave Deng the nod. Could he really be worse, Mao seemed to be asking himself, than all the other evil ministers who had let him down?†

Economics replaced ideology as the main topic in part of the press. "Stability, unity, development of the economy"—a Deng slogan—became a catch cry, almost as "study the dictatorship of the proletariat" had been in the spring.

An agriculture conference was one of several meetings on the economy that reflected a businesslike mood which reached its peak in the autumn of 1975. Deng spoke, as did a second-rank figure with a background in Hunan agriculture, Hua Guofeng.

Jiang Qing also appeared at the podium. At the NPC she failed to become minister of culture, but now she was able to dispense some cultural advice to farmers.

People's Daily published only the Deng and Hua speeches. Mao blocked a plan to publish his wife's. "Shit!" he wrote on the text when Hua brought

*Kukrit himself recalled that the place where he met Zhou "didn't look like a hospital." And Zhou was wearing a Mao badge, unusual in 1975; even in 1971, when the influence of the Cultural Revolution was much fresher, I noticed that Zhou wore only a "Serve the People" badge.

†The Deng-Mao relationship seemed a little awkward when Kukrit visited Mao in mid-1975. "Deng was sitting in a far corner, very prim and proper.... He never said a word." After cursing Nancy Tang, in a friendly way, as untrustworthy ("Never trust an American girl") Mao rather condescendingly nodded toward Deng and said, "But he's all right, you can trust him." Deng then "burst into a beatific smile."

it to him. "Barking up the wrong tree! Don't publish the talk."

He also criticized his Yanan sweetheart for an interview she had given to an American scholar, Roxane Witke, in which Jiang Qing indulged herself and revealed prior indulgences. He apparently flew into a rage when he read a transcript of her vain, wild chatter to Professor Witke.

Mao's feelings toward Jiang Qing were able to trigger two earthquakes in China's political system. The first was his upbraiding of the left; this gave the ball to Deng. The second was yet to come.

* * *

As Mao declined, and Zhou was absent in hospital, interpreters seemed to become the focus of foreign leaders' visits to South and Central Lakes.

"His lips could not move as quickly as he wanted," Prime Minister Kukrit of Thailand noted after his July 1975 session with Mao, "and sometimes his voice was inaudible."

As Kukrit walked in to the study "Mao made a very loud roaring noise. . . . He shook me by the hand and made more roaring noises, until the lady interpreters and nurses and everybody arrived." Many of Mao's words the interpreters could not understand. They turned to the nurses for help. At times the nurses were at a loss; "then Mao's amah, his servant maid, was called in to listen to his words."

At the end, when Kukrit presented a gift, Mao seemed to go blank. "He began to shake the cigar box in his hands, like a baby; someone rescued it from his grasp." Mao had somehow gone. "All the wit, the knowledge, the wisdom had suddenly disappeared from his eyes. As I shook hands, he was gazing over my head. He wasn't interested."

The Chairman had to be got out of bed and dressed for many of these ghostly audiences with foreigners. His jaw hung down and gave him the look of a soul begging, clinging to its last moments.

The walk was slow and as if on stilts. He shuffled his painful feet and his straight arms swung imperceptibly from the shoulder in the way artificial limbs do. Yet Mao had lost none of his capacity to make foreigners defer to him.

"For Tam and me," said Prime Minister Muldoon of New Zealand of the appointment he and his wife had to meet Mao, "it was an awesome moment as we drove in through the gate of the Forbidden City and were ushered in to see him."*

---

*Joseph Alsop has written that Kukrit stooped down and massaged Mao's calves and ankles, but the story may have been invented by Kukrit's enemies in Thailand. Kukrit himself flatly denied to me that the incident occurred. Nevertheless the Thai leader remarked: "I talked to him as though I were his son or grandson."

He broached with Imelda Marcos, First Lady of the Philippines, the personal tragedy that lurks close to anyone who achieves high office. "The higher you get," he remarked to the tough beauty from Manila, "the more stones will be thrown at you by others."

"Nearly everyone who comes to meet me and whom I like goes home to face disaster," Mao morbidly observed to Kukrit. He meant men such as Nixon, Tanaka, Nkrumah, Heath, Sukarno, Whitlam, Sihanouk, to name seven leaders friendly to China who met reversal at home.

When Kukrit politely wished Mao a long life, Mao rejoined with a brooding: "What's the point?"

"He was an old man who still believed in his own supremacy," Prime Minister Kukrit concluded, "but if anybody were to forge his signature, or issue commands in his name, beyond the realm of his own room, he wouldn't know about it."

*   *   *

Mao's America policy had frayed at the edges since the high point of early 1973 when the two nations set up offices in each other's capitals.

The Chinese turnabout on policy toward the superpowers had seemed complete at that time, as the issue of nuclear weapons showed. Russia previously provided an umbrella of nuclear deterrence for China; Moscow claimed in 1972 that it had four times saved China from a U.S. nuclear attack. By the spring of 1973 U.S. officials hinted in private that the American link with Peking was saving China from a Russian nuclear attack!

China had changed partners, in the minds of those partners, even more perhaps than in its own.

Yet the Sino-American tie was damaged by a variety of pressures from mid-1973. Kissinger was due to come to Peking in August, but the trip was postponed, because of that month's Tenth Congress (at which Zhou was cool toward the U.S.).

Pi Lin pi Kong was merrily erecting America as one of its targets. Military voices, as we have seen, were questioning the tilt toward Washington. Vietnam, on which American bombs still rained, was carping at Peking's pro-Americanism. The Chinese envoy in Washington found it convenient to be absent from his post throughout the spring of 1974.

The decline of the Mao-Zhou partnership did not help. It exposed America policy to ultra-leftist and PLA maneuvers. It made the U.S. side wonder if China's pro-America policy would "stick."

Kissinger found Deng, Mao's new executive officer, less warm toward the U.S. than Zhou. He wondered why Deng often quoted Mao but would not even respond to questions about Zhou's condition. "A nasty little man," he even said of Deng.

In China in late 1974, Kissinger went to see Zhou in his hospital, but found the premier strangely guarded in manner, and was puzzled that although Zhou seemed in good health the meeting was abruptly terminated after a mere thirty minutes.

Still worse, Mao did not see Kissinger—the first time this had happened on all the American's visits to Peking.

Mao was south of the Yangze; even so, six other foreign leaders flew down—in virtual blindfold conditions—for an audience with him in the couple of months before and after Kissinger was in China. The point was that Mao, pro-American as he was compared with some in his Politburo, took a dim view of Kissinger's arriving in Peking direct from Vladivostok, where he and President Ford had been supping with Brezhnev.*

Some of Mao's colleagues, who had no investment in the Mao-Zhou link and who were attracted by the idea of an easing of Sino-Soviet tension, quietly threw sand into the machinery of the U.S.-China relationship during 1974.

Mao's own view of America also posed a problem. Its ambivalence came out sharply in a talk with Pompidou of France late in 1973. Détente was a hoax, he bluntly told a man who thought of himself as one of its apostles. The West was having the wool pulled over its eyes by the Soviet Union. American will power was ebbing.

Kissinger became so jittery about the prospects of the forthcoming trip by President Ford to China that when, to his great relief, Mao invited him for a chat during his October 1975 stay in Peking, the secretary of state asked Mao to *put in writing a promise to receive Ford when he came to Peking.*

Perhaps Mao was wryly amused by the utilitarian bent of the Americans—whether or not he would still be alive may have been *his* preoccupation—but he did not hesitate. He reached for a felt-tipped pen and scribbled the commitment Kissinger prayed for.

The Mao-Ford summit was a tame affair. For Ford, coming after Nixon, it was a bit like being the second man to land on the moon. The U.S. President, anxious about Ronald Reagan's challenge from the right, came to Peking with little in his briefcase. And Mao, awesome but terribly frail, seemed as unreal as the man in the moon.

Intensified cross-currents bedeviled Chinese policies. And the fall of Saigon did not liberate Sino-American relations any more than it liberated the people of South Vietnam.

"We have been defeated [in Vietnam]," Kissinger remarked ruefully to a Chinese official in the spring of 1975, "and *you* will have to deal with the

---

*Journalists covering Kissinger found in their Peking hotel rooms a map of Siberia which had Vladivostok, a city only forty miles from the Chinese border, whose Russian name means "Rule the East," marked by its old Chinese name, Hai Shen Wei.

consequences." Mao knew better than some of his colleagues just what Kissinger meant.

He met with a stream of Vietnamese leaders in the 1970s, hiding his growing anxiety about Vietnam's future relations with China as he embraced the wily, deeply anti-Chinese visitors.*

Mao encouraged the cocky Vietnamese heroes to put the struggle against the U.S. behind them and think more broadly about Vietnam's place in Asia. He made little impact. Turned off by Mao's anti-Soviet forebodings, the Vietnamese had different fish to fry.

"Vietnam is a temple with four abbots," Mao remarked to Jiang Qing not long afterward, "and anyone who gives alms and cloth is their patron." It was not long before his attitude to Vietnam resembled that of America's most bristling hawks. He would never receive a Vietnamese visitor again.

It happened that Mao, in his up-and-down pattern of health, was in vigorous form during Ford's visit.

The 110-minute talk with the President was richer in detail and longer than Mao's talk with Nixon in 1972. Mao threw his hands around in gesticulation, and rocked with laughter at one point. He seemed to sense that a U.S. President was sitting in his study for the last time, and to rouse himself for a last effort of advocacy.

And his "eyes lighted up," according to Betty Ford, when he met her daughter Susan.

But reluctance and uncertainty ate—from both sides—at the summit. It was clear to both Chinese and American officials, and to the Chinese people who saw a newsreel of the Mao-Ford meeting, that Mao did not have long to live. Neither Deng nor Ford, the two men who carried on the policy discussions, was a strong leader with a clear mandate from his domestic constituency.

---

*"We are of the same family," he declared in December 1972 to Mrs. Binh of the southern Marxist government-in-waiting. "We and you, South and North Vietnam, and also Laos and Cambodia are of the same family," he added curiously. "We support each other." Was he warning Mrs. Binh that Laos and Cambodia had their own rights as separate nations, and reminding her that China had Korea, in addition to Vietnam, as a close-by friend?

At any rate, Mrs. Binh felt sufficiently at ease to call her host "Uncle Mao."

Mao asked the Hanoi negotiators to come and see him on their way home from Paris in February 1973. For an unusually long one and a half hours he talked with Foreign Minister Trinh and Kissinger's opposite number, Le Duc Tho.

Not long afterward he met with Hanoi's two top men, Party chief Le Duan and government chief Pham Van Dong.

Again in late 1973 he received Mrs. Binh and her president, Nguyen Huu Tho. "We should . . . thank you people of South Vietnam," he said in a possible attempt to draw a distinction between south and north, "because you have fought many years."

Mao did seem to slightly favor the regime of the south, over Hanoi, as in receiving Mrs. Binh, the south's foreign minister, in December 1972, but not Truong Chinh, a Hanoi Politburo member, who visited Peking the same week.

And the two partners, while willing to lie in the same bed, were dreaming very different dreams.

The issue of Russia, which had brought Mao and Nixon together in 1972, was a barrier between Mao and Ford in 1975.

In the American view, the opening to China was an end in itself. Sino-U.S. tension in Asia had been defused; détente with China was a twin of détente with Russia.

In Mao's view, the name of the game was power and not peace. He envisaged a long struggle against Soviet global power, with the U.S. in China's corner, doing the job of resisting Russian "hegemony" which China was too weak to do alone.

So the summit was a failure for a curious reason. Ford would not budge on the Taiwan issue—main roadblock to normalization—for U.S. domestic political reasons. Mao would not refrain from criticizing U.S.-Soviet détente and telling his guests that "only the Kremlin benefits from it." The tragedy was that the bilateral problem and the strategic disagreement were not seen in combination.

Mao had once before opposed détente, in the late 1950s, in a different way but for the same reasons. Russia, not the U.S., was in those days his friend. He then saw Russia, not the U.S., as in danger of being deluded by the promise of détente. By 1975 the two superpowers had changed places.

Yet Mao's strategy looked the same, in its nationalism and its long-range vision. He did not want Russia and the U.S. to fight each other, but he did not want them to gang up together against China either. He wished them to be uneasy with each other, giving time for China to become stronger, and be a match for either—or both.

22

An Arrow Near the End of Its Flight (1976)

As the last minutes of 1975 ticked by Mao was sunk in an armchair of his outer study. The skin of his face resembled wax more than living tissue. The eyes looked vacant. Frail as Dresden china, he seemed almost as lifeless.

In from the darkness walked Julie Nixon Eisenhower and her husband David. Two young women helped Mao struggle to his feet. He tottered, then steadied himself, and the two nurses stepped back. He shook hands with the Americans before whirring cameras and blazing TV lights. The two women put him back again in his slipcovered chair.

Julie took a letter out of a Manila envelope and put it into Mao's thin, pale hand. It was written by a man who had lost office to a man who should have, but had not, lost office.

Mao stirred to life in recalling the improbable Nixon-Mao political love affair of 1972. "How is Mr. Nixon's leg?" he inquired, as if to establish a mood of nostalgia.

"When your father comes," Mao remarked of Nixon's impending second visit to China, "I will be waiting." He brought both arms down heavily to the sides of his chair to propel the words; it was his most animated sentence of the evening.*

Julie and David stumbled across a contradiction in Mao as 1976 began.

They found Mao warm toward all things American. "Chairman Mao has followed your trip," a senior Chinese figure said to the Eisenhowers as they left Shanghai for Washington. "He considers you part of his family."

---

* "I was surprised," Julie remarked of Peking's envoy to Washington, who was present in the room, "when he did not lean forward in his chair to catch every word the Chairman spoke." Instead Huang Zhen "gazed casually around the room."

Given the painful diction and the banal content, perhaps it was not so surprising. Mao seemed a mere exhibit, and the ambassador had seen the "exhibit" before.

When Mao rose to end the interview, a young girl ran a comb through his hair before a TV crew recorded the final handshake on film.

Yet the couple came upon many flourishes of ultra-leftism, some of them the work of Mao himself.

"It is nothing," Mao said to Julie and David of a militant poem that was being typeset for republication that very moment. "I wrote it in 1965." But the poem, "Well Mountain Revisited," was a grenade of leftism.

"We can clasp the moon in the Ninth Heaven," ran its apocalyptic lines, "And seize turtles deep down in the Five Seas."

The issue of *People's Daily* that reported the Mao-Eisenhower conversation also carried "Well Mountain Revisited," together with "Two Birds: A Dialogue," an equally militant poem written on the eve of the Cultural Revolution, which ended "Look, the world is being turned upside down."*

If January 1975 had brought a breeze from the left, January 1976 now saw a gale from the left. Mao was less in charge of it than he had been a year before—when he sulked while the NPC's "dialogue" came down on the side of the wrong "bird"—but he cared about it with the earnestness of an old man making his last fling.

A letter to Mao from a "worker-peasant-soldier" group at Qinghua University was the seed that led to the harvest of ultra-leftist chaff in the spring of 1976.

Written on Mao's 82nd birthday, the letter was a complaint that "the bourgeoisie" at China's famous technical university had "fanned a rightist evil wind of reversing verdicts." In other words, common sense had struck back against the nonsense of Cultural Revolution educational "reforms."

The letter reached Mao's desk in the wake of two others from a Qinghua faction of pragmatic stripe. "Unless the system is changed," the head of the school, Liu Bing, wrote to Mao, "young people will be leaving the university without being able to read a book."

Deng was behind Liu Bing. When Liu told the peppery vice-premier of the leftist complaint about a "rightist evil wind," Deng swore and vowed in defiance: "We'll make it a typhoon."

The issue was joined: "red" versus "expert." Would Mao be able to muster the strength to adjudicate?

The older Mao got, the more he believed in the conscious will of man, even as his hatred grew for the schools whose task it was to cultivate that conscious will. "The more books one reads," he allowed himself to say, "the more stupid one becomes."

He belittled professors. He told students to sleep during class and cheat in exams. He sent writers to grow rice in remote villages.

Yet Mao never lost the Confucian conviction that teachers and books

* We encountered the two poems earlier; see pages 304 and 312.

shape the world. He feared the professors even as he belittled them; the specter of a Peking version of Budapest's "Petofi Club" of 1956 haunted him for years. He could not resist reading the stories writers wrote even as he ran them down as rubbish.

Go back to his trip through Hunan in the 1920s to see the root of the tragedy. "Even if 10,000 schools of law and political science had been opened," he exulted in his *Report on an Investigation of the Peasant Movement in Hunan*, "could they have brought as much political education to the people, men and women, young and old, all the way into the remotest corners of the countryside, as the peasant associations have done in so short a time? I don't think they could."

He went on:

> "Down with imperialism!" "Down with the war lords!" "Down with the corrupt officials!" "Down with the local tyrants and evil gentry!"—these political slogans have grown wings, they have found their way to the young, the middle-aged, and the old, to the women and children in countless villages, they have penetrated into their minds and are on their lips.

Nineteen seventy-six was not 1927. Political slogans did not "grow wings" in the same way at Qinghua as when desperate peasants groped for words to summarize the evils that blighted their lives. Young Mao had seen knowledge only in relation to revolution. Old Mao could not see that "education for revolution" was a meaningless phrase for the ordinary chemistry or physics student of the 1970s.

Mao returned Liu Bing's letter without any reply. The "birthday" letter from the ultra-leftists he liked a lot; it appeared on the front page of *People's Daily* soon after he read it.

"Are you [Liu Bing] trying to drive workers, peasants, and soldiers off the campuses," ran a typical sentence in the torrent of ultra-leftist articles on education that Mao authorized, "just like pushing shit out of the bowel?"

A mini-Cultural Revolution seemed to have been launched, starting, as always, in the realm of education and culture, where it was easy to confuse words with realities.*

---

* Later in the year, Mao called in an educator, Zhang Nanxiang, who had been purged from high posts in left-wing gales. As Zhang came in, Jiang Qing, who was hovering at Mao's bedside, warned him that his report to Mao on the educational situation "shouldn't last over three minutes."

Zhang, once President of Qinghua University and now disenchanted with policy, muttered grimly that "thirty seconds will be enough for my report." He baldly summed up for Mao: "College students study the textbooks of middle schools. Their academic level is equal to that of primary school students."

Old Mao, the mischief-maker behind the educational decline, sighed and murmured: "If this situation goes on, not only will the Party fall, but the nation itself will perish."

"Enemies" appeared as if from an assembly line. Every sphere of life and work was said to be in the grip of "two-line struggle." It became fashionable to say "revolution" mattered more than "production." Officials in the Zhou-Deng camp were cowed. Foreign trade suffered.

Mouths were full of phrases about the "glories of the Cultural Revolution," as if spouting them often enough could root out the gut feeling of most Chinese that the Cultural Revolution was a disaster. The mood was set by intoxicated activists who felt, as Mao spurred them on to feel, they could "clasp the moon in the Ninth Heaven and seize turtles deep down in the Five Seas."

Was this a mere debate, good for the kids? Or was Mao trying to purge someone from the Politburo, preparing the way, as in previous such efforts, with an issues campaign in the press? Mao had given the answer on New Year's Eve.

"There will be struggle in the Party," he murmured to Julie Eisenhower.

Shaky as he was, Mao had mustered fresh strength for an effort to rescue the fading values of the Cultural Revolution. It was no accident that "Well Mountain Revisited" and "Two Birds: A Dialogue" had been written as overtures to the Cultural Revolution.

Mao was correct to suspect that the "newborn socialist things" of the 1960s had a bleak future in Deng's hands.

The Cultural Revolution had been a mere festival; it had not brought into being new structures. Mao had wanted a "serve-the-people" altruism to take hold of the populace. "A great revolution," he called the Cultural Revolution, "that touches people to their very souls and aims at solving the problems of their world outlook."

He had been searching for new political *methods*. "In the past, we waged struggles in the rural areas, in factories, in the cultural field. . . . But all this failed to solve the problem because we did not find a form, a method, to arouse the broad masses. . . . The answer was the Great Proletarian Cultural Revolution."

And Mao had wanted to get rid of colleagues who had fallen away from the Maoist virtues.

A new mentality *did* take hold of many young people in the 1960s; their awe for authority and old things was reduced. A new political method *did* unfold; mobilization of the grass roots led to a measure of direct political participation by millions who had once been passive and sullen. And Mao's enemies at the top *were* removed; half the Politburo fell in the storm of the Cultural Revolution.

Yet none of these changes endured. Youth's excitement gave way to a good deal of cynicism by the 1970s. Mass mobilization from below was not made an integral part of China's political system. And the victims of the

Cultural Revolution came back on deck as the victors of the 1970s—Deng chief among them.

Reviving the Cultural Revolution made no sense—a festival is only a festival—but one can see why old Mao, mixing up as usual his role as teacher with his role as leader, wanted to try and do so once more before he died.

Soon an event occurred that tipped the scales toward the left and gave Mao his last chance.

* * *

The pastry chef at the Peace Hotel in Shanghai worked on two fancy cakes. They were to sweeten Richard Nixon's 63rd birthday.

The vanilla cake with white and brown frosting was for Julie and David, then guests at the hotel, to eat that day. A larger one, in a silk-covered box, adorned with the characters for "Happy Birthday Mr. Nixon," was for the couple to take back to San Clemente.

As the kitchen staff prepared the cakes to be taken upstairs to the Eisenhowers' room, a messenger arrived at their door with a far from festive piece of news from Peking: Zhou Enlai was dead of cancer at 78.

Julie and David went ahead and ate their cake for breakfast. Much else on the surface of life in China seemed normal, even as the press switched from lambasting Zhou's policies to lauding Zhou. Yet the death of Zhou at this particular time was a terrible piece of bad luck for the PRC, for it gave Mao a chance to lurch around like a bull in the china shop of this fresh mini-Cultural Revolution.

Zhou's body was taken from the hospital where he died to a pavilion in the Forbidden City. In freezing cold, a silent, weeping crowd of close to a million people gazed with a jumble of feelings at the cortege with its hearse draped in black and yellow rosettes.

Mao alone among the Chinese leaders was absent from the stream of mourners who had gone to Peking Hospital to pay last respects to Zhou's body. Even the 90-year-old Zhu De came to view the slight, stiff corpse, draped in a CCP flag and surrounded by flowers and plants.

Nor did Mao attend the funeral service, at which Deng spoke fulsomely to the 5,000 top persons of China, and over which Wang Hongwen presided awkwardly, like a student who had strayed into a professors' meeting.

Mao had attended very few funerals since the 1950s, and none since Chen Yi's in 1972, yet he was probably physically capable of putting in an appearance at the service, held only a few minutes' walk from his home.

He sent a paper wreath. It was placed on one side of a boyish portrait of the man who had been China's premier for twenty-six years, with a wreath from the CCP on the other, above a casket of the remains (Zhou had asked for cremation and for his ashes to be "scattered upon the rivers and soil of our motherland.")

Perhaps Mao simply did not wish to be seen by large numbers of people. He had slipped over to the hospital to sit beside Zhou's bed during the premier's last hours. Some pang of loneliness, or even remorse, may have moved him to be the last person apart from medical workers to speak with the most durable and loyal of all his senior associates.

"Each person has but one death," wrote the ancient Chinese scholar Si Maqian, "but it can be light as a feather or heavy as Mount Tai." Zhou's death was as heavy as the great mountain in Shandong Province because, unexpectedly, it came before Mao's.

Zhou's presence could have smoothed Mao's passing. But Mao's presence could not damp down—indeed it augmented—the political flames that leaped from Zhou's ashes.

Without Zhou, and with a Mao in "King Lear" condition and "monkey" mood, a challenge by the ultra-left to Deng's brusque command of affairs was a sure bet.

Polarization, in a word, was what Zhou's death brought in the late winter of 1976. And Mao's very presence—plus his flickering predilections—loaded the dice against Deng.

When Jiang Qing went to view Zhou's body she did not remove her cap. This apparent slight, captured in a TV newsreel, caused tremors. A soldier in Shenyang threw a chair at a TV set in anger. A crowd in Canton, watching a neighborhood TV set in Peking Road, began to chant: "Beat her up."

Zhou's widow, the plain but redoubtable Deng Yingchao, greeted Deng Xiaoping with affection as he drew near to the bier. But Ms. Deng was arch toward Jiang Qing. Her manner toward Zhang Chunqiao seemed to fall between the two extremes: cordial without being warm.

Pictures were, as ever, the nearest Chinese equivalent of investigative reporting in the West; the "Party struggle" of which Mao spoke to the Eisenhowers began in earnest before Zhou's body was cold, and the TV film gave a hint of its contours.

*   *   *

With Zhou's death, Deng Xiaoping lost a key buttress for his attempt at arranging a post-Mao alignment of power.

The ultra-leftists saw a green light to go ahead and seek a quite different alignment of power. Jiang Qing would throw the dice in her biggest gamble yet. Zhang Chunqiao, a man with a broader mind and base than Jiang's, might or might not stand behind her.

Mao himself was at a tangent to it all. A "post-Mao alignment of power" was not exactly his focus of attention; he was still alive; he felt he had much yet to do.

And despite some affection for Zhou, and an absence of it for his estranged wife, Mao was in a militant mood, and irritated with Deng Xiaoping. Zhou's widow would have had small reason to embrace Mao if he had joined the group of mourners at Peking Hospital.

"Without struggle there is no progress," Mao declared in a midwinter maxim. "Can 800 million people manage without struggle?" Even as Mao was sweetly asking Julie about her father's leg, these words were being transmitted as an unmistakable message of dissatisfaction with a whole range of Deng's policies.

In old China an emperor's edict used to be placed in the mouth of a gold-painted wooden phoenix, lowered from the Gate of Heavenly Peace, taken by a mandarin of the Board of Rites on a tray decorated with clouds, copied on yellow paper and sent to every corner of China. So it was with Mao's fresh quotes.*

But if the mandarin's tray was *People's Daily* and Peking Radio, who played the part of the golden phoenix? Did Mao wish to ridicule the pragmatic line of the second half of 1975; or were the ultra-leftists acting in his name?

The new maxims were at any rate from Mao's own pen. His words had lost none of their corrosive power; his reign hung by a thread of aphorisms.

"Stability and unity do not mean writing off class struggle," ran another New Year's Mao quote that electrified the nation. "Class struggle is the key link and everything else hinges on it." The terms "stability and unity" happened to be the badge of Deng's management of affairs as he consolidated his power (with Zhou sinking toward death) from mid-1975.

These issues hung in the air like a thick fog as a round of grueling Politburo meetings began. Each molehill of a quote from Mao was made, by the contending factions, into a mountain as astonishing as the weird peaks of Guilin. A tug of war for the premiership was going on.

Deng was one candidate to replace Zhou. Zhang was the other.

The knives were out; Mao's presence was no longer enough to stay them. Deng gave a report on economic policy to the fifteen-man Politburo. Yao Wenyuan criticized it as being theoretically unsound. Someone (not Mao) grasped the nettle and proposed Deng as premier. The ultra-leftists said flatly that they would not serve under him. Jiang Qing countered by nominating Zhang, the most widely acceptable candidate her circle could put

---

* Mao himself was aware of the similarity. "Don't treat everything that has been issued as an 'imperial edict,'" he remarked at a conference in Nanning.

forward. Those who favored Deng, including the military leader Ye Jianying, managed to block Zhang's appointment as premier.

Mao's own eyes turned toward a protégé from his home province who had
never caused him any bother.

The amiable Hua Guofeng was a modest man, with every reason so far to
be so. Mao could at least trust him; it was Hua's great advantage in a poisonous atmosphere with trust in very short supply.

Hua, who came from Hunan to the national political scene only in 1969,
had fewer enemies than the battle-scarred Deng. He stood between Deng
and the ultra-leftists on some key policy issues. His style was cool in a season of hotheadedness.

Yet the services Hua had rendered to Mao, together with Mao's dislike of
most other candidates, were the amiable Shanxi-born Hua's chief assets.

He had done irrigation work in Mao's home district. He supervised the
building of the unerringly adulatory Mao Memorial in Music Mountain.
Under his authority a railroad was built to link the area with Changsha—a
lucky break for the tiny village—and a color-TV factory was placed in Music Mountain, giving attractive jobs to many of Mao's distant relatives.

Mao seemed aware that he was choosing a figure from the second rank
rather than the best available man to replace Zhou. He knew that Hua had
been called "stupid" and a "country bumpkin" by some people (possibly his
estranged wife). He countered by saying he found Hua "noble-minded and
good-mannered but not pompous."*

Mao also felt it necessary to add that Hua was *"not* stupid." And he acknowledged the problem of Hua's relative obscurity. "It is necessary to do
propaganda and give publicity to Comrade Hua," the old man instructed,
after Hua was named acting premier in February, "to make him known to
the people of the whole country step by step."

If Hua was an inoffensive compromise choice, that did not put an end to
the feuds.

Some demon in Mao wanted to struggle on even when only phantoms
were the target. "You are making socialist revolution," he wrote in a devastating pronouncement not long after Hua's promotion, "and yet you don't
know where the bourgeoisie is. It is right in the Communist Party—those in
power taking the capitalist road."

It was vintage Mao, a believer in *yin* and *yang* if not in much else, a still-
questing soul who distrusted equilibrium, who could not admire light without reminding everyone of the presence of darkness.

"He has never been a Marxist," Mao suddenly burst out of Deng. How-

---

* The phrase was a quote from a Han emperor's defense of one of his ministers.

ever difficult Deng's position was after cancer took Zhou off, these six words were the nails in Deng's political coffin for 1976.

It was easy to say, and a thousand voices now did so, that Deng had "twisted" Mao's words. He had made a list of the virtues the Chairman insisted upon—stability and unity, development of the national economy, class struggle—but Mao, it was said in 1976, had not meant that the virtues were of equal rank.

Deng, the press cried (though without naming him), had defied Mao by downgrading "class struggle" from being the "key link" to being merely one item among others. The vice-premier was an "unrepentant capitalist roader."

Mao had overreached himself, as well as the facts, in calling Deng and his friends "capitalist roaders." Some top supporters of Deng—the military leader Ye Jianying was one—were so disgusted at the attacks on the senior vice-premier that they marched out of the Politburo room and left Peking for the south, shouting that they would take no further part in the destructive proceedings and murmuring about Mao's arbitrariness.

People's Daily baldly announced (*after* Hua's elevation and Deng's disappearance from his posts) that the Central Committee was "split." How, then, could a cadre or a citizen be expected to follow instructions from "Chairman Mao and the Central Committee?"

Mao's last crusade was solving no problems, but merely adding to the problems that would crash down on China when he died. In toppling Deng, and choosing Hua, he seemed merely to be proving that he was still alive, beating off death by an arbitrary assertion of will.

*   *   *

Is it possible to align Mao the teacher and Mao the dictator?

Mao once spoke in a fascinating way about how Sun Yat-sen had given up medicine for politics. "Then he could be in control of the physicians," Mao observed. "Politicians handle ["are doctors of"] the mutual relations among men." This extremely Confucian remark expressed a highly moral view of politics.

Sun had, in Mao's view, chosen the higher course by going into politics. One could thus be a teacher on a grander plane. The raw material was nothing less than the souls of the people. What Sun did, Mao did also.

Mao had often spoken of the need for soul-searching. "Do it three times or until nobody has any more opinions," he said to the Eighth CCP Congress. The words jump at us. *Until nobody has any more opinions.*

Oneness was Mao's dream. You teach until the lesson is clear. Equally in politics. The ruler is a teacher writ large in that he draws the people together in a felt Oneness.

Hence the odd pas de deux that democracy and authority danced in Mao's mind. "Without a high degree of democracy," ran a remark of his which has mystified quite a few people, "we cannot have a high degree of centralism." Of course! Only if the masses offer up their minds can the ruler orchestrate the collective Oneness which is the moral goal of politics.

The terrible problem in all this arose in a dialogue between Mao and his nephew Mao Yuanxin. "When the policy of the Party changes," Mao said to the young man in giving him a list of dos and don'ts, "you should be clear-minded." Surely Mao must have paused, searching for something better, before uttering the term "clear-minded." What exactly *do* you do when the Party changes its mind? Do you fall in with the change of policy? Or can it be right to persist in a dissenting stance? Being clear-minded would only sharpen the dilemma.

Mao was a teacher: he did want his pupil, the Chinese nation, to be clear in its own mind. But Mao was also a dictator: there was to be only one mind.

For the Chinese people not to be of one mind was *immoral*—that was a sinister link between the didactic Mao and the power-wielding Mao.

By the 1970s this "sinister link" had produced a chronic sickness in China's political system.

The Mao of 1949 had not expected smooth sailing after "Liberation," but he mistook the nature of the coming tensions. "After several decades," he said on the eve of gaining power, "the victory of the [revolution], viewed in retrospect, will seem like only a brief prologue to a long drama." Twenty-five years later that was true.

The drama, though, was not moral, as Mao anticipated, but institutional.

Mao repeatedly sought renewal of the system through heroic acts. He continued to hanker for a deeper moral community. But this quest made sense only within Mao's personal world, not within China's social world.

The very success of Mao's revolution had produced a generation that passed him by. History does not stop still while yesterday's vision struggles to perfect itself. Mao was like a speaker addressing an audience that has left for its next engagement.

As a young man Mao fought one day with his brother. His parents had died not long before. A CCP branch was getting under way in Music Mountain. Mao, stepping into his father's shoes, was fusing family and CCP affairs. Brother Zemin objected to this. "The Communist Party," he burst out to Mao, "is not the ancestral temple of the Mao family."

The remark—what ghosts of intimate household life lurked behind it!—infuriated Mao. He grabbed a stick and tried to hit Zemin with it.

Mao did have one foot in patriarchal China. He did at times confuse the Communist Party with an ancestral temple. His search for Oneness went beyond politics as understood by younger Chinese.

Part of the pathos of the "Criticize Confucius" drive was that the role for an ideology—whether Confucius's or Mao's—had already been dropped from the "long drama." Confucius versus Mao was a feud among pedants, to the millions of Chinese for whom the future of the nation had priority over the accumulated glory of doctrine.

"Our beloved fellow countrymen," Mao wrote before winning power, "will be able to live like human beings and to choose the government they wish." But Mao had in mind a moral community rather than a democratic polity.

"People" meant a collective metaphysic to Mao, not an array of citizens with jostling interests and diverse opinions. He said "the people" came to power in 1949. There was some truth in this—his government was widely representative of ordinary people's views, and it did bring benefits to such people—yet "the people" never come to power merely by a change in who represents them.

Intellectuals were supposed to give their "hearts" to the Party during the Great Leap Forward. Peking saw the spectacle of professors walking through the streets with cardboard, silk, or velvet images of hearts, en route to present them at Party headquarters.

This was religion, not politics.

Mao did see himself as a sage whose direct ties to the masses obviated the intermediate structures which are the realm of politics in its modern sense. It was a pattern well established in old China. But truth and power fused in a sage *bestriding the modern state of the PRC* was a baleful pattern indeed—and for increasing numbers of Chinese, an unacceptable pattern.

"If we do not oppose the new formalism and new dogmatism today," Mao had said in criticism of 28B at Yanan, "the Chinese mind will be bound by the chains of another form of extremism." It had occurred.

* * *

The Boeing 707 painted with the red and black Chinese characters for the name of the PRC's airline was a novel sight at Los Angeles airport. It had come to fetch Richard Nixon, for his first major public appearance since leaving the White House.

The Boeing 707—it was the first time the Chinese government had ever sent an aircraft to pick up and fly home a private foreign visitor—landed at

Peking airport in a cool mist. Hua Guofeng, the new acting premier, stood beaming on the tarmac.

Mao and Nixon fell upon each other like old friends with great futures behind them. They talked for 100 minutes.

Nixon sat beside Jiang Qing to hear songs about the "liberation of Taiwan." He grinned in front of a lurid exhibition of the bloody omnipresence of class struggle from the age of the cave man to the age of Deng Xiaoping.

The gesture of asking the disgraced Nixon back was Mao's; it looked like one more misjudgment of an old man making decisions on the basis of slim evidence.

To many people—but not to Mao—Nixon's reappearance in such a spectacular way seemed as welcome as the smell of leaking gas at a party. Just three days away was the New Hampshire primary, in which Ford was being challenged by Reagan; the revived memory of Ford's "pardon" of Nixon was excruciating for the White House.

Even Chinese diplomats in Washington, it was later learned, pointed out to Peking that asking Nixon back "might be misunderstood." But China's fledgling America hands were overruled.

Mao wished to see Nixon. He had told Imelda Marcos, in late 1974, to tell Nixon that, and repeated the message to three subsequent visitors. The Chinese foreign ministry, in Mao's view, could like it or lump it.

Mao was never one to take pains over the nuances of other nations' domestic politics. Least of all Mao at age 82, for whom symbols were reality, for whom past memories gave meaning to the present, and for whom China was still largely its own world.

He did not ask himself—could not have seen meaning in the question— what he would feel like if the White House asked the fallen Liu Shaoqi to the U.S. for a friendly visit.

Mao wasn't trying to "rehabilitate" Nixon, as some Americans suspected. He was doing something simpler, and much more China-centered, than that.

Mao admired Nixon for his breakthrough in U.S.-China policy; why not honor him?* He felt frustrated at Ford's immobilism—what was there to lose when Ford was doing so little against Russia and so little toward China?

---

*Nixon was given head-of-government treatment equal to that accorded Ford two months before. He spent six hours in talks with Hua, and became the first foreigner to explore the mind of this man whom the world as yet hardly knew from a bar of soap. He was the first private foreigner ever permitted to offer a return banquet to the Chinese government in the Great Hall of the People.

And Mao had never understood the anti-Nixon point of view on Watergate—shouldn't rulers be permitted to rule? "Watergate was blown out of all proportion," he complained to Kukrit of Thailand. "We cannot understand why so much fuss was made of this affair," he said to Pompidou. He did not see why such a tiny mishap, as it seemed to him, could unhorse President Nixon. And he did not like the consequences, for China's interests, of the spectacle of America tearing out its own entrails.

"Too much freedom of expression" was Mao's diagnosis of the cause of the Watergate fiasco. "What is wrong with taping a conversation when you happen to have a tape recorder with you?" asked Mao, who in 1968 said he had begun to do the same thing himself. "Most people in America love playing with tape recorders," he mused. He also declared to Kukrit: "I think Nixon's downfall was caused by warmongers in the United States."

"Please write to Nixon," he said in startling simplicity to Kukrit, "and tell him that I think of him." There was puzzlement, pathos, and a deep Chinese ethnocentrism in Mao's remarks on Nixon's fall.

In asking Nixon back to China, Mao was trying to spur Ford on, more than to embarrass him. He knew little about U.S. primaries; the final timing of Nixon's trip was San Clemente's, moreover, not Peking's.

Mao was focusing on a larger question: should China reaffirm the American link, or let it wither and try to achieve détente with Russia?

When the Chinese millions saw Nixon on *People's Daily's* front page, shaking hands with the Chairman, the message was not a criticism of Ford but a confirmation of America's importance to China.

Nixon fulfilled Mao's purpose by making skeptical remarks about U.S.-Soviet détente. It was "naïve," said Nixon in a banquet speech, to believe that "the mere act of signing a statement of principles or a diplomatic conference" can secure peace. This apparent criticism of the Helsinki Conference on European Security was music to Mao's ears, if not to Ford's.

The America question and the Deng question were connected, in Mao's mind if not in reality,* as had become clear in two curious episodes the previous year.

Not long before Ford went to China, the beloved old novel *Story of the Marshes* was suddenly denounced as insidious. Mao felt the tale of peasant rebellion was "capitulationist" in spirit.

The peasant hero of *Marshes,* Song Jiang, was not a hero at all, he declared, reversing a long-standing view.

Deng (and perhaps some of his PLA friends) would be ready to "capitu-

*Deng seemed to be locked with Nixon in some trans-Pacific revolving door: when Nixon was "in" (1972), Deng was "out"; when Deng was "in" (1973–1975), Nixon was "out"; and now when Nixon was pushing back "in," Deng was "out."

late" to Moscow, it began to be whispered in Peking corridors, just as Song Jiang "capitulated" to the emperor while pretending to resist him to the end.

Deng scoffed at the strained analogies and the jumping to conclusions involved in the attack on *Story of the Marshes.* "Some people hear wind and think it's raining," he hissed.

The second episode was just as bizarre. Members of a Russian helicopter crew, seized 21 months before in northwest China, and many times declared by Peking to be "spies," were suddenly exonerated, *just after Ford limped home from Peking.* The Chinese Government said they were not spies after all, gave them a fancy banquet, and sent them unbelievably home to Moscow.

Never in the PRC's history had Peking reversed itself in that way on a spy accusation, and declared intruders to be innocent after having repeatedly called them spies. Was there more than one view of Russia in the Chinese government at the time of the failure of the Mao-Ford summit?

It seems certain that Mao disapproved of the exoneration of the Soviet helicopter crew just after Ford's lackluster visit—and it can only have been Deng, Mao's chief minister at the time, who authorized the gesture to Moscow.*

In the end the Nixon trip was not harmful to U.S.-China relations, as American newspapers said it would be, nor did it boost them much (except in the mind of the Chinese public), as Mao hoped it would do.

"Nothing is hard in this world," Nixon cried in Peking, applying a Mao poem to the prospects for Peking-Washington relations, "if one dares to scale the heights." Both men, deeply impressed with each other, seemed to be scaling personal heights, rather than bringing change to the external world.

For Nixon the trip was a mere nostalgic footnote to that of 1972. For Mao it was that, but also a grenade hurled onto the battlefield of Politburo struggle.

*   *   *

Just one week after *People's Daily* printed his first denunciation of Deng as a person ("That man's never been interested in class struggle"), Mao was

---

*Deng was suspect on many grounds, to be sure, to the Mao of 1976. But it was hardly surprising that inadequate hostility toward Moscow was a fault that Mao found in a colleague who disappointed him. It was the eleventh time Mao had fallen out in a big way with a top CCP figure. Each time the Soviet issue was present. Each time Mao took the harder line toward Moscow's views, merits, or intentions. Interestingly, Kukrit, in his talks in Peking during July 1975, found Deng—but not Mao—strong in his praise for and support of Hanoi's policies.

brought news of a quiet but intense demonstration building up half a mile away in the Square of the Gate of Heavenly Peace.

It was Spring Festival, when the dead are remembered. Wreaths and poems in honor of Zhou Enlai had appeared on the steps of the Monument to the People's Heroes. Crowds came to look at the vast display. It seemed innocent enough.

But the air was tense. Some of the poems went beyond commemorating Zhou and took a swipe at the ultra-leftists who had been so noisy in the three months since Zhou's death. Mao's early wife, Yang Kaihui, was praised in a slap at Jiang Qing. There were references to monsters, using the term *yao mo*, a play on Yao Wenyuan's name.* It was subtle, but explosive.†

A second theme was a brooding anxiety about China's overall condition. "What is the greatest problem at present?" one man cried out to the throng from the steps of the usually forbidding Great Hall of the People. "Where is China going? That is the biggest problem."

Criticism of Mao was an underlying third theme. "The day of Qin Shi-huang is done," ran one verse, evoking the emperor who was Mao's hero, often presented as a fine alternative model to the rotten Confucius. There was a hint, in the fairly youthful demonstration, of irritation at the patriarchal, arbitrary ways of Mao. "China is no longer the China of yore," one poem said in defiance, even in warning. "And the people are no longer wrapped in sheer ignorance."

This was more than a commemoration of the much-admired Zhou. It was a judicious but firm entry of a segment of public opinion into the murky saloon of Mao's court politics. The swelling scene at the monument bade fair to be a climax to the months of indirect sniping by the ultra-left at Deng as an "unrepentant capitalist roader."

In the wake of the news from the square, Mao made several decisions which followed, like a row of igniting firecrackers, one from the other.

Peking city authorities removed the wreaths from the monument. This act turned a calm memorial into a riot, which went on for fourteen hours and

---

*One poem read:
> Clear River,* shaking bridge,† and vicious waves tumble.
> Darkened sky, darkened earth, darkness spreads all over.
> When will Hsiang-yu's‡ heroic spirit descend,
> To sweep away the dense fog and bring back the light of day.

> * pun on Jiang Qing's name
> †pun on Zhang Chunqiao's name
> ‡Zhou Enlai

† There were no wreaths, Spring Festival or not, for Kang Sheng, though the leftist security chief had also recently died.

involved at least 100,000 people. People were roughed up. Vehicles were burned. One hundred people were injured and some died.

One young man, a Qinghua University student who was no doubt an admirer of the ultra-leftists, after making a short speech to the effect that Zhou had at times been guilty of "opposing Chairman Mao," had his hands tied up with wire by an angry mob, and was pushed up and down the steps of the monument until he was a bleeding mess.

The Politburo met in panic. It voted to dismiss Deng from his jobs, and to formally elevate Hua to be premier and, as first vice-chairman of the CCP (a new position), Mao's heir as leader of China. All this was Mao's handiwork.

Deng had fallen victim to unstable succession politics; to his own peremptory ways; to the bad luck of being a pragmatist out of season.

There is no evidence that Deng was behind the riot. A riot would not have occurred if the Peking mayor, surely after a nod from Mao, had not ordered the pro-Zhou wreaths removed.

What *was* clear was that opinions in the Politburo had polarized too much. A resolution of them was urgent. The government had to give the nation a quick signal of clarity of purpose.

Mao himself authorized the dismissal of Deng as the key step. Although he was apparently too ill to attend the crucial Politburo meeting, he transmitted a motion to dismiss Deng through his nephew Mao Yuanxin.

Mao even permitted himself to refer to Deng—who is a very short man—as a "dwarf."

The Politburo decision to fire Deng was said to be "unanimous." This was unbelievable. Were the PLA leaders—Ye Jianying, Xu Shiyou, and others—in favor? Did Deng vote for his own dismissal? "Unanimous" meant that no one could be allowed to go on record as having opposed Mao's proposal.

The flood of anti-Deng rhetoric bore a number of Mao trademarks. "The counterrevolutionaries lauded Deng Xiaoping," intoned *People's Daily,* "and attempted to nominate him to *play the role of Nagy.*" Mao, living in the past, still dwelt with the nightmare of the Hungarian events of 1956.

Signs existed that Mao had won a Pyrrhic victory.

- The ultra-leftists did not quite have Deng's scalp; his friends had won for him the right to remain a Party member, "so as to see how he will behave in the future."

- Deng was out, but the ultra-leftists were not in; the ambiguous figure of Hua was the man to whom Mao's ebbing power flowed after Spring Festival.

- PLA leaders, unhappy with the trend of events, scarcely bothered to hide the fact that they were biding their time, waiting for Mao to die and the leftist squall to die with him (not the army, but the leftist militia, put down the pro-Zhou riot; the PLA could have squashed it in minutes if the circumstances had been right to do so).

• Public opinion, which in a modest way came of age in China in the spring of 1976, by no means fully accepted Mao's dismissal of Deng; it began to be whispered in China that Mao might no longer know what he was doing.*

The official denunciation of Deng by name spoke the truth when it said he had "refused to repent." He did not fully fight back at Mao—he was seeking merely to preserve some ground on which to build later—but he did fight with his tongue.

"If they tell you that you're a capitalist roader," he said to his supporters in a remark that must be seen as contemptuous of Mao's mind at that time, if not of Mao, "it means you're doing a good job."

"Defend Chairman Mao." This remarkable slogan cropped up as spring limped into summer. It was odd that the supreme leader of the Chinese Revolution, now eighty-two, had to be "defended" in his own capital.

The Chinese people, often deceived by the older Mao, were starting to have a gentle revenge in the contemplation of the great man's mortality. The succession was a universal issue, accessible to all. The human condition—not "class enemies" or the maneuvers of mandarins possessing special knowledge—was the ultimate force at the bottom of the 1976 crisis.

Any person in the street understood this and could gossip about it. Mao had wielded fearsome power, but he did not possess the power to stop people from beholding his decline, and looking beyond him to a post-Mao era.

* * *

The riot, and its shattering echoes behind the closed doors of the Forbidden City, took a heavy toll of Mao. It is doubtful that he made any major decision of state after April.

Prime Minister Muldoon of New Zealand went to South and Central Lakes later that month and found the scene embarrassing. Mao could hardly keep his head from lolling against the back of his armchair. With great effort he panted out a few phrases.

"It was clear to me," said a shaken Muldoon, "that he had not long to live."

---

* One recalls the words of Cast Iron Charlie (and is tempted to imagine them on Deng's lips) when he was fired by the first Henry Ford: "The team was breaking up. The captain was a sick man, unable to call plays. The line coaches were gone. Anyone who made a brilliant play was called out."

Sometimes Mao's smooth old hand would reach out for a pad on which to scratch a couple of characters. The ideographs were clear enough, to anyone used to Mao's swirling handwriting, but not always their meaning.

"With you in charge I'm at ease," Mao wrote on a piece of paper for Hua, between his ten-minute talk with Muldoon and going back to bed. But in charge of what? Of next week's conference on pig farming? Of getting Muldoon safely home to New Zealand? Of the anti-Deng campaign? Of China's future?

"Act according to the principles laid down," Mao scratched out the same evening. Hardly surprising that a huge fight arose over just what Mao had in mind. Was he referring to past precedent in general, or to some freshly minted behest?

In May the prime minister of Singapore spent a painful few minutes with Mao. "It was not a substantial exchange," said Lee Kuan Yew of this next to last meeting Mao ever had with a foreigner. "His words were unintelligible. They had to be first deciphered by his niece [Wang Hairong], and then interpreted into English. Occasionally the niece would write them down to check the words back with him."

The Vienna neurologist Dr. Walther Birkmayer, who had previously been consulted about Mao's Parkinson's disease, flew to Peking in conditions of great secrecy during the summer. But it was not possible to do more than prolong Mao's life by a few months at most.

All of the Politburo felt anxious about how China would face its first weeks without the incomparable symbol of the PRC's very existence.

Some among the ultra-leftists were terrified of Mao's passing.

No one, however critical of him, could afford to appear anxious to hustle him off the stage before it was absolutely necessary to do so.

The members of the Politburo did not find it easy to agree on *anything* in 1975–1976, least of all on how to handle the demigod who was still the fulcrum of each of their immediate futures. So Mao stayed on the stage, grunting his lines, while senior colleagues hovered in the wings like message boys who could take no responsibility.

"Chairman Mao is well advanced in years and is still busy with his work," a junior foreign ministry official stated in June. "The Central Committee of our Party has decided not to arrange for [him] to meet foreign distinguished visitors."

It had been a very long time since a Chinese official last made a statement about Mao's personal condition. The message was clear: Mao was dying and the Chinese people, who for years had seen pictures of Mao only when he was with foreigners, would never see a live image of him again.

The decision was overdue, given Mao's painful, brief meetings with New

Zealand, Singapore, and Pakistan leaders over recent weeks. But it was a tricky one to make. And whoever made it, it was certainly not the full "Central Committee of our Party."

The ultra-left, it seems, resisted the step. For the Shanghai radicals, Jiang Qing, and others in Mao's immediate court, Mao was the maypole from which they swung.

What remained of the Politburo's pragmatic wing welcomed the decision, but these leaders were too weak to have forced the issue.

Hua no doubt led the way. The shy new premier was close enough to Mao to engineer the decision without risking a burst of Mao's ire. He was not so much a part of the ultra-left that he would let *raison d'état* be eclipsed by a last-ditch effort to hang on to Mao as a fig leaf for Jiang Qing's faction.

Did Mao himself join in, or himself make the decision? We do not know.

* * *

Mao became subject to courtiers, because he was gravely ill, and because no procedure existed to transfer his power to an agreed upon successor. That Mao would no longer receive foreign visitors did not mean that he had *resigned*.

Proximity, the gun, personal loyalty, and blood ties came to matter more than the constitution or any other rules.

Various members of the Politburo vied for access to documents or information from Mao's place. Much power flowed to Mao's long-time bodyguard, Wang Dongxing, who controlled the elite guard corps Unit 8341,* much spy work, and the administrative office of the CCP Central Committee.

So, too, family members. Mao's nephew Mao Yuanxin gravitated from Manchuria, where he was deputy commissar of the Shenyang Military Region, to be his sinking uncle's virtual chief of staff.

One day soon after taking up his post in the inner court, Yuanxin went in to tell his uncle about a disturbing poster put up by influential people in Shanghai.

Deng's praise of Zhou in his funeral oration was too high, the poster said. "The verdict should be reversed." Whatever Yuanxin's motives may have been in telling Mao about the poster, Mao is said to have uttered a clear-cut response: "The people will surely oppose any attack on Zhou Enlai," he reasoned. "The verdict on the memorial speech given at Zhou's funeral cannot be changed. The people do not support the reversal of the verdict."

A few days later the Chinese people had on their hands a new Mao quote

---

*8341 had come to comprise 35,000 to 40,000 men, two guard divisions, an independent armored regiment, and some antiaircraft, engineering, and signal battalions.

whose ambiguity illustrated the drastic problem of having a dying sage-emperor still reigning but no longer ruling.

"The people do not support the reversal of verdicts," was the quote. But what in the name of Confucius did it mean? The Chinese public, which did not know of Mao's conversation with his nephew, were told Mao meant the people didn't support *Deng's* reversal of the verdicts *of the Cultural Revolution!*

This is not to say Mao still sympathized with Deng; but the ultra-leftists were using Mao's irritation with Deng, and perhaps faking its degree, for wider purposes of their own.

Mao's name was thrown around in fierce argument even as he met with the Politburo. During one meeting, Zhang Chunqiao criticized China's import of turnkey factories as a departure from the principle of self-reliance. "All these large import items," Hua ventured, "have been approved by Chairman Mao." Zhang shouted back: "You always use the Chairman to suppress people!"

Mao evidently sat (or lay) quietly through many such fights, tipping his hand only now and then, writing down a crucial maxim later that night, asking one or another of the protagonists to come and see him as a sign of where his sympathies lay.

Jiang Qing enjoyed a season of fresh influence, in feudal style, as the dying ruler's wife. With Mao too weak to make his probable distaste for her resurgence prevail over her technical status as his wife, Jiang Qing supervised the telephone lines, kept an eye on the flow of documents, replaced interpreters she did not like with others more malleable, and generally prepared the way for a post-Mao supremacy of her circle.

The life of Mao had come full circle in its relation to feudal tradition. He began as a boy who rebelled against the Chinese past; his first marriage, at age fourteen, was an arranged one and he rejected it. He ended as a neo-emperor whose feet seemed locked into the time-honored steps of China's past; his last wife was a female consort pulling the strings from behind a tottering throne.*

The entire Politburo came to Mao's bedside for a meeting in midsummer. Some of them may have been trembling as they drove home.

"Help Jiang Qing," Mao began one sentence, as he tried to give some instructions for future policy. But the words trailed off and it was later disputed whether he added "to carry the Red Flag" or "to correct her errors."

Jiang Qing and her circle claimed he said the first, which would have

* A poster put up in Peking during a surge of bold expression two years after Mao's death was not far from the mark. Mao was "mentally out of touch with reality in his last period," wrote the irate citizen, and "family-style fascist dictatorship" sprouted.

meant succeeding Mao as Chairman of the CCP. The lady's detractors heard the second phrase and took it to be a repudiation, albeit a friendly one, of her views and ways.

"Few live beyond 70," Mao remarked to the bedroom gathering, "and as I am more than 80, I should have died already." It did not quite seem a matter for discussion. Mao, in a mood to expose the grim side of life, gazed at his silent, apprehensive colleagues. "Are there not some among you who hoped I would go to see Marx sooner?" he went on relentlessly.

Eventually Hua found his tongue: "None."

Mao demolished Hua's tact: "Really, no one? I don't believe it!"

Death seemed to have no mercy on China in 1976. As if the political earthquakes at Spring Festival were not enough, an appalling real earthquake uprooted the city of Tangshan and killed some 250,000 people in midsummer, just after Zhu De's death.

Mao insisted on being informed of every detail about the situation in Tangshan. It would be surprising if the tragedy did not give him a sense of foreboding. In rural China it has long been believed that nature's signs foreshadow political events. A severe earthquake, peasants held, meant the coming end of a dynasty and its mandate to rule. His mind encrusted with traditional themes as it was, Mao must have speculated on the same connection.

China was full of rumors, most of them to do with Mao's impending death, and the official press admitted they were out of control by editorializing against the phenomenon of rumormongering.

Before the earthquake, turtles became agitated, pandas held their heads and screamed, tigers and yaks lay down on the ground when they sensed a tremor—the animals felt nature's instability.

After the earthquake, rumors soared, banks were robbed, incivility in social relations became more frequent, workers refused to take responsibility—the people felt the polity's instability.

No matter how alarming or risky all previous lurches of line since 1949 had been, Mao's presence had always been a constant—a final source of authority, a limit on upheaval's end result.

That era was ending. No precedent existed in the PRC's life for the discontinuity that loomed; only to a sinking last emperor of a dynasty *could* Mao be compared.

*   *   *

"When the burden is too heavy," Mao once said during a conversation on war, "death is the way out." The burden became too heavy for Mao by late August. He lay in a coma.

There was time for the hagiographic pens to muster their leaden phrases.

Time for Hua Guofeng to lay plans for the succession. Time for Jiang Qing to busy herself with counterplans.*

Could he really be still alive? The physical Mao lying prone under the tall windows of the Ming dynasty pavilion seemed unreal. For all factions in the Politburo had already substituted Maoism for Mao; that way the actual 82-year-old Mao had been recycled into a dozen "Maos" shaped to suit the needs of the recyclers.

He was beyond talking about politics, though Jiang Qing and her circle, who were the least sanguine about the coming post-Mao era, tried to squeeze a final instruction from his trembling lips.

Voices outside China spoke always of the *uncertainty* that would come with Mao's death. Yet Mao's *presence* had long been the chief source of uncertainty in China; and the fact of not knowing when he would die produced one final phase of uncertainty.

His death would in some respects produce a pristine certainty for the country he had been tormenting for nearly two decades.

It was a balmy afternoon of Peking's Indian summer. At three-thirty the radio foreshadowed an announcement of the highest importance for half an hour hence. Some people working in central Peking guessed its message, for they had seen a constant flow of cars in and out of South and Central Lakes during the morning.

"Chairman Mao has left this world" (*shi shi le*).

In the early hours of that September morning, Mao found his way out. It took the government only sixteen hours—this was lightning speed by Peking standards—to tell the nation and the world.

In the Politburo it came as a relief.

At the grass roots some wept; far more were stunned.

Mao had led the CCP for longer than anyone had led a major nation in modern times. Many hundreds of millions of Chinese had no memory of a China without him.

Households hung up the PRC flag at half mast. Mao badges were worn in some numbers for the first time in years. Hundreds of thousands of people who ordinarily never bothered to read the prefabricated prose of *People's Daily* bought a copy to get full details; the newspaper multiplied its usual Peking press run by nine.

Yet the mood of the capital (even more so the rest of the country) was

---

* Her detractors said—the charges are impossible to verify—that she moved Mao heartlessly from one bed to another, to satisfy some ulterior purpose; that she squeezed $3,000 from him as he lay dying; that when death finally came she was in the middle of a game of bridge far from Peking and cursed her ill luck at fate's timing; that she rushed back to install herself at South and Central Lakes and to search for certain of Mao's handwritten documents that could be useful to her cause.

fairly calm and quotidian. There was none of the eerie sense of paralysis that enveloped Russia when Stalin died. There were no spontaneous "scenes" among the masses; people went on as usual with their work and household routine.

Death, for the Chinese, has its place in nature's order. Few Chinese felt affection for Mao that was strong enough to move them to tears.

The death announcement, "Message to the Whole Party, the Whole Army, and the People of All Nationalities Throughout the Country," was written with some emotion. "The Chinese people and the revolutionary people the world over love him from the bottom of their hearts. . . ."

Ironically, the peasant organizer who took the CCP out of the international Communist movement and tilted China toward the West was called a "great teacher of the international proletariat and the oppressed nations."

A week of mourning was proclaimed. There would be no sport or entertainment in the land of 900 million. Mao's body would lie in state at the Great Hall of the People. People great and not great would file past the bier "to pay their last respects."

That at least was what New China News Agency first stated. A small change was made to the statement before it was widely disseminated and translated. The word "last" was dropped. People would come to *pay their respects.*

The change showed that Mao's body—not to speak of the legacy of his mind—was a hot potato for the grim-faced Politburo.

Some years before, Mao had driven out to Papaoshan Cemetery and selected a grave site for himself and Jiang Qing. More than once he revisited the plot at the 886-grave cemetery in the company of Jiang Qing.

In 1976 it seemed outrageous to some of the Chinese leaders that a burial plan that involved Blue Apple should be proceeded with. Cremation and the scattering of Mao's ashes on the "rivers and mountains of China"—Zhou Enlai's instruction in his own case—would be, in the opinion of many, the most seemly solution.

But Mao had not asked for this. Moreover, it better suited some in the Politburo, including Hua, to adopt the appalling solution of mummifying Mao's body (*à la* Lenin) and putting it on view for generations yet to come to gaze upon.*

Mao may have left this world, but his political heirs, who still needed his authority, would allow no *last* respects.

Embalmers were hastily summoned from Vietnam, where they had had recent successful experience with the corpse of Ho Chi Minh, to prepare

---

* Mao was inconsistent on this subject—he once said "After I die, send my remains to Xiang Tan, Hunan"—but mummification in a mausoleum seems to be the last thing he would have wished.

Mao for a post-death physical role in Hua's effort to keep a grip upon China.

Dislike of Jiang Qing had produced the worst possible disposition of Mao's remains.

Three hundred thousand people filed past the catafalque to "pay their respects." Viewing time was reserved for foreign diplomats, a separate segment for foreign ideological friends of the CCP. Among the wreaths from this or that committee was one inscribed: "Deeply mourn the esteemed great teacher Chairman Mao Zedong, from your student and comrade in arms Jiang Qing...."*

Cables of condolence came in from 123 foreign governments. Many were musclebound with praise; the more any government had vilified Mao in the 1950s and 1960s, the more effusive was its tribute to him in 1976. Mao would have taken pleasure in the contradiction.

In New York the UN flag was flown at half mast. In Moscow *Izvestia* carried the story in two lines at the bottom of its next to last page. In Hong Kong the stock market sank. In Taiwan there were joyful celebrations.

From Toronto came a poignant word. "We have all passed our time," the 80-year-old Zhang Guotao said when asked for a comment on the death of his old rival. "Like me," the tired old man said without rancor, "Mao was a mortal being, and death is merely a question of time."

A million people came to the Square of the Gate of Heavenly Peace for the funeral rally at the end of the week of mourning. At 3 P.M. sharp, work in China stopped for three minutes. The entire 900 million (no doubt with a few exceptions) stood to attention in silence. Every siren in China—on trains, in factories, on ships—sounded off for those three climactic minutes.

With the illogic that often makes a funeral a lie, it was Wang Hongwen who stepped to the rostrum to preside. Hua spoke, in his deliberate apprentice's phrases, of Mao's greatness and Deng's evil.

Sun Yat-sen's widow stood near Hua as he prated about "capitalist roaders" in the Party being "still on the capitalist road," and about "the bourgeoisie" being lodged "right in the Communist Party."

At the end of the meeting everyone present—together with the millions watching or listening throughout China—made three solemn bows toward the enormous portrait of Mao on top of the Gate of Heavenly Peace. Then a 500-man band played the soaring anthem, "The East Is Red," whose last line calls Mao "the people's great savior."

By 4 P.M. the crowd was gone. Bicycles began to surge as usual past the Gate of Heavenly Peace, running over bits of waste paper that were the wadded-up programs from the rally. The era of Mao was over.

* Appended too were the names of Mao's children and some other relatives.

23

Epilogue

With all his faults, Mao gave China a new start, and gave the twentieth century a fascinating man of politics.

A strong Communist movement would have existed in China without Mao. He was by no means the key figure in its origins; turmoil and injustice would have guaranteed communism's strong appeal, Mao or no Mao.

Yet the CCP probably would not have won power by 1949 if Mao had not become its leader in the 1930s. Certainly a Chinese communism without Mao would have been less distinctive from other varieties of communism than it is.

Why did he succeed in winning power in the CCP and the nation, his greatest achievement? There was a personal fire in him. No one without it could have ignited with his times as Mao did with the period following the fall of China's last dynasty. He was certain of himself, and of the eventual triumph of his peasant army. That—beyond mere hunger for power—gave him a will of granite.

The power of individual character to move mountains—and God knows Mao did so—is not independent of a close relation with the social character of the time. Mao grew up in dislocated times when people cried out for a strong healing hand. It was a radical epoch. Those ready to support a determined iconoclast like Mao were thick on the ground—as seldom before and not since.

It was also a fluid epoch; the nation was like a carnival ground with a hundred sideshows all bidding for a nod from the public. Communists, Nationalists, war lords, bandits, Methodists, foreign adventurers, to name some, all jostled together in spin-drier fashion, rising and falling, forming fragile alliances, starting new schemes which died as quickly as others took their place. In such a situation the man of granite has a unique chance to crash through and change a society.

Epilogue

Mao was a gambler too, like others on the carnival ground, and he en-joyed a good deal of luck. His own body escaped the knife by a hair's breadth three or four times. He gained control of the CCP at the end of the Long March in part because his archrival had bad luck while struggling through Tibet.

In the larger swirl of events, the timing of Japan's attack on China played into Mao's hands—as it fouled up Chiang's plans. Within the bag of snakes that was the CCP leadership, Mao escaped destruction by keeping relatively distant from Moscow and its Comintern. Almost every Chinese leader who went along with Russia's poor advice lost his footing in the CCP as a result. Mao survived almost by process of Kremlinological elimination.

And it was Mao's dirty secret that he saw the necessity of—indeed he ex-ulted in—violence. He forged ahead of others in the CCP by leaving them in Shanghai and taking a gun to the countryside.

In war he did well by virtue of two traits: extreme flexibility in tactics and an ability to communicate his strategy to his followers.

Mao once called himself a center-leftist. In methods he was. True of his cunning caution toward his father on the farm. True of his constant flexible use of a "united front" in order to isolate the main enemy. True of his ten-dency to unleash the hounds of the left but to rein them in when their useful energy began to turn into useless excess.

His hatred of the right ensured that he would jump now and then toward the left. But the extreme left was not his spiritual home. He liked that niche on the spectrum from which he could oppose the right yet also curb the left, when he felt like it, with a shaft of irony or a dose of earthy realism.

"Walk on two legs," he would say. This natural sense of balance—shades of the ancient Chinese belief in the duality of soft *yin* and hard *yang*—served him well in his prime years.

He was bright and taught himself a lot from books; he also came from the hinterland of China. Each factor was equally important. In the heat of revo-lution he coolly hitched his intellect to the passions of the masses.

Mao got furious at injustice—as did many others during the twilight of old China—but he also remained sufficiently detached emotionally to ana-lyze the experiences he had.

In the end, Mao's qualities cannot be explained aside from the long-rip-ened qualities of Chinese civilization. Could the Congo produce a Mao? Could New Zealand? We cannot account for Mao's success merely by un-wrapping him as an individual psychological package. That old China pro-duced determined, rebellious, quizzical Mao is as true—and full of conse-quence—as that Mao produced new China.

His place in the history of China and the world will be large. He led a revolution that killed old China, pushed the country into a process of transformation perhaps more trenchant than any previous sudden social change in any major nation, and restored the independence and status in the world of the oldest and largest polity.

To be the dominant figure in the twentieth-century story of the world's most populous society is itself to be a titan. Mao was also among the half-dozen or so most consequential rulers in the entire three thousand years of China's recorded history.

As a unifier he ranks with the first emperors of the Sui dynasty (sixth century A.D.) and the Ming dynasty (fourteenth century A.D.). Even with his hero the whirlwind dictator Qin Shihuang, who knocked China into shape 221 years before the birth of Jesus.

As a recaster of Chinese society he outweighs the two Sui and Ming emperors—who hardly changed the social system—and can only be compared with the iconoclastic Qin Shihuang. Maybe also with Wang Mang (on the throne A.D. 8 to 23), who was a kind of early bird of socialism amid the winter of feudalism.

As a man with a doctrine, Mao surpasses any previous Chinese person of state including the Qin emperor, and perhaps should be put alongside Confucius and other sages whose words have shaped Chinese life. In some ways he stands out even among these. For he won massive influence during his own lifetime, whereas most Chinese sages became famous only after their death.

Mao bulks so large in the twentieth century because his impact was sustained through successive varied stages of China's modern convulsion. He lived long enough to be the Marx-Lenin-Stalin rolled into one of the Chinese Revolution.

More than 50 years ago he was China's Marx as he analyzed the ills of a feudal China carved up like a melon by foreign intruders. He became a Lenin as he led the rebellion that seized power by crablike encirclement from the countryside. After 1949 he put on a third hat as China's Stalin and took trowel and bricks to build a new socialist China.

Mao was not one man but five, at least. Gadfly peasant organizer who lit fires of revolt all over China. Military commander. Poet with a taste for riotous romanticism. Philosopher who gave a new moral Oriental form to Marxism. Head of a government which is the biggest bureaucracy on earth.

Mao was a man of action *and* of vision, a semi-intellectual, somewhat like de Gaulle and Churchill. This sort of actor-thinker—always influential in times of turbulence—finds history alive with compelling excitement. His first stirring of political ambition arises from confronting a beauty in the past which he believes can be recreated in the future. His special interest is how history moves. He sees both ideas and the will of extraordinary individuals as a key to history.

This kind of actor-thinker is out of sympathy with the abstract intellectual. He is military-minded; the sword lies by the history book. He loves his own nation more than the most glittering model of logical truth. He is bored with technology, uneasy at the potency of machines to change the way we live. He is not very good at economics.

Mao, Churchill, and de Gaulle were all actor-thinkers in these ways. Serious men of ideas who nevertheless failed to win approval from "real" intellectuals. Lonely men who stepped outside the library to save their nation and became, in the process, legends hardly to be distinguished from the heroes of the sagas that had nerved them to action.

For most Chinese of the mid twentieth century, the main point about Mao was that he unified China. Political unity has often been absent in this nation comparable to the whole of Europe in size and diversity. By the 1920s China had become so weak and anarchic—like a sheet of loose sand, as Sun Yat-sen lamented—that many Chinese and non-Chinese believed it intrinsically incapable of pulling itself together.

The era of Mao's rule was one of Chinese history's notable eras of unification. Dialects melted. Schools put an easily recognizable "New China" stamp on children from the Himalayas to the forests by Korea. A network of Communist organization made China's twenty-nine provinces interdependent to an unprecedented degree.

Never before in Chinese history had *any* book been read by hundreds of millions of ordinary people as was Mao's *Quotations* during the Cultural Revolution. Even as one laments the book as an intellectual straitjacket, one salutes it as a unifying force.

In Chinese eyes it is also of cardinal importance that China under Mao stood up in the world. It recovered its lofty self-image. The "sick man of Asia" rose fast enough to make parts of Asia nervous at his new vigor. No fear haunted young Mao more than that China might be wiped out by foreign assaults.

The years since 1949 have shown what the older Mao meant when he said that "the Chinese people have stood up." You have only to see the excitement on young Chinese faces when Peking announces a nuclear test. Or talk with older Chinese who, though not fond of communism, speak well of the Peking regime because its regained weight in the world sparks their pride as Chinese.

What of Mao's ideas? He made peasants for the first time the centerpiece of a Marxist plan to make revolution. More than had been done before, even by Lenin, he took imperialism to be the key fact about the world politics of his era. These were the twin pillars of his doctrine.

But Mao was also original in two other conceptions which gave character to the edifice on top of the pillars. He hated stability with a vengeance. The fixed laws of European Marxism he replaced with his pet notion that everything is in flux and always will be.

Revolution was for Mao less an event than a way of life. Endless sparks of discontent at what he saw around him, and a lust to stir the pot with the stick of change—these were the two constants in Mao's approach to politics.

Mao did not, I think, see socialism as a science at all. Marx and Engels did, and they declared all previous socialist ideas to be utopian speculation. Mao was as precise as a slide rule on the strategy of winning power. But the society he aimed for was not marked out by scientific laws.

This had the advantage that Mao was never complacent, always questing for a more human, deeply felt socialism. If Germans invented socialism as a science, Mao, at his best, softened socialism into a social morality. He wanted not only a new state, but a new type of citizen who lived for his fellows.

It had the disadvantage that old Mao did not quite know *what* pattern of society he wanted. It was as if the playing out of his father's impact upon him (predisposing him to the exertion of sheer will and to focus on enemies) sometimes overwhelmed his mother's impact (predisposing him to embrace the settled goals of a moral life).

Mao became known to the world outside China to a degree that no figure in China's 3,000 years had ever been before. This was ironic since he grew up as a country boy who seldom cast his eye beyond China. Two trips to Russia were his only foreign experiences.

He was forty-three when his meetings with Edgar Snow brought the first sustained relationship with a non-Chinese of his life. He mastered no foreign tongue.

Mao's vision and passion were limited to China for most of his life. Other countries mattered to him only insofar as they either interfered with China or possessed ideas and experience from which China could learn.

Mao, whose greatness was uncompromisingly Chinese, nevertheless intersected sharply with the world's consciousness. "Chairman Mao"—the cozy prefix may have helped to bridge the cultural gulf—became a household phrase in most countries. *Quotations* was translated on a scale that during the 1960s eclipsed the Bible. Even Confucius and his doctrines never traveled as well as that. Genghis Khan made it to Europe, in his own fashion, but he lacked a doctrine. Mao was "the first Chinese to speak to the rest of the world in plain, blunt language about issues that concern all of us. . . ."

In much of the Third World during the 1950s and 1960s, Mao was the chief personal symbol of anti-colonialism in its myriad forms. He surpassed the appeal of Sukarno, Nehru, and Nasser, because he saw that a new deal for the backward peoples required not only cursing the West, but a total, by-the-bootstraps transformation at home.

In the West we are not used to political figures of inescapable importance arising in the non-white East. A Chinese wave on the shore of world history—that was Mao's novelty. Son of the soil as he was, a China-firster to an almost geological degree, he nevertheless ended up one of the giants of this century's world politics. For overall impact he has been matched, I think, only by Franklin Roosevelt, Lenin and perhaps Churchill.

Strange in a way that this very Chinese sage—so nationalistic that he was prepared to count socialism as refuse if it did not rescue and enrich China—should fire off two of the most reverberating shots in post–World War II international politics. The breakdown of his alliance with Russia in 1960 put an end to World Communist unity. His opening of the door to America, a decade later, turned a bipolar world into a triangular one.

From the depths of his Chineseness he drew the skills to work surprises on the world.

The quarter century of Mao's rule over the PRC was not just an interlude of utopianism. It remade Chinese society. That social change runs on into the future—even as the Chinese people breathe easier in the absence of a demigod who became a misfit as he aged and China modernized.

Mao's government made a new China more socially just than old China in three ways. Rewards come mainly according to work—no longer according to birth, or land or capital possessed. So the distribution of China's national product has become one of the most egalitarian in the world, and very few fall through the net and perish through want of a dollar. And the basic tools for advancement—health care and a simple education above all—are no longer commodities purchasable only by a minority.

Under Mao, China took large steps of social modernization—the most potent form of modernization—and although the process turned out young people poles apart from Mao's world view, these moderns are the predictable products of Mao's PRC.

As he died Mao could claim for China some steps toward prosperity. Economic progress has not been as impressive as Japan's, for many reasons, but more so than India's. Despite Mao's tendency to pull up a plant in mid-growth and check on its health, the gains have been fundamental in nature, even though the rate of growth has not been rapid.

Overall, Mao left China largely self-sufficient and possessed of the sixth biggest economy in the world.

Yet Mao's record was mixed, at home especially, for as a man and a politician he had large flaws. He had strong prejudices and was not always consistent.

For all his serenity he was not an altogether secure man. To few of his colleagues did he become personally close; grudges lodged in corners of his mind; vanity lay behind his off-hand ways. He was a great leader but in many ways not an admirable character.

Mao went in for odd bedfellows. He would ally with anyone—a bandit today, a prince tomorrow—if success required it. Next morning the bandit or prince would be tossed aside like a used Kleenex.

He zigzagged because he did not follow a policy down the long corridor of implementation. He often drew back in horror at fruit from a tree planted by his own hand. He made periodic furious assaults on the very idea of bureaucracy, which in a nation of 900 million people is a bit like a gardener saying he can't stand dirt.

China sadly lacks some of the rosy traits promised by Mao's socialism. Mao wanted a "flourishing culture" for new China. But political propaganda cowed the writers and teachers. Mao looked forward to "personal liveliness" among the citizens. But he left behind a sullen populace that had learned by experience not to stick its neck out.

To a degree Mao never settled down after 1949. He never quite managed to modulate the pristine revolutionary values of the past into modes of operation for the post-victory years. He was less good as a manager than he had been as an iconoclast, teacher, and warrior.

China's recovery from economic backwardness is proving to be a long, slow process. It lags well behind the recovery from national humiliation which was the second task of Mao's revolution. This is partly because it is a gargantuan task to bring a quarter of mankind from poverty to modernity in one generation, but partly because Mao was less good at economics than he was at politics.

The man who called himself both wild tiger and tricky monkey did seem full of contradictions. He threw stones at convention all his life, yet he left the PRC bogged down in wary-eyed conformism. He liked to wallow at times in traditional waters, yet he ordered Chinese youth to the high dry land of modernity. He allotted a big role to will in history, yet he preached dialectical materialism, which bows the knee to objective historical forces.

Something in Mao rejected the flat high plateau of success. At inconvenient moments he would summon back the old values of the road.

Economic progress is the key to all Mao hoped for China—but he was often anxious at its character.

Unity and trust within the government he gaily jettisoned in order to lunge into his terrible Cultural Revolution.

A businesslike, if not intimate, relationship to Russia would have made life a great deal smoother for Peking during the last few years. But Mao could not bear to see past purity swallowed up in a Soviet-style future—so he declared Moscow the source of all evil.

Mao's contradictions did not exist, though, within a closed world of Mao the man. They became so large because China changed more than he changed, and so his relation to China's convulsions changed.

Mao's career was not cut from a single cloth. The late Mao—after de-Stalinization in Europe—was enormously different from the Mao who won power.

Marxism as an ideology self-destructs as a new social reality is brought about *by the very triumph of a Marxist party*. Mao, who had "revised" Marx and Lenin, should have realized that Maoism too would have to be revised as conditions in China changed. But he did not quite believe in his own claim—as Calvinists did not quite believe in a parallel claim—that all ideas are determined by social reality. He could not face the loss of authority that the crumbling of his ideology would bring.

The man who hated the old ended up clinging superstitiously to an ideology others began to find old.

Young Mao had been excited by Marxism; he used it masterfully to win power and bring a new era to China. Old Mao was baffled by the changed relation of that Marxist faith to the new society around him. China might have been better off if he had died twenty years earlier than he did.

"Not to have a correct political viewpoint," Mao once said, "is like having no soul." But the relation between political passion and the soul ebbs and flows.

In 1919 Mao was stirred to his depths by the tragedy of the young bride. He called for "a great wave of the freedom of love."

What of the freedom to love in the China that Mao left? One moment of adultery could bring years in jail to an adventurous granddaughter of the Changsha girl of 1919.

It is not that old Mao lost his vision of setting the Chinese people free from bondage, but that after decades of the CCP in power the emancipation of the individual woman is not, as sixty years ago, a matter of a struggle between two overall political world views.

Young Mao and his friends were gripped by deep personal convictions which were at the same time social convictions. They saw their own lives—what an age it was!—as mere fuel on a fire of revolution that would transform China and themselves at the same time. Politics in 1919 was manifestly about the happiness of the people.

The situation Mao left in 1976 was different. Individual rights no longer enjoyed an easy coincidence with large political struggles.

Mao had after all been born in 1893. His first education had been in the Confucian Classics. Most of his life had been a rural one, a life without machines, when armies prowled the hills, communications were medieval, and the elite of his generation were bending down to uplift a citizenry mired in appalling backwardness.

Mao was a modernizer; but the modernizer could not—never can—take his place in the ranks of the moderns.

China's last dynasty still stood when at age fourteen he was married off in feudal style against his will. More than half a century later dozens of heads of state trod a path to Peking, almost as pilgrims, to confer with this stay-put Buddha who never went to see them. It seemed patriarchal. It was; for Mao's personal drama as father of the Chinese Communist state had its beginnings in a patriarchal age.

He saw economic development only in terms of national power, not in terms of individual well-being—a growing preoccupation in China.

He failed to grasp the enormity, the supra-class, obliterative power, of nuclear war.

He said the Chinese peasants were "poor and blank." No limit to the superb poems that can be written on the empty page! Mao had in mind especially the backwardness of China's countryside and the suffering of its stoic people. Yet it is also true that each succeeding generation, smart or well-heeled as it may be, is poor and blank in a way that Mao did not seem to understand.

However heroic a segment of history may be, the time comes when its "page" is scrawled with marks and legends that no longer carry a message to those who come upon it. Nature turns the page and youth finds the next blank expanse a source of challenge.

The individual character of Mao the rebel synchronized with the social character of a generation angry and sad at the chaos of their country in the early twentieth century.

But the chimes of Mao's personal clock did not ring in harmony with the chimes of *later* social clocks. A mere measure of Mao's mortality? But also an explanation of why he outlived his usefulness to China.

"You must not always think that you alone are indispensable," Mao once advised an audience, "as if without you in the world, the earth would not turn, and the Party would not exist. Do you imagine that because butcher Chang dies people thereafter must eat pork covered with bristles? No need to fear for anyone's death. Whose death would really be a great loss? Marx, Engels, Lenin, Stalin—aren't they all dead? The revolution must still go on." But Mao's revolution could not really go on without Mao.

In 1978 a visitor to Shanghai prepared his camera to photograph a white plaster statue of Mao at the gate of Fudan University. "Don't do that," said a group of student leaders, rushing up. "We're pulling it down next week."

Deng Xiaoping, driving force of the Chinese government, has said Mao was 70 percent good and 30 percent bad. In private the judgment is harsher; many Chinese resent, despise, or hate Mao.

It is now quietly acknowledged that he was glorified too much at the expense of colleagues who also did much for the Chinese Revolution. That he was arbitrary in his judgments about people. That he squandered the enthusiasm of the Chinese masses by zigzags in policy. That he lost touch with public opinion in the 1970s and relied too much on relatives and courtiers.

Yet China must, and I think will, deal subtly with the legacy of Mao. China doesn't need him anymore, and yet it does.

Mao bestrode an era that needed a supreme colossus. The need has passed. Mao's "masses" can now—as his China did—stand up and flex "its" muscles. And the "it" will become "them."

The modern citizens of tomorrow will not need a great leader. They will honor Mao as a great unifier of China. They may turn to him at times for ethical adjudication, as people did to Confucius in a different age. They will not take much notice of him in designing the modern socialist China of tomorrow.

In the Politburo, fights will occur, but not in the old way. They will be less about ideology than those of Mao's era. To lose power need no longer mean to lose truth as well. Only in the person of Mao were power *(zheng)* and doctrine *(jiao)* fused. Now they will drift apart. Politics will be a bit more predictable; less theatrical; duller; less nerve-racking for the man in the street who gets damaged by its gyrations.

"Raise High the Banner of Mao Zedong's Thought," cry official voices now that Mao is safely in his crystal box. Up it goes, higher and higher, until no one can read what is written on its receding crimson threads.

Yet the banner casts a long shadow. Mao's successors have called into existence a variety of "Maos"; they will use these "Maos" as weapons in fighting China's problems and each other.

The banner itself, also an abstraction, will be needed by Mao's heirs tomorrow. To many ordinary Chinese, especially in the villages, "Chairman Mao" is the chief symbol of the PRC's identity. Hua, Deng, anyone who tries over the next years to control the vast realm that is China, will need to utilize that symbol.

The real Mao has melded with China's body, like yeast in a loaf already baked.

As 1980 began, the drama of "tiger" and "monkey" battling for supremacy within the spirit of one supreme leader looked like a thing of the past.

The future seemed to belong to the tiger who knew all about power and exulted in progress. The monkey who cast an oblique eye on human nature and had his doubts about progress was not to be seen.

And yet . . . could the Mao who was Sun the monkey king yet unleash from his mausoleum some "little devils" to pull the foundations from under any new plateau of success? Had he bequeathed the monkey's spirit to some receptive pockets of Chinese society—if not to the stability-minded Party leadership—as he in turn had inherited it from the age-old Chinese culture that shaped him?

Bibliographic Note

Key sources for this book have been Mao's own speeches and conversations and writings, most of them not officially released, and many of them only recently available; what follows is a brief guide to them, in Chinese, and where available in English translation.

A small portion of Mao's writings has been published in Peking, after much editing, as *Mao Zedong hsüan-chi,* 5 volumes. Many of his poems have appeared in *Mao chu-hsi shih-tz'u* (1963) and publications of the same title (all Peking) in 1965 and 1968.

A far fuller selection, and often more faithful to the original text, of pre-1949 items only, is *Mao Zedong chi,* ed. Takeuchi Minoru, 10 volumes, Tokyo, 1972—in Chinese with Japanese editorial matter.

Since the Cultural Revolution a stream of authentic but unauthorized writings has reached Taiwan and other places. Chief among the writings: *Mao Zedong ssu-hsiang wan-sui* (April 1967); *Mao Zedong ssu-hsiang wan-sui* (August 1969); *Mao Zedong ssu-hsiang wan-sui* (1967); *Mao chu-hsi wen-hsüan* (n.d.); *Mao chu-hsi tui P'eng, Huang, Chang, Chou fan-tang chi-t'uan ti p'i p'an* (1967?); *Mao chu-hsi chiao-yu yu-lü* (1967).

Quite a few of these writings are now available in English. On the official plane, there is a 5-volume *Selected Works;* and some additional pieces in *Selected Military Writings of Mao Tse-tung* (1966) and *Selected Readings from the Works of Mao Tse-tung* (1966); also *Mao Tse-tung Poems* (1976), a selection of thirty-nine; as well as a few other poems in *Chinese Literature, Peking Review,* and other magazines. Many poems are also translated in W. Barnstone (ed.), *The Poems of Mao Tse-tung.*

The 10-volume Tokyo work is not translated,* which means a vast body of the pre-1949 writings still must be consulted in Chinese. However, Schram has published some translations in *The Political Thought of Mao Tse-tung;* and J. Ch'en in *Mao Papers* and *Mao* (ed.).

Of the post-1949 writings, some have appeared in translation in book form: in *Mao Papers* and in Schram's *Chairman Mao Talks to the People.* Some have appeared in the quarterly *Chinese Law and Government:* 1-1, 1968; 1-4, 1968–1969;

*As I go to press, the U.S. Government has made available a translation, whose quality I have not yet been able to gauge: JPRS No. 71911-1-5, under the title *Collected Works of Mao Tse-tung.*

3–4, 1970–1971; 5–1, 1972; 5–3 and 5–4, 1972–1973; 6–2, 1973; 9–3 and 9–4, 1976–1977; 10–2, 1977; 10–4, 1977–1978; 11–4, 1978–1979. And many have been translated by the U.S. Government: U.S. Consulate-General, Hong Kong, *Current Background,* No. 891 (1969), No. 892 (1969), No. 888 (1969), and 897 (1969); U.S. Department of Commerce, JPRS, Nos. 61269-1 and 61269-2 (1974)—"Miscellany of Mao Tse-tung Thought," No. 49826 (1970)—"Series on Communist China No. 90," No. 50792 (1970)—"Series on Communist China No. 108," and No. 52029 (1970)—"Talks and Writings of Chairman Mao." The "Mao Writings Project" at Brown University has translated further items which will be published in due course.

Magazines here and there have come out with items, especially *Issues & Studies,* Taipei: 1970/3; 1970/4; 1970/1; 1972/7; 1973/12; 1973/1; 1973/9; 1973/5; 1973/7; 1973/10; 1973/8; 1973/11; 1974/5; 1974/9; 1975/2.

Records of some of Mao's talks with foreigners are interesting enough, and sufficiently available, to be mentioned here: E. Snow's *The Long Revolution; Nouvel Observateur,* 9/13/76 (Mao–Pompidou); A. Malraux's *Antimémoires; Khrushchev Remembers,* 2 vols.; J. Service: *The Amerasia Papers* and *Lost Chance in China* (ed. J. Esherick); *Le Monde,* 9/10/76 (Mao–Bettencourt); *Tokyo Shimbun,* 9/27/72 (Mao–Tanaka); *Pouvoirs* (Qui Governe La Chine), no. 3, 1977 (Mao–French group); *Sunday Times,* London, 6/12/60, 6/18/60, 10/15/61, and 10/22/61 (Mao–Lord Montgomery); *Saturday Evening Post,* 11/14/64 (Mao–French group); Kissinger's *White House Years; Sonntag,* Berlin, 12/16/56 (Mao–Gunther Weisenborn).

It would plunge you into an endless and soon unrewarding jungle if I were to list the secondary sources on Mao, or aspects of his career, which I have read. Most of the best work is contained in academic monographs, and in *China Quarterly, Modern China,* and other specialist journals; much of this is cited in my reference notes.

Of the biographies, Mao's own story to Snow, in *Red Star over China,* stands alone. The part-biography by Li Jui on the early Mao, published in Peking (see Abbreviations, p. 439) is of fundamental value. Xiao San and Xiao You are both indispensable for their knowledge of young Mao; Schram's *Mao Tse-tung* is outstanding among non-Chinese works. Throughout, I have benefited from the brilliant work of Schram on Mao's career and thought; not only his *Mao Tse-tung,* but many journal articles, all as solid as they are original. The biography itself, alas, is now partly out of date, having been written fifteen years ago; one need only note Schram's remark (p. 311) "The orientation adopted by Mao Tse-tung in late 1962 and early 1963 has continued to determine Chinese policy down to the present time"), and point to the array of Mao's writings and remarks that became available only after the Cultural Revolution, as well as material such as the memoirs of Zhang Guotao (Chang Kuo-t'ao), mentioned above and in my Reference Notes.*

Of the other biographies the best is J. Ch'en's *Mao and the Chinese Revolution;*

---

*I should also add that I have two basic disagreements with Schram. He sees Mao as fundamentally consistent throughout his life, I see much more that is ad hoc in Mao. I see his ideology being often reshaped, compromised, or even set aside, because of the practical demands of statecraft; especially I see the Mao of the late 1950s and after as fundamentally different from the Mao who grasped Marxism as a faith and the Mao who won power.

And I see Mao (even the "early" and "middle" Mao) as less of a Leninist internationalist than does Schram ("There is not the slightest doubt that Mao Tse-tung . . . is loyal to the ideal of a united world communist movement" [*Asian Survey,* June 1963]).

indeed for the period up to 1949, where it stops, it is a match for Schram. Others have points of merit (their full titles are cited in my notes): Payne (some firsthand information); Han Suyin (new interview material and some fine narrative reconstruction in her first volume); Pye (probing questions about Mao the personality); Hsiao Ying's *Wo shih Mao Zedong ti nu mi shih* (personal details); Wang Ssuch'eng's *Mao fei Zedong cheng chuan* (personal details); G. Paloczi-Horvath's *Mao Tse-tung* (comparative communism perspective); D. Wilson (ed.) *Mao Tse-tung in the Scales of History* (essays by scholars); Ssu Ma Ch'ang Feng's *Mao Zedong yü Zhou Enlai* and his *Mao Zedong p'ing ch'üan* (Mao's conflicts with colleagues); Huang Yu-ch'üan's Mao *Zedong sheng p'ing tzu-liao chien-pien* (excerpts from diverse source materials).

Very few of the other biographies in English or other Western languages (I cannot read Japanese) add much, though S. Uhallay's *Mao: A Critical Biography* is a good summary for the time it was written.*

Of the works which deal with an aspect of Mao, or with Mao within some broader context, the most worthwhile include E. Rice's *Mao's Way;* R. Solomon's *Mao and Chinese Political Culture;* F. Wakeman's *History and Will;* J. Rue's *Mao Tse-tung in Opposition, 1927–1935;* B. Schwartz's *Chinese Communism and the Rise of Mao;* the memoirs of Zhang Guotao; Witke's *Comrade Chiang Ch'ing;* Hsiao Tsoling's *Power Relations Within the Chinese Communist Movement;* Chiang Yungching's *Pao-lo-t'ing yü Wuhan cheng-ch'üan;* L. Schaffer's forthcoming *Mao Zedong and the Hunan Labor Movement;* Snow's *Random Notes on Red China;* the Chinese-language memoirs, mentioned in the notes, by Gong Chu (Kung Ch'u), Chen Changfeng, Chai Tso-chun, Liu Bocheng, Yen Ch'ang-lin; Lu Ch'iang's *Ching kang shan shang ti 'ying hsiung'—Mao Zedong wai shih;* MacFarquhar's *The Origins of the Cultural Revolution;* J. B. Starr's *Continuing the Revolution.*

*As I go to press an industrious biography by a British journalist has come to hand, D. Wilson's *Mao: The People's Emperor* (London).

Reference Notes

The aim of the Notes is to give the sources in a clear, brief, unpedantic way. References are mainly confined to direct quotations. Sometimes a reference is also given for a fact that may not appear self-evident.

I have forgone references for facts or descriptions that are known and locatable in the standard literature on twentieth-century China (e.g., in the political account on pp. 7–8) and to items that are obvious (e.g., "a passage from Mao's *Selected Works*," which is given as dating from 1927, is obviously from Vol. I, which covers that year).

Page references to books are given in all cases where the location of a passage is not obvious. In a few cases, e.g., the *Wan Sui* documents, it seemed better to give the date of the fragment, rather than a page reference; the latter is given only when the date of the item is unknown.

I have given the place and date of publication of books cited only when this information is of particular significance for the book's contents.

If a passage comes from a Chinese source that is also available in an English version (e.g., from *Mao Zedong chi,* also in *Selected Works),* a reference to the English is sometimes given for the reader's convenience; the reader should note that I have not necessarily followed the translation, or indeed the text itself, that appears in the official *Selected Works.*

In quoting Mao's verse, I have given the standard Peking translation as source, but I have frequently adjusted the wording, after consulting the Chinese text (principally *Mao chu-hsi shih-tz'u* [1963] and additional poems published in *Chung-kuo wen hsüeh* during 1978) and other available translations. At times I have followed phrasing from the following English versions: J. Ch'en's *Mao and the Chinese Revolution;* W. Barnstone's *The Poems of Mao Tse-tung,* and Rush's work mentioned under Chapter 15.

In the Notes, Chinese words are given in Wade-Giles form—*except* (in listing works in Chinese) for the names of people that appear in the body of the book in *Pinyin* form—because library catalogues and bibliographies virtually all still use that older form.

Dates and numbers of serial publications are given according to these examples:
1972/4   i.e., April 1972 (a monthly publication)
5/7/56   i.e., May 7, 1956

2–4, 1968   i.e., Volume 2, Number 4, 1968

Certain information has come from interviews with Chinese or foreigners, mainly officials—as with Gough Whitlam for Chapter 21, or Huang Hua concerning the Sian Incident, or Winston Lord for Chapter 20—but since the sources for some of these interviews cannot be named, it does not seem appropriate to give a partial list here.

Some facts and descriptions are drawn from my visits to the scenes of Mao's career: the family house and exhibition at Music Mountain; former schools, houses, and other sites in Changsha; the peasant institute and former residence in Wuhan; the peasant institute and Mao's former houses and offices in Canton; Mao's old office at a former building of Peking University; the buildings where the delegates to the CCP's first meeting met and resided in Shanghai; sites at Yanan.

ABBREVIATIONS

Publications

CB	*Current Background* (U.S. Consulate-General, Hong Kong)
Ch'en	Jerome Ch'en: *Mao and the Chinese Revolution*
CIS	China Information Service (New York office of Taipei government)
CLG	*Chinese Law and Government*
CQ	*China Quarterly* (London)
FEER	*Far Eastern Economic Review* (Hong Kong)
IAS	*Issues and Studies* (Taipei)
JPRS	Joint Publications Research Service (U.S. Department of Commerce)
KR	*Khrushchev Remembers* (1970)
KR (LT)	*Khrushchev Remembers: The Last Testament* (1974)
Li Jui	Li Jui: *Mao Zedong t'ung-chih ti ch'u-ch'i ko-ming huo-tung* (Peking); now also available in translation *(Early Revolutionary Activities of Comrade Mao Zedong),* to which page references are keyed.
LT	*London Times*
Mao Chi	*Mao Zedong chi,* 10 vols., in Chinese (Tokyo)
MC	*Modern China*
NCNA	New China News Agency (Peking)
NYT	*New York Times*
PD	*People's Daily (Jen-min jih-pao)*
PKR	*Peking Review*
Poems	*Mao Zedong Poems* (Peking, 1976)
RF	*Red Flag (Hung ch'i)*
Rice	E. Rice: *Mao's Way*
RS	Edgar Snow: *Red Star over China*
SCMM	*Survey of China Mainland Magazines*
SCMP	*Survey of China Mainland Press*
SS's *Mao*	Stuart Schram: *Mao Tse-tung*
SW	Mao's *Selected Works,* 5 vols. (Peking)
Talks	Schram, ed.: *Chairman Mao Talks to the People* (Mao speeches)
Thought	Schram, ed.: *The Political Thought of Mao Tse-tung* (Mao writings)
TLR	Edgar Snow: *The Long Revolution*

TMD   Han Suyin: *The Morning Deluge*
Wan Sui   *Mao Zedong ssu-hsiang wan-sui* (3 vols., which are designated respec-
             tively: "1967"; "April 1967"; "1969." The item is thereafter identified
             by the date of Mao's remarks, unless the date is not precisely given in
             the book, in which case a page reference is added.)
WHCM   *What's Happening on China Mainland* (Taipei)
WIT   Han Suyin: *Wind in the Tower*
Witke   Roxane Witke: *Comrade Chiang Ch'ing* (Jiang Qing)
WP   *Washington Post*
Xiao San   Xiao San (or Hsiao San, or Emi Hsiao, or Emi Xiao): *Mao Zedong
             t'ung-chih ti ch'ing-shao-nien shi-tai*
Xiao You   Xiao You (Siao Yu): *Mao Tse-tung and I Were Beggars*
Zhang   Zhang Guotao (Chang Kuo-t'ao): *The Rise of the Chinese Communist
             Party*, 2 vols. (Memoirs)

Other Abbreviations

FN   Footnote (in RT's text)
HK   Hong Kong
NY   New York
RT   The author

CHAPTER 1. PROLOGUE

Page

1   A Burmese leader to RT, Rangoon, 11/15/79.
1   Kukrit Pramoj (former prime minister of Thailand) to RT, Bangkok, 11/
     10/79.
1   (lice) *RS*, p. 79.
1   My attention was drawn to the double character of Mao's face by Robert
     Elegant's *China's Red Masters*, p. 247.
1   Smedley's *Battle Hymn of China*, p. 123; Chang Tung-ts'ai's *Sancho No-
     saka and Mao Tse-tung* (Taipei), p. 46.
2   Ganis Harsono to RT, Jakarta, 11/29/79.
2   ("bowels") Snow's *Journey to the Beginning*, p. 165.
2   (FN) B. Compton's *Mao's China*, p. 34.

CHAPTER 2. CHILDHOOD

NOTE: Facts and descriptions in this chapter have been drawn from Xiao San's
Mao Zedong t'ung-chih ti ch'ing-shao-nien shi-tai (Peking); Wang Ssu-ch'eng's
Mao Zedong cheng ch'uan (Taipei): Cheng Hsueh-chia's account in *Issues and
Studies*, November and December 1973; the Chinese pamphlet translated in *CB*,
900; Chao Yen-chang's *Tsai Mao chu-hsi ti ku hsiang* (Hankou); *Chieh-fang-chün
wen-yi*, Nos. 20–21, 1967 (*SCMP*, 614).

Page

5,6   The origin of the name Shaoshan is explained in *TMD*, p. 15.
  8   ("I hated") R. Payne's *Mao Tse-tung*, p. 30.
  9   (lunch incident) *CB*, 900, p. 10.
  9   ("If you can") *TMD*, p. 16 (trans. adjusted).
9,10   ("city," "After my return") *RS*, p. 124.
 10   (pig story) Li Jui, p. 6; Xiao San, Ch. 1, Section III, has a different version. Liu Ta-wen in *Hsinhua jih-pao*, 9/8/45, tells of Zedong giving money to a poor man.
 10   (at tombstone) Xiao You, pp. 6–7.
 11   (ox) Xiao San, p. 11.
 11   ("We made many," "From then on") *RS*, p. 128.
 12   ("ruling power," "opposition") *Ibid.*, p. 125.
 12   ("It is not") *Ibid.*, p. 125.
 12   ("I thought") *Wan Sui*—1969, 8/18/64.
 12   On the forced marriage see Ssu Ma-shu in *Tien-wen t'ai-pao*, HK, 12/20/58.
 13   ("Alas") *RS*, p. 131.
 13   Xiao San, Ch. 1, VI, says rice merchants, rather than bean merchants.
 14   ("The first hero") *CB*, 900, p. 10.
 14   ("Free Rice") Xiao San, p. 14.
 14   ("I did not") *RS*, p. 130.
 14   ("hate") *Ibid.*, p. 126; ("At the same") p. 130.
 15   (incident at dinner) Xiao You, p. 11.
 15   ("How much") *Ibid.*, p. 13.
 16   ("ordinary people") *RS*, p. 130. H. Cummins's *Mao Tse-tung: A Value Analysis* (Edmonton), a comparative study of the lives of Mao and another CCP figure, Hsiao Ke, shows the limits to Mao's intrinsic rebelliousness.
 16   Zhang, I, Ch. 1.
 16   ("Most of my") *RS*, p. 127.
 16   "Individual character" and "social character" is from E. Fromm's *Escape from Freedom*, Appendix.
 17   (laziness) *RS*, p. 126; italics by RT.

CHAPTER 3. KNOWLEDGE FOR WHAT?

Page

 18   (Wang incident) Xiao You, pp. 14–15.
 18   (taunts, and exchange with headmaster) *Ibid.*, pp. 19–22.
 19   (FN) *RS*, p. 132.
 20   (Japan) *Ibid.*, p. 133.
20,21   (book incident) Xiao San, Ch. 1, VIII.
 21   Mao's hatred of criticism was confessed in 1959, *CLG*, 1–4, 1968.
 22   ("When will you") *TMD*, p. 34.
 22   ("speechless") Xiao San, Ch. 2, IX.
 22   ("I was most") *RS*, p. 135.

Page

23   ("join the revolution") *CB*, 900, p. 10.
24   ("I could write") *RS*, p. 129.
24   ("I, being a student") *Ibid.,* p. 138.
24   ("Thinking") *Ibid.,* p. 139.
24   ("If the people") Ch'en, p. 44.
25   ("I painted") *RS*, p. 140.
25   ("My father," "Disgusted") *Ibid.,* p. 140.
25   ("I am the universe") Li Jui, p. 40.
25   ("It was better") *RS*, p. 141.
26   (with Tan) Xiao You, pp. 32–34.
26   ("Its curriculum") *RS*, p. 141.
27   (ox) Xiao San, Ch. 3, XIII.
27   ("I escaped") *RS*, p. 142.
27   (entrance exam, "I managed") *Ibid.,* p. 142.
28   ("There were many") *Ibid.,* p. 143.
28   Many details of Mao's life at FTTS are in Chou Shih-chao's article in
      Hsin kuan-ch'a (Peking), No. 2.
28   (FN) Li Jui, p. 42.
29   ("despised Liang") *RS*, p. 143.
29   (seizes Yuan) Li Jui, p. 45.
29   ("I was obliged," "Thanks") *RS*, p. 143.
30   ("A man") *Ibid.,* p. 143.
30   ("newspaper room") Li Jui, p. 23.
30   ("wasted") *RS*, p. 149.
31   ("A country") *Kung Yen,* Vol. 1, No. 1; there is a letter of Mao's (Li Jui,
      p. 83) which insists that Western thought is flawed no less than Eastern
      thought.
31   (FN) Li Jui, pp. 28–29.
31   Xiao San, Ch. 3, XVI; cf. English version (Bombay, 1953), p. 42; see, too,
      CB, 900, p. 17.
31   (down Yue Lu mountain) Li Jui, p. 30.
32   (first published article) *Hsin ch'ing-nien.* April 1917.
32   Xiao You (*Ming pao yüeh-k'an,* HK, 1968/10) has a rather far-fetched
      explanation of how "twenty-eight strokes" means "Communist"—since
      the first character for the latter term (*gong*) bears a physical resemblance
      to the characters for "twenty-eight."
32   ("I believed") *Chung-yang jih-pao,* Taipei, 11/4/72.
32   The student union, which began as the Aptitude Development Society, in-
      cluded alumni and was quite a well set up affair. See Xiao San's "Mao
      Zedong t'ung-chih tsai 'Wu-ssu' shih-ch'i," in *Kwang-hui te wu-ssu,* Pe-
      king, 1959, pp. 19ff.
32   (hawking snacks) *Hsin Hunan pao,* 7/1/50.
32,33 (Japan) *CB*, 900, pp. 21, 15.
33   (night school announcement) Li Jui, p. 61, and Terrill's *800,000,000 : The
      Real China,* p. 124.
33   (FN—"Daily Record") Lynda Shaffer's forthcoming *Mao Tse-tung and
      the Hunan Labor Movement,* p. 113.

Page

33   ("We will tell you") Li Jui, p. 64.
33   (advertisement) *RS*, p. 144; Li Jui, p. 74, says Mao got "five or six" replies; see also *IAS*, 1973/12, p. 72.
33   The putting together of the two characters "new" and "people" seems to have been inspired by phrases from the Classics—"renewing the people" in *Great Learning*, and "make new people" in *Book of History*.
33   ("There are two") Xiao San, Ch. 4, XIX.
34   ("wizard," "brain") Li Jui, p. 52.
34   (Tolstoy) *Ibid.*, p. 82.
35   (marginal quotes) *Ibid.*, p. 24.
35   (*xue wen*) Xiao San, Ch. 3, XV.
36   ("wherever") Li Jui, p. 38.
36   ("More than ever") *RS*, p. 149.
36   (eulogy) Li Jui, p. 320.

CHAPTER 4. WIDER WORLD IN PEKING AND SHANGHAI

Page

37   (on *New Youth*) *Xiao San*, p. 61.
37   (Mao's set-up in Peking) Ch'ang Kung's *Ch'in Kung chien hsueh sheng huo hui-yi*, p. 8.
37   ("I used") *RS*, p. 151.
38   ("My office") *Ibid.*, p. 150.
38   ("I tried") *Ibid.*, p. 150.
39   (trees) *Ibid.*, p. 151; for a report on Mao's passivity in Peking see *IAS*, 1973/12, p. 74.
39   (FN) Li Huang in *Ming pao yüeh-k'an*, HK, 1969/6.
40   ("I felt") *RS*, p. 149.
41   ("I saw") *Ibid.*, p. 152.
43   (FN) Li Jui, p. 27.
43   ("The movement") *CB*, 900, p. 23.
44   ("He often") Chou Shih-chao in *Kung-jen jih-pao*, 4/20/59.
44   ("Great Union") *Mao Chi*, I, pp. 57ff.
45   (union of students) *Ibid.*, I, pp. 61–62.
45   ("unexpected pleasure") *Kung-jen jih-pao*, 4/20/59.
45   (FN) Li Jui, pp. 109–110. One source (see Huang Yü-ch'uan's *Mao Zedong sheng p'ing tzu-liao chien-pien*, p. 45) says Mao was much less of a lone ranger as editor of the *Review* than Li Jui makes him out to have been.
46   Zhao case from *Hunan li-shih tzu-liao*, 8, 1959; Witke in *CQ*, 31; *Kung-jen jih-pao*, 4/20/59; *Thought*, pp. 334ff; "prisoner's cart" from Li Jui, p. 121.
47   Zhang's tyranny in Hunan is detailed in Chou Shih-chao's article in *Kwang-hui te wu-ssu*, pp. 57ff.
48   Snow called it a "trial marriage" (*RS*, p. 156), but one must note that he deleted the statement from the revised 1968 edition of *RS*. On the first

Page

child's birthdate see the article "Mao Zedong ti chia," in *Ming pao yüeh-k'an*, HK, 1967/3.

48   ("It's all") *Wen hui pao*, HK, 11/20/57.

49   ("Three books") *RS*, p. 155.

50   ("His own") *Ibid.*, p. 157.

50   ("Each one") *Wu-ssu shih-ch'i shih-k'an chieh-shao* (Peking), 1959, Vol. 1, p. 155.

50   ("The revolution") *Chieh-fang-chün wen-yi*, No. 36.

50   ("Study hard") *Thought*, p. 18.

51   On the gate of his school Mao inscribed the slogan: "The world is ours, To get things done everyone should come and join in." ("Mao chu-hsi nien ch'ing ti shih-hou," in *Kung shang jih-pao*, Cambodia, 1/13/67).

51   The ways in which Mao kept one foot in the Changsha establishment—through certain former teachers, among other means—are set out in Shaffer's forthcoming book, pp. 55ff, 65, 246–248, and *passim*.

51   According to Xiao You (*Ming pao yüeh-k'an*, HK, 1968/8 and 10) Mao had an affair with his female co-worker at the bookstore.

51   (FN) Li Jui, p. 156.

52   (few at father's funeral) *Wan Sui*—1969, 8/18/64.

53   A. McDonald has presented Mao's autonomy writings (in Chinese) in *Ho-gaku Kenkyu*, Vol. 16, No. 2 (Tokyo), and analyzed them in *CQ* 68; quotations from pp. 771, 775, 770 of *CQ*. "Judged mistaken," from Li Jui, p. 138.

53,54 (Mao-Xiao You exchange) Xiao You, p. 249.

54   (Isms and problems) *Hsin ch'ing-nien*, 1919/12 and following issues.

55   (FN) Li Jui, p. 166.

56   ("He delighted") Zhang, I, pp. 140, 141.

56   ("You could") Li Ang's *Hung-se wu-t'ai*, p. 98.

56   ("Though there be") *CQ*, 68, p. 771.

58   ("The delegates") Xiao You, p. 256.

58   ("If we work," at Hangzhou) *Ibid.*, p. 258.

CHAPTER 5. ORGANIZING

Page

59   ("Mr. Mao") *Kung-jen jih-pao*, 4/20/59.

60   (announcement) *Mao Chi*, I, pp. 81ff.

60   ("Give your," "Set out") Li Jui, p. 173.

60   For Mao's shrewdness in obtaining money for the school, see Shaffer, p. 100.

60   (FN) *Ibid.*, p. 92.

61   (on Anyuan). "Mao chu-hsi tsai An-yuan," part of "Mao chu-hsi chuan-chi," in *Chieh-fang-chün wen-yi*, No. 6, 1968.

61   (FN) *TMD*, p. 95.

62   (at blackboard) *CB*, 900, p. 25.

62   On the evolution of the Mao-Liu relationship see P'eng Shu-chih's article

Page

in *Ming pao yüeh-k'an*, HK, 1968/12. On the limits to Mao's role at Anyuan, see Shih Cheng's article in *Tzu kuo*, HK, 1968/9.

63 (change of abode) *Chieh-fang-chün wen-yi*, 3/25/68, trans. in *SCMM*,
621.

63 (Maring in Changsha) *CQ*, 45, p. 103.

63 Mao had collaborated with *Great Welfare Daily's* editor on Hunan autonomy and other issues; see Shaffer, p. 248.

63 (rickshaw pullers) *CB*, 900, p. 25.

64 ("There are no classes") *Battle Hymn*, p. 44.

64 (agent's words) H. Isaacs in *CQ*, 45, p. 104.

65 ("Workers are the mother") *Chieh-fang-chün wen-yi*, 3/25/68, trans. in
SCMM, 621.

65 ("extremist," FN—interview was by Schram) Li Jui, pp. 270, 266.

66 ("I forgot") *RS*, p. 159.

67 ("There must be") *TMD*, p. 107.

67 (FN—Hunan) Shaffer, pp. 417ff.

68 ("You'd better") SS's *Mao*, p. 73.

69 Madame Chiang Kai-shek testifies to Borodin's link with Buster Keaton
in her *Conversations with Mikhail Borodin* (1977), p. 4.

69 (FN—Borodin) *Mao Tse-tung* by O. Vladimirov and V. Ryazantsev,
Moscow, p. 47.

70 V. V. Vishnyakova-Akimova's *Two Years in Revolutionary China*, pp.
228ff. (on Ho and other aspects of Borodin's circle).

70 ("He wouldn't") *Wan Sui*—1969, 12/20/64.

70 ("busy") Zhang, I, p. 342.

70 RT has misplaced the reference to the Mao-Zhang incident en route to
Hong Kong.

71 *Mao Chi*, I, p. 98. For maximum impact when addressing peasants, Mao
would render "Knock down imperialism" (*ta tao ti-kuo chu-yi*) as
"Knock down the foreign and rich ones" (*ta tao yang ts'ai tung*); Li Jui
(Chinese), p. 248.

72 ("All work") Zhang, I, p. 380.

73 ("I had") *RS*, p. 159.

73 For an account of Mao donating sizable sums of money for children's
prizes, see Liu Ta-wen in *Hsinhua jih-pao*, 9/8/45.

73 (Mao's line to Kaihui) *Chung-kuo wen-hsüeh*, September 1978. Other
sources, (e.g., the article "Mao chu-hsi yi chia wei ko-ming shih-yeh," in
Au-men jih-pao, Macao, 4/28/67, and BBC, FE, 5617, B11, 9/17/77)
say Mao and Kaihui remained as close as ever right up until 1927.

74 ("king of the peasants.") Vishnyakova-Akimova, p. 163.

75 ("I realized") *Mao Chi*, I, p. 247.

76 *Poems.*

77 ("We have") *Mao Chi*, I, p. 151.

79 On Zhou's background see Ssu Ma Ch'ang Feng's *Mao Zedong yü Zhou
Enlai*, Introduction, and pp. 2–3.

80 ("Farmers") *TMD*, p. 119.

80 ("take") SS's *Mao*, p. 91.

Page

81   "Analysis" is in *SW*, I; "The National Revolution . . ." is only in *Mao Chi*, I, pp. 175ff; I have followed some of the brilliant analysis of Schram in his chapter of the forthcoming *Cambridge History of China*, Vols. 12 and 13.

82,83   (quotes from *Report*) *Mao Chi*, I, pp. 207ff.

84   RT visited Mao's old Wuhan sites in 1973 and examined materials at them.

85   *Poems.*

86   ("But where") *SW*, I, p. 56.

86   ("an immediate") Chiang Yung-ching's *Pao-lo-t'ing yü Wuhan cheng-ch'üan* (Taipei), p. 291.

87   (FN) Roy in *New Republic*, 9/3/51.

88   ("It's all over") *TMD*, p. 162.

89   (Mao on Borodin and Roy) *RS*, p. 165.

89   (FN) Roy in *New Republic*, 9/3/51.

89   ("we really") SS's *Mao*, p. 121.

90   (Mao exchange with Center) Schram in *CQ*, 18, p. 64, and *Mao Zedong yü Zhou Enlai*, p. 10.

CHAPTER 6. STRUGGLE

NOTE: Many of Mao's activities in this period are brilliantly analyzed in J. Rue's *Mao Tse-tung in Opposition*. I have also drawn on Hsiao's book (mentioned below) and his *The Land Revolution in China, 1930–1934*, both based closely on the available documents, on I. J. Kim's *The Politics of Chinese Communism*, D. J. Waller's *The Kiangsi Soviet Republic*, P. C. Huang's article in *MC*, 1–3, and T. Lotveit's *Chinese Communism 1931–1934*.

Page

93   (effort to kill Mao) *TMD*, p. 176.

93   ("Many Communist") *RS*, p. 163; italics by RT.

94   ("The struggle") *SW*, I, p. 80.

95   ("Conscious") *Ibid.*, II, p. 151.

96   *Li Dazhao hsüan-chi*, p. 237.

96   ("Cousin") *TMD*, p. 177.

96   Wang Ming, from his later exile in Moscow, claimed that Mao murdered the two bandit chiefs, and that "in the late 1930s" Mao confided to Wang Ming and others: "After the event, I felt that Wang Zao and Yuan Wencai died innocently as they and their troops were almost reformed." See *Meng-ku hsiao-hsi pao*, Ulan Bator, 6/15–29/74 (this memoir of Wang Ming's is unreliable, especially because of the persecution mania that colors all of its discussion of how Mao treated Wang Ming).

96   ("They are all") *SW*, I, p. 81.

96   (FN) *Thought*, p. 269.

98   (description of Mao) Kung Ch'u's *Wo yü hung-chün*, p. 124.

98   On various estimates of the initial size of the Zhu-Mao forces, see *Mao*

Page

Zedong sheng p'ing, p. 94, Lu Ch'iang's *Ching kang shan shang ti 'ying hsiung,'* pp. 8, 11, and Ssu Ma Ch'ang Feng's *Mao Zedong yü Zhou En-lai,* p. 11.

100   (FN—Mao on books) A. Bouc's *Mao Tse-tung,* p. 190.

101   (Maoping points) *Mao Chi,* II, pp. 20ff.

101   ("A base") *Hui-yi Ching kang shan-ch'ü ti tou-cheng* (Peking), p. 11.

101   ("How can") *TMD,* p. 201.

104   (on Yang Kaihui and her death) *PD,* 12/8/76 and *Eastern Horizon,* HK, 1977/3 and "Yang Kaihui lie-shih sheng p'ing," in *Kung shang jih-pao,* Cambodia, 1/9/67.

104   (description of Zizhen and Mao's match with her) Kung Ch'u, pp. 142–145.

104   On He Zizhen's background see Ssu Ma Ch'ang Feng's *Mao Zedong p'ing ch'uan,* p. 299.

105   (popular song) *Ching kang shan shang ti 'ying hsiung,'* p. 28.

105   (FN—Mao's poem) *Ibid.,* pp. 13–14.

106   (New Year's incident) Smedley's *Great Road,* p. 238.

109   ("the purely military") *Mao Chi,* II, p. 78.

109   Open criticism of Zhu by Mao is claimed in Vladimirov and Ryazantsev, p. 57. See too Ssu Ma Ch'ang Feng's *Mao Zedong p'ing ch'uan,* pp. 263–264, and (on Mao-Zhu clashes, generally) his *Mao Zedong yü Zhou En-lai,* pp. 11–12. *Also Ching kang shan ti 'ying hsiung,'* pp. 22–23.

109   ("a child") *Mao Chi,* II, p. 140.

110   (obituary) SS's *Mao,* p. 149.

110   ("a joke") Hsiao Tso-liang's *Power Relations Within the Chinese Communist Movement,* vol. 2, p. 157.

110   (FN) *Poems.*

111   When the Nationalists burst into Music Mountain, Mao's relatives took the basket of diaries, study notes, and newspaper excerpts that he had saved from his student days and burned them, as a protection against persecution. A few items were rescued from the flames and are quoted at length in Li Jui. On the desecration of the Mao graves see Liu Ta-wen in *Hsinhua jih-pao,* 9/8/45.

111   (Mao to Snow) *RS,* p. 180.

111   (on Mao and 28B) I do not follow P. C. Huang—despite the acuteness of his analysis—in believing Mao gave significant credit to 28B for opposing Li Lisan-ism; when Mao spoke this way, in 1945, he was treading too carefully with Moscow to speak the whole truth.

112   ("Oppose Book Worship") *TMD,* pp. 228–229.

112   Conflicting views of Mao's role in the Rich Field incident are in Dorrill's article in *CQ,* 37, and P. C. Huang's *Chinese Communists and Rural Society, 1927–1934* (with L. Shaffer and K. Walker.) Some survivors claimed that 20,000 died at Rich Field (*Mao Zedong yü Zhou Enlai,* pp. 30–31). Zhu De was certainly critical of Mao over the incident, referring to "you know who" as the author of its horrors (Kung Ch'u, p. 266). See also *Ching kang shan ti 'ying hsiung,'* p. 38, and *Mao Zedong sheng p'ing tzu-liao chien pien,* p. 117.

Page

113   The Jiangxi's regime's libertarianism is well analyzed in Hu Chi-hsi's "Mao Tse-tung, la Revolution et la Question Sexuelle," in *Revue Fran-çaise de Science Politique*, Vol. 23, No. 1, 1973.

115   *Poems.*

116   ("From 1931") *Talks*, p. 291.

117   (Zhou-Mao clash at Ningdu and elsewhere) Waller, p. 55, and Ssu Ma Ch'ang Feng's *Mao Zedong yü Zhou Enlai*, pp. 34–35.

117   (Fu's memoir) *Hung ch'i p'iao-p'iao*, XI.

117   ("Pay Attention to Economic Work") *SW*, I, p. 150.

118   (28B's attitude to Japan's attack) C. McLane's *Soviet Policy and the Chinese Communists*, pp. 266ff.

118   ("I'll shake") *TMD*, p. 259.

120   (officer dines with Mao) Kung Ch'u, p. 399.

120   ("diplomatic illness") O. Braun's *Chinesische Aufzeichnungen* 1932–39, p. 79.

120   Fu's memoir.

121   (Mao's bag) Ssu Ma Ch'ang Feng's *Mao Zedong yü Zhou Enlai*, pp. 60–62.

CHAPTER 7. A GRIP ON THE FUTURE

Page

123   G. Stein's *The Challenge of Red China*, p. 118.

123   (FN) *RS*, p. 196.

123   Payne's *Mao Tse-tung*, p. 140.

124   (missionary) Dick Wilson's *The Long March*, p. 93.

125   ("The whole campaign") *Ibid.*, p. 111.

126   ("He has been") *TMD*, p. 281; still, Han Suyin masks some of Zhou's conflicts with Mao: these are brought out in Ssu Ma Ch'ang Feng's books.

128   Malraux's *Antimémoires*, p. 533.

128   Chen Changfeng's *Ken sui Mao chu-hsi ch'ang cheng*, pp. 38ff.

129   ("On horseback") E. Faure's *The Serpent and the Tortoise*, p. 32.

129   *Poems.*

130   *Poems.*

132   (Lolos) Liu Bocheng et al.: *Recalling the Long March*.

132   (FN) N. Wales's *Red Dust*, p. 71.

134   (on illness) *TMD*, p. 312.

134   (furious hope) Payne, p. 156.

134   (FN) G. Alitto's *The Last Confucian*, p. 285.

135   ("arbitrary") *TMD*, p. 294.

135   ("Don't envy") *Ibid.*, p. 293.

135   Zhang, II, p. 377.

135   (pro-Mao officer's words) *Great Road*, p. 329.

135,136   (dinner) Zhang, II, p. 388.

Page

136 (among the most critical moments) Snow's *The Other Side of the River*, p. 141, and *TMD*, p. 295.

137 ("This is") *RS*, p. 214.

137 (Mao to Xu) Liu Bocheng et al.: *Hsing-huo liao-yuan* (Hong Kong), p. 233.

138 Mao described the Long March as in some respects a retreat, in talking with Malraux (*Antimémoires*, p. 528).

138 The comparison with the Exodus has been developed by Kazuhiko Sumiya in Terrill and Douglas, eds: *China and Ourselves*, pp. 189ff.

139 *Poems.*

CHAPTER 8. FIGHTING JAPAN

Page

140 Details of the situation in rural Shaanxi are drawn mainly from Snow, Smedley, and M. Selden's *The Yenan Way*.

141 Zhang Guotao (*NYT Magazine*, 8/2/53) and Liang Shuming (cited in G. Alitto's brilliant *The Last Confucian*, p. 285) spoke of Mao's wine-drinking.

141 (few foreign books) Vladimirov and Ryazantsev, p. 44.

141 Chen Changfeng, p. 85.

143 *Poems.*

143 (FN) Rice, p. 114.

144 *RS*, p. 455.

144 (Mao to Smedley) SS's *Mao*, p. 201.

145 (FN—Mao at rally) Huang Yü-ch'uan's *Mao Zedong sheng-p'ing . . .*, p. 177.

145 (Message to Elder Brother Club) *Mao Chi*, V, p. 60 (trans. by Schram). According to Vladimirov and Ryazantsev, p. 83, Genghis Khan's portrait hung beside Mao's in a room of the CCP headquarters.

145 (Chiang's speech) Snow's *Random Notes on Red China*, p. 6.

146 ("You are also") *Battle Hymn*, p. 101. See also Ssu Ma Ch'ang Feng, pp. 99–101.

146 (Mao's fury, Zhou's "We didn't sleep") Snow's *Random Notes on Red China*, p. 3; Mao's behavior at this time was also discussed with RT by Huang Hua, now foreign minister of China.

147 (FN) Rice, p. 91. On Stalin's cable see too *Chung kuo kung ch'an tang shih kao*, Taipei, vol. 3, p. 728.

149,150 Smedley's *China Fights Back*, pp. 122–123.

150 SW, II (for the texts of two of the items mentioned here; the third, *Basic Tactics*, is not in *SW*, but has been published separately in Peking).

150,151 (bodyguard's account) Chai Tso-chün's *Tsai Mao chu-hsi shen-pien*, (Wuhan), pp. 11ff.

151 (FN) Consultation on the translation with Prof. Donald Gibbs.

151 ("We are men") SS's *Mao*, p. 213.

Page

152   (three phases) *Mao Chi*, VI, pp. 79ff.

153   *Stein*, p. 106.

153   *Battle Hymn*, p. 129.

154   Wales's *The Chinese Communists*, p. 252. A somewhat different account of Mao's philandering—leading to nasty confrontations between Mao and Zizhen—has been pieced together by Ssu Ma Ch'ang Feng (*Mao Zedong p'ing ch'uan*, pp. 307ff). It is clear from all accounts that the Mao-Zizhen marriage had broken down before Jiang Qing came into the picture.

155   ("go back") Rice, p. 108.

156   (love) *Battle Hymn*, p. 122.

156   (FN) Witke, p. 155.

156   (He Yi affair) Cheng Hsueh-chia in *IAS*, 1973/11, p. 65.

157   Yang Zilie's (Mrs. Zhang Guotao) *Zhang Guotao fu-jen hui-yi lu* (Hong Kong), pp. 333ff.

157   (son's tribulations) *CB*, 900, p. 5, and D. and N. Milton's *The Wind Will Not Subside*, p. 155; there is some uncertainty as to the movements of Mao's children because the rivalry of Ms. He and Ms. Jiang has affected the purity of the evidence. It is also possible that Mao and Zizhen had a fourth, and even a fifth, child; the evidence on the matter is inconclusive.

158   According to Lu Ch'iang's *Ching kang shan shang ti 'ying hsiung,'* p. 63, He Zizhen was very well treated materially by the Shanghai city authorities.

158   (divorce not Mao's initiative) Witke, p. 160.

CHAPTER 9. THE SAGE

Page

159   (sucking in smoke) H. Forman's *Report from Red China*, p. 178.

159   C. and W. Band's *Two Years with the Chinese Communists*, p. 252.

159   *Battle Hymn*, p. 121.

159   ("He neither grasps") J. Marcuse's *The Peking Papers*, p. 287.

159   ("grotesque") *Journey to the Beginning*, p. 162.

160   (Mao's habits) *Ibid.*, p. 167.

160   (loss of temper—it was with Zhang Wentian) Zhang in *NYT Magazine*, 8/2/53.

160   (on Xu) *Two Years with the Chinese Communists*, p. 248.

161   *Battle Hymn*, p. 121.

161   ("genius") Ch'en (ed): *Mao*, p. 20.

161   ("savior") *Chieh-fang jih-pao*, Chungking, 12/14/41.

162   Epstein's *I Visit Yenan*, p. 27.

163   Social changes are explored in Selden's *The Yenan Way*.

165   (Ding Ling's words) *Battle Hymn*, p. 117.

165   ("Free Love Club") *Ibid.*, p. 119.

166   ("let our") M. Goldman's *Literary Dissent in Communist China*, p. 93.

167   *Mao Chi*, VIII, pp. 111ff.

Page

167   ("clamor") Compton, p. 23.
167   ("As soon") *Ibid.*, p. 44.
167   ("Opinions") *Ibid.*, p. 4.
168   (petty charade) Zhang, II, p. 563.
169   (FN—Wang Ming incident) D. Wilson's *Mao: The People's Emperor*, p. 250.
170   ("Theory") Compton, p. 12.
170   ("If you want") *SW*, I, p. 300.
171   ("If you have not") Compton, p. 57.
171   ("worker") *Ibid.*, p. 41.
171   ("Cooking") *Ibid.*, p. 16.
172   ("wash his face") *Ibid.*, p. 47.
172   ("babies") *Ibid.*, p. 63.
172   ("arrow") *Ibid.*, p. 21.
172   ("no beauty") *Ibid.*, p. 21.
172   ("sharp mouth") *Ibid.*, p. 65.
172   (adapting Marx) *Wan Sui*—1967, 1/18/61. One can appreciate the Chineseness of Mao's view of Marxism by recalling that M. N. Roy (and others in CCP circles) used the phase "centralized world party" to refer to the international socialist movement (Roy's *My Experiences in China*, p. 20).
173   (abstract Marxism) *Thought*, p. 172.
173   ("Consider") Compton, p. 53.
173   ("I myself") *Ibid.*, p. 58.
174   Liu Shaoqi's *On the Party*.
174   ("with great equanimity") *TMD*, p. 422.

Chapter 10. A Ripening Peach

Page

175   (movies) Payne, pp. 238–239.
176   ("democracy") J. Service's *The Amerasia Papers, passim.*
176   (FN) *NYT Magazine*, 1/30/66.
177   Hurley's visit is based on D. Barrett's *Dixie Mission;* Service; J. Eshorick, ed., *Lost Chance in China;* Theodore White's *In Search of History*, pp. 198ff; and D. Lohbeck's *Patrick Hurley*, pp. 312ff. Lohbeck, an admirer of Hurley, says the shout was a "Comanche war cry, with which he had delighted the Russian soldiers at Stalingrad."
178   ("clown") *Great Road*, p. 424.
178   ("highest") B. Tuchman, in *Foreign Affairs*, October 1972.
179   ("Duet") *Mao Zedong hsüan-chi*, p. 1133.
179   ("If you") *Ibid.*, p. 1133.
179   Barrett, p. 75.
180   J. Ch'en's *Mao Papers*, p. xxx, probes the editing out of pro-USA references.
181   ("My humble self") *NYT*, 8/27/45.

452 Notes to pages 182–197

Page

182   (opera incident) Carson Chang's *Third Force in China*, p. 140.
182   ("There are no") *SW*, IV, p. 60.
183   ("The sky") Tso Shun-sheng's *Chin san-shih nien chien-wen tsa-chi*, p. 90.
183   ("merely a corpse") *SW*, IV, p. 313.
183   (FN) Wang Ming's *Polbeka Kuk I Predatelstvo Mao Tse-tung* (Moscow), p. 201.
183   (Marshall and Mao) *TMD*, p. 463.
184   ("When two") *SW*, IV, p. 54.
185   ("Delicious") Yen Ch'ang-lin's memoirs in *Chung-kuo kung-jen*, 1960, Nos. 12, 17, 18. See also Ch'en, pp. 282ff.
185   (FN) *Wan Sui*—1969, 3/28/64.
185   (FN—on women) *Mao Zedong p'ing ch'uan*, pp. 293ff, and Wang Ssu-ch'eng's *Mao fei Zedong cheng ch'uan*, pp. 4–10; Jiang Qing's words cited in Witke, p. 449.
185   (old man; girl announcer)Yen.
185   ("If this is not done") *SW*, IV, p. 29.
186   ("Sometimes") Yen.
186   (Hu) *TMD*, p. 476.
186   ("The people") *Ibid.*, p. 477.
186,187   (U.S. military observer) *Ibid.*, p. 473.
187   ("A second front") *SW*, IV, p. 135.
187   ("They heave") *Ibid.*, IV, p. 163.
188   ("Think it over") *Ibid.*, IV, p. 296.
188   ("We cannot") Payne's *Journey to Red China*, p. 41; see also *TMD*, p. 489.
188   Xiao You, p. 251.
188   (1940s estimates) *SW*, IV, *passim*.
189   *Poems*.
189   (*Aesop's*) *SW*, IV, p. 361.
189   ("To whom") J. Archer's *Mao Tse-tung*, p. 109.
190   ("we absolutely") *SW*, IV, p. 327.
190   (Amethyst affair) *Ibid.*, IV, p. 402.
190   (Stalin's words) V. Dedijer's *Tito Speaks*, p. 331.
191   (FN—Zhou's words) Vladimirov and Ryazantsev, p. 106.
191   (Stuart's diary) S. Topping's *Journey Between Two Chinas*, p. 88.
191   ("Farewell") *SW*, IV, pp. 433ff.
192   (Stuart's diary) Topping, p. 56.
192   (Chiang on CCP) J. Melby's *Mandate of Heaven*, p. 286.
192   (FN) *SW*, IV, p. 194.
193   (Jia) *Mao Chi*, X, p. 213.
194   Melby, p. 359.
195   (Guo and Wang) Elegant's *China's Red Masters*, pp. 229–230. RT has changed "twenty years" to "thirty years" in the cited words.
195   (Yang family) *PKR*, 10/14/77. Also, on Chen Yuying, and details of the Yang family in general, see BBC, Far East, 5617, BII, 9/17/77.
197   (FN) *Tokyo Shimbun*, 9/27/72.
197   ("Will the") J. Kinoshita's "The World Viewed from China," in *Sekai*, Tokyo, 1963/9.

CHAPTER 11. "WE SHALL PUT ASIDE THE THINGS WE KNOW WELL"

Page

198   (title quote) *SW*, IV, p. 422.
198   (tank) C. Roy's *Premières Clefs pour la Chine*, p. 7.
198   ("The Chinese people") *SW*, V, pp. 15–17.
198   ("Eternal glory") *Ibid.*, V, p. 22.
199   ("did not") *Ibid.*, IV, p. 414.
199   ("The era") *Ibid.*, V, p. 18.
199   ("Acheson") *Ibid.*, IV, p. 458.
199   ("We shall") *Ibid.*, IV, p. 422.
200   (democracy) *Ibid.*, IV, p. 418.
201   ("Stalin") *Talks*, p. 191.
201   (Stalin on CCP) *KR*, p. 512.
201   (Mao's illness) Pye's *Mao Tse-tung*, p. 134.
202   (FN) J. Harrison's *The Long March to Power*, p. 435.
202   (criticism) A. Whiting's *China Crosses the Yalu*, p. 179.
202   ("Victory") *SW*, IV, p. 416.
202   (H. G. Wells) *Amerasia*, I, August 1937, p. 267.
203   (FN—dilute final surge) *SW*, IV, pp. 301, 304.
203   (pineapple) *KR*, p. 514.
204   ("The greatest genius") *Thought*, p. 429.
205   ("A world") *SW*, I, p. 47.
205   ("lane" meeting on constitution) R. Loh's *Escape from Red China*, p. 122.
205   ("When a man") *SW*, IV, p. 411.
206   ("Revolutionary") *Ibid.*, IV, p. 420.
206   (youth leaders) *Ibid.*, V, pp. 95, 96, 99.
206   ("Once") *Wan Sui*—1969, 10/24/66.
206   ("Practically") *SW*, V, p. 104.
206   (FN) *Talks*, p. 279.
207   ("total power") *SW*, IV, p. 344.
207   ("two trials") *Ibid.*, V, p. 38.
207   The evidence on the outbreak of the Korean War is analyzed in Whiting and a brilliant book using Korean sources, R. Simmons's *The Strained Alliance;* a recent excellent summary of the literature is Mineo Nakajima's article in *Australian Journal of Chinese Affairs*, No. 1; all in all, Khrushchev's remark hits the nail on the head: "Kim was the initiator. Stalin, of course, didn't try to dissuade him" (*KR*, p. 401).
207   (concerning the Indian ambassador) *PD*, 1/11/77; also a Burmese leader to RT, Rangoon, 11/15/79.
208   (FN—Barr) Melby, pp. 366–367.
208   (FN) For evidence that some wanted no intervention at all in Korea, see *Ming pao yüeh-k'an*, HK, 1967/5 (article by Hsiang Te), and *PD*, 11/6/50 (editorial).
208   (FN—Anying) Vladimirov and Ryazantsev, p. 54.
208   (Mao and Anying) *Kung-jen jih-pao*, 7/18/61.
209   ("Last year") *SW*, V, p. 78.
209   (two Americans) A. and A. Rickett, *Prisoners of Liberation*, pp. 45ff.

Page

210   ("When our") *Talks*, p. 103.
211   ("There should be") *Wan Sui*—1969, p. 546.

CHAPTER 12. REMOLDING

Page

212   ("All you had") W. Hinton's *Fanshen*, p. 207.
213   ("Why") *Ibid.*, p. 399.
214   (elimination) *SW*, V, p. 215.
214,215   (Mao and Liang) *Ibid.*, V, pp. 121ff; for Liang's influence on Mao, see Alitto, pp. 290, 322.
216   ("Outside") E. Chou's *A Man Must Choose*, p. 211.
216   Milton's words are from *Areopagitica* and Mill's from *On Liberty*.
217   (FN) *CLG*, 9–4, 1976–1977, p. 85.
217   In *Mao Papers*, p. xxvi, Ch'en discusses Mao's interesting linguistic habit of using the same Chinese word (*ta*) for both "it" and "they."
218   (Hu Feng's words) M. Goldman's *Literary Dissent in Communist China*, pp. 130, 291–292, 321; *Wen-yi pao* (1955) and *Hu Feng wen-yi ssu-hsiang p'i-p'an lun-wen hui-ch'i* (1955) contain the Hu Feng materials.
219   ("The eyes") *SW*, V, p. 177.
219   ("We don't") *Ibid.*, V, p. 299.
219   ("Because") Goldman, p. 131.
219   Ch'en in *Mao Papers*, pp. xxviii ff., learnedly probes the selections involved in the *Selected Works*.
220   (Guo on Mao's poetry) *PD*, 5/12/62.
220   ("We have") *Talks*, p. 92.
221   Zhang in *NYT Magazine*, 8/2/53.
222   Mao's remark "It's no good" is from a Yugoslav diplomatic source.
222   (hot congee) Marcuse, p. 286; see also V. Cressy-Marcks's *Journey into China* p. 188.
222   ("The higher") *Wan Sui*—1969, p. 80.
222   ("Practically") *SW*, V, p. 104.
223   (8341) *PD*, 9/8/77.
223   ("I spent") *SW*, V, p. 222.
223   Zhou Chingwen's *Ten Years of Storm*, p. 83.

CHAPTER 13. BUILDING

Page

224   ("The force") *SW*, V, p. 149.
224   ("beggars") Rice, p. 131. On Mao and Gao Gang generally, see M. Nakajima's article in *Review* (Japan Institute of International Affairs), 44, 1977, and Hsu Kwan-san, in *Ming pao yüeh-k'an*, HK, 1966/3.
225   ("Only Comrade") *WIT*, p. 62.
225   (FN—slogan) Yu I-lo in *Ming pao yüeh-k'an*, HK, 1966/2.

Page

225   ("the two colonies") *Wan Sui*—1969, March 1958.

225   (car) G. Segal in *Jerusalem Journal of International Relations,* Fall 1976, p. 103.

225   (on Gao) *KR (LT),* p. 278.

225   For evidence from Soviet sources of Gao's special links with Moscow, see Vladimirov and Ryazantsev, p. 37; and p. 77 for evidence that Gao's ordeal during Yanan Rectification may have made him resentful of Mao.

225   Mao might have moved against Gao earlier, if Manchuria's industry had not been crucial to China's war effort in Korea; on this, and Mao's relations with Moscow generally, see Cheng Hsueh-chia's *Hei Mao chih cheng,* Taipei, 1963. pp. 4, 12, and *passim.*

225   ("contacts") *WIT,* p. 63.

225   (FN—"The letter") Shanghai Radio, 3/20/68.

226   (suicide attempt) Hsiang Te in *Ming pao yüeh-k'an,* HK, 1967/5.

226   ("Man needs") *Wan Sui*—April 1967, p. 10.

227   (Khrushchev on Mao) *KR,* p. 517.

228   ("Conflict") *Ibid.,* p. 517.

228   (Mongolia) *FEER,* 5/5/78.

228   (tea) *KR(LT),* p. 279.

228   ("He really knew") *Ibid.,* p. 284.

228   (incident on balcony) Witke, p. 262.

228   ("I tried") *KR,* p. 519.

229   ("Can atom bombs") *SW,* IV, pp. 21–22.

229   ("paper tiger") *Ibid.,* IV, p. 100.

229   ("good friends") Eisenhower's *Waging Peace,* p. 445.

229   (Russian names for CCP) Witke, p. 263.

229   ("test of intention") *WIT,* p. 112.

229   ("Work on your own") Witke, p. 255.

230   ("mattress") *KR(LT),* p. 322.

230   ("Excessive") *Wan Sui*—1969, p. 454.

230   (Mao and his wife together at receptions) Interviews with Mononutu, Jakarta, 12/1/79, and with a Burmese leader, Rangoon, 11/15/79.

230   ("Certain leaders") Witke, p. 256.

231   (FN—on children's character) Ganis Harsono, interview with RT, Jakarta, 11/29/79.

232   These social observations are drawn in part from S. de Beaufort's *Yellow Earth, Green Jade* (1979).

233   ("Without sacrifices") Tung Lin's *Mao chu-hsi ko-ming te yi-chia* (a Red Guard publication), p. 10. A 1954 letter of Mao's castigated any special treatment given to his relatives—of whom he said "I love them because they are part of the ranks of the workers, also because they are my relatives." (*Ch'ing-nien yi-tai,* Shanghai, 1979/9, and *Hua-ch'iao jih-pao,* New York, 10/5/79).

233   (FN—Anying buried in Korea) *CB,* 900, p. 6.

233   (family as model) Jerome Alan Cohen in Terrill, ed., *The China Difference,* p. 256.

235   (FN) *CQ,* 62, p. 188.

Page

235   Mao's remark was quoted by Sihanouk to RT in Peking, 6/29/71. Cf. the Dalai Lama's account of a talk with Mao: "Then something made him say that Buddhism was quite a good religion, and Lord Buddha, although he was a prince, had given a good deal of thought to the question of improving the conditions of the people." (Dalai Lama's *My Land and My People*, pp. 116–117.)

235   Mononutu, interview with RT, Jakarta, 12/1/79.

235,236   U Nu's *Saturday's Son*, p. 238. Even to Nehru, Mao spoke "like an elderly uncle giving good advice" (cited in Gopal's *Jawaharlal Nehru*, II, p. 229).

236,237   (FN—on Zhou) *Ibid.*, p. 264.

237   C. Taylor's *Reporter in Red China* describes foreign state visits to Peking. Also Marcuse, p. 281.

238   ("They hugged") Ganis Harsono, interview with RT, Jakarta, 11/29/79; see also his *Recollections of an Indonesian Diplomat in the Sukarno Era*, p. 162.

238   (Sukarno's visit) *A Man Must Choose*, pp. 221ff.

239   ("He believed") *PKR*, 9/6/63.

239   (FN—War and population) *Wan Sui*—1969, p. 208.

239   (FN) Interview with a Burmese leader, Rangoon, 11/15/79.

240   ("need not be in a hurry") *SW*, IV, p. 371.

CHAPTER 14. DOUBTS

Page

241   ("Some") *SW*, V, p. 184.

242   ("Big movements") Rice, p. 127.

242   ("The CCP") *Ibid.*, p. 126.

242   (Shanghai meeting) R. Loh's *Escape from Red China*, pp. 179ff.

243   (cat story) K. Eskelund's *The Red Mandarins*, p. 150.

244   ("Each age") *SW*, V, p. 303.

245   ("They're draining") *WIT*, p. 53.

245   ("We are now") *SW*, V, p. 290.

245   ("If war") *SCMM*, 653, p. 37.

245   Mao's response to de-Stalinization, not included in his *SW*, is in *PD* 4/5/56.

246   ("We were") *Talks*, p. 101.

246   ("accomplice," "fool") *PKR*, 9/20/63.

246   (Liu's words) R. MacFarquhar's *The Origins of the Cultural Revolution*, I, p. 53.

247   (VOA and Chiang's speeches) *Wan Sui*—1969, p. 85.

247   (high salaries) MacFarquhar, p. 75.

247   ("China belongs") *PD*, 5/31/57.

247   ("Any peasant") *KR(LT)*, p. 309.

247   ("While uniting") *SW*, IV, p. 210.

248   (Stalin's boys) *China News Analysis*, HK, 11/9/56.

248   (student demonstrations) *PD*, 8/8/57; 8/17/57.

Page

248   (Fei) *Ibid.,* 3/24/57.
248   (FN) Loh, p. 301.
248   ("The present") *SW,* V, p. 393.
249   ("The driving wind") Rice, p. 145.
249   (protest at hall) *Ibid.,* p. 145.
249   ("Everyone") *SCMP* (Supplement), 208, p. 1.
250   (description of swim) *Chung-kuo ch'ing-nien pao,* 5/17/57.
250   *Poems.*
252   ("I am old") *The Case of P'eng Te-huai* (Hong Kong), p. 198.
252   ("What was done") *WIT,* p. 85.
252   (Liu's remark) *Ta tao Liu Shaoqi-fan ko-ming Liu Shaoqi-ti i sheng* (1967).
252   (FN) MacFarquhar, p. 121.
252   (Deng's remark) *Deng Xiaoping tzu-pai shu.*
252   ("Socialist democracy") Rice, p. 146.
253   (clash with Mikoyan) F. Lewis's *A Case History of Hope,* p. 183. RT's italics.
253   (FN—Mao on Gomulka) *Ibid.,* p. 182.
254   ("Certain people") *SW,* V, p. 388.
254   (FN) Faure, p. 31.
254   ("If what") *SW,* V, p. 431.
254   (Mao's urgent message) *CQ,* 43, p. 127.
254   (planned visit to Poland) Cheng Hsueh-chia's *Hei Mao chih cheng,* p. 42.
255   (doctors, artists) *WIT,* p. 94.
255,256 Mao's *Nineteen Poems* (1958).
256   (nursemaid) *PKR,* 10/14/77.
256   (Jiang Qing) Witke, p. 266.
256   (Mao's words in Moscow) *Thought,* p. 436.
257   (East European reactions to Mao) D. Zagoria's *The Sino-Soviet Conflict 1956–71,* Ch. 4.
257   ("Our socialist camp") *PD,* 11/20/57.
257   (Polish and Yugoslav comments) D. Barnett's *Communist China and Asia,* p. 362.
257   Prof. Edward Friedman has pointed out that the "east wind" formulation could have meant simply a rejection of the idea of stalemate as a permanent condition.
257   (FN) *KR (LT),* p. 290.
258   ("If the Soviet Union") *Ibid.,* p. 292.
258   (Gao) *Ibid.,* p. 288.
258   (Deng) *Ibid.,* p. 288.
259   (Kosygin) *Ibid.,* p. 289.
259   ("two swords") MacFarquhar, p. 171.

CHAPTER 15. TINKERING WITH THE SYSTEM

Page

260   Interview with a Burmese leader, Rangoon, 11/15/79.

Page

260   ("After I've stayed") *CLG*, 9–3, 1976, p. 67.

260   ("I have said") *Wan Sui*—1969, 1/11/58.

260   ("For two years") *Ibid.*—1969, 1/13/58.

261   ("germs", "washing") *Ibid.*—1969, 4/6/58, and *CLG*, 9–3, 1976, p. 51.

261   ("I am") *CLG*, 9–3, 1976, p. 37.

261   ("If young," "It's like") *Ibid.*, p. 80.

261   ("pigs") *Wan Sui*—1969, 2/2/59.

262   *Prisoner of Mao*, pp. 181, 67.

262   ("Our nation") *CLG*, 1–4, 1968, p. 12.

262   ("No one") *Ibid.*, p. 11.

262   ("Did they") *Talks*, p. 156.

263   *Poems.*

263   ("I once") *Wan Sui*—1969, 5/8/58.

264   (FN—Haeckel) J. B. Starr's *Continuing the Revolution*, p. 42.

264   ("In the Yangze") *Wan Sui*—1967, p. 145.

264   ("There is") *Talks*, p. 94.

264   ("superstition") *CLG*, 1–4, 1968, p. 16.

264   ("Those who") *Ibid.*, p. 52.

264   ("Marx") *Wan Sui*—1969, 5/8/58.

265   ("When we") *Ibid.*—1969, 5/8/58.

266   ("An old") *Ibid.*—1967, p. 125.

266   (Fei) *CLG*, 9–3, 1976, p. 49.

266   (Fan Wenlan) *Wan Sui*—1969, 5/8/58.

266   ("The proletariat") *CLG*, 9–3, 1976, p. 52.

267   ("Philosophy") *Wan Sui*—1969, May 1963.

267   ("The Way") *CLG*, 9–3, 1976, p. 31.

267   (Sun Zi) *Ibid.*, 1–4, 1968, p. 20.

267   ("China") *Wan Sui*—1969, 5/18/58.

267   ("We still") *Ibid.*—1967, p. 158.

268   ("If there are") *Ibid.*—1967, p. 129.

268   ("It was good") *Ibid.*—1969, 11/30/58.

268   ("The whole") *Ibid.*—1969, 5/18/58.

268   ("Walk") *Ibid.*—1969, 11/30/58.

268   ("It must") *Ibid.*—1969, 2/2/59.

268   ("extinction") *Ibid.*—1967, p. 148.

268   (FN—Mao to German author Weisenborn) *Sonntag*, Berlin, 12/16/56.

268   ("There are") *Wan Sui*—1969, 5/20/58; also *ibid.*—1969, 12/19/58, and *CLG*, 1–4, 1968, pp. 60ff.

269   (FN—Deng) Bouc, p. 22.

269   (sparrows) *CLG*, 9–3, 1976, p. 58.

269   (FN—contraceptives) Loh, p. 147.

270   ("My mind") *CLG*, 9–3, 1976, p. 75.

270   ("The brigades," "Everything") *Wan Sui*—1967, 2/21/59.

270   ("Whoever says") *CLG*, 1–4, 1968, p. 22.

270   ("Even if") *Ibid.*, 9–4, 1976–1977, p. 77.

271   (Mao's visit to graves) *Yang-ch'eng wan-pao*, Canton, 4/23/66.

271   *Poems;* the Peking commentary is quoted from J. G. Rush's unpublished (?) "A Scrutable Mao" (1971).

Page

272   (return to Music Mountain) *PD*, 12/22/76.
272   (Mao and Munnich) *CQ*, 43, pp. 125–126.
272   (FN—on Liu) *CB*, 834.
273   *Poems.*
273   ("Who wrote") *CB*, 851, p. 6.
274   ("I am") *Ibid.*, p. 25.
274   ("The commune") *Ibid.*, p. 24.
274   (FN—Zhang's words) *The Case of P'eng Te-huai*, p. 36.
274   ("including Mao Zedong") *CB*, 851, p. 25.
274,275   (Mao to his wife) Witke, p. 301.
275   ("You have") *CLG*, 1–4, 1968, p. 27.
275   ("I am like") *Ibid.*, p. 41.
275   ("The mess hall") *Ibid.*, p. 37.
275,276   (all quotes from Mao's speech) *Ibid.*, pp. 38, 42, 39, 26.
276   ("But I think") S. Karnow's *Mao and China*, p. 123.
276   ("In Yanan") *CB*, 851, p. 14.
276   ("And to think") *WIT*, p. 164.
276   ("Why did") *CLG*, 1–4, 1968, p. 54.
277   (FN) *Ibid.*, p. 38.
277   ("Truths") *Wan Sui*—1967, p. 207.

CHAPTER 16. RUSSIA AND BEYOND

Page

278   (tomatoes) *Wan Sui*—1967, p. 130.
279   ("We needed") *KR*, p. 521.
279   ("He wanted") JPRS, 52029, p. 29.
279   ("It's impossible to *leap*") J. Archer's *Mao Tse-tung*, p. 147.
279   (copying Russia) *CLG*, 1–4, 1968, pp. 16–18.
280   ("In my view") *Wan Sui*—1967, p. 248.
280   ("Every man") *CLG*, 9–3, 1976, p. 88.
280   ("A few") *Ibid.*, p. 83.
280   (FN) Wan Sui—1969, 12/19/58.
280   ("He is") *Ibid.*—1969, 11/30/58.
280   ("They believe") *Ibid.*—1967, p. 156.
280   ("In the universe") *Ibid.*—1969, pp. 337–338.
281   ("chill") *KR (LT)*, p. 300.
281   ("tedious," "cocks") Witke, p 263.
281   ("For the last time") *KR*, p. 522.
282   ("How many") *Ibid.*, p. 524.
282   ("All the rest") *Ibid.*, p. 524.
282   (FN—"I went") Marcuse, p. 288.
282   (FN—"study Marxism") Bouc, p. 166.
283   ("Better") *Talks*, p. 199.
283   ("usurped") JPRS, 52029, p. 14.
283   ("The Soviet Union") *Wan Sui*—1969, 5/11/64.
283   ("bastards") From a Yugoslav diplomatic source.

Page

283   (Deng) *The Wind Will Not Subside,* p. 270.

284   ("We lacked") *Wan Sui*—1969, "Soviet Political Economy."

284   ("Moscow") JPRS, 52029, p. 26.

284   ("During") JPRS, 61269–2, p. 311.

284   (FN) *Prisoner of Mao,* p. 296.

285   ("I suppose you know") *Sunday Times,* London, 6/18/60.

285   (FN) Kukrit to RT, Bangkok, 11/10/79.

285   (Africans) *Wan Sui*—1969, 6/18/64.

285   (Cuba) *Ibid.*—1969, 2/13/64.

286   ("It would be") *Ibid.*—1969, 9/4/64.

286   ("Are we") JPRS, 52029, p. 15.

286   ("accept the fact") *Wan Sui*—1969, 3/22/60.

286   *TLR,* p. 205.

287   Qian's story is told in *The China Cloud* by W. Ryan and S. Summerlin, *passim.*

287   (Mao to Malraux on six bombs) *RN: The Memoirs of Richard Nixon* (Warner) II, p. 24.

287   ("If you kill") *Wan Sui*—1969, p. 256.

287   ("Yes") *Ibid.*—1969, p. 605.

288   (both quotes on the U.S.) *Ibid.*—1969, p. 33.

288   ("Imperialism") *Ibid.*—1969, 2/13/64.

CHAPTER 17. RETREAT

Page

289   (train) JPRS, 52029, p. 24.

289   (charge against Deng) *SCMP,* 4014, 9/5/67.

290   ("come back") *CLG,* 1–4, 1968, p. 44.

290   ("We are all") *Wan Sui*—1967, p. 62.

290   ("pigs," "reality") *Ibid.*—1967, 1/18/61.

290   (Liu's words) *CB,* 834, p. 20.

291   (columnist's words) *PKR,* 5/27/66.

291   (exchange with Snow) JPRS, 52029, p. 10.

291   ("Haven't") *Ibid.,* p. 14.

291   ("Those") *Talks,* p. 167.

292   ("Somebody") *CLG,* 9–3, 1976, p. 95.

292   ("It is") *Ibid.,* p. 120.

292   *Poems.*

293   *Ibid.*

293   *Ibid.* (I follow Ch'en's translation of Lu You).

294   ("The high targets") *The Case of P'eng Te-huai,* p. 413; for other remarks by Mao on Buddhism see *CLG,* 9–3, 1976, p. 67, and *Wan Sui*—1967, 9/9/59.

294   ("Why does") *Talks,* p. 193.

294   (religious monarchs) *Wan Sui*—1969, 2/12/67.

295   (FN) Dalai Lama's *My Land and My People,* p. 121.

295   (Mao-Wang talk) JPRS, 52029.

Page

296 ("dynasties") *Wan Sui*—1969, 6/16/64.
296 (FN) *Poems*.
296 ("A while") *CLG*, 9–3, 1976, p. 117.
296 ("Planning") *Wan Sui*—1969, p. 494.
296 ("When the atomic") *Ibid.*—1969, 6/16/64.
296 (Snow's words) *TLR*, p. 194.
297 ("Each person") *Wan Sui*—1969, 6/16/64.
297 ("When I have a fever") *Ibid.*—1969, 1/24/64.
297 Mao's condition in 1964 was discussed with RT by Ganis Harsono, Jakarta, 11/29/79.
297 (hated flowers) *Wan Sui*—1969, p. 532.
297 (salary) *Ibid.*—1969, 12/20/64.
298 (FN—Liu's words) *l'Express*, Paris, 9/13–19/76.
298 (appearances of people, Zanzibari) *Wan Sui*—1969, 6/18/64.
298 ("Catch a sparrow") *Ibid.*—1969, p. 19.
299 (half a year) *Ibid.*—1969, 7/28/68.
299 ("Everything") *Ibid.*—1969, p. 477.
299 (Yangs) *PKR*, 10/14/77.
299 ("What will Peking") *Ibid.*—1969, 8/18/64.
299 ("Let me ask") *Ibid.*—1969, p. 477.
300 (rebuke of 28B) Compton, p. 40.
300 (October 1957 view) *CLG*, 9–3, 1976, p. 35.
300 (FN) *Wan Sui*—1969, p. 602.
300 ("It is important") *Ibid.*—1969, p. 602.
300 ("It would") *CLG*, 1–4, 1968, p. 90.
300 ("The advent") *Wan Sui*—1969, p. 604.
300 (class struggle, "Good men") JPRS, 52029, pp. 19, 25.
301 *Poems*.
301 (Mao–Yuanxin talk) JPRS, 52029.
302 ("We must issue") *Wan Sui*—1969, 12/20/64. Liu's name is omitted from the text available in the West, but it is hardly to be doubted that Mao was referring to Liu.

CHAPTER 18. THE FURIES OF UTOPIA

Page

303 *Antimémoires, passim*, and a somewhat different Chinese report (*CLG*, 9–3, 1976) on the Mao-Malraux talk. A reader of *Antimémoires* remarked to its author: "The only trouble is that Mao Tse-tung talks rather like Malraux"; to which Malraux rejoined: "Would you rather he spoke like Bettencourt?" (another French politician who met Mao) (J. Lacouture's *Malraux*, p. 437).
304 *Poems*.
304 ("These days") *Wan Sui*—1969, 8/18/64.
305 ("There are at least") *Ibid.*—1969, 12/27/64.
305 (Mao told Lord Montgomery Liu would succeed him) *Sunday Times*, London, 6/12/60 and 10/15/61.

Page

305   The rural ills that aroused Mao are manifest in some extraordinary documents—captured by Taiwan—that are translated in C. S. Chen's *Rural Peoples Communes in Lienchiang* (1969). The SEM itself is treated in R. Baum's *Prelude to Revolution.*

305   (FN) Baum, p. 163.

305   ("The key point") *Sekai*, Tokyo, 1967/3.

305   (Mao's decision to get rid of Liu) *CQ*, 47, p. 571.

307   ("Comrade") *PKR*, 6/2/67.

307   ("A man") Pye's *Mao Tse-tung*, p. 216.

308   (remark to Albanians) *Wan Sui*—1969, 5/1/67.

308   ("Should we") JPRS 61269–2, p. 347.

308   ("If you have") *Talks*, p. 146.

308   ("Don't peasants") *CB*, 897, p. 28.

309   ("Why") *Wan Sui*—1969, 6/6/64.

309   ("fairyland") *Ibid.*—1969, 8/18/64.

309   (Still at") *CB*, 842, p. 12.

310   (party for Strong) *The Wind Will Not Subside*, pp. 103ff.

310   (FN) *Saturday Evening Post*, 11/14/62.

311   (Kosygin's silence) K. Karol's *China: The Other Communism*, p. 350.

311   (FN—Mao's prevarication) Vladimirov and Ryazantsev, p. 89.

311   ("some" colleagues) *WIT*, p. 259.

312   (FN) *NYT*, 1/19/77.

312,313 *Poems.*

313   (Miyamoto visit) *CQ*, 35, p. 59 and *passim.*

314   ("We must overcome") JPRS, 42349.

314,315 (*People's Daily* report on swim) *PKR*, 7/29/66.

315   ("We need") *Wan Sui*—1969, 3/20/66.

315   ("When we started") *Talks*, p. 120.

315   (FN) Prof. Friedman's personal observation.

316   (Peng Zhen) Rice, p. 272.

316   (Zhu's response) *Ibid.*, p. 340.

316   ("big war lord") *WHCM*, 7/15/76.

316   (FN) *CLG*, 9–3, 1976, p. 145.

317   ("The Central") Baum in Terrill, ed., *The China Difference*, p. 169.

317   (FN—"I asked her") K. Ling's *Revenge of Heaven*, p. 317.

317   (selling posters) *The Enigma of China*, Asahi, Tokyo, p. 92.

317,318 (Mao's poster) J. van Ginneken's *The Rise and Fall of Lin Piao*, p. 76.

319   ("stop to flattery") *SW*, IV, p. 380.

319   ("You should") Rice, p. 253.

319   ("suppression") *Wan Sui*—1969, p. 650.

319   ("You should replace") *Talks*, p. 255.

319,320 (Chen Yi's words) Rice, p. 333.

320   (FN) *The China Cloud*, p. 270.

320   (Mao to Albanians) *CLG*, 9–3, 1976, p. 144.

320,321 ("Deng") *Mainichi Shimbun*, Tokyo, 1/5/67.

321   ("Let's just say") *Wan Sui*—1969, 5/1/67.

321   (FN—Deng) *IAS*, 1977/10, p. 76.

322   (Zhou's words) Rice, p. 324.

Page

322   (photo at *PD*) *Enigma*, p. 27.
323   (FN) *Collected Works of Liu Shao-ch'i*, URI, HK, preface by Zhang.
323   (Liu's words) Compton, p. 132.
324   (FN) Wang Ming in *Meng-ku hsiao-hsi pao*, 6/15–29/74.
324   (Liu's foreign policies) Rice, p. 192.
324   (Liu to Albanians) *PKR*, 5/6/66.
324   (on chaos in August 1966) *Wan Sui*—1969, 8/23/66, p. 653.
324   ("The situation") *CB*, 891, p. 75.
325   (meeting with Shanghai pair) *Talks*, pp. 277ff.
326   (Mao to Zhou) *FEER*, 10/2/69.
327   ("The rotten") *Time*, 2/3/75.
327   ("Agreed") W. Burchett in *Nation-Review*, Sydney, 9/7–13/73.
327   Guo Moruo, talking to RT in Peking, 7/6/71, quoted Mao's term "Ultra-leftist."
327   ("I have opposed") *Hung-wei chan-pao*, 4/13/67.
327   ("Marx came") *Ibid.*, 4/8/67.
327   ("He has lost") *CQ*, 40, p. 92.
327,328   ("You cannot," "If leftists," "When a war") *Wan Sui*—1969, pp. 682ff.
328   ("Can the Red Guards") *SCMP*, 4200, p. 5.
328   ("Soldiers") *PD*, 3/30/68.
328   (photo) *Ibid.*, 1/2/68.
328–330   (dawn dialogue) *Wan Sui*—1969, 7/28/68.

CHAPTER 19. A TALL THING IS EASY TO BREAK

Page

332   (opening talk to Ninth Congress) *Talks*, pp. 280–281.
332   (Mao–Chen Yi exchange) *WIT*, p. 336.
333   (FN) *Hsing-tao jih-pao*, HK, 1/18/72.
334   (Mao's letter to wife) *Chung-yang jih-pao*, 11/4/72.
334   ("old woman") *Chung-kung yen-chiu*, IV (3).
334   (Mao to Malraux) C. L. Sulzberger's *The Coldest War*, p. 11.
335   ("absolute authority") *Wan Sui*—1969, 12/17/67.
335   (Mao to wife) *Chung-yang jih-pao*, 11/4/72.
335   ("I approve") *Chung-kung yen-chiu*, 9, 1972, p. 93.
335   ("the reporters") *Talks*, p. 289.
336   ("Fear") *PD*, 8/1/69.
336   (Lin to Zhu) *WIT*, p. 339.
336   ("Don't you think") *Talks*, p. 294.
336   (Summer Palace incident) *Witke*, p. 371.
336   (broadcasts) Radio Anhui, 7/16/70, Radio Hubei, 7/17/70.
337   ("Without") *WIT*, p. 343.
337   ("If each time") *Talks*, p. 294.
337   On doubts as to Lin's leadership ability, see *Red Guard*, p. 95, and Han Suyin in *NYT*, 8/21/72.
338   ("He is like") *WIT*, p. 359.
339   (impressions of Russia) Zhang, I, Ch. 4.

Page

339   A member of the Nixon administration stated to RT that it was a letter from Nixon to Mao that led to Mao's frequent use of the word "hegemony" in the 1970s.

340   (FN) *Le Monde*, 9/10/76.

341   ("I believe") *SW*, IV, p. 100.

341   ("The ghost") *WIT*, p. 357.

342   ("surprise attack") *Talks*, p. 292.

342   (Mao and Snow) *TLR*, p. 5.

343   RT wrote at the time of Laos as the final hurdle in front of Sino-U.S. détente (*800,000,000: The Real China*, pp. 145–146); Kissinger's memoirs seem to confirm this—if the phrase "Owing to the situation at the time," in Zhou's message to Nixon of 4/21/71, is a reference to the Laos crisis. (*White House Years*, p. 714).

344   (PLA slogan) *Talks*, p. 297.

345   ("I just don't") *Ibid.*, p. 296.

345   (Mao and the officer) *Ming pao*, HK, 3/7/72.

346   ("over one hundred") Witke, p. 360.

346   ("571" blueprint) *Chung-yang jih-pao*, 4/13/72.

347   ("sleep or eat") Witke, p. 372.

347,348   (Hong Kong slogan) Domes's *China After the Cultural Revolution*, p. 121.

348   The Lin crisis is based on—in addition to the documents cited—M. Kau's *The Lin Piao Affair*, Burchett's piece in *Nation-Review*, Sydney, 9/7–13/73, C. Murphy's piece in *National Review*, NY, 6/8/73, and *Lin Biao shih-chien yüan-shih wen-chien hui pien*, Taipei.

349   (Zhou's words) *NYT*, 10/12/72.

349   ("Let him go") Murphy.

349   (contacts with Moscow charge) Domes, p. 130.

349   (Kosygin to Brandt) Murphy.

349   ("over fifty" claim) Lelyveld in *NYT Magazine*, 1/27/74.

350   (blueprint) *Chung-yang jih-pao*, 4/13/72.

350   (National Day scene) AFP story in *NYT*, 10/1/71.

352   (bugging, telegram) Witke, Ch. 15.

352,353   (secret document) Kau, p. 76.

353   (Mao to wife) *Chung-yang jih-pao*, 11/4/72.

CHAPTER 20. NIXON

Page

354   *PD*, 2/21/72.

355   (pamphlet) *Shukan Shincho*, Tokyo, 1971/12.

355   Mao confessed to Nixon that there had been resistance to his visit from the Chinese side (Kissinger's *White House Years*, p. 692).

355   ("a white flag") *NYT*, 2/23/71.

356   James Pringle of Reuters reported the calculations about Chinese news coverage.

Page

356   Guo discussed Mao with RT in Peking, 7/6/71.

357   H. R. Haldeman's *The Ends of Power*, p. 90.

357   ("I would hope") *NYT*, 2/21/71.

358   A U.S. official present discussed with RT Zhou's remarks on the communiqué.

358   (FN—on manuscripts) Kissinger, p. 1058.

358   ("I can't talk") *RN : The Memoirs of Richard Nixon*, Warner, II, p. 52.

358   (on Chiang) Kissinger, p. 1060.

359   ("I am") Lord to RT, NY, 9/27/79.

359   (Mao and Nixon on girls) *RN*, II, pp. 28–29.

359   ("Those questions," "a smile," "Actually") Kissinger, pp. 1060, 1058, 1062.

359   ("There was no") Lord to RT, 9/27/79.

359   *PD*, 2/22/72.

360   *South China Morning Post*, a *NYT* News Service story by William Hill, October 1975 (citing C.P. Li, a friend of Mao's, on Mao's overruling of Zhou).

360   (FN) Kissinger, p. 1061.

360   (J. Roots quoting Zhou) *NYT*, 2/6/72.

361   ("Which is") Fumio Matsuo in *Bungei Shunju*, Tokyo, 1978/8. Also see Kissinger, p. 1062.

362   ("Mao admired") Lord to RT, 9/27/79.

362   (FN—Mao to Pompidou) *Nouvel Observateur*, 9/13/76.

363   Kissinger's "Hitler" quip was made to a group of Harvard faculty at Cambridge, 1/19/71.

363   (Mao to Pompidou) *Nouvel Observateur*, 9/13/76.

363   (Mao to Nixon) *RN*, II, pp. 29–30.

363   Word that Mao read Nixon's article came to RT from a member of the Nixon Administration.

363   (FN) *Sonntag*, Berlin, 12/16/56.

364   Nixon's promise was quoted to RT by a high official of the Carter administration who read the transcripts of Nixon's Peking talks, and by a U.S. official present at the Nixon talks.

364   ("The English") *Wan Sui*—1969, 11/30/58.

365   (FN) Marcuse, p. 289.

365   ("I accepted") Kissinger, p. 1089.

365   (verse; translated and introduced by M. Kau and D. Lattimore) *NYT* Book Review, 6/13/76.

365   ("Nixon did not catch") *IAS*, 1975/2.

CHAPTER 21. FRACTURED VISION

Page

366   Zhang Guotao, in *NYT Magazine*, 8/2/53, quotes Mao on his three expulsions.

366   ("He taught us") H. Salisbury in *NYT*, 1/11/76.

Page

367   On Zhou's assertiveness toward Mao from 1969, see the theory of a "sixth stage" in the pair's relationship, presented by Ssu Ma Ch'ang Feng in *Mao Zedong yü Zhou Enlai*, p. 9.

367   ("unerring" and FN) both statements are cited from a Red Guard tabloid "January Storm," May 1968, in Smarlo Ma's "Zhou En-lai as I Know Him," pamphlet (undated) from *Chan-wang tsa-chih* magazine of Chih Luen press, HK.

367   (Zhou's words) W. Hinton in *Boston Globe*, 1/11/76.

367   (Xu) Domes, p. 114.

367   (FN—on 29B) *WIT*, p. 342.

369   (Little Bean's death) *Hsiang-kang shih-pao*, 2/20/74.

369   (printed pro-Lin sentiments) *WP*, 4/11/74.

370   (Schumann) Witke, p. 365.

370   ("We have to") *Ts'an-k'ao tzu-liao*, Taipei, 8/16/72, p. 2.

371   (Tanaka) *Tokyo Shimbun*, 9/27/72.

371   ("disaster" and "trouble") Huang Hua to RT, NY, 11/10/72.

372   (Tanaka on Zhou) *WHCM*, 6/15/74.

372   ("Some comrades") *IAS*, 1974/6.

373   Only after Zhou's death did *PD* (1/8/76) reveal that his cancer was diagnosed as early as 1972.

373,374   (Deng's return) "Deng Xiaoping ti cheng hai fu-ch'en," in *Ch'i-shih nien-tai*, HK, 1977/3.

374   ("too harsh") CIS, 74-091.

374   (Deng's letter) *Ch'i-shih nien-tai*, 1977/3.

375,376   (Congress) *PKR*, 9/7/73.

377–381   Mao-Whitlam meeting is based on interviews with Whitlam (Canberra, during December 1978, and at other times), Fitzgerald (Canberra, during January 1979, and at other times), and Chinese officials.

380   (Mao to Pompidou) *Nouvel Observateur*, 9/13/76.

380   (FN) *IAS*, 1975/2.

381   ("Every seven") *PD*, 11/30/73. Cf. Mao's remark in 1966 that a Cultural Revolution would be necessary "every seven or eight years." (*IAS*, 1973/1).

382   (FN—Zhang's letter) *PD*, 8/10/73.

382   (FN—"Are we children") *Ibid.*, 12/28/73.

382   ("clown") *Ibid.*, 1/30/74.

382,383   (on music) *Ibid.*, 2/14/74 (*SCMP*, 5559, p. 24).

383   ("shit") *Ibid.*, 10/7/74. The quote may be found in *Mao Chi*, VI, p. 135.

384   ("Water") *WIT*, p. 381. On *pi Kong* see too *Ming pao*, HK, 10/28/76.

384   ("Nowadays") *PD*, 2/14/74.

385   (refusal to attend meeting) *Daily Telegraph*, London, 12/18/74.

385   (Bhutto) *PD*, 5/12/74.

385   (FN) *Ibid.*, 5/8/74 (Senghor), 2/26/74 (Boumediene), 2/23/74 (Kaunda), 3/26/74 (Nyerere), 4/3/74 (Khieu), 5/19/74 (Makarios).

385   ("I am not very well") *NYT*, 5/14/74.

386   (FN) Prof. Edward Friedman drew my attention to Zhou's trip to Changsha, which he learned of from a caption at an exhibition that he saw in China.

Page

386   Kissinger remarks: "I am convinced—though I cannot prove it—that only illness and death saved [Zhou] from an assault by what was later called the Gang of Four, tolerated if not backed by Mao." (*White House Years*, p. 1059).

386   *Kwang-ming jih-pao (Brilliant Daily)*, 7/23/74.

387   ("It is better") "Ssu-jen pang ti shang t'ai ho hsia t'ai," in *Ch'i-shih nien-tai*, 1976/12. See too *Ming pao*, HK, 10/28/76.

387   ("expounder") *PD*, 7/16/74.

388   ("She is," FN, "Jiang Qing speaks") *Ch'i-shih nien-tai*, 1976/12.

388   ("I am too," "I do envy") *Ch'i-shih nien-tai*, 1976/12, and *Ming pao*, HK, 10/28/76 and 10/29/76.

388   (Jiang's speech) *IAS*, 1975/7.

389   (FN) Kissinger, p. 1063.

390   (FN—Deng's words) *WHCM*, 4/30/76.

390   (FN—Mao to Montgomery) *Sunday Times*, London, 10/15/61.

390   (Deng and Wang trip) *Ch'i-shih nien-tai*, 1977/3.

391   (NPC documents) *PKR*, 1/24/75.

391   (Mao's talk with Wang) *Ch'i-shih nien-tai*, 1976/12. See too *Ming pao*, HK, 10/26/76.

391   (Liu's objection to Zhang as defense minister) CIS, 76–384.

392   (Mao on Deng) *NYT*, 5/5/75.

392   (FN on Zhang) *IAS*, 1979/1.

392   (poem) Butterfield in *NYT Magazine*, 8/1/76.

393   ("Study well") *PD*, 2/9/75.

393   (Zhang) *RF*, 1975/4.

393   (Yao) *Ibid.*, 1975/3.

393,394   (Kukrit and Zhou) Kukrit to RT, Bangkok, 11/10/79.

394   (Politburo meeting) "Tsai Kwangchow hsun-pieh 1976," in *Ch'i-shih nien-tai*, 1977/2.

394   (FN on Deng) Kukrit to RT, Bangkok, 11/10/79.

394   Episode over Jiang's speech is discussed in Terrill's *The Future of China*, p. 55, and *Ming pao*, HK, 10/27/76.

395   (Jiang Qing–Witke talk) *Ming pao*, HK, 10/27/76.

395   ("His lips") *CQ*, 64, p. 811.

395   ("roaring noise," "gift") Kukrit to RT, Bangkok, 11/10/79.

395   R. Muldoon's *Muldoon*, p. 128.

395   (FN on Kukrit's alleged gesture) J. Alsop in *Reader's Digest*, 1975/12; denial, Kukrit to RT, Bangkok, 11/10/79.

396   Mao's words to Mrs. Marcos were related to RT by a member of the Philippine government.

396   (Mao to Kukrit) *CQ*, 64, p. 811, and Kukrit to RT, Bangkok, 11/10/79.

396   (Moscow's claim) *FEER*, 1/8/72.

396   (less warm) Reston in *NYT*, 1/26/75.

396   ("nasty little man") Butterfield in *NYT Magazine*, 8/1/76.

397   (Kissinger's hospital visit to Zhou) Reston in *NYT*, 12/6/74.

397   (FN) *Ibid.*, 11/30/74.

397   (Mao to Pompidou) *Nouvel Observateur*, 9/13/76.

397   (Mao's written promise to Kissinger) *Newsweek*, 12/8/75.

Page

397   (*"We* have been") J. Alsop in *Reader's Digest*, 1975/12.
398   (FN—"We are," "Uncle Mao") *PKR*, 1/5/73.
398   (FN—"We should") *Ibid.*, 11/23/73.
398   (Mao's words to Jiang Qing) *IAS*, 1975/7.
398   (Betty Ford's report) *South China Morning Post*, 12/4/75.

CHAPTER 22. AN ARROW NEAR THE END OF ITS FLIGHT

Page

400,401   Julie N. Eisenhower's *Special People*, pp. 153ff.
401   *PD*, 1/1/76.
401   (letters to Mao) *WHCM*, 1/31/76.
401   ("typhoon") van Ginneken, p. 309.
401   ("The more books") *Wan Sui*—1969, 1/3/65.
402   ("Petofi") *PD*, 5/28/67.
402   *(Report) SW*, I, p. 47.
402   ("birthday" letter) *PD*, 12/30/75.
402   ("shit") *Ibid.*, 12/4/75.
402   (FN) CIS, 77–881.
403   ("There will be struggle") *Special People*, p. 161.
403   ("souls") *PD*, 11/6/67.
403   ("a form, a method") NCNA, 4/27/69.
404   (cakes) *Special People*, pp. 184–185.
404   The account of events surrounding Zhou's death is based on interviews with diplomats then in Peking.
405   (Mao cites Si Maqian's words) *SW*, III, p. 227.
405   (TV scenes) *Ch'i-shih nien-tai*, 1972/12.
406   (cites Mao's earlier mid-winter maxim) *PD*, 5/15/76.
406   (FN) *Wan Sui*—1969, 1/11/58.
406   ("Stability and unity") *PD*, 1/1/76.
406   (ultra-leftists refusing to serve) C. Hollingworth in *Daily Telegraph*, London, 2/19/76.
407   (on Mao Memorial) *IAS*, 1976/3.
407   (remarks on Hua) *Ch'i-shih nien-tai*, 1977/2.
407   ("You are making") *PD*, 3/10/76.
407   ("Marxist") *Ibid.*, 3/10/76.
408   (twisting Mao's words) *Ibid.*, 2/17/76.
408   ("split") *Ibid.*, 2/17/76.
408   (Sun) *Wan Sui*—1969, 5/20/58.
408   ("Do it") JPRS 52029, p. 4.
409   ("democracy," Yuanxin) *Ibid.*, pp. 6, 48.
409   ("victory") *SW*, IV, p. 374.
409,410   (Zemin incident) *Wan Sui*—1969, 6/16/64.
410   ("human beings") *SW*, IV, p. 152.
410   ("hearts") *WIT*, p. 108.
410   ("chains") Compton, p. 36.

Page

410–413 (accounts of Nixon visit) *PD*, 2/24–27/76 and *NYT*, 2/23–27/76.

411 "might be misunderstood" comes from Chinese diplomats' conversation with RT.

411 Marcos's message reported by Safire in *NYT*, 2/9/76.

412 (Mao to Kukrit) *CQ*, 64, p. 811 and Kukrit to RT, Bangkok, 11/10/79.

412 (Mao to Pompidou) *Nouvel Observateur*, 9/13/76.

412 ("naive") *PKR*, 2/27/76.

412 Mao had often referred positively to Song Jiang, as in "On Contradiction" (1937), "The Chinese Revolution and the Chinese Communist Party" (1939), and as recently as his reply to General P'eng at Mount Lu in 1959.

413 ("wind") *PD*, 4/8/76.

413 ("Nothing") *LT*, 2/26/76.

413 ("That man's") *PD*, 3/28/76.

414 (FN) Leo O. Lee translated the poem.

414 ("What is") *Christian Science Monitor*, 4/6/76.

414 ("The day") *PD*, 4/8/76.

414 ("China is no longer") *Ibid.*, 4/8/76.

415 (young man) *LT*, 4/6/76.

415 In 1979 Hua stated that both his elevations, of February 1976 and April 1976, were the personal actions of Mao, ratified by the Politburo (*PKR*, 10/19/79).

415 (Mao's authorization) *PD*, 4/8/76.

415 (transmittal of motion) *Ch'i-shih nien-tai*, 1977/2.

415 ("dwarf") Report of Helen Foster Snow's trip to China, *NYT*, 2/6/79.

415,416 ("unanimous," "and attempted," "refused") *PD*, 4/8/76.

416 ("Defend") *Ibid.*, 4/10/76.

416 *Muldoon*, p. 128.

417 ("With you in charge") *PD*, 12/17/76.

417 ("It was not") Letter of Prime Minister Lee Kuan Yew to RT, 11/28/79.

417 (Birkmayer) *CQ*, 67, p. 676.

417 ("Chairman Mao is well advanced") *WHCM*, 6/30/76.

418 (FN on 8341 unit) *Ibid.*, 6/30/76.

418 (Yuanxin's talk with Mao) *Ch'i-shih nien-tai*, 1977/3. See also *Ming pao*, HK, 10/29–30/76.

419 ("The people do not support") *PD*, 3/10/76.

419 (Politburo meeting) *Ch'i-shih nien-tai*, 1977/2.

419 ("Help") van Ginneken, p. 318. Other information on the bedside meeting is in BBC Summary of World Broadcasts, Far East, 5335, 10/12/76, and *Ming pao*, 10/26–30/76, and *NYT*, 10/7/76. As to the alternative versions of Mao's "Help Jiang Qing" remark, it is quite possible that he uttered both, seemingly contradictory, endings to the sentence.

420 ("When the burden") *Wan Sui*—1969, 6/16/64.

421 (FN) *Ch'i-shih nien-tai*, 1976/12 and *Le Monde*, 11/19/76.

421 Account of events surrounding Mao's death based on interviews with diplomats then in Peking.

Page

422   (pay their respects) *PKR*, 9/13/76.

422   (grave site) *China News*, Taipei, 11/5/75.

422   (FN—"After I die") BBC, Far East, 5335, 10/12/76.

423   (wreath) *CQ*, 68, p. 880.

423   (Zhang's words) *LT*, 9/11/76.

423   (report of funeral) *PD*, 9/19/76.

CHAPTER 23. EPILOGUE

Page

425   Some of his escapes are recorded in *RS*, and in Chen Chang-feng's *Ken sui Mao chu-hsi ch'ang cheng.*

425   The analysis of Mao's military skills draws on the ideas of Professor Jacques Guillermaz of Paris.

425   (center-leftist) Terrill's *800,000,000: The Real China*, p. 68.

427   ("the Chinese people have stood up") Mao's words were contained in his prior text, "On the People's Democratic Dictatorship," *SW*, V. p. 15.

429   ("the first Chinese") D. Wilson, ed., *Mao Tse-tung in the Scales of History*, p. 3.

431   ("soul") Snow's *The Other Side of the River*, p. 158.

432   ("poor and blank") *Wan Sui*—1969, p. 34.

433   ("You must not") *Ibid.*—1969, 6/16/64.

433   The visitor to Fudan, a Japanese, related the incident to RT, his former teacher.

Index

Acheson, 192, 199
"Advice to Boys and Girls on the
    Marriage Problem," 46
Aesop's Fables, 189
Africa, and Mao, 152, 236, 285, 298
"Against the Second 'Encirclement'
    Campaign," 115
Alsop, Joseph, 395n
Amerasia, 179
Amethyst (frigate), 190
Analects of Confucius, 9
"Analysis of the Classes in Chinese
    Society," 81
Anarchism, in 1920s, 54–55
    in Cultural Revolution, 325–326, 330
Anti-Bolshevik Campaign, 112
Anti-Japan National Salvation
    Association, 147
"Antis" drives, 217–218
Antonioni, Michelangelo, 382
Anyuan Workers Club, 62
Army, revolutionary, Mao joins, 23–24
Art, Mao's Yanan policy on, 167
Art of War (Sun Zi), 267, 295–296
"Ascent of Mount Lu," 273
Atomic bomb. *See* Nuclear weapons
Autumn Harvest Uprising, 88–91, 92
Awakening, 42

Bai Xiangguo, 389n
Band, Claire and William, 159
Bandaranaike, Prime Minister, 369
Bandung Conference, 234
Barr, David, 208n
Barrett, David, 176, 178–180, 194
Basic Tactics, 150

Bettencourt, André, 340n
Bhutto, 385
Binh, 398n
Birkmayer, Walther, 417
Bo Gu, 111–112, 116, 120, 169, 172,
    174
    and Long March, 122–136
"Bombard the Headquarters," 319
Book of History, 31
Book of Poetry, 33, 45
Book of Rites, 191
Book of Songs, 296
Borodin, Mikhail, 69, 70, 88, 89, 153
Boumediene, 385n
Brandt, Willie, 349
Braun, Otto, 119, 120, 153, 188
    and Long March, 122–131
Brezhnev, Leonid, 286, 338, 341, 343,
    397
Brilliant Daily, 386–387
Buddhism, 8, 11, 12, 16, 18, 36, 170n,
    294–295
Bulganin, Nikolai, 228, 259, 278

Cai Chang, 43, 166
Cai Hesen, 31, 34, 37, 39, 43, 51
Cai Tingkai, 118–119
Canton-Hankou railroad, strike, 65
Capitalists, takeover of businesses from,
    242–243
    capitalist-roaders, 321, 407–408
Capital of Peace (Ningdu) conference,
    117
Central Work Conference, 344
Changsha, Peng's march on, 110–111
"Changsha," 76

Chaplin, Charlie, 175
Chen Boda, 242, 324n, 329, 343
Chen Changfeng, 128, 141–142
Chen Duxiu, 41, 50, 56, 57, 64, 65, 67n,
    70, 84, 87–88, 89, 94, 95, 96, 99,
    296
Chennault, Claire, 177
Chen Yi, 98n, 319–320, 326, 327, 332,
    368–369, 404
Chen Yuying, 196, 256
Chen Zaidao, 368n
Chiang Kai-shek, 38, 70, 78, 79, 80,
    110, 111, 161, 168, 198, 203, 215,
    219, 227, 242, 248, 280, 345, 356,
    358, 425
    anti-communist campaigns, 84–88,
        114–120
    captured by Mao, 146–147
    and civil war, 184–194
    and Long March, 123–133
    united front with CCP, 142–149,
        176–184
China's Destiny (Chiang), 187
China Youth Association, 39n
Chinese Communist Party (CCP)
    at Anyuan, 61–62
    and Autumn Harvest Uprising, 88–
        91, 92
    Central Committee, 79, 291, 342
    Labor Secretariat, 61
    Li's leadership ends, 110–111
    Mao becomes leader, 126
    Mao becomes national functionary,
        68
    membership, 1948, 193
    Party Center, 97
    peasant branch at Music Mountain,
        75
    Peasant Department, 79
    Rural Department, 242
    and 28B, 111–112
    united front with Nationalists, 142–
        149, 176–184
    see also Communist Party Congress
Chongqing, Chiang and Mao meet at,
    181–183
Chronicles with Imperial
    Commentaries, 26
Churchill, Winston, 161, 190, 242, 337,
    426–427, 429
"The Cigarette Tax," 71
Civil War, 184–194

Coal miners at Anyuan, Mao organizes,
    61–62
Collier's, 209–210
Communist Manifesto, 48
Communist Party Congress
    First, 55–58, 102
    Second, 66–67, 102
    Third, 67, 71, 102
    Fourth, 72–73, 102
    Fifth, 86–87, 102, 107–108
    Sixth, 102, 107
    Seventh, 173–174
    Eighth, 239n, 251–253, 261n, 263–
        264, 265, 268, 333, 380, 408
    Ninth, 332–334, 380
    Tenth, 375–378, 380, 396
    see also Chinese Communist Party
Communist Youth League, 113, 252
Confucius and his ideas, 8–10, 20, 29,
    45, 66, 94, 172, 199, 216, 220, 223,
    234, 250, 262, 275, 381, 390, 401–
    402, 410, 428, 432
    campaign against, 382–387, 390, 396,
        410
Constitution
    party, 174, 332, 375–376, 391
    state, 224, 391
Construction workers, strike, 1922, 63
Cooperatives, 244
Council of People's Commissars, 119
Counterrevolutionaries, rooting out of,
    213–214
"A Critique of Miss Zhao's Suicide,"
    46
Cultural Bookstore, Changsha, 51–52,
    86
Cultural Revolution, 308–331, 332,
    333, 334, 335, 343, 344, 352, 355,
    368, 375, 382, 393, 394, 401, 403–
    404, 419, 427

Dadu River, crossing of, 132–133
Dalai Lama, 295n
Darwin, Charles, 26, 378
De Gaulle, Charles, 162, 217, 240n,
    283, 287, 303, 334, 426–427
Delegation of Petitioners for the
    Dismissal of Zhang, 47
Democracy, and Mao, 99–100, 176, 409
Demonstrations in 1956, 248
    in 1976, 414–415
Deng Tuo, 291n

Deng Xiaoping, 226n, 245, 249–250, 251, 252, 258, 269n, 283, 289, 290, 297, 301, 313–314, 333, 370, 391, 396, 398, 403–419, 433, 434
  in Cultural Revolution, 316–322
  rehabilitation, 373–374, 379, 385, 390, 392, 394
Deng Yingchao, 157 (Zhou Enlai's wife), 405
Desai, Morarji, 238
Ding Ling, 42, 165, 166, 167, 248
Dixie Mission, 175–176
Doctrinairism, 253
Dream of the Red Chamber, 193, 295
Du Fu, 295
Dulles, John Foster, 236, 286, 341, 354, 363, 364, 382, 389

Eastern Miscellany, 60
East Mountain Higher Primary School, 18–22, 75, 100, 112, 172, 216
Economic development, 244–245, 429–430, 432
Education Bureau, 52
Education Promotion Society, 51
Eighth Route Army, 147, 149, 150
8341 unit, 223, 418
Eisenhower, David, 400–401, 405
Eisenhower, Dwight D., 281, 360
Eisenhower, Julie Nixon, 400–401, 405
Elder Brother Club, 12, 13, 145
Elections, in Yanan, 163–164
  Mao on, 206n
Encyclopaedia Britannica, 196
Engels, Friedrich, 54, 428, 433
Epstein, Israel, 162
The Essence of Christianity (Feuerbach), 215
Explanation of Difficulties (Han Fei), 296

Famine, and food riots, 1906, 13
Fan Wenlan, 266
"Farewell Leighton Stuart," 191, 201
"Farewell to the God of Plague," 263
Faure, Edgar, 254n
Fei Xiaotong, 248, 266
Feuerbach, Ludwig, 215
First Front Army, 123
First Middle School of Hunan, 26
First Teachers Training School (FTTS), 27–34, 51, 59, 75

Fitzgerald, Stephen, 377, 386n
"Five Antis" campaign, 217–218
"571 Plot," 345n, 346, 350
Five Year Plan, First, 220–221, 232, 241, 281
Food riots, and famine, 1906, 13
Food shortage, 13, 14, 269
Ford, Betty, 398
Ford, Gerald, 397–399, 411, 412, 413
Ford, Susan, 398
Foreign Affairs, 363
"Four Firsts," 306
Fourth Front Army, 133–136
Fu, Nelson, 108, 117, 120, 125, 134

Gang of Four, 388n
Gao Gang, 224–227, 258, 277, 283, 291, 300, 324n
Gayn, Mark, 176n
Geneva Conference on Indochina 1954, 234
Genghis Khan, 143, 144, 145, 429
Golden Sands River, crossing of, 131
Gomulka, Wladyslaw, 232, 253
Grable, Betty, 175
Graceful Xiang Printing Company, 45
The Grapes of Wrath (film), 175
"The Greatest Friendship," 204n
Great Heroes of the World, 20, 21, 26
Great Leap Forward, 260–263, 268–271, 274, 278–280, 282, 290, 315, 368, 410
Great Proletarian Cultural Revolution. See Cultural Revolution
"Great Union of the Popular Masses," 44, 66
Great Welfare Daily, 46, 47, 59, 63, 197
Green, T. H., 29
Guang Xu, 19
Guide, 71, 77, 79, 82, 84
Guo Moruo, 195, 220, 356
Gu Tian Resolutions, 109
Gu Yenwu, 21

Haeckel, Ernst, 264n
Haig, Alexander, 356
Hai Rui Dismissed from Office, 290–291, 308, 325
Haldeman, H. R., 357
Han Fei, 296, 386
Han Gaozu, 388

Han Wudi, 21, 143
Han Yu, 29
Health Book Society, 54
Heath, Edward, 363, 385n, 396
Heaven Asks, 53
Hegemony, 339
He Long, 110, 120, 122, 124
He Shuheng, 52, 55n, 56
He Yi, 156–157
He Zizhen, 104–105, 106, 114, 122,
    123, 129, 166, 230
    separation from Mao, 154–158
History of Socialism (Kirkup), 49, 51
Hitler, Adolf, 119, 173, 363
Ho Chi Minh, 70, 281, 341, 422
House arrest, 1934, 120, 122
How to Be a Good Communist (Liu), 305
Hua Guofeng, 272, 334, 394, 407, 411,
    415, 419, 420, 421, 422, 423, 433,
    434
Huang Hua, 191
Huang Xing, 22
Huang Yongsheng, 344–345, 346
Huang Zhen, 400n
Hu Feng, 218–219
Hu Hanmin, 70, 72, 99, 107
Hunan Federation of Labor, 62
Hunan Peasant Union, 82
Hunan Province Library, 26–27
Hunan Provincial Council, 42
Hunan Self-Cultivation University, 59–
    60
Hunan United Association of All
    Circles, 45
Hunan University, 41
Hundred Flowers Campaign, 246–249,
    261, 315
Hungary, events of 1956, and Mao,
    254, 255, 257, 272, 276, 290, 402,
    415
Hu Qiaomu, 324n
Hurley, Patrick, 177–180, 181
"The Hurley-Chiang Duet Is a Flop,"
    179
Hu Shi, 38, 43, 54
Hu Zongnan, 186

"The Immortals," 255–256
Imprecorr, 110
In Opposition to Party Formalism, 171
Intellectuals
    Mao as semi-intellectual, 24, 164,
        216, 308, 426

Intellectuals *(cont'd)*
    Mao's Yanan policy toward, 164–168
    in 1956, 246–247, 248
    see also Cultural Revolution
International Woman's Day, 166
Izvestia, 423

Japan
    and Manchurian Incident, 118
    Mao and, 20, 33, 113, 127, 136, 138,
        139, 142, 152, 168, 236, 340, 365,
        371–372
    war with, 150, 152, 425
Japanese Communist Party, 313–314
Jiang Qing, 155–156, 158, 160, 165,
    166, 169n, 185, 196, 208, 228,
    229–231, 256, 274–275, 276, 281,
    282, 297, 307, 309, 310, 315, 318,
    329, 334, 336, 342, 347, 352, 353,
    355, 376, 382n, 383, 384, 387, 394,
    395, 398, 402n, 405, 406, 411, 414,
    418–423
    anti-Zhou activities, 388–391
Ji Pengfei, 134
Joffe, Adolf, 67
Johnson, Lyndon, 222, 240, 337
Journalism Society, Peking University,
    38, 39
Journal of the New People, 20
Journey to the West, 8, 294, 314

Kadar, Janos, 254
Kang Sheng, 245, 329, 414
Kang Youwei, 20, 23, 34, 199
Kant, Immanuel, 29
Kaunda, Kenneth, 385n
Kautsky, 49, 327
Khieu Samphan, 385n
Khrushchev, Nikita, 202, 203, 225, 230,
    240, 245–246, 247, 251, 271, 286,
    312, 324, 327
    at Moscow summit conference, 256–
        259
    visits with Mao, 227–229, 278–282
Kim Il-sung, 207, 211, 233n, 281
Kirkup, 49, 51
Kissinger, Henry, 343, 344, 372, 388–
    389, 397–398
    and Nixon's first China visit, 355–
        363
Know Shame, 33
Kollantai, 165

Korean War, 207–211, 213–214, 235, 252, 260, 276, 360, 361
Kosygin, Aleksei, 259, 282n, 286, 304, 310–311, 338, 341, 349
Kou tou, 5, 12
Kropotkin, Prince Peter, 40, 44
Kuai Dafu, 329, 330, 333
Kukrit, Prime Minister, 285n, 393–394, 395, 396, 412, 413n
Kuomintang. *See* Nationalist Party

Labor Circles, 52
Land law, 204
"Land of Peach Blossoms" (Tao), 273
Land policy, in Yanan, 163
   during civil war, 192n
   after 1949, 212, 213, 244
Lan Ping (Blue Apple). *See* Jiang Qing
Le Duan, 398
Le Duc Tho, 398n
Lee Kuan Yew, 417
Lei Feng, 336
Lenin, Nikolai, 40, 49n, 62, 80, 115, 144, 167, 170, 200, 205, 233, 246, 259, 262, 264, 275, 298n, 327, 339, 376, 422, 426, 428, 429, 433
Liang Qiqiao, 20, 23, 29, 34
Liang Shuming, 134n, 214–215
Liberalization, 1956, 244
Liberation, 165
Liberation Army Daily, 229, 306, 307, 309
Li Dazhao, 38, 45, 48, 50, 54, 56, 57, 64, 77, 86, 95, 96
Li Desheng (Mao's pseudonym), 185
Li Lisan, 33, 62, 64, 65, 66, 69, 70, 72, 85, 112, 114, 116, 134, 188, 203, 220, 251
   as CCP head, 97–111
Li Min (daughter), 185, 231, 307
Li Na (daughter), 158, 185, 231, 307, 352
Lin Biao, 98n, 100n, 109, 131, 154, 161, 226n, 276, 297, 305–306, 311–312, 315, 316, 318, 319, 321n, 328, 329, 332, 338n, 339, 367, 368, 369, 370, 374, 376, 379, 384
   decline and fall, 334–337, 342–353
Lin Liguo, 345, 347, 348, 350
Lin "Little Bean," 348–349, 369
Li Taibo, 29
Literary Currents, 307, 308, 310, 316
Liu Bang, 54

Liu Bing, 401, 402
Liu Bocheng, 391
Liu Shaoqi, 52n, 62, 64, 65, 66, 80, 85, 147n, 151, 174, 184n, 188, 203n, 226, 227, 242, 243, 246, 249, 251, 252, 255, 270, 272, 274, 289, 290, 310, 329, 330, 333, 337, 339, 370, 390n, 392, 411
   and Cultural Revolution, 319, 321–325
   differences of outlook with Mao, 322–324
   feud with Mao, 298–305
Liu Xiang, 83
Li Xiannian, 355
Lolos, Mao's treatment of, 132
Long March, 120–121, 122–137, 224, 380, 425
Lord, Winston, 358–359, 362
Luding Qiao (The Bridge that Lu Built), 133
Lu Dingyi, 324n
Luo Ruiqing, 311, 394
Lu You, 293, 294

MacArthur, Douglas, 207, 208–210
Makarios, 385n
Malaria, Mao's flareups of, 108, 117, 120, 134
Malenkov, Georgi, 203
Malraux, André, 128, 287, 303–304, 308, 334, 356
Manchuria
   Gao Gang affair, 224–226
   Soviet control of, 202
Manchurian Incident, 118
Mao Anqing (son), 68, 157–158, 196, 208, 231
Mao Anying (son), 63, 157–158, 196, 208–209, 233n
Mao Fuxuan, 74
Maoism, 162, 168–173, 428
Mao Xinhai, 74
Mao Yuanxin (nephew), 231, 301, 382n, 409, 415, 418
Mao Yuanyao, 74
Mao Yueqiu, 74
Mao Zedong
   and A-bomb, 286–287
   and Americans, post-WWII, 175–184, 190–192, 194; *see also* United States
   "Antis" drive, 217–218

Mao Zedong *(cont'd)*
  as "B-52," 346, 350, 375
  becomes head of state, 196–199
  becomes Marxist, 47–50
  birth, 2, 4
  body training, 31
  childhood in Music Mountain, 4–15
  children, 63, 68, 157–158, 196, 208–209, 231, 233n
  cuts pigtail, 23
  death, 2, 420–423
  declining years, 381, 391–396, 400–410, 414–420
  and Dixie Mission, 175–176
  and Maoism, 162, 168–173, 428
  and economic development, 242–245, 429–430, 432
  education: at East Mountain Higher Primary School, 18–22; in economics, 25; at First Middle School of Hunan, 26; at First Teachers Training School, 27–34; self-study, 14–15; at South Bank, 8–9
  as emperor, 3, 212, 223, 274n, 290–291, 298, 406
  family life, 10–14, 299; with Jiang, 155–156, 229–231; and Long March, 122–123; on Music Mountain, 73–74, 84; on Well Mountain, 103–104
  and First Five Year Plan, 220–221
  Ford visit to, 398–399
  foreign visitors to, 235–240, 370–373, 377–381, 383, 385, 395–398, 400–401, 411, 416–417
  health, 134, 183n, 226; malaria, 108, 117, 120, 134; Parkinson's disease, 185, 297, 417
  image of, 161–162
  Khrushchev's visits with, 227–229, 278–282
  and Korean War, 207–211
  marriages: at age 14, 12, 16; to He Zizhen, 104–105; to Jiang Qing, 158; to Yang Kaihui, 48, 63, 68
  meets Chiang at Chongqing, 181–183
  military life, 2, 23–24, 32; and Autumn Harvest Uprising, 88–91, 92; civil war, 184–194; and Long March, 120–121, 122–137; march on Changsha, 110–111; move to Rich Metal, 106–107; and

Mao Zedong: military life *(cont'd)*
  Nationalist encirclement attempts, 114–115, 119–120; and united front against Japan, 118, 142–150; on Well Mountain, 93–105
  Moscow visits, 201–202, 256–259
  Nixon visits, 354–365, 410–413
  at Peking University, 37–40
  personal and physical characteristics, 1–2, 15–17, 19, 34–36, 55–56, 70–71, 128–129, 159–161, 195, 297
  poetry, 2, 36, 76, 85, 105n, 115, 129, 130, 139, 143, 189, 250, 255–256, 263, 271, 273, 292–293, 301, 304, 312–313, 318, 365, 392, 426
  political life: at Canton, 67–68, 69; at Changsha, 42–43, 51–52, 53–55; and labor movement, 61–66; and peasants, 74–76; and 28 Bolsheviks, 111–112, 115–117, 121, 124, 126; and united front with Nationalists, 68–71, 75–80, 85–89, 142–147; at Wuhan, 84–87; at Yanan, 162–167
  political writings, 22–23, 32; in Changsha, 43–47, 52–53; on civil affairs, 117; in *Guide,* 71, 79, 82; Gu Tian Resolutions, 109; *In Opposition to Party Formalism,* 171; on military ideas, 150–153; on peasants, 81–84; in *Political Weekly,* 72n, 77; of speeches, 222–223; in Yanan, 150–152
  as rebel, 15, 17, 318
  relations with father, 4–5, 10–11, 14, 16, 163, 164, 271, 425
  relations with mother, 11–12, 17, 36, 164, 271
  and revisionism, 253, 300–301, 431
  runs away from home, 9–10
  and shelling of Quemoy and Matsu, 280
  as student activist, 32–34; in Hunan, 41–43; in Peking, 37–40, 47–49
  swimming, 6, 31, 250, 260, 261, 314–315
  as teacher, 33; at Hunan Self-Cultivation University, 59–61; of nation, 173, 409; of peasants, 74–75, 78, 84; at Xiu Ye, 51
  visits Music Mountain, 271–272, 392
  wander and study tour, 31–32
  and Yanan Way, 140–141

Mao Zedong (cont'd)
    see also Chinese Communist Party;
    Communist Party Congress;
    Cultural Revolution; Great Leap
    Forward
Mao Zejian (adopted sister), 52, 63, 73,
    74, 103, 111
Mao Zemin (brother), 11n, 12, 36, 52,
    61, 64, 73, 74, 77, 103, 129, 295,
    301n, 409–410
Mao Zetan (brother), 11, 36, 52, 60,
    73, 103, 122, 156
March
    on Changsha, 110–111
    Long, 120–121,122–137, 224, 380, 425
    on Nanchang, 110
    from Well Mountain to Rich Metal,
    106
Marco Polo Bridge Incident, 147
Marcos, Imelda, 396, 411
Maring, 63, 66–67, 80
Marshall, George C., 180, 183–184,
    191, 203
Marx, Karl, and Marxism, 40, 42, 44,
    48–49, 54, 65, 80, 82, 94, 101–102,
    170, 172, 173, 205, 244, 246, 264,
    268, 284, 299, 327, 426, 428, 431
May Fourth movement, 40, 42, 54, 59,
    61, 71, 94
McCarthy, Joseph, 210n, 219
Melby, John, 194
"Methods of Teaching in the
    Countryside," 78
"Methods of Work," 316
Mif, Pavel, 111, 112
Mikoyan, Anastas, 246, 253
The Militant, 85
Mill, John Stuart, 26, 216, 247
Milton, John, 216
Miyamoto, Kenji, 313–314
Mononutu, Ambassador, 235, 236
Montesquieu, Baron de, 26
Montgomery, Lord, 285, 390n
Moscow
    Mao's visit to, 1949, 201–202
    summit conference, 1957, 256–259
Muldoon, Prime Minister, 395, 416–417
Munnich, Prime Minister, 272
Music Mountain (Shaoshan)
    Mao's childhood in, 5–6
    food shortage in, 14
    Mao leaves, 14–15
    returns, 271–272, 392

"Music Mountain Revisited," 271

Nanchang, march on, 110
Nanning, conference in, 260,406n
National Day celebrations, 228, 322,
    337, 350–351, 385
Nationalist Party (NP), 67–68
    attempts encirclement, 114–115, 117,
    120–121
    Congress, 69, 77–78
    Land Committee, 85
    Organization Department, 69
    Peasant Department, 70, 72, 77, 78
    Propaganda Department, 77
    united front with CCP, 142–149,
    176–184
    Western Hills Group, 77, 78
National People's Congress, 224, 385,
    391, 392n
"The National Revolution and the
    Peasant Movement," 81–82
National Soviet Congress
    First, 115
    Second, 119
Negotiation, Chiang and Mao, 181–183
Nehru, Jawaharlal, 237, 238–239, 257,
    429
New Age, 60
New China Daily, 181
New Culture, 42
New Democracy, 200
New Democratic Youth League, 206
New Education, 52
New Hunan, 45
Ne Win, 347
New Life, 52
New People's Study Society (NPSS),
    33, 37, 47, 50, 51, 54
New Voice, 42
New Youth, 30, 32, 37, 38, 40, 41, 49,
    52, 54
Nguyen Huu Tho, 398n
Nie Yuanzi, 329, 330, 333, 336n
Nineteenth Route Army, 118
Nixon, Richard, 145, 338, 342–343,
    372, 373, 396, 399, 400, 404
    China visits, 354–365, 410–413
North China Daily, 194
Northern Expedition, 79, 80, 82, 86
"The Northward March" (Du Fu), 295
Nosaka, Sanzo, 1
Nuclear weapons, 296, 379, 427
    China explodes A-bomb, 286–287

Nuclear weapons *(cont'd)*
  H-bomb, 320
  Khrushchev-Mao talks on, 227, 229, 258, 281
Nyerere, 385n

Ochab, 253
"Ode to Plum Blossom," 293
On Policy, 345
On Practice, 170
On Protracted War, 150–152, 273
"Oppose Book Worship," 112
Outer Mongolia, sovereignty, 202
An Outline of the Capitalist System, 55

Pang (blacksmith), 13–14
Paulsen, F., 30, 36
"Pay Attention to Economic Work," 117
Peasant associations, 71–72
Peasant Movement Training Institute, 72, 77, 84
"The Peasant Question in China," 78
Peasant unions, 74, 82
Peking, Mao captures, 194–196
Peking University, 37, 38, 51, 164, 195, 214n, 246, 270, 333
Peng Dehuai, 100n, 105–106, 110, 111, 188, 209, 245, 252, 282, 290, 291, 294, 295, 300, 306, 308, 338, 342, 343, 367
  criticizes Mao, 273–277
Peng Pai, 72, 74, 78, 84
Peng Zhen, 251n, 252, 309, 314, 319, 324n
People's Daily, 194, 195, 209, 218, 219, 220, 237, 242, 246, 247, 263, 287, 309, 314–315, 321, 322, 325, 326, 328, 342, 351, 354, 359, 372, 375, 381, 382, 383, 387, 390–391, 394, 401, 402, 406, 412, 413, 415
People's Liberation Army (PLA), 195, 197, 199, 221, 224, 232, 274, 276, 285, 306–309, 326, 328, 330, 333–336, 343–347, 352, 355, 367–369, 372–373, 384–385, 415–416
  and civil war, 184–194
  and Korean War, 207, 209, 211
People's Republic of China (PRC)
  beginnings, 199–207
  Khrushchev's visit with Mao, 227–229, 278–282
  in 1950s, 231–234
  tenth anniversary, 281

People's Republic of China *(cont'd)*
  when Mao died, 429–432
Pham Van Dong, 398n
Philosophy Society, Peking University, 38
Phouma, Souvanna, 235
Poetry, 2n, 36, 76, 85, 105n, 115, 129, 130, 139, 143, 189, 250, 255–256, 263, 271, 273, 292–293, 301, 304, 312–313, 318, 365, 392, 401, 403
Politburo, 127, 136, 226, 244, 249, 284, 289, 312, 320, 351, 373, 387, 392, 394, 403, 406, 415, 417–419, 421, 422, 433
Political Weekly, 77n
Politics, Mao's Yanan policy on, 167
Pompidou, Georges, 362n, 363, 380, 397, 412
Popular Daily, 51, 52
Pravda, 227
Problems of Chinese-American Relations, 355
Problems of Strategy in the Anti-Japanese Guerrilla War, 150

Qian Xuesen, 287, 320n
Qin Shihuang, 21, 143, 234, 302, 414, 426
Quemoy and Matsu, crisis over, 280
Quotations from Chairman Mao, 306, 307, 317, 318, 335, 427, 428
Qu Qiubai, 87, 89, 90, 97, 111, 122

Rains of Hunan Poetry Club, 54
Rao Shushi, 225, 226
Razak, 385n
Reading, 8, 10–11, 12–13, 26–27, 176n, 196
Reagan, Ronald, 411
Rebelliousness, in childhood, 15–17
Red Army
  born, 98
  captures Zunyi, 125–126
  march from Well Mountain to Rich Metal, 106
  on Well Mountain, 98–105
  see also People's Liberation Army (successor name)
Red Detachment of Women, 355
Red Flag, 289, 382
Red Guards, 316–318, 325–330, 336, 337, 357
Red Star Over China (Snow), 82, 154
Reform Movement of 1898, 20

Ren Bishi, 184n
"Reply to a Friend," 292–293
Report on an Investigation of the Peasant Movement in Hunan, 82, 83, 84, 85, 94, 173, 402
Resist Japan University, Yanan, 168
Revisionism, 253, 288, 300, 313, 431
Revolutionary Committee, 328
Riot, at Spring Festival 1976, 414–415
Rogers, William, 355
Romance of the Three Kingdoms, 8, 15, 21, 37, 41, 132, 143n
Roosevelt, Franklin D., 161, 173, 176, 177, 179, 190, 361, 429
Rousseau, Jean Jacques, 26, 167, 206n
Roy, M. N., 87n, 89, 239
Rusk, Dean, 363
Russian Affairs Study Group, 52

"Sacrificial Eulogy," 36
Schistosomiasis, 263
Schmidt, Helmut, 312n, 363
School for Cadres Children, Yanan, 168
Schumann, Robert, 370
Selassie, Haile, 351
Selected Works, 53, 82, 83, 173, 180, 204, 205, 219, 222, 234
Senghor, 285
Service, John S., 176, 179
Settling Accounts Movement, 212
Sex as bone of contention in Yanan, 165
   in Kiangxi, 113–114
   Mao's attitude to, 43
Shanghai Commune, 325
Shi Dakai, 132
Sihanouk, Prince, 235, 294, 350, 373, 396
Si Maqian, 405
Six Crises (Nixon), 357
Smedley, Agnes, 1, 2, 64, 144, 149–150, 153–154, 156, 159, 161, 166, 222
Smith, Adam, 26, 63
Snow, Edgar, 29, 48, 82, 111, 123n, 140, 144, 154, 159, 286, 291, 296, 297, 315n, 321, 342, 354, 428
Snow, Lois, 342
"Snow," 143, 181, 296
Socialism: From Utopian to Scientific (Engels), 54
Socialist Education Movement (SEM), 305, 324

Socialist Youth Camps, 52, 54, 55
Society for the Study of Wang Fuzhi, 30, 60
"Solitary Anger" (Han Fei), 386–387
Song Jiang, 13, 412–413
South East Asia Treaty Organization, 227
Souvanna Phouma, 235
Soviet Republic of China, 115–116
Soviet Union, 45n, 49, 52, 56, 79–80, 121, 142, 158, 172, 174, 179, 190, 221, 237, 246, 349, 425, 431
   border clashes, 337–338, 341
   deStalinization, 279
   Mao's trips to, 201–204, 256–259, 428
   relations deteriorate, 278–284
   Treaty with, 202
   see also Khrushchev, Nikita; Stalin, Joseph
Spencer, Herbert, 26
Spirit of '76 (airplane), 354, 358
Spring Festival riot 1976, 414–415
Stalin, Joseph, 80, 89, 146–147, 161, 170, 190, 207, 210, 225, 246, 247, 248, 272, 422, 426, 433
   Mao's relations with, 201–204
   Soviet condemnation of, 245–248
Stein, Gunther, 123, 153
Stilwell, Joseph, 176, 177, 179
Story of the Marshes, 4, 8, 9, 13, 15, 41, 92, 95, 98, 116, 128, 412–413
Strauss, Franz Josef, 363, 391
Strength of the People, 22, 32
Strong, Anna Louise, 192, 229, 310
Stuart, Leighton, 190–192
Student union, Mao's leadership of, 32–33
Study and Criticism, 382, 383
"A Study of Physical Culture," 32
Sukarno, 231, 235n, 238, 396, 429
Sun, the monkey king, 314, 324, 434
Sun Yat-sen, 7, 22, 24, 27, 34, 67, 68, 69, 72, 75, 77, 83, 198, 408, 427
   his widow, 257n, 322, 423
Sun Yat-sen (gunboat), 78
Sun Yat-sen University, 112
Sun Zi, 267, 295
System of Ethics (Paulsen), 30, 36

Taiping rebels, 7, 132
Taiwan, and Mao, 192, 199, 202n, 207, 208, 209, 210, 229, 268, 279–280, 284, 360, 364, 378, 411

Talks at the Yanan Forum on Literature and Art, 168, 218–219
Tan, 26
Tanaka, Prime Minister, 197n, 371–372, 396
Tang, Nancy, 394n
Tan Yenkai, 51
Taoism, 25, 27, 55, 245, 266
Tax policy, in Yanan, 113
"Ten Great Relationships," 244
Third Teachers Training School, 63
Third World, relationships with, 152–153, 235–240, 284–286
Thought Reform Movement, 214, 217
"Thoughts on March Eighth" (Ding), 166
"Three Antis" campaign, 217–218
Three Generations (Kollantai), 165
Treaty of Friendship, Alliance, and Mutual Assistance, 202
Trinh, 398n
Truman, Harry, 209, 210n, 213, 343, 361
Truong Chinh, 398n
28 Bolsheviks (28B), 111, 115, 116, 117, 142, 147–148, 162, 171, 172, 267, 274, 300, 367n, 410
    and Long March, 124–135
"Two Birds: A Dialogue," 312, 401, 403

Unions, Mao organizes, 61–65
United Front, of Mao, 68–71, 75–80, 85–89, 142–147, 162–167, 247
United Nations, 351
United States, Mao and, 21, 53, 138, 175–177, 178, 180–184, 190–192, 194, 268, 287–288, 310–311, 338, 340, 396–397
U.S. News and World Report, 209
United Students Association of Hunan, 42, 43, 45, 51
U Nu, 235, 236, 237n
Upward Strife, 42

Vietnam, and Mao, 310, 312, 340, 360–361, 398, 413n
Von Falkenhausen, General, 119
Von Seeckt, General, 119

Wales, Nym, 132n (Snow's wife), 154
Walking tour, 31–32
A Walk in the Sun (film), 175

Wang (librarian), 195
Wang Dongxing, 418
Wang Hairong (niece), 294–295, 301n, 358, 374, 381, 417
Wang Hongwen, 376, 377–378, 380, 381, 387, 389, 390, 391, 393n, 404, 423
Wang Jingwei, 70, 77, 78, 86
Wang Mang, 426
Wang Ming, 111–112, 116, 118, 119, 148, 169, 172, 174, 183n, 222, 251, 324n
Warm Tide, 42
Washington, George, 21, 144
Weekly Critic, 45
Weisenborn, Gunther, 363n
Well Mountain, Mao at, 93–105
"Well Mountain Revisited," 304, 401, 403
Wen (cousin), 19, 20
White, Paul Dudley, 347, 351
Whitlam, Gough, 350n, 377–381, 396
Why Lean to One Side?, 202
Wilson, Harold, 363
Witke, Roxane, 156n, 395
Women's Bell, 42
Words of Warning in an Age of Prosperity, 13
Workers Association, 54
Wu Gang, 255–256
Wu Han, 291n, 308
Wu, Lily, 154

Xiang River, battle of, 123, 125
Xiang River Daily News, 23, 24
Xiang River Review, 43, 44, 45n, 51
Xiang You, 32, 54
Xian Incident, 146–147
Xiao San (Emi), 112–113, 161
    as school friend of Mao, 19–35
Xiao You, 112, 188, 293
    as student friend of Mao, 19–58
Xie Fuzhi, 329
Xiu Ye (FTTS primary school), 51, 59
Xu Haidong, 137
Xu Shiyou, 367, 368, 415
Xu Teli, 160

Yanan, Mao policy in, 160–168
"Yanan Forum on Literature and Art," 167, 218
Yanan *Talks,* 168, 218, 219
Yanan Way, 140

Yan Fu, 26
Yang Changji, as Mao's teacher, 29–38, 48, 83, 95, 99
Yang Kaihui, 39, 48, 49, 51, 52, 60, 63, 65, 68, 73, 74, 84, 93, 104, 105, 111, 114, 156, 195, 196, 231, 255, 256, 272, 299, 414
Yao Wenyuan, 308, 309, 319, 325, 329, 333, 393, 394, 406, 414
Ye Chun, 334, 345, 348
Ye Jianying, 355, 407, 408, 415
You Chi, 32
Young People's Library, 51
Youth Society, 54
Yuan Shikai, 24, 27
Yuan (the Big Beard), 29, 32, 34
Yudin, P. F., 222

Zhang Chunqiao, 325, 333, 391, 393, 394, 405, 406, 407, 414n, 419
Zhang Fei, 275
Zhang Guotao, 16, 18, 38, 57, 64, 66, 67n, 69, 70–71, 115, 148, 168–169, 174, 186, 221, 323n, 339, 343, 353n, 423
  and Long March, 128–137
Zhang Jingyao, 42, 45, 47, 51
Zhang Mutao, 168–169
Zhang Nanxiang, 402n

Zhang Tiesheng, 382n, 392n
Zhang Wentian, 127n, 272, 274, 276
Zhang Xueliang, 146–147
Zhang Zuolin, 86, 146
Zhao (Miss), 46, 48, 431
Zhen Zhang, 39
Zhong Hanhua, 368
Zhou Chingwen, 223
Zhou Enlai, 1, 2, 21, 40, 78, 79, 86, 89, 100n, 117, 122n, 126, 153n, 204n, 227, 228, 230, 234, 235, 236, 237n, 243, 283, 297, 333n, 334, 354, 355, 358–364, 396–408, 414, 415, 418, 422
  and civil war, 178–191
  and Cultural Revolution, 317–328
  and Lin Biao's fall, 340–351
  status, 1970s, 366–391
Zhou Yang, 324n
Zhu De, 2, 98–99, 127, 148, 153n, 159, 161, 168n, 178, 184n, 194, 222, 226, 245n, 249, 273, 274, 276, 277, 291, 316, 336, 369n, 404, 420
  tension with Mao, 101, 109, 136–137, 226, 316
  joint command with Mao, 98–126
Ziegler, Ronald, 356
Zunyi, capture of, 125–126
Zunyi conference, 126–127, 135

About the Author

Ross Terrill was raised in rural Australia, of schoolteacher parents; he attended Melbourne University (where he received first-class honors in history and political science), worked in the Student Christian Movement, and served in the Australian Army. Arriving in the United States in 1965, he became an American citizen in 1979, and is today one of the Western world's leading authorities on China.

Terrill has moved within a triangle of academia, journalistic writing, and public life. After finishing his Ph.D. thesis at Harvard, which won the Sumner Prize, he taught for eight years on the Harvard faculty in the areas of political thought, Chinese politics, and international relations. While Associate Professor of Government and Director of Student Programs at the Center for International Affairs, he wrote the distinguished biography *R. H. Tawney and His Times* (1973), as well as numerous journal articles.

As a foreign correspondent, Terrill has written for the *Atlantic Monthly, The New Republic, Foreign Affairs,* and newspapers including *The New York Times, Los Angeles Times, Washington Post,* and *Chicago Tribune,* and he has won the National Magazine Award for Reporting Excellence and the George Polk Award for Outstanding Magazine Reporting. Abroad, his articles appear regularly in the *International Herald Tribune* (Paris), *Bulletin* (Sydney), *Die Zeit* (Hamburg), *Asian Wall Street Journal* (Hong Kong), *Yomiuri* (Tokyo), and *Straits Times* (Singapore). He has been a confidant of political figures in Australia and the United States, has testified before various committees of the U.S. Congress, and addressed leading forums in various countries.

An inveterate traveler, Terrill has made some twenty-five trips through the Far East, as well as many in Eastern and Western Europe. He first went to China as a wandering student in 1964, returning there in 1971 (a journey that resulted in the classic *800 Million: The Real China*),1973, 1975, 1978, and most recently in 1980. His books include *Flowers on an Iron Tree* (1975), *The Future of China* (1978), and several edited volumes, among them *China and Ourselves* (1970) and *The China Difference* (1979).

Terrill lives in Cambridge, Massachusetts, where he is a Research Associate at Harvard's Center for East Asian Research, and a contributing editor of the *Atlantic Monthly.*